How to Do
Everything™

Genealogy

Fourth Edition

How to Do
Everything™

Genealogy

Fourth Edition

George G. Morgan

Mc Graw Hill Education

New York   Chicago   San Francisco
Athens   London   Madrid   Mexico City
Milan   New Delhi   Singapore   Sydney   Toronto

Library of Congress Cataloging-in-Publication Data

Morgan, George G., 1952–
  [How to do everything with your genealogy.]
  How to do everything : genealogy / George G. Morgan. — Fourth edition.
    pages cm
  ISBN 978-0-07-184592-2 (alk. paper)
  1. Genealogy. 2. United States—Genealogy—Handbooks, manuals, etc. I. Title.
  CS16.M69 2015
  929.1072'073—dc23

                                                                    2014046320

McGraw-Hill Education books are available at special quantity discounts to use as premiums and sales promotions, or for use in corporate training programs. To contact a representative, please visit the Contact Us pages at www.mhprofessional.com.

How to Do Everything™: Genealogy, Fourth Edition

7 8 9 10   LCR   21 20 19

ISBN   978-0-07-184592-2
MHID   0-07-184592-5

Sponsoring Editor Roger Stewart	**Technical Editor** Drew Smith	**Composition** Cenveo Publisher Services
Editorial Supervisor Janet Walden	**Copy Editor** William McManus	**Illustration** Cenveo Publisher Services
Project Manager Kritika Kaushik, Cenveo® Publisher Services	**Proofreader** Madhu Prasher	**Art Director, Cover** Jeff Weeks
Acquisitions Coordinator Amanda Russell	**Indexer** Claire Splan	**Cover Designer** Jeff Weeks
	Production Supervisor Jean Bodeaux	

This book is dedicated to the memory of my cousin,
Penny Frank Hahn
(1945–2014)

(Courtesy Dez Merrow Photography)

About the Author

George G. Morgan (Odessa, FL) is president of Aha! Seminars, Inc., and is recognized as a genealogical expert. He is a popular speaker at genealogical conferences across the United States at national, state, and local conferences, as well as in Canada and the United Kingdom, and on genealogical cruises. His range of genealogical interests and speaking topics is among the most diverse among the genealogical speaking community.

George is the prolific author of eleven previous landmark genealogy books, including *The Official Guide to Ancestry.com*, *Genealogical Research in the Major Repositories of London*, and the best-selling *Advanced Genealogy Research Techniques* written with co-author Drew Smith. He writes regular columns for the *Association of Professional Genealogists Quarterly* and *Family Tree Magazine*, his articles are regularly featured in *Family Chronicle* and *Internet Genealogy*, and his articles and columns have appeared in magazines and at websites in the United States, the United Kingdom, Canada, China, and Singapore.

George also delivers webinars for expanding eager audiences of genealogists and librarians who crave instructional materials to help them locate records, understand their content, evaluate information, and integrate this all into the context of their ancestors' lives.

About the Technical Editor

Drew Smith, MLS, has been a librarian at the University of South Florida (USF) Tampa Library since 2007, and was previously an instructor for the USF School of Library and Information Science (now the School of Information). He is a respected and popular speaker at local, state, and national conferences. He has written numerous articles for genealogical magazines, and is currently the "Rootsmithing with Technology" columnist for the Federation of Genealogical Societies' *FORUM* magazine. Drew is the author of the book *Social Networking for Genealogists*, published in 2009 by Genealogical Publishing Company. In 2013 he was selected to serve as the first Chair of the Family History Information Standards Organisation (FHISO). Since 2007 Drew has been the President of the Florida Genealogical Society of Tampa. He is a past Director of the Federation of Genealogical Societies and a past Secretary of the Association of Professional Genealogists (APG).

George and Drew together produce The Genealogy Guys[SM] Podcast, the longest-running genealogical podcast, published online at **http://genealogyguys.com** and enjoyed by thousands of listeners around the world.

Contents at a Glance

Contents

Preface

This is a golden age for conducting our family history investigations. It is important that genealogical exploration include *both* traditional *and* electronic research. We still need to visit or work with physical facilities such as libraries, archives, courthouses, and other locations because only a small percentage of documents are on the Internet. However, the technology to assist genealogists is growing faster than ever. Information, in the form of indexes and original documents digitized by the tens of millions, is being added to the Internet each month. Newspapers and city directories that were printed on fragile, non-archival paper stock are being scanned and electronically indexed at an astonishing rate. Billions of photographs, including vintage pictures from personal family collections, are also being digitized, labeled, and placed online at a variety of websites. Cemeteries are being canvassed and photographed by volunteers around the world and are being placed online.

I wrote the first edition of this book because I felt that no other introductory book about genealogy went into enough detail about getting started with your family history research and then progressed beyond the basics. Over the last decade, no other how-to genealogy book has been published with as much information and as many illustrative graphics as this book, and this fourth edition is no exception.

I always wanted a genealogy how-to book that addresses records in the United States, Canada, England, Wales, Scotland, Ireland, and Australia. This book provides that. Research in the primary English-speaking countries is essential, especially if you are trying to research backward and "cross the pond." Understanding one type of record in one location can help you draw analogies in another location, therefore more quickly grasping the importance of the content and the contextual implications of a new record.

What This Book Covers

This new, fourth edition of the book continues the premise of providing a solid foundation for genealogical research. It also includes discussions of many different record types of genealogical importance created and available in English-speaking countries, the physical repositories and/or online resource facilities where they may be found and accessed, and a wealth of logical research methodologies. The figures and tables throughout complement the text, providing samples and details for your future reference.

Genetic genealogy research has rapidly evolved since the third edition, and this book reflects the most recent testing that is available, and discusses tools and references for getting the most of your genetic genealogical results. It also includes up-to-date information about social media, which has become an important part of the collaboration between genealogists.

New to this edition is an up-to-the-minute discussion of a number of mobile genealogy apps for the iPhone and Android operating systems. These are in addition to the mobile apps available for many of the genealogical database software programs that run on desktop, laptop, and tablet computers.

Regardless of your experience and expertise, I know that you will find something helpful at the turn of every page in the book. Don't discount a particular concept or description presented. Instead, use the contents of the book as a structured review. You'll learn *or relearn* the basic rules of genealogical evidence and how to use your "critical thinking skills" to evaluate the source materials that you find. You will learn to look more deeply into basic record types, such as vital or civil records and censuses, and you will discover and understand other, more advanced record types that perhaps you have never used. You will undoubtedly encounter "brick walls" that may stymie your research. Yes, they can be frustrating, but they don't have to bring your research to a standstill. When you reach an impasse, return to the chapter(s) that includes information about records that are likely to provide you with answers. Alternate record types are nearly always available to provide another source of information. You may also find help to circumnavigate your brick walls in the book, *Advanced Genealogy Research Techniques* (McGraw-Hill, 2013), which I wrote with my partner Drew Smith. In it we explore many ways of approaching daunting research problems.

You are embarking on a fascinating genealogical research odyssey that may last the rest of your life. Along the way you will meet many wonderful people and visit some fascinating places. You also will come to know your ancestors and their families as real people—*and* as close personal friends. It is my fervent hope that your research will be successful and that your family tree will prove to be a fruitful source of information to help you better understand your family origins. I also hope that you will share the stories with your family, friends, and other genealogists. I know from more than 50 years of personal experience that you'll have an exciting and gratifying journey. I continue to learn something new each and every day, and I know that you will too.

Happy hunting!
George G. Morgan

Acknowledgments

Every book is a labor of love, but it also is hard work. A book about genealogy certainly involves complicated research, analysis and descriptions of materials, and discussions of successful research methodologies. The author also must rely on other people in order to bring the book to fruition. I would be remiss if I didn't extend my sincere thanks to the generous people who helped me on many levels.

This is my fifth book for McGraw-Hill. The publication team could not have been more helpful, supportive, and professional in every way. I first want to thank Roger Stewart, editorial director at McGraw-Hill Professional, for his friendly counsel throughout the writing and production process. His intelligence and wit have helped to inspire me. Amanda Russell is the editorial coordinator who has juggled the details and cheerfully answered so many of my questions.

Janet Walden is the editorial supervisor who efficiently reviewed and coordinated the editing of my manuscript. She certainly helped smooth the final product.

Drew Smith has been the technical editor for all four additions of this book. His meticulous attention to the technical details has been wonderful. He has helped ensure that the URLs included are correct and current. Furthermore, I have to thank him for his help with the chapter on DNA for genealogy. He is an expert, and I keep learning more from him every day.

I want to thank Bill McManus, the copy editor who has worked on the second, third, and fourth editions of this book. That continuity, his great editorial skills, and the very logical questions he has posed throughout the process have resulted in a more highly polished book.

I also want to thank the following people for sharing documents, photographs, and images for use in the book: Susan Jones, Peter Frank, Lourdes Sanchez Merrow, Karen Roth, Drew Smith, and Jeff Smith. Their contributions are great complementary materials for the book. Thanks to Ed Zapletal at Moorshead Magazines, Ltd., for allowing me to include the material I had written about the Genealogical Proof Standard in the book. Thanks to Diane Haddad at *Family Tree Magazine* for allowing the use of their great genealogy forms.

I would like to thank Drew, Karen, Penny, Peter, and Carey for their moral support through the writing process. And finally, a big thanks to my many, many genealogy friends around the world who so generously share their knowledge, experience, and warm support.

PART I

Begin Your Family History Odyssey

1

What Is Genealogy?

HOW TO...

- Understand the difference between genealogy and family history
- Assess what constitutes a family
- Consider the different motivations of genealogists
- Incorporate documentary hearsay, and genetic evidence

We live in fast-paced times and are inundated by information of all types. Our jobs and other influences often take us far away from where we were born and where our families may still live. Since geographic distances can impose communication breaks between us and other family members, it is normal for us to sometimes feel the need to know more about ourselves and to reconnect with the history of the people in our families and with the simpler times, places, and events in which they lived.

Genealogy is fast becoming one of the most popular hobbies in the English-speaking world. This is becoming more evident with the huge audience responses to recent television series such as *Who Do You Think You Are?* in the United States, the United Kingdom, and elsewhere, *Genealogy Roadshow, Faces of America,* and Finding Your Roots in the United States, and other genealogy-related television programs produced and broadcast elsewhere. Baby Boomers, as they reach retirement age, are finally finding the time to trace their family history and are becoming immersed in their research.

Understand the Difference Between Genealogy and Family History

Don't be intimidated by the term "genealogy." The word is derived from Latin and Greek and simply means the study of a line of descent. And genealogy is nothing new. The aristocrats in ancient China carefully documented their male family lines in genealogies referred to as *jia pu*. Egyptian royalty detailed their familial histories and relationships, and these are often documented in hieroglyphics carved into stone or on clay tablets or painted onto wet plaster (see Figure 1-1).

FIGURE 1-1 The Saqqara Tablet contains a list of Egyptian pharaohs. It was found in the tomb of a priest by the name of Tjenry, who lived during the reign of Ramesses II.

It was important for royalty and aristocratic families in Europe to document their family lines in order to determine the rights of succession and the validity of an heir to inherit. The terms *genealogy* and *family history* are often used interchangeably. While they may seem similar, there actually is a distinction between them:

- Genealogy is the scholarly study of a family's line of descent from its ancestors, during which one develops an understanding of the family's historical context and documents its history and traditions.
- Family history is the study of a family's history and traditions over an extended period of time and may involve documenting some or all of the facts.

A family historian may seek to trace and document specific family members or a branch of the family, and to perhaps write a family history. A genealogist, on the other hand, typically has a much broader view of the family. He or she traces an entire or extended family structure, including brothers, sisters, aunts, uncles, and cousins. This includes both their ancestors (the persons from whom they are descended) and their own descendants. The genealogist actively seeks documentary evidence of many types to prove and verify facts about the family. In addition, the genealogist seeks to place family members and ancestors into geographical, historical, and social context in order to better understand their lives. The genealogist also documents the sources of all the evidence he or she finds, using standard source citations.

In actuality, those of us who are eager to learn as much as possible about our families and our ancestors will combine both genealogy and family history research. This approach will provide us with detailed biographical information to actually bring these people's lives into focus.

Assess What Constitutes a Family

The simplest concept of a traditional nuclear family has been considered to include a father, a mother, and children. However, a modern family can consist of any number of combinations of individuals:

- A single parent and one or more children
- A stepparent and one or more children

- A grandparent and one or more children
- One or more grandparents, or a father-in-law or mother-in-law, living with the family
- An aunt or uncle, and perhaps cousins
- One or more foster parents
- A same-sex couple, perhaps with one or more either natural children or ones that the couple has adopted
- Any family unit with adoptees

As you can see, the living arrangements are many, and the interpersonal relationships between the people in a household can be complex. People don't always have to be related by blood to be components of a "family." However, these are still family groups that need to be represented, as they exist, and need to be documented as part of your family history.

Motivations for Genealogical Research

We *are* the product of our ancestry in many different ways. Certainly genetics play a critical part in our physical makeup, determining our physical characteristics and potential susceptibility to medical conditions, both physical and mental. However, the circumstances of place, time, physical environment, education, economics, experiences, family group dynamics, social influences, and interactions with the personalities of our family members and friends also distinctly influence our development. These other influences will all contribute to the overall person that we become. The family stories and traditions that we have observed and that have been passed from generation to generation contribute to our sense of kinship and belonging. It is no wonder that we want to explore, maintain, document, and preserve these stories and traditions. Documentary evidence is still the most significant resource used in genealogical research, but genetic genealogy has rapidly become another component in the genealogist's toolkit. We will examine and discuss all of these types of research evidence throughout the book.

Why are so many people interested in their family history? There are certainly many motivations for genealogical research. Here are the most common ones:

- **Create a sense of belonging**   Some people trace their ancestry to help understand their place in the family.
- **Document family traditions**   The term *family tradition* has multiple meanings for genealogists. In one sense, it refers to such things as why a particular holiday is celebrated, why certain foods are or are not eaten, or why members dressed in particular clothing or styles. Family tradition can also refer to family stories that are passed on from one family member to another. You might refer to these as the "family legends."

- **Join heritage or lineage societies**   Some people study and document a family's direct line of descent in order to link to some famous group of people. Often this is done in order to join one or more of the lineage or heritage societies, such as the Daughters of the American Revolution, the General Society of Mayflower Descendants, or the First Fleet Fellowship.
- **Research ethnic origins**   There is a great deal of interest in tracing the place of origin of a family line, the racial origins, or religious background.
- **Document medical history**   Many people may research their family members' data for reasons such as to discover the family's medical history. This may help project possible longevity or provide clues to susceptibility to specific medical conditions that recur in a family line.
- **Locate heirs**   Some people, including family members and legal professionals, perform research to trace living people who are descended from specific individuals. This may be done to reconnect family members or to trace individuals who may be entitled to inherit from an estate.
- **Locate birth parents**   Adoptees frequently are interested in identifying and perhaps connecting with their birth parents. Adoption laws in some places seek to protect the identities of birth parents by preventing anyone from accessing original birth records without approval of a court of law.
- **Pursue paternity/maternity claims**   Genealogical research, including genetic tests, is used to establish and document relationships between children and their birth father or mother. This may provide documentary proof for use in civil court cases.
- **Document ownership of property**   There are many people who are interested in the history of their property or home. They may therefore perform genealogical research into land and property records, census documents, and other historical materials in order to determine the names and biographical information of the people who previously may have owned the property.
- **Conduct historical or social research**   Scholars and historians often perform genealogical research in order to learn more about a particular area's historical background and the people who lived there.
- **Perform background research**   Authors frequently investigate details about places and individuals living in a place at a particular time as background for their books or magazine articles. Writers and producers of video productions, particularly biographical and historical documentaries, perform background research in order to ensure that details are correct.

You can now begin to understand that there are many types of people who are doing research of a genealogical or family history nature. They are ordinary citizens of all ages, historians, sociologists, anthropologists and archaeologists, legal personnel and paralegals, land and property clerks, government officials, adoptees, and potential heirs. It also includes people like us who are interested in learning more about our ancestors and their places in history. Whatever *your* reasons for tracing and investigating your own family's history, your search will lead you on a fascinating and exciting journey of discovery. Don't be surprised if your quest lasts a lifetime.

Documentary, Hearsay, and Genetic Evidence

The term *evidence* is one we will discuss a great deal throughout the book. As a genealogist or family history researcher, you are always looking for details about individuals. These details can come in many forms. Human beings love to write about themselves, and their administrative governments delight in gathering statistical information. Paper records that were created at various times during our ancestors' lives, by both them *and* other people, constitute documentary evidence. They may include letters and notes, diaries, and other written materials written by your ancestors and their families or friends. They may also include more formal documents generated by government authorities for a wide variety of purposes. These might include census records, birth, marriage, or death documents, land and property documents, court records, wills and probate records, and many more. Figure 1-2 shows a marriage record from a county marriage book from 1866.

Hearsay evidence is that which is typically shared verbally between individuals. A prime example might be a family story passed from generation to generation. ("Family tradition has it that Grandfather Holder fought in the Civil War.") This type of evidence is typically considered much less reliable than other types because the facts can become distorted with the retelling of the story over time.

DNA testing has become an important part of the genealogical research process over the last decade. Its reliability in proving genetic familial relationships provides methods for confirming documentary evidence already collected or identifying matches with other related family members.

All of these types of evidence provide details about your ancestors and their lives. Some pieces of evidence are more reliable than others. In some cases, you will find that some information found on the Internet is reliable, but that other online information may be problematic in some respect. You will learn more in the coming chapters, however, about many different kinds of evidence and how to use your critical thinking skills to effectively evaluate them, so that they help build your knowledge of your family.

Now that you have a better understanding of what genealogy is, let's get started on our genealogical journey!

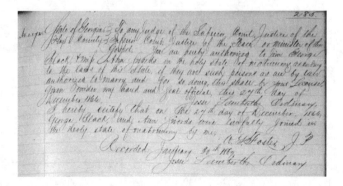

FIGURE 1-2   A marriage record from Floyd County, Georgia, documenting the matrimony between George Black and Ann Swords on 27 December 1866.

2

How Do I Get Started?

HOW TO...

- Start at the beginning with yourself and work backward in time through your ancestors
- Discover sources of information in your own home
- Understand what types of records and materials can help you learn more
- Interview all your relatives
- Begin to organize what you find

Most people begin their family history odyssey in a very casual way. You may have seen a photograph or heard a story about some member of the family and found it interesting, and you wanted to learn more about that person or their immediate family. You probably asked more questions, or you began to seek more information in the form of letters and postcards, additional photographs, or some other type of material. Perhaps you even wrote down what you learned in some chronological order so that you could get a clearer understanding about the person or their family.

My own genealogical research began on a cold, snowy January day in my North Carolina hometown when I was nine years old. While snowfall was not unusual, a six-inch accumulation was rare indeed. There was no school scheduled for several days, and I spent the days at the home of my aunt, Mary Allen Morgan, and my grandmother, Minnie [*sic*, Laura Augusta] Morgan while my parents worked. Both women had a strong sense of family and history, especially my grandmother, who was 88 at the time. She was the daughter and granddaughter of prominent physicians in Mecklenburg County, North Carolina. She was also the great great granddaughter of two North Carolina Revolutionary War patriots. One of these was John McKnitt Alexander, the secretary of the group of citizens in Mecklenburg County who formed the provincial committee that crafted and signed the fabled Mecklenburg Declaration of Independence on 20 May 1775. The other was Major John Davidson, a Revolutionary War military leader after whose family Davidson College was named.

On that snowy day, the three of us gathered at a handmade drop-leaf table dating back to the 1740s and these ladies proceeded to educate me about our family history. Using a roll of brown parcel paper, a ruler, and pencils, we began drawing a family tree. Fortunately for me, my grandmother was a packrat and had saved generations' worth of materials. To construct our family tree, we used family Bibles, one of which bears a publication date of 1692 in Edinburgh, Scotland; family letters, postcards, and Christmas cards dating back to the late 1930s; a group of old deeds and wills; and *The History of Mecklenburg County from 1740 to 1900* by J. B. Alexander, published in 1902. My grandmother was born in January 1873, and she readily related family stories and anecdotal information dating back to her own childhood. She talked about her parents, about her brothers and sisters, and about the current events of her time. Her recollections of inventions and her perspectives of the times through which she lived were fascinating. Needless to say, I became hooked, and subsequent visits involved my appeals to both my grandmother and my aunt to "Tell me about when you were a little girl." I have since spent more than five decades in my own quest for more and more information about all branches of my family's origins and history. A day does not go by that I don't locate a new piece of evidence or discover something I might have missed in the past. It truly is a journey of discovery each and every day.

Start at the Beginning: Yourself and Your Family

You will want to start your own genealogical journey with yourself and what you know, and then work your way backward in time. Along the way you will want to collect documentation to verify every fact *and* keep track of where and when you obtained every piece of this evidence. (We will discuss types of evidentiary documents throughout the book and the process of documentation in more detail in Chapter 4.)

A typical research path for you to follow would begin with the following information:

Yourself   Obtain a copy of your own birth certificate. This document provides you with the date and location of your birth, sometimes even the time of birth, and often includes information about your physical characteristics at birth, such as weight, length, and hair and eye color. It also may indicate the names of your parents, their race (and/or nationality), their ages at the time of the event, the name of the physician or midwife attending the birth, and possibly additional details. The content of a birth certificate will vary depending on when and where the document was created. Later certificates may contain more information.

- Birth certificates can be obtained in the United States from county health departments, state bureaus of statistics, or other governmental agencies. Check the VitalRec.com website at **http://vitalrec.com** for information about each state and territory and where to make contact to locate and obtain document copies.

- The Births and Deaths Registration Act of 1836 was passed in England by Parliament. As a result, civil registration of births, marriages, and deaths in England and Wales began on 1 July 1837. The General Register Office (GRO), a division of Her Majesty's Passport Office, holds a copy of all of these registrations centrally. The GRO website is located at **http://www.gro.gov.uk/gro/content/certificates/default.asp**. You can order copies of all these certificates there. A central index is held at The National Archives (TNA) in Kew, in south-west London. Local County Records's Offices (CROs) across England and Wales also hold copies of their records registered since 1837. The indexes to the civil registrations of births, marriages, and deaths are also available through Ancestry.com in the UK at **http://www.ancestry.co.uk**, findmypast **http://www.findmypast.com**, FreeBMD at **http://www.freebmd.org.uk**, and MyHeritage at **http://www.myheritage.com**.
- The National Records of Scotland (NRS) is located in Edinburgh and is the contact point for birth, marriage, and death certificates. You may check their website at **http://www.nrscotland.gov.uk** for more information.
- The General Register Office (GRO) for Ireland in Dublin is the depository for many birth, marriage, and death records and other documents. You will want to visit their website at **http://www.welfare.ie/en/Pages/General-Register-Office.aspx** and click the link labeled Research.
- The General Register Office of Northern Ireland (GRONI) is the repository for many different record types, including birth, adoption, marriage, civil partnership, and death certificates. These can be ordered for various time periods at the nidirect government services website at **http://www.nidirect.gov.uk/gro**.
- In Canada, the responsibility for the civil registration of births, marriages, and deaths lies with each province or territory. The Library and Archives Canada (LAC) website at **http://www.collectionscanada.gc.ca** provides links to a vast collection of Canadian genealogical resources grouped into categories, including links to provincial and territorial archives, libraries, and other repositories.
- Like Canada, responsibility for civil registration in Australia lies with the state or territory. The Society of Australian Genealogists (SAG) has produced an excellent web page concerning Australian civil registration at **http://www.sag.org.au**.
- If you are researching vital records or civil registration in other countries, you may want to use your favorite Internet search engine and enter the type of document and the name of the country. As an example, I entered the phrase **"death certificate" + singapore** and was rewarded with a link to the Immigration & Checkpoints Authority (ICA) and its web page at **http://www.ica.gov.sg**, at which I located a link to "Birth/Death registration services," and then to the eXtracts Online system that allows you to submit online applications to search for and obtain birth and death extract applications since 1872. (See **https://extracts.ica.gov.sg/extracts/index.xhtml**.)
- Another excellent reference for you when seeking vital records or civil registration records worldwide is Thomas J. Kemp's book, *International Vital Records Handbook* (6th edition), published by Genealogical Publishing Company (2013).

Your Parents   Learn as much about your parents as possible. Obtain copies of their birth certificates, their marriage license, and any other documents possible. Your mother's maiden name will appear on birth and marriage documents, school records, and sometimes others, and will be an essential part of your research. Please note that her maiden name may not appear on a marriage document for a second or subsequent marriage. Ask questions to learn where your parents grew up, where they went to school, where they lived at every point in their lives, what religious affiliation they have had and the names and addresses of the religious institutions they attended, where they were married, what jobs they may have had, what their hobbies and interests are, and anything else you can learn. Take copious notes along the way because this may be the only opportunity you have to gather these important family details. Obtain a copy of the death certificate if a parent is deceased, and seek to obtain copies of any obituaries and funeral notices. You will learn a great deal about all of these documents later in the book.

Siblings   Obtain a copy of the birth certificate for each of your brothers and sisters. In addition, obtain any other documents that may have been created for them. Your lives are inextricably linked, and the information you learn about them may reveal other research paths for you.

Aunts and Uncles   Your research will extend to your parents' siblings as well. You will want to learn as much about their family groups as you can. After all, the family structure and dynamics can be important in learning more about the factors that influenced your life. In addition, other family records may have passed to those families rather than to yours.

Cousins   Regardless of the family relationship with your cousins, close or distant, try to learn as much about them as possible. They are tangible extensions of your family's line too.

Grandparents   Obtain copies of documents for your parents' parents too. You are also tracing your line of descent from these people and want to know as much as possible about them.

Continue expanding outward as far as you can to learn about other family members, their spouses, their parents, and their children. Don't worry if you can't locate information or obtain all the documents on everyone. This is an ongoing process and, as you progress through this book, you will learn more about how to extend your research reach and locate more and more information. Part of what we do, as genealogists, is to fill in gaps in the informational puzzle in order to create a larger picture.

Discover Sources of Information in Your Own Home

Your quest for family information should begin in familiar territory. Start with what you know and work backward in time. It is probable that you have in your own home or in the homes of your parents, grandparents, and other family members any number of resources that can help you document your family. Take time to consider the following home source materials that you might find around your home and what information they may provide.

Vital Records and Civil Registration Records

There are a large number of different documentary records that record milestone life events. They include birth certificates, marriage licenses and certificates, civil partnership documents, divorce decrees, and death certificates issued by governmental agencies. Among the death certificates are included records of stillbirths, although these documents may not be readily accessible.

In the United States, these documents are typically referred to as vital records. Throughout the current and former nations of the British Commonwealth, they are referred to as civil registration records, or BMDs (birth, marriage, and death records). The term "civil registration records" is also used to designate these types of government-issued records in many other areas of the world, including Central Europe, Mexico, Central and South America, Africa, the Philippines, and elsewhere.

Examples of a birth certificate and a death certificate are shown in Figures 2-1 and 2-2.

The vital or civil registration records documents issued by governmental entities may or may not contain completely accurate information. A death certificate, for example, will provide the details of an individual's death, such as name, date, gender, cause of death, and the location where the death occurred. This data may or may not be 100 percent correct; however, it is considered to be the official record of the death. Likewise, a coroner's report or the report of an inquest will provide what is deemed the official report on the death.

Other information found on a death certificate, such as the individual's date of birth, parents' names, occupation, and other personal data unrelated to the death, may or may not be correct. A family member or some other individual who may be familiar with the deceased typically provides this information to the official who is completing the form, and that informant may or may not have had accurate details. In addition, the person completing the form may have made errors in recording or transcribing the information provided. As a result, the details unrelated to the individual's death should be viewed with some skepticism until you have verified them with other independently created sources that were created at or near the time of the event, such as a birth, occurred. We will discuss this in greater detail in Chapter 4.

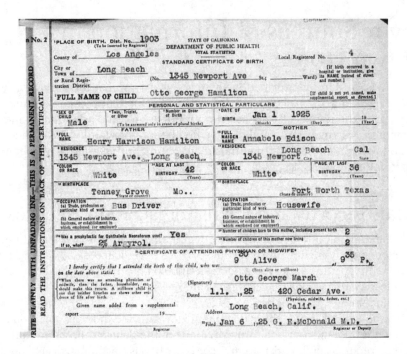

FIGURE 2-1   Birth certificates can provide essential clues for date and location of birth, names of parents, and other facts.

Religious Records

Ecclesiastical records are often found in the home. Certificates of baptism, christening, and confirmation or records of a bar mitzvah or bat mitzvah may be found among family papers. Documents of marriage issued by the church, as opposed to a government-issued marriage license or certificate, may be among the family's treasured documents. Look also for church programs or bulletins issued at the time of and/or commemorating an important occasion, because these may contain names of relatives and other information. These events may also be recorded in the religious organization's files or archives, along with more detailed accounts of the events and participants. Other congregation publications might include a commemorative congregational history, photographs, newsletters, and other materials.

Personal or Family Bible

Pages containing birth, marriage, death, christening, confirmation, baptism, and other events are commonly included in Bibles. Your ancestors or family members may have entered detailed information themselves. You also may find other materials tucked inside a Bible, such as letters, postcards, greeting cards, newspaper clippings, photographs, obituaries, funeral cards, bookmarks, and other items considered special or important to the owner. These may provide invaluable clues to other locations

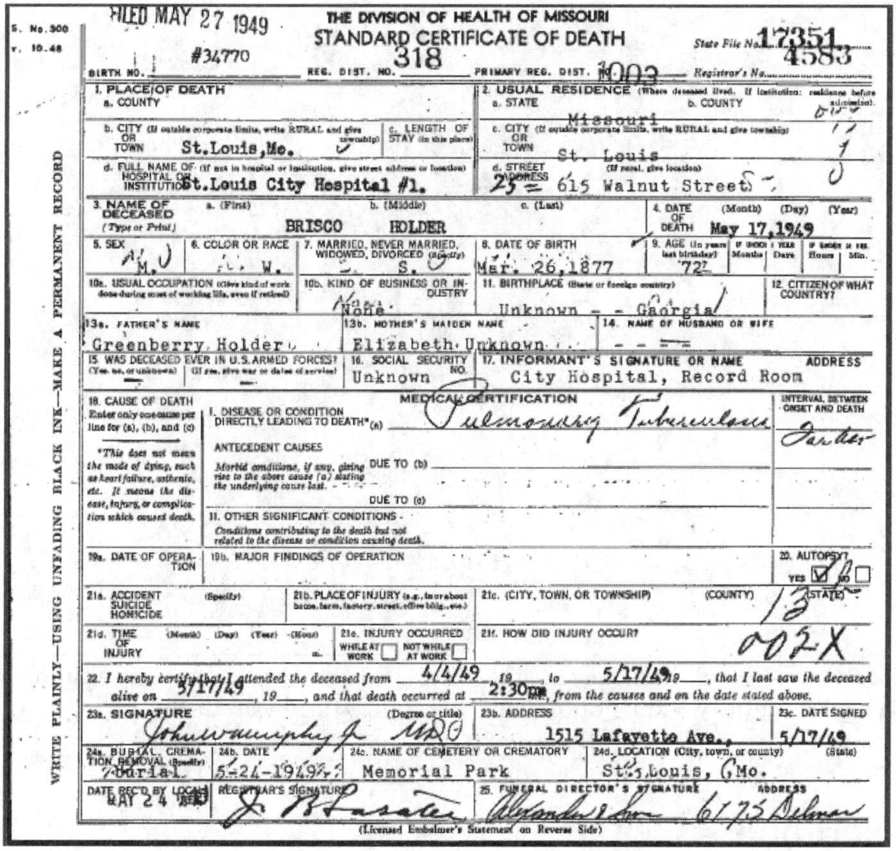

S. No. 300
R. 10-48
FILED MAY 27 1949
THE DIVISION OF HEALTH OF MISSOURI
STANDARD CERTIFICATE OF DEATH
State File No. 17351
4583
BIRTH NO. #34770
REG. DIST. NO. 318
PRIMARY REG. DIST. NO. 1003
Registrar's No.

1. PLACE OF DEATH
a. COUNTY
b. CITY OR TOWN (If outside corporate limits, write RURAL and give township) St. Louis, Mo.
c. LENGTH OF STAY (in this place)
d. FULL NAME OF HOSPITAL OR INSTITUTION (If not in hospital or institution, give street address or location) St. Louis City Hospital #1.

2. USUAL RESIDENCE (Where deceased lived. If institution: residence before admission)
a. STATE Missouri
b. COUNTY
c. CITY OR TOWN (If outside corporate limits, write RURAL and give township) St. Louis
d. STREET ADDRESS (If rural, give location) 615 Walnut Street

3. NAME OF DECEASED (Type or Print) a. (First) BRISCO b. (Middle) c. (Last) HOLDER
4. DATE OF DEATH (Month) (Day) (Year) May 17, 1949
5. SEX M.
6. COLOR OR RACE W.
7. MARRIED, NEVER MARRIED, WIDOWED, DIVORCED (Specify) S.
8. DATE OF BIRTH Mar. 26, 1877
9. AGE (In years last birthday) 72
10a. USUAL OCCUPATION (Give kind of work done during most of working life, even if retired)
10b. KIND OF BUSINESS OR INDUSTRY None
11. BIRTHPLACE (State or foreign country) Unknown - - Georgia
12. CITIZEN OF WHAT COUNTRY?
13a. FATHER'S NAME Greenberry Holder
13b. MOTHER'S MAIDEN NAME Elizabeth Unknown
14. NAME OF HUSBAND OR WIFE - - -
15. WAS DECEASED EVER IN U.S. ARMED FORCES? (Yes, no, or unknown) (If yes, give war or dates of service)
16. SOCIAL SECURITY NO. Unknown
17. INFORMANT'S SIGNATURE OR NAME ADDRESS City Hospital, Record Room

MEDICAL CERTIFICATION
18. CAUSE OF DEATH Enter only one cause per line for (a), (b), and (c)
I. DISEASE OR CONDITION DIRECTLY LEADING TO DEATH* (a) Pulmonary Tuberculosis
INTERVAL BETWEEN ONSET AND DEATH
ANTECEDENT CAUSES
Morbid conditions, if any, giving rise to the above cause (a) stating the underlying cause last.
DUE TO (b)
DUE TO (c)
*This does not mean the mode of dying, such as heart failure, asthenia, etc. It means the disease, injury, or complication which caused death.
II. OTHER SIGNIFICANT CONDITIONS - Conditions contributing to the death but not related to the disease or condition causing death.
19a. DATE OF OPERATION
19b. MAJOR FINDINGS OF OPERATION
20. AUTOPSY? YES NO
21a. ACCIDENT SUICIDE HOMICIDE (Specify)
21b. PLACE OF INJURY (e.g., in or about home, farm, factory, street, office bldg., etc.)
21c. (CITY, TOWN, OR TOWNSHIP) (COUNTY) (STATE)
21d. TIME OF INJURY (Month) (Day) (Year) (Hour) m.
21e. INJURY OCCURRED WHILE AT WORK NOT WHILE AT WORK
21f. HOW DID INJURY OCCUR?
22. I hereby certify that I attended the deceased from 4/4/49, 19__, to 5/17/49, 19__, that I last saw the deceased alive on 5/17/49, 19__, and that death occurred at 2:30 pm, from the causes and on the date stated above.
23a. SIGNATURE (Degree or title) MD
23b. ADDRESS 1515 Lafayette Ave.
23c. DATE SIGNED 5/17/49
24a. BURIAL, CREMATION, REMOVAL (Specify) Burial
24b. DATE 5-24-1949
24c. NAME OF CEMETERY OR CREMATORY Memorial Park
24d. LOCATION (City, town, or county) (State) St. Louis, Mo.
DATE REC'D BY LOCAL REG. MAY 24
REGISTRAR'S SIGNATURE
25. FUNERAL DIRECTOR'S SIGNATURE ADDRESS 6175 Delmar
(Licensed Embalmer's Statement on Reverse Side)
WRITE PLAINLY—USING UNFADING BLACK INK—MAKE A PERMANENT RECORD

FIGURE 2-2 A death certificate provides detailed information about a person's death.

where family information may be found. In one family Bible, I found a page listing the wedding guests at my grandmother's first wedding on 2 February 1898. (See Figure 2-3.) Another page revealed a listing of the bridegroom's death just five months later from "that dreaded disease typhoid fever." (See Figure 2-4.)

Photograph Albums

Family albums may contain photographs and many other types of family memorabilia. If you are very fortunate, someone will have labeled the photos with the name(s) of the subject(s), the location, and the date on which the picture was taken. If not, be prepared to spend time with other family members and try to identify and label the pictures. This can be an enjoyable experience for everyone and especially rewarding for you as a genealogist. Photographs are keys to understanding your family's history and can be used to help place your ancestors and family members in geographical, social, and historical context.

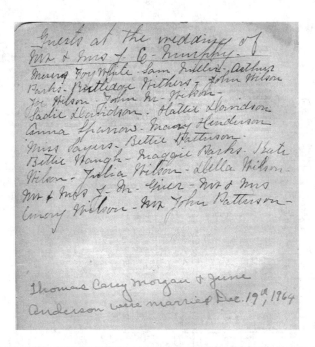

FIGURE 2-3   A personal Bible may include interesting details, such as this example in which the guests at the wedding of Mr. and Mrs. J. E. Murphy are listed.

Scrapbooks

A scrapbook often presents a chronicle of life events for an individual or for an entire family group. Newspaper clippings can point you to additional sources for more information and documents. Programs of recitals, plays, sports events, and other occasions may reveal a family member's talents or interests. Obituaries, such as the one shown in Figure 2-5, are full of family history pointers and are often included in scrapbooks or memory books. While an obituary may be undated and the newspaper in which it was published might not be known, the value of the clues found in the obituary can be enormous.

Letters and Postcards

Family correspondence is an important chronicle of life events. Letters may provide first-hand accounts of births, graduations, weddings, funerals, and other family occasions. You may uncover details about a person's everyday life, trips they made, their problems and concerns, and news about other family members. Here you may learn more about personal characteristics and family relationships than anywhere else. A return address in the body of a letter, such as in the example shown in Figure 2-6, on

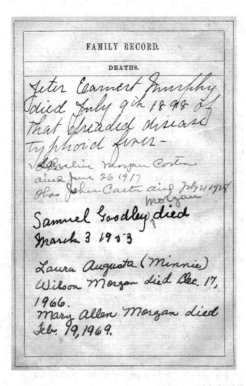

FIGURE 2-4   Jeter Earnest Murphy, the bridegroom at the marriage documented in Figure 2-3, died of typhoid fever just five months and one week after the wedding.

the original envelope, or on a postcard may provide an invaluable clue to locating other records about these family members at the time the communiqué was mailed.

Postcards can also contribute significant information. A vintage picture postcard sent by an ancestor or family member may include a photograph of some feature of their hometown on the face side, and this provides a great visual image of the place where they lived. A postcard sent while on a vacation or family trip may include names of places visited and individuals met, even in the form of a dated postmark. These may provide clues to point you in the direction of records about those people.

Diaries and Journals

Everyday life events and often an individual's innermost thoughts are to be found in diaries and journals. Our ancestors often spent more time recording the details of their lives than we do today, and these cherished volumes can be real treasure troves for the family historian. Even a calendar or appointment book can paint the picture of a person's daily life, and someone's personal telephone book can be invaluable for tracing other relatives and friends, along with their records.

F. M. Stocks, Pioneer
Resident of Atlanta,
Dies at Residence

Francis M. Stocks, a pioneer resident of Atlanta and one of the city's most prominent men, died at 4 o'clock Wednesday afternoon at his home on Piedmont road at the age of 68 years.

Mr. Stocks came to Atlanta in 1880, was founder and proprietor of the Stocks Coal company, and conducted a prosperous business for 38 years. He was a Christian gentleman and a member of the Walker Street M. E. church since he first came to Atlanta. He was always ready to give to charitable work and to help those in need.

Mr. Stocks had a slight stroke of paralysis seven years ago, when his wife died, and has never been himself since. In April he had his second stroke, and he had been very low until his death Wednesday.

He is survived by five children, Thomas F. Stocks, Miss Nellie Stocks, Mrs. Gerald G. Hannah, Mrs. Alvis M. Weatherly of Birmingham, and Mrs. W. Watts Morgan, and two brothers, James D. Stocks and William H. Stocks.

Funeral arrangements will be announced later.

FIGURE 2-5 Obituaries, such as this one, are often found in scrapbooks. This one provided important details of the arrival in Atlanta, employment, cause of death, place of interment, and names of other family members.

Sept. 26-44
526 Grafton Ave
Dayton 6 - Ohio

Dear Della -
Your letter came while I was in Hospital, two weeks ago — Had Two Blood Transfusions and am considerably better than

FIGURE 2-6 A return address on a letter, its envelope, or a postcard from a family member may point to the geographical area where they lived and where other documents are to be found.

Accounting journals for a family farm or business may paint a detailed picture of the lifestyle of the family at the time, the crops and livestock they raised, the costs of supplies and clothing, and weather patterns, to name a few. During the time of slavery in the United States and elsewhere, the names of slaves may have been listed, along with information about their births, marriages, deaths, and other events, in a farm or plantation ledger.

Family Histories

An ancestor or another member of the family may already have prepared an historical account of a portion of the family's history. That doesn't mean that your work is already done for you, by the way. It merely means that you have a ready-made path to follow and to re-prove the facts and hypotheses already set forth by the other researcher. Your predecessor investigator may have made errors, incorrectly analyzed some piece of evidence, or drawn the wrong conclusions. It is therefore important that you recheck the information by *personally* examining the evidence, evaluating the facts, and developing your own hypotheses.

Local Histories

Don't overlook books, manuscripts, pamphlets, and other materials that focus on the area where your ancestors and family members have lived. These may be in the family collection because of the area and also because information about the family may be included. In J.B. Alexander's *The History of Mecklenburg County from 1740 to 1900*, published in Charlotte, North Carolina, in 1902, I was rewarded not only with a biographical sketch of my great-great-grandfather, Isaac Wilson, M.D., but also with probably the only surviving photographic image of the man. Figure 2-7 shows two facing pages from that book.

Baby Books

The joy of the arrival of a child is recorded in baby books in great detail by parents, guardians, grandparents, and others. You may find that baby books contain photographs, descriptive notations, receipts, snippets of hair, and a diverse group of materials that may provide clues to other types of evidence. They may even include information about the names of previous generations or a simple family tree. The baby book page shown in Figure 2-8 includes photographs that show a couple at the church at which their daughter was baptized. The location and the date of 2 December 1945 may direct you to church records. Those, in turn, may provide you with the child's date of birth and more details about the parents. The father created the artwork and labeling on the page. You may find important clues to other materials and their locations in these little books that have been kept by the family.

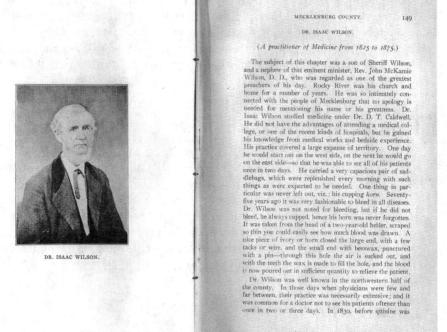

FIGURE 2-7   Local histories may provide ancestors' biographical details found nowhere else.

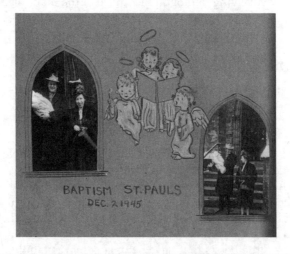

FIGURE 2-8   Baby books contain photographs, documents, and informative notations that may lead you to other materials.

Marriage Books and Photograph Albums

A wedding provides an ideal occasion for the gathering of families and for the creation of often-vivid records. Matrimonial registers signed by attendees, photograph albums, wedding gift lists, thank-you card lists with names and addresses, and other records may provide excellent resources for your further research. You also may find the original marriage license or church-issued marriage certificate, and copies of other documents from the couple's religious institution(s) to help document the event. These can often lead you back to the congregational membership rolls, and these can frequently be used to trace family members' movements from place to place over time.

Funeral Books and Memorial Cards

Mortuaries and funeral homes have long provided families of the deceased with a funeral or memory book. These can be rich in untapped detail. The name of the deceased and the dates of birth and death are included, as well as the date and place of any services, and the place of interment. A copy of death notices, obituaries, and funeral notices may be included. The register of persons who attended the visitation or wake will include family members' names and signatures, confirming their presence at the time. An examination of the register may help you reveal the married names of female relatives. In addition, the list of active and honorary pallbearers, as shown in Figure 2-9, should be studied to determine if family members were tapped to participate.

Cards such as the one shown in Figure 2-10 are often distributed at funerals and memorial services. They may commemorate the vital dates of the deceased and/or provide the text for a prayer to be read in unison by participants in the service. The name and location of the funeral home or religious institution that may be printed on the card can provide contact information to potentially locate additional material.

Identification Documents

You might find a number of identification documents that you can use as evidence in your research. A driver's license or passport confirms date of birth, age, physical characteristics, and residence. A Social Security card in the United States can provide an account number that can then be used to obtain a copy of the person's SS-5 application form for a Social Security number. Health service cards, insurance cards, alien registration cards, identity cards, driver's licenses, and other types of identity papers from a variety of sources can provide leads to their issuers for other potentially informative data.

Immigration Papers

On admission to a new country, an immigrant is typically issued some piece of documentation to prove his or her identity. Depending on the country and the

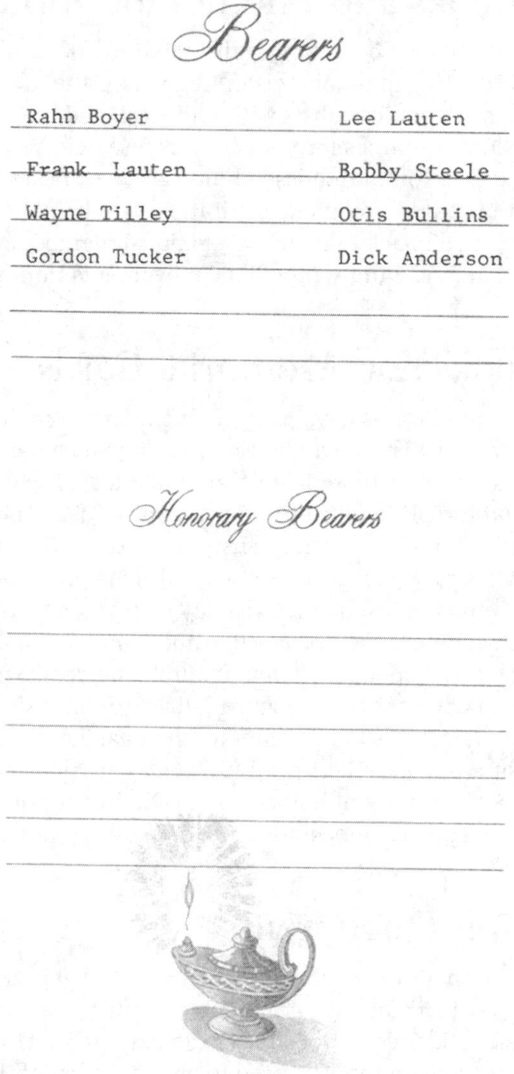

Bearers

Rahn Boyer	Lee Lauten
Frank Lauten	Bobby Steele
Wayne Tilley	Otis Bullins
Gordon Tucker	Dick Anderson

Honorary Bearers

FIGURE 2-9 A page from a funeral book shows the names of pallbearers.

historical time period, this may have been as simple as a letter or as formal as a visa, passport, alien registration card, or another document. In addition, vaccination records may also be located among immigration papers that point to the place of vaccination in the previous country of residence.

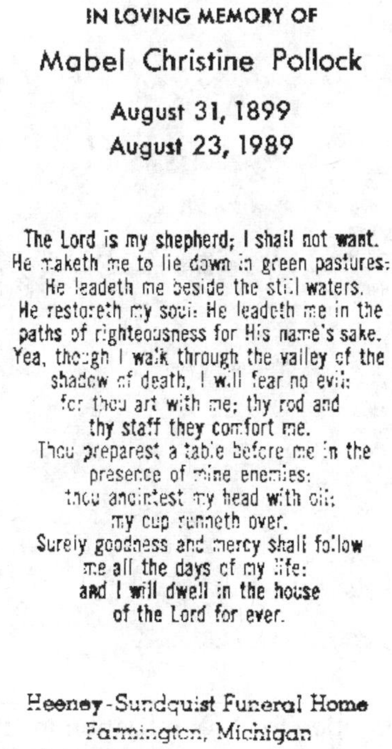

IN LOVING MEMORY OF

Mabel Christine Pollock

August 31, 1899
August 23, 1989

The Lord is my shepherd; I shall not want.
He maketh me to lie down in green pastures:
He leadeth me beside the still waters.
He restoreth my soul: He leadeth me in the
paths of righteousness for His name's sake.
Yea, though I walk through the valley of the
shadow of death, I will fear no evil:
for thou art with me; thy rod and
thy staff they comfort me.
Thou preparest a table before me in the
presence of mine enemies:
thou anointest my head with oil;
my cup runneth over.
Surely goodness and mercy shall follow
me all the days of my life:
and I will dwell in the house
of the Lord for ever.

Heeney-Sundquist Funeral Home
Farmington, Michigan

FIGURE 2-10 A memorial or prayer card may include the name and contact information of a funeral home or church.

Naturalization Papers

Many immigrants took the necessary steps to renounce their original citizenship to become citizens of their new country. Some countries have required multiple documents to facilitate the process. In the United States, for example, an immigrant would swear an oath renouncing any allegiance to any foreign "power, sovereign, or potentate" and then sign a Declaration of Intention document. This was done at a courthouse and was the first step in the process to indicate his or her plan to seek citizenship. After a specific waiting period, the person would file a Petition for Naturalization to initiate the paperwork to verify his or her good residency and employment record, and to formally request to become a naturalized citizen. While the process and the names of the documents vary in different countries, the process is similar.

The applicant or petitioner usually maintains copies of each document associated with their naturalization process and, finally, of the citizenship document. Figure 2-11 shows a United States Certificate of Naturalization. Not only are these treasured

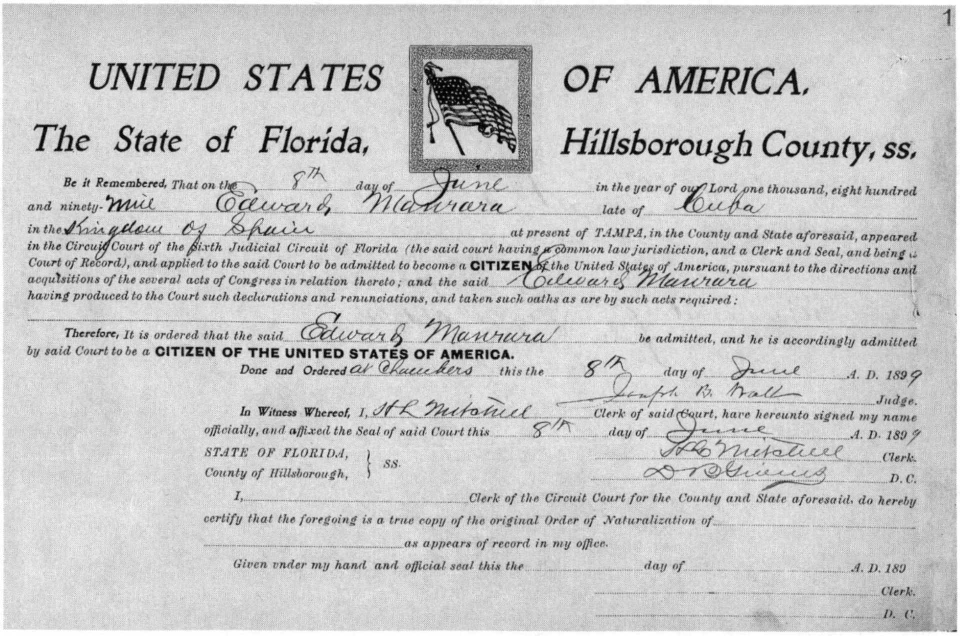

1

UNITED STATES OF AMERICA,

The State of Florida, Hillsborough County, ss.

Be it Remembered, That on the 8th day of June in the year of our Lord one thousand, eight hundred and ninety-nine Edward Manrara late of Cuba in the Kingdom of Spain at present of TAMPA, in the County and State aforesaid, appeared in the Circuit Court of the Sixth Judicial Circuit of Florida (the said court having a common law jurisdiction, and a Clerk and Seal, and being a Court of Record), and applied to the said Court to be admitted to become a CITIZEN of the United States of America, pursuant to the directions and acquisitions of the several acts of Congress in relation thereto; and the said Edward Manrara having produced to the Court such declarations and renunciations, and taken such oaths as are by such acts required:

Therefore, It is ordered that the said Edward Manrara be admitted, and he is accordingly admitted by said Court to be a CITIZEN OF THE UNITED STATES OF AMERICA.

Done and Ordered at Chambers this the 8th day of June A. D. 1899

Joseph B. Wall Judge.

In Witness Whereof, I, H L Mitchell Clerk of said Court, have hereunto signed my name officially, and affixed the Seal of said Court this 8th day of June A. D. 1899

STATE OF FLORIDA, } SS.
County of Hillsborough, }

H L Mitchell Clerk.
D. C. Givens D. C.

I, ________ Clerk of the Circuit Court for the County and State aforesaid, do hereby certify that the foregoing is a true copy of the original Order of Naturalization of ________ as appears of record in my office.

Given under my hand and official seal this the ______ day of ______ A. D. 189

________ Clerk.

________ D. C.

FIGURE 2-11 The completed Petition for Naturalization for Edward Manrara, dated 8 June 1899, in Hillsborough County, Florida, made him a U.S. citizen. (Courtesy of the University of South Florida Digital and Special Collections.)

documents, but they also provide evidence of citizenship that entitles the person to citizenship privileges such as the right to vote in elections.

Land Records

Land and property records provide evidence of land ownership and residence. These are among the most numerous and yet perhaps the least used documents available for genealogical research. They include land grants, deeds, mortgages, agreements of sale, leases, mortgages, abstracts of title, land contracts, bonds, tax notices, tax bills, homestead documents, liens, legal judgments, dower releases, easements and releases, surveys, and other documents. Some of these property instruments provide significant details for your research. For example, the transfer of land from someone who has died may actually include the date of the owner's death, and this can be beneficial, especially if no other formal death documentation was required at the time of the death. A deed may also list the married name of a daughter whose marriage record and married name you may not otherwise be able to locate.

Military Records

Documents related to military service come in a wide range of record types and formats, depending on the location, the time period, the branch of the service, and the type of military unit. Draft registration cards such as the one shown in Figure 2-12, enlistment documents, military service statements, disability certificates, discharge papers, separation papers, and pension records are common. Commendations, medals, ribbons, decorations, uniforms, swords, firearms, and other weapons are more tangible evidence of military service that can point you to official service records.

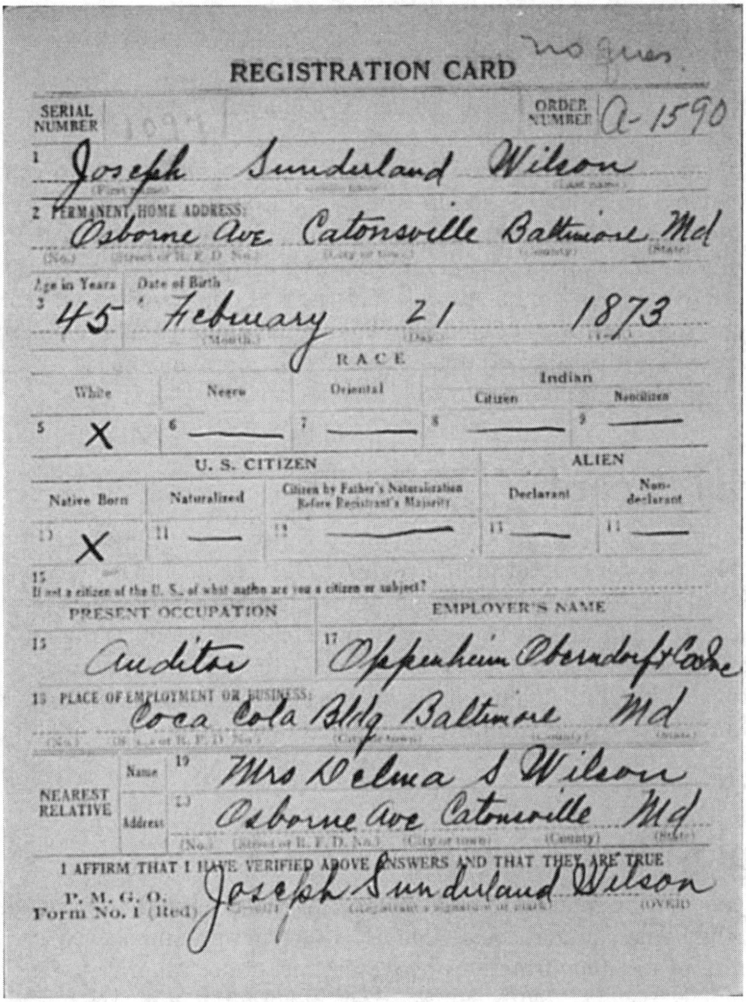
REGISTRATION CARD

SERIAL NUMBER 1097 — ORDER NUMBER A-1590

1 Joseph Sunderland Wilson

2 PERMANENT HOME ADDRESS: Osborne Ave Catonsville Baltimore Md

Age in Years 3 45 — Date of Birth 4 February 21 1873

RACE

White	Negro	Oriental	Indian: Citizen	Indian: Noncitizen
5 X	6 —	7 —	8 —	9 —

U. S. CITIZEN: Native Born	Naturalized	Citizen by Father's Naturalization Before Registrant's Majority	ALIEN: Declarant	Non-declarant
10 X	11 —	12 —	13 —	14 —

15 If not a citizen of the U. S., of what nation are you a citizen or subject?

PRESENT OCCUPATION: 16 Auditor — EMPLOYER'S NAME: 17 Oppenheim Oberndorf & Co

18 PLACE OF EMPLOYMENT OR BUSINESS: Coca Cola Bldg Baltimore Md

NEAREST RELATIVE — Name: 19 Mrs Velma S Wilson — Address: 20 Osborne Ave Catonsville Md

I AFFIRM THAT I HAVE VERIFIED ABOVE ANSWERS AND THAT THEY ARE TRUE

P. M. G. O. Form No. 1 (Red) — Joseph Sunderland Wilson (Registrant's signature or mark) (OVER)

FIGURE 2-12 Military records such as this World War I draft registration card provide details such as birth date, residence, employer, and contact person.

Military regimental histories may also be in the family possession, as may be correspondence between the service person and his or her military branch and with other friends from service. These materials are rich in information that may help you learn more about a person and his or her military life.

Directories

City directories, telephone directories, professional directories, alumni lists, personal telephone and address books, and similar items may be found in the home. These may include names, addresses, birthdates, ages, and other details about family members.

Religious Publications

Newsletters, church bulletins, and other religious publications present a detailed chronology of the congregation's activities. You may find your ancestor's or family member's life events announced there, as well as news of their involvement in congregational activities. Copies are often kept for sentimental value by one or more family members and are therefore often found at home. Remember that the presence of a family member's name in one or more of these publications suggests that there are probably membership records available in the congregation's offices. Transfer of membership from one congregation to another is often well documented in the church membership rolls, and this may lead you to previous places of residence, church congregations, and potentially to other records.

School Records

Enrollment forms, homework papers/reports/projects, report cards, transcripts, diplomas, honor rolls, fraternity and sorority documents and jewelry, yearbooks and annuals, school photographic portraits, awards, and other materials may be found at home. (See Figure 2-13.) They represent information about family members from a specific period of time. Don't overlook these great resources and the insights they may provide. In addition, alumni directories and other correspondence may provide names and addresses of administrative offices that you may potentially contact for additional information.

Employment Records

Employers may be reluctant to release records concerning their employees. However, around the home you may locate materials such as apprentice agreements or indentures of servitude from long ago. More recent documents may include résumés, pay vouchers, paycheck stubs, union cards and other documents, life and health insurance policies, severance papers, retirement or pension documents, a Social Security (or Railroad Retirement Board) card, a medical care or prescription benefit

LILLIAN BLUE
Gibson, N. C.

Π Θ Μ

Student Council, '24, '25; Secretary Student Body,
'24, '25; Y. W. C. A. Cabinet. '23, '24; Fire Marshal, '23,
'24, '25; Dramatic Club, '23, '24, '25; Walking Lieutenant
'21, '22, '23, '24, '25.

"She strives best who serves most."

When a responsibility comes Lillian's way she assumes
it and does her duty, earnestly and well. She has been
a capable secretary of the Student Council, and an
inspiring example to the rest of us. She is the kindest
hearted girl in school and mothers us all.

MARTHA LEE BORDEN
Goldsboro, N. C.

Σ Φ Κ

President of Senior Class, '25; Vice-President of
Sigma Phi Kappa Society, '24, '25; President of Cotillion
Club, '25; Vice-President of Junior Class, '24; Associate
Editor of *Voices of Peace*, '25; President of Preparatory
Class, '22; Choral Club, '21, '22, '23, '24, '25; Secretary
of Sigma Phi Kappa Society, '24; Secretary of Sopho-
more Class, '23; Commencement Marshal, '24; Statistics,
'23, '25.

*"All the gladsome sounds of nature borrow
sweetness of her singing."*

You have only to look at her picture to know that she
possesses irresistible personal charm. She possesses
not merely charm, however, but ability as well, for
Martha Lee has been for years a strong member of the
Class of '25. Peace will miss her, but we know she will
make a success in the musical world for has she not a
lovely voice—and a Victrola?

Thirty-one

FIGURE 2-13   A college yearbook, such as Peace Institute's 1925 *Lotus*, may yield
important biographical information about your ancestor's participation in school activities.

card, a National Health Service identification card, or other employment-related materials. Don't overlook employee newsletters that have been saved; there might be a mention of your ancestor or family member in that specific issue.

Search for the Less-Than-Obvious Items

In addition to all of the items listed in the preceding sections, don't overlook household items that may contain important clues. Engraved jewelry and silverware may speak volumes to you. For example, an 18-karat gold locket holding tiny photographs of an elderly couple and engraved with the dates "1856–1906" provided the clue I needed to identify them as one set of my great-grandparents. These are the only surviving pictures of these ancestors that I have been able to find. Embroidered samplers, needlework, and quilts often include names and dates. Plaques, coats of arms, and personalized souvenirs offer other information. And don't overlook heirloom furniture and pictures, because you never know what may be incorporated into the design or concealed inside or underneath them.

It is important to investigate *all* the materials at home that may provide information or clues to your family's history. Search through books, letters, papers, trunks, suitcases, boxes, baskets, drawers, chests, attics, basements, crawlspaces, closets and cupboards, garages and sheds, and everywhere else you can imagine. As you discover each new piece of evidence, keep track of where and when you located it. While that may seem unimportant now, it is definitely a worthwhile part of your documentation and may reveal another clue to you in the future. Consider placing each document that you find in an archival-quality envelope, folder, or polypropylene sheet protector sleeve along with a note (on acid-free paper) indicating the name(s) of the person(s) about whom the item concerns, the date you located it, and where you located it. (We will discuss the importance of documenting your source materials in more detail in Chapter 4.)

Interview All Your Relatives

You never know where you will find that next piece of information. It could be as close as the family member sitting right beside you or it could be a distant cousin with whom you've never spoken. Your job is to learn as much as you can—*now*! Many a genealogist or family historian has lamented having waited too late to talk with parents and grandparents. However, it is never too late to make contact with uncles and aunts, cousins, and family friends to learn as much as you can. You also may find that the "missing" family Bible isn't really lost; it may be in the possession of another relative after all.

Genealogy is a lot like journalism. You are seeking information from a variety of sources, asking questions, gathering facts and speculation alike, tracking down documentation, researching your sources, evaluating what you find, and producing hypotheses. If you do your job in a scholarly manner, you may be rewarded with factual proof as well as a better understanding of your family's story, person by person.

A good researcher learns how to ask questions, both of themselves and of others. Good interviewing skills are an essential part of your research, and it takes time to become an expert. There is an art to successfully conducting an interview with another family member but, with a little advance preparation and organization, you can become a pro in no time.

An interview need not be an "interrogation" so much as a friendly discussion. You will ask open-ended questions that require more elaboration than just a "yes" or "no" response. You want to get your relative to share knowledge and experiences in a friendly, non-threatening environment. A two-way conversation can be a mutually satisfying experience, blazing a trail for a stronger relationship—and more information—in the future.

Examples of some open-ended questions might include

- Where and when were you born?
- What were your parents' names?
- What were the full names of your brothers and sisters?
- When and where were they born?
- What was it like growing up during the Great Depression?
- What were some of your experiences in school?
- Who was your first date, and where did you go?
- What jobs have you had, and what were they like?
- What kind of trips did you take when you were younger, which was your favorite, and why?
- What do you know about your grandparents, and what can you tell me about them?
- What can you tell me about your aunts and uncles?

It is important to realize that there may be sensitive issues in the family that people are uncomfortable about and prefer not to discuss. Scandals, shame, secrets, lies, embarrassment, humiliation, and disgrace are all reasons for reluctance or refusal to discuss a person, place, time, or event. Two powerful emotions are pride and the desire to protect the family reputation. Let me give you four examples involving refusals of family members to talk about the past:

- Both of my grandmothers were concerned that no one be aware of their ages. One refused to tell anyone the year of her birth and left instructions in her will that only her date of death be inscribed on her gravestone. The other shaved years from her age at each census until, in 1930, she had "lost" 16 years.
- A woman of Native American descent refused to discuss her parents. She was ashamed that she was an Indian, and she followed the example of her mother who denied or masked her ethnic origin.
- One woman was shocked to learn that she had been born out of wedlock and that the woman she thought was her older sister was, in fact, her mother. When asked about this by the family genealogist, she not only refused to discuss the matter but also made the genealogist swear never to repeat the scandalous information to anyone else in the family. She wanted to protect her own children and other family members from the scandal of illegitimacy.

- Imagine the surprise of the genealogist who discovered that her grandmother had made the family fortune in a most unusual way. "Granny" always said she didn't want to talk about her husband, and that he was a worthless man who left her before her daughter was born. The genealogist located her grandmother in the 1910 United States census in Chicago, listed as a boarder in the home of two sisters, Minna and Ada Everleigh. Further historical research revealed that the Everleigh sisters were the proprietors of one of the most famous brothels in Chicago and that Granny had been an "employee" there.

As you can see, there may be many reasons why family members are reluctant to discuss the past and other family members. However, don't leap to any conclusions. Some people are just not the talkative type.

Social media has made tracing and making contact with other people significantly easier. As an example, my paternal grandmother's brother died in an automobile accident in December 1916, and the family lost track of his widow and children. I conducted research on this woman using census records, city directories, digitized newspapers, and other documents. I was able to locate information on her children and grandchildren by tracing names through series of obituaries. I was able to identify one of the descendants as a member of Facebook and have since made contact with her and exchanged additional information. We will discuss social media in great detail in Chapter 15.

Consider Several Types of Interviews

Most people think of an interview as a face-to-face encounter between two or more individuals. An interview, however, can take one of several forms. In fact, some of the best interviews I've ever conducted with relatives have been done by telephone, and in multiple sessions. Consider the following types of interviews as possibilities for obtaining information from your family members:

- **Face-to-face interview**   This technique involves setting a time and place that is convenient to everyone involved.
- **Family gatherings**   A family reunion, a holiday dinner, a graduation, a wedding or funeral, or just a simple visit with other relatives can stimulate informal conversations from which stories and important family details can be learned.
- **Telephone conversations**   The telephone can be used to schedule and conduct either a casual interview or a more formal, in-depth interview. Use a "phone visit" as an occasion to ask one or two questions at a time. By establishing ongoing telephone communications with a relative, you not only build and strengthen the relationship between you and the relative, but also can continue asking questions about details over time as you proceed with your research.
- **Virtual interviews**   Use Skype (**http://www.skype.com**) or another Internet-based facility to conduct audio or video interviews with your relatives.
- **Written questionnaires**   Use postal mail or email to gather family information. Some researchers prepare open-ended questions in document form and send these to relatives. Beware of sending a lengthy questionnaire, though. Few people

are willing to spend a lot of time responding to dozens of questions. A few shorter sets of questions posed over an extended period of time often yield a better response rate. If you choose to use postal mail for your survey, be sure to enclose a self-addressed, stamped envelope (SASE) to encourage replies.

- **Requests for corrections**   Two effective tools used by genealogists to gather information are the family tree chart, commonly referred to as a pedigree chart, and the family group sheet. We will discuss these in more detail in Chapter 4. However, these are the documents that genealogists prepare to organize their family data and present it in report format. You may choose to send a copy of the documents to relatives, along with a SASE. Request that they add to and/or make corrections to the information you have compiled. Be sure to ask for photocopies of any documents they may have that corroborate the facts they provide, and always offer to reimburse them for the cost of their copying, postage, and mileage. Be sure to follow up by sending them a thank-you note and an updated copy of the forms.

When preparing your list of questions, leave plenty of space in between them for responses. You will appreciate this when you are conducting an oral interview, and it encourages mail and email respondents to fill in the blank space with their commentary.

You may be surprised at the information gleaned during the oral interview process. I've located family Bibles, marriage certificates, deeds, letters, journals, and a host of other documents this way. Most important, however, has been the wealth of stories I've heard. These tales help bring the family members and their experiences to life. A first cousin related to me a story that her mother told her about two of our retired great-aunts and a train trip they made to Savannah, Georgia, to buy fresh crabs. They made the trip by day, purchased a bucket of live crabs, and then returned to the train station to take a sleeper train back home, booking an upper and a lower berth. During the night, one aunt awoke to use the bathroom. When she returned to her berth, she decided to reach up and pinch her sister's behind. Her sister burst from her berth yelling, "Good heavens! The crabs are loose!" Other passengers were awakened by the racket and peered out of their berths, only to see a woman race to the end of the train car and pull the emergency brake to stop the train. Not only is this a hilarious story, but also it provides some insight for me into the relationship of the two sisters and one's love of practical jokes.

Schedule Interviews for Best Results

It is important to respect your relative's time. It is inconsiderate and rude to show up unannounced to ask a lot of questions for which your relative is unprepared, especially if he or she has another commitment. Your best course of action, regardless of whether you would like to conduct a face-to-face, telephone, or virtual interview, is to make contact in advance and schedule a mutually convenient time for your session. Be prepared for the question, "Well, what is it you want to know?" Before you even make the appointment, you should have decided what information you hope to learn and have an idea of the questions you want to use to elicit the information.

By identifying the topics you want to discuss and letting the family member know in advance, he or she can mentally prepare for your interview. The person also might like to gather together photographs, Bibles, papers, and other items to show you. By contacting an elderly first cousin in advance and telling her I was interested in her parents and grandparents, I was rewarded with an opportunity to see my great-grandparents' Bible, letters they had written during their courtship, and pieces of heirloom furniture I had not known existed.

If you would like to record the interview, be sure to ask permission in advance. Remember that recording devices can be intimidating and distracting, and can make your subject self-conscious and nervous. If you detect any reluctance on the part of your subject, either in advance or at the time of the interview, don't record it. Be prepared to instead take good notes during the conversation.

Ask the Right Questions

Know something about the person you plan to interview *before* you make the appointment and *before* you arrive or call to conduct the interview. The last thing you want to do is waste anyone's time, and you want to make the most of the time you have together. That means understanding the person's place in the family structure, where they were geographically located, what other family members he or she would likely have known, and what materials might have come into their possession. Your primary goal should be to learn about the people and their lives. If there are materials that might document their life events, it is a bonus to be able to see them. It is most important, however, to learn *about* the people and their lives so that you can place them into geographical, historical, and sociological context. This will help you anticipate what records might exist to document their lives, where those records were created, and where they may be found today.

Your family's origins and background certainly will determine the questions that you will ask. There are many, many places on the Internet where suggested lists of family history interview questions have been published. There are many free articles at Ancestry.com's Learning Center at **http://www.ancestry.com/cs/HelpAndAdviceUS**. Enter a topic keyword in the Search box at the top of the page to locate pertinent articles.

Use the Right Equipment for Your Interviews

You should be properly prepared to capture the information you are about to receive. Here are some basic pieces of equipment you will want to take with you to the interview:

- Paper and pencils or pens
- Audio/voice recorder or video recorder
- Conventional or digital camera
- Extra film
- Extra batteries
- Portable scanner

If you obtained permission in advance to record the interview, you will want to have checked the operation of the recorder in advance. The smaller the recording device, the less intrusive it will be. Be sure you know how to use it and that it is in good working condition before you leave home. When you arrive for the interview, ask again if it is okay to record. If it is not, pack up and move the recorder out of the interview area so that it is not a distraction. If your relative agreed to recording, though, you should be prepared to quickly and efficiently set up the equipment. Perform a sound check on the recording volume before you start, and place the microphone closer to your subject than to yourself. You want a clear recording of the responses and, even though you may not be able to hear all your questions and comments, you should be able to easily relate your subject's responses to your original questions.

Take one or two family items with you to help encourage conversation. I often use an old family photograph as a prop. I ask questions such as, "Can you tell me where and when this picture was taken, and can you help me identify the people in it?" This single question may be the icebreaker you need and the catalyst to open the floodgates of recollection. It literally can be worth the proverbial thousand words.

If you own or can borrow a laptop computer and a portable scanner, consider taking them with you as well. Family members may have Bibles, documents, photographs, and other items that can be copied on site. You will find that most of your relatives, regardless of how close they feel to you, are reluctant to let the family treasures out of their possession for any period of time. Some items can be photographed clearly enough using a digital camera with a higher megapixel resolution so as to provide a clear and legible image. However, a scanner always provides the best quality image for your records.

Set the Tone of the Interview

It is important in a face-to-face interview especially, but also in a telephone interview, to establish a comfort level for your relative and for yourself. Make sure that there is plenty of time available and that it is a pleasant environment. Interruptions should be kept to a minimum if possible. A third person sitting in on an interview can be a distraction and may prevent the person you are interviewing from opening up to you. Your interviewee may feel uncomfortable or reluctant to discuss people, events, and personal topics with another person present.

Start the interview with a few minutes of lighthearted conversation to set the tone of your time together. Share something with your relative about your life, news of the family, or some other item that might be of mutual interest. It helps break the ice and make your subject feel more at ease. When you begin the actual interview, however, make a tangible transition to that part of the session. In a face-to-face interview, you can do this by straightening yourself in your chair, opening your notebook, setting up a voice recorder (if your subject has already agreed to being recorded), or making some other visible transition. If conducting a telephone interview, make the shift with a comment such as, "Well, I don't want to take up a lot of your time, so why don't we get started?" Use your common sense and tact about what is the right method of transitioning with each relative.

Think of yourself as a friendly, non-threatening journalist. Ask open-ended questions that require a response. "Where were you born and when?" is a good starter. You want to learn names, places, and dates, but you also want to know about the people in your relative's life: parents, brothers, sisters, grandparents, aunts, uncles, cousins, nephews, nieces, friends, teachers, ministers, librarians, and anyone else who may have influenced his or her family and life.

There may be topics that are sensitive and uncomfortable to discuss. Don't press the issue. Move on to the next question. The answer to the question may come up in another way, at another time, and perhaps from another relative, but for the present you should let the subject drop. Being pushy and insistent can raise barriers between you and your relative that may interfere with the remainder of the interview and with the relationship between you as well.

Keep the interview short, no longer than one to two hours. Be alert to signs of fatigue. If you notice that your subject is beginning to tire, especially older relatives, be considerate and suggest that you continue later. A break may be sufficient, but scheduling another session may be a better option. In the interim, both you and your relative will have time to digest what you have already discussed. You may revise your list of questions as a result, and your relative will have time to regroup and perhaps locate photographs and other materials he or she feels will be of interest to you.

Don't Forget the "Thank You"

After the interview, be sure to thank your relative for the time together and for sharing so much wonderful family history with you. Make another appointment, if appropriate, to meet again and talk. After you return home, consider sending a thank-you note expressing your appreciation. Building these personal relationships in small ways like this is important. The connections you make are personally gratifying for both of you, and you never know what genealogical dividends they will pay in the future.

Begin to Organize What You Find

As you collect originals or copies of documents, photographs, family artifacts, and the exciting information gleaned from interviewing your relatives, you soon may feel overwhelmed at the volume of materials you are compiling. You're probably wondering what you're going to actually do with all this "stuff."

It is important to keep track of where and when you actually obtained the information and materials, and that will become part of the documentation process we'll explore in Chapter 4. It also is a good idea to develop a filing system early in your research process. Consider creating a large file folder or three-ring binder for each family surname (last name) you identify. Start with your own surname, moving on to your father's surname if it differs from yours, and then your mother's maiden surname. Continue on to the surnames of each of your four grandparents, your eight great-grandparents, and so on. You may also be interested in setting up files for the spouses of your brothers and sisters, aunts and uncles, cousins, and on and on. I use binders for my filing system, and I file all the records for a surname (such as Morgan) in one binder. Within that binder, I file documents by given name (first name or forename) and then middle name(s) of each person, and then I file the documents for each of these individuals in chronological sequence. I also file each document in an archival-safe, polypropylene sheet protector. These protective sleeves are available at every office supply store and will help preserve the condition of the documents you obtain.

This is a starting point in your organization process, and your own filing system can be customized to your own research and reference needs. We will discuss organization and preservation in extensive detail elsewhere in the book. In the meantime, you can get started so that the job won't seem so overwhelming later.

Get Started!

The starting point for your genealogical research begins with yourself and moves backward to your parents and beyond, as well as to your siblings and their families. Start with what you know and then move on to the unknown territory, actively seeking information and documentation along the way. The more data you obtain and the better you get to know about your family members' lives, the better prepared you are to venture further and learn more. Step by step, you will work your way further back in time and learn more about your ancestry. Placing your ancestors into context with the places and time periods in which they lived, and understanding the social and historical factors that influenced them, will bring these people to life for you. You are, after all, a direct product of these people, their genetic makeup, their circumstances, and the life decisions they made. As you learn more, you will become more self-aware of why you are the person you are, and you'll find yourself wanting to learn even more. Few things are more thrilling than touching a marriage certificate signed by your ancestors 150 years ago or holding an old Bible that was lovingly used by an ancestor. It won't be long before you have joined the tens of millions of other family historians around the world who are involved in the thrill of the research chase and the excitement of discovery.

3

Balance Traditional, Electronic, and Genetic Research

HOW TO...

- Be a modern genealogical researcher
- Understand traditional research
- Discover documentary evidence and where it is found
- Learn about different types of electronic resources
- Include DNA testing in your research
- Integrate traditional, electronic, and genetic research

You are sure to have seen television shows and movies about police detectives investigating a crime. They are looking for evidence of all sorts to determine how it happened in a particular situation, and to substantiate their case with solid proof. Genealogy researchers are doing much the same thing. They are always looking for materials to help learn more about their ancestors' families. Like police crime scene investigators, we refer to those materials that we discover about our ancestors as "evidence." Throughout this book we will discuss different types of evidence sources in great detail. That will help you evaluate and analyze the evidence more accurately, and to reach reliable hypotheses about your family members.

There has never been a better time to be involved with genealogy. It hasn't been that many years ago that genealogy and family history research was essentially a print-based process. Researchers visited libraries and archives to check books, periodicals, microfilm and microfiche, and other holdings to determine what evidence might be located in other places, and then they would write letters to request lookups and copies of documents. They would travel to courthouses and other repositories to locate, access, and view original documents. They might also have visited a nearby Church of Jesus Christ of Latter-day Saints (LDS) Family History Center (FHC) to consult the catalog of the Family History Library (FHL) in Salt Lake City, Utah, in order to identify potentially helpful records that had been microfilmed.

They would ask the volunteers at the FHC to order the microfilm or microfiche from Salt Lake City, pay a rental fee, and then use the microform materials at the FHC. The other alternative was to physically travel to facilities where records were held or where evidence might be found. In addition, a researcher might have sent a written query to a genealogical publication, such as the now defunct *Everton's Genealogical Helper*, to broadcast his or her interest in locating information about a specific individual. This kind of research was time-consuming and potentially very expensive. The wait for responses to letters and inquiries and the arrival of microform materials seemed interminable. As a result, the pace of the genealogical research progress was very slow.

The late 1970s and 1980s saw the development of dial-in Bulletin Board Services (BBSs) on which people connected to discuss common interests. Genealogy was a big use of BBSs, and online chats for general genealogical research topics, as well as location- and record-specific topics, became very popular. As time passed, commercial online services were introduced, including CompuServe, GEnie, Delphi, Prodigy, and America Online, and these capitalized on the high level of interest in family history research.

The origins of the Internet date back to the 1960s. The National Science Foundation provided funding in the 1980s for a U.S. backbone network for use by scientists and academicians. By 1990, the general public began using this network to connect with multiple network sites on a single dial-in connection. Tim Berners-Lee, a British scientist, formulated the concept of the World Wide Web, and in 1993 the first graphical web browser was introduced. The addition of graphic images to Internet web pages revolutionized communications, marketing, research, and so much more.

For genealogists, the Web has facilitated the publication of digitized original documents, indexes, photographs, newspapers, manuscripts, and many other resources. It has unquestionably accelerated our research possibilities and reach. Millions of new document images and indexes are added to the Internet each month, not the least of which is the ongoing project by FamilySearch to digitize and make available on the Internet its billions of microfilmed document images.

Undoubtedly, not every record that was ever created will be digitized, indexed, and made available online during our lifetimes. That means that we still must rely on physically locating and accessing the original documents that we need as evidence using traditional research methods. Nevertheless, the unprecedented rate at which new materials are being added to websites truly makes this a golden age for genealogical research.

Be a Modern Genealogical Researcher

There are really three main categories of resources available to help us locate and access evidence today:

- **Original source documents and printed materials** This category includes original documents in such places as courthouses, churches, cemeteries, public record offices, government facilities, and a host of other facilities. One-of-a-kind resources such as manuscripts and loose papers may also yield important information that contributes to our research knowledge. Books, magazines, and newspapers found in libraries and archives or in personal collections are also critically important. They may provide unique information or they may point you to original source materials.

- **Internet-based source materials**   This category encompasses a broad range of materials, including free and commercial database websites, message boards, mailing lists, reference sites, libraries' and universities' websites, government websites, and a host of other online reference and educational facilities.
- **Genetic genealogy materials**   The introduction of DNA testing in recent years has produced a scientific category of evidence that is being used in genealogical research. It can be used to verify the research already done on paper and/or can help identify potential familial matches.

Your job is going to involve access to and evaluation of *all* of these types of materials in your research. You will always be working each type of information in tandem with the others. Let's explore each of these categories in more detail.

Understand Traditional Research

Traditional research was and still is the central form of genealogical investigation, and it is essential for acquiring documentary evidence. In Chapter 4, we will discuss in detail the concepts of primary vs. secondary information and original vs. derivative sources. The most reliable evidence of an event is an original document created at or very near to the time the event occurred. It is not something transcribed or taken from a word-of-mouth account, because the details may have inconsistencies or may be incorrect. If you are unfamiliar with the concepts of primary vs. secondary information and original vs. derivative sources, feel free to skip ahead to the corresponding sections in Chapter 4 and then come back to this section.

Traditional research entails looking for clues that direct you to concrete documentary evidence about your ancestors and their family members. If you have watched any of the several *CSI: Crime Scene Investigation* series or comparable police dramas on television, you know that building a reliable case means searching for original evidence, studying it, evaluating it in relation to other facts or evidence, developing a hypothesis (or more than one), and substantiating the hypothesis with a strong body of original evidentiary proof. Does that sound complicated? Well, it is and it isn't. Yes, your research should be done in a scholarly manner and must incorporate strong original evidence. However, this will quickly become second nature to you, and soon you will be enjoying every aspect of "the thrill of the chase."

Discover Documentary Evidence and Where It Is Found

Traditional research will always involve working with a wide variety of materials. These include but are not limited to the following:

- Books, journals, magazines, and newsletters
- Manuscripts

- Maps
- Indexes
- Histories
- Biographies
- Newspapers
- Documents from many traditional locations and sources

Books, Journals, and Periodicals

Printed books will always be an important source of genealogical information in your research. These are available at libraries and archives, at bookstores and newsstands, and through online booksellers' sites. You will find books that contain everything from how-to information, such as this book, to transcribed records, to published images of original records.

Journals, magazines, and newsletters published by genealogical and historical societies, as well as commercial magazines, may provide details and/or case studies containing information about your ancestor or some facet of his or her life. There are sure to be articles about life in a particular community in which your ancestor lived. Therefore, even if your ancestor is not named, you can gain insights into what life was like in that place at a particular point in time. The findmypast databases include the Periodical Source Index (PERSI), a facility created by the Allen County Public Library in Fort Wayne, Indiana. PERSI (**http://search.findmypast.com/search/periodical-source-index**) indexes genealogical society publications from the United States and elsewhere, with more than 6 million citations.

Some older historical books are being electronically scanned and indexed, and these are appearing at a number of online sites such as Ancestry.com (**http://www.ancestry.com**; see Figure 3-1), HeritageQuest Online (available through institutional subscriptions at some public libraries), WorldVitalRecords.com (**http://www.worldvitalrecords.com**; see Figure 3-2), Family History Books (**https://books.familysearch.org/primo_library/libweb/action/search.do?vid = FHD_PUBLIC**) of FamilySearch, Google Books (**http://books.google.com**), GenealogyBank (**http://www.genealogybank.com**), and other websites. These are typically every-word searchable and can provide you with access to resources otherwise available only at a remote library or archive.

You will always want to invest time in researching the collections found in libraries, archives, and genealogical societies. Many of these organizations have also digitized and indexed materials and placed them online. These facilities can provide clues to guide you to the original evidentiary records that you want to examine in your research.

Manuscripts and Oral Histories

Original, one-of-a-kind handwritten manuscripts and typescripts are seldom found anywhere but inside a library or archive. You can often find these cataloged by the library or archive in which they are held. An unpublished family history may contain a wealth of information and clues that can lead you to genealogical treasure. However,

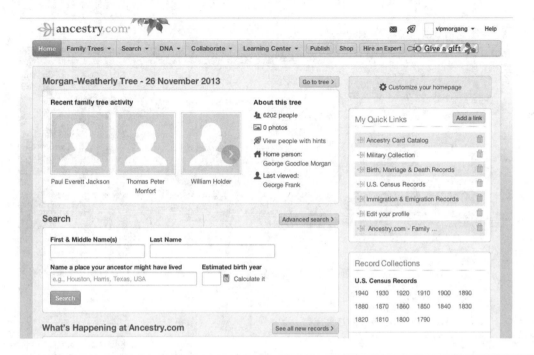

FIGURE 3-1   Main page of Ancestry.com

don't expect a manuscript to have been microfilmed or digitized. While some have been digitized and others may be digitized in the future, you will more than likely need to travel to the repository where the manuscript is stored in order to access it.

There are several important online tools for locating manuscripts:

- **British Library manuscripts**   The manuscript collections of the British Library are an important part of Britain's national heritage of manuscripts and other documentary materials. These are described in detail in the library's online reference webpages, beginning at **http://www.bl.uk/reshelp/ findhelprestype/manuscripts/msscollect/manuscriptscollections.html**. The page link labeled Manuscripts – Other Libraries & Institutions (**http://www .bl.uk/reshelp/findhelprestype/webres/manuscriptsotherinst/index.html**) points to other repositories around the country *and* abroad where important manuscript collections are held.
- **Manuscripts Online**   Manuscripts Online is a facility formed through a collaboration in the UK between six universities in England and Ireland. It provides a search engine to access electronic content dating from the years 1000 to 1500. (**http://www.manuscriptsonline.org**)
- **The National Archives (UK)**   The National Archives in the UK, also referred to as TNA, has consolidated its reference catalog of materials in its collection and to archives across England and Wales in 2014. The new catalog is called Discovery, and can be accessed at **http://discovery.nationalarchives.gov.uk**. It contains

FIGURE 3-2   US Book Collection search page of WorldVitalRecords.com

descriptions of more than 32 million records held by TNA and more than 2,500 other archives across the country.

- **National Library of Australia**   The manuscripts in this collection document the history and activities related to the formation of Australia, its territories, and some surrounding areas. The individual states and territories hold additional manuscript materials that may also be of interest. (**http://www.nla.gov.au/ what-we-collect/manuscripts**)
- **National Union Catalog of Manuscript Collections (NUCMC)**   NUCMC is an electronic catalog produced and maintained by the Library of Congress. Its mission is to describe archival and manuscript collections held by repositories located throughout the United States and its territories, and to promote bibliographic access to the nation's documentary heritage. (**http://www.loc.gov/coll/nucmc**)

In addition to manuscripts, oral history collections are being added to archives and libraries around the world. Don't overlook the possibility that recorded oral interviews may include important details about the time and places where your ancestors lived. These can provide excellent information to place your ancestral family in geographical and time context. Oral histories may be available in both recorded and transcribed formats. Check with public and academic libraries to determine what they have among their holdings and how to access them.

Maps

Geography is an integral part of genealogical research. It is essential to understand the location where your ancestor lived, where the geopolitical boundaries were, how the boundaries may have changed during and since your ancestor's residency there, and what governmental body had jurisdiction of the area at a specific time. While many historical maps have been digitized and are on the Internet, most exist only in library collections, archives, university special collections, or the holdings of individuals or organizations (such as the Library of Congress, whose collection includes the map shown in Figure 3-3).

Indexes

There are thousands of published indexes to original records of genealogical importance. P. William Filby's epic and ongoing publication, *Passenger and Immigration Lists Index*, remains the most important reference for identifying information about immigrants to the American colonies and the United States. *Germans to America* is another important reference. However, there are indexes to original documents worldwide. The Civil Registration registers of births, marriages, and deaths for England and Wales, for instance, cover the period from July 1837 to 2006, and more recent registrations are accessible up to 18 months prior to the current date. Indexes to names in censuses, bride and groom marriage indexes, land and property indexes, military service records and awards, and hundreds of other record types have been published. These indexes provide guidance to direct you to the original records, and you can then order copies and examine the exact content for yourself.

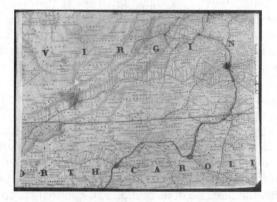

FIGURE 3-3   Map showing Col. John Singleton Mosby's route through Virginia and North Carolina during the U.S. Civil War. (From the Library of Congress collection.)

Histories

History books and other historical accounts, such as diaries and journals, may exist only in printed form or as a manuscript. These accounts can provide you with the context of a place and time in which your ancestor lived. In some cases, a local history may provide the only evidence of your ancestor's presence and activities in an area. You can learn about the activities in which your ancestor may have participated and about events that may have affected your ancestor's life.

Biographies

Biographies and autobiographies of individuals are important sources of information and provide clues to original materials. Typically found in library collections, you can use these publications as you would a history book. A biography or autobiography provides the historical context for a time period and describes people, places, locations, and events. For example, while your ancestor's name may never be mentioned, a biography of a military leader under whom your ancestor served will likely provide a chronological account of military engagements and details about the living conditions. This information is helpful in understanding that portion of your ancestor's life and the events that influenced him or her and other people.

Newspapers

A newspaper chronicles a community, incorporating news and events about people from all walks of life. Original newspapers are not frequently retained in storage, for a number of reasons. They are certainly a fire hazard, and their physical composition may produce other by-products that can be harmful to public health. Additionally, newsprint from the late 19th century forward is highly acidic in content, and the acid and lignin can contaminate other materials, causing them to discolor and deteriorate.

Many newspapers have been microfilmed before the originals were destroyed. This is excellent news for researchers. However, unless the newspaper has been indexed in some way, your research will depend on knowing dates or date ranges of issues; otherwise, you may have to comb through image after image on many rolls of microfilm or many sheets of microfiche. These microform records are often found in a library or historical archive in or near the place of publication. Copies may also be held in a regional, state, provincial, or national library or archive. You will need to visit that repository to access these records.

More recently, voluminous quantities of newspaper titles are being digitized, both from the original paper and from previously microfilmed records. Most are being indexed using optical character recognition (OCR) software, thereby making them searchable. Tens of millions of historical newspaper pages are being scanned each year.

Many public, state, regional, territorial, and national libraries and archives are actively engaged in identifying historical newspapers, digitizing and indexing them, and making them available on the Internet. The Chronicling America collection of the Library of Congress (**http://chroniclingamerica.loc.gov**), shown in Figure 3-4, includes massive collections of digitized newspapers

Online subscription sites such as GenealogyBank (**http://www.genealogybank .com**) provide access to many digitized and searchable newspaper collections available. The British Newspaper Archive (**http://www.britishnewspaperarchive .co.uk**) provides access to more than 8 million pages of more than 250 newspapers. Ancestry.com has a collection of newspapers, and findmypast, in partnership with the British Library, has made available more than 200 newspaper titles covering the period from 1710 to 1953. The findmypast collections also feature newspapers from the United States, Canada, Ireland, and some other international locations (see Figure 3-5). Other historical newspaper titles, such as those digitized and indexed by ProQuest and other commercial entities, may be available to you through public and academic libraries.

It is important to remember, however, that because of the varying quality of the microform images from which the digitized images were taken, and the limitations of the OCR scanning capability, there may be unavoidable indexing errors.

FIGURE 3-4   Main page of the Chronicling America collection at the Library of Congress website

FIGURE 3-5   An image from the findmypast British Newspapers online database collection showing an account of a will in the *Hull Daily Mail* on 20 June 1941

Documents from Many Traditional Locations and Sources

Your research for original documents or exact copies will take you to many places. This book will help lead you to specific repositories in various locations in order to access those documents. Among them are government offices, health departments, police records repositories, coroners' offices, land and property offices, civil, criminal, and probate courts, churches and religious offices, military records storage repositories, cemeteries and cemetery offices, manuscript collections, libraries, archives at all levels, schools and universities, genealogical and historical societies, and many more. The documents will be unique unto themselves. You will learn more about many types of documents and working with them throughout this book.

Learn About Electronic Research Materials

There has been a great acceleration in the availability of genealogical information in recent years. The Internet has greatly facilitated access to original source documents and printed materials. Reference sites and online catalogs have facilitated our ability to quickly locate what might be available, to inquire, and to more quickly access those materials.

Online genealogical subscription services have certainly proliferated on the Internet. These include Ancestry.com (**http://www.ancestry.com**), Fold3 (**http://www.fold3.com**; see Figure 3-6), MyHeritage (**http://www.myheritage.com**; see Figure 3-7), Mocavo (**http://www.mocavo.com**; see Figure 3-8), and many others around the world. New online resources debut each year. Others may be acquired by other companies and folded into their service offerings. And some may simply founder and disappear.

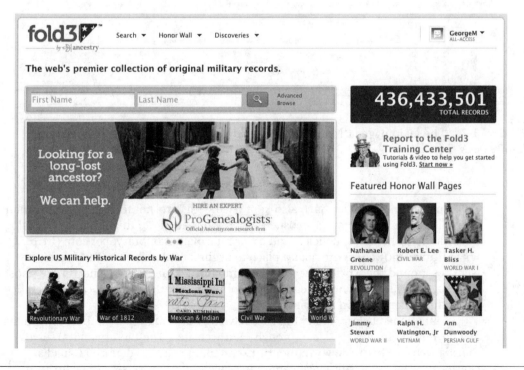

FIGURE 3-6   The main page at Fold3 provides access to the largest collection of digitized U.S. military records.

FIGURE 3-7 The main page at MyHeritage provides access to billions of records and family trees.

Libraries and archives have also kept pace with Internet technology. Essentially every library or archive has a website that provides access to their electronic catalog, descriptions of holdings, policies, and other information. LibrarySpot.com (**http://www.libraryspot.com**) provides a place to begin locating libraries' and archives' websites around the world. The Online Computer Library Center, Inc. (OCLC) hosts WorldCat (**http://www.worldcat.org**), another excellent tool for locating specific books and other items in libraries.

As mentioned before, many libraries have digitized materials in their collections and have made them accessible through their websites. The Library and Archives Canada website (**http://www.collectionscanada.gc.ca**) has digitized Canadian census records, and has produced an impressively informative set of how-to and reference resources in its Genealogy and Family History area at **http://www.collectionscanada.gc.ca/genealogy/index-e.html** (see Figure 3-9). The diversity of digitized records that are accessible through libraries' websites is phenomenal.

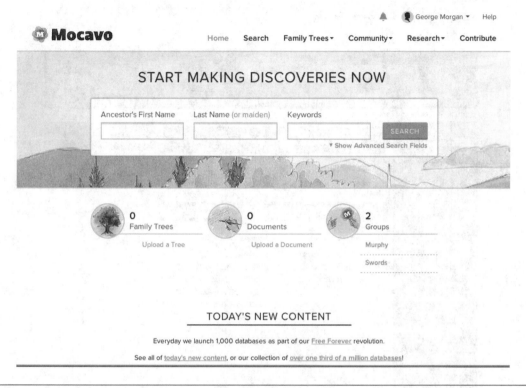

FIGURE 3-8   The main page at Mocavo, the large, free genealogy search engine

In addition to the websites maintained by libraries and archives, these institutions frequently subscribe to important database services. Some of these may be genealogy-specific, while others, such as historical newspapers and obituary databases, may be fully searchable and provide access to invaluable information to help further your research. Many of these are typically accessible from your remote computer with the use of your library card number. Other databases may be accessible by visiting the public or academic library itself.

Your favorite web browser software provides you with access to resources worldwide: digitized documents and photographs, newspapers, digitized historical map collections, cemetery information and transcriptions, online newsletters and magazines, and much, much more. We'll explore these further later in this chapter and elsewhere in the book.

FIGURE 3-9 The Genealogy and Family History page at the Library and Archives Canada

Understand Electronic Research Materials

You will find that there are many different types of electronic research resources, and that keeping them straight may sometimes be difficult. If you understand the difference between them and what they can provide, it will become easier to decide which resource(s) will be your best tool(s) to use for specific types of research. Let's explore the major kinds of electronic resources you will use. We'll cover all of these in more detail later in the book.

Email and Mailing Lists

One of the most ubiquitous electronic tools in use today is email. It provides a rapid and inexpensive way to communicate with one or lots of people at once. Email allows you to send and receive textual communiqués and to attach files, such as word processing documents, spreadsheets, digital photos, audio files, videos, and data files, from many software applications.

Electronic mailing lists are a commonly used resource, allowing many people to subscribe and to send and receive messages sent by other subscribers. There are thousands of genealogy-related mailing lists, each with a specific topical purpose. There are surname lists, lists for specific geographical areas, lists concerning locating and working with specific record types, ethnic and religious lists, and lists on a wide variety of other topics.

Message Boards

Electronic message boards are similar to mailing lists, providing a means for exchanging information with others (see Figure 3-10). A message board, however, resides on the Internet, and you must proactively read it and/or post messages to it. The best genealogy message boards are those at Ancestry.com (**http://boards.ancestry.com**). GenForum (**http://genforum.com**) was also a prolific message board until September 2014 when Ancestry.com, its owner, retired the facility as active and discontinued the ability to post new messages there. The messages have all been archived, however, and are still searchable. Some other genealogy websites may also provide messaging facilities. (Some message boards also may be set up to notify you via email when there is a new message. However, email doesn't play a role in posting to and working with message boards.)

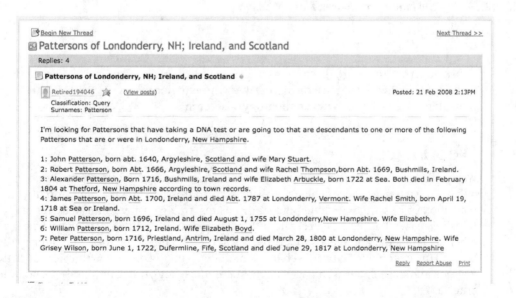

FIGURE 3-10   A message board posting concerning the Pattersons of Londonderry, NH, Ireland, and Scotland

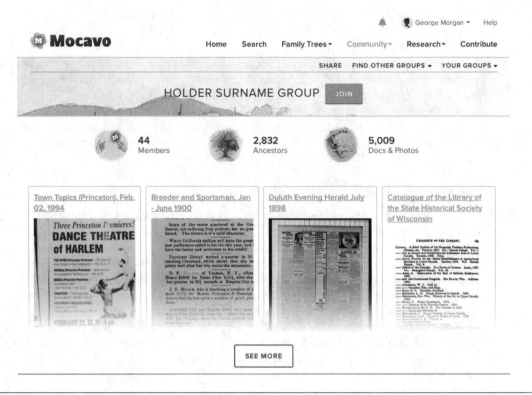

FIGURE 3-11 Surname group area from Mocavo

In addition, there are discussions of geographical areas, surnames, and record types at such places as Mocavo (**http://www.mocavo.com**; see Figure 3-11) and Genealogy Wise (**http://www.genealogywise.com**).

Web Pages

Web pages on the Internet contain a wealth of information, and there are literally billions of web pages accessible by visiting web addresses known to you or that you read about. These may include personal websites, free websites, and subscription websites, as well as blogs, wikis, and other resources. (We will discuss blogs, wikis, and other social media and electronic resources at the end of this chapter and later in the book.) However, your favorite web browser allows you to connect with Internet search engines and to seek out web pages using site names, keywords and phrases, and other criteria.

Compilations, Directories, and Specialized Indexes

There are many websites that have compiled various types of materials for your reference. RootsWeb, a subsidiary of Ancestry.com (**http://www.rootsweb.ancestry .com**), provides many how-to materials, access to mailing list resources, family trees submitted by other researchers, and a variety of online tools. Cyndi's List of Genealogy Sites on the Internet (**http://www.cyndislist.com**; see Figure 3-12) is a compilation of more than 330,000 categorized links to genealogical sites on the Internet. It is *the* starting point for locating all types of research resources. Linkpendium (**http://www .linkpendium.com**) provides well over 10 million links to location and surname materials on the Internet. The USGenWeb Project (**http://www.usgenweb.org**) and the WorldGenWeb Project (**http://www.worldgenweb.org**) are two all-volunteer collections for United States and international genealogical information and resources, respectively. Find A Grave (**http://www.findagrave.com**; see Figure 3-13) is a massive collection of more than 116 million records of cemetery and interment information from around the world that have been transcribed by individuals and entered into a free online database.

FIGURE 3-12   The main page at Cyndislist.com

FIGURE 3-13   The main page at Findagrave.com

Search Engines

The compilations and indexes provide excellent information when you know what you are looking for, but the use of a search engine can exponentially expand your research. Experienced users of the Internet often have one or more favorite search engines such as Google (**http://www.google.com**) or Bing (**http://www.bing.com**). Fortunately there also are genealogy-specific search resources. Mocavo (**http://www.mocavo.com**) is the world's largest free genealogy search engine.

Subscription Internet Sites for Genealogy

There are many subscription genealogy sites on the Internet, all of which combined provide access to literally tens of thousands of databases. These databases include indexes to records, digitized and indexed original document images, scanned and searchable books and newspapers, and a host of other great resources. Leaders in this area are Ancestry.com (**http://www.ancestry.com**), Archives.com (**http://www.archives.com**), Fold3 (**http://www.fold3.com**), findmypast (**www.findmypast.com**), MyHeritage (**http://www.myheritage.com**), and WorldVitalRecords (**http://www.worldvitalrecords.com**), among others.

Blogs

Blogs are journals published online about many topics. One great place to locate genealogy-specific blogs that might be of interest to you is Chris Dunham's Genealogy

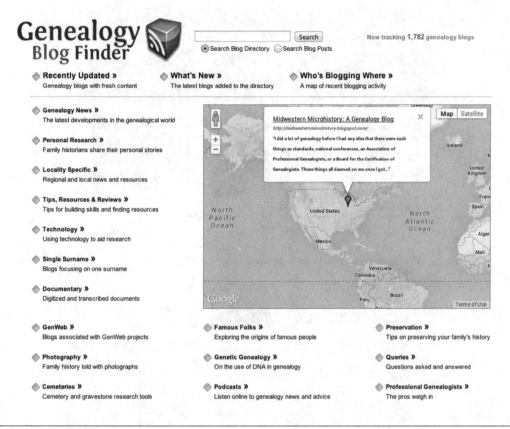

FIGURE 3-14   The Genealogy Blog Finder is a great place to find blogs for all areas of your genealogy research.

Blog Finder (**http://blogfinder.genealogue.com**; see Figure 3-14). In addition, the GeneaBloggers website (**http://geneabloggers.com**) also offers, in its Genealogy Blog Roll area, a searchable collection of almost 3,000 genealogical blogs. There are blogs about national and ethnic origins, religious information, genetic genealogy, software programs, news and events, and many more topics discussed by bloggers worldwide.

Podcasts and Videocasts

Podcasts are audio programs that are recorded and published on the Internet. You can listen to them at their website, download and listen to them on your computer or MP3 player/iPod, or burn them to a CD. I am co-host, with my partner Drew Smith, of *The Genealogy Guys Podcast* (**http://genealogyguys.com**; see Figure 3-15). Other genealogy podcasts include the *African Roots Podcast* (**http://africanrootspodcast.com**),

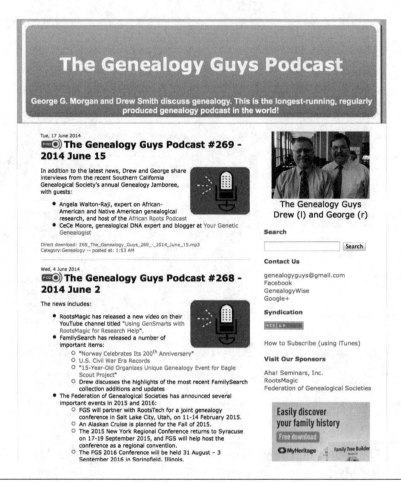

FIGURE 3-15 The main page of the Genealogy Guys^{SM} Podcast website

the *Genealogy Gems Podcast* (**http://www.genealogygemspodcast.com**), and the *Irish Roots Cafe* (**http://www.irishroots.com**). Each of these (and others) provides news, research tips, interviews, book reviews, and/or other features.

The video equivalent of a podcast is referred to as a "videocast" or "vodcast." You will find genealogy videos at YouTube (**http://www.youtube.com**) by searching for keyword **genealogy**.

Webinars

Webinars are live seminars presented on the Internet, and they are often recorded for later download and enjoyment. Genealogy webinars are presented on a wide variety of subjects. Ancestry.com presents webinars about using Ancestry.com and Family

Tree Maker database software, and past webinars have been recorded. RootsMagic (**http://www.rootsmagic.com**) offers webinars about its product and about research topics. Genealogy webinars also are being offered by the leading genealogical speakers and by some genealogical societies. The Southern California Genealogical Society, the Illinois State Genealogical Society, the Wisconsin State Genealogical Society, and others offer webinars that are presented live and recorded for later access. You must register in advance to participate in a live webinar, and a logon ID is provided before the event. Other societies are jumping on the bandwagon to offer webinars as part of their regular meetings in order to provide educational variety for their members.

Streaming Video from Conferences

Organizers for major genealogical conferences are now offering live streaming video of select sessions from their conferences. These sessions are typically also recorded for later access. The sessions require advance registration, and a logon ID is provided. There may or may not be a cost to access a live streaming session, but if there is, it is usually a nominal fee. Some of the conferences that have today provided streaming video include RootsTech, the National Genealogical Society, and the Southern California Genealogical Society.

Include DNA Testing in Your Research

Genetics has grown increasingly popular with genealogists as a means of corroborating their paper research findings and/or identifying potential matches with other researchers. There are several companies performing DNA tests and maintaining sites on the Internet to facilitate researchers' ability to connect and collaborate with other researchers with whom they have matches. However, DNA is just another tool that can be incorporated into your research strategies. We will be talking about DNA and genetic genealogy in much greater detail in Chapter 13.

Integrate Traditional, Electronic, and Genetic Research Findings

The overview I have shared with you in this chapter is sure to have piqued your interest in the many kinds of resources that are available. Hopefully, you now have a better understanding of the differences between so-called "traditional," "electronic," and genetic resources. If you thought, "Wow! I can do it all on the Internet!" you would be completely wrong. While there *is* a great deal of material on the Internet and the quantity is increasing every day, there is much, much more that is not there. Your research must incorporate *and* combine traditional research and resources *with* electronic resources, and you can also add DNA test results to your research.

This chapter has prepared you to learn about each of the resources discussed throughout the book. Chapter 4 will expand on this chapter, and you'll learn all about how to effectively analyze and organize the evidence you've already found at home. We will then discuss in the following chapters many of the most important record types and resources available to you in researching your family history.

You are already well on your way to building the solid foundation for effective genealogy and family history research that will serve you well on this journey of discovery. Read on!

4

Analyze and Organize Your Family Information

HOW TO...

- Understand the Genealogical Proof Standard
- Recognize and evaluate original vs. derivative sources
- Avoid errors in derivative sources
- Evaluate primary vs. secondary information
- Apply critical thinking skills to your genealogical research
- Place your ancestors into context
- Format names, dates, and locations correctly
- Work with pedigree charts
- Work with family group sheets
- Create source citations for your data
- Select a family tree format

Gathering your family information is fun and exciting. Your research will lead you to many adventures. You will learn a great deal about your family members' origins and their activities. Placing them in geographical, historical, and social context will also pique your interest in maps, histories, and many other topics. I enjoy "the thrill of the chase" because I always learn something new and I meet such interesting and generous people along the way.

So far in the book we've defined what genealogy and family history are, and we've discussed how to get started. I hope you've done some investigation with materials that you've found around the house: family or individual Bibles, certificates, receipts, letters and postcards, photographs, family heirlooms, scrapbooks, baby books, school records, newspaper clippings, and so much more. We've also talked about the difference between traditional, electronic, and genetic resources.

Your research will certainly lead you to many repositories and expose you to a wealth of different record types. You will acquire original documents, photocopies of original documents, and digitized versions of original documents as you conduct your research. These allow you to *personally* examine and analyze the information they contain. You will also encounter indexes and transcriptions that can point you toward the original documents, and you will want to follow the leads to obtain or access the originals.

It can be frustrating to remember what you thought you had seen on a document and not be able to find that document when you want to examine it again. It therefore is important to organize and file the materials you find in your genealogical quest so that you can find them quickly when you need them. These documents will provide the evidence you need to analyze an ancestor's life and to better understand the person.

Later in the book, we'll discuss how to go about selecting the genealogy database software program that best suits your needs. Using one of these specialized programs is invaluable for storing your data and generating reports. Before you make that decision, though, there are some essential concepts that form the foundation for all the research and analysis you do. In this chapter, you will learn about the indispensable methodologies for identifying and properly analyzing the evidence you discover, whether that be documents, books, periodicals, manuscripts, photographs, microfilm, cemetery markers, or oral stories. My goal is to help you understand these points and to prepare you to maximize your effectiveness throughout your investigative research process.

Understand the Genealogical Proof Standard

The pieces of information you obtain are referred to as "evidence," and each item needs to be individually examined to determine what kind of evidence it is, when and where it was created, who created it, why it was produced, and what it describes or documents. You also want to know in what form you have found the evidence.

Genealogists have developed over time the standards for evaluating the evidence that they locate. Each piece of evidence is unique. The type of record and contents are going to vary, and the quality and reliability of the evidence need to be assessed. In other words, how good is the evidence that you have discovered?

The Board for Certification of Genealogists (BCG), one of the bodies to perform certification of the competency of professional researchers in the United States, classified the standards for genealogical proof between 1997 and 2000. BCG defined the Genealogical Proof Standard (GPS) and identified five components:

- A thorough search in source materials that might answer or resolve the resource question. The term "reasonably exhaustive search" is frequently used to describe one's strong research into as many applicable resources as possible.
- The use of informative citations for each informational or evidentiary source item that contributes to the answer to the research question. Source citations should be complete and accurate so that anyone reading them can successfully locate the source material for their personal review and evaluation, and so that the quality of the source can be evaluated.

- The analysis, comparison, and contrast of relevant source materials so as to consider and weigh their value as evidence in determining the answer to the research question.
- The careful review of evidence, including conflicting evidence pertaining to the same "fact," and resolution of those conflicts with a hypothesis or answer to the research question.
- A written statement describing the answer to the research question, and how each piece of evidence supports that answer. The written statement may consist of narrative text, a list of facts, or a combination of the two formats.

The five component parts are dependent on one another and support one another. For example, a reasonably exhaustive search into multiple record types that might be used to establish a marriage date for a couple might include

1. A "reasonably exhaustive search" into marriage-related records in a specific geographical area, including county marriage record books in a courthouse, online marriage indexes at one or more online database sites, inquiries into religious institution records, witness accounts, as well as references in U.S. federal census records that might indicate how long the couple has been married. Newspaper articles concerning an engagement, the nuptial ceremony, and subsequent anniversary commemorations can also contribute to the documentation.
2. Creation of meaningful source citations for each item to document the research path for retracing the research and for deciding the credibility and accuracy of the source as it pertains to the marriage event.
3. Analysis of all the information sources and weighing their strengths and weaknesses as authoritative evidence to support a hypothesis regarding the marriage.
4. Review of incomplete or contradictory pieces of evidence, and expansion of the research to identify other sources that resolve conflicts or provide corroboration of one or more pieces of evidence.
5. A written statement of the answer to the question about the marriage date, which includes discussions of specific pieces of evidence, source citations concerning their origins, the weight placed on each item, and a description of how each piece was analyzed.

Recognize and Evaluate Original vs. Derivative Sources

Another important consideration in your research is whether the evidence you find is an *original* or a *derivative* source of information. By that, I mean that the material is either an original document *or* has been taken (derived) from some other source. Derivative source material might include such things as word-of-mouth accounts, information transcribed from other materials, information extracted or abstracted

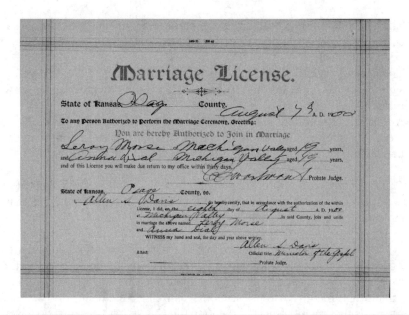

FIGURE 4-1   A marriage license can be a strong source of information. The upper portion of this document is the license; the bottom portion is the "return," which was completed by the official performing the marriage. The document was then returned to the clerk for registration. This marriage certificate is from Osage County, Kansas, from August 1900.

from the original sources, or anything else that is not the genuine, original source created at or near the time of the event or piece of information being documented.

The original sources you use are indeed the actual documents or other materials created for the purpose of recording something. A marriage certificate, such as the one shown in Figure 4-1, would certainly be an original source document, but a marriage entry in the courthouse register would not. An exact photocopy, a microfilm image, a photograph, or a scanned document image can be considered equivalent to the original source.

Derivative sources are a different story. Anytime someone copies or transcribes something, there is a possibility that an error may be introduced. In the course of your genealogical research, you will work with many different materials. Sometimes it is impossible to obtain a photocopy or an exact image of the material. As a result, you will spend time copying the information in the original by hand. What you are doing is "deriving" information from the original source, regardless of whether it is a document, a tombstone, an engraved piece of jewelry, or another original source item.

Understand Types of Derivative Sources

Genealogists know that there are three basic types of derivative sources: a transcription, an extract, and an abstract. Let's discuss the attributes of each of these materials.

Transcription

A transcription is an exact written copy of an original source material. The operative word here is "exact." That means that you are working from the original and are copying its content exactly, word for word, and preserving the spelling and punctuation precisely as it appears in the source document. Since it is possible for you to make transcription errors, it is important that you carefully check your work to ensure that you don't omit anything or introduce any additional words or characters, and that you don't make any alteration to the content or intent.

If you find that you must make a personal notation in the transcription for clarity, enclose it in square brackets and precede your text with the italicized Latin word *sic*. There are two types of things that might commonly appear in square brackets in the transcription. The use of [*sic*] alone usually means that the transcription is exactly as it appears in the original, even though it might look like an error to the reader. The use of [*sic*] followed by a comma and some additional text is usually a transcriber's notes to provide some additional information, such as spelling out an abbreviation, providing a proven fact documented by other solid evidence, or otherwise clarifying the information immediately preceding the [*sic*] notation. *Sic* is a Latin word for "thus" and should be italicized.

As an example, you might encounter a name spelled as Lizzy in a document and you might know from another piece of proof and evidence that the real given name was different or spelled differently, in which case you might notate the different spelling as follows: [*sic*, Elizabeth].

Consider the situation in which a will for a certain man included a list of his six children. The list included "John, Paul, Edward, Polly, Ann, and Elizabeth." If you transcribed these names and omitted the comma between John and Paul, you or a subsequent researcher might read your transcription and conclude that there were only five children instead of six. A conclusion might be drawn that the first listed son's name was "John Paul" rather than the two names, John *and* Paul. This could be confusing for you and for any other researchers reading your supposedly accurate transcription.

Extract

In the case of a lengthy document, you might decide to copy only portions of the original that pertain specifically to an individual you are researching. An extract is similar to a transcription except that, instead of copying the entire document, you excerpt and copy only *portions* of the original. You still copy the content of the section(s) in which you are interested, word for word, and preserve the spelling and punctuation as it appears in the original source document. However, you might omit portions that you feel are unimportant to your research.

Extracting from original source materials is a common practice. It also is a cause of many errors. An index of names and other information created from original documents can really be an extract or an abstract. People sometimes, in their haste to gather information, make transcription errors or omit important details, which may adversely impact their work and that of other researchers who access and use it. You can protect the integrity of your own research by using extracts, such as indexes, to direct you to the original source material. It is always good to obtain a copy of the entire original source document, whenever possible. You can evaluate the document's contents yourself, and you may find at a later date that you would like to refer to the original to reconfirm your work, provide a copy to another researcher, or look for additional details that may have seemed irrelevant to your earlier research.

Published extracts can be especially problematic in some cases. Remember that, when an extract is prepared, much material can be left behind. The loss of details, language, spelling, and punctuation can adversely impact your *or someone else's* research. In the case of African-American research, for example, an extract of a slaveholder's last will and testament may omit the names of slaves bequeathed, sold, or freed from slavery and under the terms of the will. Those details may be unimportant to one of the slaveholder's descendants. However, descendants of the slaves would be *very* interested in the existence of their antecedents' names in the will. As a result, the extract would be useless to the African-American researcher unless he or she traced the genealogy of the slaveholder and personally examined the original of the will.

It is important to indicate in your work that what you have copied is, in fact, an extract from the original document. This will communicate to you or to other researchers reviewing your work that there is, in fact, more content in the original document.

Abstract

Another type of derivative work is the abstract. Unlike the transcription or extraction, an abstract does not seek to preserve the content of the original source. Instead, an abstract merely *describes* the content of the original source. It contains far less detail than even an extract and may list only what the researcher feels is pertinent to his or her research. An abstract represents the researcher's interpretation of the original material. It may enclose in quotation marks exact text to indicate verbatim material copied from the original document. An abstract of a slaveholder's last will and testament might consist of only the family and heirs of the slaveholder, and might altogether omit any mention of the slaves.

Depending on the knowledge, insight, and skill of the researcher, the information derived from the original and documented in the abstract may contain errors. His or her interpretation, hypothesis, and/or conclusion may be correct but, then again, it may be flawed as a result of taking information out of its original documentary context. This is another reason why someone reading that abstract will want to personally examine the original will.

Information on the Internet

A tremendous amount of information is published on the Internet. Remember that copying and transcribing information from a document to a web page may introduce any number of errors. As a result, you should always consider that what you find on the Internet is a derivative source of information. You will find this to be true of text and indexing. You will *always* want to personally examine the original document for yourself. Professional and volunteer indexers with the best of intentions who read original documents and enter data to create indexes to make them searchable make mistakes. Handwriting is often extremely difficult to read and interpret, and this often causes confusion and indexing errors. This, coupled with simple typing errors, makes working with materials on the Internet problematic.

The images of original documents that you find on the Internet should be considered identical to the original. They may have been digitally photographed or digitized from documents previously microfilmed. Your careful personal examination of a digitized image can therefore be considered the equivalent of traveling to the repository and examining the original source document.

Keep this in mind whenever you are working with material on the Internet. Maintain a healthy skepticism of text-based information, and always seek an exact copy of the original document for personal examination.

Avoid Errors in Derivative Sources

As you can see, there potentially are problems with each of these forms of derivative sources. If errors are introduced at any point by a researcher, an indexer, or a transcriber, these often are disseminated to other researchers. As a result, an error may be perpetuated and, because it appears again and again in many researchers' work, the error may come to be considered "fact." You therefore want to use extreme caution when you encounter other people's transcription, extraction, and abstraction work. Again, always try to obtain a copy of the original source so that you can personally examine it. Your hypotheses and conclusions may differ from those of another researcher. By personally reviewing and analyzing the original document, you can apply your *own* knowledge and insight into your own family's ancestry, and your own knowledge of specific records and record types, in reaching your own conclusions.

You will certainly do your own share of derivative work, and fortunately there are some excellent forms available on the Internet. Among the best are those at Ancestry .com at **http://www.ancestry.com/trees/charts/researchext.aspx**. Here you will find a Research Extract form, as well as census forms for the U.S. federal census population schedules, 1790–1940; UK censuses, 1841–1911; and various Canadian censuses. *Family Tree Magazine* provides another excellent collection of forms at **http://www.familytreemagazine.com/freeforms**. You can also find any number of forms for extracting and abstracting wills, deeds, property descriptions, and other documents by searching on the Internet. The forms are especially helpful as guides to help ensure that you capture critical information.

Evaluate Primary vs. Secondary Information in Original Records

It is always important to weigh the evidence. A highly important consideration in your research is to recognize what may *or may not be* accurate information included in a whole variety of resources. You will quickly learn that not every source of information is equal and that some materials are more reliable than others. That means that you will personally evaluate every piece of evidence, regardless of the source, and analyze its strength and value.

In many cases, a piece of documentary evidence is generated as the result of some event: birth, marriage, death, sale of property, voter registration, taxation, court action, probate process, or some other occasion. Sometimes, though, a record is created before the fact and the event never takes place, as in the case of marriage bonds or marriage licenses issued where the marriage never occurred, tombstones created for an individual who was never buried in the plot, and agreements of sale that were never executed. Are these valid pieces of evidence too? Of course they are, because they were created to represent intent. Even if the intended action never occurred, the piece of evidence places the person(s) involved in a certain place at a specific point in time and tells you something about his or her life. It may lead you to another clue or another piece of evidence.

When evaluating the records of your ancestors' lives, you must always consider the source of the information. When and where was it created? Who created it? Why was it created? Is the information included correct? Information from source materials can be grouped into two categories: *primary information* and *secondary information*. There are very distinct differences.

Primary information was created at or very near the actual event being recorded and is therefore more likely to be accurate. Secondary information was typically created after the fact and, because of the lapse of time and memory and type of information, tends to be less reliable than primary information. Some source materials contain *both* primary *and* secondary information. Let's explore some of the most common types of documentary evidence and evaluate the quality of the information.

Birth Certificates

An example of a source of primary information is an original, photocopy, or scanned image of a birth certificate, such as the one shown in Figure 4-2. The information on this document is typically provided at or just after the time of birth and was completed for the purpose of recording the event. The details about the child's birth date, time, and location are primary information; the age of the parents, however, is considered secondary information because their births occurred years before. You would search for birth records of the father or mother to confirm their birth information.

An amended birth certificate, such as one issued later that changes the information recorded at the time of the birth, may have been intended to provide more accurate or complete information than that which was entered on the original document. Amended birth certificates are also issued for adopted children. There may indeed be other, less correct information placed on those documents just because they were created later. Civil registration birth certificates in England and Wales, for example, included an additional field on the form for children whose names had not been decided at the time of birth. Rather, the child's name may not have been declared until the child was christened. At that time, a parent would return to the registrar's office and provide the child's name to be added to the certificate.

NORTH CAROLINA STATE BOARD OF HEALTH
BUREAU OF VITAL STATISTICS

CERTIFICATE OF LIVE BIRTH

1443

REGISTRATION DISTRICT No. 79-80   REGISTRAR'S CERTIFICATE No. _____   BIRTH No. 132—

1. PLACE OF BIRTH		2. USUAL RESIDENCE OF MOTHER (Where does mother live?)	
a. COUNTY Rockingham b. TOWNSHIP Reidsville		a. STATE N.C. b. COUNTY Rockingham	
c. CITY OR TOWN Reidsville Is Place of Birth Within City Limits? YES [X] NO [ ]		c. CITY OR TOWN Madison Is Place of Res. Within City Limits? YES [X] NO [ ]	
d. FULL NAME OF HOSPITAL OR INSTITUTION (If NOT in hospital or institution, give street address or location) Annie Penn Memorial Hospital		d. STREET ADDRESS or R.F.D. NO. Box 363	

3. CHILD'S NAME (Type or Print)	a. (First) George	b. (Middle) Goodloe	c. (Last) Morgan
4. SEX Male	5a. THIS BIRTH SINGLE [X] TWIN [ ] TRIPLET [ ]	5b. IF TWIN OR TRIPLET (This child born) 1st [ ] 2nd [ ] 3rd [ ]	6. DATE OF BIRTH (Month) (Day) (Year) Aug. 24, 1952

FATHER OF CHILD

7. FULL NAME	a. (First) Samuel	b. (Middle) Thomas	c. (Last) Morgan	8. COLOR OR RACE White
9. AGE (At time of this birth) 42 YEARS	10. BIRTHPLACE (State or foreign country) Alamance Co.N.C.	11a. USUAL OCCUPATION Bookkeeper	11b. KIND OF BUSINESS OR INDUSTRY	

MOTHER OF CHILD

12. FULL MAIDEN NAME	a. (First) Sarah	b. (Middle) Edith	c. (Last) Weatherly	13. COLOR OR RACE White
14. AGE (At time of this birth) 41 YEARS	15. BIRTHPLACE (State or foreign country) Rome, Ga.	16. CHILDREN PREVIOUSLY BORN TO THIS MOTHER (Do NOT include this child)		

17. INFORMANT'S NAME AND RELATION TO CHILD	a. How many OTHER children are now living?	b. How many OTHER children were born alive but are now dead?	c. How many children were stillborn (born dead after 20 weeks pregnancy)?
Mother	1	0	0

I hereby certify that this child was born alive on the date stated above. at 1:50 A.M. P.M.	18a. SIGNATURE Ernest Reynolds	18b. ATTENDANT AT BIRTH M.D. [X] MIDWIFE [ ] OTHER (Specify)
	18c. ADDRESS Reidsville,N.C.	18d. DATE SIGNED
19. DATE REC'D BY LOCAL REG. Sept. 9, 1952	20. REGISTRAR'S SIGNATURE	21. DID MOTHER HAVE BLOOD TEST FOR SYPHILIS YES [X] NO [ ]

FOR MEDICAL AND HEALTH USE
(This section MUST be filled out)

22a. LENGTH OF PREGNANCY 40 Weeks	22b. WEIGHT AT BIRTH 7 LBS. 7½ OZS.	23. IS MOTHER MARRIED? YES [X] NO [ ]	HAS MOTHER INSPECTED CERTIFICATE FOR ACCURACY OF INFORMATION? YES [X] NO [ ]

FORM No. 13
Rev. 1/49

I hereby certify that this is a true and correct copy which appears on record in the Office of the Register of Deeds of Rockingham County, North Carolina, in Book _39_, Page _1443_.

Witness my hand and official seal, this the _17th_ day of _April_ 1979.

Irene Pruitt, Register of Deeds

By: _____
Ass't./Deputy Register of Deeds

FIGURE 4-2   Birth certificates provide essential clues for date and location of birth, names of parents, and other facts.

A delayed birth certificate, which is one issued some time after the event—probably for someone born before birth certificates were issued, born at home with the benefit of a midwife, or whose records were destroyed in a courthouse or other repository—is always a source of secondary information. That is because all of the proof of the date of birth is acquired later and usually from secondary materials.

Marriage Certificates

Another example of a source of primary information is a marriage certificate. Prior to a marriage, a couple usually must have obtained a license to marry, and a government office typically issued the license. When the marriage was performed, the person officiating at the ceremony signed and dated the license to indicate that the marriage had been completed according to law. The signed license was then returned to the government office for issuance of the official marriage certificate. The signed license is commonly referred to as a "marriage return," and a clerk transcribed the information contained in the document into a marriage book. As the marriage book was filled, it was typically alphabetically indexed in two sequences: by the groom's name and by the bride's name. A marriage document transcribed into a marriage book in a courthouse, such as the one shown in Figure 1-2 (Chapter 1), would be considered a derivative source even though the information was copied into the book shortly after the event. That is because it has been transcribed, or copied by hand, and there is the possibility that the clerk made a transcription error. The entry of an incorrect maiden name on my great-grandparents' marriage record caused me to spend years searching for the possibility that my great-grandmother had been married before.

Death Certificates

Some documents can emphatically be a source of *both* primary *and* secondary information. A death certificate is considered a source of primary information for details concerning a person's death, such as the date, time, and location, the name of the mortuary or funeral home that handled the funeral arrangements, and the intended place of interment or disposition of the remains. However, the death certificate is a source of secondary information for all other details, such as the date of birth of the decedent, his or her birthplace, the names of the parents and spouse, the decedent's occupation, and other information. A government official or coroner completed the information on the death certificate in order to certify the death. Someone else, such as a relative or friend, provided that information to the government official or coroner and he or she may not have had adequate knowledge of these details or accurate facts. That person is referred to as the "informant." The death certificate shown in Figure 4-3 contains a great deal of information. Sometimes you may even see a death certificate on which some data fields are left blank or are marked "unknown" or "N.K." (Not Known).

Be suspicious of the quality of information you find on a death certificate provided by an informant if you see some information, such as parents' names, left blank or notated as "unknown."

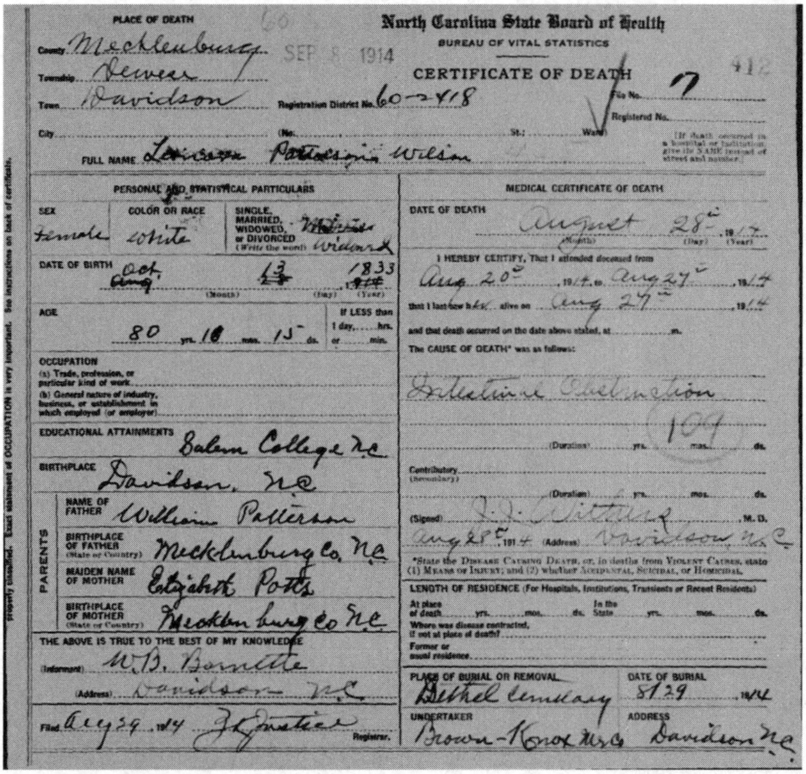

PLACE OF DEATH
County Mecklenburg SEP 8 1914
Township Dewees
Town Davidson Registration District No. 60-2418
City (No. St.; Ward)
FULL NAME Louisa Patterson Wilson

North Carolina State Board of Health
BUREAU OF VITAL STATISTICS
CERTIFICATE OF DEATH
File No. 7
Registered No.
(If death occurred in a hospital or institution give its NAME instead of street and number.)

PERSONAL AND STATISTICAL PARTICULARS
SEX female
COLOR OR RACE white
SINGLE, MARRIED, WIDOWED, or DIVORCED (Write the word) Widowed
DATE OF BIRTH Oct 13 1833 (Month) (Day) (Year)
AGE 80 yrs. 10 mos. 15 ds. If LESS than 1 day, ... hrs. or ... min.
OCCUPATION (a) Trade, profession, or particular kind of work. (b) General nature of industry, business, or establishment in which employed (or employer)
EDUCATIONAL ATTAINMENTS Salem College N.C.
BIRTHPLACE Davidson, N.C.
PARENTS
NAME OF FATHER William Patterson
BIRTHPLACE OF FATHER (State or Country) Mecklenburg Co. N.C.
MAIDEN NAME OF MOTHER Elizabeth Potts
BIRTHPLACE OF MOTHER (State or Country) Mecklenburg Co. N.C.
THE ABOVE IS TRUE TO THE BEST OF MY KNOWLEDGE
(Informant) W. B. Barnette
(Address) Davidson N.C.
Filed Aug 29 1914 J. G. Justice Registrar.

MEDICAL CERTIFICATE OF DEATH
DATE OF DEATH August 28 1914 (Month) (Day) (Year)
I HEREBY CERTIFY, That I attended deceased from Aug 20 1914, to Aug 27 1914
that I last saw her alive on Aug 27 1914
and that death occurred on the date above stated, at ... m.
The CAUSE OF DEATH* was as follows:
Intestine Obstruction
(109)
(Duration) ... yrs. ... mos. ... ds.
Contributory (Secondary) (Duration) ... yrs. ... mos. ... ds.
(Signed) J. J. Withers M.D.
Aug 28 1914 (Address) Davidson N.C.
*State the DISEASE CAUSING DEATH, or, in deaths from VIOLENT CAUSES, state (1) MEANS OF INJURY; and (2) whether ACCIDENTAL, SUICIDAL, or HOMICIDAL.
LENGTH OF RESIDENCE (For Hospitals, Institutions, Transients or Recent Residents)
At place of death ... yrs. ... mos. ... ds. In the State ... yrs. ... mos. ... ds.
Where was disease contracted, if not at place of death?
Former or usual residence.
PLACE OF BURIAL OR REMOVAL Bethel Cemetery
DATE OF BURIAL 8/29 1914
UNDERTAKER Brown-Knox Mrs Co
ADDRESS Davidson N.C.

FIGURE 4-3 A death certificate can contain both primary and secondary information. Data about the death, the mortician, and the planned place of interment is considered primary information. Other details may be considered secondary information and can therefore be less reliable.

Every piece of information that does not directly relate to the event for which the source document was prepared should be considered secondary information. You certainly can use secondary information as a clue or pointer to other primary information that verifies or refutes what is on that death certificate.

Let's examine three other examples of sources of secondary information that might contain errors.

Obituaries

An obituary is a written notice of the death of an individual. It typically includes the name of the person, where they lived, the date of death, and information about any planned funeral or memorial service. An obituary may also include biographical information, as well as the names of surviving family members and/or people who

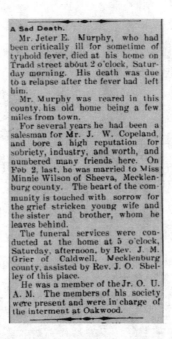

A Sad Death.

Mr. Jeter E. Murphy, who had been critically ill for sometime of typhoid fever, died at his home on Tradd street about 2 o'clock, Saturday morning. His death was due to a relapse after the fever had left him.

Mr. Murphy was reared in this county, his old home being a few miles from town.

For several years he had been a salesman for Mr. J. W. Copeland, and bore a high reputation for sobriety, industry, and worth, and numbered many friends here. On Feb 2, last, he was married to Miss Minnie Wilson of Sheeva, Mecklenburg county. The heart of the community is touched with sorrow for the grief stricken young wife and the sister and brother, whom he leaves behind.

The funeral services were conducted at the home at 5 o'clock, Saturday, afternoon, by Rev. J. M. Grier of Caldwell, Mecklenburg county, assisted by Rev. J. O. Shelley of this place.

He was a member of the Jr. O. U. A. M. The members of his society were present and were in charge of the interment at Oakwood.

FIGURE 4-4 An obituary can contain important biographical information, and can provide clues to other records, but it may also contain errors.

preceded the individual in death. There are a number of places where errors may be introduced in an obituary, starting with the informant who provided the information to the writer of the notice. He or she may provide incorrect or incomplete information because they didn't know the details or because they were distraught. The person taking down the information, such as a funeral home employee or a newspaper copy desk clerk, may omit a word, alter a fact, or introduce spelling or punctuation errors. A newspaper publisher may create errors in the typesetting process, or an editor may either miss catching an error or introduce a mistake. Each person handling the information may potentially contribute to the possibility of errors. The result might be a severe error that leads you on a wild-goose chase. Obituaries published on the Internet are no exception. The example shown in Figure 4-4 contains extensive biographical details, including Mr. Murphy's age, the street on which he resided, and his place of employment. Important clues to his recent marriage information, the cemetery in which he was buried, and the acronym of a fraternal organization to which he belonged point to other possible documentary evidence.

Cemetery Markers

Tombstones such as the one shown in Figure 4-5, grave markers, and memorial plaques placed in cemeteries, mausoleums, and elsewhere may provide clues to sources of primary and/or secondary information. They should always be considered a secondary source. Some are simple and others are more elaborate and may contain

FIGURE 4-5   Cemetery markers can provide birth and death information but should always be considered a secondary source.

great quantities of information. The name and dates on a marker can lead you to search for documents such as birth and death certificates, church or religious records, military records, obituaries, land and property records, wills and probate documents, and other materials.

Some markers may even be adorned with medallions commemorating military rank or membership in some organization. This information may lead you to other records.

More elaborate markers, like the one shown in Figure 4-6, may provide more information. This stone indicates that Harry was the youngest son of "Benj. & Isabella Green." His date of death is shown as "Oct. 10, A.D. 1871" and his age as "8 years and 6 months." This detailed information provides a link to the parents' information and would encourage you to seek details concerning the child's date of birth and the cause of his death.

FIGURE 4-6 An elaborate marker for Harry Green at Bonaventure Cemetery, Savannah, Georgia.

Like obituaries, though, gravestones and memorial plaques are created based on information provided to the creator of the marker and may contain erroneous information. It is not unknown for a stone carver to make a mistake. For example, the surname on one gravestone in an old cemetery in downtown Tampa, Florida, is misspelled. Instead of replacing the stone, however, someone returned to carve a slash mark through the incorrect letter and inscribe the corrected letter above. A marker in the historic cemetery in St. Marys, Georgia, was incorrectly carved, and the stonecutter used a stone cement to fill the incorrect letter and then re-carved it. The error is still visible on the stone. Remember that the stone carver is only inscribing what was provided and that he, too, can introduce errors.

Another problem with tombstones is that, unless you were involved with the purchase or placement of a marker on a grave, you may have no idea when the stone was created or installed. Families could not always afford to install a marker for a grave. As a result, it may have been years or decades before a stone was ordered and installed. (The cemetery office may have a record of the manufacturer of the marker and when it was installed at the site.) While the information you see is "set in stone," always seek corroboration elsewhere of the facts engraved or cast there.

Bible Entries

It is a natural assumption for us to make that what is entered in the family Bible is correct, but these entries can be misleading as well. Remember that birth, marriage, death, and other entries could have been made at any time. There are several items to look for when examining entries made in a Bible that may indicate that they are not primary information:

- *Always check the publication date of the Bible.* If the date of any entry predates the publication date, you know that it was added later and is therefore secondary information.
- *Examine the handwriting carefully.* The fact that the handwriting is identical doesn't mean much, especially if this was a personal or family Bible. One person may have been the family scribe. However, if you can identify the owner of the handwriting for the entries and can determine that entries were made prior to that person's birth *or* for a logical period when he or she could not have made the entry, you may conclude that the information is secondary in nature.
- *Examine the ink used in the entries.* If all the entries appear to have been made with the same pen and ink, it is possible that someone added a group of entries at one time and not as they occurred. Another tip-off is if any entries for events with dates that precede 1945 are made using a ballpoint pen—they are definitely secondary information. Why? Because the ballpoint pen was not invented until 1938, was introduced during World War II for military use, and was not sold commercially until 1945.

Apply Critical Thinking Skills to Your Genealogical Research

As you have seen, the examination of source materials can tell you a great deal. Personal analysis is a key activity in determining the strength of the evidence you discover. You are acting like an investigative journalist or a crime scene investigator, investigating the scene, the events, the people, and the story. You should always ask the questions about *who, when, where, what, how,* and *why* of your ancestor's life events. In addition to merely reporting the story, you will analyze information and evidence, and develop realistic hypotheses. Like a journalist, you have the equipment, knowledge, skills, and a structured methodology to apply to your investigation. Your job is to bring all of these factors together for the purpose of identifying, classifying, and analyzing the evidence you find.

One thing you will do in your genealogical research is to employ your critical thinking skills to the evaluation of the evidence you find. You do this when you read news articles, assessing the information presented and analyzing it for veracity and reliability. Using the same skills is imperative in your work because you have to determine what information you have and the quality or reliability of the evidentiary sources. There are five basic evaluation criteria you will use, and these should be applied to everything you evaluate, from printed resources to electronic and Internet materials to physical objects and heirlooms.

A component of your critical thinking skills is the knowledge and experience you have gained during your life, coupled with a healthy dose of common sense. The understanding you will acquire as you continue encountering and working with new and different types of genealogical source materials will make you more sensitive to analyzing the evidence. You cannot take anything for granted, but should instead measure the evidence by the five criteria listed here:

- **Origin**   Always question where the material originated, when it was created, who created it, and why. Determine if you are working with an original piece of evidence or an exact facsimile, such as a photocopy, microfilm, or scanned image. If you have a piece of derivative source material, you must determine whether it is a transcription, an extract, or an abstract of the original. Try to gain access to the original source material whenever possible so that you can personally examine and analyze it.
- **Quality and accuracy**   The origin of the source material goes a long way toward determining the accuracy of the material. However, recognize that mistakes can be made even in original materials. For example, a census taker could misspell a name on the form he or she is completing. Determine whether the information can be verified or refuted by other evidence and, if so, by what other specific pieces of evidence and how reliable (or faulty) that material might be.
- **Authority**   Is the creator or author of the material an authority or expert? How do you know? Have you checked his or her credentials or reputation? Is the information hearsay or is it fact? Is the information you are examining a

hypothesis or a proven truth? Again, it is important to consider whether the material being analyzed is an original or derivative source and whether it is primary or secondary information.

- **Bias** Is there any possibility that what you are evaluating is influenced by any bias? Does the creator or author have another agenda? It is possible that you are dealing with partial truth in some instances, especially where individuals' accounts of events are concerned. There may be a reason to lie or to mask the truth. Examples might include a child born out of wedlock; a person misrepresenting his or her age due to vanity or a desire to legally marry, or to qualify for or avoid military service; or a concern about the perception of being descended from a particular ethnic or religious group. How do you know that you have not discovered purposely bogus information?

- **Sources** Evaluate the sources from which you have obtained the information. This relates back to origin, quality and accuracy, authority, and bias. However, if you obtain information from another researcher, carefully examine the sources he or she cites, and be prepared to verify absolutely everything that person has cited.

With all of this in mind, you should maintain a healthy skepticism in your investigation. Be wary of information that seems too good to be true, and remember that some data can be the subject of interpretation. Someone else's analysis of evidence may differ from yours for a variety of reasons. You or another person may have different perspectives of other people's lives and events, and that may influence the hypotheses and conclusions that are drawn. Try to keep an open mind, but also apply your critical thinking skills to the analysis of each piece of evidence you find.

You can expect to encounter some brick walls in your research. This book will teach you ways of approaching apparent dead ends and circumventing brick walls in your research, and how to use alternative research strategies and substitute record types in the process. You may also want to read the book *Advanced Genealogy Research Techniques*, which I co-authored with Drew Smith. In it we present many research strategies and lots of examples of how to work around brick walls in your research.

Place Your Ancestors into Context

English poet John Donne is famous for his *Meditation XVII*, in which he states, "No man is an island, entire of itself." He asserts that all of mankind is interconnected, and all are a part of one another's history and activities. This is as true in our genealogical research of the past generations as it is of today. Our ancestors lived in specific places and time periods, and they witnessed and participated in events and activities as surely as we ourselves do.

It is essential during your research process to learn as much about your ancestors' lives and times as possible so that you can better understand them. That means learning about the geography of the places where they lived, including where the jurisdictional boundaries of their state, province, country, or territories were drawn.

You also must become a student of the history of the places and times in which your ancestors lived. This will help you understand what their lives were like and perhaps the motivations for some of their actions. The history of the area where they lived will also help you understand who created certain types of documents at that time and the reasons for the private type of information contained in those documents.

Major cataclysms as well as ordinary events shaped the lives of our ancestors. Consider, for example, the Potato Famine in Ireland in the 1840s, which, according to some sources, caused more than 1.5 million starving Irish citizens to migrate to North America. Or perhaps the rule of *primogeniture*, under which the oldest son inherited the land of his father and may have forced one or more younger sons to leave home to make his own way in the world. Your ancestor may have become an apprentice in order to learn a trade. Political oppression or a war may have caused your ancestors to seek refuge in another place. Your investigation of the place, history, culture, and climate where your ancestors lived and where they may have migrated will serve you well in understanding their lives, what records may have been created by and about them, and where these materials may now be located.

Format Names, Dates, and Locations Correctly

Gathering information about your family is one thing; recording it in a consistent format that can be understood and used by others is quite another. Genealogists use a number of standardized forms for this purpose, and genealogy database software programs can produce printed versions of these forms as a result of data entered into and stored in their programs. Let it suffice to say that genealogists have standards for the entry of data. Let's discuss each type of data and the standards that are universally used. Figure 4-7 demonstrates how information should be properly formatted.

Record Names

People's names are entered on genealogical forms and in genealogy database programs using their first name (also referred to as a given name or forename), full middle name(s), and surname (last name). It is also important to include notations that help differentiate between different individuals, and to add a suffix such as a Senior (Sr.) or Junior (Jr.) or a III, IV, or V. In addition, you could use the suffix field to indicate a royal title, such as Prince of Wales, Duke of Alba, or Duchess of Cambridge.

A woman's name is always recorded with her first name, her middle name, and her maiden surname. It is not unusual to find different ways used to indicate the maiden name of the married woman in printed materials such as family histories or newspaper stories. You may see a woman's married name followed by a notation of

Ancestors of Laura Augusta (Minnie) Wilson

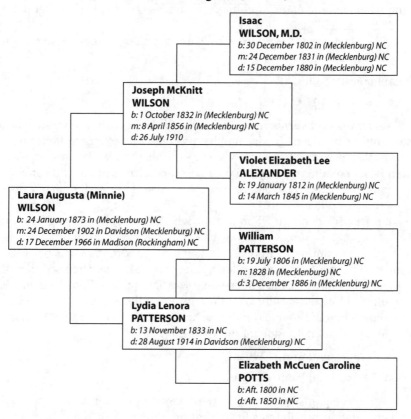

Isaac
WILSON, M.D.
b: 30 December 1802 in (Mecklenburg) NC
m: 24 December 1831 in (Mecklenburg) NC
d: 15 December 1880 in (Mecklenburg) NC

Joseph McKnitt
WILSON
b: 1 October 1832 in (Mecklenburg) NC
m: 8 April 1856 in (Mecklenburg) NC
d: 26 July 1910

Violet Elizabeth Lee
ALEXANDER
b: 19 January 1812 in (Mecklenburg) NC
d: 14 March 1845 in (Mecklenburg) NC

Laura Augusta (Minnie)
WILSON
b: 24 January 1873 in (Mecklenburg) NC
m: 24 December 1902 in Davidson (Mecklenburg) NC
d: 17 December 1966 in Madison (Rockingham) NC

William
PATTERSON
b: 19 July 1806 in (Mecklenburg) NC
m: 1828 in (Mecklenburg) NC
d: 3 December 1886 in (Mecklenburg) NC

Lydia Lenora
PATTERSON
b: 13 November 1833 in NC
d: 28 August 1914 in Davidson (Mecklenburg) NC

Elizabeth McCuen Caroline
POTTS
b: Aft. 1800 in NC
d: Aft. 1850 in NC

FIGURE 4-7   A pedigree or ancestor chart showing formatted names, dates, and locations

her maiden name, prefaced with *nee* or *née*. For example, a married woman's name may be represented as:

Mrs. Carolyn Penelope Mason, *née* Weatherly

Mrs. Mary Martha Knox, *nee* Wilson

Another method of representing a maiden name is to include it in the full name stream and italicize it or to include it in brackets. You may therefore see it written as follows:

Mrs. Carolyn Penelope *Weatherly* Mason

Mrs. Mary Martha [Wilson] Knox

While the use of any of these formats is acceptable in a text environment, the use of first name, middle name, and maiden name is the standard format to be used in genealogical situations.

While it is not mandatory to do so, some genealogists capitalize the surname, as in the following examples:

Green Berry HOLDER

Laura Augusta WILSON

Capitalization of surnames is most often done in written text, such as letters, emails, online message boards, mail list postings, and other communiqués, because it causes the surnames to be easily seen. Genealogy software programs also offer the option when creating reports and charts to capitalize surnames. If someone is reading a written document, the capitalized surname stands out and is clearly differentiated from a first or middle name.

Another consideration when dealing with names is how to represent nicknames. It is not unusual for someone to be given a nickname or diminutive of a name by which they are commonly known. My paternal grandmother was born Laura Augusta Wilson but, from infancy, was called by the name Minnie. She used that name throughout her life. Her husband's name was Samuel Goodloe Morgan, and he was commonly addressed as Sam. When representing these situations on ancestral charts, it is standard practice to enclose the nickname or diminutive in quotation marks following the first and middle names. For example:

Laura Augusta "Minnie" Wilson

Samuel Goodloe "Sam" Morgan

By preserving this important piece of name information when you find it used, you increase your possibilities for finding additional records for the individual. Remember that a person may be known and recorded in formal or official documents with their full birth name, with their birth first name, middle initial, and surname, or simply by initials and a surname. However, they may be known and recorded in more casual or informal materials by their nickname and surname. You may be surprised to find a nickname used where you might instead expect to find the full name. Nicknames are often used in obituaries so that the reader can easily identify the person whose death is being reported. It is not unusual, too, that a nickname or diminutive version of the name is used on a grave marker.

Genealogy database software programs usually accommodate the entry of a nickname or diminutive. The programs will also allow you to enter the suffix Sr., Jr., II, III, etc. These name features are then displayed as part of the full name on the individual's record in the program, and can be included on charts and reports that are produced. For example, one of my cousins is represented as follows in my database:

Alvis Morrison "Al" Weatherly III

This makes it very clear that this man is the third in a series of people named Alvis Morrison Weatherly, and that he is commonly known as Al.

Here is one final note about titles of address for individuals. You may want to include some title that an individual has earned or been given. You might want to enter Dr., Rev., Maj., the Honorable, or some other title of distinction. Most genealogy database programs allow you to enter titles of individuals as a prefix to the name. That information will also appear in your database and on reports.

Record Dates

The United States uses a format for dates that is different from the format used in almost every other part of the world. Whereas most Americans usually write a date in the format June 12, 1905 (or 6/12/1905), in their documents and correspondence, much of the rest of the world writes it as 12 June 1905 (or 12/6/1905). To prevent possible confusion, you always want to use the DD MONTH YYYY format for all of your genealogical work, where the word name for the month is used. You will find that using this standard makes communicating with other genealogists worldwide easier.

Record Locations

When conducting your research, you will find that boundaries, place names, and political/governmental jurisdictions have changed throughout time, often more than once. It is important for you to seek records in the correct place. That means learning what governmental or other official entity had jurisdiction over a place at the time your ancestor lived there and at the time a specific record was created. It also means working with both contemporary and historical maps. For example, some of my early Morgan ancestors settled in the mid-1750s in what was then Orange County, Province of North Carolina, in the American colonies. Today, the exact area in which they settled is divided into Caswell and Person Counties in the State of North Carolina.

The way in which you record locations in your research should reflect the name of the place, the county, parish, or other geopolitical area in which it was located, and the state, province, and country. Yes, country jurisdictions changed too. In those cases, it is important to also include the country name. Some examples are shown in Table 4-1. (You may also enter counties or provinces, separated by commas or enclosed in parentheses.)

Certainly be careful to record the correct geopolitical entity for the location *at the time the event occurred*. This is essential because that is the place where the records were recorded and where they are probably still archived. For example, if I wanted to record the marriage of one ancestor in that area in North Carolina, in 1761, I would record the birth location in the following manner:

Reuben MORGAN   24 August 1761   Orange County, Province of North Carolina, British America

The marriage date of his son, which occurred in the same community after the formation of Caswell County in 1777, would be recorded as follows:

William MORGAN   22 December 1783   Caswell County, North Carolina, USA

TABLE 4-1   Examples of How to Properly Format Location Names

Location	Record It As
Madison, North Carolina	Madison, Rockingham County, North Carolina, USA
Rome, Georgia	Rome, Floyd County, Georgia, USA
Montreal, Canada	Montreal, Québec, Canada
Barkham in Berkshire, England	Barkham, Berkshire, England
Cottingham in the East Riding district of Yorkshire, England	Cottingham, East Riding, Yorkshire, England

The difference in the county name distinguishes the fact that the event occurred under a different governmental jurisdiction. In the course of my research, I determined that Caswell County was formed on 8 April 1777 from a northern portion of Orange County. Therefore, if I want to obtain a copy of Reuben's marriage record, I would contact or visit the Orange County courthouse in Hillsborough, North Carolina, whereas I would visit the Caswell County courthouse in Yanceyville, North Carolina, for William's marriage record. It is acceptable to abbreviate a state, province, or country as long as you use an acknowledged abbreviation. You will note in the first example above that I did not list the country as USA but did so in the second example. That is because there was no official United States of America until the Declaration of Independence was signed on 4 July 1776. (Some of my ancestors and relatives continue to live in the same exact location to this day. What was once Orange County became Caswell County, and then an act was passed by the North Carolina legislature in 1791 to split the four Eastern districts of Caswell County off to become Person County, effective on 1 February 1792. It is important to make note of those jurisdictional and boundary changes so that you always search in the right place for records of events that occurred at a specific point in time. For my family, my research has taken me to the courthouses of all three counties.)

Suffice it to say that it is vitally important to properly identify the right location *and* to record it as part of your records. If you are researching your ancestry in Germany, you will want to study history of the states, duchies, kingdoms, and states and their periods to help determine where to search for specific records pertinent to when your ancestors lived there. Let me give you a strong example.

If you are researching Polish ancestors, you will most definitely need to study Poland's history. The Kingdom of Poland was established on 18 April 1025. It became part of the Polish–Lithuanian Commonwealth in 1569. It was invaded and partitioned by the Russian Empire, the Kingdom of Prussia, and the Austrian Hapsburg Monarchy during the 18th century, ultimately resulting in the dissolution of the Commonwealth in 1795. It was not until the conclusion of World War I in 1918 that Poland became independent again as the Second Polish Republic. However, invasions of the country by Germany and Russia at the beginning of World War II ended its independence again. Poland became the communist People's Republic of Poland as part of the Soviet Union. It was not until the 1980s that the Solidarity movement emerged (Independent Self-governing Trade Union "Solidarity") under the leadership of Lech Wałęsa. Semi-free elections were held in 1989, and it became the Republic of Poland on 13 September 1989.

As you can see, the turbulent history of Poland means that different governmental entities had control of the creation of civil records. Roman Catholic Church records in Poland may provide a more consistent body of information over time. Those are being digitized and indexed by FamilySearch. It is important to determine the place where your ancestors may have lived so that you can most accurately determine what government had authority at the time and created records, and to trace the location of those materials.

Work with Pedigree Charts

Now that you know how to collect, evaluate, and analyze evidence, and know how data is to be formatted, it's time to learn about the forms that genealogists use for entering their data. *Family Tree Magazine* (at **http://www.familytreemagazine .com/freeforms**) and Ancestry.com (at **http://www.ancestry.com/download /charts#ancchart**) have developed a wide array of genealogical charts for use in gathering and recording data. All of these are available as PDF files and are free to download. I urge you to visit both these sites and review each of the free forms that these companies offer. You're sure to find a layout for each that you like.

One of the basic genealogy forms we use is known as a *pedigree chart*, and is sometimes known by other names, such as "ancestral chart" or "family tree chart." These forms come in a variety of styles and typically represent three or more generations. Let's begin our discussion by looking at some examples. *Family Tree Magazine* provides their version of the pedigree chart at **http://familytreemagazine .com/upload/images/PDF/ancestor.pdf** (see Figure 4-8).

Pedigree charts are used to represent multiple generations of direct ancestry. The downloadable chart shown in Figure 4-8 can be used to represent five generations. Others you might locate through retail stores or on the Internet may represent three or more generations. Some versions may be used to represent as many as 10, 12, 16, or more generations. These latter specimens are usually intended for showy displays, but some genealogists will use the larger format as a working document in order to have their direct family lineage shown on a single sheet.

Let's use your own family as an example and use *Family Tree Magazine*'s Ancestor Chart form as a worksheet. Remember I said you should start with yourself? That's what you do here. Enter as much information as you have and enter it in pencil so that you can change it later as needed. Fill in *your name* on the line in the center of the left side of the page. Remember that you should enter a woman's surname using her maiden name. Under your name on line 1, enter your date of birth (in the format of DD MONTH YYYY such as 24 August 1985), the place of your birth (in the format

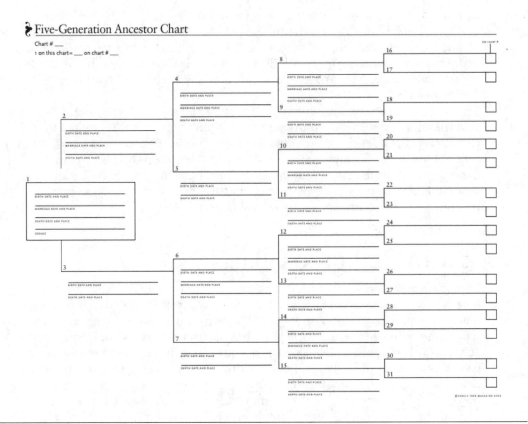

FIGURE 4-8 Family Tree Magazine's Ancestor Chart (pedigree chart)

of City, County, State, Country or appropriate format), the date of your marriage to the person listed below you, if appropriate, and the place of the marriage. Enter your surname in all capital letters (uppercase) so that it will always be easy to see. If you are married, you may fill in your spouse's name on the line below. We will assume that you are not yet deceased, of course, so you can leave the areas for date of death and location blank.

The next blocks above and below your entry are used to represent your father (at the top) and your mother (below). Enter the birth, marriage, and (if applicable) death dates and locations your parents. Please note that marriage information is always listed on pedigree charts under the male, assuming the parents were married. Enter your mother's name using her first, middle, and maiden name, and enter her maiden name in capital letters. You may not yet have all the names or other information. That's the purpose of genealogical research.

The next column consists of blocks to represent your grandparents—your father's father and mother and your mother's father and mother. Fill in these people's names and any vital information you know.

The next column contains blocks represent your great-grandparents. Fill in as many names, dates, and locations as you can. The last column contains blocks for the names of your great-great-grandparents and boxes labeled "See Chart #".

You have probably discovered already that you have gaps in your family knowledge. You may also be unsure about some of the information you entered. That's okay, though. That's why we typically enter the data in pencil, so that we can change or correct it as we locate more evidence. (Remember that when you use a database program, you will be able to enter data, edit it, and generate reports that include formatted charts like this.)

The boxes for chart numbers allow you to cross from this chart to others that allow you to enter details on your great-great-grandparents and earlier generations. This provides a way for you to organize and navigate through charts for multiple generations. For example, you may have obtained information on your great-grandparents' parents and beyond. Since you don't have enough room on this chart to represent them, you will need to complete a new pedigree chart for those persons. Let's say you start a new chart for your great-grandfather's ancestors. On the new chart, his name will be listed on the line on the left, just as your name was listed on the first chart. His spouse will be entered below, and his parents' (your great-great-grandparents) names will be entered on the lines in the next column, and so on. You may label this as **Chart 2**. Label the first chart you completed **Chart 1**. Now, cross-reference them as follows:

- Beside your great-grandfather's name on Chart 1, enter the number **2** (for Chart 2).
- In the upper-left corner of another blank chart, enter the number 2. Where it is labeled "1 on this chart = _____ on chart #. _____," enter for the first blank your great-great-grandfather's number "16", and put "1" in the second blank. This tells you that the person in the number 1 position on this chart is number 16 on Chart 1.

You have now cross-referenced the charts for easy navigation back and forth. You will want to create a binder to hold your pedigree charts. File the chart that begins with your own generation on top, followed by other generations in chart number sequence.

Work with Family Group Sheets

While the pedigree or ancestral chart represents a single thread of descent, a *family group sheet* (or *family group record*) is a representation of a complete family unit: father, mother, and all children. You potentially will prepare a family group sheet for every family unit you document. An example of Ancestry.com's Family Group Record document is shown in Figure 4-9, and a free downloadable version is available at Ancestry.com at **http://c.mfcreative.com/pdf/trees/charts/famgrec.pdf**. Some family group sheets include spaces for recording the sources of the information that you have found.

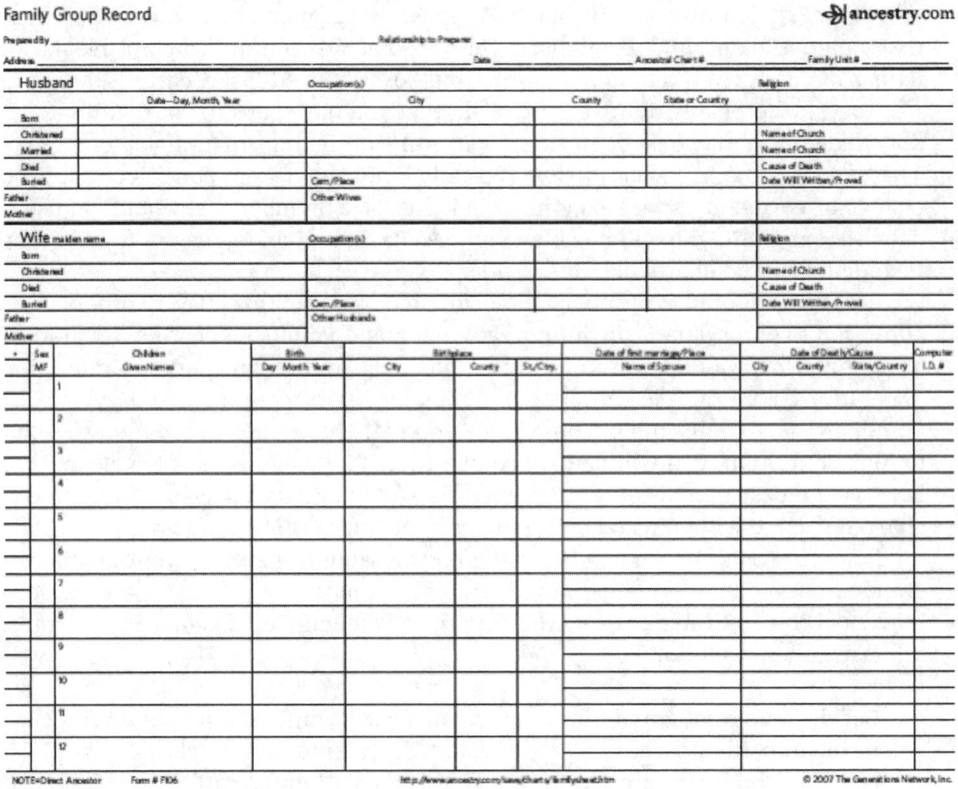

FIGURE 4-9 Ancestry.com's Family Group Record form

The Source Summary for Family Information from Ancestry.com at **http://c.mfcreative.com/pdf/trees/charts/soursumm.pdf** can be used in conjunction with their Family Group Record document to keep track of the origin of the evidence you use to document the facts. Please take a few minutes to download and print copies of these sheets now.

The family group sheet begins by asking for the name of the preparer and that person's address and other information. In the event you share a copy of this form with another person, he or she will be able to contact you with questions or to share their research with you. You also have a place at the top of the form to cross-reference this sheet to a pedigree chart.

This form contains space for substantially more information than the pedigree chart, but the sources and types of information are pretty self-explanatory. You will note, though, two interesting columns for the children. The first is one with an asterisk (*) at the top, representing whether or not the father and mother are direct ancestors. Remember, some children in a family unit may be from another marriage and may have been adopted by the new spouse. The other column is for Computer

ID. You may decide to cross-reference this chart with entries in a computer program, and this column could facilitate that effort.

What if you have the name of one person and not the name of his or her spouse? What if you only know a wife's first name and not her maiden name? What if you know there was a child but you don't know his or her name? Leave the information blank, or add a question mark, backslashes (//), or some other notation to indicate missing data. You can always return to enter it when you locate it.

Take a few minutes to complete a family group sheet for your own parents' family unit, and include information about your siblings and yourself. Any facts you don't know can be left blank for now. You can come back to complete them later when you have located documentation for those facts.

You now have a good idea about recording information on a pedigree chart and a family group sheet. However, there are always exceptions in families that need to be recorded. Let's examine three such circumstances that you may encounter.

Record Multiple Family Units with a Common Spouse

What do you do when a spouse died or a couple divorced and a spouse remarried? How do you represent that? The answer is that you create a new family group sheet for the new family couple and for their family unit. Children produced from this union are included on this separate sheet.

How to Handle Non-traditional Family Units

There have always been family units operating without the benefit of marriage. And with an increasing number of same-sex marriages or civil unions taking place in many places worldwide, there now is also a need to record those family units and relationships. Whatever the arrangement and whoever the people are, it is important to record the family unit "as is." Therefore, when you record two individuals in a relationship, portray it on a family group sheet. If there was no marriage, indicate it as **NONE**. Most genealogy database programs today now allow you to represent a relationship status with such codes as "friends," "married," "partners," "single," "private," "other," or "unknown." You should be honest about relationships where known unless the publication of such knowledge would be detrimental or hurtful in some way. If there are children produced from a nontraditional pairing, show them as you normally would, as issue from the union.

How to Record Adopted Children

A common question is how to record adopted children on a family group sheet. Should you include them? The answer is, of course, an emphatic yes. Adopted children are part of the family unit, regardless of the identities of their birth parents. The adopted child's birth parents, if known, can be recorded in the notes section of your family group sheet or in the notes area of a genealogy database program. However, the adoption formalizes the legal relationship between the child and his or her adoptive parents and should become the primary family relationship represented in your records.

Most genealogy database software programs allow for the identification of a child's relationship to its parents. The Family Tree Maker program (produced by Ancestry.com), for example, provides values of Natural, Adopted, Step, Foster, Related, Guardian, Sealed, Private, and Unknown.

Remember that adoption may be a sensitive topic for the adoptee, his or her parents, or some other family members. You will therefore want to be considerate about publishing the information outside the family circle. That does not mean you shouldn't record it in your records. However, many of the genealogy database programs allow for the omission of the parent-child relationship information when reports are produced or data files are created.

Create Source Citations for Your Data

When you were in school and preparing term papers, you were probably required to prepare a bibliography of your source materials. You may also have used footnotes and endnotes for individual fact or quotation references. This is the scholarly way to document research because it provides details for the reader or subsequent researcher to retrace your work. It also allows the reader to evaluate the quality of your conclusions based upon the types of sources that you used as evidence.

Source citations are more than just "busywork." As you collect information, evidence, documents, and other materials for your family history research, it is essential to record where you found them. You want to provide a record for yourself and any other genealogical researcher so that he or she can retrace your steps, locate the material you used, and personally examine it. Even in cases where other researchers don't retrace your steps, they will still want to know what kinds of sources you used. Your interpretation of data may be different from someone else's. The fact that you may actually be looking for different information may influence what you search for, what you believe is important, and the way you interpret it in your family's application. One seemingly insignificant name to you in an ancestor's last will and testament may be just the "missing link" that another researcher has been seeking for years.

Your source citations will generally follow standard bibliographic citation standards for books, journals, magazines, newspapers, and similar printed sources. Students and researchers know that there are several citation formats for these kinds of materials, but typically the style used by genealogists resembles the standards of the Chicago Style, which is commonly used among historians. Chicago Style, as documented in the most current edition of *The Chicago Manual of Style*, provides an appropriate general framework for genealogical source citations to typical printed material (books, journals, magazines, newspapers, etc.). The structure of your source citations should contain all essential information that will help another researcher identify and locate the source material you used, even if your citations do not adhere exactly to a standard style. The following are examples of some of these common source materials.

Many genealogists find that *The Chicago Manual of Style* doesn't include citation formats for commonly cited genealogical sources. For example, tombstones, embroidered samplers, and engraved jewelry frequently provide essential sources of information. Fortunately, Elizabeth Shown Mills has written the definitive reference for genealogical source citations. Her book, *Evidence Explained: Citing History Sources from Artifacts to Cyberspace*, is the accepted standard used in the United States' genealogical community.

Book

Mills, Elizabeth Shown. *Evidence Explained: Citing History Sources from Artifacts to Cyberspace*. 2nd ed. Baltimore, MD: Genealogical Publishing Co., 2009.

Magazine Article

Morgan, George G. "Tracing Frances Lamb Mims Wilson: A Case Study." *Internet Genealogy Magazine*, December/January 2014.

Newspaper Article

Pilarczyk, Jamie. "Learning History's Lessons." *Tampa Tribune*, 10 September 2008. B3.

Newspaper Article on the Internet

Malesky, Betty. "Genealogy Today: Promoting rights of genealogists." *Green Valley News & Sun*, 26 June 2014. < http://www.gvnews.com/lifestyle/genealogy-today-promoting-rights-of-genealogists/article_95107a06-f8b0-11e3-aeb0-001a4bcf887a.html >. Accessed 26 June 2014.

Family Bible (One-of-a-Kind)

Family data, Morgan Family Bible, *The Holy Bible*, new edition (New York, NY: Christian Book Publishers, Inc., 1921); original owned in 2014 by George G. Morgan (106 E. Hunter Street, Anytown, FL 33333).

Print materials such as those shown in the previous examples make up a sizeable portion of reference material for genealogists. However, we also work with an amazing array of materials, including letters, postcards, journals, diaries, deeds, census records, birth certificates, marriage licenses, christening and baptismal records, bar and bat mitzvah records, wills, probate packets, obituaries, ships' passenger lists, naturalization records, medical records, tombstones, engraved jewelry, furniture, embroidered samplers, and much, much more. We work with all types of media as well: paper, microfilm, microfiche, CD-ROMs, computer files, databases, photographs and slides, PDF files, scanned images, records found on the Internet or exchanged electronically in such media as email and data files, blogs, wikis, podcasts, webinars, social media, and in other online virtual environments.

The essential components of every citation are the name of the author or creator, a title or description of the source, where the source was published and who published it, and the date of creation or publication. In addition, if the source is a rare or one-of-a-kind item, it is important to include the place where it resides and/or where you accessed it. Here are examples of just a few more sources used in genealogical research and appropriate citation formats for them.

Cemetery Marker (Large Cemetery)

Green Berry Holder tombstone; section New Front Addition, Terrace 1, Lot #1, Myrtle Hill Cemetery, Rome, Floyd County, Georgia, USA; transcribed by the writer on 14 July 1998.

Cemetery Marker (Small Rural Cemetery)

Caroline Alice Whitefield Morgan Carter tombstone, Cooper Cemetery, Caswell County, North Carolina (Ridgeville township, Latitude 36° 17' 15" North, Longitude 79° 12' 02" West), photographed by George G. Morgan on 24 August 2011.

Microfilm of U.S. Federal Census

Green B. Holder household, 1870 U.S. census, Subdivision 141, Floyd County, Georgia, page 102, line 22; National Archives micropublication M593, roll 149.

Email Message

Mary A. Morgan, "Your Great-grandmother Patterson," email message from < mam@ auntmary190505.com > (106 E. Hunter Street, Madison, NC 27025) to author, 14 June 2011.

Blog

Seaver, Randy. "Genea-Musings," online < http://www.geneamusings.com/ >. "Rabbit Trail - Where Was Aaron Seavers Land in Grand Blanc, Michigan," downloaded 26 June 2014.

The amount of information included varies with the type of source material you use, what it provides, and, in some cases, where it is physically located. You will want to learn all about citing your sources so that you can do a scholarly job.

The more information you locate, the more important it is to have clearly documented the sources. You will soon learn from personal experience that it is often impossible to recall the origin of a particular piece of information. Source citations are invaluable when retracing your own research and are essential as documentation for other researchers' use in trying to retrace and verify your work.

You will always want to perform effective and scholarly research on your family history. That means identifying and using the best possible source materials you can locate, analyzing them carefully, weighing the evidence, formulating reasonable hypotheses, and drawing realistic conclusions. It combines all the skills discussed so far in this chapter, and these comprise the basic rules of genealogical evidence.

Select a Family Tree Format

Throughout this chapter, I've discussed the mechanics of collecting, analyzing, recording, and citing sources for your family history data. Now is the time to start considering just how to record and display your data.

As you read the title of this section, you probably are thinking, "How can there be more than *one* format of a family tree?" Actually, there are a number of different ways to view family data, and each one can help you analyze what you have discovered in perhaps a different way. Genealogists also have their own preferences about which display format they use. For example, you should know that there are two major family tree display formats: the *standard chart* format and the *fan chart* format. The standard format shown in Figure 4-10 presents a vertical, linear view of two generations. The double, parallel lines linking individuals indicates their marriage or union.

The same data can be displayed in a fan chart format, as shown in Figure 4-11 starting with the focus individual and his or her spouse, and additional generations' information extending in semicircular bands by generation.

As you are working with your family genealogy, you will find it useful to be able to create both ancestor and descendant tree views. An *ancestor chart* starts with one individual as its focal point and presents a picture of that person's ancestors. A *descendant chart* starts with an individual and shows his or her descendants. The number of generations represented on any chart is your option. Genealogical database programs can produce a number of different reports, and you can specify as many generations as you would like to see and to include as much or as little information as you like. At the very minimum, however, you should include each individual's name, date of birth, date of marriage (if any), and date of death (if deceased). The location of each of these events is important for tracing the evidence of the event from the right repository, and you may therefore want to include that data as well.

In addition to the standard and fan formats of the ancestor and descendant chart formats, there are some other formats as well. An *hourglass tree* combines the features of both the ancestor and descendant tree views. In Figure 4-12, my great-grandfather Rainey Baines Morgan is the focal individual, with his wife, Caroline Alice Whitefield [sometimes spelled Whitfield], shown at his side and their union being indicated with the double lines linking them. Rainey's parents, Goodloe W. Morgan and Mary L. Woods, and his two sets of grandparents, Reuben Morgan and Mary Merritt, and William Woods and Mary Farley, are shown above him as his ancestors. Rainey's three sons, Samuel G. Morgan, William R. Morgan, Sr., and John A. Morgan, are shown as descendants, and their respective wives are shown beside them, again with the unions represented by double lines.

All of the tree formats previously discussed really are just that: tree formats. They are called trees because they begin somewhere with a root individual and branch out from there. The format that you will encounter most for representing lineal family relationships is the pedigree chart that we discussed earlier in the chapter. It is an ancestral tree representation, but is by far the most commonly used representation in day-to-day genealogy work.

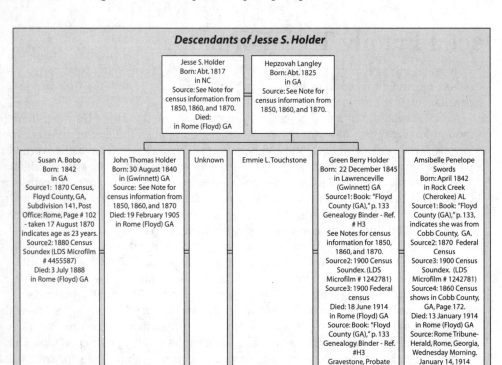

Descendants of Jesse S. Holder

Jesse S. Holder	Hepzovah Langley
Born: Abt. 1817 in NC	Born: Abt. 1825 in GA
Source: See Note for census information from 1850, 1860, and 1870.	Source: See Note for census information from 1850, 1860, and 1870.
Died: in Rome (Floyd) GA	

Susan A. Bobo	John Thomas Holder	Unknown	Emmie L. Touchstone	Green Berry Holder	Amsibelle Penelope Swords
Born: 1842 in GA. Source1: 1870 Census, Floyd County, GA, Subdivision 141, Post Office: Rome, Page # 102 - taken 17 August 1870 indicates age as 23 years. Source2: 1880 Census Soundex (LDS Microfilm # 4455587) Died: 3 July 1888 in Rome (Floyd) GA	Born: 30 August 1840 in (Gwinnett) GA Source: See Note for census information from 1850, 1860, and 1870 Died: 19 February 1905 in Rome (Floyd) GA			Born: 22 December 1845 in Lawrenceville (Gwinnett) GA Source1: Book: "Floyd County (GA)," p. 133 Genealogy Binder - Ref. # H3 See Notes for census information for 1850, 1860, and 1870. Source2: 1900 Census Soundex. (LDS Microfilm # 1242781) Source3: 1900 Federal census Died: 18 June 1914 in Rome (Floyd) GA Source: Book: "Floyd County (GA)," p. 133 Genealogy Binder - Ref. #H3 Gravestone, Probate packet	Born: April 1842 in Rock Creek (Cherokee) AL Source1: Book: "Floyd County (GA)," p. 133, indicates she was from Cobb County, GA. Source2: 1870 Federal Census Source3: 1900 Census Soundex. (LDS Microfilm # 1242781) Source4: 1860 Census shows in Cobb County, GA, Page 172. Died: 13 January 1914 in Rome (Floyd) GA Source: Rome Tribune-Herald, Rome, Georgia, Wednesday Morning. January 14, 1914

FIGURE 4-10 A standard, two-generation family tree chart. (Generated from the author's copy of the RootsMagic genealogy database program.)

Blank pedigree charts, as you have seen, can be downloaded from the Internet. They also can be purchased online and at genealogical meetings and conferences in many formats, and range from as few as 3 generations to as many as 12 or more. These can be completed manually. Genealogy database software programs can also produce pedigree charts whose contents and formats you can customize.

You will want to experiment with the various formats to determine which one you like best and/or which one best represents your family data. Although it is time-consuming to complete a family tree chart by hand, many people do just that. Sometimes they create a display-quality tree using graphics, photographs, and calligraphic text. These can be framed and displayed as family heirlooms.

On the other hand, you will find that there are a number of genealogy database software programs available. You enter your data and source citations, even photographs, and can produce a variety of customized, computer-generated reports. Those reports include pedigree charts, family group sheets, and family trees in the standard, fan, hourglass, and other formats. Some of these databases also facilitate writing and publishing a quality family history, while others can produce HTML files containing your family data for web pages.

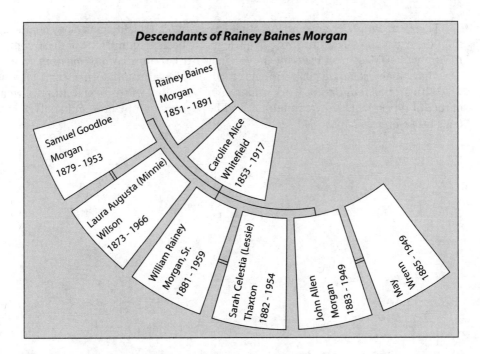

FIGURE 4-11 Sample of descendants chart in fan format. (Generated from the author's copy of the RootsMagic genealogy database program.)

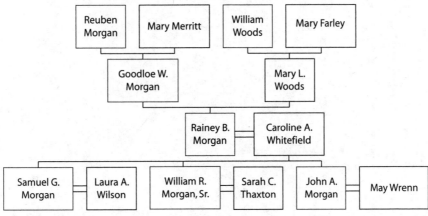

FIGURE 4-12 An hourglass family tree chart. (Generated from the author's copy of the RootsMagic genealogy database program.)

There are a number of companies that will print high-quality genealogy charts for you from the data you extract from your genealogy database program. One of these companies is Family ChartMasters in Pleasant Grove, Utah (**https://familychartmasters.com**). They have many standard chart formats or can develop a custom format chart for you.

With all this foundation work under your belt now, let's proceed into the wealth of record types, what they can tell us, and how you can interpret and analyze them. Let's move on to Chapter 5.

5

Place Ancestors into Context and Locate Their Basic Records

HOW TO...

- Place your ancestors into context
- Become a student of history
- Establish your ancestor's location at every point in their life
- Use maps to locate the *right* place to research
- Locate birth, marriage, death, and divorce records
- Identify and locate parish records for christenings, marriage banns, and burials
- Locate domestic partnership and civil partnership records
- Deal with suspected name changes

The most basic record types for establishing an ancestor's locations and life events are birth, marriage, and death records. Recent years have seen passage of legislation to permit civil partnership and domestic partnership records for opposite sex and same-sex couples. In other cases, records of the dissolution of marriage may exist. Government census records are another type of documentary evidence that can be used to verify your ancestor's location at regular intervals, and we will discuss these in great detail in Chapter 6. In the meantime, the use of the personal records of individuals and couples form a framework for other research of a person's life. Once you establish an ancestor's location in a specific place at a given point in his or her life, you can pursue your research for other documents and evidence to expand your knowledge and understanding of that person.

This chapter focuses on how to place your ancestors into historical, geographical, and sociological context so you can be most effective in understanding and using records about their lives. A simple yet extremely effective methodology for the proper use of maps and gazetteers to help locate records is also presented. We will also discuss the fundamental records that document the three most common types of modern personal records that may be available: birth certificates, marriage licenses

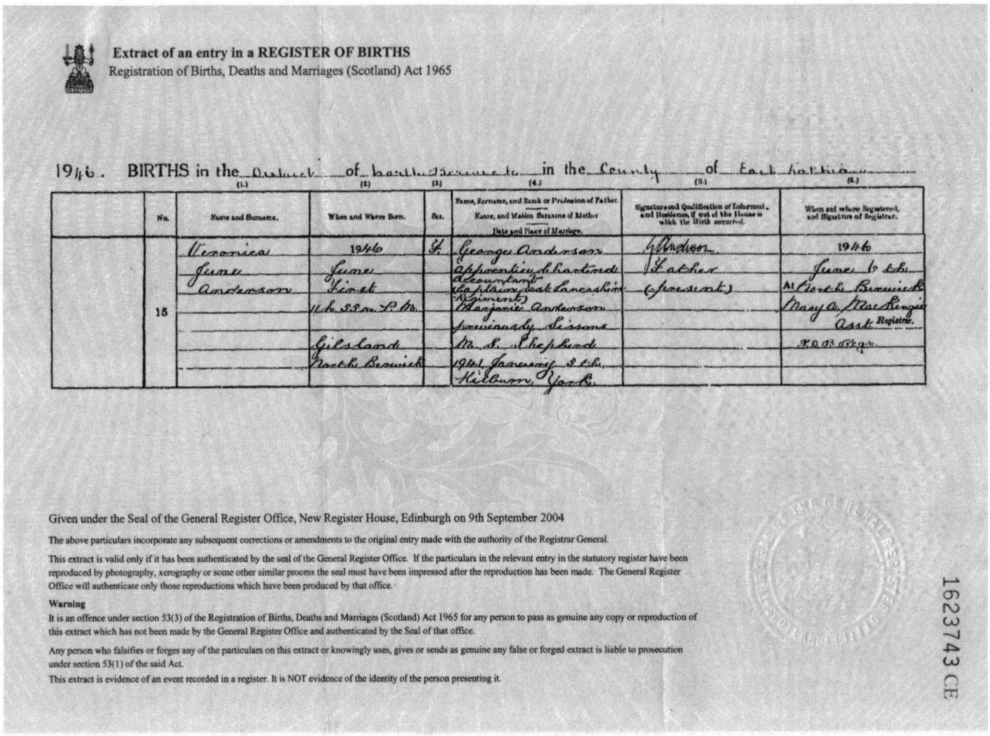

Extract of an entry in a REGISTER OF BIRTHS
Registration of Births, Deaths and Marriages (Scotland) Act 1965

1946. BIRTHS in the District of North Berwick in the County of East Lothian

	No.	Name and Surname.	When and Where Born.	Sex.	Name, Surname, and Rank or Profession of Father. Name, and Maiden Surname of Mother. Date and Place of Marriage.	Signature and Qualification of Informant, and Residence, if out of the House in which the Birth occurred.	When and where Registered, and Signature of Registrar.
	15	Veronica June Anderson	1946 June First 11h. 55m. P.M. Gilsland North Berwick	F.	George Anderson apprentice Chartered Accountant (Captain East Lancashire Regiment) Marjorie Anderson previously Sissons M.S. Shepherd 1941 January 8th Kilburn, York.	G. Anderson Father (present)	1946 June 6th At North Berwick Mary A. MacKenzie Asst. Registrar.

Given under the Seal of the General Register Office, New Register House, Edinburgh on 9th September 2004

The above particulars incorporate any subsequent corrections or amendments to the original entry made with the authority of the Registrar General.

This extract is valid only if it has been authenticated by the seal of the General Register Office. If the particulars in the relevant entry in the statutory register have been reproduced by photography, xerography or some other similar process the seal must have been impressed after the reproduction has been made. The General Register Office will authenticate only those reproductions which have been produced by that office.

Warning
It is an offence under section 53(3) of the Registration of Births, Deaths and Marriages (Scotland) Act 1965 for any person to pass as genuine any copy or reproduction of this extract which has not been made by the General Register Office and authenticated by the Seal of that office.

Any person who falsifies or forges any of the particulars on this extract or knowingly uses, gives or sends as genuine any false or forged extract is liable to prosecution under section 53(1) of the said Act.

This extract is evidence of an event recorded in a register. It is NOT evidence of the identity of the person presenting it.

1623743 CE

FIGURE 5-1 Certified copy of a birth entry from Scotland

and certificates, and death certificates. Examples of documents from the United States, the United Kingdom (like the one from Scotland shown in Figure 5-1), and Canada are included to provide a better understanding of what these documents can offer.

Let's now concentrate on methodologies for placing your ancestors' lives into context and get started locating these records.

Place Your Ancestors into Context

Our ancestors were real people. They lived in exact locations during particular time periods. They were subject to the laws and regulations of their governments and were influenced by other people and events, just as we are today. Their curiosity and interest in the world around them was keen. Like the people shown in Figure 5-2, they actively sought out the news of the day, sometimes even traveling considerable distances to obtain a newspaper. They lived in a community and interacted with their family members, friends, neighbors, and other people in the area. The climate

FIGURE 5-2   Our ancestors were interested in the news of the day.

influenced their lifestyle, and the social, political, and economic environment most certainly influenced their lives. The types of governments and their organization, leadership, and regulations imposed a structure under which they lived as well. All of these factors contributed to the types of records that may have been created for and about your ancestors.

Your ancestor who was a farmer was dependent on weather and a market for his or her crop in order to survive and prosper. He may have farmed most of the year but worked elsewhere in the winter months to sustain an income. Another ancestor who lived in a town or city typically would have been exposed to news, new technologies, clothing fashions, and other developments more rapidly than his rural counterpart. Still another ancestor who was conscripted or enlisted for military service would have received special training and was assigned to duties in a specific geographic area. He also may have traveled a great deal and been exposed to new areas, different cultures, and introduced to many new things. All of these would have influenced his perspective of the world and may have altered his future actions.

Consider, for example, an Irish family in the mid-1840s who was impacted by the Potato Famine. Starving and economically devastated, the father may have sought relief for himself and his family by emigrating from Ireland to America. By studying the history of Ireland during that period, you can better understand the physical, political, and economic factors that motivated someone to want to emigrate elsewhere. By also studying the history of America at that time, and the specific area to which the family immigrated, you can gain an appreciation for what drew the family there: jobs, opportunity, cost of living, and climate, joining people they already knew, to name but a few. Similarly, an American farming family in the Dust Bowl area of the United States during the Great Depression of the 1930s may have abandoned its land and moved westward to California in search of employment in order to stave off destitution and starvation.

As you can see, it is impossible to research your ancestors in a vacuum. It is important to place them into geographical *and* historical context, and that means studying history, geography, economics, sociology, meteorology, and other factors documented in all sorts of materials. These may provide you with insights into their lives and into their motivations for making some of the decisions they made.

Become a Student of History

The study of your family's story also becomes a study of history at all levels. I've found that making the connection between my ancestors and the history of the places and times in which they lived has brought that history to life. It also has helped me get to know them as individuals. My ancestors came alive for me beginning on the snowy day spent with my aunt and grandmother in January 1962, and expanded when I heard stories that they and other relatives shared about family members and their experiences. As a result, my interest in and appreciation for history, geography, and my family heritage was sparked forever. No longer were historical facts studied at school merely a memorization of places, dates, and famous people's names. The exploration of *my* family's history encouraged me to place *them* in a particular place and time, and give consideration to what the impact of events and ideas in the area at that time might have had on them. I reflected on what *their* participation in those events, and *their* interactions with their contemporaries, might have been. No matter their station in life, they have come alive for me. Learning more about them continues to be an exciting and enlightening experience!

My brother located some letters a few years ago that were written between 1900 and 1902 by the woman who was to become my paternal grandmother and that were addressed to my grandfather. One poignant letter dated Thursday, 19 September 1901, stated that she, her mother, and two sisters had been up late the night before sewing black armbands for her father and brothers. The family had then attended a special church service that day in Charlotte, North Carolina, in honor of President William McKinley, who had died on 14 September of wounds sustained from an assassin's bullets on 6 September at the Pan-American Exposition in Buffalo, New York. It was a national day of mourning, and the church service they attended coincided with McKinley's funeral service in Canton, Ohio. This letter contains a personal expression of shock and grief that was echoed in newspaper accounts of the time.

Your research will take you to many interesting places where you will discover a wealth of information about your family. There is no doubt that you will become fascinated with contemplating what your ancestors' lives must have been like as you read and learn more about history.

Family Histories

Someone may have written a history of your family or an historical account that includes details about your family. Unless one of your ancestors was an eminently famous person whose biography would be of interest to a wide audience, you will find that most family histories are either self-published by the author or privately published. Sometimes an author produces only a few copies of the family chronicle in manuscript form and perhaps donates a copy to the local public library. These gems can be invaluable resources and point you to all sorts of information. However, it is important to use your critical thinking skills to evaluate the content and the source materials. Don't accept any "fact" at face value, even if the family history was compiled and written by Uncle John or Cousin Mary. Research and verify everything for yourself. You may find that all of their information is correct and well researched and that the source evidence was meticulously cited. However, there is no substitute for examining the source materials yourself and forming your own conclusions.

County and Local Histories

Histories written about a limited area, such as a town, county, province, territory, or parish, can provide important details in your research. *The History of Mecklenburg County from 1740 to 1900* by J. B. Alexander, originally published in 1902 by the Observer Printing House in Charlotte, North Carolina, proved a goldmine for my family research. I learned a great deal about the history of Charlotte and the surrounding area, which a number of my ancestors helped settle in the early 1700s. Included were articles concerning agriculture, commerce, and economics through the years, and these helped me visualize my ancestors' environment. Other articles discussed specific churches, their histories, and their congregations. Modes of travel, clothing, and medical treatments were described. However, of special interest to me were biographical sketches of several of my ancestors, including my great-great-grandfather, Isaac Wilson, M.D., for whom a photograph was included. (See Figure 5-3.) To my knowledge, this is the only surviving photographic image of my ancestor, who was born on 30 December 1802 and died on 15 December 1880. Imagine my excitement at learning specific details about him, such as the fact that he was considered a "progressive physician" who practiced between 1825 and 1875. I learned that he eschewed the practice of cupping, in which a cupping glass was used to increase the blood supply to an area of the skin.

My great-great-grandfather organized and participated in both shooting matches and fox hunting. I also learned that he was a justice of the peace and that he officiated at many weddings. This was the first place I learned that he was married three times. Based on what I gleaned from this book, I set off on research to verify the information using other records and newspaper accounts and found the written account to be extremely accurate.

County heritage books have become popular in the United States and elsewhere over the years. These are primarily compilations of information about places, events, and families whose roots have been based in that area. Organizers solicit articles from area citizens and descendants. Recognize that a great deal of this information may

DR. ISAAC WILSON.

FIGURE 5-3   This photograph of the author's great-great-grandfather, perhaps the only surviving photograph of the man, was discovered in a county history published in 1902.

be hearsay or family myth, and may have been written by persons who were neither researchers nor historians. Every fact should therefore be carefully scrutinized and personally verified for accuracy.

There are a variety of places where you can find local histories. Towns and cities celebrating centennials, sesquicentennials, bicentennials, and other milestone anniversaries often publish booklets commemorating the extended history of the area. Articles and photographs may include your ancestors and other family members. In addition, local newspaper and magazine coverage may include similar genealogical treasures. Don't overlook these resources in your search for family information.

Churches and synagogues preserve many types of records and also can be a source of local historical information. Commemorative books and albums are common and may include names, photographs, and other details that may be useful.

The local or county genealogical and historical societies are essential research resources. They may have unique photographic and documentary materials relating to your family that can be found nowhere else. In addition, these groups undertake transcription and preservation projects. These may involve compiling materials, creating indexes, and generating reports or articles for their newsletter or journal.

Such projects might include compiling histories of local businesses, canvassing and indexing cemeteries, and transcribing tax rolls and jury lists. They also may possess diaries, journals, photographs, and correspondence files of local residents. You never know what they have until you ask.

The local public library and nearby academic libraries may have originals or copies of documentary information of local historical value. Besides the privately published family histories or one-of-a-kind manuscripts mentioned earlier, these repositories might also maintain file cabinets (known as "vertical files") with miscellaneous documents such as correspondence and obituaries. Newspaper clipping files may also contain collections of articles related to specific subjects and people. Some libraries' special collections have acquired unusual sets of records. The library at the University of South Florida in Tampa's Special Collections has acquired the earlier records of several local mortuaries/funeral homes, the marriage books and marriage licenses for Hillsborough County, naturalization records dating from circa 1890 to 1915, and many other historical documents about the area. The special collections department of public and academic libraries and archives should therefore be explored through their online catalogs and in person.

State and Provincial Histories

Learning about local history is important, but be sure to learn about state and provincial histories as well. These provide a broader perspective of the historical role played by a town or other geopolitical entity. This can lead you to a better understanding of the events and influences in your ancestor's life.

Historical and genealogical societies, as well as lineage and patriotic organizations, might provide excellent resources for your research. Libraries of all types hold books about state or provincial history, particularly state libraries and archives. One of my favorite websites is LibrarySpot.com at **http://www.libraryspot.com**. Here you will find links to all types of libraries in the United States, links to national libraries in more than 100 countries, and many reference resource links. The UK Public Libraries site at **http://dspace.dial.pipex.com/town/square/ac940/weblibs.html** provides a compilation of links to public libraries in the United Kingdom. Discovery, the new online catalog at The National Archives (TNA) in the UK now provides access to the holdings in their collection and of more than 2,500 archives across the country. There are more than 9 million records available for download at this writing. Discovery is accessible at **http://discovery.nationalarchives.gov.uk**. Library and Archives Canada has created a web page of Canadian library websites and catalogs at **http://www.collectionscanada.gc.ca/gateway/s22-200-e.html**. State, provincial, and national libraries and archives provide extensive materials about history. Many of these facilities also house and preserve original sources, as well as printed, microfilmed, and scanned images. Such collections include

- Library of Congress at **http://www.loc.gov**
- Library and Archives Canada at **http://www.collectionscanada.gc.ca**

- The National Archives (of the United Kingdom) at **http://www
  .nationalarchives.gov.uk**
- National Archives of Australia at **http://www.naa.gov.au**

Using your favorite search engine and entering terms such as "national library" or "national archive" and the name of the country can help you locate many more such national sites.

National and World History

The influences of national and international events were important factors in the lives of our ancestors, their families, and their communities. The perspective of history gives us the opportunity to better understand our forebears' place in it. You may think that events in France in the late 1700s had little impact on the American continents, but you would be incorrect. On the contrary, following its devastating defeat in the Seven Years' War against Britain (1756–63), France was eager for revenge against the British. When the American Revolution erupted, statesman Benjamin Franklin traveled to Paris and met with French government officials, and the two countries entered into a treaty on 6 February 1778. Franklin met with King Louis XVI and Queen Marie Antoinette on 20 March 1778 to confirm that treaty, and with that the French entered into an agreement to provide aid and support to the American colonies. Following the American Revolution, the French helped broker the signing of the Treaty of Paris at Versailles on 3 September 1783, in which Great Britain recognized the independence of the United States of America. (See Figure 5-4.)

In another treaty, signed on 30 April 1803, the United States successfully completed the negotiations for the Louisiana Purchase from France at a price of approximately $15 million. The area comprised more than 800,000 square miles extending from the Mississippi River in the east to the Rocky Mountains in the west. In addition to the impact to North America of this negotiation, the French also occupied Spain in the early 19th century. That occupation severed commerce between Spain and its colonies in Central and South America. Between 1808 and 1826, the Spanish lost all of Latin America, with the exception of Cuba and Puerto Rico. Emulating the example of their neighbors to the north in the new United States, the Spanish colonies rebelled and ultimately claimed their own independence.

Another important event in France in the late 1780s was the formation of a group, the Société des Amis des Noirs (Society of the Friends of the Blacks), who met in Paris in early 1788 to campaign against the French slave trade. On 4 February 1794, slavery was abolished in the French colonies. The news spread across the Atlantic and slaves were freed in those colonies. The action did not go unnoticed in Britain, the United States, and elsewhere. By 1807, the slave trade in all British colonies was abolished and, in that same year, the United States Congress passed legislation prohibiting the importation of slaves into the country and its territories. Slave smuggling persisted through 1862 until President Abraham Lincoln's Emancipation Proclamation

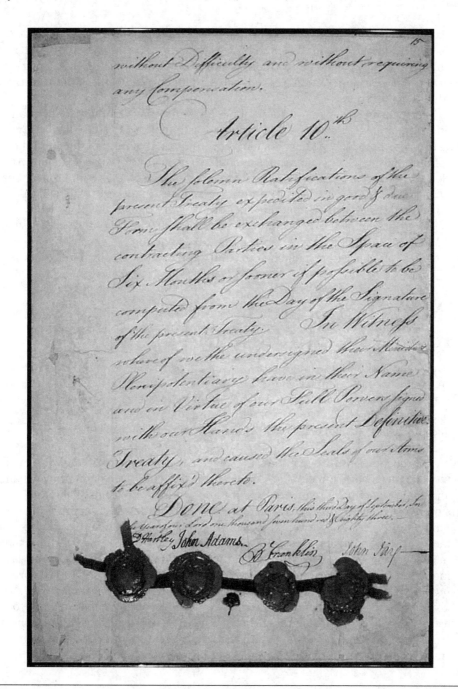

FIGURE 5-4   Signatures on one of two original copies of the Treaty of Paris, signed on 3 September 1783

abolished all forms of slavery in the Southern states, effective on 1 January 1863. The 13th Amendment to the United States Constitution was passed by Congress on 31 January 1865 and adopted on 6 December of that year, ending slavery and involuntary servitude in the United States and greatly expanding the civil rights of African-Americans.

As you can see, events on a national level may have had far-reaching and enduring impacts elsewhere. That is why it is important to study history and to consider how all world events may have impacted your ancestors and their contemporaries during their times and later. The actions of the Société des Amis des Noirs described previously can be said to have impacted persons of French, Spanish, English, North American, South American, and African descent. You will find that it is imperative to learn something about the history of both the place where your ancestors originally lived *and* the places to which they immigrated. There is definitely a push-pull influence involved that, if you invest the time to explore histories, may provide a much clearer understanding and appreciation of your heritage.

Use Maps to Locate the *Right* Place to Research

Maps, like the one shown in Figure 5-5, are an essential part of our everyday life. We consult them to plot travel routes as we move from place to place, check them to determine correct postal codes, and use them in a wide variety of other ways. We find maps today printed on paper, on the Internet, and in computer software programs, and the use of Global Positioning System (GPS) technology is becoming more widespread.

Throughout history, maps have changed again and again. Boundaries have moved, towns have come under different jurisdictions, place names have changed, and some places have ceased to exist for any number of reasons. Therefore, we cannot simply use contemporary maps as references for locating records. We must use a number of types of historical maps in our genealogical research. In order to determine the *right* place to look for records and other evidence, it is essential to understand the geographical history of an area. Many genealogists hit "dead ends" and waste inordinate amounts of time because they either fail to understand the importance of properly using maps in their research or they don't possess the skills to use them.

If you are not familiar with the many different types of maps and how you can use them for your genealogical research, a good book is available on the subject. *Walking with Your Ancestors* by Melinda Kashuba (Betterway Books, 2005) provides a strong overview of many types of maps and how to use them.

Avoid Wasted Time and Energy

Imagine the frustration of having planned a vacation that included research at a courthouse in a particular area, only to discover when you arrived that the information

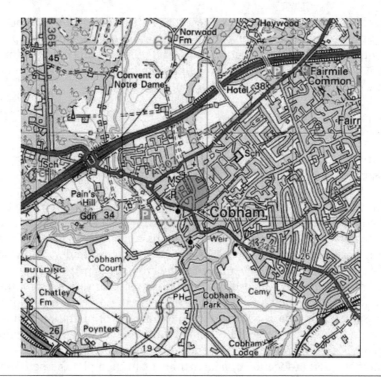

FIGURE 5-5   Historical Ordnance Survey map of Cobham, Surrey, England

you were seeking was actually located in another county's courthouse. It happens all too frequently, especially when a person fails to determine beforehand where his or her ancestors lived *and* which county had jurisdiction over the area at that time.

Perhaps expending the time and expense of a research trip is an extreme example, but it does happen. Certainly, as we conduct research from the comfort of our homes, we do the same kind of work and may waste time by searching for records in the wrong place. However, there are many other ways we can waste time and money researching the wrong materials. You want to avoid the following types of errors:

- Researching in the wrong books
- Checking the wrong census areas
- Using the wrong indexes and other finding aids
- Writing to the wrong courthouse
- Researching the wrong geographical areas and records in databases and on the Internet
- Traveling to the wrong location

Worse yet, you could actually be researching the wrong ancestors! When your family has a common name and there are people of the same name in the area, it is entirely possible to latch onto the records of one individual whose details seem "almost right." You might then spend a great deal of time tracing that person's records until you encounter names, places, dates, and other evidence that definitively tell you that you've been on a wild goose chase. Don't think it can't happen to you? It has happened to the best of us.

Use Maps for Multiple Purposes

Maps are a necessity in our genealogical research. They help us locate roads and streets, towns, cities, counties, parishes, states, provinces, territories, countries, landmarks, waterways, oceans, continents, islands, and more. Contemporary and historical maps, such as the one shown in Figure 5-6, help us determine the geopolitical jurisdictions in place at a specific time. They provide a visual representation of the spatial relationships between physical locations, and can help us place our ancestors' physical location into perspective. This can help us better understand where they might have been in relationship to events occurring around them.

I often use historical maps from the 16th to 19th centuries to plot the possible migration paths followed by my own ancestors in the American colonies and the early United States. This means having studied the history of migration routes north and south as well as across the Appalachian Mountains. That investment of time in that research has allowed me to use evidence of a person being in one location at one time and being in another location at a later time. I can then plot the potential migration routes for ancestors between two points and anticipate what their journey entailed at that time. Using colored markers, I draw on a map the probable routes that they

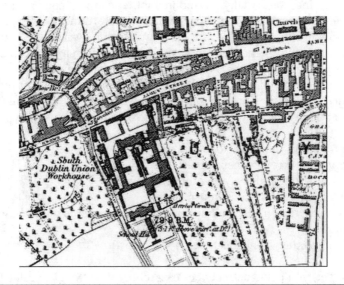

FIGURE 5-6   Map of the workhouse in South Dublin, Ireland, in 1849

may have taken, based on prevailing migration routes at the time. I can then begin researching any interim stops they may have made and the records that may have been created and left behind in those locations. The process has been remarkably successful, and I'd like to share it with you.

Use a Methodology That Works

I have worked with maps for many years and have found a practical methodology for working with maps and other related resources that can improve your success at locating the *right* place to search for records.

Step 1: Start with a Contemporary Map

Obtain a good current map of the area where you believe your ancestors lived in the past. There are many excellent map resources available, including bound atlases, printed individual maps for areas, and maps available from motoring associations such as the American Automobile Association (AAA) and its counterparts in other countries. In addition, highway department maps at a local, county, or other administrative area level provide excellent detail, including secondary and tertiary roads, natural landmarks, churches and cemeteries, and other features. Whatever maps you use should include contemporary boundary lines.

You probably won't want to use cheap maps and atlases because they often do not contain as much detail as you would like; they also sometimes contain errors or omit important features. Maps on the Internet services also are sometimes less accurate than you would like, and seldom contain the detail you might need, especially boundary lines. Beware of driving directions from these sites, and always compare two sets of driving instructions for conflicting information. Consider the creator of the map, their authority and expertise, the purpose of the map, and the accuracy.

On your good contemporary map, follow this progression and make notes as you proceed:

1. Locate the place you seek.
2. Note the name of the specific county or province in which it is located today.
3. Make specific notes of the place's location within the contemporary boundaries.
4. Note surrounding towns or cities and their direction and distance from your site.
5. Make note of other surrounding topographic features of the landscape such as waterways, mountains, and shorelines, and their physical position and distance in relation to the place you located.

It is possible that the place you are searching for isn't listed on the map. Perhaps it is too small or is an unincorporated area, or perhaps the place has been renamed or no longer exists. What do you do? Never fear, there are other resources available to you. Local histories are invaluable in helping locate these places. However, one of the best tools you can use is a *gazetteer*, also referred to as a *place name dictionary*. There are many of these available for different parts of the world, both printed and Web-based. For United

States research, I have become addicted to using the book *American Place Names of Long Ago* by Gilbert S. Bahn. The work is based on a portion of *Cram's Unrivaled Atlas of the World*, published in 1898, and whose U.S. information was based on the 1890 U.S. federal census returns. I also use *A Genealogical Gazetteer of England*, compiled by Frank Smith, which includes names of locations as they existed prior to 1831.

Among the best Internet-based gazetteers are the following:

- United States Geological Survey Geographic Names Information System (also referred to as the USGS GNIS), a massive searchable database of United States national mapping information. Located at **http://geonames.usgs.gov/pls/ gnispublic**, the GNIS allows you to search by name and location, and to narrow your search to a specific feature type. I often find this facility indispensable in locating somewhat obscure cemeteries. The results include latitude and longitude, as well as links to a number of mapping services that can be used to display maps. Figure 5-7 shows an image from the GNIS in Google Maps.

- The Atlas of Canada, located at **http://atlas.nrcan.gc.ca/site/english/index .html**, provides access to its Gazetteer Map Service and allows you to search for place and feature names. You can narrow your search to a specific province and territory and/or feature type. In addition, however, the site contains links to collections of different maps, including a large number of historical maps covering

Click red balloon: to see feature detail. Drag red balloon: to find coordinates of any point. Refresh page: to restore original point(s).

FIGURE 5-7 GNIS in Google Maps (Satellite view) showing Woodland Cemetery in Madison, Rockingham County, North Carolina

the history of Canada, outline maps, and an archive of images from various editions of the *Atlas of Canada*, going back to the first edition published in 1906.

- The Geoscience Australia Place Name Search facility, hosted by the Australian government and located at **http://www.ga.gov.au/place-names**, is a compilation of more than 370,000 geographic names provided by members of the Committee for Geographical Names in Australasia.
- The Gazetteer for Scotland at **http://www.scottish-places.info** is an excellent resource for locating towns and features in Scotland. It also provides an historical timeline feature. In addition, facilities were recently added to allow you to work with areas using either the old Scottish counties or the modern council areas. The former facility is based on the full text of Francis H. Groome's *Ordnance Gazetteer of Scotland*, published in 1885. It also includes an historical map layer that includes maps of all the county and parish boundaries, overlaid with 19th-century six-inch Ordnance Survey maps.
- GENUKI at **http://www.genuki.org.uk** has compiled a wealth of helpful resources. Their gazetteer at **http://www.genuki.org.uk/big/Gazetteer** is quite comprehensive, covering the whole of England, Ireland, Wales, Scotland, and the Isle of Man.
- If you are seeking an online gazetteer facility for another country or locale, you can always use your favorite web browser and enter search terms like the ones shown here:

  gazetteer [insert country/province name here]

You may be rewarded with search results that you can explore online.

You also should consider using the reference resources available to you in libraries of all types. Reference librarians at public and academic libraries are trained to respond to research inquiries from patrons and can direct you to map collections, atlases, and gazetteers. State and national libraries and archives are another resource, and many of them handle reference question requests via telephone and email.

Step 2: Locate and Examine Historical Maps

Your next step is to determine the time period during which your ancestors lived in the area. Locate an historical map of that area from that time period. (See Figure 5-8.) If you are researching your ancestors in the United States, you might want to consult the *Map Guide to the U.S. Federal Censuses, 1790–1920*, by William Thorndale and William Dollarhide. This book provides maps of every state for each of the decennial censuses taken between 1790 and 1920. Each map shows the current counties and their boundaries and the counties in existence at the time of the census and their boundaries. This is an excellent tool for a high-level comparison between the contemporary and historical geopolitical boundaries in the United States. (These maps are part of the U.S. Federal Census collection of the HeritageQuest Online database available through many libraries and archives. You can access the maps when using the Browse facility.) You can follow up with a search for and consultation of detailed historical maps of the area from the period. This is the procedure you should follow for other countries and locales as well.

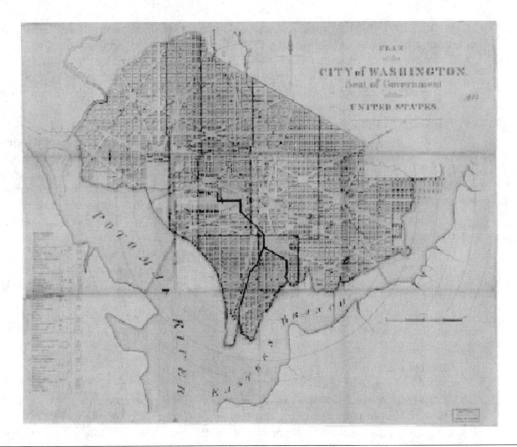

FIGURE 5-8 Historical map of Washington, DC, dated 1822

Another good map reference book for American research is *The Family Tree Historical Maps Book: A State-by-State Atlas of U.S. History, 1790-1900* by Allison Dolan (Family Tree Books, 2014). It provides excellent full-color maps from different periods that can give you a visual perspective of the development of states and territories over 200 years. There is a timeline of key dates in each state's history.

Locate the place you found on your contemporary map in Step 1. Compare it to historical maps from before and after the dates in which your ancestors lived in the area. Make note of the surrounding towns and landmarks you found on your contemporary map and locate these on the historical map. This can be crucial when you are looking for places that changed names or disappeared. More important, though, is to carefully note the administrative boundaries, such as state, province, county, or parish. If the place you are researching was located in another county at the time your ancestors were there, for instance, you will be seeking to locate records in *that* county's repositories and not in that of the current county's repositories. There are some rare cases in which records are transferred to new jurisdictions, such as when new counties are created and the most recent property lists and tax lists are transferred. It is therefore important to keep this in mind when asking about the availability of records in and from the original government offices.

Step 3: Fine-tune Your Search Location

The examination of maps is an important factor in locating the *right* place to research records, but there is another step you should perform. While the *Map Guide to the U.S. Federal Censuses, 1790–1920* is an excellent reference work, it provides detail only at the ten-year intervals at which the federal censuses were taken. You may need to determine a more exact date for when the administrative area was formed. Let's look at two examples.

The Pennsylvania county of Wyoming (see Figure 5-9) was formed in 1842 from Luzerne County. If you were looking for marriage records of your Wyoming County ancestors from 1840, you would seek them in Luzerne County, while if they were married in 1843, you would look in Wyoming County. I was able to determine the county formation dates through use of *The Family Tree: The Essential Guide to American County and Town Sources* (Family Tree Books, 2010), published by the editors of *Family Tree Magazine*. I might also search the Internet for information concerning the formation of Wyoming County and its parent county. One of the best resources for this type of information is the FamilySearch Wiki at **https://familysearch.org/**

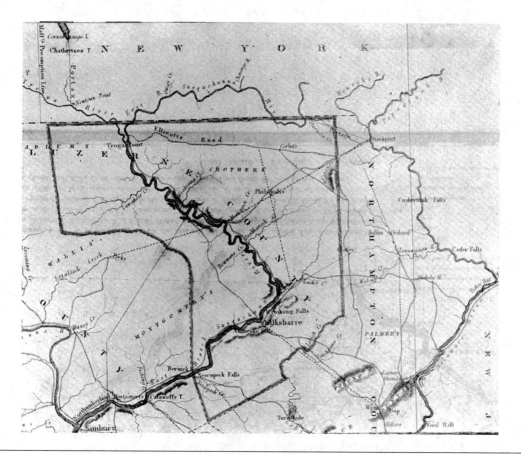

FIGURE 5-9   Historical map of Wyoming County, Pennsylvania, dated 1791

learn/wiki/en/Main_Page. It contains more than 79,000 extensive articles about geographical locations, genealogical records, and research advice at the time of this writing, and is still expanding.

Geopolitical boundaries across Europe have changed time and time again. Poland provides perhaps the most vivid example of boundary changes. The country was partitioned between Austria, Prussia, and Russia in 1772 and each country annexed a portion of Poland. In 1793, Russia and Prussia signed a Second Partition Treaty and more of Poland was seized. In 1795, Russia effected yet a third partition and obtained part of the remainder of Poland. While some of the records from these periods may still exist in Polish archives, others would have been created and archived by the other national governments. And, since the Kingdom of Prussia no longer exists, what would have happened to all of those records? Jumping forward to 20th-century Poland, the invasion by the German army on 1 September 1939 began yet another period of division. The Germans and the Russians partitioned and divided Poland yet again. Figure 5-10 shows boundary changes for Poland in the 20th century. As you can see, your research of Polish ancestral records would be dependent on the historical time period, the partitioning of the country, and the governmental jurisdiction at the time, as well as a number of other factors.

There are many historical map collections online that you will delight in using. Here are just a few examples:

- The Perry-Castañeda Library Map Collection at the University of Texas at Austin (**http://www.lib.utexas.edu/maps/index.html**)

FIGURE 5-10   Map showing boundary changes of 20th century Poland

- David Rumsey Map Collection (**http://www.davidrumsey.com**)
- Library of Congress American Memory Map Collections (**http://lcweb2.loc.gov/ammem/gmdhtml/gmdhome.html**)

You can often find excellent historical maps of a given area by using your favorite web browser. Simply type **historical map** followed by the name of the place for which you want a map. If the place name is two or more words, enclose the place name in quotation marks. Here are several examples of searches.

> historical map germany
> historical map "north carolina"
> historical map españa

You will notice in the last example that I used the native spelling for Spain. I did that because some content on the Internet may be named or labeled with the country's name as spelled there. A little creative search strategy work such as that can often pay dividends in search results.

Step 4: Identify the Records Created and Their Current Location

It is important to read about the types of records created at the time and their purpose. You also will need to determine if they still exist and where they are located. The type of record often dictates its ultimate fate. Some records are of such a nature that, once they have served their purpose, they are discarded or destroyed. Others are of such importance that they are maintained for an extended period of time or permanently.

The Family Tree Sourcebook gives detailed descriptions of record types created in each of the United States, the dates when record-keeping for various record types began, and where these records are most likely to be housed today. I say "most likely" because there is the possibility that records may have been relocated for any number of reasons.

When researching in England, you will want to learn about The National Archives in Kew, Richmond, Surrey, and at **http://www.nationalarchives.gov.uk**. It is the repository of all official documents for England and many for Wales. The General Register Office for Scotland (GROS) in Edinburgh, and at **http://www.gro-scotland.gov.uk**, is your starting point to learn what is available there, while the General Register Office in Roscommon, Ireland, at **https://www.welfare.ie/en/Pages/General-Register-Office.aspx**, provides the same types of information for Ireland. The General Register Office of Northern Ireland is the repository for many different record types, including birth, adoption, marriage, civil partnership, and death certificates. These can be ordered for various time periods at the nidirect government services website at **http://www.nidirect.gov.uk/gro**.

The combined Library and Archives Canada site, at **http://www.collectionscanada.gc.ca**, is accessible in both English and French. It offers excellent, well-organized information about available records, and the website is being reorganized as of this writing. The National Archives of Australia site at **http://www.naa.gov.au** likewise presents information about its record keeping and details about available resources.

In addition to all of the places previously mentioned, The Church of Jesus Christ of Latter-day Saints (LDS), whose members are often referred to as "Mormons," has the largest genealogical library in the world. Their website at **https://familysearch.org** is filled with interesting resources, and you will want to visit the FamilySearch Wiki mentioned earlier to access articles about each specific area where your ancestors lived to learn what records were created and may still be available.

Step 5: Contact the Repository to Obtain Copies of Records

Once you have determined the *right* place to search for and locate records, make contact with that facility. *The Family Tree Sourcebook* provides excellent contact information for facilities in U.S. states and counties/parishes that can help you locate existing records. Older materials are sometimes relocated, are stored off-site in another location, have limited or prohibited access due to legislation or governmental restrictions, or have been lost or destroyed. It is therefore a good idea to make contact with the repository of record to determine what they really have, how accessible the materials are, and how to access or obtain copies. This is especially important if you are planning a research visit. You will want to learn the days and hours of operation, what personal access is permitted, any costs for copies, and method of payment accepted. If records are in off-site storage, you will want to determine how you can gain access to them. This may require filing a special request for retrieval of older archived records so that you can work with them when you arrive. In other cases, an off-site storage location may be staffed, and you may be able to make an appointment to visit.

Whenever you make contact with a facility, you can avoid some dead-ends by being prepared and by asking open-ended questions. Over the years, I've found that preparing a written set of the questions I want to ask is a way to make certain that I cover everything necessary and all the contingencies. Try this method yourself and I'm certain you will find it helpful.

Begin by performing some advance research so that you know the names of the persons for whom you are seeking records, what type of records you want, and the correct time period. You should include nicknames and any other names by which a person may have been known. Be certain to use the maiden name of a woman if you are seeking marriage records or other documents created before her wedding date. One distant cousin I always knew to be called "Sudie" was actually born Susan Elizabeth Wilson. It was under her nickname that I found her in some records, and under her birth name that I found her in others.

Open-ended questions are those that require more than a "yes" or "no" answer. For example, if you ask a clerk if their facility has the marriage records from 1902 and he or she responds in the negative, what do you do? Your next question should be, "Can you tell me if those records exist and, if so, where I might be able to locate them?" Otherwise, the clerk may or may not volunteer that information. On the other hand, you might phrase your initial question as, "I'm looking to find a marriage record from 1902. I am hoping that your office has them here or, if not, can you tell me where they are and how to access them?" Your question in this format calls for a response that can lead to a more in-depth conversation.

Maps Can Equal Success

Libraries, archives, courthouses, records offices, government offices at all levels, museums, churches, other physical repositories, and the Internet can all be used to obtain maps. As you can see, this methodology for effectively locating and using maps will substantially improve your chances for success in locating the *right* place for finding your ancestors' records and other evidence. With this in mind, let's proceed to learn about locating some official documents.

Locate Birth, Marriage, and Death Records

The most basic and yet most important records you can locate for your ancestors are ones that record their birth, marriage, and death information. (See Figure 5-11.) These are generally referred to in the United States as "vital records" because they record the vital life events. They are referred to as civil registration records in many other places. One of my English friends refers to these as the "hatch, match, and dispatch" records. Other records that fall into the same category would include divorce decrees and supporting documents, and civil partnership records. Stillbirth records may also exist, and may take the form of a death certificate or a separate document. What makes all these records so important to a genealogist is that they not only confirm your ancestor or family member in a specific place at a given point in time, but also potentially connect that person to other family members.

The originals, exact copies, or other official certifications of these records may be in your family's possession, and you just need to ask family members for access to

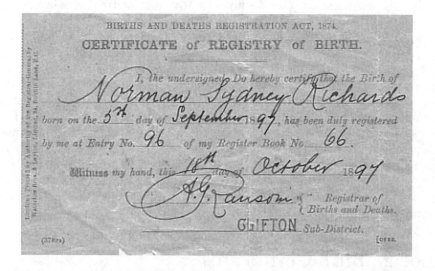

FIGURE 5-11   Certificate of Registry of Birth from the United Kingdom, dated 18 October 1897

them. However, in most instances and especially in cases of older births, marriages, and deaths, you will have to determine if the records were commonly created at the time and, if so, where they are located. You then will have to expend effort to obtain copies of them, either by mail, email, telephone, or personal visit to the repository where they are held. Some records may have been digitized and made available online in subscription databases or at government websites.

It is important to recognize right away that you may not be able to obtain copies of some records. Creation of a birth certificate, for example, may not have been required at the time your ancestor was born. In the United States, you may find that some of the counties in a particular state began creating official birth records earlier than others. Kentucky counties, for instance, began creating birth records as early as 1852. In contrast, the North Carolina legislature did not pass legislation requiring counties to create birth and death records until 10 March 1913, and it was not until 1920 that all counties were in full compliance with the law.

Civil registration was implemented in England and Wales on 1 July 1837 and required the registration of births, marriages, and deaths within a prescribed time frame. Prior to that, ecclesiastical parishes were required to record christenings, marriages, and burials. Civil registration legislation was not passed in Scotland until 1854. In Ireland, compulsory civil registration of non–Roman Catholic marriages began on 1 April 1845. The registration of births, deaths, and all marriages began on 1 January 1864. Civil registration began in Canada in the mid-1800s but its implementation varied by province and territory. In Australia, the government of each colony or state implemented civil registration independently. Tasmania was the first, keeping records beginning in 1838, and the Australian Capital Territory was the last, beginning in 1911.

In some cases, laws may limit access to originals or copies of birth records to the individual for whose birth the document was created and/or to his or her parents. Certain information on death certificates may also be masked when copies are created, in order to preserve the privacy of the surviving family members and to prevent the release of information that might be used to steal an identity.

Keep in mind that these three types of records—birth, marriage, and death records—can be used to establish the location of your ancestor or family member at a specific place at a point in time. By extension, that helps you begin locating other records created in the same vicinity, which can expand your knowledge of that person and his or her extended family. Those might include census documents, city directories, property and tax records, church records, cemetery records, wills and probate records, and many more. When official birth, marriage, and death records are not available for whatever reason, you will need to consider locating alternative record sources to establish the same or similar information. We will discuss this later in the chapter and throughout the book.

Locate Birth Certificates

The first document created for many people was a birth certificate such as the one shown in Figure 5-12. We all have had parents and the vast majority of us alive today

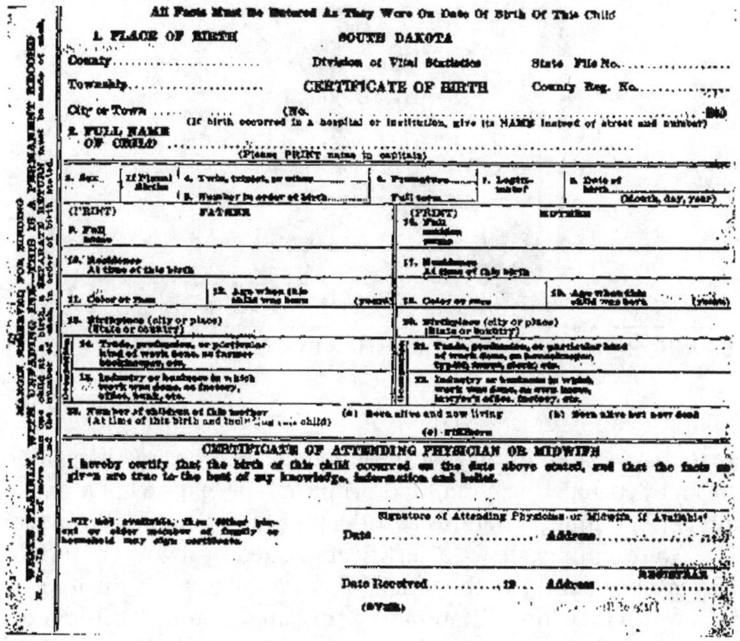

All Facts Must Be Entered As They Were On Date Of Birth Of This Child

1. PLACE OF BIRTH

SOUTH DAKOTA

County........................ Division of Vital Statistics State File No..................

Township...................... CERTIFICATE OF BIRTH County Reg. No..................

City or Town .... (No. .... St.)

(If birth occurred in a hospital or institution, give its NAME instead of street and number)

2. FULL NAME OF CHILD ....

(Please PRINT name in capitals)

3. Sex | If Plural Births | 4. Twin, triplet, or other | 5. Number in order of birth | 6. Premature / Full term | 7. Legitimate? | 8. Date of birth (Month, day, year)

(PRINT) FATHER | (PRINT) MOTHER

9. Full name | 16. Full maiden name

10. Residence At time of this birth | 17. Residence At time of this birth

11. Color or Race | 12. Age when this child was born (years) | 18. Color or race | 19. Age when this child was born (years)

13. Birthplace (city or place) (State or country) | 20. Birthplace (city or place) (State or country)

14. Trade, profession, or particular kind of work done, as farmer bookkeeper, etc. | 21. Trade, profession, or particular kind of work done, as housekeeper, typist, nurse, clerk, etc.

15. Industry or business in which work was done, as factory, office, bank, etc. | 22. Industry or business in which work was done, as own home, lawyer's office, factory, etc.

23. Number of children of this mother (At time of this birth and including this child) (a) Born alive and now living (b) Born alive but now dead (c) Stillborn

CERTIFICATE OF ATTENDING PHYSICIAN OR MIDWIFE

I hereby certify that the birth of this child occurred on the date above stated, and that the facts as given are true to the best of my knowledge, information and belief.

Signature of Attending Physician or Midwife, if Available*

Date .... Address ....

REGISTRAR

Date Received ...., 19... Address ....

FIGURE 5-12 Blank birth certificate form from South Dakota

were probably born with the benefit of some medical attention. And typically there was a record made of the birth in the form of a birth certificate and/or a hospital or other medical record. A birth certificate is an important document because it is used to verify identity. From a genealogist's perspective, it can be the basis for beginning research in a specific geographic area for other family members and for a wide variety of other records.

You will need to determine *where* the person was born in order to determine if there is a birth certificate from that time. The methodology for using maps to locate the *right* place to search for records is especially helpful.

The Family Tree Sourcebook, for example, can be used to determine for the United States, state by state, and county by county, when official birth records began to be kept by the government offices in those areas, as well as where to seek them. The FamilySearch Wiki at **https://familysearch.org/learn/wiki/en/Main_Page** also provides excellent information about the creation of and access to all types of vital records and civil registrations.

Birth certificates come in many formats, with different titles, and contain different amounts of information. At a minimum, you can expect to find the name of the child, the parents' names, the child's date of birth, the child's gender, the location where the birth occurred (or was registered), the name of the attending physician or midwife, and the signature of the registrar. Other information likely to be found on birth records includes the child's birth weight and length, the precise time of birth,

FIGURE 5-13   Certificate issued in 1942 attesting to a Canadian birth entry in Ontario in 1875

and the parents' racial or ethnic background and their occupations. More recent birth certificates may include the child's footprints and perhaps even a photograph. You will find a number of examples of birth certificates in the graphics throughout this chapter. Figure 5-13, for example, shows a certificate issued by a government office in 1942 that confirms a birth entry in the official files dating to 1875. Birth records in different parts of the world may look different and contain different levels of detail, but their intent was to formally record a birth. The Dutch birth certificate shown in Figure 5-14 is a good example of this.

You may also come across an amended birth certificate from time to time. These are used to change or correct information entered on the original birth certificate. A typical reason for the issuance of an amended certificate is to change or correct the name of the child or its parents. Amended birth certificates are also used in cases of adoption. At the time of the legal adoption, particularly that of an infant or small child, a magistrate orders the creation of an amended birth certificate. This document includes the names of the adopting parents and replaces the original birth certificate in all file locations. The original, which lists the natural or birth parents, is typically removed in U.S. locations and placed in a court file with the adoption records. In most cases, these records are sealed by the court and may require a judicial order to gain access to them. The amended birth certificate is clearly marked to indicate that it is amended and, in the case of adoption, that there was an adoption that caused its creation.

Birth civil registration forms provide a space for the later addition of a child's name. The name might not be selected until the time of christening, for example. The child's forename may therefore be added to the original document or an amended birth certificate may be issued at a later date.

Delayed birth certificates are not uncommon. Governments may, in lieu of an original birth certificate, issue these. In cases in which birth records were not created at the time of a person's birth, or where the original records have been lost or destroyed, the governmental office will issue a substitute document. Typically, the applicant needs proof of birth for identification purposes in order to obtain a passport or a visa, or to apply for pension benefits. The person completes an application and presents him- or herself in a governmental facility, and supplies several alternative forms of proof. These might include a family Bible, school enrollment records, church

FIGURE 5-14 An original Dutch birth certificate dated 1886

records, military service records, employment records, and affidavits from other people who were alive at the time of the applicant's birth and who can confirm that the applicant is indeed the correct person. These alternative proofs, all of which are usually sources of secondary information, are reviewed. If they are deemed sufficient, a delayed birth certificate is issued and is considered the legal equivalent of an original birth record. An example of a delayed birth certificate is shown in Figure 5-15.

Alternative records can, of course, be used as evidence of the birth. Remember that you must use your critical thinking skills to evaluate these materials and determine whether they are original vs. derivative sources and/or contain primary vs. secondary information. You need to determine whether these materials are sufficient to *prove* the fact in question, in this case, a birth. Some of the many types of alternative records you might be able to use include the following:

- Baby books created by the parents of other family members might document information about the birth.
- Christening or baptismal records, such as the one shown in Figure 5-16, may be found in family documents or obtained from a church. These typically contain the person's name, date of birth, parents' names, and sometimes names of other family members and godparents.

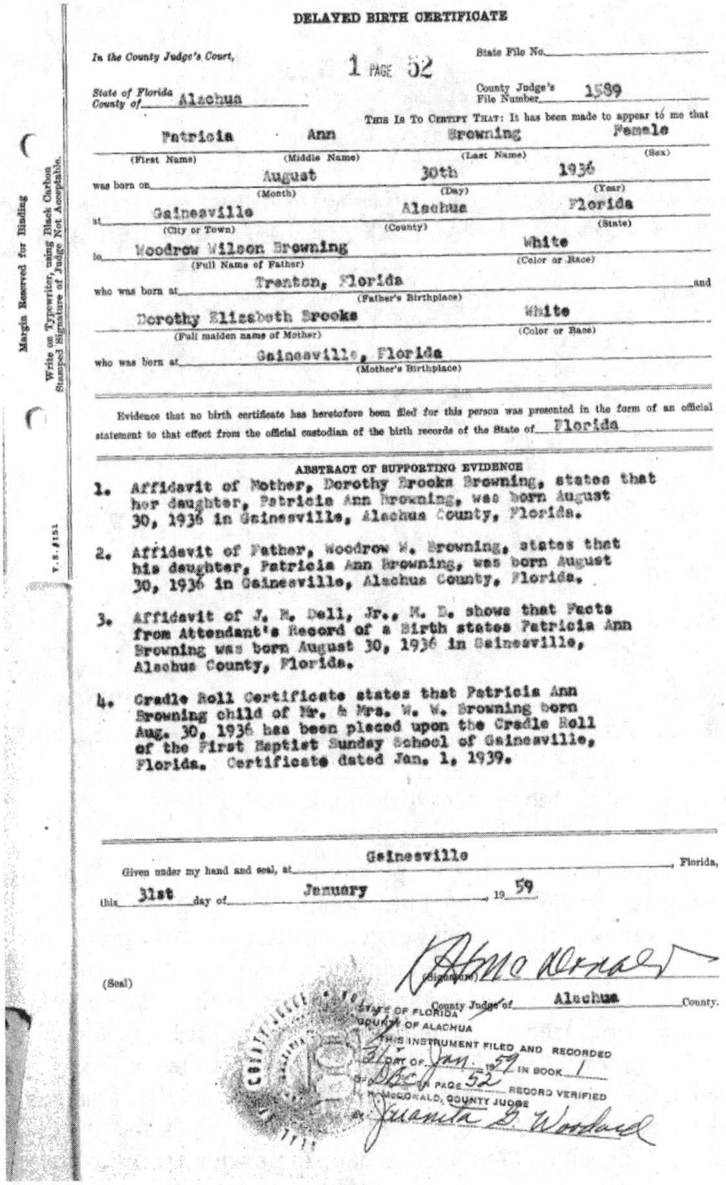

DELAYED BIRTH CERTIFICATE

In the County Judge's Court,

State File No.

1 PAGE **52**

State of Florida
County of **Alachua**

County Judge's
File Number **1589**

THIS IS TO CERTIFY THAT: It has been made to appear to me that

Patricia **Ann** **Browning** **Female**
(First Name) (Middle Name) (Last Name) (Sex)

was born on **August** **30th** **1936**
(Month) (Day) (Year)

at **Gainesville** **Alachua** **Florida**
(City or Town) (County) (State)

to **Woodrow Wilson Browning** **White**
(Full Name of Father) (Color or Race)

who was born at **Trenton, Florida** and
(Father's Birthplace)

Dorothy Elizabeth Brooks **White**
(Full maiden name of Mother) (Color or Race)

who was born at **Gainesville, Florida**
(Mother's Birthplace)

Evidence that no birth certificate has heretofore been filed for this person was presented in the form of an official statement to that effect from the official custodian of the birth records of the State of **Florida**

ABSTRACT OF SUPPORTING EVIDENCE

1. Affidavit of Mother, Dorothy Brooks Browning, states that her daughter, Patricia Ann Browning, was born August 30, 1936 in Gainesville, Alachua County, Florida.

2. Affidavit of Father, Woodrow W. Browning, states that his daughter, Patricia Ann Browning, was born August 30, 1936 in Gainesville, Alachua County, Florida.

3. Affidavit of J. R. Dell, Jr., M. D. shows that Facts from Attendant's Record of a Birth states Patricia Ann Browning was born August 30, 1936 in Gainesville, Alachua County, Florida.

4. Cradle Roll Certificate states that Patricia Ann Browning child of Mr. & Mrs. W. W. Browning born Aug. 30, 1936 has been placed upon the Cradle Roll of the First Baptist Sunday School of Gainesville, Florida. Certificate dated Jan. 1, 1939.

Given under my hand and seal, at **Gainesville**, Florida,

this **31st** day of **January** 19 **59**

(Seal)

County Judge of **Alachua** County.

STATE OF FLORIDA
COUNTY OF ALACHUA
THIS INSTRUMENT FILED AND RECORDED
31 DAY OF Jan 59 IN BOOK 1
PAGE 52 RECORD VERIFIED
McDONALD, COUNTY JUDGE
BY Juanita D. Woodard

Margin Reserved for Binding
Write on Typewriter, using Black Carbon
Stamped Signature of Judge Not Acceptable.

V.S. #151

FIGURE 5-15 A delayed birth certificate is often issued when no original was created. Alternative proofs are presented to the government for review.

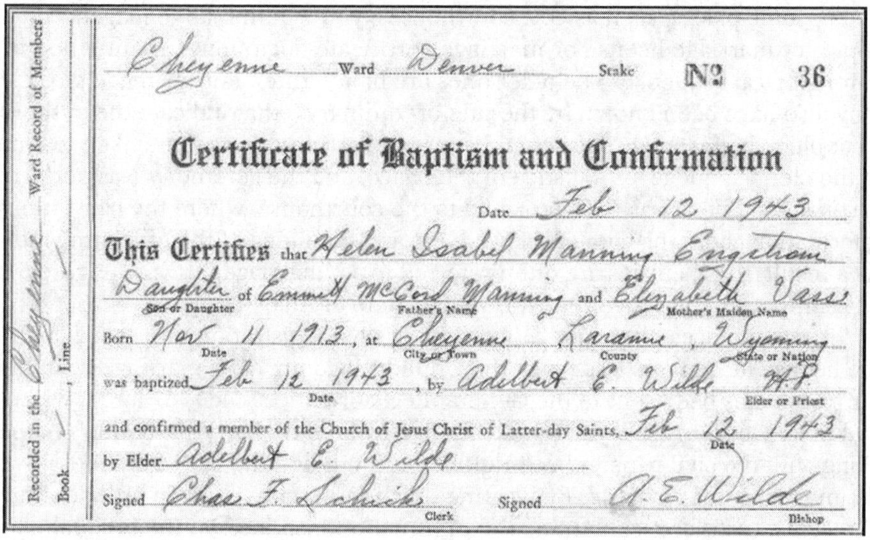

Recorded in the Cheyenne Ward Record of Members

Book 1, Line

Cheyenne Ward Denver Stake No. 36

Certificate of Baptism and Confirmation

Date Feb 12 1943

This Certifies that Helen Isabel Manning Engstrom

Daughter (Son or Daughter) of Emmett McCord Manning (Father's Name) and Elizabeth Vass (Mother's Maiden Name)

Born Nov 11 1913 (Date), at Cheyenne (City or Town) Laramie (County), Wyoming (State or Nation)

was baptized Feb 12 1943 (Date), by Adelbert E. Wilde H.P. (Elder or Priest)

and confirmed a member of the Church of Jesus Christ of Latter-day Saints, Feb 12, 1943 (Date)

by Elder Adelbert E. Wilde

Signed Chas. F. Schick (Clerk) Signed A. E. Wilde (Bishop)

FIGURE 5-16 Certificate of Baptism and Confirmation from 1943

- A birth announcement published in a newspaper or a church publication may provide clues to the date and location of primary birth records.
- The family Bible may contain entries recording names and dates of birth.
- Letters, journals, and diaries of members of the immediate or extended family may contain information about a birth.
- Affidavits from witnesses at or near the time of the event are useful in obtaining delayed birth certificates but may be helpful to you as well.
- Medical records, although not generally released to persons other than the patient and his or her immediate family members, may provide a date of birth. Medical practitioners often maintained their own records of deliveries they performed.
- School enrollment records are a good secondary source of birth information. Data may be obtained by making a request of the school administration officials, who may provide photocopies or written responses to specific questions.

Another part of your investigative process also involves using your knowledge of history, geography, and your family, and coupling that with your creative thinking to consider what other types of record and materials might provide evidence of the event.

Find Marriage Licenses and Certificates

Marriage records are among some of the oldest records kept. The earliest ones are typically found in religious institutions, but others can be found among the many places where civil registration records are located. They are often indexed for easy reference, both in groom and bride sequence by surname and then given name.

In some places, such as U.S. courthouses, you will find large ledgers containing copies of marriage license or marriage certificate documents, maintained in chronological sequence. The older ones are handwritten entries made by a clerk (who may also have been known by the title of "ordinary") that indicate the authorization of a couple to be married. The actual license or certificate was then taken to a member of the clergy, a judge, or a justice of the peace, and the ceremony was performed. The original document was then returned to the courthouse, where the clerk transcribed information about the date of the wedding and the name of the officiating individual. As a result, these entries are often referred to as "marriage returns." Figure 5-17 shows an example of a marriage return from the State of Alabama.

In other places, there are civil offices or civil registration offices at which the license to wed was issued. In the United Kingdom, each marriage document ultimately has been sent to the General Register Office (GRO), where it was recorded and filed. Quarterly indexes were compiled by groom's name and bride's name, along with the civil register book number or letter and the page number on which the marriage was recorded. By locating this information, you can order online from the GRO a certificate containing the information inscribed on the original marriage document on file.

In some cases, you may find the original documents in a government office, or you may obtain a copy of the document or a certified document, such as the one shown in Figure 5-18, attesting to the content of the marriage entry.

Marriage laws have varied over time in different places. The legal age at which an individual could enter into a marriage contract may have been 16, 18, or some other age. Exceptions to these laws may have been made with the express permission of one or

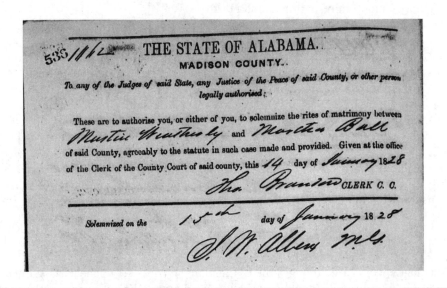

FIGURE 5-17   This marriage license from 1828 was returned to the county clerk of Madison County, Alabama, after the ceremony for registration and filing. It is the marriage record for one set of the author's great-great-grandparents.

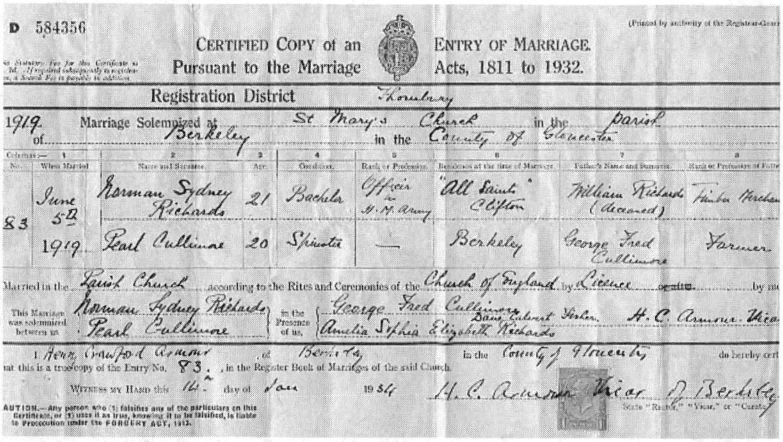
D 584356

CERTIFIED COPY of an ENTRY OF MARRIAGE
Pursuant to the Marriage Acts, 1811 to 1932.

Registration District Thornbury

1919. Marriage Solemnized at St Mary's Church in the parish of Berkeley in the County of Gloucester

No.	When Married	Name and Surname	Age	Condition	Rank or Profession	Residence at the time of Marriage	Father's Name and Surname	Rank or Profession of Father
83	June 5th 1919	Norman Sydney Richards	21	Bachelor	Officer H.M. Army	"All Saints" Clifton	William Richards (deceased)	Timber Merchant
		Pearl Cullimore	20	Spinster	—	Berkeley	George Fred Cullimore	Farmer

Married in the Parish Church according to the Rites and Ceremonies of the Church of England by Licence

This Marriage was solemnized between us: Norman Sydney Richards, Pearl Cullimore. In the Presence of us: George Fred Cullimore, Amelia Sophia Elizabeth Richards. H. C. Armour, Vicar

I, Henry Crawford Armour, of Berkeley in the County of Gloucester do hereby certify that this is a true copy of the Entry No. 83, in the Register Book of Marriages of the said Church.

WITNESS MY HAND this 14th day of Jan 1934 H. C. Armour Vicar of Berkeley

FIGURE 5-18 This Certified Copy of an Entry of Marriage was issued by the GRO as legal documentation of a marriage that took place in Gloucester, England, in 1919.

both of the parents of a minor. In addition, laws dictating the permissibility of marriage between couples who shared a certain consanguinity, or blood relationship, were generally closely adhered to. For example, a person might not be permitted by law to marry his or her sibling, first cousin, uncle or aunt, or another similarly close relative.

Marriage licenses are common across the world. What differs, however, are the formats and the amount of information contained on them. The typical marriage record will include the names of the two parties being wed, the date and location, the name or signature of the person who officiated, and often the names or signatures of at least two witnesses. Other records may include far more details, such as the ages or even the dates of birth of the bride and groom, their marital status (single, spinster, widow, widower), the names of their parents, the filing date and location, and the name or signature of the clerk or ordinary. English marriage registrations even include the addresses of the bride and groom. Others may include the occupation of the fathers of the couple.

The elaborate marriage certificate shown in Figure 5-19 appears to have been issued by the church rather than by a governmental office, as there is no registration information on it. The couple's names are Germanic, and the bride's name, Adolphine M. Reeb, is followed by the notation, "geb. Kleinknecht." The "geb." is an abbreviation for the German word *geborene*, which is the feminine of the German word for *born* or, in this context, *née*. This notation indicates that Kleinknecht was the bride's maiden name, and that she had been married before. Also note that another member of her family, Theodor (or Theador), signed the document as one of the witnesses.

The earliest marriage documents recorded royal or noble marriages. Over time, marriage documents became more common and were issued and recorded by churches. These were all handwritten, often in florid script or calligraphy. Later ones used standardized forms. Still others can be found that are extremely ornate, with elaborate artwork, gold or silver leaf, wax or metallic seals, and affixed with ribbons.

FIGURE 5-19 This elaborate marriage certificate, dated 20 April 1881, was probably issued by a church.

There are other records that can be used to help prove a marriage or the intent to marry. The following list includes a number, but certainly not all, of the kinds of alternative record types you might use to help document a marriage:

- Marriage banns are a public announcement, read out on at least three successive occasions in a parish church, of a declaration of intent to marry. These may be documented in church minutes, bulletins, and other publications. Figure 5-20 shows a page from an English parish church's marriage banns in 1796. Before the use of formal marriage certificates, marriage banns found in church records may be the only indication that a couple intended to marry.
- Marriage bonds were sworn by the groom and witnessed as a declaration of the intent to solemnize a marriage.
- Newspaper announcements of engagements and accounts of the marriages can provide clues to the date and place of a wedding that you can then follow up to locate primary documents.

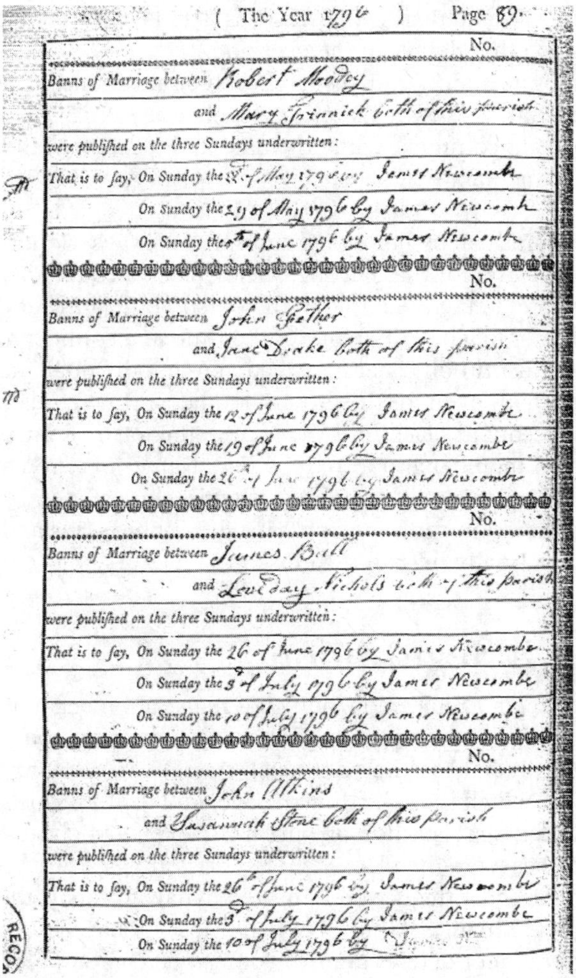

FIGURE 5-20   Marriage banns were announced or published on several successive Sundays to make public a couple's intention to wed.

- A wedding invitation is an excellent indicator of intent that you may use to help locate a primary marriage record. Remember that dates on a preprinted invitation may have been changed due to unforeseen circumstances.
- Marriage ceremonies performed in a religious institution are typically recorded in their records.
- Civil marriages performed in a city hall or other government office will be found recorded in these governmental offices' files.
- Bible entries may contain marriage information but should be verified with other records.

- Letters, journals, and diaries may discuss details of a wedding, the persons who attended, and other details of the occasion.
- Printed announcements, notices in church publications, or newspaper accounts of milestone anniversary celebrations, such as a 25th, 50th, or 75th wedding anniversary, are pointers back to the date and location of the original event and original documentary evidence.

Marriage records can be helpful in a number of ways. Certainly, they are sources of primary information for the marriage. They place a couple in a specific place on a particular date. Using the name of the person officiating at the ceremony, you may be able to refer to a city directory of the time and connect him (or her) with a specific religious institution. That may lead you to individual and family records for the bride and perhaps even for the groom. Membership records may then point you to previous and subsequent places of residence in the form of entries in church minutes where transfers of membership were recorded. Names of parents and witnesses may connect you with other family members, friends, and collateral relatives, too. These are examples of how you can use your critical thinking skills and your creativity to identify other potentially helpful records.

Before Civil Registration

Earlier in the chapter, I indicated when civil registration began in England and Wales, Scotland, and Ireland. I also mentioned that those records produced in Canada and Australia are usually held by the provincial, state, or territorial offices. Prior to the effective dates on which those birth, marriage, and death records were required, laws typically required the registration of similar life events in church parish registers.

Parish churches were the places where christenings, marriages, and burials were typically recorded. Individuals were required by law to report these events to the Church of England/Anglican Church parish priest so that they could be recorded within a certain number of days after the occasion. The Catholic churches also maintained their own registers in their parishes. These are ecclesiastical records, and the entries in England and Wales were therefore written in Latin until the early 1700s, and later in English. That means that you may need to brush up on your Latin language skills in order to read and understand some of these older records. After the implementation of civil registration, however, the parish churches continued to keep these records for their own purposes.

Many parish records have been microfilmed over time, and these are being digitized, indexed, and placed on the Internet at various places. Here are some of the most prominent websites at which you will find parish records online:

- **Ancestry.com** Parish registers and other ecclesiastical records are available for England and Wales, Scotland, Ireland, and Canada at **http://www.ancestry.com** and its various international websites.
- **FamilySearch** Parish registers and other ecclesiastical records are available for England and Wales, Scotland, and Ireland, and other countries around the world are available at **https://familysearch.org**.

- **Findmypast** This site at **http://www.findmypast.com** includes some parish registers.
- **MyHeritage** Parish registers and other ecclesiastical records are available for England and Wales, Scotland, Ireland, Canada, Italy, Mexico, Australia, and many other countries worldwide are accessible at **http://www.myheritage.com**.
- **ScotlandsPeople** This site at **http://www.scotlandspeople.gov.uk** provides access to birth, marriage, and death records (statutory records), Old Parish Registers, and Catholic Parish Registers and other Catholic documents.

Research Divorce Records

Records of a divorce are far less numerous than marriage records, and so you would think they would be easier to locate. Unfortunately, though, that is not always true. Some courthouses, record offices, and government facilities have done an excellent job indexing the divorces by the names of the husband and wife. Their documents are usually organized in an orderly filing system. In other government offices, the divorce documentation may be filed only under the name of the plaintiff—the person who sued for divorce. Others, however, may simply have filed divorce petitions and decrees in chronological sequence. These filing systems, and a lack of cross-referencing indexes, can make your job problematic and may require you to spend hours paging through sheaves of papers. Even if the courthouse or clerks have not been as organized or diligent in their filing, there are other possibilities.

Make certain before you undertake a search for divorce records that you determine which court would have handled the process for the period in time when the divorce likely occurred. For example, in one place and time a divorce might have been handled by a civil court, while in another place the hearings may have been held and the dissolution of the marriage may have been finalized in a family court, a high court of justice in the family division, a superior court, a chancery court, or some other judicial division. Figure 5-21 shows an example of a bill of divorce handed down by a chancery court in 1846. Knowing in advance what the laws were at the time *and* the court of law that handled marriage dissolutions at the time can be crucial to your success.

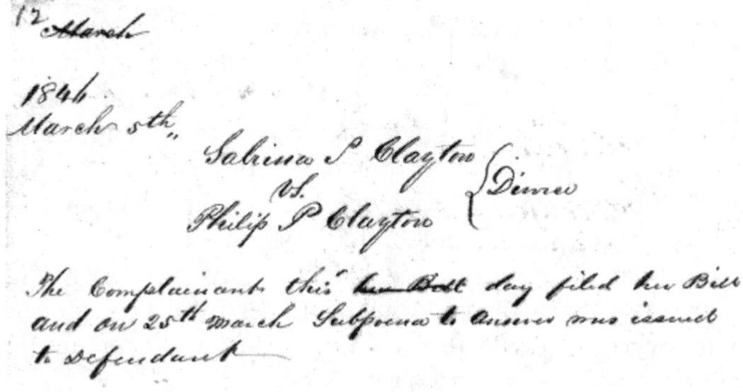
12 March

1846
March 5th,
Sabina S. Clayton
vs.
Philip P Clayton
Divorce

The Complainant this day filed her Bill and on 25th March Subpoena to Answer was issued to defendant

FIGURE 5-21 Simple bill of divorce dated 5 March 1846 found in chancery court records

Contact the court that would have handled the divorce petition or suit before you make a trip there. If an index of documents does not exist, request a search of the minutes books of the appropriate court. The minutes books are well indexed to facilitate the location of pertinent documentation relating to a specific case. The clerk can pull the document that references previous court hearings and actions in the case, and help the magistrate quickly familiarize himself with the case particulars. You may have greater success by obtaining the dates of the filings and hearings in the court minutes, and then going directly to the records if they are filed in chronological sequence.

Early records were handwritten, and reading the clerk's penmanship may be a challenge. Later records are typewritten and easier to read.

Locate Death Certificates

The sheer volume of records created as a result of a contemporary individual's death can be enormous. However, you may find that records from earlier times may be nonexistent. The creation and existence of these records will depend on a number of factors. Did the government require them to be kept? Who was responsible for creating them: the government or the church, or both? What information was to be included? Where were these records stored and for what duration? Were there natural or manmade catastrophes that caused records to be lost or destroyed? How will you find out what is and is not available?

A common death record is the death certificate. While a death registration was common in England and Wales from 1837, in the United States the issuance of an official, government-issued death certificate was not required until much later. In fact, a death certificate was not required in many states until the first two decades of the 20th century. Again, *The Family Tree Sourcebook* can help you determine when records were kept in a specific U.S. state and where they may be found. Please remember that a death certificate is a source for *primary information* about the death itself but is decidedly a source for *secondary information* about the decedent's birth, parents' names, spouse, and other facts. This other information should be corroborated with other primary evidence documentation.

Death records come in many forms. The form familiar to most people in the United States is the death certificate, and the format and amount of information included varies by location and time period. Other documents, however, serve a similar or identical purpose for genealogists because they are, after all, official documentation of a death. These might include a coroner's report, an autopsy, the final report of an inquest into the cause of death, or a ruling on evidence of an actual or assumed death presented to a judge or jury. This latter situation would include, among others, a case in which a person has disappeared and, after some period of time, is declared dead by a court of law. You also may encounter or obtain a document that acts as a certified copy of an original death certificate or that certifies the official death entry in the government's records. Figure 5-22 shows an example of a certified copy of a death entry document from the United Kingdom.

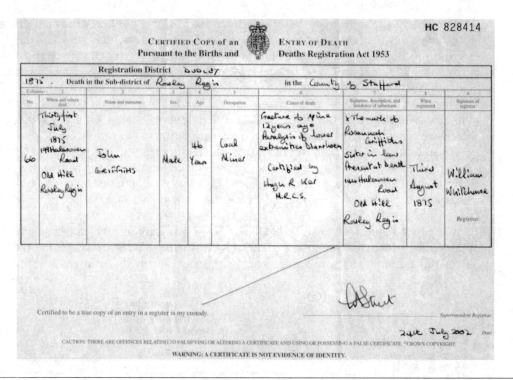

FIGURE 5-22   Certified Copy of an Entry of Death document from Staffordshire, England, for 1875

You will remember from our discussion of sources that a death certificate can be a source of both primary *and* secondary information. Since a death certificate is an official record of a person's death, it is usually created at or very near the time of death in order to record the event. There also are instances of amended death certificates being issued in order to correct or add to information entered on the original document.

The veracity of the information on a death certificate will depend on where the information originated. Information about the identity of the decedent and the death itself are usually obtained from medical, law enforcement, forensic, and other professional persons. It is their job to gather and report the correct information. You would therefore place a significant amount of credence in their data and, if placed on a certificate created at or very near the time of death, consider it to be good primary information. The name of the mortuary is generally accurate, and the intended place of interment or disposition of cremains is an excellent clue for more documentary information.

Other information found on a death certificate may not be as reliable as that gathered by the professionals. Someone who supposedly knew something about the deceased may have provided the other details included on a death certificate. Another family member or friend is usually solicited to provide the information, and he or she is referred to as the "informant." The informant may or may not know the answers to all the questions that are asked and, on the spur of the moment, may provide what he or she "thinks" is correct. The informant may also be distraught over the death and too distracted to accurately recall details. As a result, there are many errors entered on death certificates. Unless the informant has direct, first-hand, and accurate knowledge of facts, the information provided can only be assumed to be secondary in nature. Everything should therefore be verified or corroborated with other evidence sources before you accept those items of information as fact.

As an example, let's examine the death certificate presented in Figure 5-23. The name of the person may or may not be correct, depending on the source of the information. The informant provided information concerning the decedent's date and place of birth, parents' names, marital status, name of spouse, occupation, place of residence, and other data.

When you request a copy of a death certificate, you may receive an exact copy of the original document, such as a photocopy. However, it is also possible that the official office from which you order a copy will issue a certified document attesting

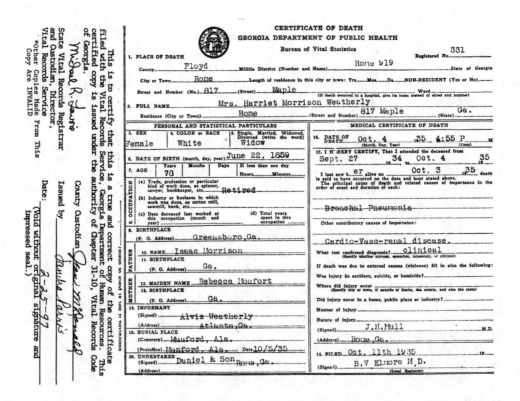

FIGURE 5-23 Certified copy of a death certificate for the author's great-grandmother from Floyd County, Georgia, issued in 1935

to be information correctly copied from the original death registration document. Figures 5-22, 5-23, and 5-24 are examples of certified copies, the first from the GRO in the United Kingdom and the other two from the United States. These copies commonly contain far less information than the original document. Remember that an exact copy of the original is your better resource, and that transcription errors might be made despite all caution. If you order a copy of a marriage or death record, request an exact copy of the original rather than a transcribed certified copy, if possible.

Other source materials for determining date of death and other family details include newspaper obituaries (a veritable wealth of clues!), burial permits, transit permits, medical records, family Bibles, tombstones and other types of cemetery markers, cemetery/sexton records, religious records, mortuary and funeral home records, and wills and probate records, just to name a few.

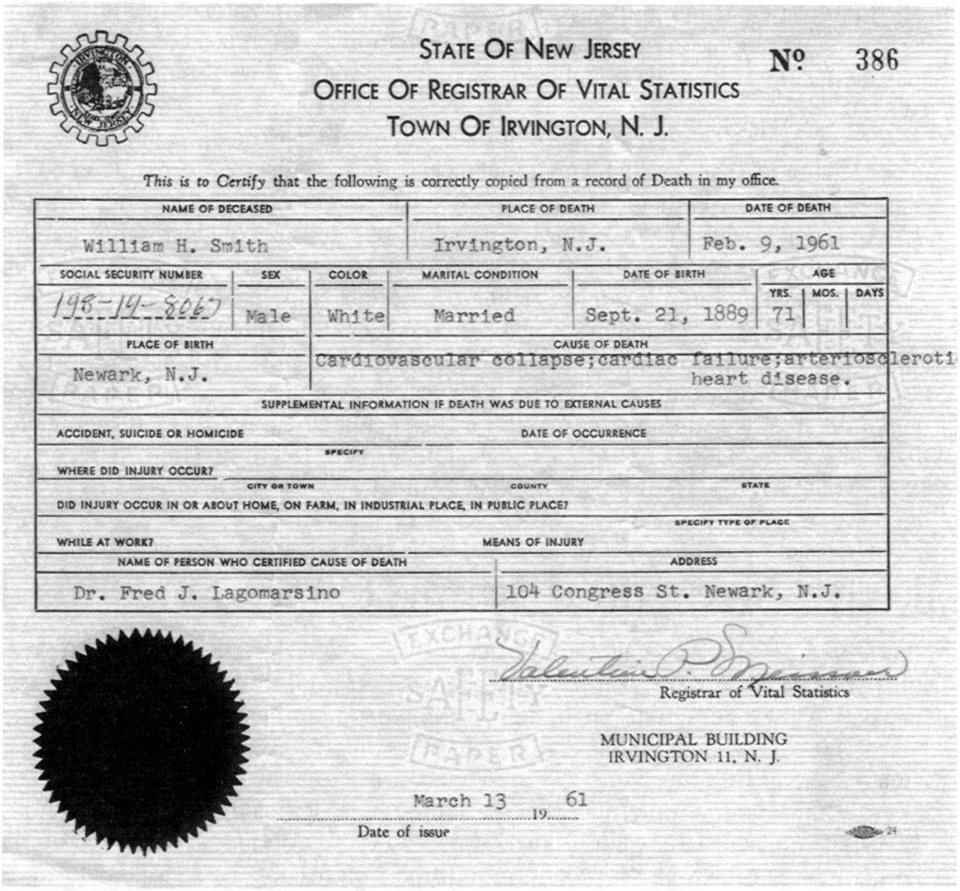

STATE OF NEW JERSEY
OFFICE OF REGISTRAR OF VITAL STATISTICS
TOWN OF IRVINGTON, N. J.

Nº 386

This is to Certify that the following is correctly copied from a record of Death in my office.

NAME OF DECEASED	PLACE OF DEATH	DATE OF DEATH
William H. Smith	Irvington, N.J.	Feb. 9, 1961

SOCIAL SECURITY NUMBER	SEX	COLOR	MARITAL CONDITION	DATE OF BIRTH	AGE YRS.	AGE MOS.	AGE DAYS
198-14-8067	Male	White	Married	Sept. 21, 1889	71		

PLACE OF BIRTH	CAUSE OF DEATH
Newark, N.J.	Cardiovascular collapse; cardiac failure; arteriosclerotic heart disease.

SUPPLEMENTAL INFORMATION IF DEATH WAS DUE TO EXTERNAL CAUSES

ACCIDENT, SUICIDE OR HOMICIDE (SPECIFY) — DATE OF OCCURRENCE

WHERE DID INJURY OCCUR? CITY OR TOWN — COUNTY — STATE

DID INJURY OCCUR IN OR ABOUT HOME, ON FARM, IN INDUSTRIAL PLACE, IN PUBLIC PLACE? (SPECIFY TYPE OF PLACE)

WHILE AT WORK? — MEANS OF INJURY

NAME OF PERSON WHO CERTIFIED CAUSE OF DEATH	ADDRESS
Dr. Fred J. Lagomarsino	104 Congress St. Newark, N.J.

Registrar of Vital Statistics

MUNICIPAL BUILDING
IRVINGTON 11, N. J.

March 13 19 61
Date of issue

FIGURE 5-24 Certified copy of a death record from New Jersey, issued in 1961

Locate Domestic Partnership and Civil Partnership Records

There are several alternatives to traditional ecclesiastical marriages. Some of our ancestors simply began living together. Statutory law may not have governed their relationship, but it may have been recognized under something called "common-law." Some places have recognized a "common law husband" and a "common law wife" in legal matters. The term refers to a domestic partner in a union created by mutual agreement and public behavior rather than by ecclesiastical or civil ceremony. You may therefore encounter the term in legal documents such as deeds and probate records period

A more recent development has involved government legislation for two more formally recognized domestic unions. These include domestic partnership agreements and civil partnership documents.

A domestic partnership agreement might be drawn up to formalize the legal recognition of a long-standing cohabitation situation by an opposite sex couple. This may be desirable because it applies particularly to real and personal property in a court of law.

A civil partnership is more formal than a domestic partnership agreement, and it legally has the force of a civil marriage. It may be used to formally record a marriage performed in a government office or in an ecclesiastical setting. The English Parliament passed the Civil Partnership Act of 2004 and this enabled same-sex couples to legally wed and to enjoy the same rights of property ownership, parenthood, life insurance recognition, next-of-kin rights in hospitals, and other benefits. One of the first couples to wed under the new law was Sir Elton Hercules John and David James Furnish, whose certified extract of the record is shown in Figure 5-25. There is also a formal process there for dissolving these partnerships, similar to divorce, and documentation is generated. Research for these civil partnership records will take you to government offices, such as the General Record Offices in England, Scotland, and Ireland, and to equivalent offices in other countries.

Deal with Suspected Name Changes

There may come a time that your ancestor "disappears" from the records. The two most obvious reasons are that the person has either relocated to another location or has died. A third possibility might be that the person has changed his or her name. Researching a suspected name change can be confusing and challenging, but let's consider the possibilities.

It is important to remember that surnames were not used in many places until the 17th century or later. People simply adopted them, in many cases based on the name of the place where they were from or their profession; there was no formal process used and probably no documentation created. Our earlier ancestors may have taken on new names without going to a court to do so.

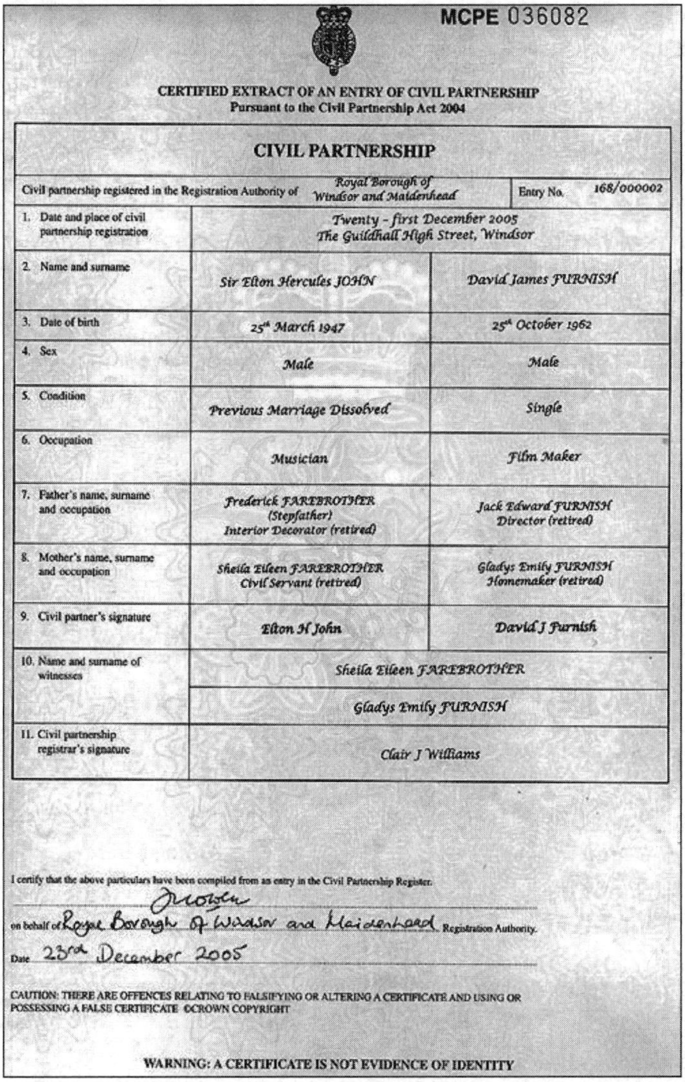

MCPE 036082

CERTIFIED EXTRACT OF AN ENTRY OF CIVIL PARTNERSHIP
Pursuant to the Civil Partnership Act 2004

CIVIL PARTNERSHIP

Civil partnership registered in the Registration Authority of Royal Borough of Windsor and Maidenhead — Entry No. 168/000002

1. Date and place of civil partnership registration	Twenty - first December 2005 The Guildhall High Street, Windsor	
2. Name and surname	Sir Elton Hercules JOHN	David James FURNISH
3. Date of birth	25th March 1947	25th October 1962
4. Sex	Male	Male
5. Condition	Previous Marriage Dissolved	Single
6. Occupation	Musician	Film Maker
7. Father's name, surname and occupation	Frederick FAREBROTHER (Stepfather) Interior Decorator (retired)	Jack Edward FURNISH Director (retired)
8. Mother's name, surname and occupation	Sheila Eileen FAREBROTHER Civil Servant (retired)	Gladys Emily FURNISH Homemaker (retired)
9. Civil partner's signature	Elton H John	David J Furnish
10. Name and surname of witnesses	Sheila Eileen FAREBROTHER	
	Gladys Emily FURNISH	
11. Civil partnership registrar's signature	Clair J Williams	

I certify that the above particulars have been compiled from an entry in the Civil Partnership Register.

on behalf of Royal Borough of Windsor and Maidenhead Registration Authority.

Date 23rd December 2005

CAUTION: THERE ARE OFFENCES RELATING TO FALSIFYING OR ALTERING A CERTIFICATE AND USING OR POSSESSING A FALSE CERTIFICATE ©CROWN COPYRIGHT

WARNING: A CERTIFICATE IS NOT EVIDENCE OF IDENTITY

FIGURE 5-25 Certified copy of the civil partnership record in England for Sir Elton Hercules John and David James Furnish, 21 December 2005

Some of the United States state laws now or in the past allowed a name change according to common law, simply by using a new name, so long as the person is not intending to mislead. However, a legal change of name in more recent times typically has involved registration of the new name with a court of law. This is typically the first of many steps because the new name must then be filed with other government offices and with every place with which the person has some legal relationship.

The change of a person's surname can occur in multiple ways. A woman's surname may change at her marriage. If that marriage is dissolved by divorce, she may file a petition with the court to resume use of her maiden surname. A man may change his surname only by petitioning a court. In the United States, some states prohibit a man from changing his surname. If you suspect that one of your ancestors may have changed their name, you should conduct some research into the laws of that location for the time period that you expect a name might have been changed. Then check the records in the appropriate court in the jurisdiction where the person lived to determine if there was, in fact, a legal change of name. Don't be surprised if you find that legal name changes in a specific governmental jurisdiction were not performed/ allowed until the early part of the 20th century. Furthermore, since a person legally changing their name must notify many government offices, businesses, and individuals, some notifications may never have been accomplished, and some records may have listed the old name long after the legal change was filed.

Summary

We've covered a great deal of territory in this chapter. By now, you should have a well-grounded feel for how to conduct scholarly research. You also have some excellent new methodologies to help ensure your success. Chapter 6 will take you into a thorough examination of census records, which in turn can lead you to a wealth of other records that will add context and details to your understanding of your ancestors' lives.

6

Use Census Schedules and Records to Locate Your Ancestors

HOW TO...

- Locate and access census records in the digital age
- Understand and work with United States census records
- Discover the history of the English, Scottish, and Irish censuses
- Learn more about the census in Canada
- Locate information about censuses in other places
- Gain access to census records

Among the most important records that exist for confirming the presence of an ancestor at a particular place at a specific point in time are census records. A *census* is defined as an official count of a population carried out at regular intervals. Censuses have been taken for many centuries in many countries and territories. Enumerations of populations were conducted for purposes of taxation, determination of legislative representation, analysis of trends in population growth and movement, and other planning purposes.

Census records are the documents most frequently used by genealogists, and their use continues to accelerate and grow. This is especially true with the availability and expansion of Internet-based databases containing digitized census document images and searchable indices.

We are going to focus on the available census records in the United States, the British Isles, and Canada in this chapter. Unfortunately, early Australian census records have been destroyed by the government and no known copies exist.

Certainly other countries have taken censuses at various times and, if you are interested in learning more about them and accessing extant records, you can use your web browser to locate archives and other repositories in which the records may be located. Other census indexes, transcriptions, and images may be accessible at various websites. For example, Ancestry.de at **http://www.ancestry.de**, the German genealogy subscription database, contains some German census records (Volkszälung) such as the image shown in Figure 6-1.

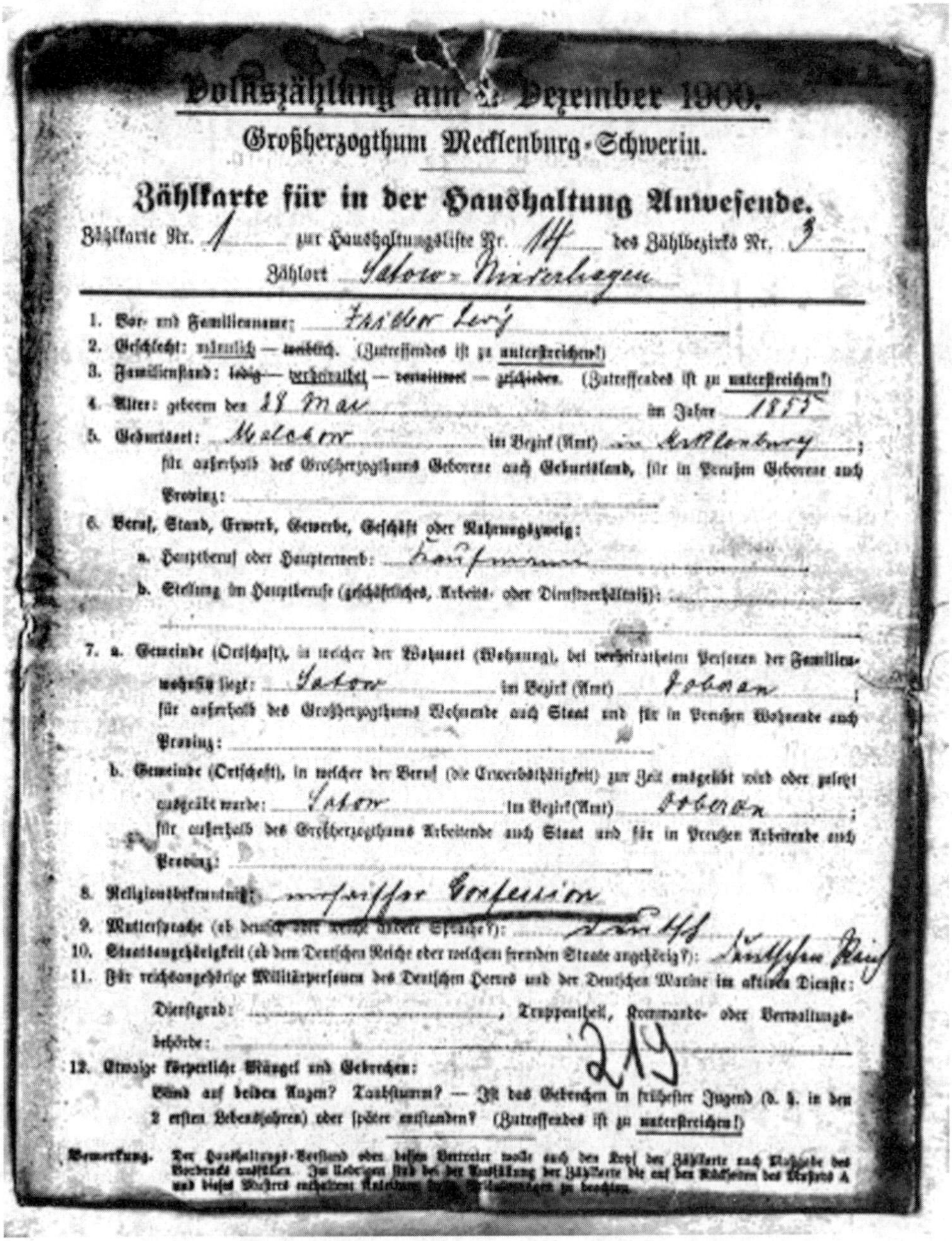
Volkszählung am 1. Dezember 1900.

Großherzogthum Mecklenburg-Schwerin.

Zählkarte für in der Haushaltung Anwesende.

Zählkarte Nr. 1 zur Haushaltungsliste Nr. 14 des Zählbezirks Nr. 3

Zählort

1. Vor- und Familienname:
2. Geschlecht: männlich — weiblich. (Zutreffendes ist zu unterstreichen!)
3. Familienstand: ledig — verheirathet — verwittwet — geschieden. (Zutreffendes ist zu unterstreichen!)
4. Alter: geboren den ... im Jahre ...
5. Geburtsort: ... im Bezirk (Amt) ...; für außerhalb des Großherzogthums Geborene auch Geburtsland, für in Preußen Geborene auch Provinz:
6. Beruf, Stand, Erwerb, Gewerbe, Geschäft oder Nahrungszweig:
   a. Hauptberuf oder Haupterwerb:
   b. Stellung im Hauptberufe (geschäftliches, Arbeits- oder Dienstverhältniß):
7. a. Gemeinde (Ortschaft), in welcher der Wohnort (Wohnung), bei verheiratheten Personen der Familienwohnsitz liegt: ... im Bezirk (Amt) ...; für außerhalb des Großherzogthums Wohnende auch Staat und für in Preußen Wohnende auch Provinz:
   b. Gemeinde (Ortschaft), in welcher der Beruf (die Erwerbsthätigkeit) zur Zeit ausgeübt wird oder zuletzt ausgeübt wurde: ... im Bezirk (Amt) ...; für außerhalb des Großherzogthums Arbeitende auch Staat und für in Preußen Arbeitende auch Provinz:
8. Religionsbekenntniß:
9. Muttersprache (ob deutsch oder welche andere Sprache?):
10. Staatsangehörigkeit (ob dem Deutschen Reiche oder welchem fremden Staate angehörig?):
11. Für reichsangehörige Militärpersonen des Deutschen Heeres und der Deutschen Marine im aktiven Dienste: Dienstgrad: ..., Truppentheil, Kommando- oder Verwaltungsbehörde:
12. Etwaige körperliche Mängel und Gebrechen: Blind auf beiden Augen? Taubstumm? — Ist das Gebrechen in frühester Jugend (d. h. in den 2 ersten Lebensjahren) oder später entstanden? (Zutreffendes ist zu unterstreichen!)

Bemerkung. Der Haushaltungs-Vorstand oder dessen Vertreter wolle auch den Kopf der Zählkarte nach Maßgabe des Vordrucks ausfüllen. Im Uebrigen sind bei der Ausfüllung der Zählkarte die auf den Rückseiten des Vordrucks A und dieses Musters enthaltenen Anleitungen ... zu beachten.

FIGURE 6-1 A German 1900 census record

Locate and Access Census Records in the Digital Age

In order to access census records for various locations and time periods in earlier times, genealogists had to visit an archive and tediously work with original census books. The 20th century saw the microfilming of many census records by respective countries' governments. In addition, the Church of Latter-day Saints (LDS) sent photographic teams across the world, beginning in 1938, to locate, access, and photograph records. This included census documents. Their photographs were placed on microfilm, and these films were available at the LDS library facilities in Salt Lake City, Utah, and through rentals at LDS Family History Centers throughout the world. Indexes to some censuses were prepared, as you will learn in this chapter. Some of these indexes were published in book form for researchers' use in libraries and archives. Others were published in microform format, and some of these were published on diskettes and CD-ROMs. With the arrival of the so-called "digital age," microfilmed census documents have often been digitized and the images placed online in databases. Those databases have often been indexed for rapid access.

As great as that all sounds, you will not always find that entire countries' historical census record images have been captured. We are fortunate that most of the extant original census documents for the United States, the United Kingdom, Ireland, and Canada were preserved and microfilmed over time. The governments of these respective nations are prohibited by privacy laws from making census records accessible to the public until proscribed time periods have passed. The United States has a 72-year privacy law, for example, and the most recent federal census records available to the public at this writing are from the 1940 census. (The 1950 census records will not be available until 2022.) The most recent available census for England and Wales is the 1911 census. The 1901 census is the most recent available for Scotland. The most recent available Canadian census dates from 1921. In recent years, the microfilmed census documents have been digitized, indexed, and placed online at such sites as Ancestry .com (**http://www.ancestry.com**), Ancestry.ca (**http://www.ancestry.ca**), Ancestry .co.uk (**http://www.ancestry.co.uk**), Archives.com (**http://www.archives.com**), FamilySearch (**https://familysearch.org**), Fold3.com (**http://www.fold3.com**), findmypast (**http://www.findmypast.com**), MyHeritage (**http://www.myheritage .com**), and the Library and Archives Canada (**http://www.bac-lac.gc.ca**).

The digitization and indexing of these census records, however, does not mean that literally everything is available online. Some documents have been misplaced, damaged, and/or intentionally destroyed. In other cases, some of the microfilmed census documents may not have been digitized yet. This means that you may sometimes find gaps that may confound your research, and you may need to seek out alternate records to verify that your ancestors were in a specific location at a particular point in time.

Other countries' census records may exist in fragments, and these may or may not have been microfilmed and subsequently digitized and placed on the Internet. You may be able to locate census records that have been placed online by using your favorite web browser and searching for the name of the country and the word census. I suggest using Google Translate (**https://translate.google.com**) to translate the word "census" into the native language for the searches, and even use the name of the country in its native language. Here are some examples:

France census: France recensement
Germany census: Deutschland Volkszählung or Deutschland zensus

Another possible help would be to use the Google search engine for the particular country whose census information you want to find. There are more than 150 different country versions of Google. For example, if you were searching for German census records, you might use the German version of Google at **http://www.google.de**. You can then review the search results for a specific time period. You can determine in advance the years and locations in which census enumerations were conducted by visiting the FamilySearch Wiki and searching for "German census." The wiki will include, in many cases, links to existing websites at which you might find descriptions, extracts, and even indexed census images. You can visit the site at **http://www.checkdomain.com/list.html** to obtain the two-letter Internet country code/domain name. While Google does not have a version of its search engine for every country, you can try entering **http://www.google.[xx]** (where **xx** is replaced by the country code) to see if there is a version of the Google search engine for that native country.

As we discuss census records, be aware that they can be a source of primary information to help establish a person's location in a specific place at a certain point in time. Even that is suspect at times, as you will see. All other information on a census document should definitely be considered secondary information, and should be verified and corroborated with other evidence sources whenever possible. Some of the reasons why this information may be secondary include

- Names entered on the census forms may have been nicknames or diminutives of first names/forenames. Initials may also have been used.
- The census enumerator may have misheard the response to the question or entered wrong information.
- The respondent at the residence may not have known the information.
- The respondent may have misremembered details about events that occurred many years ago, such as years married, age at marriage, age or birth date, year of arrival in the country, whether naturalized, or other data.
- The enumerator may not have interviewed a member of the household, but instead asked a neighbor about the family.
- There may have been errors introduced in transcribing data from the original copy of the census schedule to second and perhaps third copies.

These are the primary reason that we find errors and misinformation in census records. Therefore, it becomes important to verify the data with other sources of evidence. Keep this in mind as you work with census documents, and maintain some skepticism about possible secondary information.

Understand and Work with United States Census Records

In the United States, the federal government has taken censuses every ten years, beginning in 1790 and continuing to the present. (A federal census was taken in 1885 for five states and territories and was intended to supersede the results of the 1880 census for those areas. Refer to Table 6-1 further in the chapter for the 1885 census and the areas affected.) A number of state and territorial censuses also have been conducted periodically, and these can supplement your use of federal census records in American research. In addition, Native Americans on reservations were enumerated every year from 1885 to 1940.

Prior to 1790, a few of the original 13 colonies performed partial or complete enumerations of citizens for their own purposes. Some of these records still exist and, in order to locate them, it is a good idea to contact the respective state archive or state library to determine what might have been created, what might still survive, and where to locate the materials. Online sites for digitized images of U.S. census records include Ancestry.com (**http://www.ancestry.com**), Archives.com (**http://www .archives.com**), FamilySearch (**https://familysearch.org**), findmypast (**http:// www.findmypast.com**), Fold3.com (**http://www.fold3.com**), HeritageQuest Online, and MyHeritage (**http://www.myheritage.com**). (Please note that HeritageQuest Online is a database that is only available to libraries as an institutional subscription.) Not all census documents have been digitized, however; some may be available only in original paper records at the U.S. National Archives and Records Administration (NARA at **http://www.archives.gov**) or in a microfilmed format.

The United States Constitution, which took effect on 4 March 1789, established the taking of a national census on a regular basis. Article I, Section 2 specifically called for a census to be taken every ten years. Direct taxation of the population to support the federal government's operation was to be based on census information. The Constitution stated that each free person counted as a whole number, including those bound for service for a term of years, and that free males would be taxed and could vote. Indians living on treaty land were excluded from direct taxation and voting. Other, non-free persons (slaves) were to be counted as three-fifths of a free person for legislative representation. An Indian who joined the white population was to be considered a "free person" and could vote. The entire text of the Constitution is available at the Library of Congress' website at **http://memory.loc.gov/ammem/ collections/continental** and an extensive article about the Constitution is available at **http://en.wikipedia.org/wiki/United_states_constitution**.

Federal censuses have been taken every decade from 1790 through 2010. An official Census Day was established for enumerators to ask questions "as of" that date. The official United States Census Day for each census is shown here:

1790	2 August
1800	4 August
1810	6 August
1820	7 August
1830 through 1900	1 June
1910	15 April
1920	1 January
1930 through 2010	1 April

The enumerators, or census takers, were given a deadline by which time they were to accomplish their work, instructions to follow, and a set of questions to be used. Census forms for the 1850 to 2000 censuses are available at the Integrated Public Use Microdata Series (IPUMS) website of the Minnesota Population Center at the University of Minnesota, located at **http://usa.ipums.org/usa/voliii/tEnumForm .shtml**. The enumerators' instructions for the 1850 through 1950 censuses can be found at **http://usa.ipums.org/usa/voliii/tEnumInstr.shtml**. Refer also to the website at **http://usa.ipums.org/usa/voliii/tQuestions.shtml** for only the questions for 1850 through 1950 and for both the questions and the instructions for the 1960 through 2000 censuses.

Assistant marshals of the U.S. judicial districts performed the earliest census enumerations, from 1790 through 1870. At the time of the 1790 census, there were 16 federal court districts. These represented each of the original 13 states and Vermont, which was included in the first census even though it didn't become a state until 1791. The 2 additional districts comprising the 16 represented the area of Virginia that became Kentucky and the area of Massachusetts that became Maine. These marshals performed the census enumerations in addition to their ordinary duties. They were poorly paid for their work and often had to purchase paper, pens and ink, horse feed, and other supplies with their own funds. They had little incentive to do a good job. They sometimes erred in the areas in which they were assigned. When they failed to reach the state and county boundaries they were assigned to enumerate, or when they enumerated past these boundaries, the result was either omitted residents or duplication of other marshals' enumerations. During these decades, Congress provided funding for the enumeration time period and a subsequent tabulation only. This funding was appropriated in the Congressional session prior to the enumeration year.

It is important to note that the early federal census forms from 1790 through 1840 contained only the names of the heads of household, with the other members of the household represented numerically in categories organized by age, gender, and race. Figure 6-2 shows an example of the 1820 census, which recorded this type of enumeration.

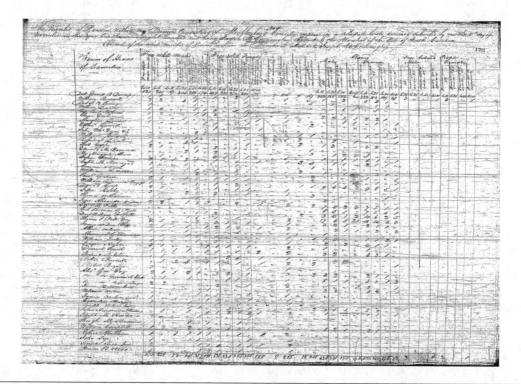

FIGURE 6-2 The 1820 U.S. federal census contained only the names of the heads of household and included numerical counts of persons by age group, gender, and free or slave status.

The first central Census Office was established and opened in 1850 in Washington, D.C., with the purpose of centralizing the coordination of the taking of a decennial enumeration. It was not until the 1850 census that the names of all persons within a household were listed. When the enumeration by the marshals was complete, the documents were sent to Washington and the final tabulation and reporting was performed. When these activities were finished, the office was disbanded and all census activity was discontinued until preparation for the next census. The same process was used for both the 1860 and 1870 censuses.

A Congressional act established and provided funding for a permanent Census Office beginning with the 1880 census. That year marked significant changes to the U.S. federal census process in a number of ways. For the first time, the assistant federal marshals were removed from the process. The Census Office hired employees to conduct the enumerations, devised formal Enumeration District maps and descriptions of the areas to be enumerated, revised the enumeration instructions, and revised the census forms (or census schedules, as they are called).

The most common of the federal census documents is the Population Schedule, a sample of which from 1880 is shown in Figure 6-3. These and other schedule documents are discussed next.

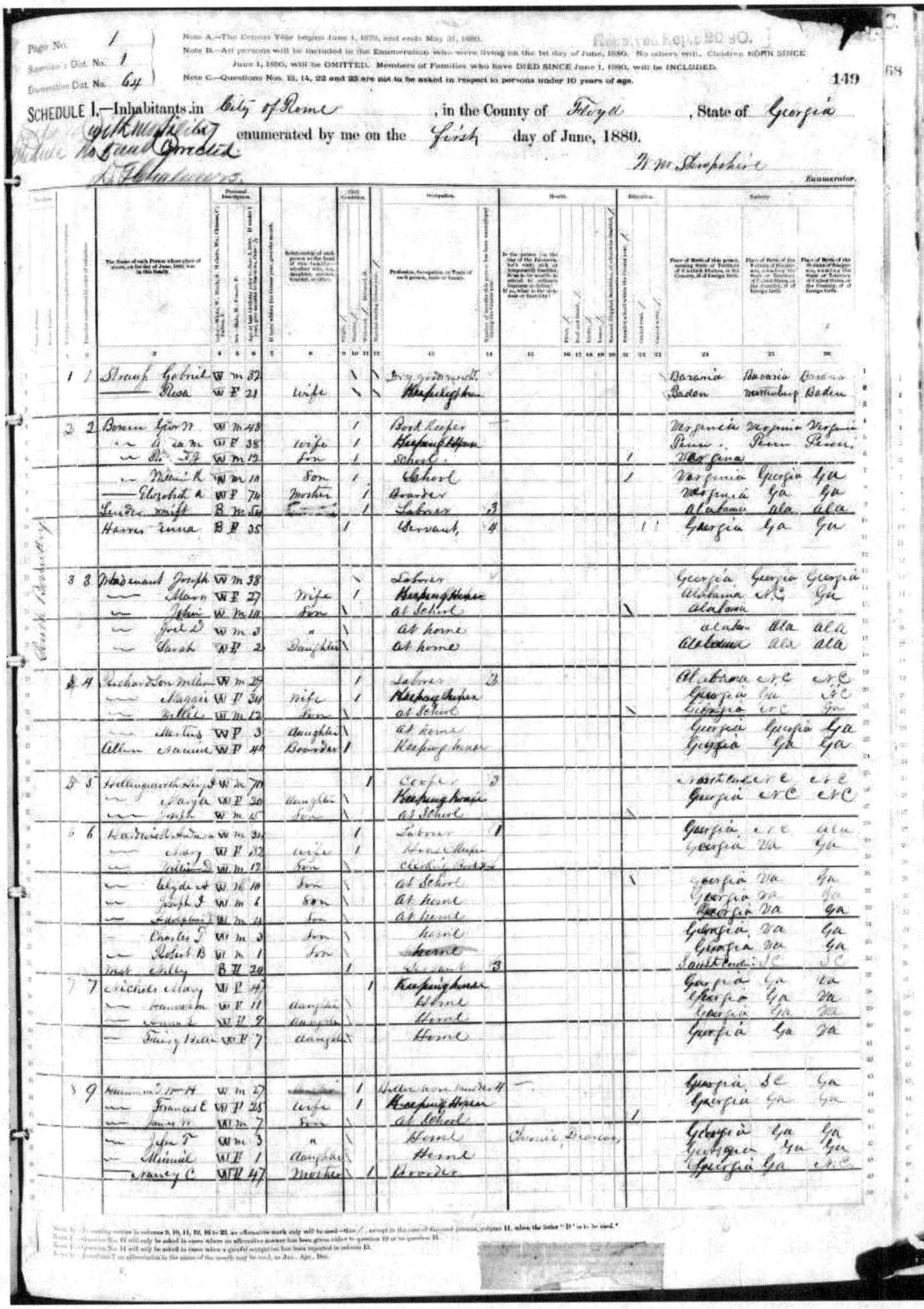

FIGURE 6-3 An 1880 U.S. federal census Population Schedule for Floyd County, Georgia

The 1880 census marked another significant change in the Population Schedule. While the 1850 census called for the names of all inhabitants to be listed on that document, the 1880 census required that each inhabitant's name *and* their relationship to the head of household be included. This is a very important addition for genealogists. Table 6-3 at the end of this chapter defines for each federal census each of the census forms, or schedules, used for each enumeration year, and what information can be found on each schedule.

Understand Originals vs. Copies of Census Documents

I mentioned earlier that errors might have been introduced during the transcription of information from the original census forms to copies. It is therefore important to know that there have been requirements for different numbers of copies to be made of the original documents created as part of the census enumeration process. From 1790 through 1820, the enumerators provided their original copies to the district court by which they were employed. As part of this process, the states sent only summary data to Washington, D.C., and kept their original census documents. The summaries for 1790 through 1810 were destroyed during the War of 1812 when the British burned Washington, D.C.

In 1830, Congress passed legislation that required the states to send all pre-1830 original documents to Washington, D.C. Some states had lost or destroyed their originals. Some states complied with the federal order while others, unfortunately, sent nothing or only partial documentation. As a result, you may find that no census materials exist for certain states for certain years, or that only incomplete records exist.

If you examine Table 6-1, you will notice that for census years 1830 through 1885, copies of the original census schedules for each state (not summaries) were sent to Washington, D.C., and not the original documents, which were kept by the states. It is important to note that for 1790–1820 the census schedules that ultimately ended up in the possession of NARA are the originals returned by the states as a result of the 1830 legislative directive. Documents submitted for the 1830 through 1885 censuses were *transcribed* copies of the original documents completed by the enumerators. The copies are transcriptions and, by their very nature, are prone to the possible introduction of transcription errors. In the case of the 1870 census schedules, a transcription of a transcription was actually sent to Washington. That doubled the possibility of the introduction of transcription errors. The census documents sent to Washington for all subsequent enumerations were originals.

All of the digitized U.S. documents that you find online for the 1790 through 1930 censuses at sites such as Ancestry.com (**http://www.ancestry.com**), Archives .com (**http://www.archives.com**), FamilySearch (**https://familysearch.org**), Fold3.com (**http://www.fold3.com**), findmypast (**http://www.findmypast.com**), HeritageQuest Online, and MyHeritage (**http://www.myheritage.com**) were

TABLE 6-1 U.S. Federal Censuses, Number of Copies, and Disposition

Year	Enumerator	# Copies Prepared	Sent to Washington
1790	Assistant Marshal	1 original	Summary sent; originals requested in 1830
1800	Assistant Marshal	1 original	Summary sent; originals requested in 1830
1810	Assistant Marshal	1 original	Summary sent; originals requested in 1830
1820	Assistant Marshal	1 original	Summary sent; originals requested in 1830
1830	Assistant Marshal	• 1 original • 1 copy prepared by clerk	Copy sent
1840	Assistant Marshal	• 1 original • 1 copy prepared by clerk	Copy sent
1850	Assistant Marshal	• 1 original • "Clean copy" was prepared by Assistant Marshals and sent to state secretary of state ("state copy") • Secretary of state prepared complete copy for federal government ("federal copy")	"Federal copy" sent
1860	Assistant Marshal	• 1 original • "Clean copy" was prepared by Assistant Marshals and sent to state secretary of state ("state copy") • Secretary of state prepared complete copy for federal government ("federal copy")	"Federal copy" sent
1870	Assistant Marshal	• 1 original • "Clean copy" was prepared by Assistant Marshals and sent to state secretary of state ("state copy") • Secretary of state prepared complete copy for federal government ("federal copy")	"Federal copy" sent
1880	Census Office	• 1 original • 1 copy was prepared by district supervisor	Copy sent

TABLE 6-1   U.S. Federal Censuses, Number of Copies, and Disposition

Year	Enumerator	# Copies Prepared	Sent to Washington
1885	Census Office and State Enumerators	• 1 original for CO, FL, NE, and the Dakota and New Mexico Territories • 1 copy	Copy sent
1890	Census Office	• 1 original • No copy	Original sent (most were destroyed by fire and water)
1900	Census Office	• 1 original • No copy	Original sent
1910	Census Bureau	• 1 original • No copy	Original sent
1920	Census Bureau	• 1 original • No copy	Original sent
1930	Census Bureau	• 1 original • No copy	Original sent
1940	Census Bureau	• 1 original • No copy	Original sent

produced from microfilmed images of the NARA documents. All of those census documents were microfilmed in the 1930s as part of the federal Works Progress Administration (WPA) assignments. The 1940 census documents were never microfilmed, and they were digitized directly from the census schedules before their release to the public in 2012. Therefore, whenever you work with census images on microfilm and in online databases, remember that the "copy censuses" may be prone to a higher error rate than the originals because some are transcribed copies of the original schedules. Transcription errors may have been introduced.

Use Strategies to Work with Population Schedules

The census Population Schedule is the most comprehensive of the U.S. federal census documents, and contains entries for each household. The completeness and accuracy of the enumeration was, of course, dependent on the quality of the work performed by the enumerator, the answers provided by the respondent, and any transcription work done to generate a copy or copies.

Certainly there are omissions in any census. This can be the result of an enumerator missing a residence for whatever reason. An important strategy for every genealogist when working with census records is to locate the family you are researching in one census, and to make note of three to six other families on either side of your family. The reason you will do so is to create a reference group for researching other census years. If you find your family in one census and cannot locate them in the next, check any indexes for that census and look for the neighbors next to them in the previous or subsequent censuses. If you can find the neighbors but your family is not there, there are four possibilities:

- The enumerator omitted or skipped your family's residence.
- Your family was not home, or refused to participate, when the enumerator called.
- Your family moved.
- Your family was deceased, which is more probable when there was only one family member at that location or if the family members were elderly at the time of the previous census.

Another important strategic consideration is that families who lived next door or close to one another, especially in the earlier times, may have intermarried. A check of marriage records in the area may reveal a marriage between families, in which case your "missing" family member may have relocated to live with the newly married couple. I have found numerous examples in my own family ancestry in which a husband died and the wife relocated to live with a son or daughter and their family. Don't be surprised to find a mother-in-law living with her daughter and son-in-law, and even buried in their cemetery plot.

Perhaps the best advice I can give you when doing your genealogical research is to learn how to *misspell* your family members' names. Heaven knows, they misspelled them and so did the other people who created records about them. Consider the many spellings of the surname of SMITH. There are SMITH, SMYTH, SMYTHE, SMIT, SCHMIT, SCHMIDT, and even extended spelling versions of the names such as SMITT, SMITTY, SMITHERS, and many more. One of my ancestors, John Swords, has military service and pension records from the Revolutionary War filed under the spellings of SWORDS, SOARDS, and SORDS, and that doesn't include several other errors in indexes other people have prepared. You can prepare yourself for your research in any type of records by considering the spelling of the surnames, and even the given names, and by preparing a list of alternate spellings and possible misspellings. Using the list, make sure you look for these spellings in census indexes and schedules, or any other records of genealogical importance. By doing so, you can avoid missing records for your own family. Remember, too, that the people who index the digital census images may have introduced errors. The enumerator's handwriting may have been unclear or the indexer may simply have misspelled or omitted a name.

Don't Overlook the 1885 Census

The enumerations for the U.S. federal census were scheduled to be performed every ten years. Following the 1880 census, however, some states and territories complained that there had been errors and that their populations had been undercounted. As a result, they argued that their congressional representation that was based on census population data had been compromised. Congress agreed that it would share 50 percent of the cost with any state or territory desiring another census enumeration. Only five states and territories took advantage of this federal offer and, in 1885, a special census was taken for these areas:

- Colorado
- Dakota Territory (only a part survives)
- Florida (four counties missing)
- Nebraska (two counties missing)
- New Mexico Territory (four counties missing)

Ancestry.com has digitized and indexed the surviving 1885 federal census documents. Each of these areas' documents are titled as a state census even though the federal government paid half of the expense and the format forms were identical to those used by the 1880 federal census. The only differences were in the header, which stated that this was an 1885 census, and that the enumerations were performed in June of 1885.

You should be aware that a number of states conducted their own censuses halfway between the federal enumerations. Some of those were done in addition to the federal enumerations of the five areas listed previously. We'll discuss state censuses a little later in the chapter.

Use Substitutes for the 1890 Census

The 11th census of the United States, taken in 1890, was different from all others before or since. The Population Schedule included information on only one household per form. It also included a special Veterans and Widows Schedule on which Union soldiers, sailors, and marines, or their surviving widows, were to be enumerated. Again, Congress only financed one copy of the census documents, as it did for all later censuses. States or counties wishing to obtain a copy for their own records would have had to pay for a transcription for their own files. There is no known request having been received for a state or county copy. All original copies of the census documents were sent to the Census Office.

The federal government, recognizing that the tabulation of the 1890 census schedules would be an enormous job, called for a competition to be held for a mechanized method of processing the data to be collected. Herman Hollerith, who had been working on data entry and tabulation machines for a number of years, entered and won this competition. His system utilized punch cards created by use of a manual keyboard resembling a telegraph key. Clerks were able to process an average of 700 cards per day, after which tabulators tabulated an average of 2,000 to 3,000 families per day. As a result, there were over six million persons counted by Hollerith's machines in a single day!

Once the census was complete, the original documents were placed in cartons and stored. In 1896 or 1897, the Census Office destroyed all but the Population Schedules and the Union Veterans and Widows Schedules. The Population Schedules were stored in the basement of the Commerce Building in Washington, D.C., and the Veterans and Widows Schedules were stored on an upper floor. Around 5:00 P.M. on 10 January 1921, a fire broke out in the basement of the building. Records that were not destroyed by flames had been inundated with water from the firefighters' efforts. The documents were relocated to another storage location but, unfortunately, no salvage was ever performed on the documents. The entire remainder of the 1890 census was destroyed in either 1934 or 1935.

The 20-year gap in census records between 1880 and 1900 can seem, at first glance, devastating to your research. However, there are other types of records that can be used as a substitute for this lost census. You will need to use some creativity and refer to reference resources that still exist. These include

- City directories
- Jury rolls
- Voter registration cards and lists
- Land and property records, including plat maps and tax lists
- Newspapers and journals

Use More than Just the Population Schedules

The primary type of census document used by the U.S. federal government is the Population Schedule. As we have discussed, the amount of information requested and entered on the Population Schedules varied over time. All surviving documents that were created through 1930 and that were accessioned to NARA have been microfilmed and are available from NARA in Washington, D.C., and at many of NARA's regional branch locations. In addition, copies of the NARA microfilm are available through the Church of Jesus Christ of Latter-day Saints' (LDS) Family History Library (FHL) in Salt Lake City, Utah, and can be ordered for use in the LDS Family History Centers (FHCs) around the world. Many have also been made available at Ancestry.com and other online genealogy database sites. Additional schedule forms were used at various times, and these include the following types of schedules:

- **Slave Schedules** Used in 1850 and 1860 to determine the numbers, vital statistics, and living conditions of slaves. The slaveholder's name, number of slaves, the slaves' age, gender, and color are listed (B = Black; M = Mulatto). Columns are also included for: Fugitive from the State; Number manumitted; Deaf & dumb, blind, insane, or idiotic; and Number of Slave houses (this last column was used only in 1860). The slaveholders' names can be cross-referenced to the Population Schedules on which they were listed. (See Figure 6-4.)
- **Mortality Schedules** Used in the 1850 through 1885 censuses to determine how many persons died in the 12 months prior to Census Day, their vital statistics, duration of illness, and cause of death. (See Figure 6-5.)

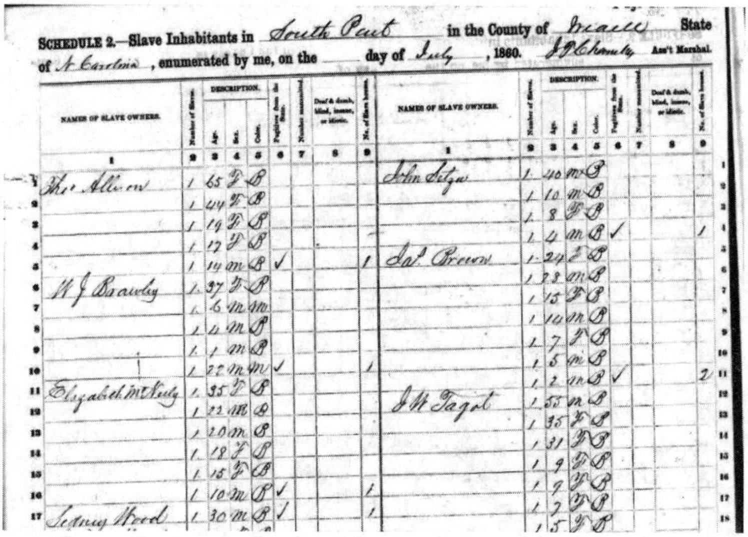

FIGURE 6-4 Portion of a 1860 Slave Schedule for Iredell County, North Carolina

- **Union Veterans and Widows Schedule (also titled as Special Schedule, Surviving Soldiers, Sailors, and Marines, and Widows, Etc.)** Used in the 1890 census to enumerate the Union veterans of the U.S. Civil War and widows of Union soldiers. (This is the only substantial surviving fragment of the 1890 census.) The upper portion of the document identifies the name, company, and rank of the veteran, and the name of the regiment or vessel. It includes the dates of enlistment and discharge, and the length of service. The lower section of the document includes the post office address, disability, and any pertinent comments. (See Figure 6-6.)

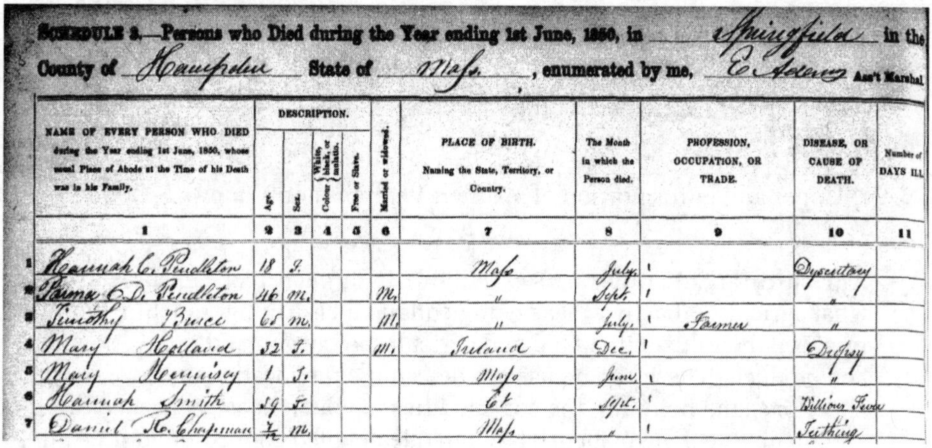

FIGURE 6-5 Portion of a Mortality Schedule from the 1860 U.S. federal census for Springfield, Hampshire County, Massachusetts

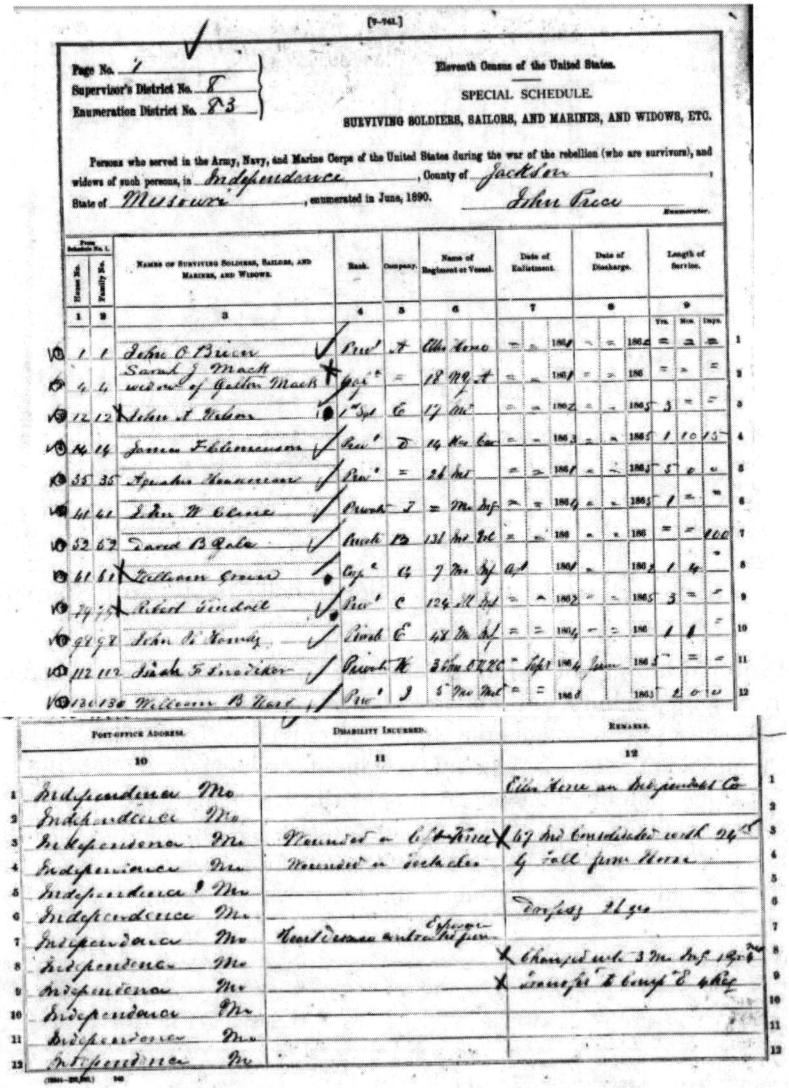

FIGURE 6-6 Upper and lower portion of a Union Veterans and Widows Schedule

- **Agricultural Schedules** Used in the 1840 through 1880 censuses to determine what agricultural activity was being conducted (farming, ranching, forestry, mining), the value of the land and agricultural output, and production in some key products. These can be used to determine the location and size of an ancestor's land holdings, the commodities in which he was engaged in producing, and the livestock he owned. They provide detailed context of your farming ancestor's life. Many of these agricultural schedules for some states are available at Ancestry.com in a database collection titled "Selected U.S. Federal Census

Non-Population Schedules, 1850–1880" at **http://search.ancestry.com/search/ db.aspx?dbid = 1276**. The information varies from census year to census year, but the detailed data provides a keen insight into the activities on the property in the year prior to the census date. This can provide you with contextual information about your farming ancestor and the family members and their lives at that time.

- **Industry and/or Manufacturing Schedules**   Used in the 1810 through 1910 censuses to determine the industrial and manufacturing activity and output, value of products, and other data. Many of these schedules have been lost or the federal government intentionally destroyed them. Images of the surviving schedules are mostly poor quality. Some of these schedules for some states are available at Ancestry.com in a database collection titled "Selected U.S. Federal Census Non-Population Schedules, 1850–1880" at **http://search.ancestry.com/search/ db.aspx?dbid = 1276**.

- **Defective, Dependent, and Delinquent Classes Schedules**   Used only in the 1880 census. This was a seven-page document that was completed when the enumerator received a response about one of these types of persons on the Population Schedule. The enumerator could also, through personal observation, make an entry onto the appropriate schedule form for one of the seven classes as defined as follows:
  - **Schedule 1**   Insane (included persons in asylums or living at home)
  - **Schedule 2**   Idiots (included mentally handicapped persons living in institutions or at home)
  - **Schedule 3**   Deaf-mutes (included persons in schools or living at home)
  - **Schedule 4**   Blind (included persons in schools or living at home)
  - **Schedule 5**   Homeless children (in institutions such as orphanages and residential church schools)
  - **Schedule 6**   Prisoners (included persons incarcerated in jails or prisons)
  - **Schedule 7**   Paupers and indigent persons (included persons living in workhouses, almshouses, and the homeless)

  Some of these schedules for some states are available at Ancestry.com in a database collection titled "U.S. Federal Census - 1880 Schedules of Defective, Dependent, and Delinquent Classes" at **http://search.ancestry.com/search/ db.aspx?dbid = 1634**. Other schedules for other areas may be available on microfilm from the Family History Library in Salt Lake City, Utah.

- **Social Statistics Schedules**   Used in the 1850 through 1870 censuses. Important information about towns, counties, or states can be gleaned from these schedules. They include information that can be used as a resource to locate specific types of institutions in these years, and trace any surviving records. They include
  - Real estate values and taxes
  - Colleges, academies, and schools
  - Crops
  - Libraries
  - Newspapers and periodicals published
  - Churches, affiliation, number of people the building will accommodate, and value
  - Fraternal organizations and lodges
  - Pauperism, crime, and average wages

The U.S. Indian Census Rolls were taken for Native Americans every year from 1885 to 1940. They were prepared and submitted by Indian agents or superintendents in charge of Indian reservations. There is not a census for every tribe or every reservation for each year. Only those persons who maintained a formal affiliation with the tribe are listed on the rolls. In the later years of 1935, 1936, 1938, and 1939, only supplemental information was included on the census documents. In particular, only additions and deletions were recorded. The content on the other census rolls typically included the name of the Indian agency or reservation, the name(s) of the tribe being enumerated, and the date of enumeration. The name of each individual (Indian and/or English) is listed, along with the person's gender, age, birth date, relationship to the head of the family unit, marital status, and possibly other details. In later years, the degree of Indian blood may also be listed. Family groups are typically listed together. (See Figure 6-7.)

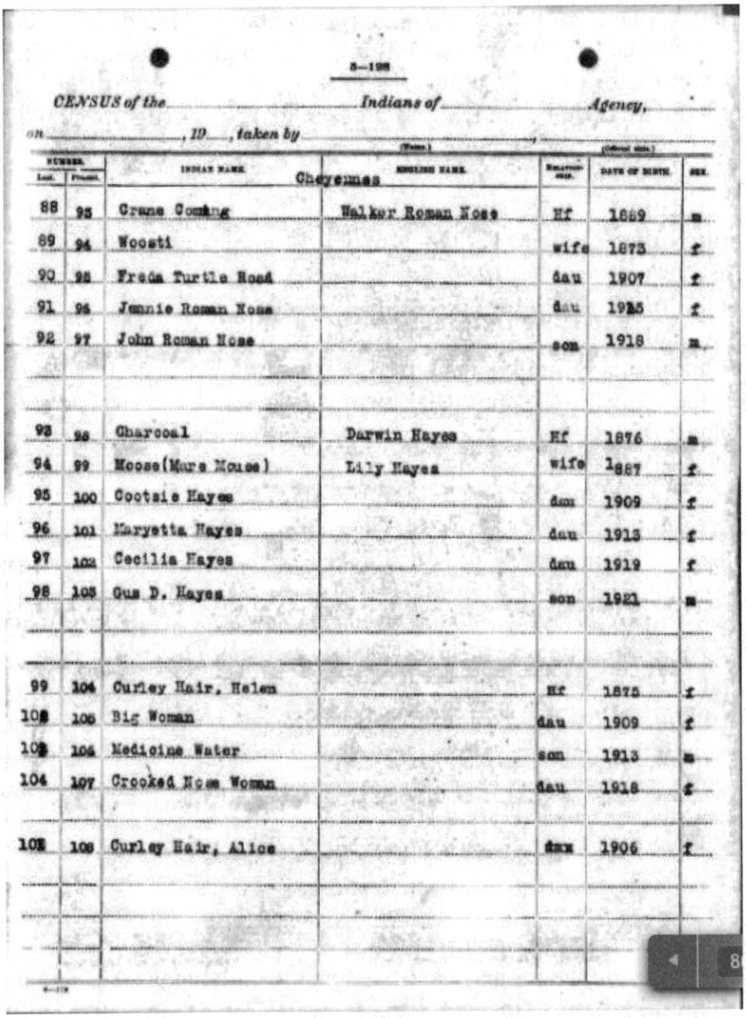

NUMBER Last	NUMBER Present	INDIAN NAME	ENGLISH NAME	RELATION-SHIP	DATE OF BIRTH	SEX
			Cheyennes			
88	93	Crane Coming	Walker Roman Nose	Hf	1869	m
89	94	Woosti		wife	1873	f
90	95	Freda Turtle Road		dau	1907	f
91	96	Jennie Roman Nose		dau	1915	f
92	97	John Roman Nose		son	1918	m
93	98	Charcoal	Darwin Hayes	Hf	1876	m
94	99	Moose (Mare Mouse)	Lily Hayes	wife	1887	f
95	100	Cootsie Hayes		dau	1909	f
96	101	Maryetta Hayes		dau	1913	f
97	102	Cecilia Hayes		dau	1919	f
98	103	Gus D. Hayes		son	1921	m
99	104	Curley Hair, Helen		Hf	1875	f
100	105	Big Woman		dau	1909	f
101	106	Medicine Water		son	1913	m
104	107	Crooked Nose Woman		dau	1918	f
105	108	Curley Hair, Alice		dau	1906	f

FIGURE 6-7 Page from an Indian Roll for the Cheyenne from 1920

In addition to all the census schedules, beginning with the establishment of the Census Office for the 1880 census, the area to be canvassed by each enumerator was more clearly defined. The Census Office designated what were known as Enumeration Districts, or EDs. These were defined and represented with textual descriptions and/or ED maps to define the boundaries for each group of enumerators reporting to a district supervisor. Figure 6-8 shows the ED map for a portion of Detroit in the 1930 census. The enumeration districts defined on ED maps sometimes coincided with political areas or voting precincts, but not always. ED maps exist for federal census areas from 1880 through 1940, and are accessible on microfilm published by NARA. These microfilms can be used at all NARA facilities and the Family History Library. Ancestry .com has published the digitized U.S. Enumeration District Maps and Descriptions for 1940 at **http://search.ancestry.com/search/db.aspx?dbid = 3028**.

Earlier in the book, I told you about the importance of maps in your research, and provided you with a strategy for using maps to find the *right* place to locate your ancestors and their records. The censuses can provide you with another opportunity to use different types of maps. An ED map is helpful if you know your ancestors' address and where in the area that address is situated. Once you know the ED in which your ancestors and their family members lived, you greatly improve your

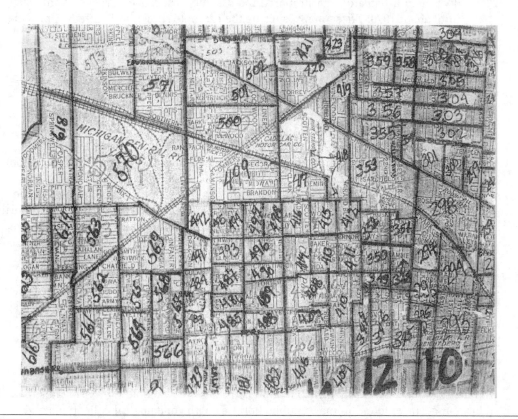

FIGURE 6-8 1930 Enumeration District map showing an area of Detroit, Michigan

chances of quickly locating the right census page(s) to find them, even if the surname was misspelled. There are other resources you can use to help you with this:

- **City directories** are name and address listings published on a fairly regular basis in towns and cities, and were used to help people locate one another. Some of these directories include both individual persons and businesses.
- **Telephone directories**, like city directories, can be helpful in locating addresses. The first telephone directory published in the United States dates from 21 February 1878 in New Haven, Connecticut. The first British telephone directory was published on 15 January 1880 in London. The local public library in the area may have copies of all directories that you can access.
- **Land and property records**, which we will discuss in a later chapter, typically include deeds, indentures, tax rolls, lien papers, and other records indexed by name for easy location by the property clerk, tax assessor, and other government officials. These can provide the names and addresses of the owners, and the governments' maps of property for taxation purposes can be compared with ED maps to help quickly establish a family member's location.
- **Sanborn Fire Insurance Maps** were used in the United States to clearly document urban areas for property and casualty insurance purposes from 1867 until about 1970. These maps, such as the example shown in Figure 6-9, provide street-by-street details concerning the buildings, the materials used in their construction, the use of the building, and other information. Additional maps of subareas provide extensive detail down to the actual shape of an individual building and its construction materials. Sanborn maps of some commercial sites even show interior layouts. You can use a Sanborn map in conjunction with directories and land and property records, and compare it against an ED map in order to quickly home in on an ancestor's census records.

Many public and academic libraries may have printed and bound copies of Sanborn maps in their collections covering their respective areas. The Digital Sanborn Maps 1867–1970 database is distributed as an institutional subscription database by ProQuest, LLC. Environmental Data Resources, Inc. or their affiliates hold copyrights for Sanborn Maps. You may therefore want to check with the libraries to determine if they provide access to the maps of an area that you might like to research and/or to the database.

Some of the Sanborn maps published prior to 1923 may have been digitized and placed online by various entities. (Materials published in the United States before 1923 are typically no longer covered by copyright laws, and are considered to be in the public domain. However, please make sure that you read and understand any copyright statements that appear on these websites so that you do not infringe on any copyrights.)

Use Census Finding Aids to Locate Your Ancestors

Indexes to the 1790 through 1870 federal censuses are available for most states in book form and can be found in many public libraries with genealogical collections and in academic libraries with genealogical and governmental documents collections.

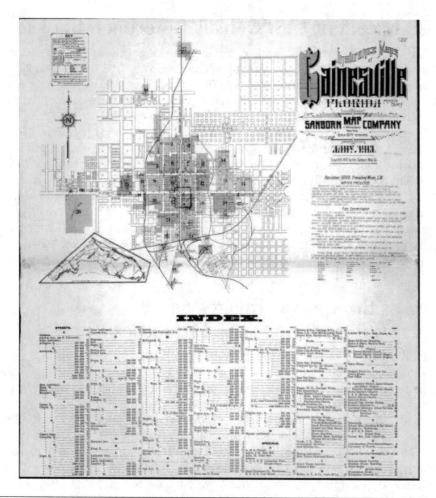

FIGURE 6-9 One sheet of the 1913 Sanborn Fire Insurance Map for Gainesville, Florida

Online subscription databases offering access to U.S. federal census indexes include those at Ancestry.com (**http://www.ancestry.com**), Archives.com (**http://www.archive.com**), FamilySearch (**https://familysearch.org**), findmypast (**http://www.findmypast.com**), Fold3.com (**http://www.fold3.com**), HeritageQuest Online, MyHeritage (**http://www.myheritage.com**), and through many libraries and archives. At the time of this writing, no online service provides access to every census schedule type or to all of the ED maps. These online database services provide links to actual census Population Schedule document images. Ancestry.com provides additional indexes for the 1885 federal census enumeration conducted in and for the five states and territories mentioned earlier and in Table 6-3 at the end of this chapter.

Use Excellent U.S. Census Reference Books

William Thorndale and William Dollarhide's book *Map Guide to the U.S. Federal Censuses, 1790–1920* (Genealogical Publishing Company, 1987; reprinted 2007) is an excellent resource for locating places in the correct state and county for each of the U.S. federal censuses. There were also some censuses taken in colonial times, which may have been documented and/or microfilmed by state archives. (These maps are available as part of the HeritageQuest Online database via the Census Browse function.) Ann S. Lainhart's book *State Census Records* (Genealogical Publishing Company, 1992; reprinted 2008) is a valuable reference on this subject. Three other excellent books regarding the U.S. federal censuses are William Dollarhide's *The Census Book: A Genealogist's Guide to Federal Census Facts, Schedules and Indexes* (Heritage Quest, 1999), Kathleen W. Hinckley's *Your Guide to the Federal Census for Genealogists, Researchers, and Family Historians* (Betterway Books, 2002), and Loretto D. Szucs and Matthew Wright's *Finding Answers in U.S. Census Records* (Ancestry Publishing, Inc., 2001).

Access the Census Images on Microfilm and in Online Databases

Federal census records for the years 1790 through 1930 were microfilmed decades ago and are available through your nearest LDS FHC. These censuses' microfilm has been digitized and indexed and made available at multiple sites on the Internet. As mentioned before, the 1940 census was never microfilmed but was digitized directly from the original paper documents. That means that the surviving records from the 1790 to 1940 censuses' schedules, with a very few exceptions, are accessible online.

U.S. census records from the 1950 and later U.S. enumerations are protected through the Privacy Act and are not made publicly available for 72 years.

Ancestry.com (**http://www.ancestry.com**) has compiled the most complete online indexes for the U.S. federal censuses to date and has digitized a majority of the surviving census schedules. These are available through Ancestry.com's U.S. Discovery, World Explorer, and World Explorer Plus paid subscription collections, or through Ancestry Library Edition, the institutional database subscription accessible at many public libraries and archives. Ancestry.com's collections include Population Schedules, Slave Schedules, Mortality Schedules, Defective, Dependent, and Delinquent Schedules, some Agricultural Schedules (1850 through 1880), some Industrial/Manufacturing Schedules (1850–1880), some Social Statistics Schedules (1850–1880), the Indian Censuses (1885–1940), and the Enumeration District Maps (for 1940 only). Figure 6-10 shows the result of a search at Ancestry.com in the 1930 census records, and you will note a link to view the actual census page for this person.

ProQuest has digitized the federal census Population Schedules for 1790 through 1940, and made them available through access to its HeritageQuest Online databases. Searchable indexes are only available at the time of this writing for census years 1790 through 1820, 1860 through 1920, 1930 for only Connecticut, Delaware, Maryland, Texas, and Virginia, and 1940. HeritageQuest Online is only available by institutional

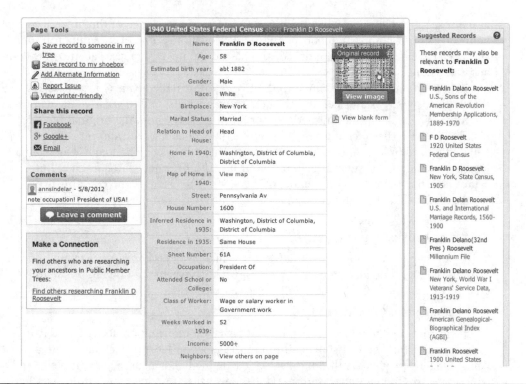

FIGURE 6-10   Partial search result record from the 1940 U.S. federal census for Franklin D. Roosevelt and his family from Ancestry.com with a link to the census image

subscription, and you will find that many public libraries have subscriptions. As a library cardholder for one of those libraries, you may be able to remotely access the HeritageQuest Online databases from your home computer.

FamilySearch (**https://familysearch.org**) is, at the time of this writing, in the process of digitizing and indexing its extensive microfilm records. The U.S. federal census Population Schedules for 1790 through 1940 are complete as of this writing, as are the Slave Schedules and Mortality Schedules of 1850. More records are expected to be available in digital form with indexes over time.

MyHeritage at **http://www.myheritage.com**, findmypast at **http://www .findmypast.com**, and Archives.com at **http://www.archives.com** also provide access to U.S. federal census records.

Don't Forget to Search State Censuses

In addition to the federal censuses, at certain times a number of the individual states have conducted their own census enumerations. These most frequently occurred halfway between the decennial federal enumerations—in other words, at the half-decade mark. These records, many of which have been microfilmed and are stored at the respective state's archive or library, can provide evidence of the presence of your ancestor or family member in a particular location. Some of these microfilmed censuses have been digitized, indexed, and placed online as databases at Ancestry.com and elsewhere.

Ann S. Lainhart compiled an authoritative reference titled *State Census Records*, which details which states conducted their own censuses, and in what years, whether the records have been microfilmed and/or indexed, and where the original records reside. The book, because it was published in 1992, does not list Internet sites at which digitized images and indexes of state census records can be found. One way of locating such digitized records is to use your favorite Internet search engine. Enter **"state census"** followed by the name of the state. If the state name contains two words, enclose those in quotation marks. Here are two examples:

"state census" iowa
"state census" "new mexico"

If you happen to know a specific year in which a state's census was taken and you want to search for details about that, you may add a year to the end of your search terms. For example, I entered the following search:

"state census" florida 1935

I was rewarded with search results that provided information about Florida's state censuses (and voter lists), beginning in 1845 when Florida became a state and continuing every 10 years through 1945. I learned which censuses are complete, and which ones are fragmentary. Multiple links to websites provided me with research paths to continue my searches.

Understand and Work with British and Irish Census Records

The first modern census in Great Britain was taken in order to determine the makeup of the population and its activities. There had been a period of poor harvests and food shortages. A substantial number of agricultural workers also had joined the military services and therefore could not be involved with working the land.

The Census Act 1800 (41 George III, cap. 15) was enacted and called for a full population enumeration of England, Wales, and Scotland beginning in 1801. The act also called for an enumeration to be conducted every ten years thereafter. A census has been performed ever since, with the exception of 1941, when all government funding and activity were directed toward the war effort.

In order to determine the livelihoods of the citizens in the 1801 census, questions were asked that elicited responses to help divide the population into three categories: those involved with agriculture, those working in manufacturing and trade, and those engaged in other types of employment. The population of England and Wales in 1801 was almost 9 million, and the population of Scotland was a little over 1.6 million. No names were requested, although a few officials did include names in their documents. The questions asked in 1801 included

- How many inhabited and uninhabited houses are located within the parish, and how many families live in the inhabited houses?
- How many persons are living in the parish, how many are males, and how many are females? (Military personnel and seamen in military service or on registered vessels were not to be included.)
- How many persons are involved with agriculture, with manufacturing or trade, with handicraft, or in other types of employment?
- How many persons' baptisms and burials have there been within the parish in 1700, 1710, 1720, 1730, 1740, 1750, 1760, 1770, 1780, and in each subsequent year up through 31 December 1800, and how many were there of each gender?

The process of conducting this first census was extensive. Standardized forms were distributed to all households and were to be completed based on persons in a residence as of the census night, 10 March 1801. (See Table 6-2 for census dates.) The information was gathered by enumerators and attached to a copy of the Census Act 1800, and the enumerators presented the documents to a high constable or other officer and swore an oath as to the accuracy of the information. The returns were gathered by the official, endorsed, and submitted with a list of the names of the enumerators to a town clerk or clerk of the peace. The returns were then summarized into statistical reports, which were then submitted to the Home Office by 15 May 1801.

A similar format with comparable questions was used in the 1811, 1821, and 1831 enumerations. In 1811, a question was added to determine why a house was unoccupied. In 1821, a question was added to elicit ages of men in order to help determine how many men were able to bear arms. It was also in 1821 that Ireland was first included in the census, and its population at that time was calculated to be over 6.8 million. The 1831 census included more-detailed questions concerning economic conditions.

The 1841 census was the first to record the names of the inhabitants, their gender, and their age (the person's age was rounded down to the lower five-year increment for persons over the age of 15), and therefore is the earliest British census used by most genealogists and family historians. In addition, these census documents were sent to a central government location for tabulation and reference. For that reason, they were preserved and it has been easier to access and digitize the documents.

The 1851 census included those persons living on vessels in inland waters or at sea (including the Royal Navy and Merchant Navy). In addition, persons serving abroad with the armed forces, those working with the East India Company, and British subjects residing overseas were enumerated.

Between 1861 and 1891, there were few changes in the format and questions asked on the census. The most important additions from a genealogical perspective, however, were the addition of questions concerning the languages spoken. This question was added for enumeration in Scotland beginning with the 1881 census and for the enumeration of Wales beginning with the 1891 census. It is shown in the last column on the example census form in Figure 6-11.

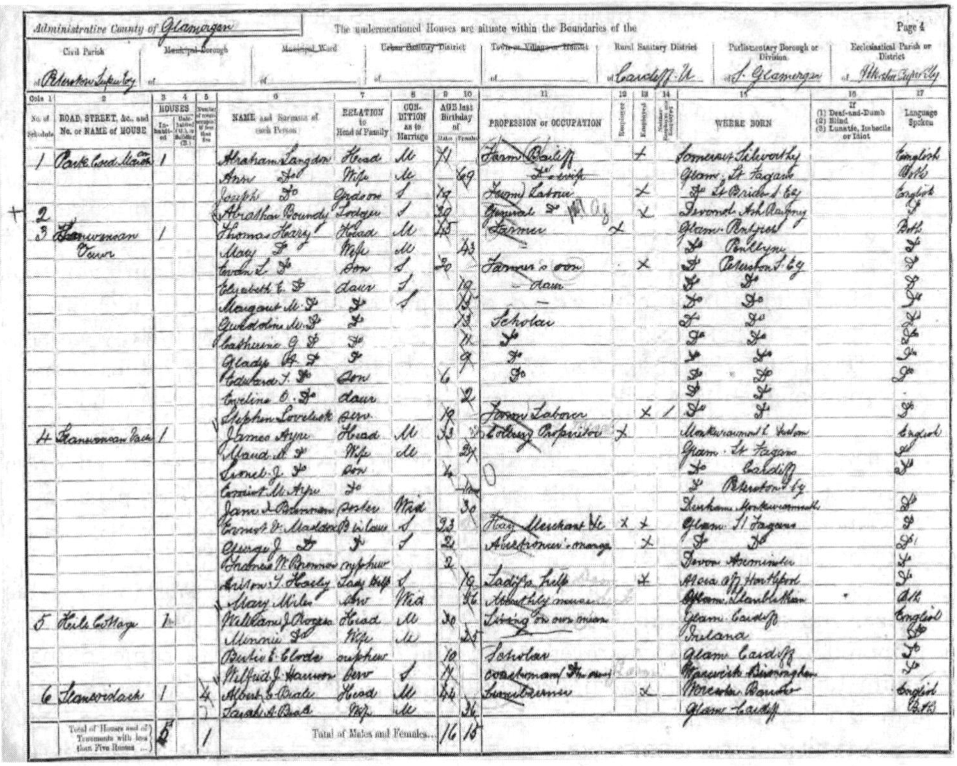

FIGURE 6-11 1891 census form created in the parish of Peterston-super-Ely in Cardiff, South Glamorgan, Wales

The 1901 census included questions to elicit more precise responses. A good introduction to the British census information can be found in the guide at The National Archives website at **http://www.nationalarchives.gov.uk/records/ research-guides/census-returns.htm**. Census records' contents are protected in the United Kingdom for a period of 100 years. The 1911 census information was released in digital image format in 2010 with some information redacted. The digitized census images were re-released in January 2012 with the redacted information restored. The National Archives, part of which was previously known as the Public Record Office (PRO), is custodian of the census records for England and Wales, as well as for the Channel Islands and the Isle of Man. Separate enumerations for Scotland and Ireland were taken, and these records are in the possession of the General Register Office for Scotland (GROS) at **http://www.gro-scotland.gov.uk** and at The National Archives of Ireland at **http://www.nationalarchives.ie**, respectively. As mentioned in Chapters 1 and 3, the GROS website says, "From 1 April 2011, the General Register Office for Scotland merged with the National Archives of Scotland to become the National Records of Scotland (NRS). This website will remain active until it is replaced in due course by a new website for NRS." The website of the new entity is **http://www .nrscotland.gov.uk**. The UK census indexes and images for 1841 through 1901 are accessible through subscription online at **http://www.ancestry.co.uk** and at Origins .net at **http://www.origins.net**. The 1911 census was released after some controversy in Parliament concerning early release of the census and possible violation of promised privacy. An index and transcriptions of parts of this census are accessible at the time of this writing at a pay-per-view site, **http://www.1911census.co.uk**, with more transcriptions being added over time.

Work with England's and Wales' Census Records

The British government, like that of the United States, defined an "as of" date for use by the respondents, and this date is also referred to as the "census night." The individual household schedule was to be completed based on the persons who were in the household during the period of Sunday night to Monday morning on the dates listed in Table 6-2.

It is important that you take into consideration the "as of" date when considering the information found in a census schedule with other genealogical evidence. For example, you might wonder why a person's age is listed as 41 in the 1841 census and only as age 50 in the 1851 census. If you examine the dates in Table 6-2, you will notice that the 1851 census was taken more than a month earlier than the one the previous decade. You could hypothesize that the respondent's birthday fell after 30 March and up to and including 6 June of 1800. Based on that theory, you could

TABLE 6-2   Census Enumeration Dates for British Censuses 1801–1911

Year	Census Date
1801	Monday, 10 March
1811	Monday, 27 May
1821	Monday, 28 May
1831	Monday, 30 May
1841	Sunday, 6 June
1851	Sunday, 30 March
1861	Sunday, 7 April
1871	Sunday, 2 April
1881	Sunday, 3 April
1891	Sunday, 5 April
1901	Sunday, 31 March
1911	Sunday, 2 April

then begin searching in other records for evidence of the person's date of birth. This kind of analysis and thought process can help you focus your research more acutely.

If the head of the household did not properly complete the census form, the enumerator was supposed to have called at the house and requested the additional information. If the person was illiterate, blind, or for some other reason unable to complete the schedule, the enumerator was to have conducted an interview, asked the questions, and completed the document himself.

Descriptions of the enumeration districts can be extremely helpful in locating your ancestors' records. The example shown in Figure 6-12 is from the 1891 census of England and Wales and shows the registration district of Spilsby and the sub-district of Alford in Lincolnshire.

Learn the Status of Irish Census Records

The Irish government took an independent census in 1813, and then censuses were taken every ten years from 1821 through 1911. Due to the Irish Civil War, no census was taken in 1921, but the next census was conducted in 1926. The censuses were

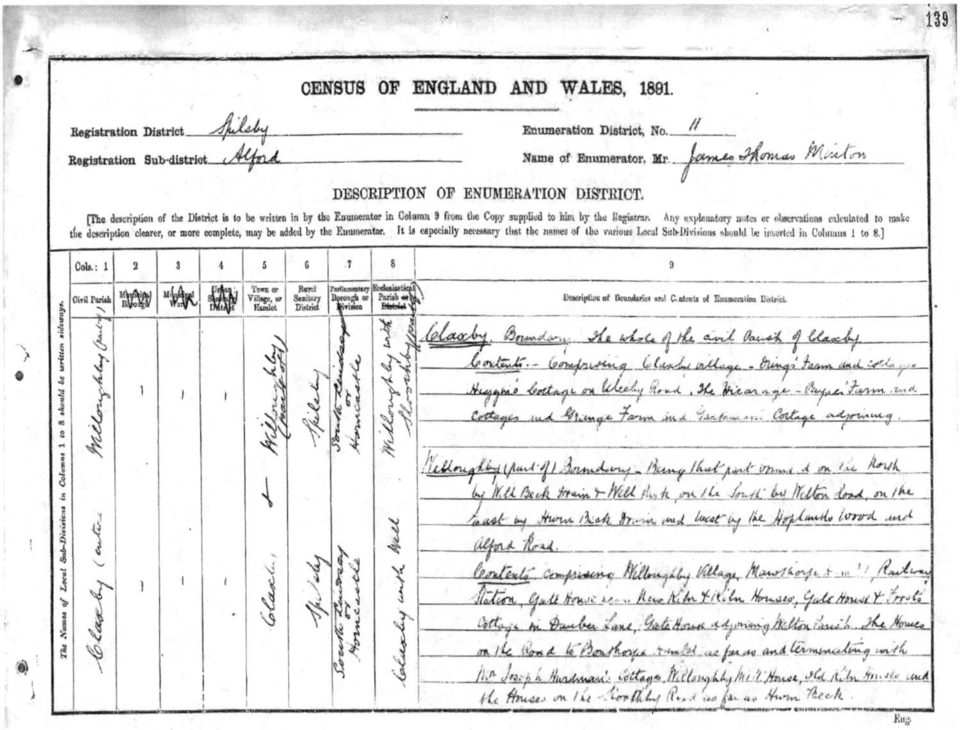

FIGURE 6-12   An 1891 form containing the description of the enumeration district

taken in 1936 and 1946 and, from 1946 to 1971, the census was taken every five years. Since 1971, the census has been conducted every ten years.

Unfortunately, the Irish census records have not fared well over time. The 1813 census no longer exists. Most of the census information from the 1821 through 1851 censuses was destroyed by fire at the Public Records Office at Four Courts during the Battle of Dublin in 1922, and the censuses from 1861 and 1871 were destroyed by government order shortly after the data was compiled and summarized. The 1881 and 1891 censuses were pulped during World War I because of a paper shortage. The surviving materials have been microfilmed by the LDS, and these films can be obtained through the LDS Family History Library in Salt Lake City, Utah, and through the LDS Family History Centers worldwide. The census returns for the whole of Ireland for 1901 and 1911 are almost complete, and can be viewed online at the National Archives of Ireland at **http://www.census.nationalarchives.ie**.

As a result of the loss of so much of the Irish census material, census substitutes can sometimes be used as alternate evidence sources of residence, age, and other information. These include Old Age Pension Records; Tithe Applotment Books (1823–1838); Griffith's Primary Valuation (1848–1864); and other, later land and property records. Irish Census Finder at **http://www.censusfinder.com/ireland.htm** is particularly useful for locating Irish census fragments and substitutes for the 19th century Irish censuses.

Use Quality Reference Materials When Working with British and Irish Census Records

There are excellent resources available for your reference when working with British census records. The best written reference concerning the 1801–1901 censuses is Edward Higgs' *Making Sense of the Census Revisited: Census Records for England and Wales, 1801–1901: A Handbook for Historical Researchers*, published in London by University of London, Institute of Historical Research in 2005. The book provides an excellent history and perspective of the enumerations of that period. Another excellent book is *Census: The Expert Guide* by David Annal and Peter Christian, published by The National Archives [UK] in 2008. And yet another book is *Tracing Your Ancestors Using the Census: A Guide for Family Historians* by Emma Jolly, published in 2013 by Pen & Sword Books, Ltd.

Indexes of censuses have been prepared by a variety of organizations. One excellent starting point is the GENUKI website at **http://www.genuki.org.uk**, which is concerned with UK and Ireland genealogy. Another is the BritishIslesGenWeb Project, which is a subsidiary part of the WorldGenWeb Project at **http://www.worldgenweb.org**. The BritishIslesGenWeb Project can be accessed at **http://www.britishislesgenweb.org**, from which you can visit a number of county or island sites where information about and links to census resources can be found.

Access the Census Records for Britain and Ireland

We've already mentioned a number of resources for gaining access to census records for England, Wales, Scotland, and Ireland, but let's recap:

- The England and Wales manuscript returns of the 1841 to 1911 censuses are in the possession of The National Archives (formerly known as the PRO). These have been microfilmed and are available for review at The National Archives, at larger libraries with genealogical materials, and through the LDS Family History Library and LDS Family History Centers. (You can locate the FHC closest to you by conducting a search through the LDS FamilySearch website, specifically using the search template at **https://familysearch.org/Eng/Library/FHC/frameset_fhc.asp**.) These census images for 1841 to 1911 are digitized and indexed at **http://www.ancestry.co.uk**. The 1911 census index and transcriptions are accessible at **http://www.1911census.co.uk**.
- Surviving Irish census records have been microfilmed. The 1901 records for Northern Ireland are available on microfilm through the Public Record Office of Northern Ireland (PRONI) or through the LDS FHL and FHCs as described previously. You can learn more about the 19th century records at **http://www.proni.gov.uk**. The 1901 and 1911 censuses for all of Ireland can be viewed online at the National Archives of Ireland at **http://www.census.nationalarchives.ie**.
- Scotland's census records are in the possession of the General Register Office for Scotland (GROS) and can be accessed at the National Archives of Scotland (NAS) in Edinburgh. Census records have been microfilmed and the microfilm can be accessed at NAS, at larger libraries with genealogical collections that have purchased the film, or through the LDS FHL and FHCs as described previously. Learn more about the NAS holdings at **http://www.nas.gov.uk**. In addition, the GROS and brightsolid online publishing have partnered to create and maintain a pay-per-view website called ScotlandsPeople at **http://www.scotlandspeople.gov.uk**. The site provides searchable indexes to birth, marriage, and death entries in the statutory indexes, old parish registers, and Catholic registers for various years. In addition, indexed census images are available from 1842 to 1911. To respect privacy of living people, Internet access has been limited to birth records over 100 years old, marriage records over 75 years old, and death records over 50 years old. Ancestry.co.uk has digitized and indexed the census records of Scotland from 1841 to 1901 but does not include the 1911 images as of the time of this writing.

Access the Records of the 1939 National Identity Card Registration

In addition to the decennial censuses, a "mini-census" of a sort was conducted in 1939 when, in preparation for war, a National Registration Bill was quickly introduced in Parliament, passed, and granted royal assent. National Registration Day was set at

29 September 1939 and enumerators visited households across the nation to gather information for identity cards. Approximately 46 million cards were issued. You can request information from the identity registration books by visiting the following websites and completing a request form:

- England and Wales   **http://www.hscic.gov.uk/register-service**
- Scotland   **http://www.gro-scotland.gov.uk/famrec/how-to-order-an-official-extract-from-the-1939-national-identity-register.html**
- Northern Ireland (a Freedom of Information request)   **http://www.proni.gov.uk/index/about_proni/freedom_of_information/making_an_foi_request_about_public_records.htm**

Understand and Work with Canadian Census Records

Canada's history is a fascinating study of many people: French, English, Aboriginal, and a mélange of religions, ethnicities, and cultures. The first census in what became Canada was conducted in 1666 by Jean Talon. This enumeration recorded the name, age, marital status, and occupation of each of the 3,215 inhabitants of New France. Between 1666 and the first official Canadian census in 1871, there were no less than 98 different colonial and regional censuses conducted, most of which were performed for purposes of taxation and military conscription. Over time, new questions were added to gather more information about building structures, livestock, crops, firearms, and churches. Religious affiliation—Catholic or Protestant—became another area of interest, and it became important to enumerate other groups, such as the Acadians, Indians (or "First People" as they are referred to), and Blacks. Census returns prior to 1851 are incomplete for most areas.

The Canadian census returns after 1851 used a Population Schedule form for the enumeration by name of every individual in a household, and that schedule was usually accompanied by a separate Agricultural Schedule that included information about the acreage, land use, buildings, crops, livestock, and valuation.

Library and Archives Canada (LAC) at **http://www.collectionscanada.gc.ca** is the repository for most of the census materials, including those from before Confederation in 1867. However, some of the original documents for New Brunswick, Nova Scotia, and Prince Edward Island prior to 1871 are still in the possession of the provincial archives or libraries. Learn about the LAC census holdings on microfilm in its "Catalogue of Census Returns on Microfilm, 1666–1901" at **http://www.collectionscanada.gc.ca/databases/census-microfilm-1666-1901/index-e.html**. The LAC has digitized 1901, 1906, 1911, and 1916, and recently converted all the images to PDF format. Ancestry.com's Canadian subscription website, at **http://www.ancestry.ca**, has digitized and indexed the 1861 to 1921 censuses and many of the provincial and territorial censuses.

Explore the Depth of the 1871 Census for Canada

The first official national census was conducted in 1871 and was part of the British North America Act in 1867, which created the Canadian Confederation. The Act stated, "In the general Census of the Population of Canada which is hereby required to be taken in the Year One thousand eight-hundred and seventy-one, and in every Tenth Year thereafter, the respective Populations of the Four Provinces shall be distinguished."

This first census requested a vast amount of information from the respondents and for that reason is extremely important for genealogical researchers whose ancestors and family members lived in Canada at that time. There were nine schedules used to collect information:

- **Schedule 1** Population Schedule by name of every living person
- **Schedule 2** Schedule with the name of every person who died within the previous 12 months
- **Schedule 3** A return listing all public institutions, real estate, vehicles, and implements
- **Schedule 4** Agricultural return for cultivated produce, such as crops, fruits, and plants
- **Schedule 5** Agricultural return for livestock, animal products, furs, and homemade fabrics
- **Schedule 6** Return of industrial manufacturing
- **Schedule 7** Return of products of forest resources
- **Schedule 8** Return for shipping concerns and fisheries
- **Schedule 9** Return for mining and mineral products

You can relate the information found on surviving Schedules 3, 4, 5, 7, 8, and 9 to the name of a person whose name is listed on Schedule 1, the Population Schedule. By doing so, you can expand your knowledge of what that person's economic livelihood entailed, of the extent of their holdings, and of the success or failure of the operation, and you also gain a perspective of the lifestyle of the person or family unit.

The 1881 census eliminated the schedule of industrial manufacturing. Unfortunately, though, only the Population Schedules exist. They have, however, been microfilmed and subsequently digitized.

The 1891 census returned to nine schedules again, but only the Population Schedules survive. These have been microfilmed and subsequently digitized.

By the time the 1901 census was to be conducted, Canada consisted of British Columbia, Manitoba, Ontario, Quebec, New Brunswick, Nova Scotia, Prince Edward Island, and two territories: Yukon Territory and the Northwest Territories. Census enumeration areas generally, but not always, corresponded to electoral districts. It is important for you to refer to enumeration area descriptions to help you home in on your family members' locations.

Enumeration was conducted by door-to-door interviews, with enumerators individually visiting each house and asking the questions of the "head" of the household. Enumeration was to be completed within 30 days of 31 March 1901. The census commissioners were forced to revise the schedules, however, before being able to compile and send the completed forms to the census office. By the end of August, the central census office in Ottawa had received 98 percent of the forms. The original schedules for British Columbia schedules were lost when the steamer *Islander* sank on 15 August 1901. The census in British Columbia therefore had to be taken all over again, and this delayed the final tabulation of the census data.

In 1955, the Dominion Bureau of Statistics, at the direction of the Public Records Committee, destroyed the original documents from the 1901 census. Fortunately, however, all of the population records (Schedule 1) and most of the buildings, land, church, and school records (Schedule 2) have been preserved on microfilm, although the quality of the filming is uneven and some images are unreadable. Some instances of the additional schedule forms used can be found among the microfilmed records.

The good news is that Library and Archives Canada has digitized the microfilm images and made them available for browsing at its website (**http://www.bac-lac .gc.ca/eng/census/1901/Pages/1901.aspx**) in a searchable database by geographic location. Census districts and maps also are accessible online, which, as you've already learned, can be invaluable in helping you quickly locate your family. A search of the database for the census records for a province and then a geographical area will return a search results list with records like the one shown in Figure 6-13. It provides you with details about the specific location of the records associated with that place. It also indicates the Record Group (RG) under which Library and Archives Canada has classified and catalogued the records, as well as the reel number for use in accessing the microfilm from which the digital image was produced.

In 1905, the Census and Statistics Act received Royal Assent and defined that a general census would be taken in Canada in 1911 and every ten years thereafter. It also declared that a population and agriculture census was to be taken in Manitoba, Saskatchewan, and Alberta in 1906 and every ten years thereafter. As a result, the following two schedules were prepared and the enumeration was conducted:

- Population and livestock
- Agriculture

As was done for the 1901 census, microfilm was created of the original records, but the original documents were destroyed in 1955. Library and Archives Canada also has digitized the microfilm images and made these available on its website.

1

Province/Territory:	Ontario
District Name:	ESSEX (North/Nord)
District Number:	59
Sub-district Name:	Windsor (City/Cité)
Sub-district Number:	I-1
Schedule:	2
Notes:	Ward/Quartier No. 1
Reference:	RG31 , Statistics Canada
Microfilm Reel Number:	T-6466
Finding Aid Number:	31-40
	The following images are associated with this entry.
	Associated images: ☑

FIGURE 6-13 Search results from the online index to the 1901 census at the Library and Archives Canada website

Locate Additional Information on the Censuses

Census records can provide you with a huge amount of information and many clues to research. As I've mentioned before, it is important to become a student of history and to learn about the places where your ancestors and family members lived, the time period in which they lived, the documents that may have been created at the time for whatever purposes, which documents have survived, where the surviving materials are located, in what format(s) they exist, and how to gain access to them.

You have seen examples in this chapter of census materials that were created for various purposes. Some have survived while others have been lost to fire or through other causes. Transcripts may have been made or original documents may have been microfilmed, and then the originals may have been destroyed. In many cases, census documents have been digitized, indexed, and made available on the Internet. You may be able to conduct "armchair genealogy" over the Internet from the comfort of your own home to access images. In other cases, you may have to visit a library or an LDS Family History Center in order to access microfilm copies of document images or to access some databases available as institutional subscriptions. Other times, you may have to schedule a trip to visit the repository where original documents reside.

Your challenge is to actually track down the documents in whatever form they may exist, and determine how you can access them. And that does, indeed, mean studying the history of the documents. Fortunately for all of us, the Internet provides a wealth of knowledge we can use in our quest. I often use my web browser and a search engine to learn more about available documentary materials. As an example, when searching for information about Canadian census materials for 1906, I entered the following in the search engine:

canada census 1906

I was rewarded with a huge number of search results, not the least of which was one near the top of the list that happens to be the authoritative site on the subject: Library and Archives Canada's website for the 1906 census, at **http://www.bac-lac.gc.ca/ eng/census/1906/Pages/about-census.aspx**.

Take the time to study each column of a census document. You may find additional information that can act as clues to other evidence and resources to aid your understanding of your ancestor and his or her family.

Learn to use the Internet effectively to search and locate information that may be of historical value to your research. In addition, learn how to use online catalogs of libraries, archives, and other facilities so that you can determine what publications may be available to help in your search.

By this time, you have become very knowledgeable indeed about the process of genealogical research and about placing your ancestors into geographical and historical context. The next chapter will take you into some more advanced record types to help you further trace and understand your ancestors and family members. You're on your way now with perhaps the most exciting journey you will ever make. Let's move right ahead!

TABLE 6-3   U.S. Federal Census Records Content, 1790 Through 1940

Census Year	Type of Document	Columns for Information	Comments
1790	Population Schedule	• Head of household • Number of free white males (by age range) • Number of free white females (by age range) • Other free persons and slaves	Name of the head of household was the only name listed.
1800	Population Schedule	Same as 1790 Population Schedule	
1810	Population Schedule	Same as 1790 Population Schedule	
1810	Manufacturing Schedule	• Name of owner, agent, or manager • Type of business • Commodity produced • Value of output • Number of employees	These schedules may be of interest if family operated a manufacturing concern. All 1810 schedules are lost.
1820	Population Schedule	Same as 1790 Population Schedule, plus the following: • Head of household • Number of free white males (by age range) • Number of free white females (by age range) • Number of slave males (by age range) • Number of slave females (by age range) • Number of free colored males (by age range) • Number of free colored females (by age range) • Aliens • Disabilities (deaf, dumb, blind, insane)	
1820	Manufacturing Schedule	Same as 1810 Manufacturing Schedule	Some schedules are missing or lost.
1830	Population Schedule	Same as 1820 Population Schedule, plus questions on Alien status	
1830	Manufacturing Schedule	Same as 1810 Manufacturing Schedule	Some schedules are missing or lost.

(Continued)

TABLE 6-3 U.S. Federal Census Records Content, 1790 Through 1940

Census Year	Type of Document	Columns for Information	Comments
1840	Population Schedule	Same as 1830 Population Schedule, plus the following: • Number involved in variety of trades • Number in school • Number over 21 who can read and write • Number insane • Age and name of Rev. War veterans	
1840	Agricultural Schedule	• Name of owner, agent, or manager • Number of acres of improved and unimproved land • Detailed information about crops, timber, mining, livestock, honey, and other commodities	Submitted to Secretary of the Interior to catalog and evaluate the utilization of farmland. Excellent insight into family life.
1840	Manufacturing Schedule	Same as 1810 Manufacturing Schedule (mostly statistical information and of very limited use)	Some schedules are missing or lost.
1850	Population Schedule	• Head of household • All names, ages, gender, and race • Occupation • Real estate value • Place of birth • Married in last year • Literacy • Deaf, dumb, blind, insane	First census to include the names of every person in the household.
1850	Slave Schedule	• Name of slave holder • Number of slaves • Age, gender, and color • Fugitive from a state? Which state? • Number manumitted • Deaf, dumb, blind, insane, or idiotic • Number of buildings in which housed	Slave names are seldom listed, but some are included.

TABLE 6-3   U.S. Federal Census Records Content, 1790 Through 1940

Census Year	Type of Document	Columns for Information	Comments
1850	Mortality Schedule	• Deceased's name • Whether widowed • Gender, age, and color (white, black, mulatto) • Birthplace • Month of death • Occupation • Cause of death • Number of days ill	Information on those who died during 12 months prior to Census Day.
1850	Agricultural Schedule	Same as 1840 Agricultural Schedule	
1850	Industry Schedule	Same as 1810 Manufacturing Schedule, but was retitled Industry Schedule in 1850–1870	Some schedules are missing or lost.
1850	Social Statistics	Included the following: • Cemeteries within town borders (names, addresses, descriptions, maps, and other data) • Churches, a brief history, affiliation, and membership statistics • Trade societies, clubs, lodges, and other social institutions	Can be used as a resource to locate specific types of institutions in these years, and trace any surviving records.
1860	Population Schedule	Same as 1850 Population Schedule	
1860	Slave Schedule	Same as 1850 Slave Schedule	
1860	Mortality Schedule	Same as 1850 Mortality Schedule	
1860	Agricultural Schedule	Same as 1840 Agricultural Schedule	
1860	Manufacturing Schedule	Same as 1810 Manufacturing Schedule	Some schedules are missing or lost.
1860	Social Statistics	Same as 1850 Social Statistics	

(Continued)

TABLE 6-3   U.S. Federal Census Records Content, 1790 Through 1940

Census Year	Type of Document	Columns for Information	Comments
1870	Population Schedule	Same as 1850 Population Schedule, plus the following: • Whether or not parents were of foreign birth • Month of birth if within this year • Month of marriage if within year	
1870	Mortality Schedule	Same as 1850 Mortality Schedule, plus parents' places of birth	
1870	Agricultural Schedule	Same as 1840 Agricultural Schedule	
1870	Manufacturing Schedule	Same as 1810 Manufacturing Schedule	Some schedules are missing or lost.
1870	Social Statistics	Same as 1850 Social Statistics	
1880	Population Schedule	1880 Census Contents: • Head of household • All names, ages, gender, and race • Relationship • Marital status • Occupation • Deaf, dumb, blind, insane • Illness or disability • Literacy • Birthplaces (person & parents) • Month of birth if within the year	• First census to include relationship of every resident to the head of household. • Parents' birthplace information provides information for tracing ancestral records.
1880	Mortality Schedule	Same as 1870 Mortality Schedule, plus the following: • Where disease was contracted • How long a resident of the area	
1880	Agricultural Schedule	Same as 1840 Agricultural Schedule	
1880	Manufacturing Schedule	Same as 1810 Manufacturing Schedule	Destroyed by act of Congress.
1880	Social Statistics	Same as 1850 Social Statistics	

TABLE 6-3   U.S. Federal Census Records Content, 1790 Through 1940

Census Year	Type of Document	Columns for Information	Comments
1880	Defective, Dependent, and Delinquent Classes Schedules	Seven separate schedules to be compiled by the enumerator: • Schedule 1—Insane Inhabitants • Schedule 2—Idiots • Schedule 3—Deaf-Mutes • Schedule 4—Blind Inhabitants • Schedule 5—Homeless children (institutions) • Schedule 6—Inhabitants in Prison • Schedule 7—Pauper and Indigent Inhabitants	Includes inmates of asylums, orphanages, poor houses, almshouses, prisons, and other institutions, as well as those who the enumerator observed.
1885	Population Schedule	Same as 1880 Population Schedule	Special census for which the federal government agreed to share 50 percent of the cost with any state or territory desiring another census. Only five states/territories took advantage of this offer: • Colorado • Dakota Territory (only a part survives) • Florida (four counties missing) • Nebraska (two counties missing) • New Mexico Territory (four counties missing)
1890	Population Schedule	Same as for 1880 Population Schedule, plus the following: • Ability to speak English • Rent or own home • Years in country, and if naturalized • Number of children born and number still living • Whether Civil War veteran or surviving spouse (in which case a separate schedule also was completed—see below)	Each family was listed on a single sheet. • Population Schedules destroyed by fire and water at Commerce Building in January 1921. • Originals destroyed in mid-1930s.

(Continued)

TABLE 6-3 U.S. Federal Census Records Content, 1790 Through 1940

Census Year	Type of Document	Columns for Information	Comments
1890	Mortality Schedule	Same as 1880 Mortality Schedule	Destroyed in 1896 or 1897.
1890	Surviving Soldiers, Sailors, and Marines, and Widows, etc. Schedule	• Name of veteran or surviving spouse • Age • Branch of service (Army, Navy, Marines) • Duration of service • Date of enlistment and discharge • Rank, company, regiment, and vessel • Disability	• Survived the 1921 fire. • Union veterans only, but a few Confederates are included. • Partial returns; some counties missing. • Originals destroyed in mid-1930s.
1890	Agricultural Schedule	Same as 1840 Agricultural Schedule	Destroyed in 1896 or 1897.
1890	Manufacturing Schedule	Same as 1810 Manufacturing Schedule	Destroyed in 1896 or 1897.
1900	Population Schedule	Same as 1890 Population Schedule, plus the following additional information: • Exact month and year of birth (only 1900) • Number of years married	This was the first census to enumerate U.S. citizens abroad.
1900	Agricultural Schedule	Same as 1840 Agricultural Schedule	
1900	Manufacturing Schedule	Same as 1810 Manufacturing Schedule	Destroyed by act of Congress.
1910	Population Schedule	Same as 1900 Population Schedule, plus the following additional information: • Year of arrival in United States • Whether veteran and, if so, of which war (only on the 1910 census)	
1910	Agricultural Schedule	Same as 1840 Agricultural Schedule	
1910	Manufacturing Schedule	Same as 1810 Manufacturing Schedule	Destroyed by act of Congress.

TABLE 6-3   U.S. Federal Census Records Content, 1790 Through 1940

Census Year	Type of Document	Columns for Information	Comments
1920	Population Schedule	Same as 1910 Population Schedule, plus the following additional information: • Native tongue	Question regarding whether a veteran (on 1910 census) was not included.
1930	Population Schedule	Same as 1920 Population Schedule plus the following additional information: • Whether owns a radio • Year of naturalization • Whether veteran and, if so, of which war	Indians schedules often found at end of state or county returns.

1940	Population Schedule	Similar to 1930 Population Schedule plus the following additional information:
		
		• Place of birth
		• Residence on 1 April 1935
		• Person 14 years and over – Employment Status
		• Occupation/Industry
		• Income in 1939
		• Birthplace of father and mother
		• Mother tongue
		• Veterans information
		• Social Security information
		• Women who have been married:
		  • Married more than once?
		  • Age at first marriage
		  • Number of children born (excluding stillborn)	

1940	Housing Schedule		Has not survived.
1940	Farm Schedule		Has not survived.
1940	Irrigation Schedule		Has not survived.
1940	Infant Schedule		Has not survived.

(Continued)

TABLE 6-3 U.S. Federal Census Records Content, 1790 Through 1940

Census Year	Type of Document	Columns for Information	Comments
		Native American Censuses	
1885 through 1940	Indian (or Native American) Schedule	Name of each individual in household (Indian and English)	These censuses were taken on federal Indian reservations every year from 1885 to 1940.
		Relationship to head of household	
		Age, gender	
		Marital/tribal status	
		Occupation	
		Land ownership	

PART II

Expand Your Research

7

Extend Your Research with Advanced Record Types

HOW TO...

- Use religious records to trace your family
- Obtain and analyze mortuary and funeral home records
- Read between the lines in obituaries
- Discover the wealth of information in cemetery records
- Get inside your ancestor's mind using wills and probate records
- Use historical newspapers to learn about your ancestor's life events
- Consider other institutional records

You've learned a great deal about your family so far by locating and using home sources, birth, marriage, and death records, and census resources. Along the way, you also have built a foundation for all of your future genealogical research. You now know how important it is to place your family into context, to conduct scholarly research, to analyze every piece of data you uncover, and to properly document your source materials.

You've made a lot of progress so far and you now know a tremendous amount about the most commonly used records used by genealogists. However, those records are just the beginning of the multitude of different records available in which you can discover more details about your family's rich history. There literally are hundreds of different documents, record types, and artifacts that may yield information of value in developing the context of your forebears' lives.

This chapter discusses some of the more important evidence associated with your ancestors, their religion, and information sources concerned with the end of their lives. These materials can provide a treasure trove of details and clues for you. You just need to know what they are, where to look, how to access the records, and how to properly analyze them. Remember that not everything is available on the Internet. Most records are stored in courthouses, libraries and archives, churches, government offices, and many other places, and have never been photographed or digitized. You will always need to combine these traditional research resources with electronic research on the Internet and in electronic databases. You will learn to apply your critical thinking skills to the evidence and formulate reasonable hypotheses, sometimes circumventing the "brick walls" that we all invariably encounter.

Use Religious Records

Religious records are those that relate to a church or some similar established religious institution. Organized religion has provided a source for scholarly philosophical and theological study and writing throughout the centuries. Religious groups also have variously maintained documents concerning their operations, administration, and membership reaching far back into our history. As a result, religious records of many types can provide you with rich genealogical details and clues to other types of records.

There are a number of challenges you will face in your search for and investigation into these ecclesiastical records. Let's discuss these challenges first, and then we'll explore some of the types of records you might expect to find.

Locate the Right Institution

It is usually an easy task to contact the place of worship for yourself, your parents, and your siblings. The knowledge of the religious affiliation and where the family members attend worship services is pretty easy to come by. However, as we move backward in time, this information may become obscured. You may make the assumption that your ancestors belonged to the same religious denomination as your family does today, and you may be making a serious error.

Not every member of a family necessarily belongs to the same religious group. My maternal grandmother's family provides an excellent example. Her father belonged to the Presbyterian Church and her mother to a Primitive Baptist congregation. Among their six sons and six daughters, I have found them to be members of two Presbyterian, three Baptist, one Methodist, and one Christian Science churches, all in the same town. In addition, some of these people changed churches. Most notable was the entry I found in the membership roll of the First Presbyterian Church of Rome, Georgia, dated 31 October 1926, for one of my great-aunts. It read "Seen entering Christian Science Church" and her name was lined out. That clue pointed me to the Church of Christ, Scientist, where I learned that she had formally become a member of its congregation earlier in October.

In some cases, prior to or upon marriage, one spouse may change his or her religious affiliation to that of the other spouse. A change of first name or forename may also occur when the person joins the new church. Some religious groups, such as Catholics, want the children of a matrimonial union raised in their faith, and formal religious instruction and conversion is common.

Determining the religion of an ancestor or other family member is an important part of your research because there may be any number of records to provide more information for your research and pointers to other records. You cannot assume that everyone who lived in England or Wales was a member of the Church of England, that everyone who lived in Scotland was a member of the Church of Scotland, or that everyone who lived in Ireland was either Catholic or Protestant. In all these areas, other religious congregations were common, including Baptist, Methodist, Presbyterian, Lutheran, Quaker, Jewish, Muslim, Sikh, Hindu, and Buddhist. You also cannot assume that the only religions in Germany were Catholicism and Lutheranism. You will find Mennonite, Baptist, Anabaptist, Methodist, Seventh-day Adventist, and Orthodox churches, as well as Muslim, Buddhist, Sikh, Hindu, and Bahá'í Faith groups.

Look for clues to the religion of a person in the name of the *clergy* who performed marriage ceremonies for the person and the spouse, for the person's parents, and for any siblings. Clergy names are typically found on marriage licenses issued by government offices, such as the one shown in Figure 7-1 and the one shown in Figure 5-17 in Chapter 5. These documents are referred to as "marriage returns," as they have been returned to the courthouse or civil registration office to be registered as complete. Certificates of marriage created by churches, such as the one shown in Figure 7-2, may be found among family papers. Look, too, at obituaries for the names of officiating clergy at funerals and memorial services. It is often easy to determine in local historical records and city directories the religious affiliation of the clergyperson and the organization to which he or she was attached. This can provide an important link to membership rolls and to records of life events associated with the congregation.

A member of clergy, justice of the peace, or other person authorized by local government to perform marriage ceremonies may have done so for your ancestor. Identifying and tracking a member of clergy is one way to determine the religious institution with which that person was affiliated and to learn more about the bride and/or groom. There are several ways to do this. First, check for the clergy person's name in the local city directory from the time of the marriage. The directory may show the person's address and may also indicate the religious institution with which he or she was affiliated. If no affiliation is listed, you may want to locate a map of the time period, locate the address on the map, and check to see what churches are nearby. Another resource to investigate is a local newspaper. Religious institutions typically have a listing or advertisement in the newspaper to announce times of worship services and other activities. These listings are typically grouped together in the paper with those from other religious institutions in the area. They may include the name of the clergy person. This may be the clue that you need to connect the bride and/or groom to that church. You will definitely want to make contact with the church and find out what membership records might exist. An entry on the membership roll of the church may tell you if your ancestor's membership was transferred from another church and, if so, the name and address of that church. This provides another clue as to a previous place of residence, and this can be traced for individuals, their siblings, their parents, and other family members. This strategy may help you map a migration path backward in time for the family members.

If your ancestor's marriage ceremony was performed not by a member of clergy but by a member of the civil government, you may have to work a little harder to determine if your ancestor belonged to a congregation in the area. Your job is to determine the *right* institution to which your ancestor belonged. You may already

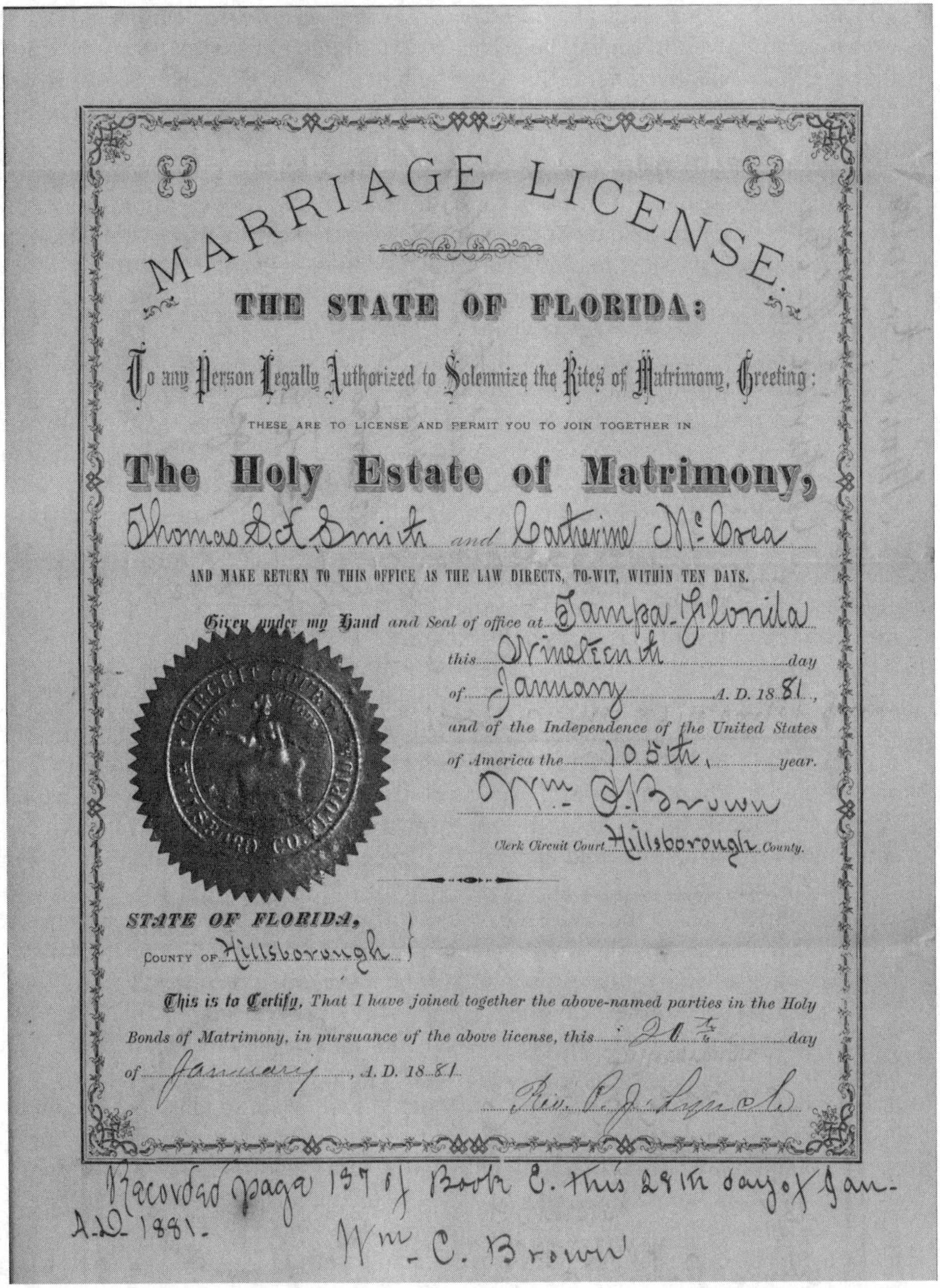

MARRIAGE LICENSE.

THE STATE OF FLORIDA:

To any Person Legally Authorized to Solemnize the Rites of Matrimony, Greeting:

THESE ARE TO LICENSE AND PERMIT YOU TO JOIN TOGETHER IN

The Holy Estate of Matrimony,

Thomas S. L. Smith and Catherine McCrea

AND MAKE RETURN TO THIS OFFICE AS THE LAW DIRECTS, TO-WIT, WITHIN TEN DAYS.

Given under my Hand and Seal of office at Tampa Florida

this Nineteenth day

of January A. D. 18 81,

and of the Independence of the United States

of America the 105th, year.

Wm. C. Brown

Clerk Circuit Court Hillsborough County.

STATE OF FLORIDA,

COUNTY OF Hillsborough

This is to Certify, That I have joined together the above-named parties in the Holy Bonds of Matrimony, in pursuance of the above license, this 20th day

of January, A. D. 18 81.

Rev. P. J. Lynch

Recorded page 137 of Book C. this 29th day of Jan. A.D. 1881.

Wm. C. Brown

FIGURE 7-1 A marriage license issued by the civil government office is then completed by an officiating clergy member or someone else authorized to perform the ceremony.

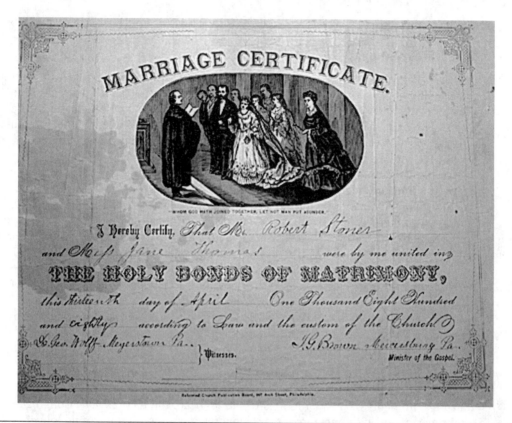

FIGURE 7-2   Marriage certificate issued by a church showing the name of the officiating clergy

know or suspect the religious denomination of your ancestor. If the community in which your ancestor lived has multiple congregations of the same denomination, you may have to contact or visit each one in order to determine if your ancestor was a member. Depending on the time period in which your ancestor lived in the area, you may also need to research local histories to determine which specific religious groups existed at the time and formed congregations. Your best strategy, however, may be to start with the congregation located closest geographically to where your ancestor or family lived, and work outward. You may also have to escalate your search to an administrative or similar jurisdictional level to locate records for defunct congregations. For example, records for the congregation of a Catholic church that merged with another may have been transferred to the person's new chosen church. Alternatively, the records may have been moved to another diocese location or to some other place. Be prepared to escalate your inquiry for a defunct church's records to a higher administrative office. This means doing a little more research into the structure of the religion and its jurisdictional structure. Be sure to also contact the local public library, historical museum, and the local genealogical and historical societies because they may have knowledge of church closures, mergers, and records transfers.

Determine What Records the Institution Might Have Created

Once you have determined the religious affiliation of your ancestor, it is important to learn about the organization. Some groups are meticulous about documenting their affairs and their membership information, while others are less inclined. The Quakers (Society of Friends) and the Catholic Church, for example, generally maintain thorough documentation of the church business and have created detailed documents about each member, including records for birth, baptism, christening, marriage, death, other sacramental and personal events, and even tithing records. Other denominations or congregations may not have maintained such comprehensive records, and the documents that survive can often be far less detailed or revealing.

Invest some time in learning about the history of the denomination to which your ancestor belonged and types of records it may have created at the time your ancestor might have been a member. This will give you a foundation for your research. You will begin to learn what types of records to request when you make contact with the particular church or organization, where they were created and by whom, what information is likely to be contained in them, and where they were kept. A good starting point is a search in Wikipedia at **http://www.wikipedia.com**, followed by a web search for the name of the religion.

Locate the Records Today

Your most immediate consideration is where to locate the records *now*. Congregations sometimes merge with one another, or a congregation may find it can no longer sustain itself financially, and therefore dissolves. A congregation may also have expanded so much that it outgrew its facility, and records storage may have become a problem. What happens to the records?

Your understanding of the history and organization of the denomination can go a long way in helping you locate records. Your study will also help you identify the types of records that were created. For example, some Christian denominations may mark a person's first communion with a ceremony and issue a certificate such as the one shown in Figure 7-3, while others may only record the event in membership records. While an existing church location may have all of its records dating back to its founding, those records may not necessarily be located on-site at that church. They may be stored in a rectory, parsonage, or vicarage. Records may have been moved to another church of the same denomination in the area, to a central parish or diocesan office, to a regional or national level administrative office, or to a storage site.

A good strategy for determining the location of historical records is to contact the clergy or secretary at the specific house of worship. Having learned what records might have been created, you can ask about their availability and request access to or copies of them. If the records have been moved or sent elsewhere, ask for the name and address of a contact and then follow that lead.

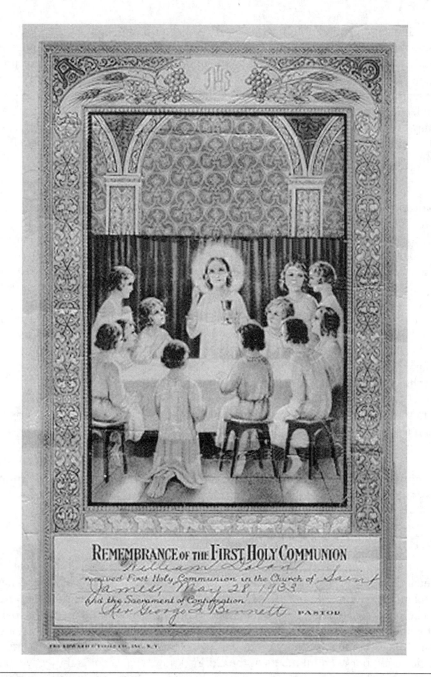

FIGURE 7-3   Certificate of a first communion

If a congregation no longer exists or you can't find it, contact the local public library and any academic libraries in the area and ask the reference department to assist you in tracing the group and its records. The local, county, state, or provincial genealogical and historical societies are additional resources you should enlist in your research. Their in-depth knowledge of the area and religious groups can be invaluable. Indeed, they may have copied or transcribed indexes, and some ecclesiastical records may even have come into their possession. Again, don't overlook making contact with a higher administrative area of the religious organization. The personnel should be able to provide you with details of the group's history and of the fate of a "missing" congregation's records.

Parish registers in England, Wales, Scotland, and the Channel Islands were in danger of damage or loss during World War II. German bombing raids often focused on churches as targets. Many of the original parish records were evacuated from the churches to other places of safety. Many of these were ceded to archives or universities for permanent safekeeping, and the older records may have remained there after the war. Locating the parish registers is a key to locating an ancestor's christening, marriage, or burial record prior to the implementation of civil registration in England and Wales in 1837 and in Scotland in 1855. An excellent resource for determining which parish registers exist, the years they cover, and their location is the book *The Phillimore Atlas & Index of Parish Registers*, 3rd edition, by Cecil R. Humphery-Smith (The History Press, 2003). The book contains detailed maps of every county in England, Wales, and Scotland, including their parishes, and a detailed table of physical locations of the records as of the time of the original publication in 1984.

Parish clergy in the Church of England were required from the time of Elizabeth I to transcribe the christening, marriage, and burial entries from their parish registers and send a copy to their bishop. Many of these Bishop's Transcripts are now in the possession of the County Record Office (CRO) in the county where the parish was located at the time. Please note that county boundaries have changed over the centuries. You will want to research histories and historical maps to determine the correct CRO from which to seek information.

Gain Access to the Records

Another challenge can be gaining access to or obtaining copies of the ecclesiastical records you want. Religious groups are, in effect, private organizations and have a right and an obligation to protect their privacy and that of their members. Most are willing to help you locate information about your ancestors and family members, particularly if you do most of the work. Remember that not all church office personnel are paid employees; some are simply members volunteering their time. Not all members of the office staff, nor even members of the clergy, know what records they have and what is in them. The old books and papers in their offices may just be gathering dust in a closet or file cabinet. Few of these materials are indexed, such as the document shown in Figure 7-4, which was found among a sheaf of loose papers tucked into a cardboard box in a church office cabinet. It often takes a considerable effort to go through such documents and locate information that may relate to your family.

The Session of the Tinkling Spring Church desires to record its
gratitude to Almighty God for the long life and useful service of its
senior Elder, W. F. Brand who departed this life May 28, 1932. Mr Brand
was elected to the eldership March 22, 1896 and gave many years of valuable service until incapacitated by the infirmities of old age. He died
at the age of ninety-two, and for thirty-six years was an honored Elder
of this church.

Be it resolved that this note be recorded in our minutes, and a copy
sent to the family.

John C. Siler Moderator.

R. H. Thompson Clerk.

FIGURE 7-4   This loose document from the minutes of a church session commemorating
the life and service of a member was found in a box, and it was never indexed.

Be prepared to offer to help the person you contact in the church office. You may
have to describe the types of record you are seeking and where they might be located.
Any reluctance you encounter may be a result of the person's lack of knowledge and
experience, lack of time, the cost of making and mailing copies for you, or some other
reason. Be kind, patient, and friendly, and offer all the help you can. Be prepared to
reimburse all the expenses and to make a donation to the congregation.

You will find that a substantial number of parish records from England, Wales,
Scotland, and Ireland have been digitized and indexed and are now at online database
websites. We discussed a number of these in Chapter 5. These include such places as
Ancestry.com (**http://www.ancestry.com**), FamilySearch (**https://familysearch.org**),
findmypast (**http://www.findmypast.com**), MyHeritage (**http://www.myheritage
.com**), and ScotlandsPeople (**http://www.scotlandspeople.com**), among others.

Interpret, Evaluate, and Place the Records into Perspective

Once you obtain the documents you want, your next step is to carefully read and
review them. I recommend reading them several times in order to absorb and
comprehend the information they contain. Interpretation can be a real challenge,

particularly if the handwriting is poor, the copies are dim or damaged, or the document is written in a language you do not understand. Many church records are written in Latin, particularly those of the Catholic Church and those of the early Church of England. You may encounter Jewish documents written in Hebrew or other languages, Russian Orthodox Church documents written using the Cyrillic alphabet, and documents from other religions written in any number of foreign languages. Old English script and German Fraktur both resemble calligraphy and their character embellishments can be particularly difficult or confusing to read. Other older or archaic handwritten materials may be difficult or nearly impossible to decipher. You will want to consider obtaining books on the subject of paleography (the study of ancient writings and inscriptions; also spelled palaeography) and using the skills or services of interpreters. Two particularly good books are *Palaeography for Family and Local Historians* (2nd Revised edition) by Hilary Marshall (The History Press, 2010) and *Reading Early American Handwriting* by Kip Sperry (Genealogical Publishing Company, 1998; reprinted 2008). A good book for working with Latin documents is *Latin for Local and Family Historians* by Denis Stuart (The History Press, 2010).

The National Archives (TNA) in England has developed several online tutorials at **http://www.nationalarchives.gov.uk/records/reading-old-documents.htm** that will instruct you about reading old documents. There are six tutorials: *Palaeography*, *Latin Palaeography*, *Beginners' Latin*, *Advanced Latin*, *Currency Converter*, and *Roman Numerals*.

As with the other documentary evidence you have obtained, be prepared to carefully evaluate the contents of the documents. Consider the information provided and use it to add to the overall chronological picture you are constructing of your ancestor or family member. Let's now look at specific ecclesiastical records.

Consider a Variety of Religious Records

Your research will present you with a vast array of potential information sources from religious organizations. The following is a list of some of the records you may encounter. Some are more common than others, and the list certainly will vary depending on denomination, time period, and the specific congregation.

- Administrative records
- Baptismal certificates
- Bar mitzvah or bat mitzvah records
- Birth records
- Bishop's Transcripts
- Building plans and related documents
- Certificates of membership
- Christening records
- Church bulletins
- Clergy appointments
- Committee minutes and reports

- Communion records
- Confirmation records
- County Record Office files
- Divorce and annulment records
- Donation and tithing records
- Excommunication records
- Fellowship group records
- Hearings and inquiries
- Lists of elders and deacons
- Marriage records
- Meeting minutes
- Membership rolls

- Missionary records
- Newspapers and journals
- Parish registers
- Photographs

Any of these documents can provide clues about your ancestor's or family member's life. Don't overlook the fact that membership records and meeting minutes also may record the previous place of membership for an individual. I was successful in tracing my maternal grandfather from the church in which he was a member at the time of his death, back through three other churches in which he was a member, to the church in which he was baptized more than six decades before, all through their membership records. A church bulletin, such as the one shown in Figure 7-5,

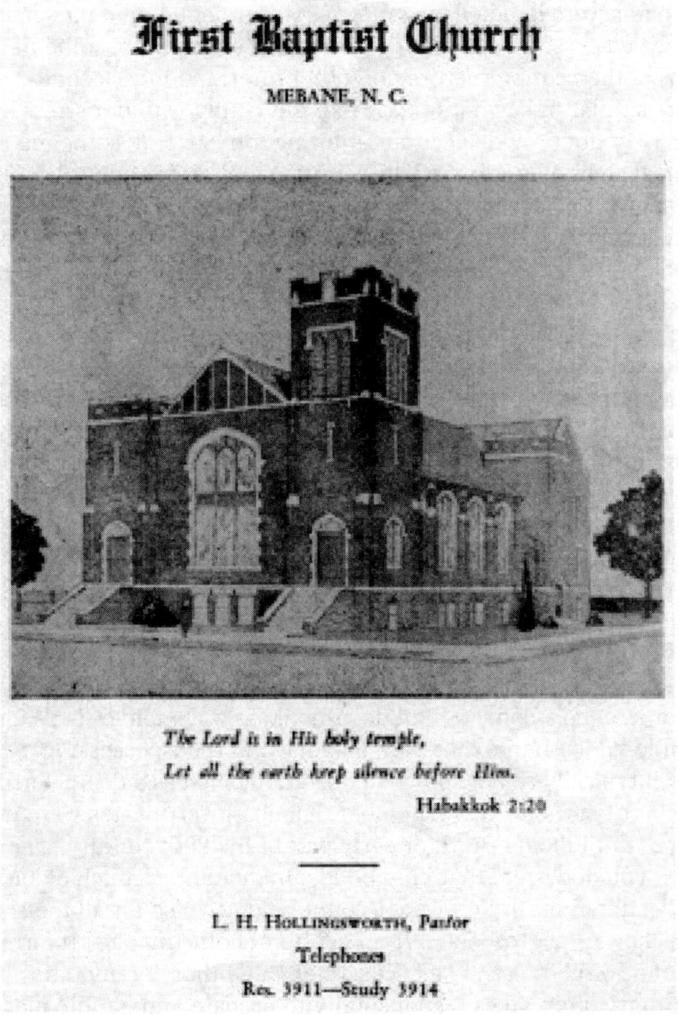

First Baptist Church

MEBANE, N. C.

The Lord is in His holy temple,
Let all the earth keep silence before Him.
Habakkuk 2:20

L. H. HOLLINGSWORTH, Pastor
Telephones
Res. 3911—Study 3914

FIGURE 7-5 Church bulletins share news about individuals and may point to other types of church records.

provided details of the election of another family member to the position of head deacon. And another church had among its records a photograph of a grandfather at the groundbreaking ceremony for a new church building. You never know what you will find in the records of religious organizations.

Obtain and Analyze Mortuary and Funeral Home Records

Among some of the most detailed records compiled about a person are those that are created at the time of his or her death. The records of an ancestor or family member whose remains were handled by a mortuary or funeral home may hold many important clues. As we discussed with death certificates in Chapter 5, some of the information on them is of the primary nature and other information is secondary. Funeral home records are similar in several ways. First, the family is under stress at the time of the death and may not provide accurate information. Second, someone else acting as an informant, such as a less immediate family member, friend, or hospital employee, may not know the answers to questions being asked. Third, the person taking down the information may have misheard or incorrectly written the information. If that person took handwritten notes and later typed them, that transcription process may also have introduced more errors. It is important, for all of those reasons, that you verify the information you find in these records with original sources or sources of primary information.

As with religious records, it is important to do some research in advance to determine whether a mortuary's services were used and, if so, which mortuary it was. A mortuary or funeral home performs a variety of functions, and someone usually selects the specific services desired for the person who is deceased. The activities of the mortuary or funeral home may include providing a simple coffin or a fancy casket, embalming and cosmetic preparation, clothing the corpse, writing an obituary, arranging for or conducting memorial services, providing transportation for the deceased and the family, contacting pallbearers, arranging for interment or cremation, and other, more specialized services. As a result, mortuaries and funeral homes collect a great deal of information. This may be summarized on a single card, on one or more sheets of paper, or may be a collection of documents in a file folder. Let's discuss some of the most common documents that they may have in their possession.

You will typically find a copy of a document such as a death certificate or coroner's report (or both) in their file. Remember that death certificates were not required in many places until the late 19th or early part of the 20th century. Therefore, don't be surprised if you don't find that kind of documentation in much older files. Another common document is an itemized accounting or invoice for all the services provided. Figure 7-6 shows a page of detail from a funeral home invoice. Information about the selection of a coffin or casket, a burial vault, and other commodities is often included.

A mortuary often takes responsibility to prepare and handle placement of obituaries in newspapers and other media, and that information or a copy of the obituary information may be included in the file.

Ray Funeral Home
119 NORTH MARKET STREET · MADISON, NC 27025 · (919) 548-9606

PAID
_12-20-93_
FORBIS & DICK
FUNERAL SERVICE

December 22, 1993

MR. CAREY MORGAN
3606 CALYX CT.
GREENSBORO, NC 27410

The Funeral for EDITH WEATHERLY MORGAN on November 21, 1993

We sincerely appreciate the confidence you have placed in us and
will continue to assist you in every way we can. Please feel free
to contact us if you have any questions in regard to this statement.

THE FOLLOWING IS AN ITEMIZED STATEMENT OF THE SERVICES, FACILITIES,
AUTOMOTIVE EQUIPMENT, AND MERCHANDISE THAT YOU SELECTED WHEN MAKING
THE FUNERAL ARRANGEMENTS.

SELECTED SERVICES OF FUNERAL DIRECTOR AND STAFF:
Local Removal . . . . $ 90.00
Embalming . . . . $ 300.00
Other Preparation . . . . $ 75.00
Director and Staff . . . . $ 760.00
SELECTED USE OF FACILITIES AND EQUIPMENT:
Other Use of Facilities . . . . $ 120.00
Use of Visitation Room . . . . $ 120.00
Equip. for Church Service . . . . $ 120.00
SELECTED USE OF AUTOMOTIVE EQUIPMENT:
Hearse . . . . $ 100.00
Family Vehicle . . . . $ 80.00
Utility Van . . . . $ 80.00
Service Vehicle . . . . $ 80.00

        FUNERAL HOME SERVICE CHARGES . . . . $ 1925.00

SELECTED MERCHANDISE:
Lexington Maple . . . . $ 2765.00
Continental . . . . $ 994.00
Register Books . . . . $ 25.00
Acknowledgement Cards . . . . $ 10.00
Rita Barber #6749 . . . . $ 100.00

THE COST OF OUR SERVICES, EQUIPMENT, AND MERCHANDISE
THAT YOU HAVE SELECTED. . . . . $ 5819.00

AT THE TIME FUNERAL ARRANGEMENTS WERE MADE, WE ADVANCED CERTAIN
PAYMENTS TO OTHERS AS AN ACCOMMODATION. THE FOLLOWING IS AN
ACCOUNTING FOR THOSE CHARGES.

EDITH WEATHERLY MORGAN
Page 1

FIGURE 7-6   Detailed invoice page from a funeral home invoice

Look for copies of a cemetery deed and a burial permit, depending on the time period, place, and type of burial. The cemetery deed may be in the possession of the cemetery office or the cemetery administrator; the county recorder of deeds sometimes issues cemetery lot deeds, and so that becomes another place you can check. You will occasionally find other materials, including correspondence and photographs.

Mortuaries and funeral homes are private companies and, as such, are not required to provide copies of their business documents to genealogists. An owner or administrator may decline to provide access to you for reasons of business privacy or to protect the confidentiality of family information. They also are not required to retain and preserve records in perpetuity.

Many mortuaries and funeral homes over the years have been sold or have gone out of business. Their records may have been transferred to a new owner, placed in storage, lost, or destroyed. You may need to work with libraries, archives, and genealogical and/or historical societies to determine the disposition of records from a defunct mortuary or funeral home. Some may have been donated to and preserved in the special collections of libraries. For example, the records of several funeral homes in Tampa, Florida, now reside in the Special Collections of the University of South Florida Tampa Library. These include cards and books from those facilities, such as the card shown in Figure 7-7 and the two-page record shown in Figures 7-8 and 7-9.

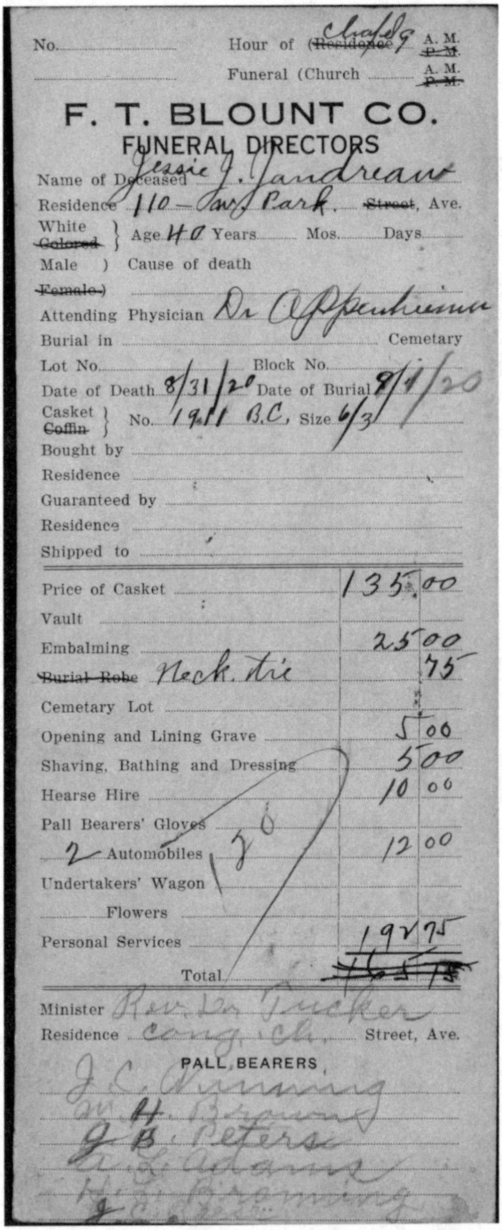
No. Hour of (Residence) Chapel 9 A.M. P.M.
Funeral (Church A.M. P.M.

F. T. BLOUNT CO.

FUNERAL DIRECTORS

Name of Deceased Jessie J. Jandreau
Residence 110 — Park Street, Ave.
White / Colored } Age 40 Years Mos. Days
Male / Female) Cause of death
Attending Physician Dr
Burial in Cemetary
Lot No. Block No.
Date of Death 8/31/20 Date of Burial 9/1/20
Casket / Coffin } No. 1911 B.C. Size 6/3
Bought by
Residence
Guaranteed by
Residence
Shipped to

Price of Casket	135.00
Vault	
Embalming	25 00
Burial Robe Neck tie	75
Cemetary Lot	
Opening and Lining Grave	5 00
Shaving, Bathing and Dressing	5 00
Hearse Hire	10 00
Pall Bearers' Gloves	
2 Automobiles	12 00
Undertakers' Wagon	
Flowers	
Personal Services	
Total	192 75

Minister Rev. Dr. Tucker
Residence Cong. Ch. Street, Ave.

PALL BEARERS

J. B. Peters

FIGURE 7-7 Funeral home information card from 1920

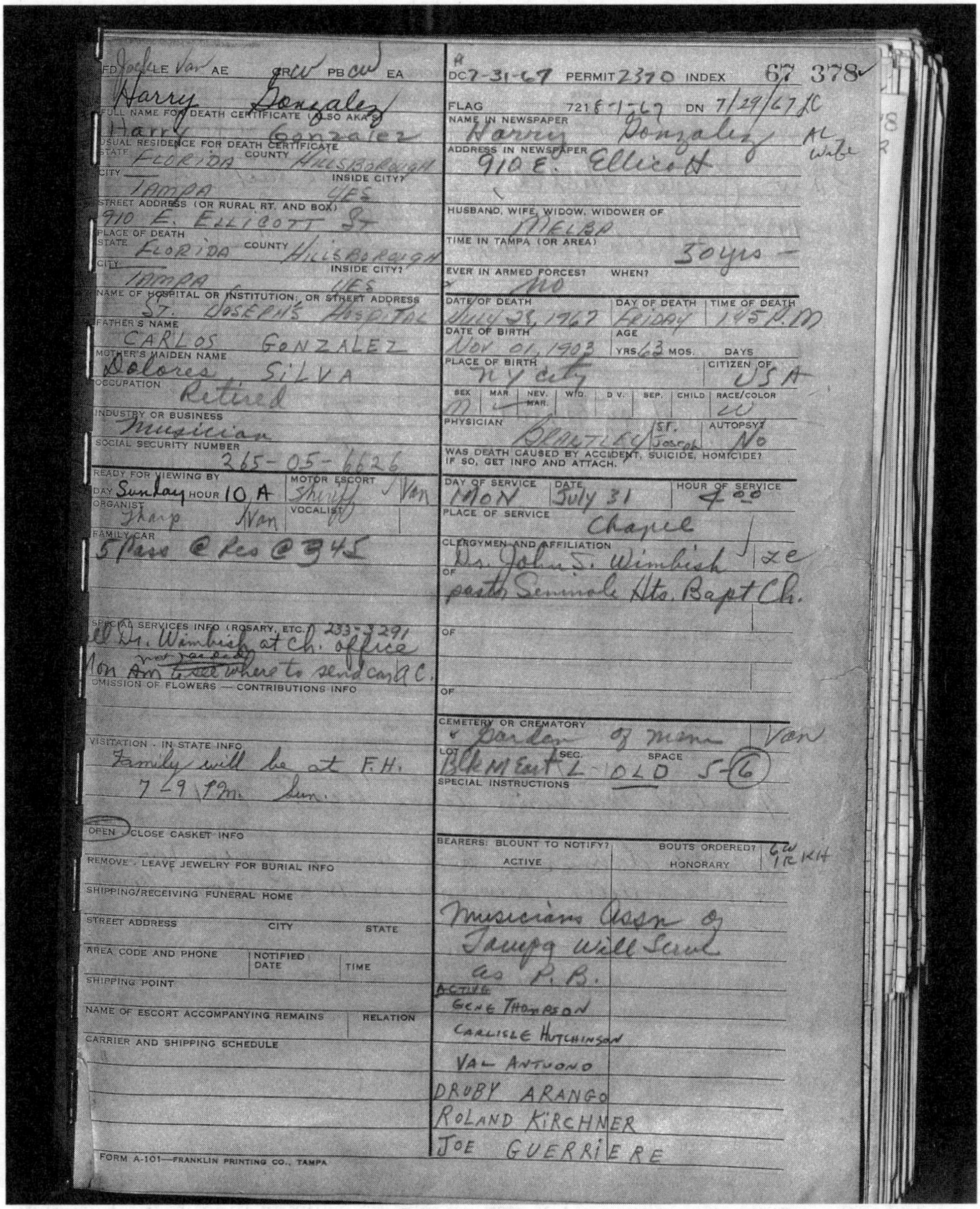

FD Joelle Van AE GRCW PB CW EA
Harry Gonzalez
FULL NAME FOR DEATH CERTIFICATE (ALSO AKA'S)
Harry Gonzalez
USUAL RESIDENCE FOR DEATH CERTIFICATE
STATE FLORIDA COUNTY HILLSBOROUGH
CITY TAMPA INSIDE CITY? YES
STREET ADDRESS (OR RURAL RT. AND BOX) 910 E. ELLICOTT St
PLACE OF DEATH
STATE FLORIDA COUNTY HILLSBOROUGH
CITY TAMPA INSIDE CITY? YES
NAME OF HOSPITAL OR INSTITUTION, OR STREET ADDRESS ST. JOSEPH'S HOSPITAL
FATHER'S NAME CARLOS GONZALEZ
MOTHER'S MAIDEN NAME Dolores SILVA
OCCUPATION Retired
INDUSTRY OR BUSINESS Musician
SOCIAL SECURITY NUMBER 265-05-6626
READY FOR VIEWING BY DAY Sunday HOUR 10 A
MOTOR ESCORT Sheriff Van
ORGANIST Tharp Van
VOCALIST
FAMILY CAR 5 Pass @ Res @ 3 45
SPECIAL SERVICES INFO (ROSARY, ETC.) 233-3291
Dr. Wimbish at Ch. office
Mon Am not decided where to send car R.C.
OMISSION OF FLOWERS — CONTRIBUTIONS INFO
VISITATION - IN STATE INFO
Family will be at F.H. 7-9 P.M. Sun.
OPEN CLOSE CASKET INFO
REMOVE - LEAVE JEWELRY FOR BURIAL INFO
SHIPPING/RECEIVING FUNERAL HOME
STREET ADDRESS CITY STATE
AREA CODE AND PHONE NOTIFIED DATE TIME
SHIPPING POINT
NAME OF ESCORT ACCOMPANYING REMAINS RELATION
CARRIER AND SHIPPING SCHEDULE
FORM A-101—FRANKLIN PRINTING CO., TAMPA

DC 7-31-67 PERMIT 2370 INDEX 67 378
FLAG 7218-1-67 DN 7/29/67 RC
NAME IN NEWSPAPER Harry Gonzalez
ADDRESS IN NEWSPAPER 910 E. Ellicott
HUSBAND, WIFE, WIDOW, WIDOWER OF MELBA
TIME IN TAMPA (OR AREA) 30 yrs
EVER IN ARMED FORCES? WHEN? No
DATE OF DEATH July 28, 1967 DAY OF DEATH FRIDAY TIME OF DEATH 1 45 P.M.
DATE OF BIRTH Nov 01, 1903 AGE YRS 63 MOS. DAYS
PLACE OF BIRTH N Y city CITIZEN OF USA
SEX M MAR NEV. MAR. WID. D.V. SEP. CHILD RACE/COLOR W
PHYSICIAN Bratley St. Joseph AUTOPSY? No
WAS DEATH CAUSED BY ACCIDENT, SUICIDE, HOMICIDE? IF SO, GET INFO AND ATTACH.
DAY OF SERVICE MON DATE July 31 HOUR OF SERVICE 4 00
PLACE OF SERVICE Chapel
CLERGYMEN AND AFFILIATION Dr. John S. Wimbish
OF pastor Seminole Hts. Bapt Ch.
OF
OF
CEMETERY OR CREMATORY Garden of Memories Van
LOT Blk M East L SEC. OLD SPACE 5-6
SPECIAL INSTRUCTIONS
BEARERS: BLOUNT TO NOTIFY? BOUTS ORDERED?
ACTIVE HONORARY
Musicians Assn of Tampa will serve as P.B.
ACTIVE
GENE THOMPSON
CARLISLE HUTCHINSON
VAL ANTUONO
DRUBY ARANGO
ROLAND KIRCHMER
JOE GUERRIERE

FIGURE 7-8 Page 1 of a funeral home record from 1967

You may need to contact the government offices that handle corporate licensing to determine when a funeral home or mortuary was sold or went out of business. That office may also be able to tell you about details of the transfer of ownership and new licensing, and this can point you toward the possible disposition of older records.

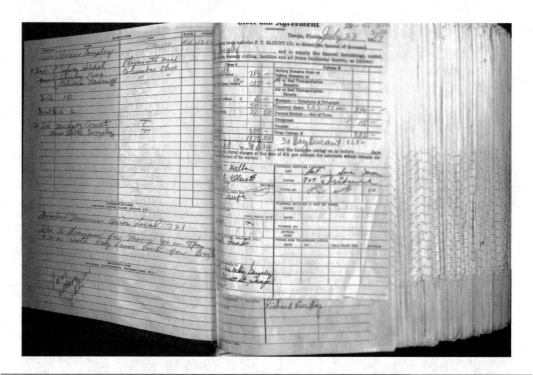

FIGURE 7-9 Page 2 of a funeral home record from 1967

Read Between the Lines in Obituaries

We're all familiar with obituaries and death notices, those announcements of people's deaths that appear in the newspaper and other media, and also on the Internet. These published gems often contain a wealth of biographical information in condensed form. You can gather a lot from reading what is printed *and* from reading between the lines.

An obituary is definitely a source of secondary information, derived from one or more persons or documents. You will definitely want to confirm and verify every piece of data listed there. The accuracy of the information included should always be considered questionable because errors can be introduced at any point in the publication process. The informant for the information may or may not be a knowledgeable family member, or the person may be under the stress of the occasion and provide inaccurate details. The person who takes down the information may introduce an error, a newspaper employee may transcribe something incorrectly, and an editor may miss a typographical error.

Some of the information and clues you can look for in obituaries include the following:

- Name and age of the deceased
- Date, location, and sometimes cause of death

- Place of residence
- Names of parents and siblings
- Names and/or numbers of children and grandchildren
- Places of residence of living relatives
- Names of and notes about deceased relatives
- Where and when deceased was born
- When deceased left his/her native land, perhaps even the port of entry and date
- Naturalization date and location
- Place(s) where deceased was educated
- Date(s) and location(s) of marriage(s), and name of spouse(es) (sometimes maiden names)
- Religious affiliation and name of congregation
- Military service information (branch, rank, dates served, medals, and awards)
- Place(s) of employment
- Public office(s) held
- Organizations to which he/she belonged
- Awards received
- Events in which he/she participated
- Name and address of funeral home, church, or other venue where funeral was to occur
- Date and time of funeral
- Name(s) of officiating clergy
- List of pallbearers
- Date, place, and disposition of remains
- Statement regarding any memorial services
- Directions regarding donations or memorial gifts

I use obituaries as pointers to locate record sources of primary information. I certainly use them to help corroborate other sources of evidence, and to help verify names, dates, and locations of events. They may include the names and locations of other family members at the time of the death, and may identify alternative research paths to get past some of the "dead ends" I may have encountered.

One of my most successful uses of obituaries occurred when researching a great-grandmother. I had tried unsuccessfully for years to trace back and identify her parents. In 1998 I finally visited the town where she lived and was able to access the actual original 1914 newspaper in which her obituary was printed. The obituary included the names of three surviving sisters whose married names I had not known. Two of the three were dead ends, but records for the third sister and her husband were easily located. I transferred my research attention to her and pretty quickly was able to trace her, and then identify and locate the parents in other records. I then used a will to "connect downward" and prove that my great-grandmother was one of their children. Suddenly the doors opened and, within a matter of months, I had fleshed out my great-grandmother's entire family *and* traced my lineage back to a great-great-great-grandfather who had fought in the American Revolution. I obtained copies of his military service and pension records from NARA. (These Revolutionary War military records were all later digitized and made available at Fold3 at **http:// www.fold3.com**.)

Locate and Delve into Cemetery Records

Most people's perception is that a cemetery is a lonely place, devoid of any activity other than the interment of remains and the visits by families and friends. However, if you have ever participated in the process of making arrangements for a family member, spouse or partner, or a friend, you know that there can be a lot of paperwork involved. And where there is paperwork, there are pieces of potentially valuable genealogical evidence. Some of these materials are accessible to you, the researcher, and others are not. However, let's examine the processes involved with handling the death of an individual and the documentation that may have been created.

Cemeteries are much more than graveyards. They are representations in a local area of the society, culture, architecture, and the sense of the community. Many genealogists and family historians arrive at a cemetery, wander around looking for gravestones, copy down the names and dates, perhaps take a few photographs, and then leave, thinking they have found all there is to be found. In many cases, they have merely drifted past what might have been a treasure trove of evidence and clues.

It is important to know that a tombstone or other type of marker isn't necessarily the only record to be found in or associated with a cemetery. You should also recognize that these memorial markers are not necessarily accurate sources of *primary information*. That is because the markers are not always created at or near the time of death, and incorrect information may have been provided and/or inscribed. While a marker may have been placed within a short time of the interment, you cannot always determine if that is the case. In other cases, a marker may have been installed in a place in which the decedent was not interred. These markers are known as *cenotaphs*. Also, understand that the information carved on a tombstone or cast in a metal marker is actually a transcription of data provided, and that one or more errors may have been made. For example, there is a granite marker in an old cemetery in St. Marys, Georgia, on which an incorrect name was carved. Rather than replace the entire stone, the stonecutter used a composite stone paste to fill in the incorrect letter. After the paste set, the correct letter was carved. Unfortunately, the flaw is still visible on the stone (see Figure 7-10). I have seen many "tombstone typos" over the decades.

Someone or some organization owns and/or is responsible for a cemetery. A visit to the local city government office that issues burial permits, to the office that handles land and tax records, or to the closest mortuary can usually provide you with the name of the owner or a contact individual. The next step is to make contact with the person or agency responsible for the maintenance of the cemetery. That may be an administrator or sexton, and this contact may yield important information.

Cemeteries typically consist of lots that are subdivided into plots into which persons' remains are interred. Someone owns the physical lot and has authorized the burials there. If a government is involved, there may have been a burial permit or similar document created to allow a grave to be opened and an individual's remains to be interred. A crematory's information concerning the commitment of the cremains to a columbarium niche may also be included. Other documents may well have been created, and they may have been given to the cemetery administrator or sexton for inclusion in the cemetery's files. Churches with graveyards usually are responsible for

FIGURE 7-10 Grave marker showing a stonecutter's error and correction

the files of information concerning burials there. Making contact with the organization responsible for the cemetery may help you obtain copies of documents that are available nowhere else. Let me give you a few examples.

When I was searching for the burial location of my great-grandparents, Green Berry Holder and his wife, Penelope Swords, I knew from discussions with family members that they were buried in Rome, Georgia, in the Myrtle Hill Cemetery. I contacted the Rome city administrative offices to determine who was responsible for the cemetery's administration and maintenance. I was directed to the Rome Cemetery Department, which is responsible for five municipal cemeteries. I made a call and spoke with the sexton of Myrtle Hill Cemetery. He was able to quickly pull the records for Green Berry Holder while we were on the telephone and told me the following:

- The date of the original purchase of the cemetery lot
- The identification information of the lot (lot number and location)
- The names of each person buried in the lot, their date of death, their ages, and the dates of their interments
- The date on which two plots in the lot were resold to the owner of an adjacent lot

I also asked about a great-uncle, Edward Ernest Holder, whom I believed was also buried in that cemetery. There was, in fact, a joint grave marker for him and his wife, shown in Figure 7-11, although his year of death was missing. I had assumed that

FIGURE 7-11 Grave marker inscribed with the author's great-uncle's name (right) with no death date

he was buried there; however, the sexton told me that only his wife was interred in this cemetery. It turned out that my Great-Uncle Ed actually was buried in another municipal cemetery on the other side of town beside another woman, Vita Fulcher Holder. (See Figure 7-12.) I learned that he had a *second* marriage about which neither I nor anyone else in the family was aware.

Based on the information the sexton was able to provide, I had much better details to research my family members interred in both of the cemeteries. I also had information about dates of death that I took to the Floyd County Health Department. There I was able to obtain copies of all the death certificates. I also headed to the county courthouse for a marriage record for my Great-Uncle Ed's second marriage and to the library to work with microfilmed newspapers, looking for marriage announcements and obituaries. Had I located the obituary of the great-uncle earlier, I would have known he was buried in the other cemetery *and* that his second wife survived him.

These clues led me to others, including the name of the current owner of the local funeral home that handled most of the family members' funerals over the decades, to church records in multiple congregations, to land and property records, to wills and estate probate files, and more.

An on-site visit to the cemetery sexton's office also provided me the opportunity to see the physical files maintained there. My great-grandmother, Penelope Swords Holder, died prior to Georgia's requirement that counties issue death certificates. However, there were copies of a burial permit, and a note to the sexton from my great-grandfather asking that my great-grandmother be buried in a specific plot adjacent to one of their grandchildren. In addition, the sexton checked an ancient interment ledger and found recorded there the cause of her death—pneumonia. This was important because, in the absence of a death certificate, the entry confirmed the family account of the cause of her death.

FIGURE 7-12   Gravestones for the author's same great-uncle (left) and his second wife, Vita Fulcher Holder (right), in Eastview Cemetery in Rome, Georgia.

There are other documents that you may find in a cemetery's office. These include requests for burial, such as the one shown in Figure 7-13, and requests to open a grave, such as the one shown in Figure 7-14. A permit, such as the one shown in Figure 7-15, is often required in order to control and keep track of the movement of the remains, and a burial permit is often another source of local tax revenue.

Transit permits are used to facilitate the movement of human remains from one political jurisdiction to another. Two examples are shown in Figures 7-16 and 7-17. These documents are usually completed in multiple copies. The original document accompanies the body to the place of final interment; the issuing governmental office retains another copy (or coupon); and other copies may be provided to the transportation carrier(s) en route. A transit permit may contain a significant amount of information about the deceased, including the age, address, cause of death, the names of the physician and coroner, the name of the undertaker, and the mode of transportation.

Some transit permit formats provided very little information. Transit permits were used when shipping bodies of soldiers back home from other locations, and a copy may be found in the mortuary records, in cemetery files, and in surviving military personnel files.

The Mount Sinai Hospital.

New York, July 27 - 03

Sir:

You will please bury the Corpse of

NAME	AGE	OCCUPATION, &c.	DISEASE	DIED
Malie Schmer	9 y.	Schoolgirl	Endocarditis Pericarditis	July 25/1903

Grave No 162 Sect. X Resident.

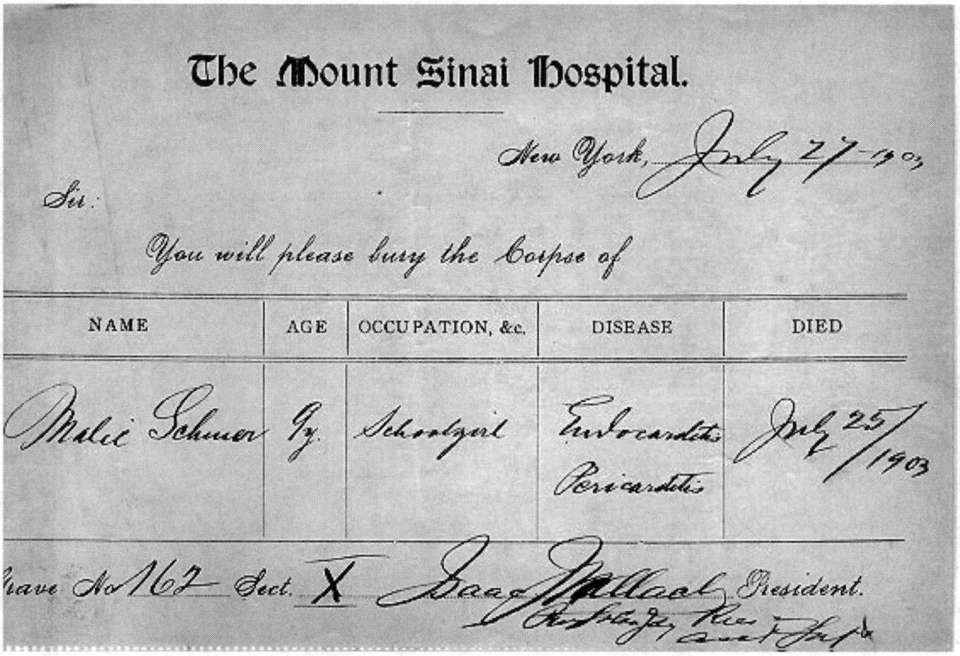

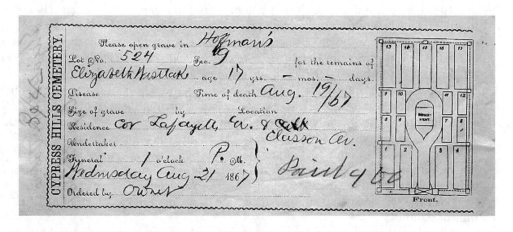

FIGURE 7-13 A request for burial found in a cemetery file

CYPRESS HILLS CEMETERY.

Please open grave in Hoffman's

Lot No. 524 Sec. 9 for the remains of

Elizabeth Mostak age 17 yrs. — mos. — days.

Disease Time of death Aug. 19/67

Size of grave by Location

Residence Cor Lafayette Av. & Classon Av.

Undertaker

Funeral 1 o'clock P. M.

Wednesday Aug 21 1867

Ordered by Owner

Paid 4.00

Front.

FIGURE 7-14 A cemetery's form requesting the opening of a grave

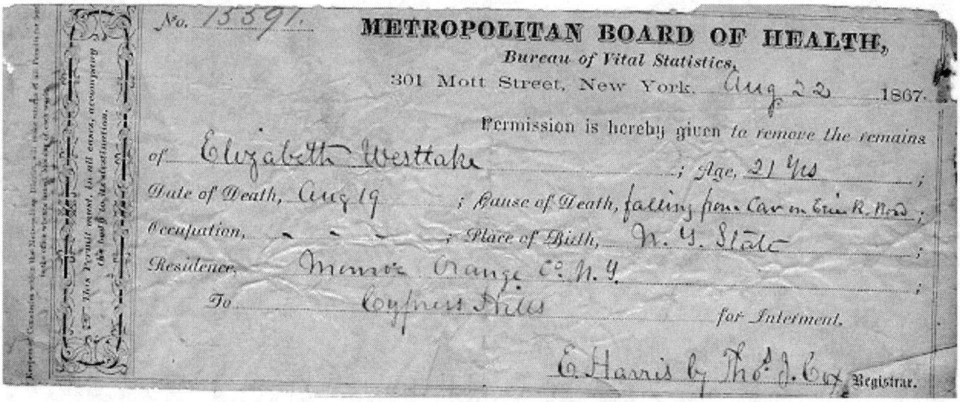

No. 15591.
METROPOLITAN BOARD OF HEALTH,
Bureau of Vital Statistics,
301 Mott Street, New York, Aug 22 1867.
Permission is hereby given *to remove the remains*
of Elizabeth Westtake ; *Age,* 21 Yrs ;
Date of Death, Aug 19 ; *Cause of Death,* falling from Car on Erie R. Road ;
Occupation, — ; *Place of Birth,* N. Y. State ;
Residence Monroe Orange Co. N. Y. ;
To Cypress Hills *for Interment.*
E. Harris by Thos J. Cox Registrar.

FIGURE 7-15 A permit allowing removal of remains from New York, 1867

Search for burial and transit permit records in the county or municipal district in which the death occurred. Depending on the location, they may or may not have survived in the issuing governmental office.

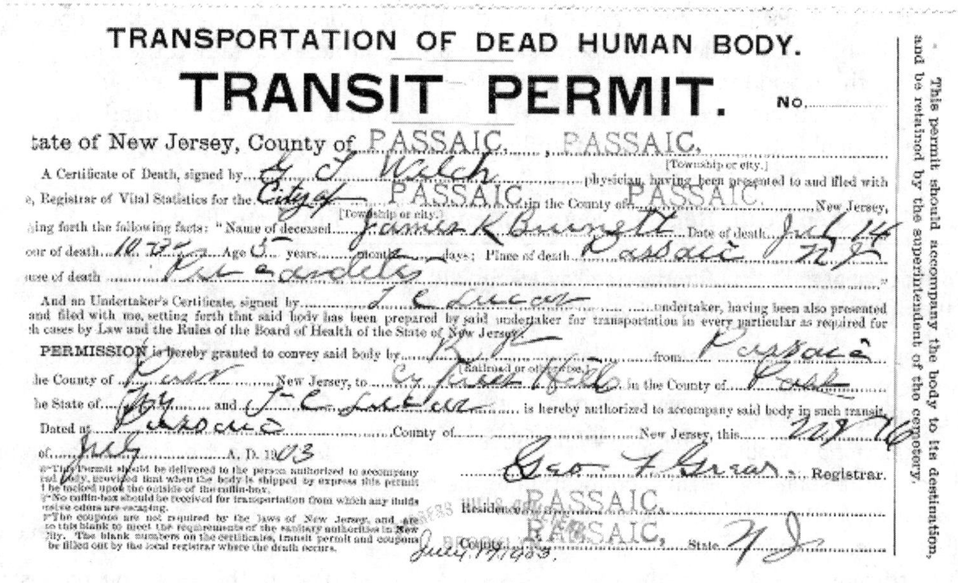

TRANSPORTATION OF DEAD HUMAN BODY.
TRANSIT PERMIT. NO.
State of New Jersey, County of PASSAIC, PASSAIC. [Township or city.]
A Certificate of Death, signed by G. T. Welch physician, having been presented to and filed with the Registrar of Vital Statistics for the City of PASSAIC [Township or city.] in the County of PASSAIC, New Jersey, setting forth the following facts: "Name of deceased James K Burnett Date of death Jul 14
Hour of death 10 Age 5 years months days; Place of death Passaic N. J.
Cause of death ..."
And an Undertaker's Certificate, signed by ... undertaker, having been also presented and filed with me, setting forth that said body has been prepared by said undertaker for transportation in every particular as required for such cases by Law and the Rules of the Board of Health of the State of New Jersey.
PERMISSION is hereby granted to convey said body by ... [Railroad or otherwise.] from Passaic
the County of Passaic New Jersey, to Cypress Hill in the County of ...
the State of N.Y. and ... is hereby authorized to accompany said body in such transit.
Dated at Passaic County of ... New Jersey, this ...
of July A. D. 1903
Geo. F. Grear Registrar.
This Permit should be delivered to the person authorized to accompany the body, provided that when the body is shipped by express this permit be tacked upon the outside of the coffin-box.
No coffin-box should be received for transportation from which any fluids or offensive odors are escaping.
The coupons are not required by the laws of New Jersey, and are attached to this blank to meet the requirements of the sanitary authorities in New York City. The blank numbers on the certificate, transit permit and coupons to be filled out by the local registrar where the death occurs.
Residence PASSAIC
County PASSAIC, State N. J.
July 17 1903.
This permit should accompany the body to its destination, and be retained by the superintendent of the cemetery.

FIGURE 7-16 This 1903 transit permit contains many details that can be investigated.

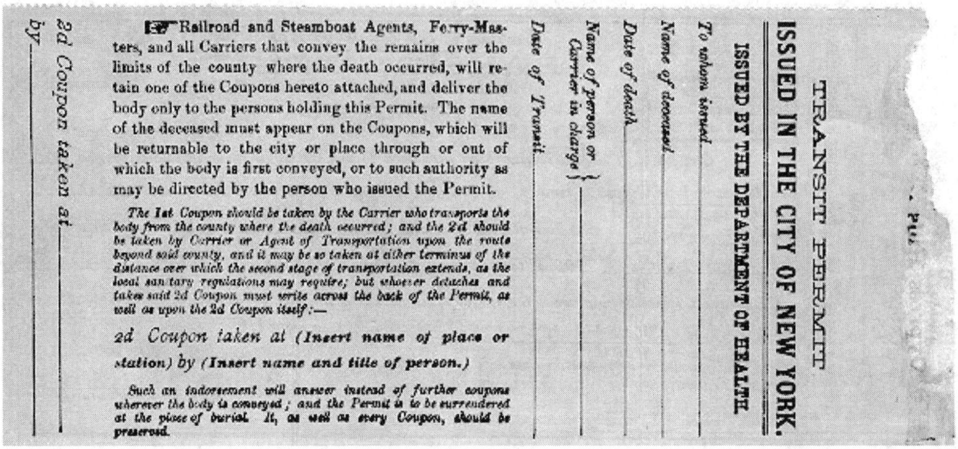
TRANSIT PERMIT

ISSUED IN THE CITY OF NEW YORK.

ISSUED BY THE DEPARTMENT OF HEALTH.

To whom issued __________

Name of deceased __________

Date of death __________

Name of person or Carrier in charge __________

Date of Transit __________

☞ Railroad and Steamboat Agents, Ferry-Masters, and all Carriers that convey the remains over the limits of the county where the death occurred, will retain one of the Coupons hereto attached, and deliver the body only to the persons holding this Permit. The name of the deceased must appear on the Coupons, which will be returnable to the city or place through or out of which the body is first conveyed, or to such authority as may be directed by the person who issued the Permit.

The 1st Coupon should be taken by the Carrier who transports the body from the county where the death occurred; and the 2d should be taken by Carrier or Agent of Transportation upon the route beyond said county, and it may be so taken at either terminus of the distance over which the second stage of transportation extends, as the local sanitary regulations may require; but whoever detaches and takes said 2d Coupon must write across the back of the Permit, as well as upon the 2d Coupon itself:—

2d Coupon taken at **(Insert name of place or station)** *by* **(Insert name and title of person.)**

Such an indorsement will answer instead of further coupons wherever the body is conveyed; and the Permit is to be surrendered at the place of burial. It, as well as every Coupon, should be preserved.

2d Coupon taken at __________

by __________

FIGURE 7-17 This City of New York transit permit includes less information, but can still provide clues to locating a death certificate and other records.

Search for Other Death-Related Documents

Death certificates, obituaries, and burial permits are not the only documents relating to death that you may locate that contain genealogical information. Nor are mortuaries, funeral homes, crematoria, and cemeteries the only places to look for these documents.

Table 7-1 includes a number of important documents, data that they may contain, and where you may search for them.

You can now see that there may be many records related to the death of an individual and these should certainly be considered as resources to be explored.

TABLE 7-1 Other Death-Related Documents and Where to Locate Them

Type of Document and Description of Its Use	Information You Likely Will Find in the Document	Where You Are Likely to Locate the Document
Death Certificate—Used to document a death. It is an excellent source for *primary information* about the death, but a source of *secondary information* for all other information. Death certificates may not exist in many places prior to 1900. Consult *The Family Tree Sourcebook* for specifics in the U.S.	Date and place of death Name of mortuary or funeral home handling body Name and location of the place of interment	County department of health County courthouse Government offices of health or vital statistics Mortuary or funeral home records Files of the cemetery administrator or sexton

TABLE 7-1   Other Death-Related Documents and Where to Locate Them

Type of Document and Description of Its Use	Information You Likely Will Find in the Document	Where You Are Likely to Locate the Document
Coroner's Report—Used to document cases of unusual, suspicious, or accidental death.	Date and place of death Cause of death Name of mortuary or funeral home handling the body Name(s) of investigating official(s) Final determination	Office of the coroner or medical examiner Courthouse with jurisdiction over location of death at the time Probate court records Other court records
Transit Permit—Used to document the movement of the deceased's remains from one political jurisdiction to another, i.e., state to state or country to country.	Date and place of death Cause of death Sometimes includes the address and age of the decedent Name and location of the originating mortuary or funeral home Name and location of the destination mortuary or funeral home Sometimes includes the name and location of the place of interment	Government office of the place of origin of the body's departure County department of health County courthouse State department of health or vital statistics Mortuary or funeral home records Files of the cemetery administrator or sexton
Burial Permit—Used to record the opening of a grave and allow the interment of remains. This may be issued by the governmental entity that had ownership and administrative control of the cemetery.	Name of the deceased Date and place of death Name of cemetery Interment location (lot and plot identity, tomb or mausoleum identity, or columbarium identity) Scheduled date of interment Name and location of mortuary or funeral home Sometimes includes name of the person or company authorized to open and close the grave Authorizing agency, signature, and date of issue	Issuing agency, usually the owner or administrator of a municipal-, county-, state-, or federal-owned/operated cemetery Files of the mortuary or funeral home Files of the cemetery administrator or sexton for the cemetery For military service personnel, may find a permit for a burial in a military cemetery in the individual's military personnel file

(Continued)

TABLE 7-1   Other Death-Related Documents and Where to Locate Them

Type of Document and Description of Its Use	Information You Likely Will Find in the Document	Where You Are Likely to Locate the Document
Interment Ledger—Used in some cemeteries in older times to record interments.	Name of the deceased Date of death Sometimes includes the cause of death and location Location of interment in the cemetery Date of interment	Office of the cemetery administrator or sexton for the cemetery
Cemetery Lot Deed or Land Title—Used to record the sale of a cemetery lot and sometimes the sale of individual plots.	Name of purchaser Name of seller Date of the sale Location and description of the lot (or plot) Amount paid for the parcel	Office of the cemetery administrator or sexton for the cemetery May also be recorded in county clerk's office along with other property records May find a copy in the files of the mortuary or funeral home that handled the arrangements, particularly if this was the first interment in the lot
Obituary—Used to publicly announce a death, location, and date(s) of arrangements.	Name of deceased Date and location of death Extensive or abbreviated information about the person's life, survivors, and other personal information Date and location of funeral or other services Location of interment	Newspapers, church bulletins and newsletters (local and regional), union and fraternal organization publications, professional publications Libraries and archives with microfilmed holdings of the above publications Internet-based obituary transcriptions

TABLE 7-1 Other Death-Related Documents and Where to Locate Them

Type of Document and Description of Its Use	Information You Likely Will Find in the Document	Where You Are Likely to Locate the Document
Public Notices—Used to advertise a death, and both to announce the collection of debts for the estate and to request presentation of claims.	Name of deceased Date of death and residence Name of administrator Sometimes includes place of death and place of interment if different from place of residence	Newspapers Libraries and archives with microfilmed holdings of the newspapers Estate and probate packets Probate court minutes
Cemetery Canvasses and Gravestone Transcription Projects—Compilations and publications to record the interments in a cemetery or other place of interment for posterity.	Any information inscribed or cast onto a tombstone or other grave marker May or may not be all-inclusive, including epitaph May or may not include photographs May or may not be published	Genealogical societies in the area and at the state level Historical societies in the area and at the state level Libraries and archives Genealogy society periodicals, which can be located using the Periodical Source Index (PERSI) online at **http://www.findmypast.com** and in HeritageQuest Online and can be ordered from genealogical libraries using interlibrary loan
County and Local Histories—Used to record information of historical significance in a specific geographical area.	May contain a variety of information about individuals, families, ethnic groups, and other facts to help you locate religious, public, private, and family places of interment.	Genealogical societies in the area and at the state level Historical societies in the area and at the state level Libraries and archives
Military Histories and Regimental Histories—Used to record information of historical significance relating to a specific military event or military unit.	May contain a variety of information about individuals serving in the military, their families, ethnic groups, and other facts to help you locate religious, public, private, family, and military places of interment.	Genealogical societies in the area and at the state level Historical societies in the area and at the state level Libraries and archives

(Continued)

TABLE 7-1 Other Death-Related Documents and Where to Locate Them

Type of Document and Description of Its Use	Information You Likely Will Find in the Document	Where You Are Likely to Locate the Document
Military Service Papers—Used to document the military service and pension information for an individual.	May contain a variety of information about an individual and his or her military service. May also include information about death benefits paid and interment in a military cemetery in the U.S. or abroad.	Military service and pension files (different locations) American Battle Monuments Commission website (for WWI, WWII, Korean War, and Vietnam War) at **http://www.abmc.gov** Fold3.com (**http://www.fold3.com**)
Funeral or Condolence Books—Provided by the mortuary or funeral home to allow persons visiting the family of the deceased to sign their name and write a message.	May contain a variety of information, but also may specify date and location of interment.	Home sources/family effects
Websites—Many websites contain information related to places of interment.	The Internet contains a wealth of information concerning deaths and interments, and using a search engine can be of some assistance.	Ancestry.com databases **http://www.ancestry.com** BillionGraves **http://billiongraves.com** FamilySearch **https://familysearch.org** Find A Grave **http://www.findagrave.com** Fold3.com **http://www.fold3.com** MyHeritage **http://www.myheritage.com** RootsWeb databases **http://www.rootsweb.ancestry.com** USGenWeb Project **http://www.usgenweb.org** WorldGenWeb Project **http://www.worldgenweb.org** Historical newspaper databases available through libraries

Get Inside Your Ancestor's Mind Using Wills and Probate Records

Wills and probate packets can be extremely interesting and revealing collections of records. A person's last will may be one of the most honest statements about his or her relationships with other family members and friends. The probate packet's contents may also provide detailed information and insights into the person that you may never find anywhere else.

Understand the Meaning of a Will and Testament

Let's first discuss some of the terminology that you are likely to encounter. A *will* is a legal document in which a person specifies the disposition of his or her property after death. The person who makes the will is called the *testator*, and the will may also be referred to as the *last will and testament*. You may encounter the term *testatrix* in older wills, which indicates that the person who created the will was a female.

At the time a testator dies, he or she is referred to as the *decedent* or the *deceased*. The process of proving a will's authenticity or validity is called *probate*, taken from the Latin word *probatim* or *probare*, which means, "to examine." The legal body responsible for reviewing and examining materials related to the handling of an estate in the United States is the *probate court*. In England and Wales, the body responsible was the *prerogative court* prior to 1857, the Court of Probate between 1857 and 1875, and, after 1875, the High Court of Justice (originally, the Probate, Divorce and Admiralty Division, and now the Family Division). In Scotland, the probate process is called *confirmation*. In the United States, you might engage a *lawyer* (or *attorney*) to assist with the probate process, while in England, Wales, Scotland, Ireland, and some other places the person is referred to as a *solicitor*.

The person appointed by a court to oversee or administer the affairs of the estate during the probate process is known as the *executor*. In older times, the term *executrix* was used to indicate that an executor was a female. Alternatively or in conjunction with an executor, one or more *administrators* may be appointed.

Persons or entities owing money or other assets to the deceased person's estate are generally referred to as *debtors*, while persons or entities to which the estate owes money or other assets are referred to as *creditors*.

Depending on the size of the estate and/or the amount of detail to which the testator went, a will may be a short document or a lengthy one. A will does not need to be drawn up by a lawyer or solicitor; an individual may write his or her own. The term *holographic will* is used to designate a will that has been entirely handwritten and signed by the testator. This is considered a legal document so long as the testator signs it. Usually, however, it is advisable to have two or more witnesses to the signing of the document. This makes the probate process, or the proving of the will, simpler because it assures that the signature or mark of the testator is genuine.

If the testator decides to change the will after it is made and signed, a new will can be drawn up, signed, and witnessed. Sometimes, if there are minor changes or if there is an expedient required, a *codicil* can be drafted and signed. A codicil is simply a supplement to a will, usually containing an addition or modification to the original will. A codicil is often created in cases when there is a need to make immediate changes before a new will can be drawn up.

Understand the Probate Process

Roman law significantly influenced legal processes throughout Europe, and particularly in Britain. Furthermore, Medieval English law and legal customs influenced laws in the United States, Canada, and Australia. The terms "will" and "testament" originally referred to separate portions of an individual's estate, and the documents were usually separate documents handled by separate courts. A "will" was originally used to dispose of one's real property, or real estate, and the "testament" was used to bequeath personal property.

A study of history in England and Wales reveals that, from the 13th century until 1857 (with the exception of the period of the Interregnum, 1649 to 1660), ecclesiastical courts handled the probate process. These courts usually dealt only with nobility and wealthy landowners, while the landholder handled matters concerning his tenants.

Over time, the testator's will and testament documents evolved into a single instrument, the "last will and testament," and this practice spread to other places. The courts used to probate of an estate also significantly changed over time from ecclesiastical courts to civil government courts. The Court of Probate Act of 1857 established a civil court, the Principal Probate Registry (**https://www.gov.uk/ wills-probate-inheritance**), which was formally established on 11 January 1858. A Principal Registry, which under the Matrimonial Causes Act 1857, also served as the Court for Divorce and Matrimonial Causes. It was attached to the Court of Probate in London, together with a number of District Registries throughout England and Wales.

If you are researching wills and probate in Britain and Ireland, an understanding of the history of the process, the courts, their jurisdictions, and the documents' contents in England, Wales, Scotland, and Ireland is essential.

Probate law in the United States, Canada, Australia, and certain other countries is based on the English model. In the United States, though, the use of the singular last will and testament document is generally found to be the historical norm. This is the type of probate process we will explore in this section. Of course, there are exceptions and special circumstances as with any legal documentary process. However, in the interest of clarifying the probate process, let's focus on a rather straightforward definition.

A person's last will and testament is intended to express his or her wishes for what is to be done with his or her body and possessions after death, as illustrated in the case of Isaac Mitchell, whose will is shown in Figures 7-18 and 7-19. In cases where the testator had strong religious beliefs, there may be heavy religious overtones to the document. A person's will typically includes instructions concerning the disposition of the body, funeral directions, and/or memorial instructions. A will may be revoked through the creation of a new will, through creation of a codicil, or by destruction of the will itself. As mentioned earlier, a codicil can be used to revoke and/or amend specific sections of a will without the person having to write an entirely new will. It can be used to append additional, supplemental instructions to an existing will. In all cases, however, the testator must sign the will or codicil, and the signing of the document should be witnessed by at least two other persons. Witnesses' signatures provide the court with a way to confirm the veracity of the testator's signature. A notary public, or some other official who legally attests to a signature, can sometimes serve as a witness to the document, especially in modern times.

The probate process is a legal procedure intended to certify that a person's estate is properly disposed of, and the process has changed very little over the past centuries. Where there is a will and it is presented to a court to be proved, there is usually an orderly procedure that takes place. In cases where a person dies without having written or left a will, also known as dying *intestate*, a court may become involved in making sure that the person's estate is correctly valued, divided, and distributed to appropriate beneficiaries.

While there may be some special conditions of a will or codicil that add additional steps to the process, here's how a simple probate process works:

1. The testator makes his/her will and any subsequent codicil(s).
2. The testator dies.
3. Someone acting on the testator's behalf presents the will/codicil(s) to a special court of law dedicated to the probate process. The court and its judge or magistrate are concerned with the body of law devoted to processing estates. (Minutes and notes concerning the estate and any probate court proceedings related to the estate are recorded throughout the process and should never be overlooked in your research of the estate.)
4. The will/codicil(s) is/are recorded by the court. The persons who witnessed the testator's signature are called upon to testify or attest to, in person or by sworn affidavit, that they witnessed the actual signature to the document(s). This is part of the "proving" of the will—that it is the authentic document on which the testator signed his/her name.
5. The court assigns an identifying code, usually a number, to the estate and enters it into the court's records. A probate packet is created for the court into which all documents pertaining to the settlement of the estate are placed.
6. If the will or codicil(s) named one or more persons to act as the executor and/or administrator of the estate, the court issues what is referred to in the United States as "letters testamentary" and in Britain and other countries as "grant of representation." If the person designated by the testator as executor cannot or will not serve, the court designates/assigns one or more other persons to act in that capacity. This document identifies the person(s) as authorized agents of the court to act on behalf of the estate in conducting business related to settling all claims.
7. Potential beneficiaries named in the will/codicil(s) are identified and contacted. If any are deceased, evidence to that effect is obtained and, if the testator's intent expressed in the will indicates that others besides the deceased beneficiaries are to benefit from the estate instead, they are identified and contacted.

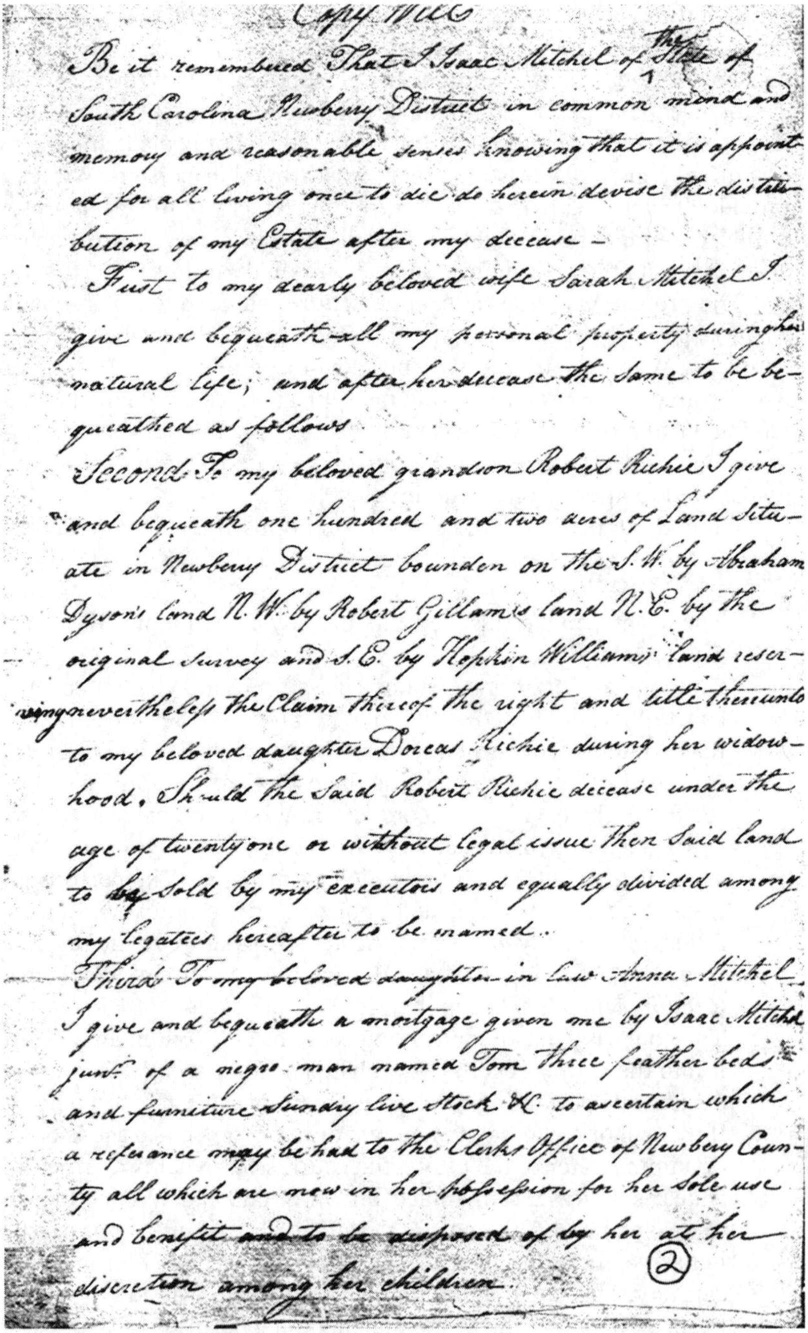

Copy Will
Be it remembered That I Isaac Mitchel of the State of
South Carolina Newberry District in common mind and
memory and reasonable senses knowing that it is appoint
ed for all living once to die do herein devise the distribution of my Estate after my decease –
First to my dearly beloved wife Sarah Mitchel I
give and bequeath all my personal property during her
natural life; and after her decease the same to be bequeathed as follows
Second To my beloved grandson Robert Richie I give
and bequeath one hundred and two acres of Land Situate in Newberry District bounded on the S.W. by Abraham
Dyson's land N.W. by Robert Gillam's land N.E. by the
original survey and S.E. by Hopkin Williams land reserving nevertheless the Claim thereof the right and title thereunto
to my beloved daughter Dorcas Richie during her widow-
hood. Should the Said Robert Richie decease under the
age of twentyone or without legal issue then Said land
to be Sold by my executors and equally divided among
my legatees hereafter to be named.
Third To my beloved daughter in law Anna Mitchel
I give and bequeath a mortgage given me by Isaac Mitchel
junr. of a negro man named Tom three feather beds
and furniture Sundry live Stock &c. to ascertain which
a referance may be had to the Clerks Office of Newberry County all which are now in her possession for her Sole use
and benefit and to be disposed of by her at her
discretion among her children.
(2)

FIGURE 7-18 Page 1 of the will of Isaac Mitchell of Newberry District, South Carolina, taken from the copy transcribed into the county will book

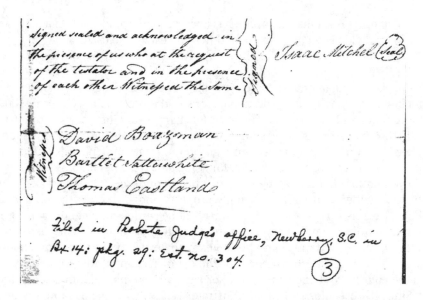

FIGURE 7-19   Page 2 of the will of Isaac Mitchell of Newberry District, South Carolina, showing the signature area with the testator's signature, the signatures of the witnesses, and the probate clerk's filing reference details

8. The executor and/or administrator publishes a series of notices, usually in newspapers circulated in the area where the testator lived, concerning the estate. Persons having claims on or owing obligations to the estate are thereby given notice that they have a specified amount of time to respond.

9. The executor and/or administrator conducts an inventory of the estate and prepares a written list of all assets, including personal property, real estate, financial items (cash, investments, loans, and other instruments), intellectual property, copyrights or patents, and any other materials that might be a part of the estate.

10. The executor and/or administrator will settle any debts, outstanding claims, or obligations of the estate, and then prepares an adjusted inventory of the deceased's assets. This document, along with any supporting materials, is submitted to the probate court and becomes a permanent part of the probate packet or a state packet/file.

11. The court clerk reviews all the documentation for completeness and submits it to the probate judge for review. The probate court rules that the estate is now ready for distribution to beneficiaries.

12. Inheritance taxes and other death duties are paid.

13. The estate is divided and distributed and, in some cases, beneficiaries are required to sign a document confirming their receipt of their legacies.

14. Following the distribution, the executor and/or administrator prepares a final statement of account and presents it to the court.

15. The court rules that the estate has been properly processed, that all assets have been divided and distributed, and that the estate is closed.
16. The probate packet is filed in the records of the probate court.

Special arrangements specified in wills and codicils, such as trusts and long-term bequests, may require additional steps in the process. In some cases, the final settlement of an estate may be deferred for many years until certain conditions are satisfied. A *trust*, for instance, sometimes called a *testamentary trust*, may require the establishment of a separate legal entity, and the estate may not be settled until a later date. A trust may be used to provide for some surviving beneficiary, such as a widow/widower, minor children, aging parents, or someone else. Some testators leave wills that skip a generation, perhaps leaving property and/or monies to grandchildren, in which case a trust is established that may not be settled for a generation (or more) and may require extended administration and management. In the case of any estate whose settlement extends to multiple years, the executor and/or administrator must prepare annual accounting reports for the court. Receipt of these reports is entered into the court record and copies of reports usually are placed into the probate file.

Since the executor and/or administrator typically publishes more notices in the press as a public notice that all claims against the deceased's estate should be presented and all debts owed to the estate are to be presented by a specific date, you will be looking in the local newspapers and other publications about the area in addition to court minutes and files.

Learn What a Will Can Tell You—Literally and by Implication

Some of the most interesting insights into an individual's personality and his or her relationships with other family members can be found by looking at probate records. A wife may have been provided for through a trust. It is not unusual in older wills to see a bequest such as, "To my beloved wife, Elizabeth, I leave her the house for her use for her lifetime, after which it is to be sold and proceeds divided between my children." One of the most detailed bequests I've seen stated, "I leave my wife, Addie, the bed, her clothes, the ax, the stove, and the mule." You may think he was being stingy, but his bequest may have been quite generous, depending on the time period. In the mid-19th century, from when this testator's will dates, the wife was entitled to live in the house for the remainder of her life unless she remarried, and so her residence was protected. The law also dictated that the man owned all the personal property. The bed may have been the most valuable piece of furniture in their possession and so was a generous bequest. By specifying her clothes, he guaranteed that she would retain ownership of those and that those would not be liquidated. The ax was important so that she could chop firewood for the stove, and therefore heat the house and cook her food. The mule provided her with help in cultivating the land and a form of transportation. You can see why it is important to consider the contents of a last will and testament in the context of the place and time.

Farther back in time and in different places, you may find that laws sometimes dictated that the eldest son inherited all of the estate, a custom known as the *law of primogeniture*. Sometimes the eldest son is not listed in the will at all because this law dictated that all real property automatically came to him. In other cases, the eldest son may be named and may be given a double share of the otherwise equally divided estate. In some cases, the testator may apply the rule of primogeniture in order to accomplish some goal, such as keeping an estate from being divided. *Ultimogeniture*, also known as *postremogeniture* or junior right, is the tradition of bestowing inheritance to the last-born. Ultimogeniture is much less common than primogeniture.

You will often see a father leave his daughter's share of his estate to her husband. Why? Often it was because a woman was not allowed to own real property or because it was felt that she could not manage the affairs of the bequest. Sometimes, because a father may have settled a dowry on his daughter when she married, the father's bequest may be a smaller one than to other, unmarried sisters, or even nonexistent. This may be done in order to make them equal in their overall share of the father's estate, regardless of the time when they may have received some gift or bequest.

A father who did not possess a large estate may have made arrangements for the placement of a son as an apprentice or indentured servant. This was a common means of guaranteeing the care and education of a son when there would not have been enough from the estate to support him. If you find such a statement in a will, investigate court records for the formalization of the arrangement. The guardian became responsible by law for the apprentice or servant. In addition, you may find documents related to apprenticeship or indenture among the property records of the county. These are typically indexed by grantor (seller) and grantee (buyer or recipient), and so a search of the father's name as a grantor may make locating copies of these contractual documents comparatively simple.

The absence of a specific child's name in a will may or may not indicate that he or she died before the testator. The omission may indicate that the child had moved elsewhere and had not been heard from for some considerable time. It might also indicate some estrangement, especially if you can determine that the child was, in fact, still alive at the time of the death. Otherwise, it is more likely that the testator would leave an equal part to that child and the court would probably have charged the executor with locating the child. You should investigate each of these possibilities.

It also is possible that, before a will was prepared and signed, an individual may have personally prepared an inventory of his or her possessions or may have engaged the services of an appraiser. Such an inventory could help determine the value of items of real and personal property and therefore facilitate the decisions concerning how to divide them in an equitable fashion.

Examine the Contents of a Probate Packet

You may be amazed at what is or isn't in a probate packet. Some courts are meticulous in their maintenance of the packets, in which case you may find vast numbers of diverse documents. Other courts are less thorough, and documents may have been misplaced, incorrectly filed, lost, or even destroyed. It is important when examining probate packets and related files to also review probate court minute books for details. (I once found a missing document from one ancestor's probate packet filed in the packet of another person's packet whose estate was heard the same day in court. It had been misfiled.) The most common items found in a probate packet are the following:

- **Will** These documents are the core of a probate packet and include names of heirs and beneficiaries, and often the relationship to the deceased. Married names of daughters are great clues to tracing lines of descent, and names of other siblings might be located only in these documents.
- **Codicil** Look for these amendments to a will as part of the probate packet. They also are noted in the minutes of the probate court, along with the judge's ruling on the validity of the will and the changes included in the codicil. Figure 7-20 shows the first codicil to the will of John Smith of Chelsea, London, making an additional bequest of £1,000 to a neighbor, revoking the bequest of an automobile to his grandson, and calling for the sale of the car and the distribution of the proceeds to a daughter.
- **Letters testamentary** Look for a copy of the letters testamentary or letters of administration document in the probate packet. If it isn't there, look in court records. The name(s) of the executor/executrix and/or administrator may well be different from the person named in the will. You will want to determine the actual person(s) and their relationship (if any) to the deceased. It may be important to know if and why the named executor did not serve. Was the person deceased or

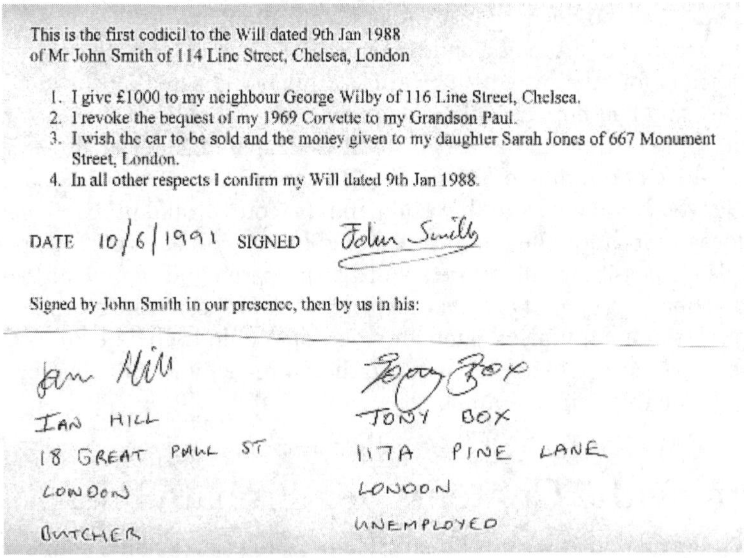

This is the first codicil to the Will dated 9th Jan 1988
of Mr John Smith of 114 Line Street, Chelsea, London

1. I give £1000 to my neighbour George Wilby of 116 Line Street, Chelsea.
2. I revoke the bequest of my 1969 Corvette to my Grandson Paul.
3. I wish the car to be sold and the money given to my daughter Sarah Jones of 667 Monument Street, London.
4. In all other respects I confirm my Will dated 9th Jan 1988.

DATE 10/6/1991 SIGNED *John Smith*

Signed by John Smith in our presence, then by us in his:

IAN HILL
18 GREAT PAUL ST
LONDON
BUTCHER

TONY BOX
117A PINE LANE
LONDON
UNEMPLOYED

FIGURE 7-20 Codicil of John Smith

did he or she decline to serve? Entries in the probate court minutes may answer these questions.

- **Inventory or appraisal of the estate**   The inventory reveals the financial state of the deceased, and this is a good indicator of his/her social status. The inventory of personal property, such as the example shown in Figure 7-21, provides indicators to the person's lifestyle. The presence of farm equipment and livestock may indicate the person was a farmer; an anvil and metal stock might point to blacksmithing as a profession; hammers, chisels, nails, a level, and other tools may reveal carpentry. In an 18th-century estate inventory, the presence of books indicates education and literacy, and the possession of a great deal of clothing and shoes indicates an elevated social position. The inclusion of slaves, as shown in the inventory in Figure 7-22, is indicative of a position of some wealth. This document provides priceless information for someone who is researching African American ancestry. There are many indicators that may direct you to other types of records. You may even find items listed in an estate inventory that confirm family stories, such as military medals, tools of a trade, jewelry, and other artifacts.

- **List of beneficiaries**   A list of persons named may differ from the list of names in the will. Beneficiaries may be deceased, they may have married and changed names, they may not be locatable, their descendants or spouses may become inheritors, and so on. This list will tell you much about the family.

- **Records of an auction**   Sometimes all or part of an estate was auctioned. Sometimes assets were liquidated to pay bills or to raise money for the surviving family. Auction records reveal much about estate contents and their value. It was common for relatives to participate as bidders/purchasers at an estate auction, and you may find people with the same surname (or maiden name) as the deceased. These may be parents, siblings, or cousins you will want to research.

- **Deeds, notes, bills, invoices, and receipts**   There may be a variety of loose papers in the probate packet that point to other persons. Deed copies point you to land and property records and tax rolls. Names appearing on other papers may connect you to relatives, neighbors, friends, and business associates whose records may open doors for you.

- **Guardianship documents**   Letters and other documents relating to the guardianship and/or custody of widows and minor children are common in probate packets and/or in probate minute books. There may be nothing found in earlier family court documents, and the information in probate court files may be the only documentation of the legal appointment of guardian(s). Figure 7-23 shows a petition for the appointment of a guardian for minor children, and Figure 7-24 shows a combination petition for and granting of guardianship from probate court records in 1911.

- **Accounting reports**   Reports filed with the probate records can provide names of claimants and entities holding estate debts, including names of relatives.

- **Final disposition or distribution of the estate**   A final estate distribution report is of vital importance. You may find the names and addresses of all the beneficiaries, what they received from the estate, and signed documents confirming their receipt. This will ultimately point you to the locations where you will find other records for these persons.

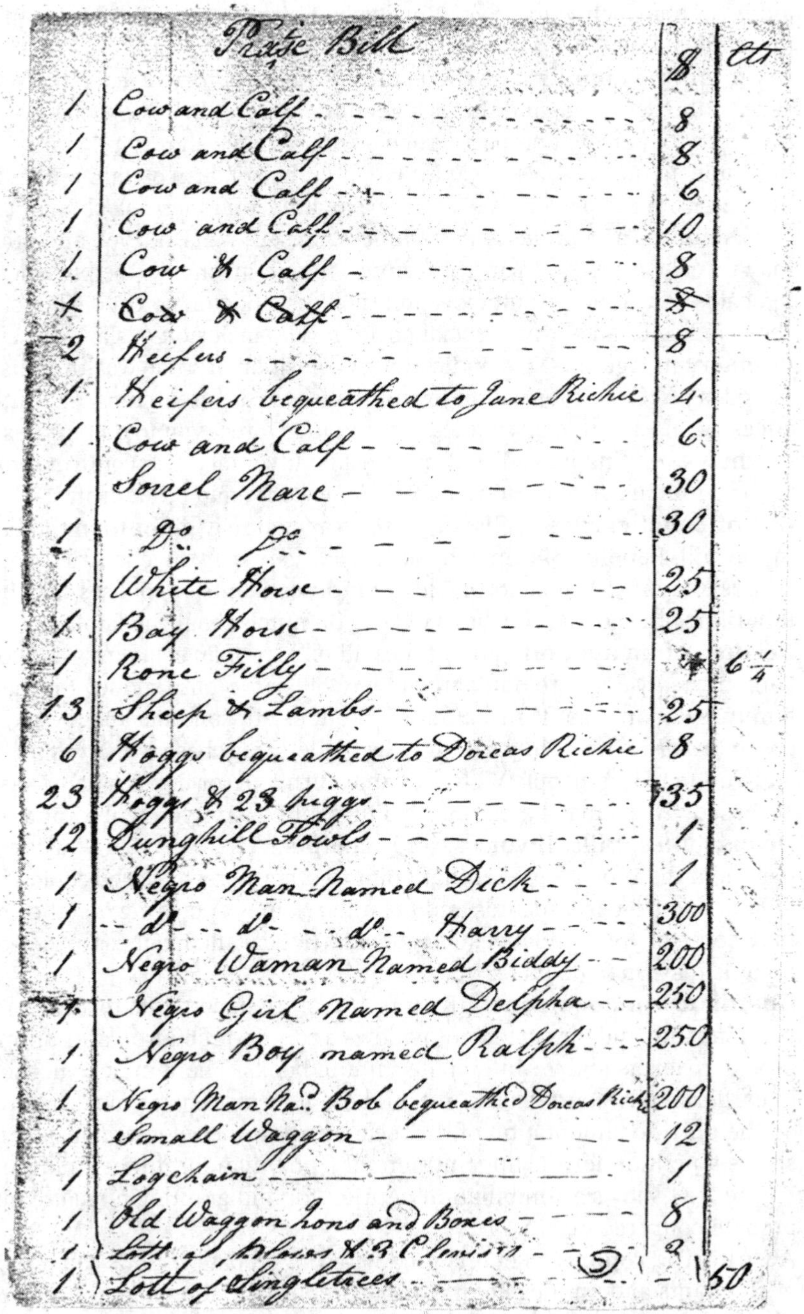

Prise Bill

		$	cts
1	Cow and Calf	8	
1	Cow and Calf	8	
1	Cow and Calf	6	
1	Cow and Calf	10	
1	Cow & Calf	8	
1	Cow & Calf	8	
2	Heifers	8	
1	Heifers bequeathed to Jane Richie	4	
1	Cow and Calf	6	
1	Sorrel Mare	30	
1	Do Do	30	
1	White Horse	25	
1	Bay Horse	25	
1	Rone Filly		6¼
13	Sheep & Lambs	25	
6	Hoggs bequeathed to Dorcas Richie	8	
23	Hoggs & 23 piggs	35	
12	Dunghill Fowls	1	
1	Negro Man Named Dick	1	
1	do do do Harry	300	
1	Negro Woman Named Biddy	200	
1	Negro Girl named Delpha	250	
1	Negro Boy named Ralph	250	
1	Negro Man Nad Bob bequeathed Dorcas Rich	200	
1	Small Waggon	12	
1	Logchain	1	
1	Old Waggon hons and Boxes	8	
1	Lott of ploues & 3 Plimises	2	
1	Lott of Singletrees		50

FIGURE 7-21 Estate inventory of a wealthy Southern man's estate file

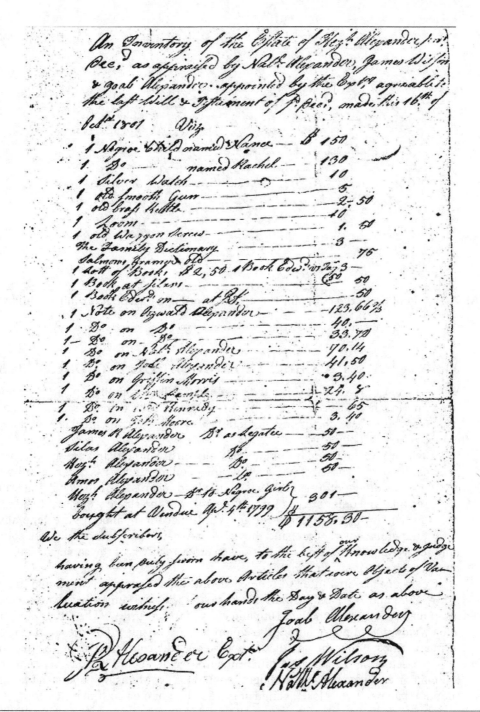

FIGURE 7-22 Estate inventory dated 1801 that includes the names of slaves

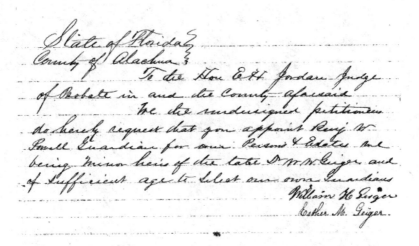

FIGURE 7-23 Petition to the court for the appointment of a guardian for minor children

Watch for Clues and Pointers in the Probate Packet

You will almost always find clues and pointers in wills and probate packet documents that point to other types of records. As such, you will soon come to recognize that you must work with these documents in tandem with other documents. Let's discuss some of these clues and pointers.

A will or probate file may contain information about land and property, as well as personal property. These references can direct you to other areas of the courthouse or other government offices. You may go into land records, tax rolls, civil and criminal court records, and other areas. If any of the assets of the estate were auctioned, check for public or government auction records. Records of auctions are generally a part of the probate packet too, and they also may have been entered into the court minutes. Here you may find connections to other relatives of the same surname who purchased items at an auction.

Guardians are appointed to protect the interests of children (as shown in Figures 7-23 and 7-24) and, in some cases, young widows. Remember that in many locations as recently as the late 19th and early 20th centuries, if the father died and left a widow and minor children, the children were considered by the courts to be "orphans." Most often, the guardians appointed by the court were male relatives of the deceased or of the spouse. A different surname of a guardian may be a clue to the maiden name of the widow. Begin looking for guardianship papers and possibly adoption papers. If you "lose" a child at the death of one or both parents, start searching census records (beginning with the U.S. federal census of 1850 and the U.K. census in 1851) for the child being enumerated in another residence, particularly

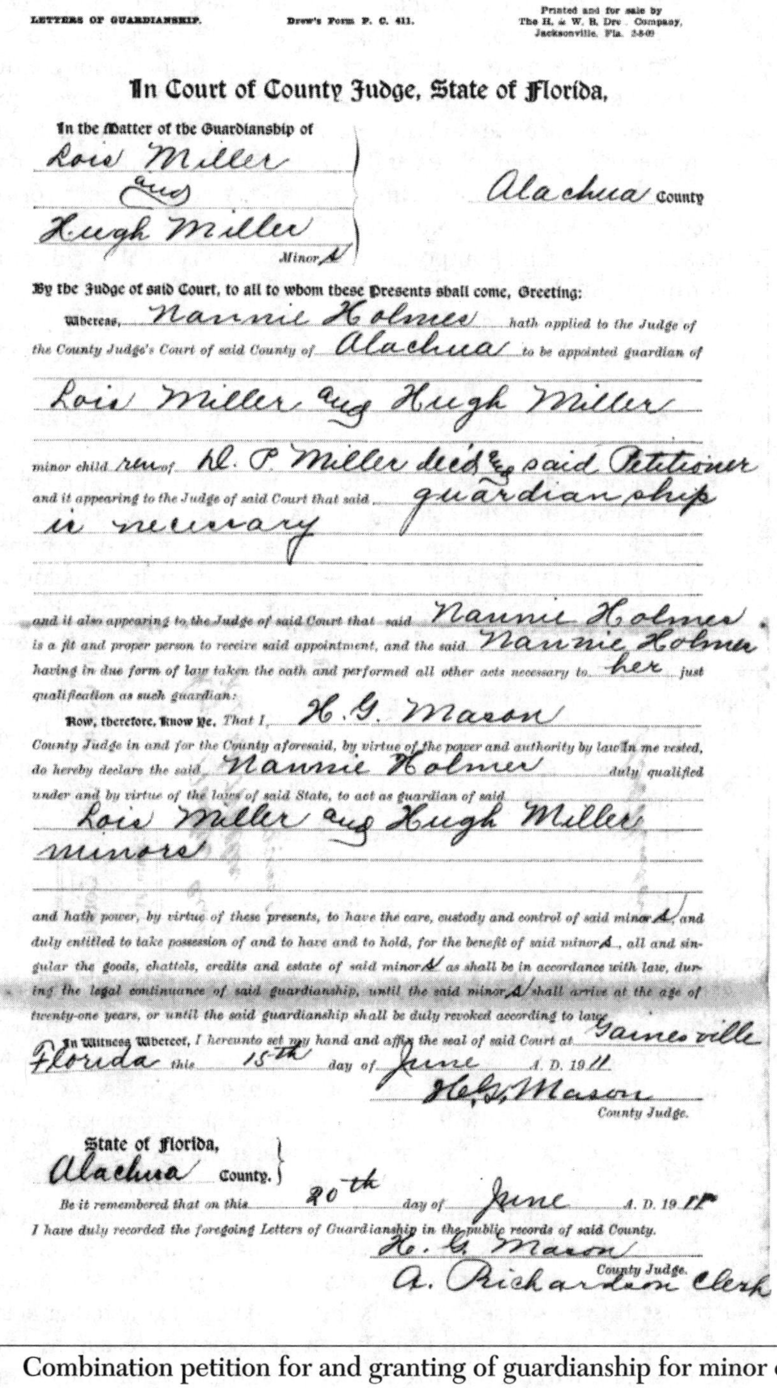

LETTERS OF GUARDIANSHIP. Drew's Form P. C. 411. Printed and for sale by The H. & W. B. Drew Company, Jacksonville, Fla. 3-8-09

In Court of County Judge, State of Florida,

In the Matter of the Guardianship of Lois Miller and Hugh Miller Minors — Alachua County

By the Judge of said Court, to all to whom these Presents shall come, Greeting:

Whereas, Nannie Holmes hath applied to the Judge of the County Judge's Court of said County of Alachua to be appointed guardian of Lois Miller and Hugh Miller minor children of H. P. Miller dec'd and said Petitioner and it appearing to the Judge of said Court that said guardianship is necessary

and it also appearing to the Judge of said Court that said Nannie Holmes is a fit and proper person to receive said appointment, and the said Nannie Holmes having in due form of law taken the oath and performed all other acts necessary to her just qualification as such guardian:

Now, therefore, Know Ye, That I, H. G. Mason County Judge in and for the County aforesaid, by virtue of the power and authority by law in me vested, do hereby declare the said Nannie Holmes duly qualified under and by virtue of the laws of said State, to act as guardian of said Lois Miller and Hugh Miller minors

and hath power, by virtue of these presents, to have the care, custody and control of said minors and duly entitled to take possession of and to have and to hold, for the benefit of said minors, all and singular the goods, chattels, credits and estate of said minors as shall be in accordance with law, during the legal continuance of said guardianship, until the said minors shall arrive at the age of twenty-one years, or until the said guardianship shall be duly revoked according to law.

In Witness Whereof, I hereunto set my hand and affix the seal of said Court at Gainesville Florida this 15th day of June A. D. 1911.

H. G. Mason
County Judge.

State of Florida, Alachua County.

Be it remembered that on this 20th day of June A. D. 1911 I have duly recorded the foregoing Letters of Guardianship in the public records of said County.

H. G. Mason
County Judge.
A. Richardson Clerk

FIGURE 7-24 Combination petition for and granting of guardianship for minor children in a relative's home. If a death certificate exists for the parent, check the name of the informant; if that person was close enough to provide information about the deceased, he or she could possibly have been named as a guardian for minor children. In the absence of relatives, the county, parish, state, or province may have committed the child to an orphanage, orphan asylum, or a poorhouse. Leave no stone unturned. Check the respective court minutes and files for the year following a parent's death for any evidence of legal actions regarding a child. You might be surprised to find lingering legal references to the support of children.

Witnesses to wills can be important. By law, they typically cannot inherit in or benefit from a will; however, they may be relatives of the deceased. It is not uncommon to find an in-law as a witness. Bondsmen involved in the settlement of an estate were often relatives. If the wife of the testator was the executor of the estate, it was not unusual for the bondsmen to be *her* relatives. (If you do not know the maiden name of the wife, check the surnames of the bondsmen carefully because one of them may have been her brother.)

You will almost always find an inventory of the estate in the probate packet. The executor or administrator of the estate is charged by the court to determine the assets, the debts, and the receivables of an estate in order to properly determine what needs to be done to divide or dispose of it. The inventory often paints a colorful picture of the way of life of the deceased. The type of furniture listed and the presence or absence of books, farm equipment, livestock, and real and personal property listed in the inventory all tell us what type of life and what social status the person enjoyed—or did *not* enjoy.

Obviously, there are many things to consider when reviewing wills and probate packet contents. Just a few of the many things to consider are the location, the laws in effect at the time, the religious affiliation of the testator, the size of the estate, and the presence or absence of a spouse, children, siblings, and parents.

Remember Why You Really Want to Examine Documents Yourself

There are many ways to obtain information about a will or probate packet. Since most of us cannot afford to travel to all the places where our ancestors lived, we may need to do some "mail order" business, writing or emailing for copies of courthouse records.

One of the problems with will and probate documentation published in books, magazines, periodicals, and on the Internet is that it may represent the interpretation of someone *else* who has looked at the documents. Unless that person is also a descendant of your ancestors, they may not have the family knowledge and insight that you have. You also don't know whether they have transcribed the document *verbatim*; it might have been correctly transcribed, but you can't be sure unless you review it yourself. Even worse, materials that have been extracted or abstracted often omit details that might be of significant importance to your research. As an example, one will that I examined listed nine children's names, some of which were double-barrel names, such as Billy Ray and Mary Lou. The insertion of extra commas in the transcription, extract, or abstract of these two children's names could easily turn these two children's names into *four* children—and wouldn't that play havoc with your research efforts?

Study the wills carefully for names of children. Don't make any assumptions. One of my friends researched her great-great-grandfather's family and was convinced that there were seven children in the family. That was until she studied the actual will of the great-great-grandfather. In the will, the names Elizabeth and Mary had no comma between them. This led her to suspect that there was one daughter named Elizabeth Mary, rather than two daughters. Further investigation of marriage records in the county contradicted the one-daughter theory because she found that there were individual marriage records for each of the two daughters, one married a year after her father's death and the other two years later. Further, Elizabeth and Mary and their respective spouses settled on land that had been part of their father's holdings and they appeared there on subsequent census records.

Locate and Obtain Copies of Wills and Probate Documents

Wills, testaments, codicils, and other probate documents can be found in a variety of places. It is important to start in the area in which the person lived and make contact with the courts that had jurisdiction at that time, if they still exist. Most of these documents will still reside in the area in which they were created. You may find that some original probate documents have been digitized and made available on the Internet, some of which may be indexed and searchable by testator name. However, most probate-related documents may be accessible only by visiting the courthouse or other repository where they are held. It is also important to remember that wills are not filed by the date on which they were written or by the date of death of the testator. Rather, they are filed by the date on which they were introduced in the probate court and entered into the probate process.

Probate documents may be encountered in many forms. The original documents may still exist and may be filed with the records of the court that handled the process. Look for court minutes and other evidence of the proceedings. Many courts and administrative offices have microfilmed their court records. Microfilm provides for compact storage of these voluminous records while preserving the originals. Microfilm also allows for the economic duplication of the records for access and use in multiple locations, and makes printing and copying simple and inexpensive.

In England, older wills were at one time handled by different levels of ecclesiastical courts that no longer exist. These include the Prerogative Court of Canterbury and the Prerogative Court of York. From the 11th century until 1858, church courts handled the entire probate process. They were responsible for the probate of wills, granting letters of administration, and hearing cases regarding probate disputes. Their jurisdictions sometimes overlapped and their administrative powers were not always clear. In addition, English wills that required the probate of an estate containing multiple pieces of land could be complicated if the parcels were in multiple church administrative districts. In those cases, a level of ecclesiastical court whose administrative level included all of the districts in which the lands were located handled the probate process. Those early ecclesiastical records were written in Latin and may present you with difficulty, both with the language used *and* the ancient handwriting style. It is important to understand the structure of the jurisdictions in the specific time period you are researching before undertaking a search for your English ancestor's will. It was not until 1858 that civil courts began handling probate and a more standard approach was put in place. The National Archives (TNA) in the United Kingdom holds wills that were handled between 1384 and 12 January 1858 and Death Duty Registers from 1796 to 1903, and most of these are searchable online at **http://www .nationalarchives.gov.uk/records/wills.htm**. (See the search aid document at **http://www.nationalarchives.gov.uk/documents/records/ifa-wills-and-admins-1383-1858-death-duty-registers-1796-1903.pdf** for details.) TNA also houses a wealth of other court records. You can search the website to learn more about what is available and how to access the records.

Ancestry.com at **http://www.ancestry.com** offers indexes, abstracts, images for many areas of England, Wales, Ireland, and some documents from the Prerogative Courts of Canterbury and of Ireland.

Findmypast at **http://www.findmypast.com** at this writing provides access to images and/or probate documents for Cheshire, London, West Kent, and the British India Office.

FamilySearch at **https://www.familysearch.org** provides the largest number of digitized wills and probate-related documents on the Internet. Most of these have not been indexed by name. However, browsable digital images are grouped together as they were microfilmed in their native repository. That means that you can usually narrow your browsing to types of records and dates for a particular location. In many cases, the court assigned a reference number or code to a will and maintained an index. Use any such indexes, because they may simplify your ability to locate specific wills. Don't overlook probate court minute books, as they reference specific documents and the dates on which they were introduced before the court.

The Origins.net website at **http://www.origins.net** has a collection called the National Wills Index containing more than 4 million wills and probate records, including those of the Prerogative & Exchequer Courts of York Probate Index, spanning the years 1688 to 1858.

ScotlandsPeople at **http://www.scotlandspeople.gov.uk** has made accessible in digital format more than half a million Scottish wills and testaments from different areas and dating variously from between 1513 and 1925. See Figure 7-25. These are free to search, but you have to buy credits to view and print.

Efforts are certainly underway to make information about wills and probate records available to citizens. Individual counties, municipalities, and courts may have digitized records and/or created indexes and placed these on the Internet. Check the governmental website for the area or contact the responsible court by telephone or email to determine what might be available to you online.

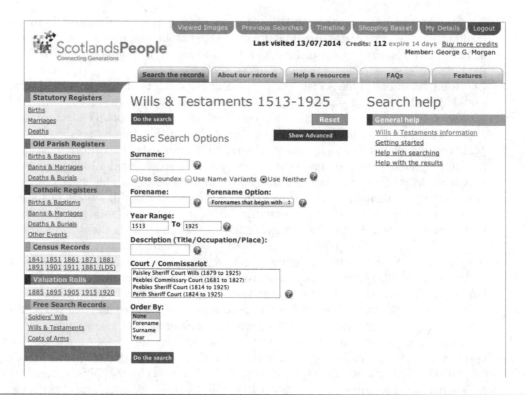

FIGURE 7-25   The ScotlandsPeople website provides this search template to locate wills, administrations, and probate documents, which you can then view and print.

Obtain Information from the Social Security Administration and Railroad Retirement Board

The Social Security Administration (SSA) was established by an act of the U.S. Congress in 1935, in the depths of the Great Depression. President Franklin D. Roosevelt's administration was hard at work trying to help the United States recover economically through a number of social and financial programs. One area that required attention was that of old-age pensions. Older Americans were at significant risk of financial ruin during the Depression, and old-age pensions were primarily only available from some state and local governments. Many of those pension programs were faltering or had collapsed, and Congress was under pressure from the administration and from the public to take action.

The Social Security Act of 1935 established a national program for Americans over the age of 65 to receive benefits, and defined the structure and criteria for participation of those people in the work force and their employers to contribute to their retirement security. The program would not begin for several years and credit would not be given for any service prior to 1937.

In the meantime, railroad employees clamored for a program that would provide credit for prior service *and* an unemployment compensation program. Legislation passed in 1934, 1935, and 1937 established the Railroad Retirement program for employees of the U.S. railroads (more about that later in this section).

At the beginning of the Social Security program, in order to determine which persons would immediately be eligible to receive unemployment benefits, the SSA used the 1880 U.S. federal census as a reference to help verify the ages of recipients. The SSA formed a special branch called the Age Search group to handle this function for persons who could not provide proof of their age. That branch still exists today to perform the same function. The Age Search group quickly determined that searching the 1880 census Population Schedules for a single person's enumeration listing was a highly laborious process. The SSA therefore commissioned the creation of an indexing system to assist in the search process. It was at that time that the Soundex coding system was developed for this program, and the first index was created for the 1880 census. Index cards were prepared by a group of employees of the Works Progress Administration (WPA), and these cards were created only for households in which there were children aged ten and under. After the 1880 census was Soundexed, indexes were prepared for many entire households in the 1900, 1910, 1920, and 1930 censuses. The original Soundex cards were microfilmed by NARA and, before the census records were digitized and indexed on the Internet, the Soundex microfilms were an effective tool for locating households.

In order to pay retirement pension benefits to an applicant, the SSA required that applicant to prove his or her age eligibility. While the Soundex system was used by the Age Search group, the person applying for benefits had to: a) have applied for and been assigned a Social Security number (SSN); b) prove his or her identity; and c) provide evidence of his or her age. (Persons with disabilities who could not work also later became eligible for Social Security benefits, and their requirements were the same.)

Social Security numbers (SSNs) were assigned to individuals by SSA offices in each state and territory. Each geographical division (state and territory) was assigned a block of numbers. As is still the case today, the SSN consists of three groups of digits. The first three digits represent the **Area Number**, which indicates the geographical location in which the assignment was made. (However, as of 25 June 2011, the first three numbers are no longer associated with a geographic area for newly assigned numbers). The next two digits represent a **Group Number**. Within each area, the group numbers include 01 to 99 but are not assigned in consecutive order. For administrative reasons, group numbers issued first consist of the *odd* numbers from 01 through 09, and then *even* numbers from 10 through 98 are used. The last group of four digits is a sequentially assigned serial number. These numbers are assigned at the time that the applicant has completed the SS-5 application form, such as the one shown in Figure 7-26, to obtain a SSN.

When a beneficiary dies, it is a legal requirement to notify the SSA so that it can immediately stop payments and, if the payment has been made, to take steps to effect the recall of all or a portion of that payment. A benefit check for the last partial month of the person's life must be returned, and the SSA has a procedure for handling the final payment. The SSA now requires a copy of a death certificate or other form of written proof of death. The SSN is permanently retired from use.

The SSA's records were maintained on paper until the early 1960s. At that time, data from the SS-5 forms of all known living persons with SSNs (along with the last known residential address) and information from all new applicants' SS-5

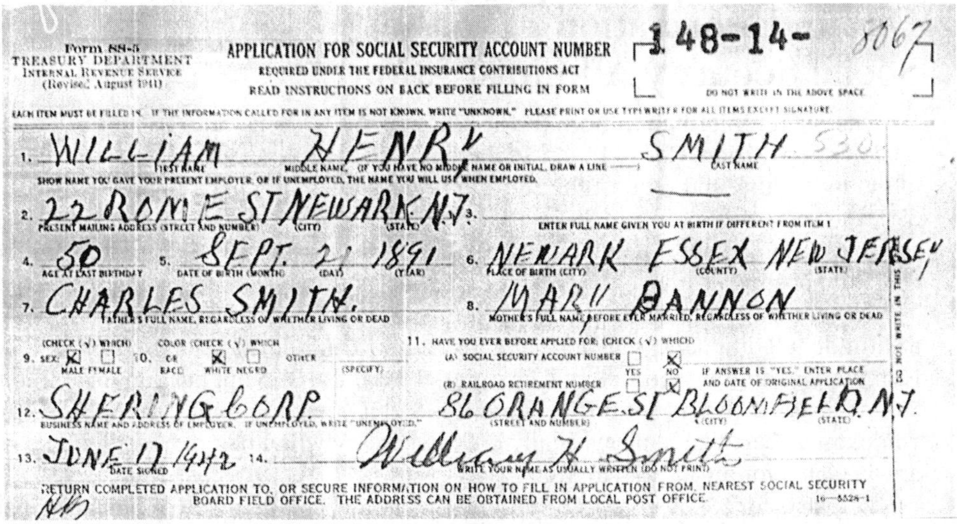

Form SS-5
TREASURY DEPARTMENT
INTERNAL REVENUE SERVICE
(Revised August 1941)

APPLICATION FOR SOCIAL SECURITY ACCOUNT NUMBER
REQUIRED UNDER THE FEDERAL INSURANCE CONTRIBUTIONS ACT
READ INSTRUCTIONS ON BACK BEFORE FILLING IN FORM

148-14- 5067

DO NOT WRITE IN THE ABOVE SPACE

EACH ITEM MUST BE FILLED IN. IF THE INFORMATION CALLED FOR IN ANY ITEM IS NOT KNOWN, WRITE "UNKNOWN." PLEASE PRINT OR USE TYPEWRITER FOR ALL ITEMS EXCEPT SIGNATURE.

1. WILLIAM (FIRST NAME) HENRY (MIDDLE NAME. (IF YOU HAVE NO MIDDLE NAME OR INITIAL, DRAW A LINE ———) SMITH (LAST NAME)

SHOW NAME YOU GAVE YOUR PRESENT EMPLOYER. OR IF UNEMPLOYED, THE NAME YOU WILL USE WHEN EMPLOYED.

2. 22 ROME ST NEWARK N.J. (PRESENT MAILING ADDRESS (STREET AND NUMBER)) (CITY) (STATE) 3. ENTER FULL NAME GIVEN YOU AT BIRTH IF DIFFERENT FROM ITEM 1

4. 50 (AGE AT LAST BIRTHDAY) 5. SEPT. 21 1891 (DATE OF BIRTH (MONTH) (DAY) (YEAR)) 6. NEWARK ESSEX NEW JERSEY (PLACE OF BIRTH (CITY) (COUNTY) (STATE))

7. CHARLES SMITH. (FATHER'S FULL NAME, REGARDLESS OF WHETHER LIVING OR DEAD) 8. MARY BANNON (MOTHER'S FULL NAME BEFORE EVER MARRIED, REGARDLESS OF WHETHER LIVING OR DEAD)

9. SEX: MALE [X] FEMALE [ ] (CHECK (√) WHICH) 10. COLOR OR RACE: WHITE [X] NEGRO [ ] OTHER (SPECIFY) (CHECK (√) WHICH)

11. HAVE YOU EVER BEFORE APPLIED FOR: (CHECK (√) WHICH) (A) SOCIAL SECURITY ACCOUNT NUMBER YES [ ] NO [X] (B) RAILROAD RETIREMENT NUMBER YES [ ] NO [X] IF ANSWER IS "YES," ENTER PLACE AND DATE OF ORIGINAL APPLICATION

12. SHERING CORP. 86 ORANGE ST BLOOMFIELD N.J. (BUSINESS NAME AND ADDRESS OF EMPLOYER. IF UNEMPLOYED, WRITE "UNEMPLOYED.") (STREET AND NUMBER) (CITY) (STATE)

13. JUNE 17 1942 (DATE SIGNED) 14. William H. Smith (WRITE YOUR NAME AS USUALLY WRITTEN (DO NOT PRINT))

RETURN COMPLETED APPLICATION TO, OR SECURE INFORMATION ON HOW TO FILL IN APPLICATION FROM, NEAREST SOCIAL SECURITY BOARD FIELD OFFICE. THE ADDRESS CAN BE OBTAINED FROM LOCAL POST OFFICE.

DO NOT WRITE IN THIS SPACE

FIGURE 7-26 A photocopy of the SS-5 application form of William Henry Smith, with the SSN assigned by the Social Security Administration

forms were entered into a computer database. In addition, the SSA began maintaining benefit information by computer and entering death information as notifications of the deaths of recipients were received. Beginning in 1962, the Social Security Death Master File began to be produced electronically on a regular basis. Initially, it contained only about 17 percent of the reported deaths, but that increased to more than 92 percent in 1980, and now represents nearly 100 percent of the deaths. Concerns about identity thefts using SSNs of deceased individuals caused the U.S. Congress in 2013 to pass legislation that will limit public access to an individual's information for three years following his or her death. The Death Master File has since come to be known as the Social Security Death Index, or SSDI, and is accessible for free at **https://familysearch.org/search/collection/1202535**, Ancestry.com/RootsWeb.com at **http://ssdi.rootsweb.ancestry.com**, MyHeritage at **http://www.myheritage.com**, and other places on the Internet. Genealogists with family members in the United States have used this valuable tool to locate the place of last residence or benefit payment in order to locate other records.

There are four criteria for a person's information to be included in the SSDI:

- The person must have had a Social Security number assigned to him or her.
- The person must be deceased.
- The person must have applied for and received a Social Security benefit payment.
- The person's death must have been reported to the Social Security Administration.

If a person was assigned a SSN and is deceased, but never received a benefit of any sort, he or she will not be found in the SSDI. For these persons, and for those persons who died prior to the computerization of the SSA records, you can still obtain a copy of their SS-5 application form from the SSA.

Obtain Information from the Social Security Administration

You can obtain information from the Social Security Administration about a deceased person's application. Contact the SSA and provide the full name, address, and birth date of the individual, and request the SS-5 application form. If you can provide the person's SSN, the cost of obtaining an SS-5 at this writing is $27; if you cannot furnish the SSN, the cost is $29. Please note that Congressional legislation in 2013 has prohibited the SSA from posting deaths to the SSDI for a period of three years following the death.

You can also request a copy of a printout from the SSDI database known as a Numident. Numident is an acronym for Numerical Identification System. The Numident is nothing more than data entered from the SS-5 application form into the SSA database. The price of this document is $16 if you can provide the SSN or $18 if you cannot. Certified copies, usually only necessary when being presented in a court, are available for an additional $10.

Requests for SS-5 forms and Numident printouts can be made online at **https://secure.ssa.gov/apps9/eFOIA-FEWeb/internet/main.jsp** or sent by mail to:

Social Security Administration
OEO FOIA Workgroup
300 N. Greene Street
P.O. Box 33022
Baltimore, Maryland 21290-3022

Your request to the SSA for a copy of the application (SS-5) for a person who never received a benefit and for whom the SSA wasn't notified of the death may be denied. However, if you can supply evidence of the person's death, such as a copy of a death certificate or coroner's report, you can appeal the decision and request to receive the copy of the person's SS-5 form.

Obtain Information from the Railroad Retirement Board

The U.S. Railroad Retirement Board (RRB) is the administrative body for the railroad workers' retirement pension benefits system. The Railroad Retirement program is similar to Social Security but is administered by the RRB in Chicago, Illinois. Up until 1963, persons who worked for a railroad in the United States at the time they applied for a SSN were assigned a number beginning with Area Numbers between 700 and 728. Therefore, if you locate any document that lists a SSN whose first three digits are in that numbering range, you will know that the person worked for the railroad industry at the time he or she was assigned the number. You also will know to check first with the RRB for records.

A person who worked exclusively in the railroad industry will apply for and receive old-age pension benefits from Railroad Retirement. An individual who worked for both the railroad industry and elsewhere would have contributed to both a Railroad Retirement pension account and to Social Security during his or her working career.

At the time of retirement, the person had to apply for a retirement pension benefit from either one or the other, but not both plans.

The RRB records you obtain may be more detailed, including earnings reports, copies of designation of beneficiary forms, and perhaps more. You can learn more about requesting these documents at the Genealogy page of the RRB website at **http://www.rrb.gov/mep/genealogy.asp**.

Requests can only be sent to the RRB by mail at the time of this writing. The address to which you would send your request, along with a check for $27 made payable to the Railroad Retirement Board, is

Congressional Inquiry Section
U.S. Railroad Retirement Board
844 North Rush Street
Chicago, Illinois 60611-2092

Use Historical Newspapers to Learn About Your Ancestor's Life Events

Newspapers chronicle a community's life and record the cultural, social, political, commercial, and agricultural conditions. Vast collections of newspapers have been microfilmed over time. Many of these, as well as surviving newsprint documents, are in the process of being digitized and every-word indexed, and are being made available online.

Historical newspapers that are being made available online are accessible in several ways. First, there are individual newspapers made available by their publishers. These are typically the more recent newspapers, from around 1985 to present. Accessing these historical papers may or may not require a fee. Two centralized websites that can be used to locate contemporary newspaper publishers and access them are OnlineNewspapers.com at **http://www.onlinenewspapers .com** and the Internet Public Library's newspaper section at **http://www.ipl.org/ div/news**. The Library of Congress in Washington, D.C., has an ongoing project to compile a collection of historical American newspapers from 1836 through 1922 at their Chronicling America website. This collection is freely accessible at **http:// chroniclingamerica.loc.gov**. Don't overlook digital newspaper collections that also may have been compiled by libraries and archives worldwide. In the United States, many state libraries and archives have endeavored to identify all of the newspapers in their state that were ever published, acquire copies of the newspapers or microfilm, and digitize and index those materials. The British Library at **http://www.bl.uk** announced in mid-2010 that it has begun digitizing more than 40 million pages of its Newspaper Library collection in Colindale, an area of London in the Borough of Barnet.

Next, there are databases of historical newspapers to which you can subscribe as an individual. One such example is Newspapers.com at **http://www.newspapers .com** (see Figure 7-27), which has more than 3,200 newspaper titles from the 1700s to the 2000s. The Ancestry.com subscription service at **http://www.ancestry.com** and

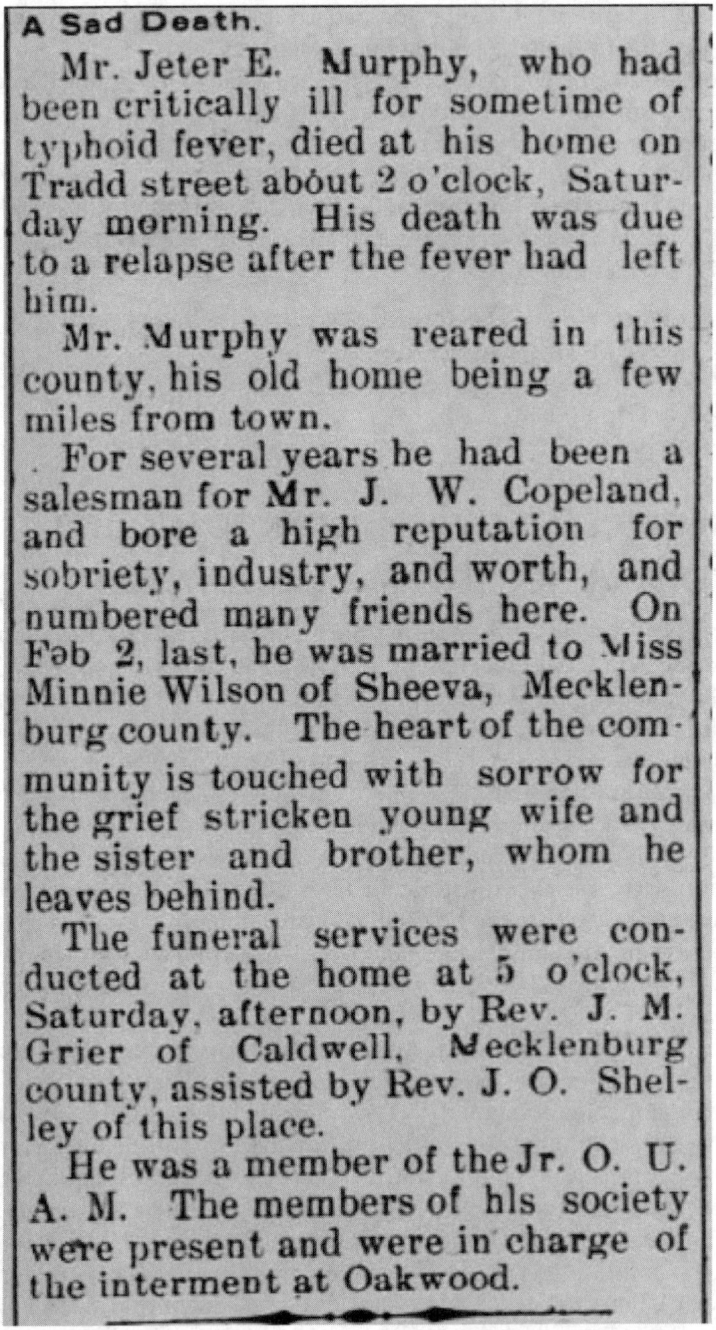

A Sad Death.

Mr. Jeter E. Murphy, who had been critically ill for sometime of typhoid fever, died at his home on Tradd street about 2 o'clock, Saturday morning. His death was due to a relapse after the fever had left him.

Mr. Murphy was reared in this county, his old home being a few miles from town.

For several years he had been a salesman for Mr. J. W. Copeland, and bore a high reputation for sobriety, industry, and worth, and numbered many friends here. On Feb 2, last, he was married to Miss Minnie Wilson of Sheeva, Mecklenburg county. The heart of the community is touched with sorrow for the grief stricken young wife and the sister and brother, whom he leaves behind.

The funeral services were conducted at the home at 5 o'clock, Saturday, afternoon, by Rev. J. M. Grier of Caldwell, Mecklenburg county, assisted by Rev. J. O. Shelley of this place.

He was a member of the Jr. O. U. A. M. The members of his society were present and were in charge of the interment at Oakwood.

FIGURE 7-27 The obituary for the author's paternal grandmother's first husband appeared in the *Carolina Mascot* (Statesville, North Carolina) on Thursday, 14 July 1898. The digitized newspaper was discovered at Newspapers.com.

some of its geographical sites also include newspapers. Findmypast at **http://www .findmypast.com** has a large collection of digitized and indexed newspapers from the United States, the United Kingdom, and around the world. Fold3.com at **http://www .fold3.com** provides access to editions of the *Atlanta Constitution*, the *Chicago Tribune*, the *San Francisco Chronicle*, and *The Times* of London. GenealogyBank at **http://www .genealogybank.com** is available for individual subscriptions and provides access to digitized newspapers from 1690 to 1977, historical books from 1801 to 1900, and historical documents from 1789 to 1980. The Irish Newspaper Archive at **http://www .irishnewsarchive.com** has digitized newspapers from across Ireland.

WorldVitalRecords.com at **http://www.worldvitalrecords.com** offers a vast newspaper collection. Another important subscription site is the Times Archive at **http://www.thetimes.co.uk/tto/archive**, which provides access to the digitized archive of *The Times* of London from 1785 through 1985.

There are digitized historical newspaper database collections that are only available as institutional subscriptions to libraries and archives. ProQuest is a major provider of historical newspaper databases, and their collections include the historical *New York Times, Atlanta Constitution, Chicago Tribune, Los Angeles Times, Toronto Star, Wall Street Journal*, and many more. The ProQuest products are available only as institutional subscriptions to libraries, and you will need to investigate libraries in your area to learn which ones provide in-house access. NewsBank, Inc., offers genealogy-specific databases such as America's GenealogyBank and America's Obituaries & Death Notices. America's GenealogyBank (**http://www.genealogybank.com**) includes digitized and indexed U.S. newspapers from 1690 to 1977 and other materials discussed previously. America's Obituaries & Death Notices includes obituaries from more recent newspapers from the 1970s and later.

You will want to check with your local public library, academic libraries, and with local archives to determine what institutional subscription databases are available. If you hold a library card and your library subscribes to a historical newspaper collection, you may have remote access from home to connect and work with some of these databases. You may otherwise visit the facility and use their online computers to access these databases.

Consider Other Institutional Record Types

You can see now how the investigative work you are doing and the scholarly methodologies you are using can begin to pay big dividends. In many of the examples I've shown in this chapter, I have tried to convey the ways that one record may provide clues and pointers to others.

As you encounter new sources of information, use your critical thinking skills to read between the lines. Consider other types of institutional records that might add to your knowledge. These could include records from employers, unions, schools, professional organizations, civic and social clubs, and veterans groups, just to name a few. Just as with cemetery offices, you never know what information might be in these organizations' files and different records.

8

Use the Many Types of Military Service Records

HOW TO...

- Expand your knowledge of military service
- Identify possible sources for military records
- Find facts in registration, conscription, and enlistment records
- Examine samples of U.S. military records
- Locate other military-related records

In the previous chapters you have learned the importance of building a firm foundation of context for your ancestors' and family members' lives using records of many types. These include the wide array of evidence materials found in the home. Records of births, christenings, marriages, divorces, deaths, and burials provide milestone life events to mark your ancestors' presence at particular locations at specific points in time. We discussed census records, and you saw that there are cases in which a census document may have included information about someone's military service record.

The period of military service is among the best documented times in an ancestor's life. Military service and pension records can reveal a great many details and place your ancestor into geographical and historical context. Fortunately for us, these records are of such important administrative value that they were created in profusion. They also were generally very well maintained throughout the period of your ancestor's service and later. Many of these records were microfilmed and have been digitized in the last several years. Others that only existed in paper format are now being digitized and indexed at a rapid rate, not only in the United States and the United Kingdom, but elsewhere as well.

The U.S. federal census of 1840 was the first to call for the name and age of American Revolutionary War veterans, and the 1890 census included a separate census schedule specifically intended to record surviving Union veterans or the widows of Union soldiers who died during or after the war. (A significant number of

Confederate veterans and widows were included.) The 1851 census in England and Wales included those persons living on vessels in inland waters or at sea, including members of the Royal Navy and the Merchant Navy. In addition, persons who were serving abroad with the armed forces and those working with the East India Company were enumerated.

As you can see, census materials may provide information about an ancestor that can spur you to search for military records. Even if you are unsure whether or not your ancestor or a family member served in the armed forces of a particular country, it is wise to invest some amount of time researching the official rosters and/or indexes to see if a familiar name appears there. You would be surprised how often people make the discovery of a military ancestor when they didn't know or think there was one. Registration and enlistment records can help link a person to other relatives, and they may provide a physical description of the individual. Military service and pension records also can provide more detailed insight into a person's life than you could imagine. There is sometimes a link between military service and other records. For example, the U.S. federal government compensated some military personnel with land rather than or in addition to paying them cash. These "bounty lands" were granted to persons in reward for their military service or for rendering goods and services to the government and/or troops. We'll discuss bounty land in more detail in Chapter 9.

You may find military-related documents and artifacts among family papers. Commendations, medals, and other awards are often cherished family treasures. Military discharge documents provided proof of service and, because military service often entitled the veteran to certain benefits, they were typically stored with important papers. Applications for pensions, medical benefits, educational benefits, and other benefits probably generated a substantial amount of correspondence. It is wise to gather and collate these materials into chronological sequence and read through them in order. You may then have another perspective to help you locate and request other materials. You may encounter other materials that may imply or point to military service and pertinent records. Some examples of these are pension statements, benefits check stubs, copies of income tax documents, obituaries, and death notices, will and probate records, tombstone carvings, and naturalization records. You may also find dog tags, medals, and souvenirs of battles that may provide clues to other military documentation.

Many genealogists fail to follow through with a search for military service records and pension files. These omissions or oversights can generally be attributed to a lack of understanding of the history of the area where their ancestors and family members lived, the military history, and events that might have played a very significant role in their lives. However, another contributing factor is that military records are not always located together. Sometimes the military service records are in one archive, the pension files are in another, and perhaps other pertinent records are in the possession of yet another governmental office. This can be confusing if you haven't taken the time to determine what records were created at a particular time, what part of the government or military used them, what they were used for, and what was done with those records when they were no longer needed. Context is important!

With all of this in mind, let's set out to become experts in the research of military records. I think you will find that these are fascinating types of records, and that they provide insights into history you never imagined.

Expand Your Knowledge of Military Service

Military service is a job and, as such, can produce a vast amount of written documentation. Census records provide information at ten-year intervals, which is a substantial span of time between milestones. Military records, on the other hand, provide a more regular form of documentation, at shorter intervals than a census does. From the date of registration, conscription, or enlistment, there will have been official military records maintained. These may include the following record types:

- Announcements/postings of promotions
- Attestation papers (UK)
- Benefits records
- Casualty reports
- Combat reports
- Death and burial records
- Discharge papers
- Draft notices (U.S.)
- Draft registration cards (U.S.)
- Duty assignments
- Educational testing and training reports/diplomas
- Enlistment forms and related documentation
- Medical records
- Military unit daily reports
- Military unit histories
- Muster rolls
- Operations reports
- Payroll records and pay stubs
- Pension applications
- Pension files containing affidavits, correspondence, payment records, and other documents
- Pension payment vouchers
- Quartermaster or provisions records
- Records of courts-martial
- Records of the awarding of medals and awards, such as those shown in Figures 8-1 and 8-2
- Service files or dossiers
- Veteran records
- Veteran's life insurance certificate

That is an impressive list of documentary evidence types. It is important to note that not every country generated or maintained this broad a range of documents, and that fewer types of records were created the farther back in history you research. Specific personnel units, too, may have required the use of additional or unique records. Still, the sheer volume of military documentation of a soldier's daily, monthly, or annual affairs can present you with a detailed insight into his or her life at that time. Remember, too, that military assignments take a person to many locations and expose

FIGURE 8-1 The Congressional Medal of Honor is the United States' highest military award.

him or her to a wide range of experiences. Military service records and discharge documents may include details of assignments' locations. The military experiences may have influenced the decisions made later in life to select a particular profession, to relocate to another area, or to take some other course of action. In some cases, a soldier, sailor, marine, merchant marine, airman, doctor or nurse, or someone in another military position may have met and married someone during his or her period of military service. Pay attention to these events and locations, and follow the leads to locate records of the spouse in his or her country of origin.

In addition to the official file contents listed previously, you may find items among materials in the home that can further your research, such as uniforms, dog tags, insignia, patches, badges, medals, ribbons, certificates and awards, correspondence, and photographs. Any of these might provide clues and pointers to military records and documentation.

FIGURE 8-2 The Victoria Cross is the United Kingdom's highest military award.

Investigate Military History for the Appropriate Time Period

Every time I visit a library, a bookstore, or an online bookseller's site, I am impressed by the vast number of books and periodicals available on the subject of military history. More and more of these publications are becoming available in electronic book (eBook) editions. There are books available about armies, navies, and every conceivable military branch. Innumerable historical accounts and examinations of military units, their engagements, and strategic analyses from the present and extending back to ancient times have been published in books, magazines, journals, and other media. There are specialty book and magazine titles that discuss the uses of horses, wagons, tanks, jeeps, ships, airplanes, helicopters, land-sea transports, landing vehicles, and other transportation modes employed in warfare. Every manner of weapon you can imagine is documented in intricate detail, from swords, scimitars, cutlasses, spears, lances, maces, sabers, knives, and bayonets to catapults, pistols, rifles, cannon, mortars, bombs, bazookas, flamethrowers, missiles, fighter aircraft, computer-assisted weapons, and other types of armaments.

You will find extensive information on the Internet about these same topics. Wikipedia (**http://www.wikipedia.com**) may be a good place to start your search because the vast majority of articles online there include source citations and hyperlinks to other sites. Remember that, whether you search in print or electronic media, you should personally review the sources cited to determine the veracity and reliability of the content.

You already know the importance of placing your ancestors and family members into geographical, historical, and social context. This is also emphatically true when it comes to researching the history of someone who may have performed some military service. You will benefit from the study of the history of the country and locale in which your ancestor lived. You will want to focus particularly on the military establishment there at the time, military service requirements, and the military conflicts in which the country and its population were engaged. This information can help you better understand what records you might expect to find. You could expect to find that a government in a time of war imposed conscription or impressments to force enrollment of personnel in the military service. In the United States in 1917 and 1918, a series of draft calls were made by the U.S. federal government to quickly build the armed forces for involvement in "The Great War" in Europe. Men in certain age ranges, such as 19-year-old Charles Ray Morrison shown in Figure 8-3, were required to present themselves at the office of their local draft board to complete a draft registration card. Knowing that every male between certain ages was required to complete a card will prompt you to attempt to obtain a copy of the record for your research. Likewise, if you had a male ancestor living in Prussia in 1816, it is important to know that compulsory military service had been imposed, even in peacetime. You might therefore want to investigate the history of Prussia, and the existence of military service records that documented your ancestor's date and place of birth and other details that might be included about him.

Sometimes you will find that individual records may no longer exist, in which case you will need to seek out alternative sources of information. State, county, parish, and local histories can be beneficial in that regard because they frequently include sections about military units that originated in the area and rosters of the people who served in them. Even if your ancestor or other family member is not listed by name, identifying the military unit(s) that originated in that area can provide important clues that might lead you to alternate materials.

Biographies of legendary military leaders, such as Vice Admiral Lord Viscount Horatio Nelson, General George Washington, General Robert E. Lee, and General George S. Patton, and others, provide minute details of their lives and military leadership. Military unit histories, analyses of battles and strategies, diaries, and memoirs are abundant. Following the U.S. Civil War and throughout the remaining decades of the 19th century, former officers and veterans penned exhaustive memoirs and historical accounts of their experiences. Some estimates are that as many as 70,000 such accounts were written and published. These narratives often contain complete rosters of the people serving with them and anecdotal materials about them. In some cases, these accounts may contain the only surviving details about the fates of individual soldiers lost in battle or to disease. Likewise, copious British military histories exist

FIGURE 8-3   Charles Ray Morrison, born in 1899, was enrolled during the United States' Third Draft Registration on 12 September 1918.

relating to many military campaigns, including the English Civil War, the Seven Years' War, the American Revolutionary War, the War of 1812, the Napoleonic Wars, the Opium Wars, the Boxer Rebellion, the New Zealand Land Wars, the Indian Rebellion of 1857, the Boer Wars, the Fenian raids, and the Irish War of Rebellion. Scores of new titles covering military histories continue to be published each year.

Historians also have chronicled military units' histories and their engagements, compiling official records and personal accounts to re-create a chronological account of events. Military-related heritage societies also have organized to honor the veterans, their families, and their descendants, and to perpetuate the history of their service. Organizations in the United States such as the Daughters of the American Revolution, the Sons of the American Revolution, the United Daughters of the Confederacy, the Sons of Confederate Veterans, and the Daughters of the British Empire foster education, caretaking activities for historical materials, maintenance of cemeteries, and publication of information relating to their respective group.

There are other organizations whose members may or may not be descendants of veterans of specific military personnel but who are interested in preserving information and materials and encouraging the study of a specific area or period. Examples of these groups include the English Civil War Society (**http://english-civil-war-society .org.uk**), the Military Historical Society of Australia (**http://www.mhsa.org.au**), the Scottish Military History Website (**http://www.scottishmilitaryresearch.org.uk**), and the United Empire Loyalists' Association of Canada (**http://www.uelac.org**). Military reenactment groups are extremely popular and provide excellent experiences for participants and spectators alike. They can help you understand what life was like at the time that your ancestor lived.

In addition, there are a number of magazines with military and historical themes to expand your knowledge, currently among them are *World War II*, *World War II History*, *Military Heritage*, *Military History*, *Civil War Times*, *History Magazine*, *Naval History*, *Canadian Journal of History*, *BBC History Magazine*, *British Heritage*, and *Journal of Australian Naval History*. You may want to purchase a copy of a magazine at a newsstand to determine if it contains information of interest or help to you. You can then subscribe to one or more publications that will contribute to your growing knowledge of the subject. These publications can help contribute to placing your military ancestors into context with their time and branches of the armed forces. You can expect to locate vast amounts of military unit information both in book and magazine form, in eBooks, and also on the Internet. Whenever you begin to research an ancestor who was or may have been in the military service, do some preliminary investigative work into the history of the area and time period, and into the records that may have been created for the military command and the personnel. Once you know what was created, you can then begin tracking down the locations where those materials may be stored and the procedures for accessing them.

Identify Possible Sources for Military Records

Military records are government documents. You will find that for a particular country or government, military records may well be distributed across a number of document depositories. This is a primary reason why it is important to study history. Military records for the period up to the Korean Conflict are held in the United States by the National Archives and Records Administration (**http://www.archives.gov**) and its National Personnel Records Center (**http://www.archives.gov/st-louis**) in St. Louis, Missouri. Later records may be in the holdings of the Department of Defense and the Department of Veterans Affairs.

In Canada, most of the military service records are held by Library and Archives Canada (**http://www.collectionscanada.gc.ca/genealogy/022-909-e.html**). In the United Kingdom, significant collections of military records, including service and pension records, are held by The National Archives (**http://www.nationalarchives .gov.uk**). Other UK military records, however, may still be in the possession of the Ministry of Defence.

The National Archives of Australia holds Army, Navy, and Air Force records (**http://www.naa.gov.au/collection/explore/defence/services.aspx**). Please note that, if your ancestor served in the military forces in other than his or her native country, the records for that service will be in the other country's possession. Let's examine each of these governments' records in some detail.

Remember that many indexes, transcripts, and abstracts of military records have been prepared. These include summary personnel records, muster rolls, casualty lists, medical reports, and many other types of records. These can point you in the direction of original, primary source documents, a copy of which you will want to obtain for your own review.

Locate Military Records in the United States

The United States, as a comparatively young nation, has a considerable military history. A vast collection of military records from colonial times still exists. You will find that the earlier the era, however, the less complete the military records may be. Documents may have been lost or destroyed, or they may simply have deteriorated before they were gathered together for archiving and preservation. You will be amazed, however, how many of the military records have been microfilmed. Many of those are in the process of being digitized, indexed, and made available online. Other military-related records that were never microfilmed are in the process of being digitized or plans are being developed to do so. A case in point is the War of 1812 pension files for veterans. These are being digitized and indexed through a fundraising project originated by the Federation of Genealogical Societies and currently in progress. All of the records are being uploaded to the Fold3.com website (**http://www.fold3.com**), where they will be accessible for free permanently.

Learn About Early Records

The earliest recorded American military conflicts are perhaps those that occurred at Jamestown in the colony of Virginia. The Native American attack on the settlement in March of 1622 killed more than 300 settlers and almost destroyed it. The English colonists retaliated and, over the next 22 years, almost decimated the Native American population in the area. Documents in the form of correspondence and historical accounts do exist from these years, which can be found among the documents both at TNA in the United Kingdom and at the Library of Virginia in the United States.

Other conflicts between the English and French colonies during the colonial period, in territory that is now split between the United States and Canada, and against the Native American tribes were numerous. However, no appreciable military documents exist *per se*. Rather, correspondence and anecdotal accounts form what historical materials exist, and these are in the hands of various archives in the United Kingdom, Canada, the United States, and some of the states' and provinces' libraries or archives. A number of histories have been published that document these conflicts.

Military forces serving in what is now the United States during the colonial era consisted primarily of European military personnel from the countries controlling specific respective areas. The Spanish governed Florida on multiple occasions, California, and some southern areas. The English governed the eastern colonies and Florida for a time. The French governed the Louisiana Territory. In addition, Mexico governed what now are the states of Texas, New Mexico, Arizona, California, Nevada, and Utah, and governed parts of what now are the states of Wyoming, Colorado, Kansas, and Oklahoma. Russia owned Alaska until it was sold to the United States on 30 March 1867.

Research Your Ancestors in the American Revolutionary War

In the early colonial period, the American colonists supplemented the British troops with local military units and militia. It was not until the mid-1700s that the 13 original colonies began to actively oppose British governance. The American Revolutionary War (1775–1783) was the first really organized armed conflict initiated by the Americans themselves, and there are unique military-related documents that were generated as a result of the clashes that occurred. There are four major sources for discovering who actually served during that war:

- Lists of veterans were compiled by each state early in the 19th century.
- Pension applications were filed by veterans, or by their surviving spouses or dependent family members, and these applications can be researched at the federal and/or state levels.
- The 1840 U.S. federal census population schedule asked for the names and ages of pensioners of the American Revolutionary War.
- Records of applicants to the Daughters of the American Revolution (DAR) detail names and other information about Revolutionary War participants. These applications may include detailed documentation, in the form of both official papers and personal materials, of the military record of members' ancestors.
- The Library of the National Society of the Sons of the American Revolution (NSSAR) holds more than 58,000 items of genealogical interest and documentation related to that period.

These are not, however, the only resources you might expect to find. Let's look at one excellent example. Let's say that you are looking for an ancestor's records relating to his military service during the period of 1775 to 1783 in what is now the United States. You will be seeking records relating to the American Revolutionary War, and you will be looking in a number of places. It is important to first of all know the state from which he served. For our example, let's choose South Carolina.

You next need to know or to investigate whether your ancestor served in the local regulators, the state militia, or the Continental Army (or a combination of the three). You therefore are going to be dealing with records originally created at the local/county, state, *and/or* national level. This makes a great deal of difference in how you approach locating any surviving records.

If your ancestor served with the local regulators, he was probably assigned to policing and protecting the area in which he lived. If he served in South Carolina's state militia, the records relating to his military service *and* his military pension, if any, would have been created and maintained at the state level. Records of regulators and state militia are most likely to be found in the South Carolina Department of Archives and History (**http://scdah.sc.gov**), in the South Carolina State Library (**http://www.statelibrary.sc.gov**), or with the genealogical or historical societies throughout the state. That is assuming, of course, that he enlisted in the state in which he lived. If you cannot find records in the state in which he lived, check surrounding states.

If your ancestor served in the Continental Army, his military service and pension records would have been generated at a higher level and would be among the records maintained at the national level today. Payroll records, such as the one shown in Figure 8-4, can show the soldier's status at regular intervals throughout his service. Records for the Continental Army would be found among the records at the National Archives and Records Administration (NARA) in Washington, D.C.

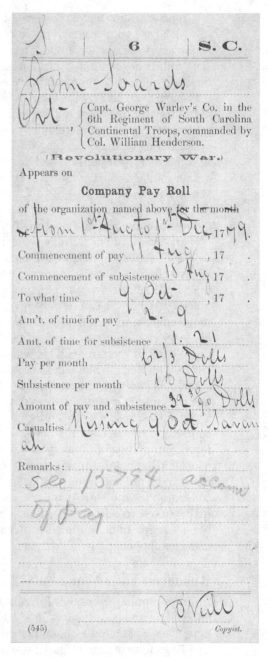

FIGURE 8-4   Company payroll record for John Soards [*sic*, Swords] for 1 August to 1 December 1779

Your ancestor may have served in one or more military units at all three levels, in which case your research might reveal records in multiple places. He may have begun service in the local regulators, for example, and then later enlisted in the state militia or the Continental Army. Similarly, he may have served his term in the state militia and then may have enlisted in the Continental Army. His unit, too, may have been sent by the state to be attached to the Continental Army. Your study of military units' history for that state's soldiers would help you understand the evolution of the participation of your ancestor's military unit and where to therefore seek existing records. You may find, as I did, that your ancestor collected a federal Revolutionary War pension and, upon its termination, applied for and was granted a state military pension for his service on behalf of the state in the Revolutionary War. What's more, all of these documents will be unique, created at different times by different government, military, or judicial officials, and therefore will contain different documents and potentially more information about your ancestor's service.

An American pension file typically includes an application for the pension, a doctor's statement, and an affidavit sworn by the applicant concerning the details of his military service. It may contain details of wounds sustained in battle and their residual effect on the person's health later in life. The personal account of the individual's service can be very revealing, and even poignant. Another affidavit was required from someone else who personally knew the applicant and could vouch for his service.

When the veteran died, his widow could apply for a continuation of her husband's pension for herself. She had to provide evidence of her marriage. For example, my ancestor Eleanor Swancy Swords applied for a continuation of her husband's pension. She submitted proof in the form of the actual family Bible pages for births, marriages, and deaths. These pages were removed from the Bible and they are among the contents of the pension file held at NARA. Children of the veteran also could apply for a continuation of the pension, and this was granted if requirements were met to establish relationship and need. Copies of the federal Revolutionary War pension files can be ordered from NARA. They also have been digitized by Fold3.com, in collaboration with NARA, and are available as part of a subscription to that service at **http://www.fold3.com**. Portions of these digitized files are also accessible through libraries with an institutional subscription to the HeritageQuest Online subscription database service.

Research Your War of 1812 Ancestors

An important development for genealogists concerns the War of 1812 pension application and bounty land files. These files had been manually indexed at NARA many years ago but the actual pension file documents had never been microfilmed. The Federation of Genealogical Societies (**http://www.fgs.org**) entered into an agreement with NARA in 2010 and began a fundraising effort to pay for the digitization and electronic indexing project for the more than 180,000 pension files held at NARA. Digitization and indexing is underway and the records are being made available for free at Fold3.com as they are completed. Diverse documents such as the one shown in Figure 8-5 can provide details of a veteran's life after the war.

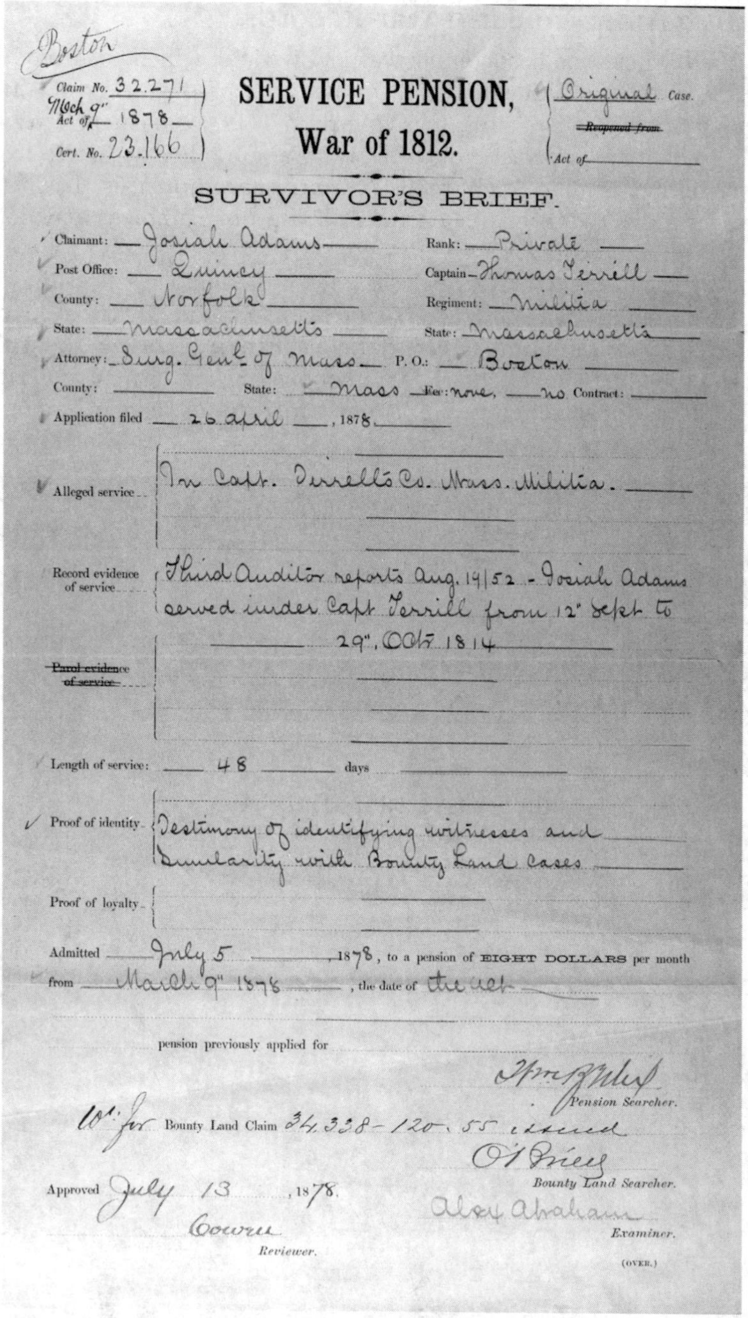

Boston

Claim No. 32.271
Mch 9" Act of 1878
Cert. No. 23.166

SERVICE PENSION,
War of 1812.

Original Case.
~~Reopened from~~
Act of

SURVIVOR'S BRIEF.

Claimant: Josiah Adams — Rank: Private
Post Office: Quincy — Captain Thomas Terrill
County: Norfolk — Regiment: Militia
State: Massachusetts — State: Massachusetts
Attorney: Surg. Genl. of Mass. — P.O.: Boston
County: — State: Mass — Fee: none, — no Contract:
Application filed 26 April, 1878.

Alleged service: In Capt. Terrell's Co. Mass. Militia.

Record evidence of service: Third Auditor reports Aug. 14/52 - Josiah Adams served under Capt Terrill from 12" Sept to 29", Oct 1814

~~Parol evidence of service~~

Length of service: 48 days

Proof of identity: Testimony of identifying witnesses and similarity with Bounty Land cases

Proof of loyalty:

Admitted July 5 1878, to a pension of EIGHT DOLLARS per month from March 9" 1878, the date of the act

pension previously applied for

Wm B Miles
Pension Searcher.

10' for Bounty Land Claim 34.338 - 120. 55 issued
O'Brien
Bounty Land Searcher.

Approved July 13, 1878.
Alex Abraham
Examiner.
Cowell
Reviewer.
(OVER.)

FIGURE 8-5 A Survivor's Brief is one of 34 document pages from the War of 1812 pension application of Josiah Adams of Massachusetts, approved 13 July 1878.

Research American Civil War Records

The United States' bloodiest conflict was its Civil War, which occurred between 1861 and 1865. The sheer volume of records produced is prodigious. NARA holds both the Union and Confederate records in its collection. Fold3.com (**http://www.fold3.com**) has digitized and placed vast groups of Civil War era military service records and pensions online. FamilySearch (**https://familysearch.org**) also has placed indexes and images in its Civil War Era Records database. State archives may hold the original state-level militia records.

You will want to search for and research your American ancestors at these online sites, as well as the Civil War Soldiers and Sailors System (CWSS) at **http://www.nps .gov/civilwar/soldiers-and-sailors-database.htm** (see Figure 8-6). This site offers indexes to the men who fought, the regiments in which they served, battles in which they fought, national cemeteries, prisoners, and Union Medal of Honor recipients.

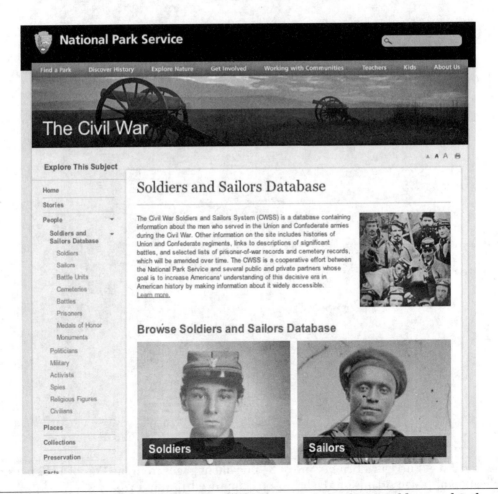

FIGURE 8-6 The main page of the National Park Service's Civil War Soldiers and Sailors Database.

Find Later Military Records

Military records of different eras also may be located in different places. Military service records in the United States are located at NARA for the period from 1775 to 1916. The United States' World War I draft registration cards were created during three calls for registration in 1917 and 1918, as shown in Table 8-1. Those draft registration cards are in the possession of the National Archives at Atlanta in Morrow, Georgia. They were microfilmed by NARA and have also been digitized and indexed by Ancestry.com (**http://www.ancestry.com**), FamilySearch (**https://familysearch.org**), and findmypast (**http://www.findmypast.com**). Understanding the history of the World War I draft registration process helped me determine that Charles Ray Morrison, shown previously in Figure 8-3, who was born in Munford, Talladega County, Alabama, on 27 March 1899, was not required to register until the Third Registration Day on 12 September 1918. I was able to locate his registration card and obtain additional personal details about him from that record. This is one example of how understanding the historical background of the period for a specific area can help you to locate records that can further your research.

You can request copies of the military service records held by NARA by completing NATF Form 86. You may request copies of military pension file records by completing NATF Form 85, or by submitting a request via the Internet. However, you will want to use NARA's eVetRecs site at **http://www.archives.gov/ veterans/military-service-records** to create a customized order form to request copies of military service records. NARA has produced tens of thousands of rolls of microfilmed military records. Their *Military Service Records: A Select Catalog of National Archives Microfilm Publications* is available in printed form but is also available in its entirety online. Visit their Publications web page at **http://www.archives.gov/ publications/genealogy/microfilm-catalogs.html**. These microfilmed records are accessible at NARA facilities, a complete listing of which can be found at

TABLE 8-1   U.S. World War I Draft Registration Calls and Age Ranges of Eligible Registrants

Registration Call and Date	Ages at that Time	Persons Born Between These Dates
First Registration Day 5 June 1917	All males between the ages of 21 to 31	5 June 1886 and 5 June 1896
Second Registration Day 5 June 1918	Males who reached the age of 21 since 5 June 1917	6 June 1896 and 5 June 1897
Supplemental Second Registration Day 24 August 1918	Males who reached the age of 21 since 5 June 1918	6 June 1897 and 24 August 1897
Third Registration Day 12 September 1918	All males aged 18 to 20 and 31 to 45 who had not previously registered	12 September 1872 and 12 September 1900

http://www.archives.gov/locations. (Be sure to check the location's website and contact the facility in advance to verify their microfilm holdings, because not all branches maintain a complete collection of all microfilm materials.) In addition, contact or visit the nearest LDS Family History Center (FHC) to determine if they can order copies of the microfilm from the Family History Library (FHL) in Salt Lake City, Utah, for your research use.

United States military service records from about 1917 to present are maintained by the National Personnel Records Center (NPRC) facility at 1 Archives Drive, St. Louis, MO 63138. Unfortunately, a fire on 12 July 1973 at its previous facility destroyed an estimated 16–18 million military personnel files. Approximately 80 percent of the U.S. Army personnel records for persons discharged between 1 November 1912 and 1 January 1960 were destroyed. An estimated 75 percent of U.S. Air Force personnel records were lost for persons discharged between 25 September 1947 and 1 January 1964. There were no duplicates or microfilm records of these records. Some of these records in files were damaged but not destroyed, and these have been re-filed. The NPRC, on receipt of a veteran's or surviving family member's request, will attempt to reconstruct a destroyed service record for an individual using other sources when possible. If you had requested copies of an ancestor's or family member's records in the past, and were told that they were destroyed by the 1973 fire, it would be wise to make another request because more materials have been recovered or reconstructed.

You can learn more about the NPRC at **http://www.archives.gov/st-louis/ military-personnel/about-ompfs.html**. Records are accessioned to NARA and become archival at the NPRC 62 years after the service member's separation from the military. There are therefore rules governing who can and who cannot access the service records. A guide is available at the website.

As you can see, there is some overlap between the military records held by NARA in Washington, D.C., and by the NPRC in St. Louis. Again, by doing some research in advance of making requests for documents or making a trip, you may avoid the expense, delays, and disappointment of coming up empty-handed because you requested material at the wrong location.

This all might be confusing if you don't take the time to understand the historical background of the period in which your ancestor lived, the military service requirements at the time, the years and military conflicts in which he or she might have participated, the branch of the military, the types of records created, and where they might be stored. For U.S. military records, the best book currently available is James C. Neagles' *U.S. Military Records: A Guide to Federal and State Sources— Colonial America to the Present*. Published by Ancestry Publishing in 1994, this book still provides excellent descriptions of the military conflicts, the records created, and where they are located. There are no Internet addresses in the book and, since its publication, some government departments have been renamed and their addresses and telephone numbers may have changed. However, the content of the book is excellent and you can use your Internet search skills to locate current governmental contact information.

Locate Canadian Military Records

Canada is a fascinating combination of French, British, and aboriginal cultures, and its history is a study of the strength and courage of individuals carving life out of a rich but often harsh wilderness. Canada's topography ranges from shorelines to plains and mountains, and its temperatures range from temperate to arctic. As a result, the study of your Canadian ancestors can be quite different depending on where they lived and in what period in time.

It is interesting to read and learn about military conflicts between the French, English, and aboriginal people, plus the clashes with the Americans to the south. In addition, Canadians have participated in both World Wars and in other military conflicts around the world. If you are researching your Canadian ancestors, written histories may provide information to augment the contextual portrait of those individuals and their families.

Search for Early Records

Library and Archives Canada (LAC) (**http://www.collectionscanada.gc.ca**) is a great source for the majority of the military records that exist, and has done an excellent job of indexing materials for ease of location. You can access these materials by visiting the main webpage and clicking the Genealogy and Family History link. Select the Military topic in the list in the middle of the page, and then choose the subtopic for the military records about which you would like to learn more. Many of the military records have been microfilmed, and links are included to complete lists of microfilm reel numbers for easy consultation.

You will also find that Ancestry (**http://www.ancestry.com** and **http://www.ancestry.ca**) includes databases of Canadian military records. Both findmypast (**http://www.findmypast.com**) and MyHeritage (**http://www.myheritage.com**) include collections of military histories and reminiscences that are searchable and which can provide clues to point you to original service records.

The earliest Canadian military records date from the colonial era and relate to records of the French Ancien Régime, records concerning British regiments that were stationed in Canada, and a variety of United Empire Loyalists resources from the time of the American Revolutionary War (1775–1783). The latter group also includes some petitions to the Crown seeking reward for their loyalty and service. Some collections are broken up into two sections, Upper Canada and Lower Canada.

Unfortunately, however, few military records of any genealogical value exist for the period prior to World War I, with the exception of records for the South African (or "Boer") War, which lasted from 1899 until 1902. Earlier records consist of little more than muster rolls and pay lists, and these contain very little information other than the name of the soldier. Most of these records also have not been indexed, which means that you will need to know the regimental unit in which your ancestor may have served.

LAC's collection of British military and naval records includes materials with references to the British army units in Canada, Loyalist regiments during the period of the American Revolutionary War, the War of 1812, Canadian militia records, and some other materials. The index to this collection and the collection itself may be available through inter-institutional loan. The index includes a short description of the document, the date, the volume number in the collection, and the page number.

The military service personnel records for soldiers who served in the South African War also are in the possession of LAC. They have been organized in alphabetical order and have been microfilmed.

Locate and Access Records from World War I

LAC holds an extensive collection of records relating to World War I, accessible from the main page at **http://www.collectionscanada.gc.ca** by clicking the Genealogy and Family History link, clicking the Military topic, and then clicking the First World War topic. The database of Soldiers of the First World War (1914–1918) consists of the Canadian Expeditionary Force (CEF), and images of each soldier's Attestation Papers, such as the one shown in Figure 8-7, are indexed and searchable.

Each CEF unit was required to maintain a daily account of its field activities from the beginning of World War I. These accounts were known as "War Diaries" and are

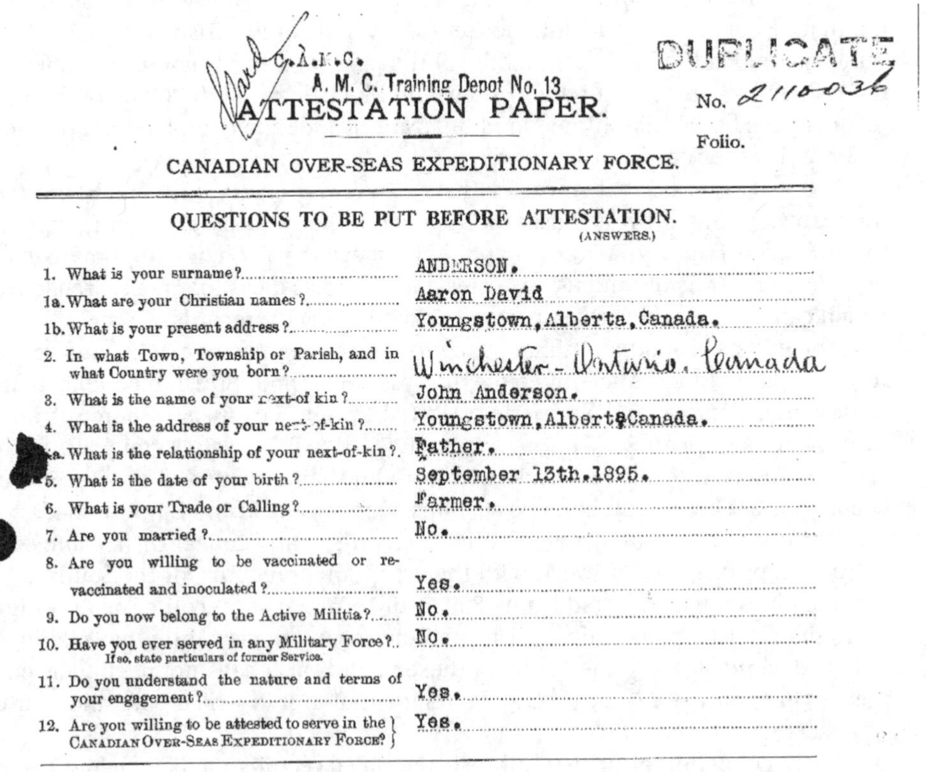

C.A.M.C.
A. M. C. Training Depot No. 13
ATTESTATION PAPER.

DUPLICATE
No. 2110036
Folio.

CANADIAN OVER-SEAS EXPEDITIONARY FORCE.

QUESTIONS TO BE PUT BEFORE ATTESTATION.

	(ANSWERS.)
1. What is your surname?	ANDERSON.
1a. What are your Christian names?	Aaron David
1b. What is your present address?	Youngstown, Alberta, Canada.
2. In what Town, Township or Parish, and in what Country were you born?	Winchester - Ontario. Canada
3. What is the name of your next-of kin?	John Anderson.
4. What is the address of your next-of-kin?	Youngstown, Albert, Canada.
4a. What is the relationship of your next-of-kin?	Father.
5. What is the date of your birth?	September 13th.1895.
6. What is your Trade or Calling?	Farmer.
7. Are you married?	No.
8. Are you willing to be vaccinated or re-vaccinated and inoculated?	Yes.
9. Do you now belong to the Active Militia?	No.
10. Have you ever served in any Military Force? If so, state particulars of former Service.	No.
11. Do you understand the nature and terms of your engagement?	Yes.
12. Are you willing to be attested to serve in the CANADIAN OVER-SEAS EXPEDITIONARY FORCE?	Yes.

FIGURE 8-7 Portion of page one of an Attestation Paper for a soldier of the Canadian Over-Seas Expeditionary Force

actually detailed unit histories. They include reports, maps, copies of orders, casualty listings, and other documents. Many of the War Diaries have been digitized and placed online, and are searchable by unit name and date. When you locate one that you wish to view, enter the collection and you will find the contents' images listed in chronological sequence by date and page. Click the link, and the document, or facing pages, will be displayed. Some images will be displayed at full size. Others may be resized using your browser to fit in its display window. If your browser has resized the image and it can be enlarged, there is a simple way to zoom in for easier reading. To zoom in on the image, move your mouse cursor to the lower-right corner of the image and pause. If it can be enlarged, a small orange box with blue arrows pointing outward from the four corners will pop up. Click that box and the image will be expanded to full size. While the contents of these War Diaries have not been indexed to make them searchable by keyword or phrase, you will find that the details of your ancestor's or family member's unit's activities will provide a clear picture of day-to-day life.

You might also want to visit the Veterans Affairs Canada (VAC) website at **http://www.vac-acc.gc.ca** for some of the best historical material about Canada's recent military past. Visit its Canada Remembers Program area (by clicking **Remembrance** on the home page), where you can search the Canadian Virtual War Memorial, a registry of more than 116,000 names of Canadians and Newfoundlanders with information about their graves and memorials. The site provides access to a searchable database of personnel information, which includes the soldier's name, date of death, service number, branch, regiment, and unit. The cemetery name, location, directions to it, and the precise burial location are included.

Another website you will want to visit is the Commonwealth War Graves Commission at **http://www.cwgc.org**, which commemorates the more than 1.7 million men and women of the Commonwealth Forces who died during World War I and World War II. Here, too, you can search by name for an individual. At this site, which represents war memorials for the entire British Commonwealth, there is even more information, including rank and nationality, as well as a link to provide details about the cemetery of interment.

The VAC also maintains the Canadian Merchant Navy War Dead Registry at **http://www.veterans.gc.ca/eng/remembrance/history/second-world-war/merchant-navy-war-dead-registry**. This database can be used to search for the names of sailors killed while serving in the Canadian Merchant Navy. It can also be used to search for the names of Canadian merchant naval vessels. You can enter the name of one of the Canadian Merchant Navy war dead, the vessel they served on, or both.

Some but by no means all of the Canadian military records are available on microfilm through the LDS Family History Centers. Microfilmed records are available for research at the LAC or through inter-institutional loan arrangements.

FamilySearch (**https://familysearch.org**) has an interesting collection at its website titled Canada, Merchant Marine Agreements and Accounts of Crew, 1890-1920. This is a browsable collection of images of documents held at the British Columbia Archives at Victoria. Included among the documents, organized by ship, are date, ship's information, provisions aboard, manifests, and signatures of the crewmembers, their ages, and birthplaces.

Search for Canadian Military Records After 1918

LAC holds personnel records for more than 5.5 million former military personnel of the Canadian Armed Forces and civilian employees of the Federal Public Service. You can request copies of records from LAC in writing, using their Application for Military Service Information form (available at **http://www.bac-lac.gc.ca/eng/discover/ military-heritage/Pages/obtain-copies-military-service-files.aspx**), an Access to Information Request Form (**http://www.bac-lac.gc.ca/eng/transparency/ atip/Pages/request.aspx**), or by letter. All requests are subject to the conditions of Canada's Access to Information Act and the Privacy Act.

Except for those who died in service during World War II, there is no public online database for the World War II personnel and service records because of access restrictions. Visit **http://www.collectionscanada.gc.ca/genealogy/022-909.007-e.html** for more information about what records are and are not accessible.

Other military records not held by LAC are referenced by links to other websites, including links to military records sites in Australia, France, Germany, Great Britain, Ireland, New Zealand, Poland, South Africa, and the United States.

Locate Military Records in the United Kingdom

Military records are of great interest in the United Kingdom because they are inextricably linked with documenting the history of Britain going back as far as William the Conqueror. You will find during your research that literally hundreds of books have been written about military conflicts that have involved Britain and its residents. The authors have used manuscripts and historical accounts of the military units and individuals, and have worked with the astonishing wealth of records that have been preserved. The Naval & Military Press, for example, is one of the largest independent booksellers in Britain, and their focus is on specialized titles concerning military conflicts. You can visit their website at **http://www.naval-military-press.com** to view or search for specific titles and subjects.

Understand the Historical Background

It is important with any research in Britain to spend time understanding the historical background of the time period and the geographical area in which your ancestors lived. This is especially true when seeking military records, because understanding the military structure at that time can help you determine what might be available and where any existing records may be located. A vast majority of military records may be in the possession of The National Archives (TNA) (**http://www.nationalarchives .gov.uk**), but some are held by other organizations. Let's start with a little history.

The English Civil War (1642–1651) is an important milestone in your military research. Prior to that period, there were no standing armies in England and Wales. Armed forces were raised as needed to fight in specific wars or for particular circumstances. Parliament raised the New Model Army, an organization of professional soldiers, in February of 1645 in order to more effectively fight the forces of King Charles I. This was the first formal army raised in England. The Union of 1707 brought England and Scotland together, and Scottish regiments became part of the British armed forces after that period.

A significant number of army documents exist starting from about 1660, and some fragmentary military records from slightly earlier can also be found. However, it is not until you begin researching military units dating from the early 1700s that you will find that large numbers of military documents have survived and have been preserved. Still, the records from these periods are records of organizations and not documents about specific individuals.

King Henry VIII's reign (1509–1547) saw the formation of the first permanent English navy. A few naval records exist dating from approximately 1617. The majority of the surviving records, however, date from about 1660 at the beginning of the reign of Charles II, the same era as those of the army.

Soldiers were organized into specific units that were known by various designations depending on the function of the organization. It helps to know that infantry troops were organized into regiments, and that subdivisions of these regiments were battalions and companies. Cavalry regiments were subdivided into squadrons, while the artillery units were subdivided into batteries. The subdivision distinctions were typically named in earlier times after their commanding officers, and it was not until the 1700s that numeric designations and a description were used to distinguish one from another. That does not mean that commanders' names were no longer used in references to the units, because you still might encounter a reference to a numeric designation along with a reference to a specific commander's group. Don't be surprised to find multiple commanders' names associated with a specific group, as there were numerous changes in leadership over time. It is therefore wise to focus on *both* a commander's name *and* a specific unit number and description. Other designations you will find for military units on active duty include armies, corps, divisions, brigades, and others. If your ancestor was an officer, there may be specific records concerning his service and command. However, if he was not an officer, it may be more difficult to locate specific records for him unless you know the unit in which he served, especially in the military records prior to the 20th century, which may not have been well organized and indexed.

If all of this seems confusing to you, don't feel that you are alone. The designations and names that were used have changed over time, and this just serves to illustrate the importance of learning more about your ancestor's origins and the military history of the era *and unit* in which he or she may have served. This can be especially important if your ancestor did not serve in the government's army but instead served in a volunteer militia.

TNA has prepared an excellent web page titled "Looking for a person?" at **http://www.nationalarchives.gov.uk/records/looking-for-person/?source = 404**. Here you can learn more about specific Army, Navy, Air Force, and many other records—by time period—that exist at TNA, what you can access online or at the archives, links to other websites, and links to TNA in-depth research guides. These resources can help you understand the types of records created, what is available, and how you might accomplish your most effective research.

Locate the Repositories Where Records Are Held

The National Archives (TNA) in Kew, Richmond upon Thames, is the best starting point for your military research. TNA was formed in April 2003 from the Public Record Office (PRO) and the Historical Manuscripts Commission (HMC). Movement of the holdings of the HMC to Kew was completed in the autumn of 2003, and everything is now housed and accessible at one location. When you are reading reference materials that refer to the PRO or the HMC, remember that these now refer to the holdings of The National Archives.

Military documents at TNA have been organized, stored, and cataloged in groups for ease of access, and a majority of these records have been microfilmed. Digitization and indexing of previously microfilmed records and other new collections have been made available at the TNA website in recent years. Therefore, TNA's holdings form a massive body of reference material that can help you learn more about and more successfully locate military documents for your British ancestor.

Military records in Britain have become more accessible in the past several years. Many of these are available on microfilm at TNA in Kew, and others have been digitized and made accessible online at **http://www.nationalarchives.gov.uk**. These resources contain exceptionally detailed history for an individual. More than 5 million military medals cards from World War I have been digitized, and copies are available for a small fee through Discovery, the online catalog at TNA at **http://discovery .nationalarchives.gov.uk/SearchUI/Home/OnlineCollections**. These cards record an individual's medal entitlement, their rank(s), their unit(s), and often the first theater of war in which they served, and they are digitized and online.

Many military records have been digitized by TNA and placed online. These include Naval Officers' Service Record Cards for more than 5,000 Royal Navy, Royal Naval Reserve, Royal Naval Volunteer Reserve, and Women's Royal Naval Service officers, Royal Air Force (RAF) service reports, RAF operations record books, RAF officers' service records, Women's RAF service records, Royal Marine service records, Household Calvary soldiers' service records, British Army nurses' service records, Women's Army Auxiliary Corps service records, and much more. At this writing, approximately 5 percent of TNA's records have been digitized. You can search the Discovery online catalog for other collections of materials and order copies.

In addition, you will find that specific governmental and civilian organizations can provide information and reference assistance. Let's look at the locations of many records.

Army Records   Army records prior to 1914 are held at TNA. Officers' records from 1914–1920 have been transferred from the Army Personnel Centre to TNA, but those from 1920 and later remain at that location. All records of enlisted personnel from 1914 and later remain there. Their website is located at **http://www.army.mod.uk/ welfare-support/23212.aspx**.

You will want to visit the Army Museums Ogilby Trust website's "Ancestor Research & Military Genealogy" pages at **http://www.armymuseums.org.uk/ ancestor.htm** to determine what is in their holdings and what may have been transferred to TNA, especially as this situation changes over time. You also will want to visit their Useful Addresses page at **http://www.armymuseums.org.uk/addr.htm** for postal, email, and website addresses that may supplement your research.

Navy Records   Naval records can be a bit more problematic to locate. Royal Navy records prior to 1914 are held at TNA, while the Ministry of Defence in Whitehall, London, retains the post-1914 records. The location of records, however, is subject to change periodically. The website for the Ministry of Defence is at **http://www .royalnavy.mod.uk**. Some good references for the location and accessibility of naval records are found at the website of the Mariners Mailing List at **http://www.mariners-l .co.uk/MarinersList.html**. In addition, be sure to check the UK Maritime Collections Strategy website at **http://www.ukmcs.org.uk** for links and access to specific sites holding maritime materials that may be of help in your research.

Ministry of Defence   The Ministry of Defence's Veterans UK website was created in 2007 and is the ideal place to begin your inquiry for personnel service records and pension information for those who served in the armed forces from World War II and later. The website at **http://www.veterans-uk.info** contains links for Service Records, Medals, and other information. The A–Z index is particularly helpful. There is a charge for record requests for family history/genealogical research purposes.

Military Museums of Note   Military museums hold fascinating collections of historical military materials that may be useful in your research. Inquiries for information and guidance usually receive prompt responses. The following list highlights some of the best of these resources:

- Imperial War Museum   **http://www.iwm.org.uk** (Be sure to enter **"family history"** in the Search box at the top of the web page. There are quite a few search results that can provide you with more information.)
- National Army Museum   **http://www.nam.ac.uk**
- National Maritime Museum   **http://www.rmg.co.uk/national-maritime- museum**
- Royal Air Force Museum   **http://www.rafmuseum.org.uk**
- Royal Marines Museum   **http://www.royalmarinesmuseum.co.uk**
- Royal Naval Museum   **http://www.royalnavalmuseum.org** (At the time of this writing, a new website was being designed for this museum. Use your favorite search engine and enter **"royal naval museum portsmouth"** to locate the current site if the URL does not work.)
- Royal Navy Submarine Museum   **http://www.submarine-museum.co.uk**

Other Helpful Resources   Don't overlook the resources of local public and academic libraries in the area in which your ancestors lived or from which they may have served. Other helpful resources in locating military records and historical materials include the following organizations:

- Federation of Family History Societies (FFHS)   **http://www.ffhs.org.uk**
- GENUKI—British Military Records page   **http://www.genuki.org.uk/big/ BritMilRecs.html**

Learn About the Types of Military Records in the United Kingdom

Military records may vary across the different branches of service. The following are document types that you may expect to locate, especially among the modern era:

- **Attestation Form**   Attestation forms were completed by most recruits when they applied to be admitted for service in the military. This is the equivalent of an enlistment form in other military organizations, such as the U.S. armed forces. The attestation form usually asked for the person's name, date and place of birth, place of residence, marital status, next of kin, occupation and/or skills, previous military service, and physical description. Later forms asked for parents' names and other information.

- **Muster Rolls and Pay Lists**   Military units tracked the physical presence of troops and their attendance using muster rolls. Regular assembly of troops included roll calls and reports of persons missing. These rolls exist by unit and can be used to verify your ancestor's presence or status in a specific location at a precise point in time. Pay records exist in various forms ranging from payroll lists to individuals' payment stubs and/or receipts.

- **Personnel Records**   These, too, vary in their existence and content over time.

- **Casualty Lists and Returns**   As a result of muster calls, observations, reports, and medical information, casualty lists were created for the military unit. Depending on the time period, individual forms may have been created to document a person's injuries or death. These can take the shape of a letter or form, and there may also be copies of correspondence in an individual's personnel or service file and/or in the military unit's files.

- **Medical Records**   Medical records may be included in an individual's personnel file, in the records of the military unit or the appropriate echelon, or may still exist in the archives of the medical facility in which the individual was treated. Summary reports were often sent to the military unit for its records, while sometimes the records are quite extensive. Figure 8-8 shows a single page from a lengthy medical summary for an English soldier wounded by shrapnel in World War II and who underwent several years' treatment for his wounds.

- **Records of Deserters**   Military life was difficult even in the best of times, and harsh conditions induced some individuals to desert. Military units maintained lists of deserters, and records were included in the individual's file. In addition, the British military published lists of deserters in public newspapers and in the *Police Gazette.* You will find that these records may be helpful if your ancestor "disappeared" from the military at a particular time.

- **Records of Courts Martial**   Military discipline has always been notoriously harsh, and a great deal has always been made of conducting and publicizing the military court martial. Detailed records of such actions are to be found in unit records and in an individual's service records. In addition, accounts of a high-profile person's court martial may sometimes be found in newspapers of the period.

- **Discharge Papers**   Discharge papers vary greatly from different periods. The earliest ones are nothing more than handwritten statements confirming the name, dates, and military unit(s) in which the individual served, signed either by an officer or clerk in the organization. Later there were pre-printed forms

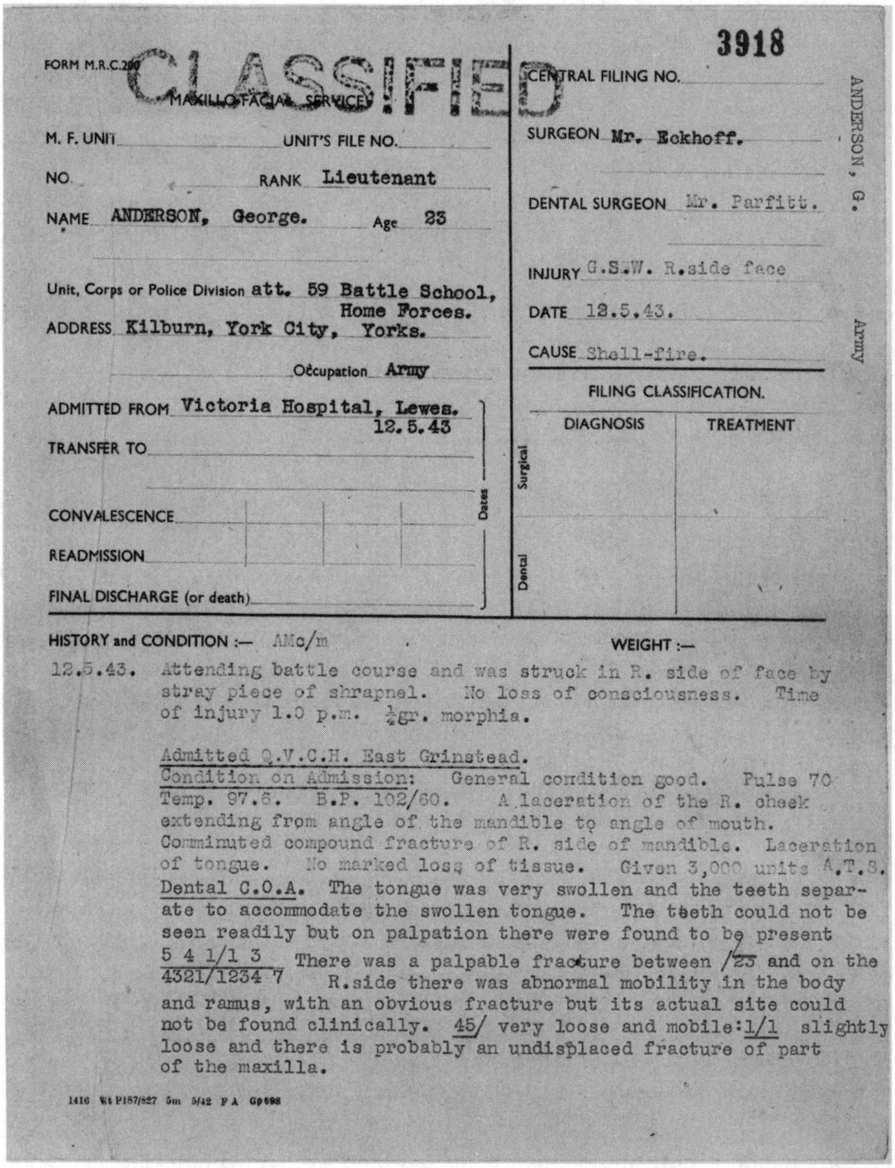

3918

FORM M.R.C.200 CLASSIFIED

MAXILLO-FACIAL SERVICE

CENTRAL FILING NO.

ANDERSON, G. Army

M. F. UNIT ______ UNIT'S FILE NO. ______

SURGEON Mr. Eckhoff.

NO. ______ RANK Lieutenant

DENTAL SURGEON Mr. Parfitt.

NAME ANDERSON, George. Age 23

INJURY G.S.W. R.side face

Unit, Corps or Police Division att. 59 Battle School, Home Forces.

DATE 12.5.43.

ADDRESS Kilburn, York City, Yorks.

CAUSE Shell-fire.

Occupation Army

FILING CLASSIFICATION.

ADMITTED FROM Victoria Hospital, Lewes. 12.5.43

TRANSFER TO ______

CONVALESCENCE ______

READMISSION ______

FINAL DISCHARGE (or death) ______

Dates

	DIAGNOSIS	TREATMENT
Surgical		
Dental		

HISTORY and CONDITION :— AMc/m

WEIGHT :—

12.5.43. Attending battle course and was struck in R. side of face by stray piece of shrapnel. No loss of consciousness. Time of injury 1.0 p.m. ¼gr. morphia.

Admitted Q.V.C.H. East Grinstead.
Condition on Admission: General condition good. Pulse 70 Temp. 97.6. B.P. 102/60. A laceration of the R. cheek extending from angle of the mandible to angle of mouth. Comminuted compound fracture of R. side of mandible. Laceration of tongue. No marked loss of tissue. Given 3,000 units A.T.S. Dental C.O.A. The tongue was very swollen and the teeth separate to accommodate the swollen tongue. The teeth could not be seen readily but on palpation there were found to be present 5 4 1/1 3 over 4321/1234 7. There was a palpable fracture between /23 and on the R.side there was abnormal mobility in the body and ramus, with an obvious fracture but its actual site could not be found clinically. 45/ very loose and mobile: 1/1 slightly loose and there is probably an undisplaced fracture of part of the maxilla.

1416 Wt P187/827 5m 5/42 F A Gp698

FIGURE 8-8 Page from the medical records of a wounded English soldier in World War II

used that provided space for the name, rank, military unit, date of birth, age, dates of service, places where the individual served and campaigns in which he had participated, awards, medals, commendations, wounds suffered, physical condition at the time of discharge, and statements concerning the individual's character and performance. Later versions of the forms used included inoculation records and other data.

- **Pension Files**   Veterans and/or their surviving spouse and/or family members were entitled to certain pension benefits. In order to obtain a benefit, a person had to make an application. This might take the form of a written petition or an appearance before a court or hearing board. Documentation is therefore likely to exist in one or more places. You may find pension records and related documents in the possession of TNA or through a specific veterans' organization. Veterans' groups and organizations that formed to assist veterans in obtaining benefits may be particularly helpful to your research. The Ministry of Defence's Veterans UK site (**http://www.veterans-uk.info**) maintains a page of web links to ex-service (veteran) organizations and registered charities.

Learn About Military Records for Ireland

Military records for Ireland and its citizens who served in the military during the time that it was under the British government will be found among those records at The National Archives. Ireland has its own Army, Navy, and Air Corps forces, and those more modern records will be in the possession of the Irish government. An excellent website to begin your research for more contemporary Irish military history and records is the Defence Forces of Ireland website located at **http://www.military.ie**.

As you can see, there are many, many avenues of research available for your search for military records in the British Isles. It is therefore important to conduct your preliminary historical research in advance so that you are better informed concerning what records may or may not be available and where to search for them.

Locate Australian Military Records

The National Archives of Australia holds records of its defense forces from the time of Federation in 1901. This includes Australian Army records from the Boer War, World War I, service between the wars, World War II, and service subsequent to World War II. The Royal Australian Navy records include two categories: service up to 1970 and service after 1970. The Royal Australian Air Force Records are also grouped into two categories: service before World War II and service after World War II. The archives also hold a number of other types of records relating to wartime service. You can learn about all of the holdings by visiting the website at **http://www.naa.gov.au**.

The Australian Ancestry.com site at **http://www.ancestry.com.au** is a genealogy database collection accessible by subscription, and it includes several military databases for Australian servicemen and servicewomen. They can be found by using the Ancestry Card Catalogue under the Search link. These include at this writing, among many others:

- **ANZAC Memorial, 1914–1918**   This database contains *The Anzac Memorial*, a book compiled to commemorate those who served in the Australian and New Zealand Army Corps (ANZAC) and died in World War I. The digitized book contains the Roll of Honour and is organized in alphabetical sequence by surname and is searchable.

- *Australia's Fighting Sons of The Empire: Portraits and Biographies of Australians in the Great War*   This book contains biographical text and photographs of thousands of Australians who served in World War I. It is digitized, indexed, and searchable. (Enter **Portraits and Biographies** in the Title box in the Ancestry Card Catalogue search template to locate it.)
- **New Zealand Army Medal Rolls, 1860-1919**   This collection is one of a number of materials published online at this site concerning individuals from New Zealand who were awarded medals, decorations, and commendations for their military service. Check the Card Catalog for other New Zealand database collections.

Another excellent site for locating information is the World War Two Nominal Roll website at **http://www.ww2roll.gov.au**. It "was created to honour and commemorate the men and women who served in Australia's defence forces and the Merchant Navy" during World War II. It contains the service details of individuals who served during the period 3 September 1939 to 2 September 1945. The number of individuals collected for the Nominal Roll includes some 50,600 members of the Royal Australian Navy (RAN), 845,000 members of the Australian Army, 218,300 members of the Royal Australian Air Force (RAAF), and approximately 3,500 merchant mariners. This database is searchable by name, service number, honor awarded, or location (within Australia or elsewhere). For each search result, you can print a certificate (see Figure 8-9), see a full explanation of all the details in the record, or request a copy of the actual records from the National Archives of Australia.

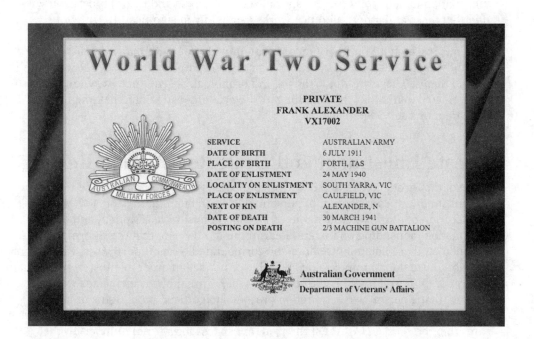

FIGURE 8-9   A certificate from the World War Two Nominal Roll website

Examine Samples of Military Records

I find that one helpful strategy in investigating military records is to examine specific representative examples of records created during the period I am researching. Army, Navy, Marine, and Army Air Corps records created during World War II in the United States all contain similar if not identical information.

Military records from the same period in the United Kingdom, Canada, and Australia will all contain information of a similar type as defined and required by their governmental organizations. Examining these materials can provide insight into just what types of data *were* recorded, and this helps me focus my search on those records as well as other locations where identical or similar data were collected. Therefore, if I am unable to locate the information in one place, I can investigate alternate research paths to possibly locate it elsewhere.

There are many reference books available that can help you learn more about military records and their contents. James C. Neagles' books, *U.S. Military Records: A Guide to Federal and State Sources, Colonial America to the Present* (Ancestry Publishing, 1994) and *Confederate Research Sources: A Guide to Archive Collections*, Second Edition (Ancestry.com, 1986), are both excellent American references. Mark D. Herber's book, *Ancestral Trails: The Complete Guide to British Genealogy and Family History*, Second Edition (Genealogical Publishing Company, 2006), contains an exhaustive study of available military records for that area. Other works, such as John J. Newman's book about U.S. World War I draft registrations, titled *Uncle, We Are Ready! Registering America's Men, 1917–1918* (Heritage Quest, 2001), provide comprehensive, definitive information to help you research specialized topic areas and record types. You will find that these and other reference works can help you significantly with your research. You just need to start investigating what is available.

Your research into military records can provide you with many details about the individual. Let's look at a number of specific examples of military records from the United States. These are not arranged in chronological sequence by when they were created, but rather in something of a logical order in which they might occur in the career of a serviceperson.

Locate Enlistment and Draft Registration Records

Some of the most detailed and descriptive records you will find are those relating to the enlistment or conscription of personnel. They contain name and address, date and location of birth, parents' names, a personal physical description, and other information, depending on the era. Bear in mind, however, that the information supplied on these documents should be corroborated with other sources. For example, it is not unusual for a minor to lie about his or her age in order to enlist in the military. It was not until well into the 20th century, when formal birth certificates were created, that a person was required to present such official proof of his or her age.

Figures 8-10 and 8-11 show both sides of a sample World War I draft registration card from the files at NARA. On the front are spaces for a serial number for the

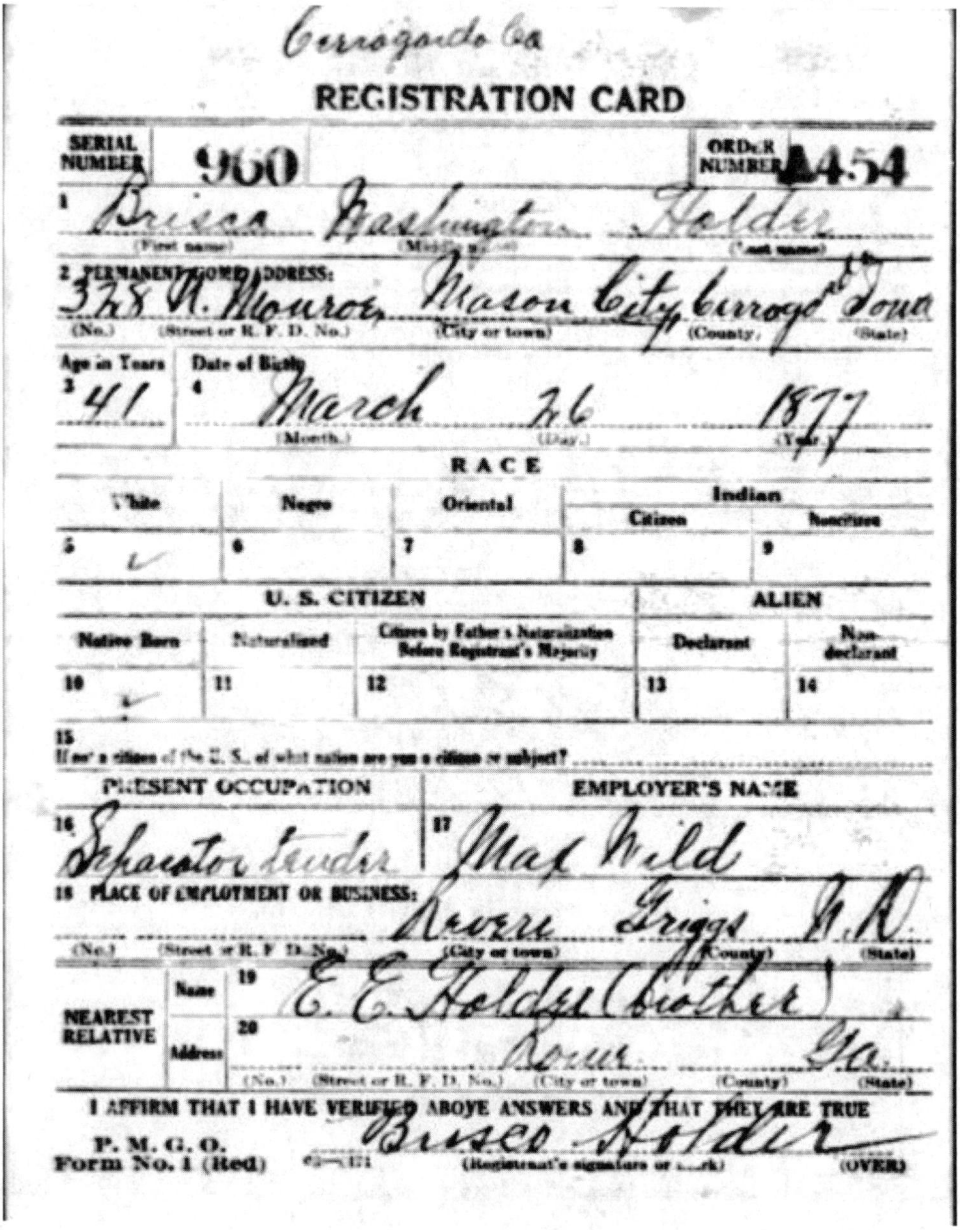

Cerrogordo Co

REGISTRATION CARD

SERIAL NUMBER 960 ORDER NUMBER A454

1 Brisco Washington Holder
(First name) (Middle name) (Last name)

2 PERMANENT HOME ADDRESS:
328 N. Monroe Mason City Cerrogordo Iowa
(No.) (Street or R. F. D. No.) (City or town) (County) (State)

Age in Years	Date of Birth		
3 41	4 March (Month)	26 (Day)	1877 (Year)

RACE

White	Negro	Oriental	Indian: Citizen	Indian: Noncitizen
5 ✓	6	7	8	9

U. S. CITIZEN: Native Born	U. S. CITIZEN: Naturalized	U. S. CITIZEN: Citizen by Father's Naturalization Before Registrant's Majority	ALIEN: Declarant	ALIEN: Non-declarant
10 ✓	11	12	13	14

15 If not a citizen of the U. S., of what nation are you a citizen or subject?

PRESENT OCCUPATION	EMPLOYER'S NAME
16 Separator Tender	17 Max Wild

18 PLACE OF EMPLOYMENT OR BUSINESS:
Revere Griggs N.D.
(No.) (Street or R. F. D. No.) (City or town) (County) (State)

NEAREST RELATIVE
Name 19 E. E. Holder (brother)
Address 20 Rome Ga.
(No.) (Street or R. F. D. No.) (City or town) (County) (State)

I AFFIRM THAT I HAVE VERIFIED ABOVE ANSWERS AND THAT THEY ARE TRUE

P. M. G. O.
Form No. 1 (Red)
Brisco Holder
(Registrant's signature or mark) (OVER)

FIGURE 8-10 Front of a U.S. World War I draft registration card

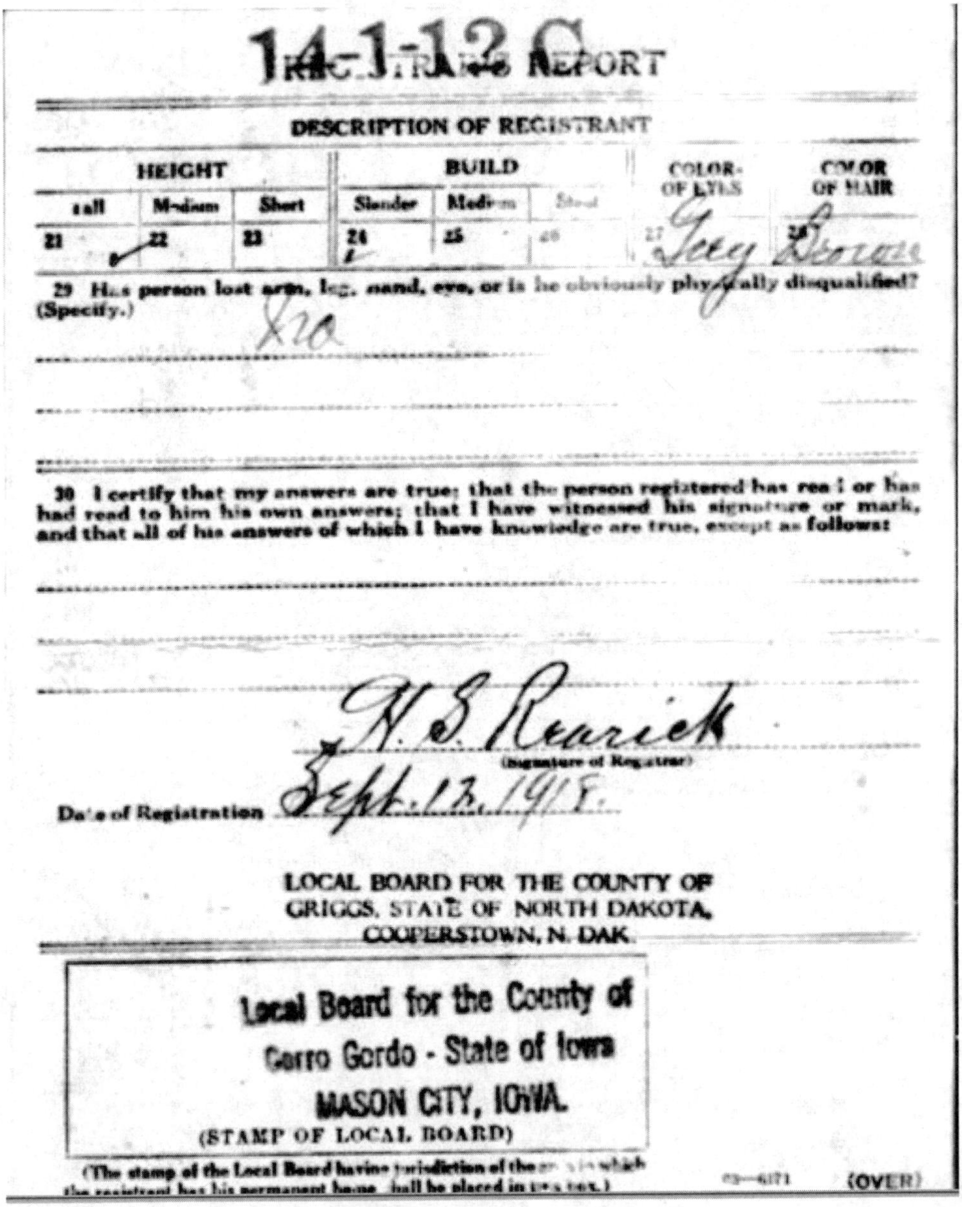

14-1-12 C

REGISTRAR'S REPORT

DESCRIPTION OF REGISTRANT

HEIGHT			BUILD			COLOR OF EYES	COLOR OF HAIR
Tall	Medium	Short	Slender	Medium	Stout		
21	22 ✓	23	24 ✓	25	26	27 Grey	28 Brown

29 Has person lost arm, leg, hand, eye, or is he obviously physically disqualified? (Specify.) No

30 I certify that my answers are true; that the person registered has read or has had read to him his own answers; that I have witnessed his signature or mark, and that all of his answers of which I have knowledge are true, except as follows:

H. S. Rearick
(Signature of Registrar)

Date of Registration Sept. 12, 1918.

LOCAL BOARD FOR THE COUNTY OF
GRIGGS, STATE OF NORTH DAKOTA,
COOPERSTOWN, N. DAK.

Local Board for the County of
Cerro Gordo - State of Iowa
MASON CITY, IOWA.

(STAMP OF LOCAL BOARD)

(The stamp of the Local Board having jurisdiction of the area in which the registrant has his permanent home shall be placed in this box.)

(OVER)

FIGURE 8-11 Back of a U.S. World War I draft registration card

registration, the registrant's name, address, date of birth, whether a U.S. citizen, nearest relative, employer's name and address, and the signature of the registrant. The back includes spaces to provide a physical description of the registrant, the signature of the registrar, and the date. The stamp of the local draft board that had jurisdiction over the area in which the applicant registered was also applied.

The information on this draft card may point you to city directory listings, a voter registration record, driver's license, land and property records, religious congregations in the area, employment records, and other records. The name of the nearest relative provides yet another research clue for you. In this case, E. E. Holder is indicated as the registrant's brother, and you might look for that name in census records, city and telephone directories, land and property records, death certificates, wills and probate records, obituaries, and other documents to locate that person in Rome, Floyd County, Georgia, and trace other family members. You might also search earlier census schedules to locate the two brothers together with their parents.

World War II draft registration records and enlistment records for U.S. soldiers, such as the ones shown in Figures 8-12 and 8-13, are becoming available online as indexes or as indexed, searchable, digitized images at such sites as Ancestry.com (**http://www.ancestry.com**), FamilySearch (**https://familysearch.org**), findmypast (**http://www.findmypast.com**), and Fold3.com (**http://www.fold3.com**).

Military Muster Rolls and Pay Records

Military units regularly muster their troops to verify attendance, issue orders, issue announcements, drill, and perform other functions. Muster roll records for a military

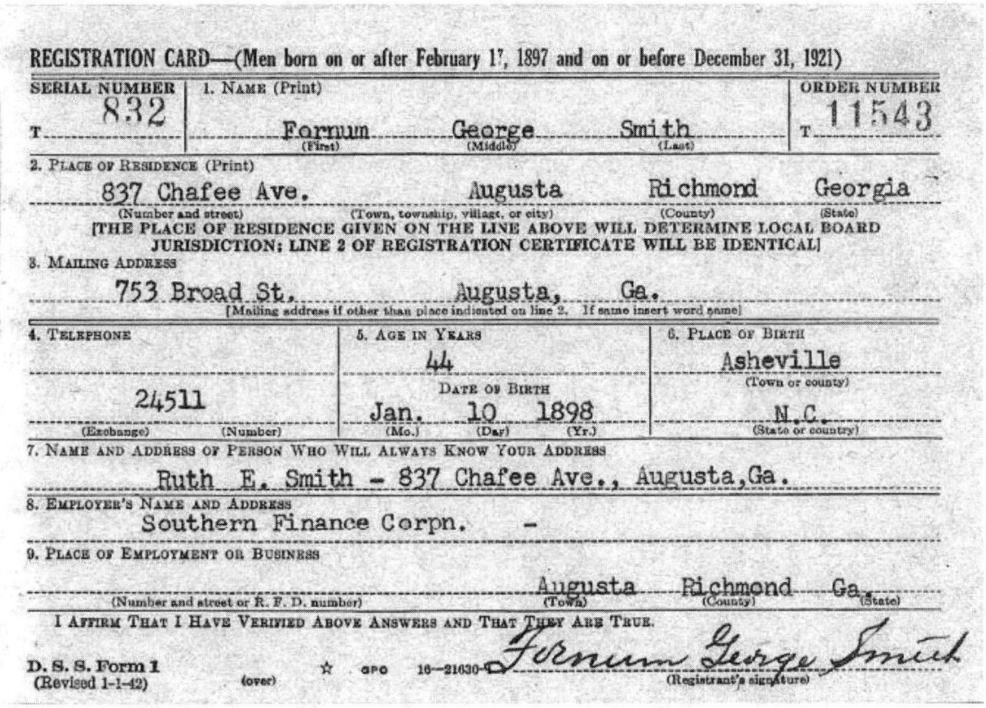

FIGURE 8-12   Digitized image of World War II draft registration card

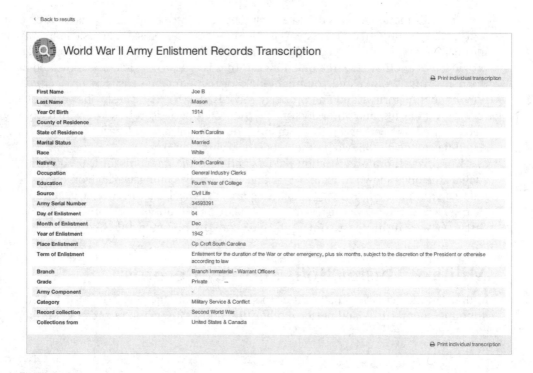

‹ Back to results

World War II Army Enlistment Records Transcription

Print individual transcription

First Name	Joe B
Last Name	Mason
Year Of Birth	1914
County of Residence	-
State of Residence	North Carolina
Marital Status	Married
Race	White
Nativity	North Carolina
Occupation	General Industry Clerks
Education	Fourth Year of College
Source	Civil Life
Army Serial Number	34593391
Day of Enlistment	04
Month of Enlistment	Dec
Year of Enlistment	1942
Place Enlistment	Cp Croft South Carolina
Term of Enlistment	Enlistment for the duration of the War or other emergency, plus six months, subject to the discretion of the President or otherwise according to law
Branch	Branch Immaterial - Warrant Officers
Grade	Private
Army Component	-
Category	Military Service & Conflict
Record collection	Second World War
Collections from	United States & Canada

Print individual transcription

FIGURE 8-13 Transcribed detail from a World War II enlistment record

unit and muster cards for individual soldiers can be found in many U.S. military service files from the colonial period forward. In addition, unit payroll records and payment stubs or receipts can provide important information to help place your ancestor at a specific place and time. The pay stub shown in Figure 8-14 for my ancestor John Swords indicates that he was paid "Three Pounds, five Shills, & eight Pence half Penny Sterling" for 43 days of military duty in 1782. Coupled with other military records, such as his sworn affidavit of service found in his Revolutionary War pension file, it is possible to link John Swords with a particular military command at that date. Further, by researching military history for that unit, I can determine where he traveled and what military action he saw.

Seek Out Educational and Training Records

Military personnel are trained to perform their jobs at an optimal level. We are all familiar with the idea of infantry troops going through their drills of marching, combat assault, hand-to-hand combat, rifle practice and marksmanship, use of artillery equipment, bivouac, flight training, seamanship, and a wide range of operations training. Military service records may contain information about the education, testing, and evaluation of an individual's skills and any specialized education or training provided. The records you may encounter in an individual's personnel files and/or the service files may include test scores, correspondence documenting successful completion of training, certificates, and diplomas. Figure 8-15 is an example of a certificate of completion of an Air Force medical training course.

Look for Military Station and Duty Assignment Orders

Personnel are assigned to specific locations and are attached to specific units. Documents are created to order the individual to report to a location and to perform explicit duties or functions. These documents are often referred to as "orders," and the individual is typically charged with delivering his or her orders to the new unit's commanding officer or clerk. A copy of the orders is retained in the individual's service file. Figure 8-16 shows an example of a Permanent Change of Station Order. Again, the information in this document can be used to verify the movement of an individual from one place to another and to help relate his or her service to the activities of the military unit at that time.

Promotions and Commissions

A successful individual may, in the course of his or her military service, be promoted to higher levels of authority and greater responsibility. In the U.S. armed forces, there is a distinction made between recruits, noncommissioned officers (also known as NCOs), and

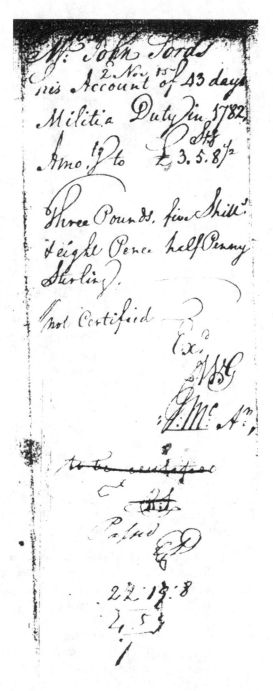

FIGURE 8-14   Image of a Revolutionary War pay record for John Sords [*sic*, Swords] military service in 1782, obtained from a NARA pension file

FIGURE 8-15 Certificate of completion of a medical training course

commissioned officers. You can learn more about the various ranks by researching the individual branches of the military service and their history at the time your ancestor or family member served. There are typically several documents associated with a personnel promotion or a commission.

A promotion of a noncommissioned officer is usually documented with a written notice to the serviceperson, a copy to every level of command under which the person serves, a copy to the person's file, and a notice posted in a unit's communication media, such as on a bulletin board, in a newsletter, or in some other venue.

An officer's commission is more formal. A congratulatory letter is delivered to the individual formally announcing the commissioning. The notification processes throughout the echelon are similar. In addition to the letter, an example of which is shown in Figure 8-17, a formal certificate like the one shown in Figure 8-18 commemorating the new appointment is created and presented to the individual.

PERMANENT CHANGE OF STATION ORDER — MILITARY

(Items preceded by an asterisk for overseas only.) (If more space is required, continue on reverse.)

1. INDIVIDUAL WP ON PCS AS SHOWN BELOW	

2. GRADE, LAST NAME, FIRST, MIDDLE INITIAL, AFSN
Private

3. SHIPPING AFSC *(Officer)*

4. CAFSC *(Airmen)*   30650A

5. ☐ OVER 4 YEARS SERVICE *(AIC Only)*

6. UNIT, MAJOR AIR COMMAND AND ADDRESS OF UNIT FROM WHICH RELIEVED
2130 Comm Sq, AFCS
APO New York 09378

7. UNIT MAJOR AIR COMMAND AND ADDRESS OF UNIT TO WHICH ASSIGNED AND DUTY STATION IF APPROPRIATE
1611 AB Gp, MATS
McGuire AFB, NJ

8. PURPOSE OF REASSIGNMENT IF OTHER THAN DUTY
Separation

9. REPORT TO COMDR., NEW ASSIGNMENT XXX
Immediately upon arrival in ConUS

10. *(Reassignment from overseas unit to CONUS unit only.)*
REPORT AT NEW ASSIGNMENT NLT_____DAYS AFTER DEPARTURE FROM CONUS PORT OF ENTRY UNIT

11. DALVP   No

12. EDCSA   3 Feb 65

13. TDY EN ROUTE *(Indicate Location or unit and address.)*

14. PURPOSE OF TDY

15. SECURITY CLEARANCE FOR PERIOD OF TDY OR COURSE OF INSTRUCTION

16. TDY REPORTING DATE

17. APPROXIMATE NO. OF DAYS

*18. LEAVE ADDRESS

*19. NEW MAILING ADDRESS *(Use upon completion of TDY, if appropriate.)* GRADE, NAME, AFSN

20. DURATION OF COURSE *(If reassignment is to attend course of instruction.)*_____WEEKS

*21. ☐ CONCURRENT TRAVEL OF DEPENDENTS IS NOT AUTHORIZED

*22. ☐ TRAVEL OF DEPENDENTS IS PROHIBITED

*23. TRAVEL OF DEPENDENTS TO A DESIGNATED POINT ☐ IS ☐ IS NOT AUTHORIZED

24. ☐ TRANSPORTATION OF DEPENDENTS AND SHIPMENT OF HHG TO TDY STATION IS NOT AUTHORIZED

*25. CONCURRENT TRAVEL OF DEPENDENTS IS AUTHORIZED *(List names of dependents and DOB of children.)*

*26. AUTHORITY FOR CONCURRENT TRAVEL

27. TRAVEL TIME WILL BE COMPUTED PER CHAPTER 26, PART 1, AFM 35-11.
TPA WITH_____DAYS TRAVEL TIME

28. _____POUNDS BAGGAGE, INCLUDING EXCESS IS AUTHORIZED

29. DISLOCATION ALLOWANCE CATEGORY

*30. MODES OF TRANSPORTATION AUTHORIZED FOR OVERSEAS TRAVEL

A. ☒ MILITARY AIRCRAFT   B. ☐ COMMERCIAL AIRCRAFT *(Category Z)*   C. ☐ MILITARY AND COMMERCIAL VESSEL   D. ☐ COMMERCIAL AIRCRAFT OR VESSEL *(Also foreign registry if US registry is not available)* RAIL OR BUS WITHIN OVERSEAS AREAS

*31. REPORT AT MATS PASSENGER SERVICE COUNTER
☒ RAF Mildenhall, England
☐ McGUIRE AFB   ☐ TRAVIS AFB
☐ McCHORD AFB   ☐ CHARLESTON AFB

*32. FLIGHT NO. OR NAME OF VESSEL
T1238

*33. PIER NO. AND ADDRESS

*34. REPORTING TIME AND DATE FOR SCHEDULED DEPARTURE
NET 1800, 2 Feb 65
NLT 2200, 2 Feb 65

35. *A. PRIOR TO TRAVEL COMPLY WITH AFM 75-4.   *B. WHILE ON LEAVE OVERSEAS COMPLY WITH AFM 35-22, AND CHAPTER 1, AFM 35-10.
  C. In the event of limited war or mobilization and individual is traveling: PCS UNACCOMPANIED-proceed as scheduled. PCS ACCOMPANIED-contact your last commander immediately for instructions before reporting to port. In the event of general war or if the CONUS is attacked report to the nearest active Air Force Installation as soon as possible.

36. REMARKS

Home of Record: Box 383, Madison, NC. Place last entered into active duty is: Charlotte, NC. AMD: MHZ WRI 3PU 0319 FN 02.

39-11

37. AUTHORITY, AFM XXX AND
AFR 35-10

38. DATE
5 January 1965

39. SPECIAL ORDER NO.
A-7

40. DESIGNATION AND LOCATION OF HEADQUARTERS
2130 Comm Sq, AFCS
APO New York 09378

41. PCS EXPENSE CHARGEABLE TO
5753500 325 P577.02 S503725 1290
2121 2141 2161 2293 2593

42. DISTRIBUTION
X

43. CUSTOMER IDENTIFICATION CODE   45 548 5776 503725

44. TDY EXPENSE CHARGEABLE TO

45. TDN   FOR THE COMMANDER

46. SIGNATURE ELEMENT OF ORDERS AUTHENTICATING OFFICIAL

John P Pribble

JOHN P PRIBBLE
2nd Lt, USAF
Asst Administrative Services Officer

AF FORM 899
AUG. 63

☆ U. S. GOVERNMENT PRINTING OFFICE — 1963-699-267

FIGURE 8-16   Permanent Change of Station Order

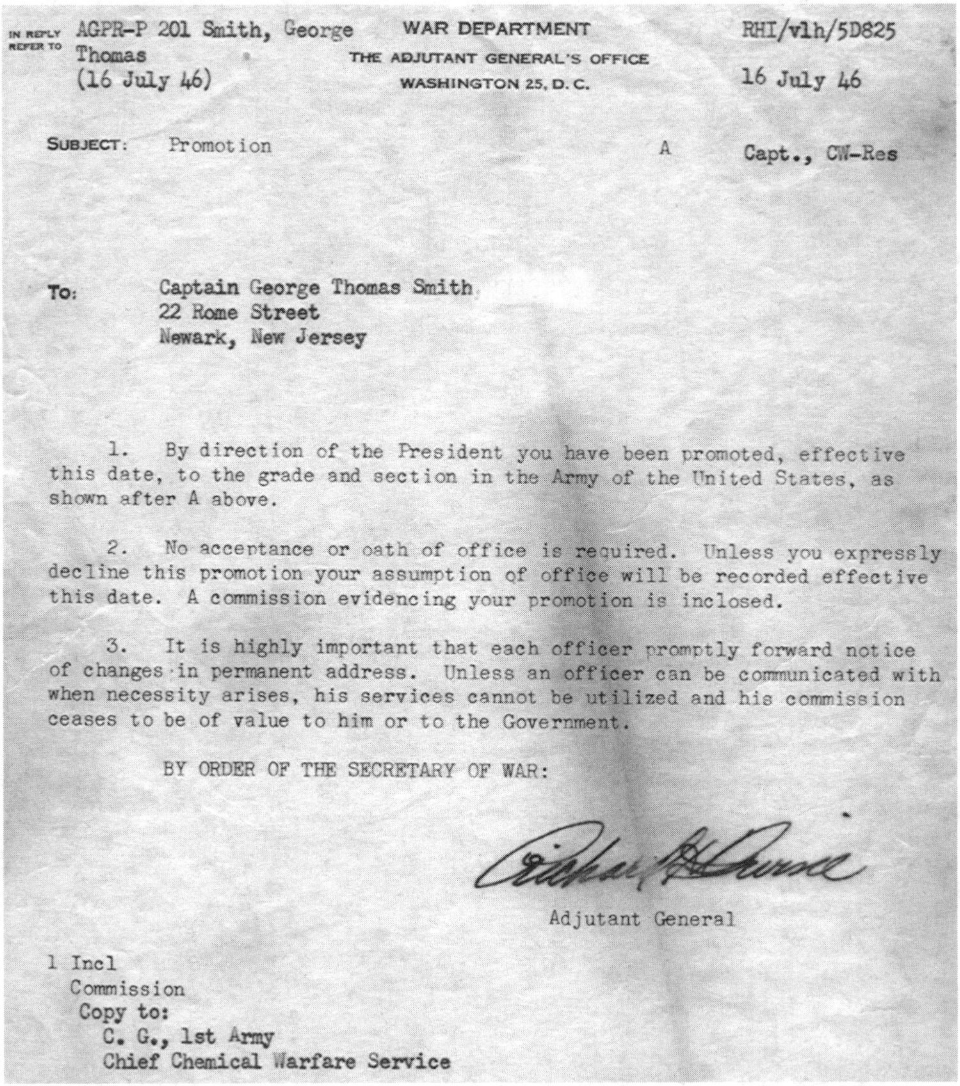

IN REPLY
REFER TO
AGPR-P 201 Smith, George
Thomas
(16 July 46)

WAR DEPARTMENT
THE ADJUTANT GENERAL'S OFFICE
WASHINGTON 25, D. C.

RHI/vlh/5D825

16 July 46

SUBJECT: Promotion   A   Capt., CW-Res

To: Captain George Thomas Smith
        22 Rome Street
        Newark, New Jersey

    1. By direction of the President you have been promoted, effective this date, to the grade and section in the Army of the United States, as shown after A above.

    2. No acceptance or oath of office is required. Unless you expressly decline this promotion your assumption of office will be recorded effective this date. A commission evidencing your promotion is inclosed.

    3. It is highly important that each officer promptly forward notice of changes in permanent address. Unless an officer can be communicated with when necessity arises, his services cannot be utilized and his commission ceases to be of value to him or to the Government.

    BY ORDER OF THE SECRETARY OF WAR:

                                        Adjutant General

1 Incl
  Commission
Copy to:
  C. G., 1st Army
  Chief Chemical Warfare Service

FIGURE 8-17   Letter notifying George Thomas Smith of his promotion to Captain

A promotion or commissioning, the awarding of medals, ribbons, clusters, and special insignia, and the awarding of a commendation and other recognition to the unit or to an individual are ceremonial occasions. The ceremony may be as simple as an announcement made at a unit formation or as formal as an occasion at which dress uniforms are worn, a military band performs, troops march in formation, rifle salutes are fired, and high-ranking officers and other dignitaries speak. In any case, records are created and become part of the military record for the individual and for the military unit.

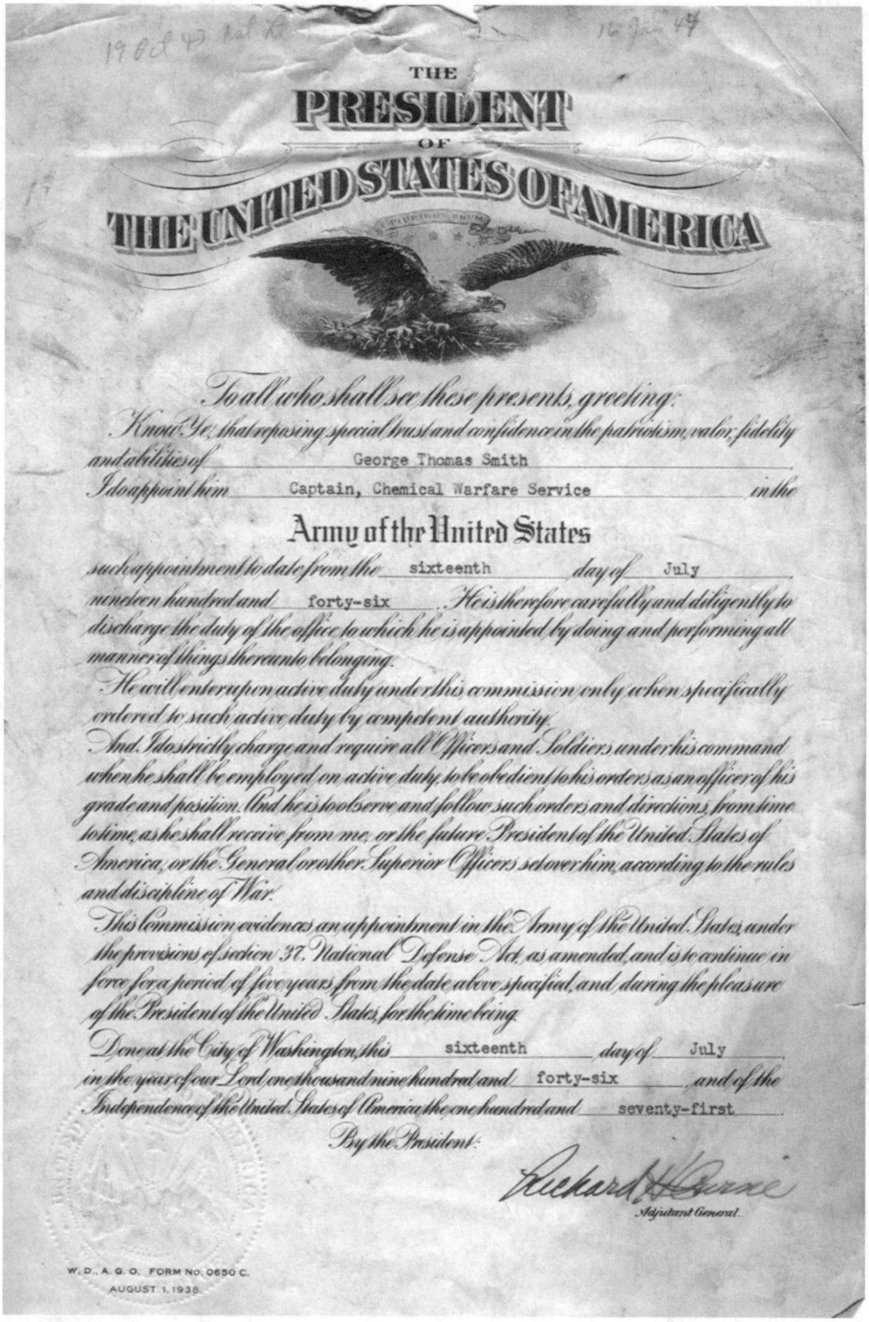

FIGURE 8-18   Certificate commissioning George Thomas Smith to Captain

Locate Military Discharge and Separation Records

You will find that the normal conclusion of an individual's military service generates a significant number of important documents. A document detailing the permanent change of duty assignment or station order may be created, along with other internal administrative documentation that may or may not be included in an individual's personnel file. There will be, however, some record of discharge or separation. These documents vary depending on the time period. Let's examine several examples.

World War I

Emil I. Hoffman's Honorable Discharge from the United States Army, dated 9 January 1919, is shown in Figure 8-19. This document is important for a number of reasons. It states that he was born in Smorgan, Russia, and that "he was 30 years of age and by occupation a Salesman" when he enlisted. Further, it describes him physically as being 5 feet 4¾ inches in height with brown eyes, brown hair, and a ruddy complexion.

On the reverse side of the Honorable Discharge certificate is his enlistment record, shown in Figure 8-20. This document is filled with great information, starting with the date of his enlistment on 27 May 1918 at Youngstown, Ohio. He was not an NCO, and he served with the AEF (Allied Expeditionary Forces) from 22 July 1918 until 24 December 1918. He was married and deemed to be of excellent character. He was vaccinated against typhoid fever and was in good health when he was discharged. A stamp in the upper-right corner and a notation indicates that he received a bronze Victory Lapel Pin on 16 September 1919. The remarks indicate that there was no A.W.O.L. or absence from duty. He also was entitled to travel pay.

World War II

The documentation changed somewhat by the time of World War II. In fact, there are even more documents that comprise the military service record and the certificates awarded to the individual.

The Honorable Discharge document and Enlisted Record for George Thomas Smith, which occupy the front and back of a single sheet and which are shown in Figures 8-21 and 8-22, are very similar to those from World War I. Another type of form used in the process was a Separation Qualification Record for Lindsay C. Royal is also shown in Figure 8-23, and it contains details about his occupational assignments, permanent address following separation, and summary text describing his assignment and activities.

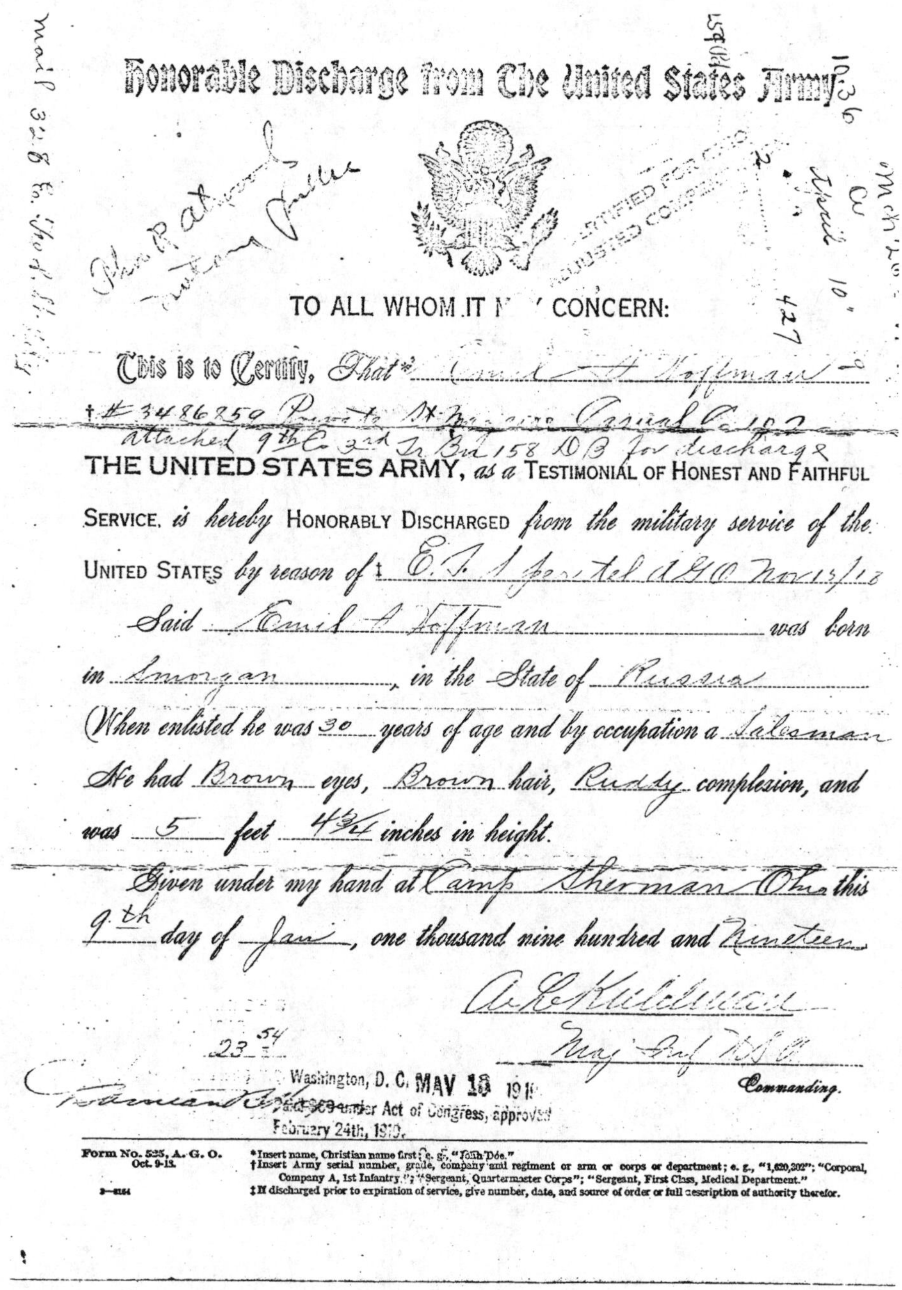

FIGURE 8-19   World War I Honorable Discharge from the U.S. Army for Emil I. Hoffman

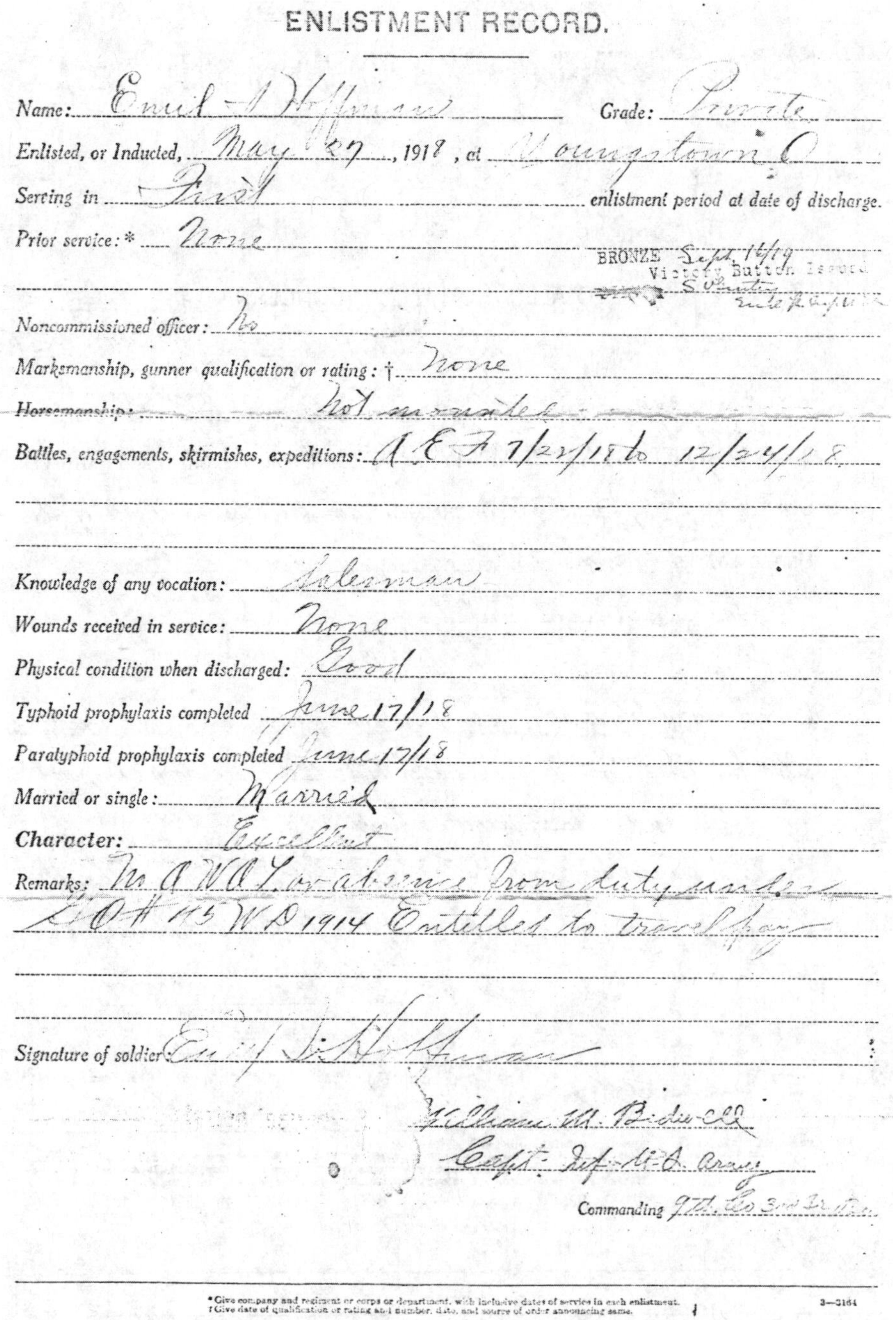

ENLISTMENT RECORD.

Name: *Emil I Hoffman* Grade: *Private*

Enlisted, or Inducted, *May 27*, 1918, at *Youngstown O*

Serving in *First* enlistment period at date of discharge.

Prior service: * *None*

BRONZE *Sept 14/19*
Victory Button Issued

Noncommissioned officer: *No*

Marksmanship, gunner qualification or rating: † *None*

Horsemanship: *not mounted*

Battles, engagements, skirmishes, expeditions: *A E F 7/21/18 to 12/24/18*

Knowledge of any vocation: *Salesman*

Wounds received in service: *None*

Physical condition when discharged: *Good*

Typhoid prophylaxis completed *June 17/18*

Paratyphoid prophylaxis completed *June 17/18*

Married or single: *Married*

Character: *Excellent*

Remarks: *No AWOL or absence from duty under*
G O # 105 W D 1914 Entitled to travel pay

Signature of soldier *Emil I Hoffman*

William M Bidwell
Capt Inf U S Army
Commanding *9th Co 3rd Bn*

*Give company and regiment or corps or department, with inclusive dates of service in each enlistment.
†Give date of qualification or rating and number, date, and source of order announcing same.

3—2161

FIGURE 8-20 World War I U.S. Army Enlistment Record for Emil I. Hoffman

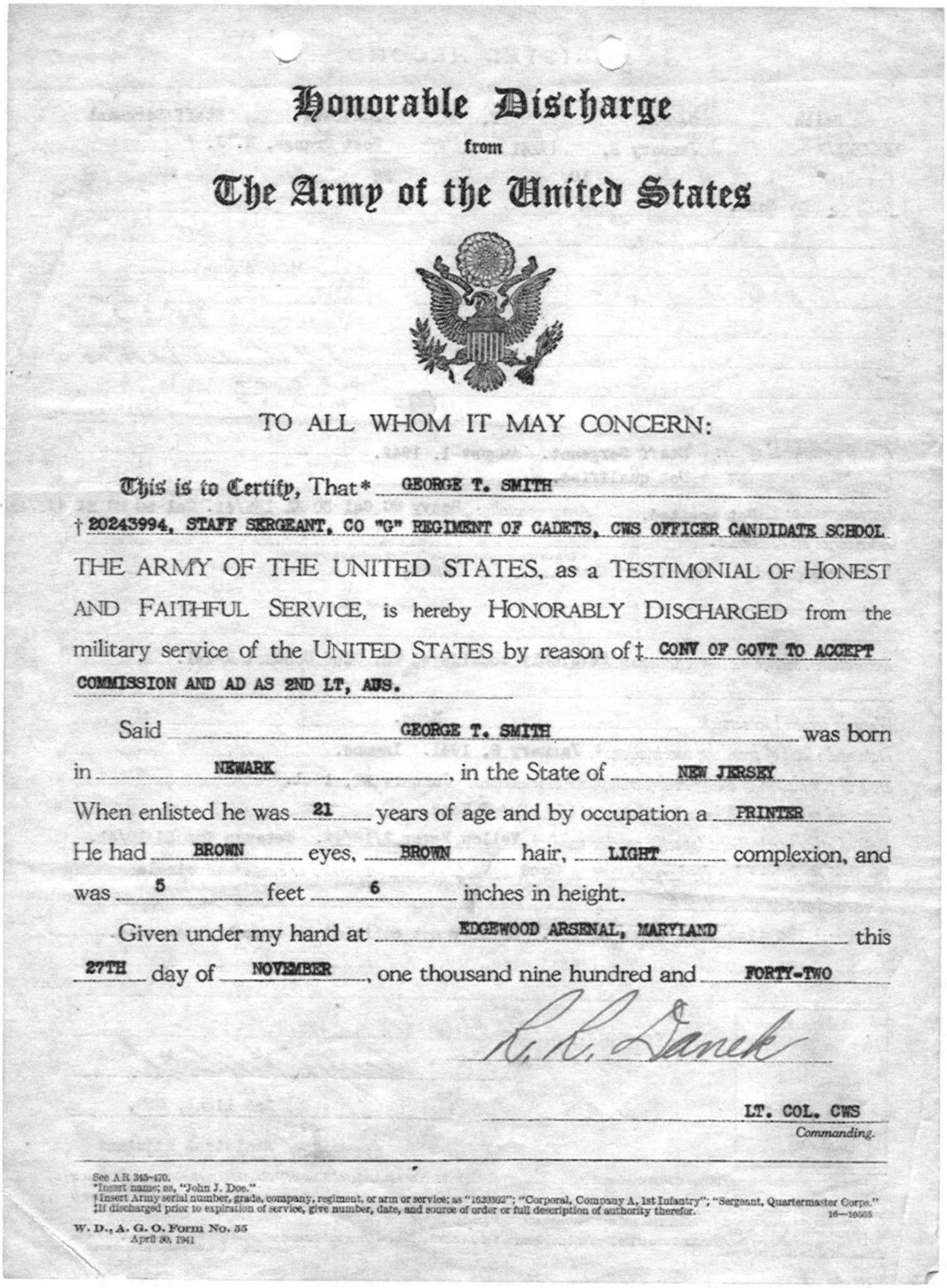

Honorable Discharge

from

The Army of the United States

TO ALL WHOM IT MAY CONCERN:

This is to Certify, That* ___GEORGE T. SMITH___

† 20243994, STAFF SERGEANT, CO "G" REGIMENT OF CADETS, CWS OFFICER CANDIDATE SCHOOL

THE ARMY OF THE UNITED STATES, as a TESTIMONIAL OF HONEST AND FAITHFUL SERVICE, is hereby HONORABLY DISCHARGED from the military service of the UNITED STATES by reason of ‡ ___CONV OF GOVT TO ACCEPT___ ___COMMISSION AND AD AS 2ND LT, AUS.___

Said ___GEORGE T. SMITH___ was born in ___NEWARK___, in the State of ___NEW JERSEY___ When enlisted he was __21__ years of age and by occupation a ___PRINTER___ He had ___BROWN___ eyes, ___BROWN___ hair, ___LIGHT___ complexion, and was __5__ feet __6__ inches in height.

Given under my hand at ___EDGEWOOD ARSENAL, MARYLAND___ this __27TH__ day of ___NOVEMBER___, one thousand nine hundred and ___FORTY-TWO___

L. L. Danek

LT. COL. CWS
Commanding.

See A.R. 345-470.
*Insert name; as, "John J. Doe."
† Insert Army serial number, grade, company, regiment, or arm or service; as "1623807"; "Corporal, Company A, 1st Infantry"; "Sergeant, Quartermaster Corps."
‡ If discharged prior to expiration of service, give number, date, and source of order or full description of authority therefor.

W. D., A. G. O. Form No. 55
April 30, 1941   16—16565

FIGURE 8-21   World War II Honorable Discharge from the U.S. Army for George T. Smith

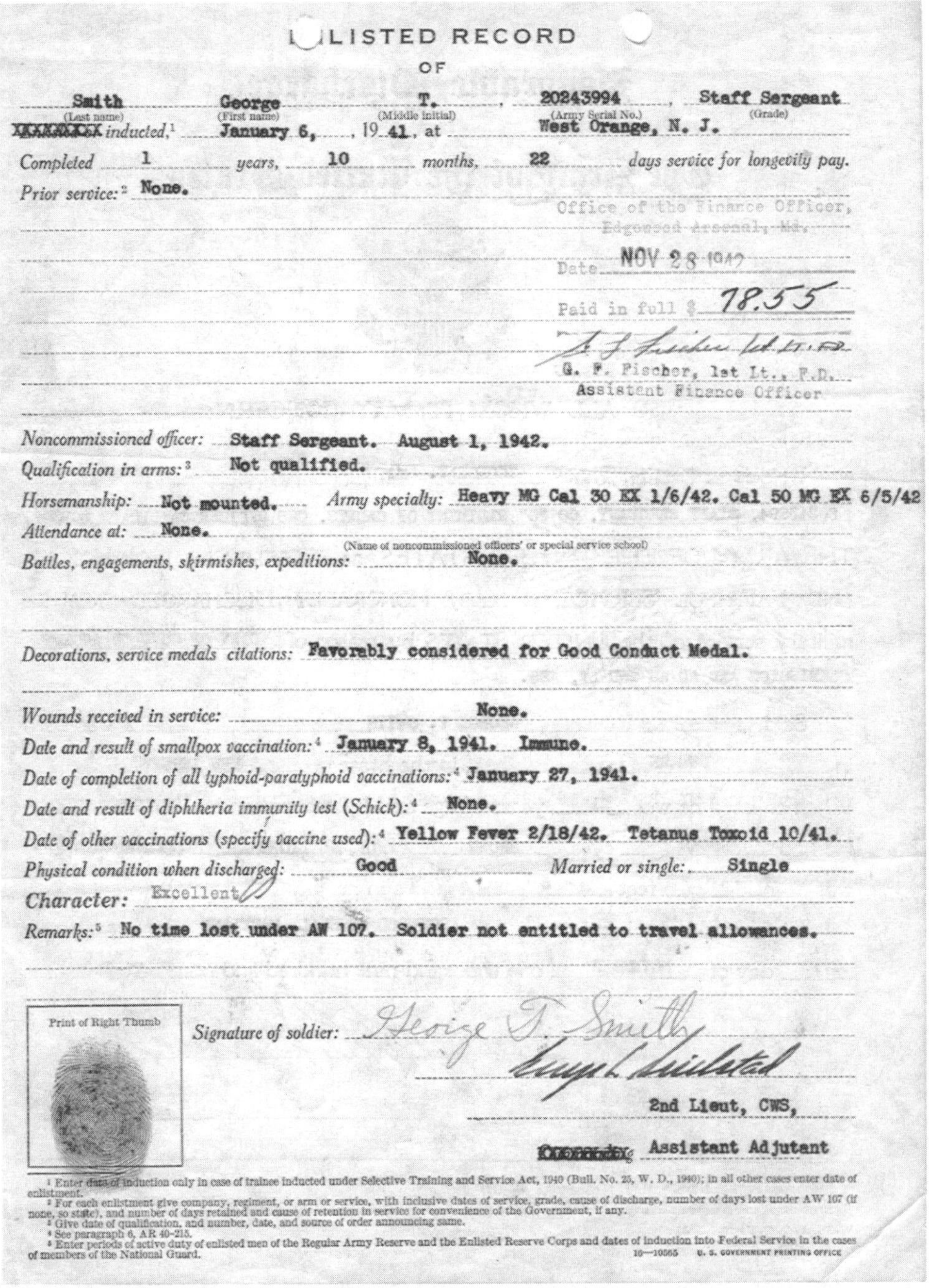

ENLISTED RECORD

OF

Smith   George   T.   , 20243994   , Staff Sergeant
(Last name)   (First name)   (Middle initial)   (Army Serial No.)   (Grade)

~~Enlisted or~~ inducted.[1] January 6, , 19 41 at West Orange, N. J.

Completed 1 years, 10 months, 22 days service for longevity pay.

Prior service:[2] None.

Office of the Finance Officer,
Edgewood Arsenal, Md.

Date NOV 28 1942

Paid in full $ 78.55

G. F. Fischer, 1st Lt., F.D.
Assistant Finance Officer

Noncommissioned officer: Staff Sergeant. August 1, 1942.

Qualification in arms:[3] Not qualified.

Horsemanship: Not mounted.   Army specialty: Heavy MG Cal 30 EX 1/6/42. Cal 50 MG EX 6/5/42

Attendance at: None.

(Name of noncommissioned officers' or special service school)

Battles, engagements, skirmishes, expeditions: None.

Decorations, service medals citations: Favorably considered for Good Conduct Medal.

Wounds received in service: None.

Date and result of smallpox vaccination:[4] January 8, 1941. Immune.

Date of completion of all typhoid-paratyphoid vaccinations:[4] January 27, 1941.

Date and result of diphtheria immunity test (Schick):[4] None.

Date of other vaccinations (specify vaccine used):[4] Yellow Fever 2/18/42. Tetanus Toxoid 10/41.

Physical condition when discharged: Good   Married or single: Single

Character: Excellent

Remarks:[5] No time lost under AW 107. Soldier not entitled to travel allowances.

Print of Right Thumb

Signature of soldier: George T. Smith

2nd Lieut, CWS,

Assistant Adjutant

[1] Enter date of induction only in case of trainee inducted under Selective Training and Service Act, 1940 (Bull. No. 25, W. D., 1940); in all other cases enter date of enlistment.
[2] For each enlistment give company, regiment, or arm or service, with inclusive dates of service, grade, cause of discharge, number of days lost under AW 107 (if none, so state), and number of days retained and cause of retention in service for convenience of the Government, if any.
[3] Give date of qualification, and number, date, and source of order announcing same.
[4] See paragraph 6, AR 40-215.
[5] Enter periods of active duty of enlisted men of the Regular Army Reserve and the Enlisted Reserve Corps and dates of induction into Federal Service in the cases of members of the National Guard.

16—10565   U. S. GOVERNMENT PRINTING OFFICE

FIGURE 8-22 WWII Enlisted Record for George T. Smith

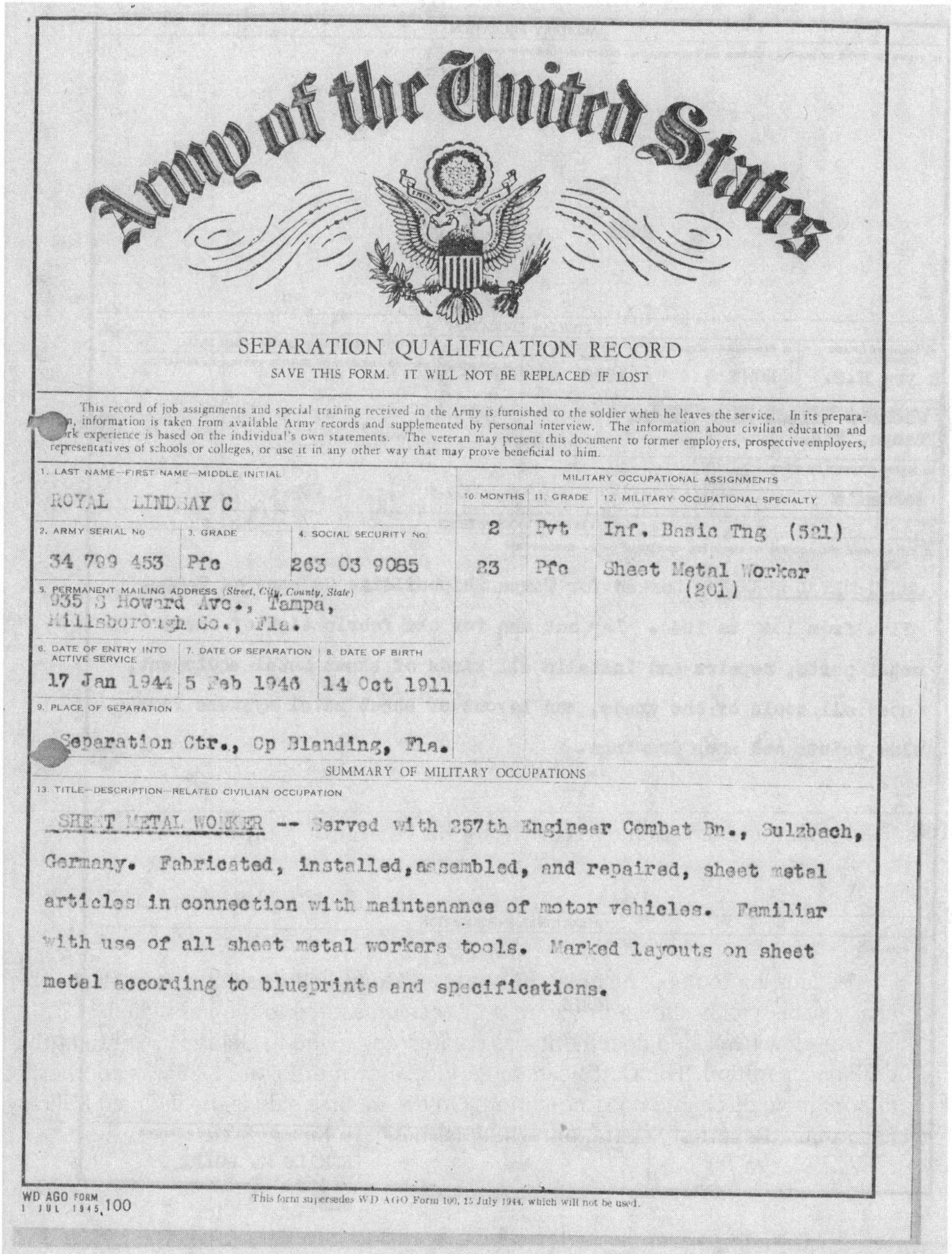

Army of the United States

SEPARATION QUALIFICATION RECORD
SAVE THIS FORM. IT WILL NOT BE REPLACED IF LOST

This record of job assignments and special training received in the Army is furnished to the soldier when he leaves the service. In its preparation, information is taken from available Army records and supplemented by personal interview. The information about civilian education and work experience is based on the individual's own statements. The veteran may present this document to former employers, prospective employers, representatives of schools or colleges, or use it in any other way that may prove beneficial to him.

1. LAST NAME—FIRST NAME—MIDDLE INITIAL			MILITARY OCCUPATIONAL ASSIGNMENTS		
ROYAL LINDSAY C			10. MONTHS	11. GRADE	12. MILITARY OCCUPATIONAL SPECIALTY
2. ARMY SERIAL No.	3. GRADE	4. SOCIAL SECURITY No.	2	Pvt	Inf. Basic Tng (521)
34 799 453	Pfc	263 03 9085	23	Pfc	Sheet Metal Worker (201)
5. PERMANENT MAILING ADDRESS (Street, City, County, State)					
935 S Howard Ave., Tampa, Hillsborough Co., Fla.					
6. DATE OF ENTRY INTO ACTIVE SERVICE	7. DATE OF SEPARATION	8. DATE OF BIRTH			
17 Jan 1944	5 Feb 1946	14 Oct 1911			
9. PLACE OF SEPARATION					
Separation Ctr., Cp Blanding, Fla.					

SUMMARY OF MILITARY OCCUPATIONS

13. TITLE—DESCRIPTION—RELATED CIVILIAN OCCUPATION

SHEET METAL WORKER -- Served with 257th Engineer Combat Bn., Sulzbach, Germany. Fabricated, installed, assembled, and repaired, sheet metal articles in connection with maintenance of motor vehicles. Familiar with use of all sheet metal workers tools. Marked layouts on sheet metal according to blueprints and specifications.

WD AGO FORM 100
1 JUL 1945

This form supersedes WD AGO Form 100, 15 July 1944, which will not be used.

FIGURE 8-23   A Separation Qualification form for Lindsey C. Royal

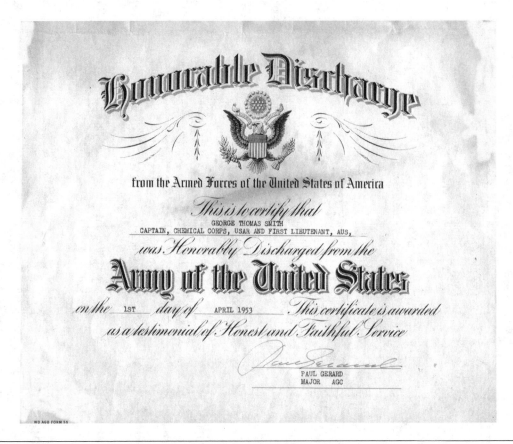

FIGURE 8-24 Honorable Discharge certificate for George T. Smith

In addition to those records, the separate Honorable Discharge certificate on heavy paper stock, shown in Figure 8-24, was presented to the individual.

Another two-sided document was created and given to George T. Smith at the time of separation. The Certificate of Service shown in Figure 8-25 was another form of honorable discharge documentation. On the reverse side is the detailed Military Record and Report of Separation, which is shown in Figure 8-26.

Army of the United States

CERTIFICATE OF SERVICE

This is to certify that

FIRST LIEUTENANT GEORGE T SMITH   CHEMICAL WARFARE SERVICE
803RD CHEMICAL COMPANY AIR OPERATIONS
BUCKLEY FIELD COLORADO

honorably served in active Federal Service

in the Army of the United States from

28 NOVEMBER 1942   *to*   27 DECEMBER 1945

Given at   SEPARATION CENTER FORT DIX NEW JERSEY

on the   27TH   *day of*   DECEMBER   *19* 45

FOR THE COMMANDING OFFICER

C H TALL LT COL INF

FIGURE 8-25   Certificate of Service for George T. Smith

CF 14A 17

MILITARY RECORD AND REPORT OF SEPARATION
CERTIFICATE OF SERVICE

1. LAST NAME - FIRST NAME - MIDDLE INITIAL		2. ARMY SERIAL NUMBER	3. AUS. GRADE	4. ARM OR SERVICE	5. COMPONENT
SMITH GEORGE T		Private	1ST LT	CWS	AUS
6. ORGANIZATION 803RD CHEMICAL COMPANY AIR OPERATIONS BUCKLEY FIELD COLORADO		7. DATE OF RELIEF FROM ACTIVE DUTY 27 DEC 45	8. PLACE OF SEPARATION SEPARATION CENTER FORT DIX NEW JERSEY		

9. PERMANENT ADDRESS FOR MAILING PURPOSES 22 ROME STREET NEWARK NEW JERSEY	10. DATE OF BIRTH 8 NOV 17	11. PLACE OF BIRTH NEWARK NEW JERSEY			
12. ADDRESS FROM WHICH EMPLOYMENT WILL BE SOUGHT SEE 9	13. COLOR EYES BLUE	14. COLOR HAIR BROWN	15. HEIGHT 5'6"	16. WEIGHT 130 LBS.	17. NO. OF DEPENDENTS 1

18. RACE			19. MARITAL STATUS		20. U.S.CITIZEN		21. CIVILIAN OCCUPATION AND NO.
WHITE	NEGRO	OTHER (specify)	SINGLE	MARRIED	OTHER (specify)	YES	NO
X				X		X	ROTOGRAVURE PRESSMAN 4-48.060

MILITARY HISTORY

SELECTIVE SERVICE DATA ▶	22. REGISTERED		23. LOCAL S. S. BOARD NUMBER	24. COUNTY AND STATE	25. HOME ADDRESS AT TIME OF ENTRY ON ACTIVE DUTY
	YES	NO			305 BOULEVARD HASBYOUCK
		X			HEIGHT NEW JERSEY

26. DATE OF ENTRY ON ACTIVE DUTY 28 NOV 42	27. MILITARY OCCUPATIONAL SPECIALTY AND NO. CHEMICAL WARFARE UNIT COMMANDER 1413

28. BATTLES AND CAMPAIGNS

NONE

29. DECORATIONS AND CITATIONS

EUROPEAN AFRICAN MIDDLE EASTERN THEATER CAMPAIGN RIBBON AMERICAN
DEFENSE SERVICE MEDAL

30. WOUNDS RECEIVED IN ACTION

NONE

31. SERVICE SCHOOLS ATTENDED CHEMICAL WARFARE SCHOOL EDGEWOOD ARSENAL MARYLAND AIR FORCE MUNITIONS SCHOOL LEICESTER ENGLAND	32. SERVICE OUTSIDE CONTINENTAL U. S. AND RETURN		
	DATE OF DEPARTURE 17 JAN 44	DESTINATION EUROPEAN TH	DATE OF ARRIVAL 28 JAN 44
33. REASON AND AUTHORITY FOR SEPARATION RELIEF FROM ACTIVE DUTY TWX AAF PDC TF2/REK/2741 25 SEP 45RR1-5 DEMOB	7 AUG 45	U S A	20 AUG 45

34.	CURRENT TOUR OF ACTIVE DUTY					35.	EDUCATION (years)		
CONTINENTAL SERVICE			FOREIGN SERVICE				GRAMMAR SCHOOL	HIGH SCHOOL	COLLEGE
YEARS	MONTHS	DAYS	YEARS	MONTHS	DAYS		8	4	0
1	5	26	1	7	3				

INSURANCE NOTICE

IMPORTANT IF PREMIUM IS NOT PAID WHEN DUE OR WITHIN THIRTY-ONE DAYS THEREAFTER, INSURANCE WILL LAPSE. MAKE CHECKS OR MONEY ORDERS PAYABLE TO THE TREASURER OF THE U. S. AND FORWARD TO COLLECTIONS SUBDIVISION, VETERANS ADMINISTRATION, WASHINGTON 25, D. C.

36. KIND OF INSURANCE			37. HOW PAID		38. Effective Date of Allotment Discontinuance	39. Date of Next Premium Due (one month after 38)	40. PREMIUM DUE EACH MONTH	41. INTENTION OF VETERAN TO		
Nat. Serv.	U.S. Govt.	None	Allotment	Direct to V.A.				Continue	Continue only	Discontinue
X			X		31 DEC 45	31 JAN 46	$ 13.75	X		

42. [RIGHT THUMB PRINT]	43. REMARKS (This space for completion of above items or entry of other items specified in W. D. Directives) ASR SCORE(2 SEP 45)75 LAPEL BUTTON ISSUED

44. SIGNATURE OF OFFICER BEING SEPARATED *George T. Smith 1st Lt CWS AC*	45. PERSONNEL OFFICER (Type name, grade and organization - signature) F P PORTER 2ND LT SIG C ASST ADJ *F P Porter*

WD AGO FORM 53-98
1 November 1944

This form supersedes all previous editions of
WD AGO Forms 53 and 280 for officers entitled
to a Certificate of Service, which will not be
used after receipt of this revision.

FIGURE 8-26 The Military Record and Report of Separation for George T. Smith

The Military Record and Report of Separation contains name, rank, serial number, military organization and occupation, permanent civilian address, date and place of birth, race, a physical description, and marital status. The detailed military history includes the locations where the individual served, decorations and citations, education and training schools attended while enlisted, areas of service outside the United States, and information about continuation of insurance. His right thumbprint was applied as another form of identity confirmation. These details provide a great deal of context about the person during his military career, regardless of length.

One additional document of interest was awarded to George T. Smith, the Army Air Forces Certificate of Appreciation for War Service, shown in Figure 8-27. I find this document particularly interesting in terms of the patriotic text that appears in the second paragraph: "Together we built the striking force that swept the Luftwaffe from the skies and broke the German power to resist. The total might of that striking force was then unleashed upon the Japanese."

An interesting development during World War II was the development of Victory Mail, also known as V-mail. The transport of paper mail between U.S. service personnel and their families in America was bulky and expensive. The Eastman Kodak Company developed the "airgraph" in the 1930s as a means of reducing the weight and bulk for two British airlines, Imperial Airways (now British Airways) and Pan American World Airways. The process involved the use of pre-formatted forms on which people addressed the letter and wrote the body of the document. The airgraph forms were photographed and stored as negatives on microfilm. At their destination, the letters were printed on photographic paper and handled through the Army Postal Services (APS).

During World War II, letters to service personnel were addressed to Army Post Office (APO) addresses. They were opened, censored, and microfilmed. At their destination, they were printed and distributed to servicemen and servicewomen. The same process was employed for letters from military personnel back to the United States. Censors read all letters and redacted any sensitive information.

As you are examining home sources, be on the lookout for V-mail documents. You can easily identify them. (See Figure 8-28.) The envelopes measure 4" × 3" and have an oval window through which the address on the letter could be seen. The letter sheet was 4" × 5" when printed from microfilm. U.S. soldiers and their correspondents between 1942 and 1945 used V-mail. Its use was not mandatory but, during that period, 556,513,795 pieces of V-mail were sent from the United States and 510 million pieces were received in the United States from military personnel abroad. V-mail and standard mail from this period may contain information to help expand your knowledge about your ancestors and family members.

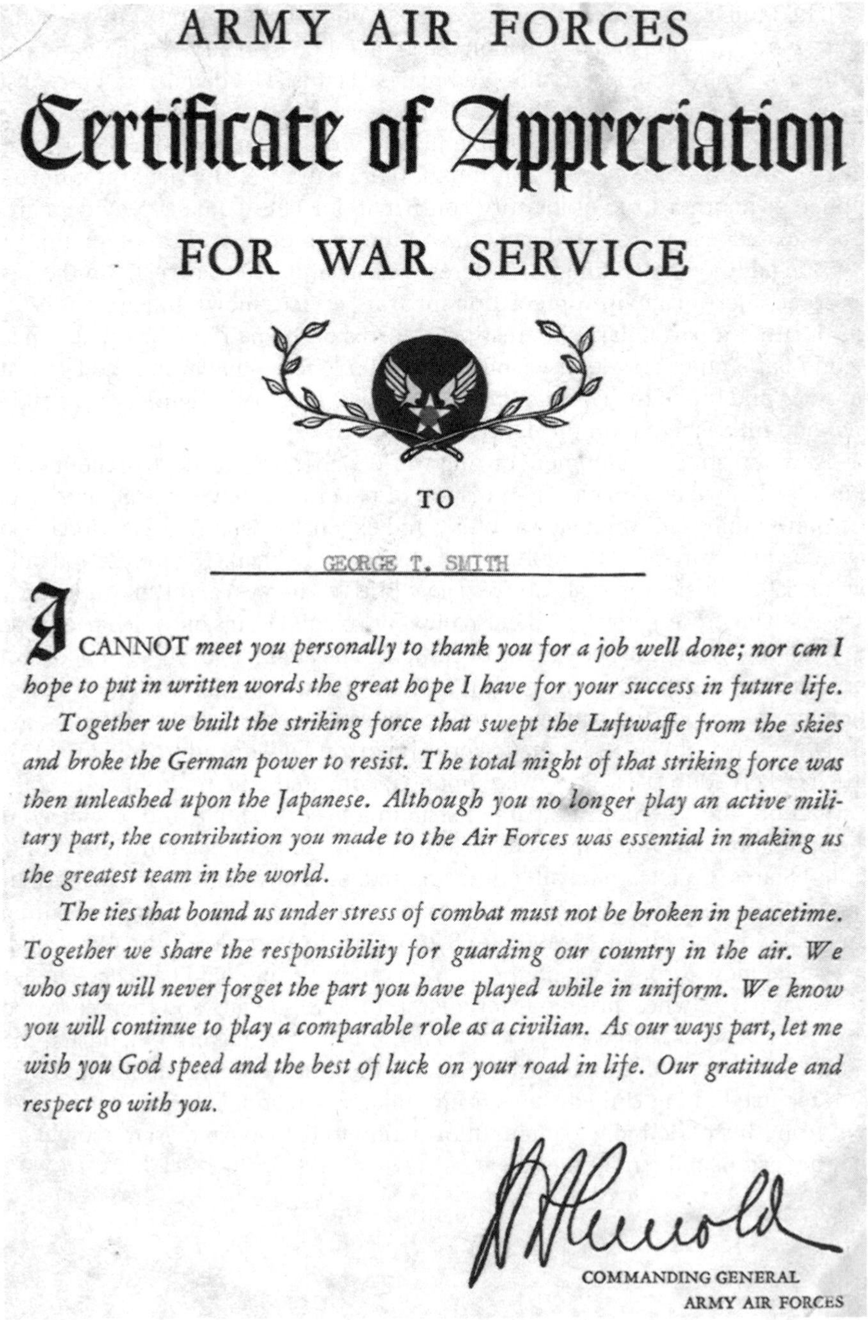

ARMY AIR FORCES

Certificate of Appreciation

FOR WAR SERVICE

TO

GEORGE T. SMITH

I CANNOT *meet you personally to thank you for a job well done; nor can I hope to put in written words the great hope I have for your success in future life.*

Together we built the striking force that swept the Luftwaffe from the skies and broke the German power to resist. The total might of that striking force was then unleashed upon the Japanese. Although you no longer play an active military part, the contribution you made to the Air Forces was essential in making us the greatest team in the world.

The ties that bound us under stress of combat must not be broken in peacetime. Together we share the responsibility for guarding our country in the air. We who stay will never forget the part you have played while in uniform. We know you will continue to play a comparable role as a civilian. As our ways part, let me wish you God speed and the best of luck on your road in life. Our gratitude and respect go with you.

COMMANDING GENERAL
ARMY AIR FORCES

FIGURE 8-27 Certificate of Appreciation for War Service presented to George T. Smith

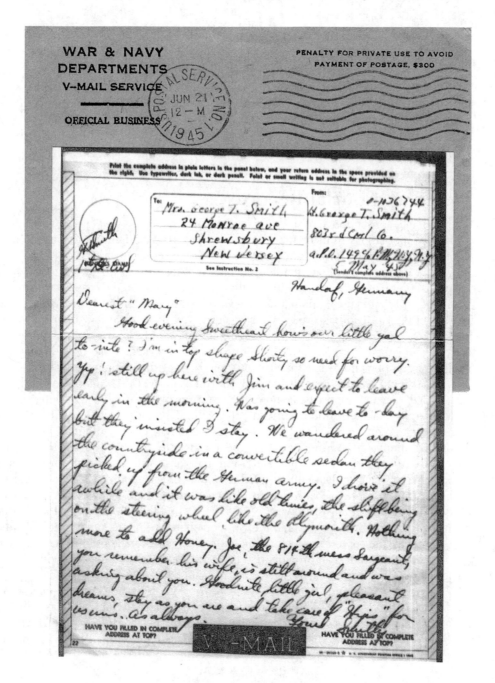

FIGURE 8-28 An example of a Victory Mail (V-mail) letter

Post–World War II

The mix of military documents changed somewhat following World War II. In 1950, a new document, the Report of Transfer or Discharge from Active Duty, was introduced for use by the U.S. military. It was used to facilitate the transfer of personnel between branches of the armed services and to provide documentation for separation and discharge. The document has become most commonly known as and referred to by its form number, DD 214, and an example is shown in Figure 8-29. In addition, a certificate of Honorable Discharge was issued.

Death and Burial Records

An inevitable consequence of military service for some is the loss of life. The U.S. military is meticulous in its communications with surviving family members and in offering support. When military personnel were killed overseas in World War II, they were interred in military cemeteries and families were contacted to determine whether to return the remains to the United States for burial. One case I have reviewed is that of 1st Lieutenant William J. Smith, who died in England in 1943. (He was the brother of George Thomas Smith, whose records are included in this chapter.) William J. Smith was initially interred in the military cemetery at Brookwood, England. After a series of detailed written communications, the family decided that his remains should stay in England rather than be returned to the United States, and the U.S. War Department arranged for permanent interment in the U.S. Military Cemetery in Cambridge, England. Figure 8-30 shows the letter received from the War Department.

Congress established the American Battle Monuments Commission (ABMC) in 1923 at the request of General John J. Pershing. Its purpose is to honor the accomplishments of the American Armed Forces where they have served since 6 April 1917, the date on which the United States entered World War I. The Commission is responsible for the establishment and maintenance of war memorials and cemeteries in foreign countries. Its website at **http://www.abmc.gov** provides access to databases of information regarding World War I, World War II, and Korean War casualties buried overseas. The site provides detailed information about the name, rank, unit, date and place of death, the cemetery in which the individual is interred, and information about services that the ABMC can provide to help honor and commemorate individuals buried in these places.

The Vietnam Veterans Memorial Wall USA website at **http://thewall-usa.com** has a searchable database of all U.S. casualties in the Vietnam War, and vast amounts of information are accessible there. A separate website exists for the United States Defense Prisoner of War/Missing Personnel Office at **http://www.dtic.mil/dpmo**.

PERSONAL DATA	1. LAST NAME - FIRST NAME - MIDDLE NAME **Private**	2. SERVICE NUMBER **Private**	3. a. GRADE, RATE OR RANK A1C E-4 · b. DATE OF RANK (Day, Month, Year) 1 OCT 63

LEGEND: Insert N/A to the items below which are not applicable

4. DEPARTMENT, COMPONENT AND BRANCH OR CLASS AIR FORCE REGAF	5. PLACE OF BIRTH (City and State or Country) MEBANE, NORTH CAROLINA	6. DATE OF BIRTH — DAY 31 · MONTH AUG · YEAR 40
7a. RACE CAUCASIAN · b. SEX MALE	c. COLOR HAIR BLACK · d. COLOR EYES GREEN · e. HEIGHT 5'10" · f. WEIGHT 147 · g. U.S. CITIZEN [X] YES [ ] NO	9. MARITAL STATUS MARRIED
10a. HIGHEST CIVILIAN EDUCATION LEVEL ATTAINED COLLEGE 2	b. MAJOR COURSE OR FIELD RELIGION	

TRANSFER OR DISCHARGE DATA

11a. TYPE OF TRANSFER OR DISCHARGE RELEASE FROM ACTIVE DUTY	b. STATION OR INSTALLATION AT WHICH EFFECTED McGUIRE AFB NEW JERSEY	
c. REASON AND AUTHORITY (SDN 411) CCG, PAR 3C, AFR 39-14	d. EFFECTIVE DATE — DAY 5 · MONTH FEB · YEAR 65	
12. LAST DUTY ASSIGNMENT AND MAJOR COMMAND 2130 COMM SQ (AFCS)	13a. CHARACTER OF SERVICE HONORABLE	b. TYPE OF CERTIFICATE ISSUED DD FORM 217AF

SELECTIVE SERVICE DATA

14. SELECTIVE SERVICE NUMBER 31 80 40 351	15. SELECTIVE SERVICE LOCAL BOARD NUMBER, CITY, COUNTY AND STATE LB# 80 REIDSVILLE (ROCKINGHAM) N. C.	16. DATE INDUCTED — DAY · MONTH · YEAR NA
17. DISTRICT OR AREA COMMAND TO WHICH RESERVIST TRANSFERRED AFRES		

SERVICE DATA

18. TERMINAL DATE OF RESERVE OBLIGATION — DAY 13 · MONTH FEB · YEAR 67	19. CURRENT ACTIVE SERVICE OTHER THAN BY INDUCTION a. SOURCE OF ENTRY [X] ENLISTED (First Enlistment) [ ] ENLISTED (Prior Service) [ ] REENLISTED [ ] OTHER: AFQT 79-85-II	b. TERM OF SERVICE (Years) 4	c. DATE OF ENTRY — DAY 14 · MONTH FEB · YEAR 61
20. PRIOR REGULAR ENLISTMENTS NA	21. GRADE, RATE OR RANK AT TIME OF ENTRY INTO CURRENT ACTIVE SERVICE AB	22. PLACE OF ENTRY INTO CURRENT ACTIVE SERVICE (City and State) CHARLOTTE, NORTH CAROLINA	

23. HOME OF RECORD AT TIME OF ENTRY INTO ACTIVE SERVICE (Street, RFD, City, County and State) BOX 383 MADISON ROCKINGHAM NORTH CAROLINA	24. STATEMENT OF SERVICE		YEARS	MONTHS	DAYS
	a. CREDITABLE FOR BASIC PAY PURPOSES	(1) NET SERVICE THIS PERIOD	03	11	22
		(2) OTHER SERVICE	00	00	00
25a. SPECIALTY NUMBER AND TITLE COMM & CRYPTO EQP SYS RPMN CAFSC 30650A	b. RELATED CIVILIAN OCCUPATION AND D. O. T. NUMBER NONE	(3) TOTAL (Line (1) + line (2))	03	11	22
		b. TOTAL ACTIVE SERVICE	03	11	22
		c. FOREIGN AND/OR SEA SERVICE	02	09	09

26. DECORATIONS, MEDALS, BADGES, COMMENDATIONS, CITATIONS AND CAMPAIGN RIBBONS AWARDED OR AUTHORIZED SAEMR SO# G-62, HQ UK COMM RGN, 1964 AFGCM SO# G-19 HQ UK COMM RGN 1964 (14FEB61 - 13FEB64)
27. WOUNDS RECEIVED AS A RESULT OF ACTION WITH ENEMY FORCES (Place and date, if known) NONE

28. SERVICE SCHOOLS OR COLLEGES, COLLEGE TRAINING COURSES AND/OR POST-GRADUATE COURSES SUCCESSFULLY COMPLETED			29. OTHER SERVICE TRAINING COURSES SUCCESSFULLY COMPLETED
SCHOOL OR COURSE	DATES (From-To)	MAJOR COURSES	
SHEPPARD AFB TEXAS	MAR 61 - NOV 61	ELECT COMM CRYPTO RPMN	GED COLLEGE
LACKLAND AFB TEXAS	DEC 61 - MAR 62	F & O MAINT TSEC/K/W-26	

VA DATA

30. a. GOVERNMENT LIFE INSURANCE IN FORCE [ ] YES [X] NO	b. AMOUNT OF ALLOTMENT NA	c. MONTH ALLOTMENT DISCONTINUED NA
31. a. VA BENEFITS PREVIOUSLY APPLIED FOR (Specify type) NONE	b. VA CLAIM NUMBER c- NA	

AUTHENTICATION

32. REMARKS BLOOD GROUP AB-POS NO TIME LOST GEN 80 ADMN 85 MECH 60 ELECT 85 DTD FEB61 PAID FOR 32 DAYS ACCRUED LEAVE NOT ELIGIBLE MGP NAC COMPLETED 11DEC61 FILED 4TH DIST OSI RE-3/93 ODSD 3FEB65 SSN: 246-56-3258

33. PERMANENT ADDRESS FOR MAILING PURPOSES AFTER TRANSFER OR DISCHARGE (Street, RFD, City, County and State) MADISON, ROCKINGHAM, NORTH CAROLINA BOX 383	34. SIGNATURE OF PERSON BEING TRANSFERRED OR DISCHARGED **Private**
35. a. TYPED NAME, GRADE AND TITLE OF AUTHORIZING OFFICER PAUL E. O'BRIEN, MAJOR USAF	b. SIGNATURE OF OFFICER AUTHORIZED TO SIGN *Paul E. O'Brien*

DD FORM 214 (8 Part) 1 NOV 55 · REPLACES EDITION OF 1 JUL 52 WHICH IS OBSOLETE · ARMED FORCES OF THE UNITED STATES REPORT OF TRANSFER OR DISCHARGE · 1

FIGURE 8-29 Report of Transfer or Discharge from Active Duty, also known as the DD 214

WAR DEPARTMENT
OFFICE OF THE QUARTERMASTER GENERAL
WASHINGTON 25, D. C.

5 January 1949

1st Lt William J. Smith, ASN 0 661 675
Plot B, Row 7, Grave 25
Headstone: Cross
Cambridge U. S. Military Cemetery

Mr. William H. Smith
22 Rome Street
Newark, New York

Dear Mr. Smith:

    This is to inform you that the remains of your loved one have been permanently interred, as recorded above, side by side with comrades who also gave their lives for their country. Customary military funeral services were conducted over the grave at the time of burial.

    After the Department of the Army has completed all final interments, the cemetery will be transferred, as authorized by the Congress, to the care and supervision of the American Battle Monuments Commission. The Commission also will have the responsibility for permanent construction and beautification of the cemetery, including erection of the permanent headstone. The headstone will be inscribed with the name exactly as recorded above, the rank or rating where appropriate, organization, State, and date of death. Any inquiries relative to the type of headstone or the spelling of the name to be inscribed thereon, should be addressed to the American Battle Monuments Commission, the central address of which is Room 713, 1712 "G" Street, N. W., Washington 25, D. C. Your letter should include the full name, rank, serial number, grave location, and name of the cemetery.

    While interment activities are in progress, the cemetery will not be open to visitors. However, upon completion thereof, due notice will be carried by the press.

    You may rest assured that this final interment was conducted with fitting dignity and solemnity and that the grave-site will be carefully and conscientiously maintained in perpetuity by the United States Government.

Sincerely yours,

Thomas B Larkin

THOMAS B. LARKIN
Major General
The Quartermaster General

FIGURE 8-30   Letter from the U.S. War Department concerning final interment of 1st Lieutenant William J. Smith

Locate Other Military-Related Records

Military records, as you have seen, can be a gold mine of detail if you know where to look. Your investment in the study of the history and geography of the areas where your ancestors and family members lived and from where they may have served in the military can prepare you for locating records much more effectively. You also will have a better comprehension of your ancestor's role in history as he or she served their country.

There are many strictly military records created by governments and archived in their repositories. Other materials, including books, eBooks, magazines, and historical materials, can expand your knowledge and help you place your military ancestors into geographical and historical context. Letters, V-mail, diaries, journals, photographs, and other materials found around the house can also provide clues to open doors. Military-related materials truly can bring your family history to life.

9

Understand and Use Land and Property Records

HOW TO...

- Locate and use land and property records in the United States
- Understand and use land and property records in Canada
- Learn about land and property records in the United Kingdom
- Locate land and property records online
- Place your ancestors into context with property records

Land and property records are among the most numerous records in existence. They can also contain some very important information about your ancestors and their families. Unfortunately, these records are also some of the most poorly understood and least used resources by genealogical researchers. The common perceptions are that a) they are cryptic and unfathomable, and b) they contain little genealogical value.

Like military records, land and property records require a bit of advance research into the history of the geographical area and the types of records that were created there at specific periods. In addition, the methods used to define boundaries and register the ownership and transfer of property also need to be understood. This is not an insurmountable problem and, once you have invested the time to learn about land and property records, you will find that they can provide a tremendous source of information. And yes, they *can and do* contain vast amounts of genealogical information to help further your research.

There are many excellent books and reference materials available to help you understand land and property records in various locations, such as libraries, bookstores, and the Internet. However, as a beginning, let's explore the basics of land and property records in the United States, Canada, and the United Kingdom. These overviews should provide you with some basic knowledge to get started in locating your ancestors' records in those places, and should give you ideas on how to approach similar research in other countries in which your ancestors lived and may have owned property.

Locate and Use Land and Property Records in the United States

The history of the United States is a colorful combination of Spanish, English, French, Dutch, Mexican, Russian, and Native American influences. Nearly every American schoolchild is taught that Christopher Columbus discovered America in 1492 and, although the place that Columbus "discovered" was not exactly a part of what we know to be the United States of today, this definitely was the beginning of centuries of colonization, conflict, and amazing expansion.

United States history makes for a fascinating study, and its settlement parallels that of Canada in many ways. You will find in the course of your genealogical research in both the United States and Canada that land and property records development is similar because of the efforts of both France and England to colonize vast areas of the North American continent. The influence of the Spanish in Florida and the southeast, in California and the southwest, and in other areas brought Spain's form of government, its religion, its governmental processes, and its forms of record-keeping with it. Each time there was a change in government, the land and property records process was impacted from the perspectives of documentation and taxation. Reregistration of land ownership was often required, and that meant that the current owner had to produce proof of title. The records, too, certainly changed in format and content.

Consider for a moment the Spanish possession of Florida in the 1500s. Spain's Catholic and Jesuit priests spent decades trying to convert the Native Americans to Christianity in that area. England, France, Portugal, and Spain all attempted to settle parts of the area. It was a bloody conflict from the outset, but the Spanish continued to colonize and settle the area. In fact, the oldest permanent European settlement in what was to become the United States is St. Augustine, Florida, established by the Spanish in 1565. The English attacked and burned the settlement several times. The Treaty of Paris was signed in 1763, ending the Seven Years' War and giving England victory over France and Spain. The treaty included provisions in which France ceded all territory east of the Mississippi River, as well as Canada, to the British. Spain also ceded Florida and other substantial territory east of the Mississippi River to England.

The British created two administrative territories in Florida: East Florida, with its capital at St. Augustine, and West Florida, with its capital at Pensacola. This action continues to influence the state to this day, as the state capital is Tallahassee, located in the panhandle of the state. During the period of British rule of Florida, residents sought proof from Spain of their ownership of land. The documents created at that time are referred to as "memorials" and "concessions," and these were actually petitions for proof of land ownership. These are written in Spanish and are among some of the earliest land documents that exist for Florida. Copies of these documents can be found variously in Florida and/or Spain.

A later treaty, the Treaty of Paris, signed in 1783, ended the American Revolutionary War. In September of that year, Great Britain signed separate agreements with both France and Spain. In the treaty with Spain, the territories of East Florida and West Florida were returned to Spain.

Spain and France also competed for possession of what we know as the Louisiana Territory, with both struggling to colonize and control this vast area. In 1800, Spain signed a secretly negotiated treaty in which it signed over its control of the entire territory to France. When the U.S. government learned that France, and not Spain, had authority over the area, it began negotiations to acquire the territory for itself. This culminated in 1803 with the Louisiana Purchase, whereby the United States acquired 828,800 square miles (2,147,000 square kilometers) of new territory.

The U.S. Army under Andrew Jackson invaded Florida during the First Indian War in 1817–18. In 1819, under the terms of the Adams-Onís Treaty, Spain ceded Florida to the United States in exchange for $5 million and the American renunciation of any claims on Spanish Texas that it might have had that resulted from the Louisiana Purchase. The two administrative regions of Florida became a single U.S. territory in 1822. The Board of Land Commissioners was established in 1822 by the U.S. government to settle all Spanish land grant claims in the territory. The records of this period are held by the Division of Library and Information Services of the Florida Department of State (**http://dlis.dos.state.fl.us**). Florida became the 27th U.S. state on 3 March 1845.

Mexico also fought for independence from Spain and gained its sovereignty in 1821. Texas declared its independence from Mexico in 1836 and won its freedom at the Battle of San Jacinto that same year. It became the Republic of Texas. After a series of conflicts with Texas, the Treaty of Guadalupe Hidalgo was signed on 2 February 1848 by Mexico and the United States. Texas became the 28th U.S. state on 29 December 1845.

The Dutch founded New Netherland, a territory that covered parts of the states of Maryland, Delaware, Pennsylvania, New Jersey, New York, Connecticut, and Rhode Island. In 1621, the Dutch West India Company received its charter. New Amsterdam, on the island of Manhattan and the site of what is now New York City, was founded in 1625. The English battled the Dutch for the area and finally received the territory in 1674. It was renamed New York.

Russia's influence is centered on Alaska, which was purchased for the United States by Secretary of State William H. Seward on 30 March 1867 for $7.2 million. It was organized as a territory on 11 May 1912, and became the 49th U.S. state on 3 January 1959.

Settlers took many Native American lands over the centuries. However, the U.S. federal government did seek to settle tribal claims through the negotiation of numerous treaties. The tribes were seldom fairly compensated, and this resulted in ill feelings and armed conflicts. The passage by Congress of the Indian Removal Act in 1830 began forced relocation and migration of Native Americans from the eastern states to what became Oklahoma and other western areas. AccessGenealogy.com has compiled an excellent collection of information about Native American records, including indexes to land allotment rolls and links to websites that host other data. Fold3.com (**http://www.fold3.com**) has digitized and indexed the Dawes Enrollment Cards and the Dawes Packets, and Ancestry.com (**http://www.ancestry.com**) has digitized and indexed the Native American enrollment cards, both of which relate directly to the relocation of the Five Civilized Tribes. The U.S. government enumerated reservations in their annual Indian Censuses of 1885 through 1940. (See Chapter 6 for more information.)

The tumultuous territorial expansion in North America throughout the centuries involved many governments. Their influences on land and property records still impact land measurement methods and record keeping to this day. This short "thumbnail" history is only one example of the kind of historical research that is important to understand as part of your preparation to conduct effective research, especially in land and property records in the areas and time periods when your ancestors arrived and lived there. You will want to study the historic events and learn more about the government(s) that had jurisdiction, the boundary changes at all levels, the records that were created, and the ultimate disposition of those particular records. This can make you a much more effective researcher of land and property records.

Learn About the Organization of State and Public Lands

Land and property research in the United States can yield vast amounts of genealogical information if you understand the organization of the materials and where to search. There are two distinct types of what I'll call "land organization" in the United States: State Land States and Public Domain Land States. Understanding the distinction between them is important because the way they are measured and recorded differs. The descriptions provided in this chapter are intended only as an introduction for you. There are many books on the subject of land records in the United States, and I would refer you to them for a more detailed study. Perhaps the best of these is E. Wade Hone's book *Land and Property Research in the United States* (Ancestry Publishing, 1997).

State Land States

The term "State Land States" refers to the fact that the land was originally controlled by the state and sold or distributed by the state itself. Any subsequent land transactions were conducted between private individuals and are therefore often referred to as "private lands." If you examine the following list, it is immediately apparent that most of the State Land States were formerly the original 13 colonies under the control of the British Crown. Others, such as Kentucky, Maine, Tennessee, Vermont, and West Virginia, were derived from an original colony. And other foreign governments controlled others, such as Texas and Hawaii. The State Land States are: Connecticut, Delaware, Georgia, Hawaii, Kentucky, Maine, Maryland, Massachusetts, New Hampshire, New Jersey, New York, North Carolina, Pennsylvania, Rhode Island, South Carolina, Tennessee, Texas, Vermont, Virginia, and West Virginia.

Following the Revolutionary War, some of the original colonies claimed extensive westward territories as part of their jurisdictions. However, with the formation of the U.S. federal government and based on individual negotiations with the states, most of the land outside what are the current state boundaries was ceded to the federal government. These lands and other territorial acquisitions by the federal government that were discussed earlier in the historical overview became what were used to create Public Domain Land States. They are also referred to as Federal Land States.

State Land States Survey Methods

The common method of land measurement in the State Land States is referred to as "metes and bounds." This scheme is based on the use of physical natural features such as rocks, trees, and waterways as reference points and the surveyor's chain as a unit of measure. Table 9-1 shows a high-level conversion from surveyors' measurements to feet and inches. You will want to refer to a complete surveyors' conversion table in another reference work.

The metes and bounds survey method dates back to the earliest colonial days, and you will find that, as a result, there are some very strangely shaped land parcels. Some surveys included the placement of stakes for use in later surveys. However, since a stake could be physically moved, a parcel of land always had to be completely resurveyed to verify the accuracy of the land holding. You will therefore find, in many surveys and land description records, references to physical features, stakes, and other people's property, as well as the use of standard surveyors' measurements. The surveyor used compass directions stated as north, south, east, west, or combinations, a compass direction in degrees, and a distance measured in surveyors' units, such as chains.

Figure 9-1 shows a surveyor's report prepared for the estate of one Eli Jones, who owned property in Caswell County, North Carolina. The report includes representations of roads and waterways, and incorporates references to roads, stakes, pointers, sweet gum trees, and other persons' properties. It uses surveyors' chain measurements to illustrate and describe the property. You will also note that, at the upper end of the drawing of the parcel, there are references to "Dower" and "Dower line." This indicates that the owner of the parcel cited was married. By law, the property could not be sold or transferred without the consent of the wife. We will discuss "dower release" shortly.

Figure 9-2 shows a detailed section from another survey report that includes a detailed metes and bounds description of the parcel of property.

TABLE 9-1   Surveyors' Measurement Conversion

Surveyors' Measure	Equivalent
1 link	7.92 inches
25 links	1 rod, 1 pole, or 1 perch
100 links	1 chain (also referred to as a Gunter's chain)
1 chain	66 feet
80 chains	1 mile
625 square links	1 square rod
16 square rods	1 square chain
10 square chains	1 square acre

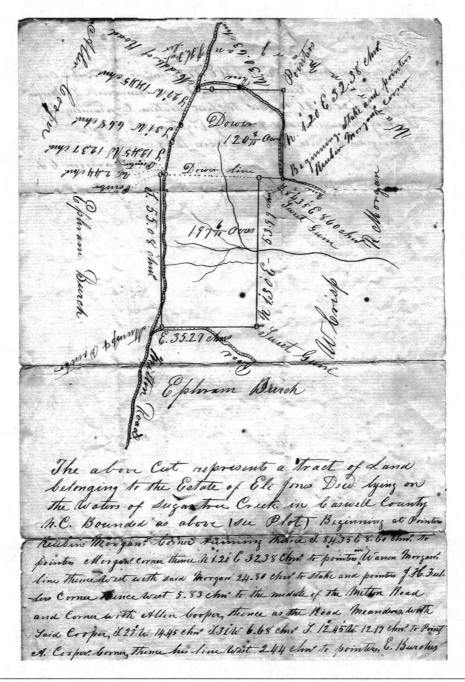

FIGURE 9-1 Survey report for a parcel of land in North Carolina that used the metes and bounds survey method

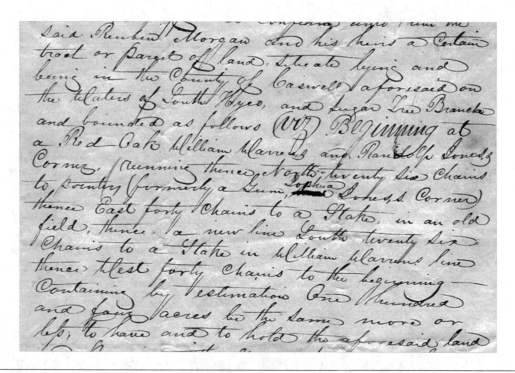

FIGURE 9-2 Detail of a metes and bounds property description from a land survey

A separate system of measurement is used in the Public Domain Land States and is known as the Public Land Survey System (PLSS), which uses units of area called "townships" and "sections." We'll discuss the PLSS in the "Public Domain Land States Records" section later in this chapter. However, be aware that a combination of metes and bounds and township systems, along with some other less widely used schemes, has been used in some areas. In Texas, for example, the Spanish land measurement method of "leagues and labors" has been used in some areas. In Louisiana, the French used the "River Lot System" of slender lots laid out perpendicular to waterways, and these are referred to as *arpents*. Ohio has used several land measurement systems depending on the area and the measurement scheme used at the time.

State Land States Records

You will find a wealth of varied and interesting land records in use in State Land States. The original process of acquiring land began with a land grant. The grant simply defined the terms under which the land would be made available by the grantor to the grantee. The terms "grantor" and "grantee" continue to be used to this day in land transactions. In order to obtain an original grant, an individual (or organization) was required to make an application. A successful application resulted in the issue of a land warrant. A land warrant is simply an official, legal order or directive for a physical land survey to be performed. The survey was conducted and returned to the appropriate land office, where it was recorded. At this point, a patent was prepared. The patent is a title document signifying that the entire acquisition process has been conducted, including the exchange of any money or other consideration. The land patent was then recorded and the title process was complete.

You will find that the subsequent land transfer process typically was continued, as property ownership moved from person to person, with the use of indentures (or agreements), a property survey, and various sale transaction documents, ultimately resulting in the preparation and recording of a deed. Figures 9-3 and 9-4 show both sides of a copy of an indenture for the purchase of a piece of property in Caswell County, North Carolina, dating from 1792. (This document is a transcription prepared by the Register of Deeds on 7 November 1838 from the Deed Book in his office, as indicated by the clerk's statement at the bottom of the second page.)

During the American Revolution, there was no formal federal government and therefore no treasury. Soldiers were paid as possible, but some were rewarded for their service with what became known as "bounty land." In many cases, the title came in the form of a land patent. There were both federal and state bounty land warrants issued, depending on the level at which the individual performed the military service. States that produced their own bounty land warrants to compensate its citizens for service were Georgia, Maryland, Massachusetts, North Carolina, Pennsylvania, South Carolina, and Virginia. A sample bounty land warrant is shown in Figure 9-5. In order to obtain bounty land, an individual had to make application and go through a documentation process to prove eligibility to receive the land. Military service or providing supplies or other aid were reasons for eligibility, so don't be surprised to occasionally find a woman's name on a bounty land application or warrant.

The number of acres granted depended on the person's rank and service. A veteran would file an application for bounty land and a warrant would be issued authorizing a land survey and later a title to be issued. Bounty land documents may be found in county records, state land offices, and/or in state archives. Bounty land warrants continued in use until 1855, with some applications that were not finalized/approved until 1858. Many U.S. federal bounty land records have been digitized and indexed by Ancestry.com (**http://www.ancestry.com**), FamilySearch (**https://familysearch.org**), Fold3.com (**http://www.fold3.com**), and HeritageQuest Online. The warrants themselves may be part of pension files.

As you can see, there are some interesting and diverse land survey schemes used in the State Land States that have their origins in their colonial past. You will want to do some preliminary research into the state and area in which your ancestors lived and owned property in order to learn what system(s) might have been in use at that time.

Measurements for Public Domain Land States

Following the American Revolution, the new federal government instituted several processes to control territorial land it acquired. There were several reasons for this. First, the government wanted to raise revenue to build its reserves and pay off debts incurred as a result of the war. Second, it wanted to compensate soldiers and other supporters from the war with land rather than money. Finally, with all of its new territory, the government wanted to encourage westward migration and settlement.

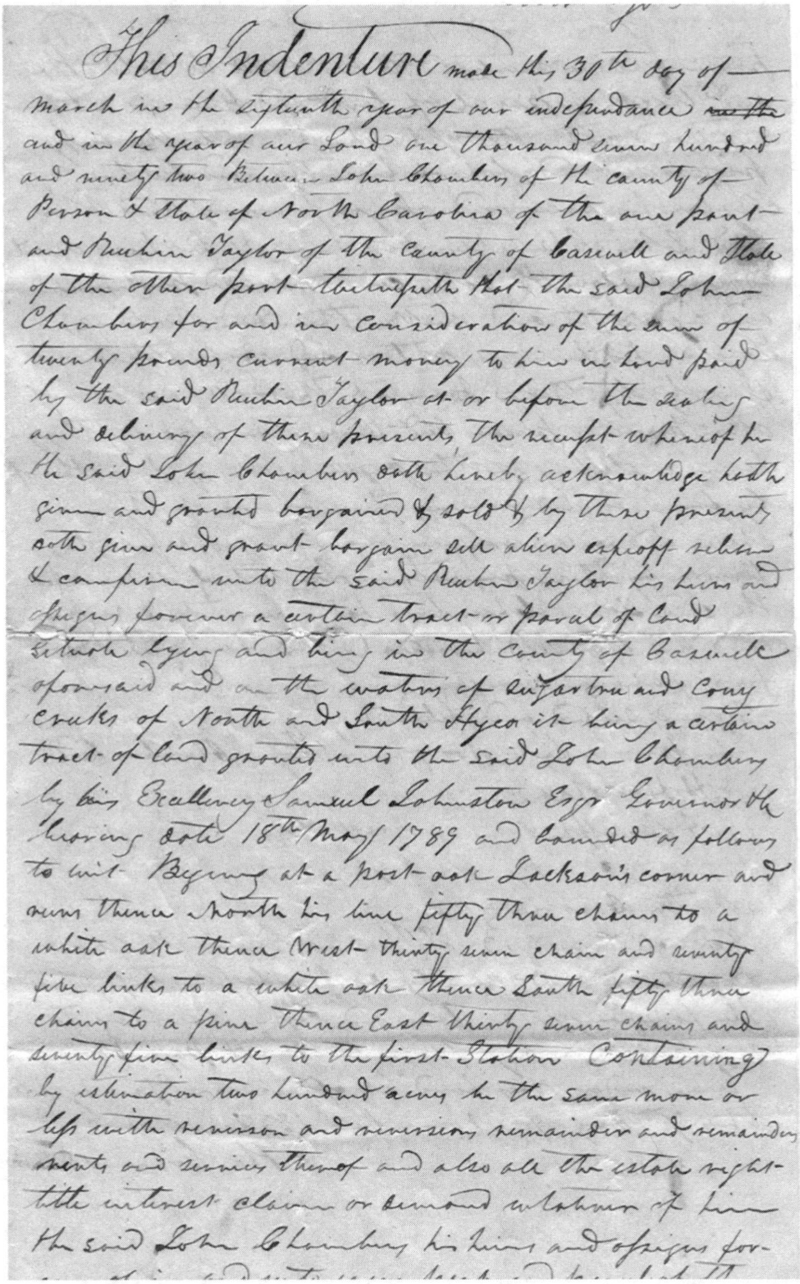

This Indenture made this 30th day of
march in the sixteenth year of our independance ~~in the~~
and in the year of our Lord one thousand seven hundred
and ninety two Between John Chambers of the County of
Person & State of North Carolina of the one part
and Reuben Taylor of the County of Caswell and State
of the other part Witnesseth that the said John
Chambers for and in consideration of the sum of
twenty pounds current money to him in hand paid
by the said Reuben Taylor at or before the sealing
and delivery of these presents, the receipt whereof he
the said John Chambers doth hereby acknowledge hath
given and granted bargained & sold & by these presents
doth give and grant bargain sell alien enfeoff release
& confirm unto the said Reuben Taylor his heirs and
assigns forever a certain tract or parcel of Land
situate lying and being in the County of Caswell
aforesaid and on the waters of Sugartree and Cony
Creeks of North and South Hyco it being a certain
tract of land granted unto the said John Chambers
by his Excellency Samuel Johnston Esqr Governor the
bearing date 18th May 1789 and bounded as follows
to wit Beginning at a post oak Jackson's corner and
runs thence North his line fifty three chains to a
white oak thence West thirty seven chains and seventy
five links to a white oak thence South fifty three
chains to a pine thence East thirty seven chains and
seventy five links to the first Station Containing
by estimation two hundred acres be the same more or
less with reversion and reversions remainder and remainders
rents and services thereof and also all the estate right
title interest claim or demand whatever of him
the said John Chambers his heirs and assigns for-

FIGURE 9-3 Front page of an indenture for the purchase of land in 1792

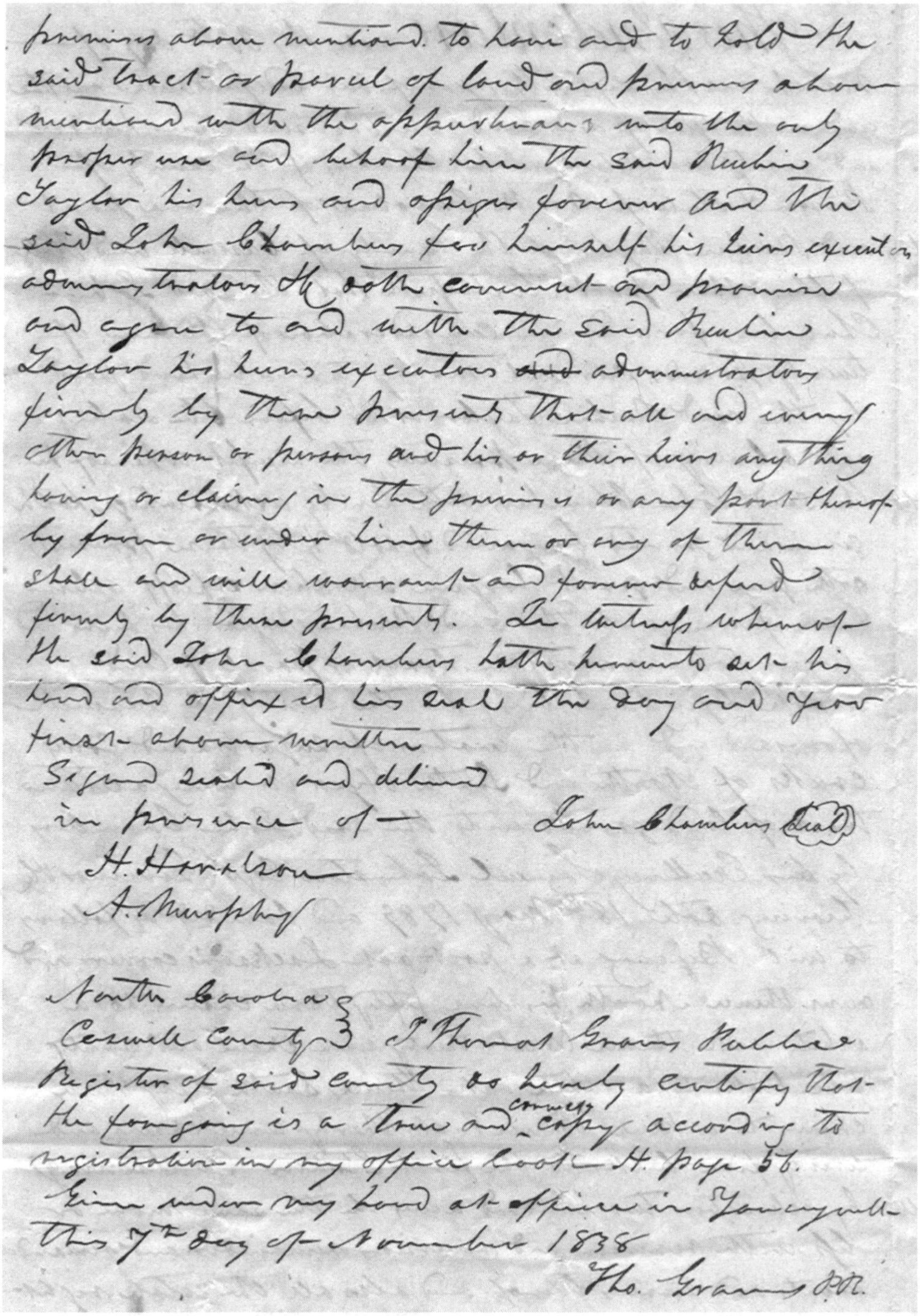
premises above mentioned. to have and to hold the
said tract or parcel of land and premises above
mentioned with the appurtenances unto the only
proper use and behoof him the said Reubin
Taylor his heirs and assigns forever And the
said John Chambers for himself his heirs executors
administrators &c doth covenant and promise
and agree to and with the said Reubin
Taylor his heirs executors ~~and~~ administrators
firmly by these presents that all and every
other person or persons and his or their heirs any thing
having or claiming in the premises or any part thereof
by from or under him them or any of them
shall and will warrant and forever defend
firmly by these presents. In witness whereof
the said John Chambers hath hereunto set his
hand and affixed his seal the day and year
first above written
Signed sealed and delivered
in presence of — John Chambers (Seal)
H. Haralson
A. Murphy

North Carolina }
Caswell County } I Thomas Graves Public
Register of said County do hereby certify that
the foregoing is a true and correct copy according to
registration in my office book H. page 56.
Given under my hand at office in Yanceyville
this 7th day of November 1838
Tho. Graves P.R.

FIGURE 9-4 Back page of the same indenture shown in Figure 9-3, showing the clerk's notation of his transcription made in 1838

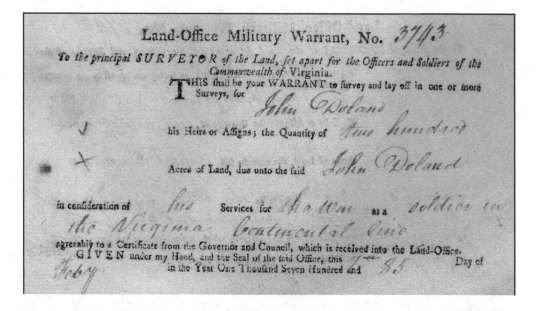

FIGURE 9-5   Bounty land warrant issued to John Doland by the Commonwealth of Virginia on 7 February 1785

As a result, documentation dating from this period is some of the richest genealogical evidence you will find. The documents may contain names of wives, marriage dates, children's names and birth dates/ages, and specific details about military service.

In order to organize these Public Domain Land areas, also known as Federal Land areas, the federal government had to establish a system of measurement so that parcels could be easily defined and recorded. Rather than using the older metes and bounds survey system that relied on the use of topographic features, the government decided to use a cartographic reference system using meridians. A *meridian* is an imaginary north–south line running from the North Pole to the South Pole. Thirty-seven principal meridians were defined over a period of time to form the basis of the Public Land Survey System (PLSS). Additional imaginary north–south lines were defined as guide meridians, and these are located 24 miles to the east and to the west of the principal meridians or of the previously established guide meridians. A horizontal line, running east to west and intersecting the principal meridians and guide meridians, is referred to as a *base line*. It is used to measure distances from north to south. These imaginary reference lines are used to facilitate a quick reference for locating a physical location.

Meridian regions are divided into tracts, each of which is approximately 24 miles wide. Each tract is subdivided into 16 townships, each of which is approximately six miles square.

You also will encounter the term "range" in your research of townships. Ranges are imaginary north–south lines within a meridian that are set six miles apart. Remember that six miles is the width of a township. A count of the number of ranges to the east or west of a meridian and to the north or south of a base line indicates a specific township. For example, if you encounter a description that indicates "T2S and R2E," this means that the township being defined or described is two townships south of the base line and two townships east of the range line.

Each township is further subdivided to provide a more finite means of locating a specific piece of property. Each township is subdivided into sections. There are 36 square sections in a township, each of which comprises approximately 640 acres. Sections are numbered from 1 to 36, with the position of the numbers being dependent on whether the township is north or south of a baseline or east or west of a range line.

A section is most often subdivided into a variety of different-sized parcels. (There are exceptions to this, particularly in Ohio and other states in which the township, range, and section scheme was not clearly in place at the time the initial surveys were performed or where specific governments dictated use of other methods.) These subdivisions of sections are typically square or rectangular in shape. That is not to say that different parcels of land might not be subdivided and shaped differently. However, land descriptions you will encounter in Public Domain Land States usually refer to townships, ranges, and sections to help define the location and size of a parcel.

There are 30 Public Domain Land States: Alabama, Alaska, Arizona, Arkansas, California, Colorado, Florida, Idaho, Illinois, Indiana, Iowa, Kansas, Louisiana, Michigan, Minnesota, Mississippi, Missouri, Montana, Nebraska, Nevada, New Mexico, North Dakota, Ohio, Oklahoma, Oregon, South Dakota, Utah, Washington, Wisconsin, and Wyoming.

Public Domain Land States Records

The land in the Public Domain Land States was distributed in a variety of ways over different time periods. Some was auctioned or sold by lottery. Initial sales of land were conducted by auction, with the land going to the highest bidder. Land offices opened and did the proverbial "booming business" in accepting applications and handling paperwork to sell land to individuals wishing to settle on undeveloped properties to the west. Land patents are the legal documents that transferred land ownership from the U.S. government to individuals.

There were a number of transactions used to transfer ownership of land from the federal government to an individual (or organization). In order to purchase a parcel of land, an individual had to be a native-born citizen of the United States or must have filed a Declaration of Intent document to initiate the naturalization process. The exception to this requirement was in the case of bounty land warrants.

The process of acquiring property usually began with the individual filing an application for a desired parcel of land. The person had to pay cash or present evidence of some form of credit. At that time, a warrant for survey was issued to accurately define the property description and to ensure that someone else did not already own the property. A completed survey report was submitted to the government and was recorded in a township plat book. The plat book consisted of a map of the township and a listing of the parcels. The surveys recorded here also included descriptions of the physical characteristics of the property, such as rocks, streams, forests, and other features.

Next, information about the transaction was recorded in the tract book. You can use the tract books' contents to point to specific townships to locate individual landowners' records. All of the paperwork created and documentation supplied so far was then gathered together and sent to the General Land Office. The materials were placed in what is commonly known as a land-entry case file and the files were reviewed. There should be a case file for every application processed, regardless of whether it was approved or rejected. The General Land Office reviewed the land-entry case file and, if approved, issued to the applicant a document referred to as a "final certificate." This indicated that all of the required steps had been taken and that a land patent for the parcel had been approved. The actual land patents were generated by the General Land Office and were sent to the local land office, where the applicant could then exchange the final certificate for the actual land patent. Figure 9-6 shows the land patent for my great-great-grandfather, John N. Swords, dated 10 August 1849, for a parcel of land in the area of Lebanon, Alabama.

There are over ten million such individual land transactions in the custody of the National Archives. They cover the 30 Public Domain Land States. The case files were filed as either military bounty land warrants, pre-1908 general land entry files, or post-1908 land entry files. The information required to access and order copies of the records will differ depending on which of these three categories the transaction falls into.

The tract books mentioned previously relate to the land entry case files and are available to help your research. These are arranged by the legal description of the land: by township, range, section, and so forth. They are divided into two geographical areas: Eastern States and Western States. For the *Eastern States*, the U.S. Bureau of Land Management (BLM) has the tract books and patents. This geographical area includes the states of Alabama, Arkansas, Florida, Illinois, Indiana, Iowa, Louisiana, Michigan, Minnesota, Mississippi, Missouri, Ohio, and Wisconsin. For the *Western States*, the tract books are located in the National Archives Building in Washington, D.C. This geographical area includes the states of Alaska, Arizona, California, Colorado, Idaho, Kansas, Montana, Nebraska, Nevada, New Mexico, North Dakota, Oklahoma, Oregon, South Dakota, Utah, Washington, and Wyoming.

The land patents for the Eastern States have been digitized and indexed by the U.S. Bureau of Land Management General Land Office (BLM-GLO). These can be searched in a database at **http://www.glorecords.blm.gov**, viewed, and printed. You also can order a certified copy of the document from that agency. The document shown in Figure 9-6 was obtained from the BLM-GLO database. The National Archives and Records Administration (NARA) in Washington, D.C., hold the tract books for the Western States.

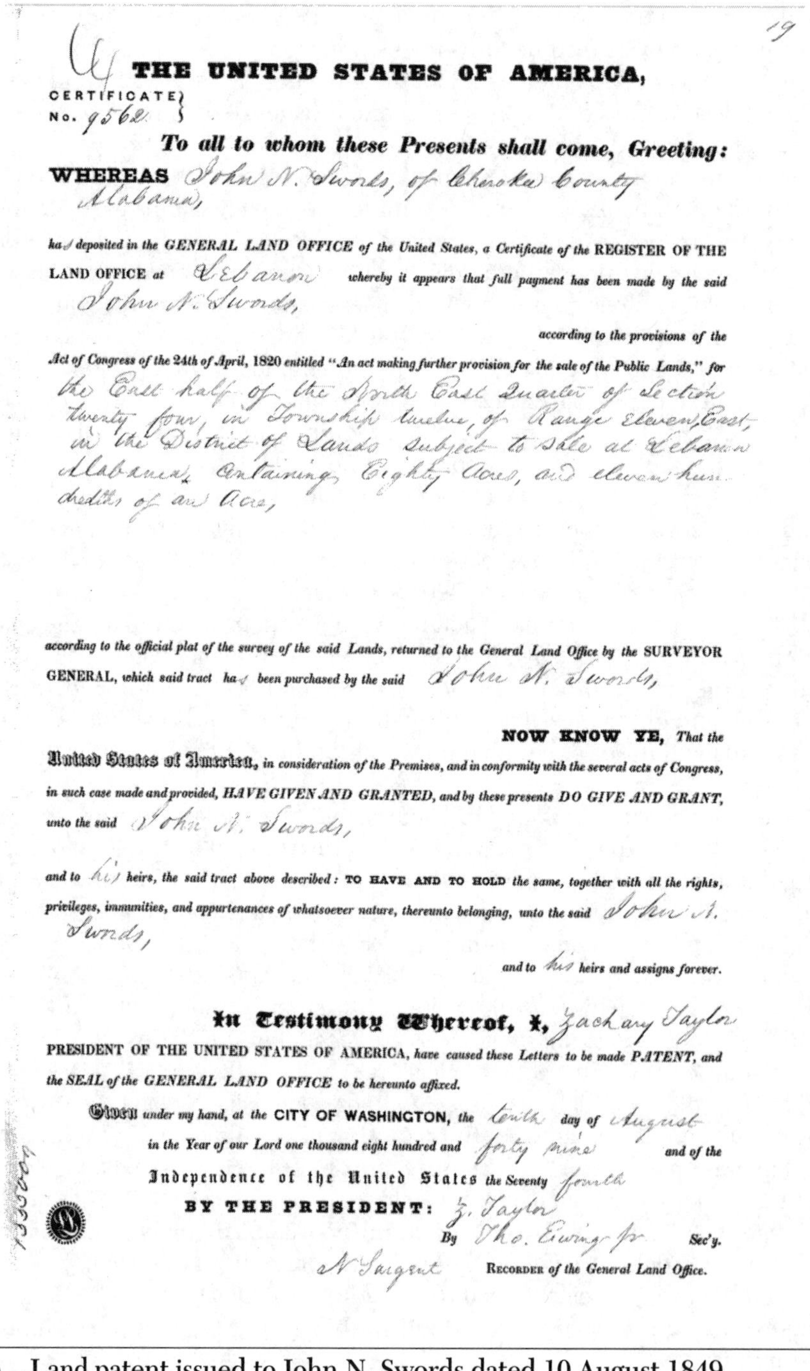

19

THE UNITED STATES OF AMERICA,

CERTIFICATE No. 9562

To all to whom these Presents shall come, Greeting:

WHEREAS John N. Swords, of Cherokee County Alabama,

has deposited in the *GENERAL LAND OFFICE of the United States, a Certificate of the* REGISTER OF THE LAND OFFICE at Lebanon *whereby it appears that full payment has been made by the said* John N. Swords,

according to the provisions of the Act of Congress of the 24th of April, 1820 entitled "An act making further provision for the sale of the Public Lands," for the East half of the North East Quarter of Section twenty four, in Township twelve, of Range Eleven, East, in the District of Lands subject to sale at Lebanon Alabama, containing Eighty Acres, and eleven hundredths of an Acre,

according to the official plat of the survey of the said Lands, returned to the General Land Office by the SURVEYOR GENERAL, *which said tract has been purchased by the said* John N. Swords,

NOW KNOW YE, *That the* United States of America, *in consideration of the Premises, and in conformity with the several acts of Congress, in such case made and provided, HAVE GIVEN AND GRANTED, and by these presents DO GIVE AND GRANT, unto the said* John N. Swords,

and to his *heirs, the said tract above described:* TO HAVE AND TO HOLD *the same, together with all the rights, privileges, immunities, and appurtenances of whatsoever nature, thereunto belonging, unto the said* John N. Swords,

and to his *heirs and assigns forever.*

In Testimony Whereof, I, Zachary Taylor PRESIDENT OF THE UNITED STATES OF AMERICA, *have caused these Letters to be made PATENT, and the SEAL of the GENERAL LAND OFFICE to be hereunto affixed.*

Given *under my hand, at the* CITY OF WASHINGTON, *the* tenth *day of* August *in the Year of our Lord one thousand eight hundred and* forty nine *and of the* Independence of the United States *the Seventy* fourth

BY THE PRESIDENT: Z. Taylor

By Tho. Ewing Jr. *Sec'y.*

N Sargent RECORDER *of the General Land Office.*

FIGURE 9-6 Land patent issued to John N. Swords dated 10 August 1849

A hotly contested issue in the United States during the first half of the 19th century was slavery, and it was one of the major issues that contributed to the U.S. Civil War. The question of which new states would be free states or slave states contributed to a decade-long delay in passage of legislation to encourage settlement, the Homestead Act. After the Southern states seceded from the Union, the slavery issue was removed from the U.S. Congress's consideration, the Homestead Act of 1862 was passed, and President Abraham Lincoln signed it into law on 20 May 1862. The new law took effect on 1 January 1863. Any U.S. citizen, or intended citizen, who was 21 years or older (male, female, and freed slaves), and had never borne arms against the U.S. government, was eligible to apply for 160 acres of surveyed government land. It was a three-part process:

1. The homesteader filed an application at a land office to lay claim to 160 acres of surveyed government land. He/she paid cash or presented a bounty land warrant, and the land office issued a receipt.
2. The homesteader had to live on the property for the next five years. He/she was required to improve the land by building at least a 12 × 14-foot dwelling and by growing crops.
3. At the end of five years, the homesteader could file an affidavit testifying that the residency and improvements conditions had been met. A witness who knew the homesteader also swore an affidavit that the witness knew him/her and affirmed that the conditions had been satisfied. The documents were reviewed by the land office and then sent to the General Land Office in Washington, D.C., along with a final certificate of eligibility for review. On approval, a land patent was issued to the homesteader.

Several other laws were enacted over the following decades. These included: the Southern Homestead Act of 1866, which addressed land ownership in the South during the Reconstruction era; the Timber Culture Act of 1873, which required the applicant to plant trees; the Kinkaid Amendment of 1904, which expanded the size of the land to 640 acres to new settlers in western Nebraska; the Enlarged Homestead Act, which passed in 1909 and which amended the Homestead Act of 1862, increasing the size of the land from 160 acres to 320 acres; and the Stock-Raising Act, which passed in 1916 and which doubled the size of the land to 640 acres.

The homestead documents are stored at NARA in Washington, D.C. At the time of this writing, a project has been completed by collaboration between the Homestead National Monument of America (located in Beatrice, Nebraska), Fold3.com (**http://www.fold3.com**), FamilySearch (**https://familysearch.org**), and the University of Nebraska-Lincoln to digitize and index the Nebraska land entry case files and place them online at Fold3.com. The Homestead Records Project will ultimately digitize and index the homestead records from all 30 Homesteading States. You can learn more at the National Park Service website for the project at **http://www.nps.gov/home/historyculture/homesteadrecords.htm**. An example of the final Homestead Certificate is shown in Figure 9-7.

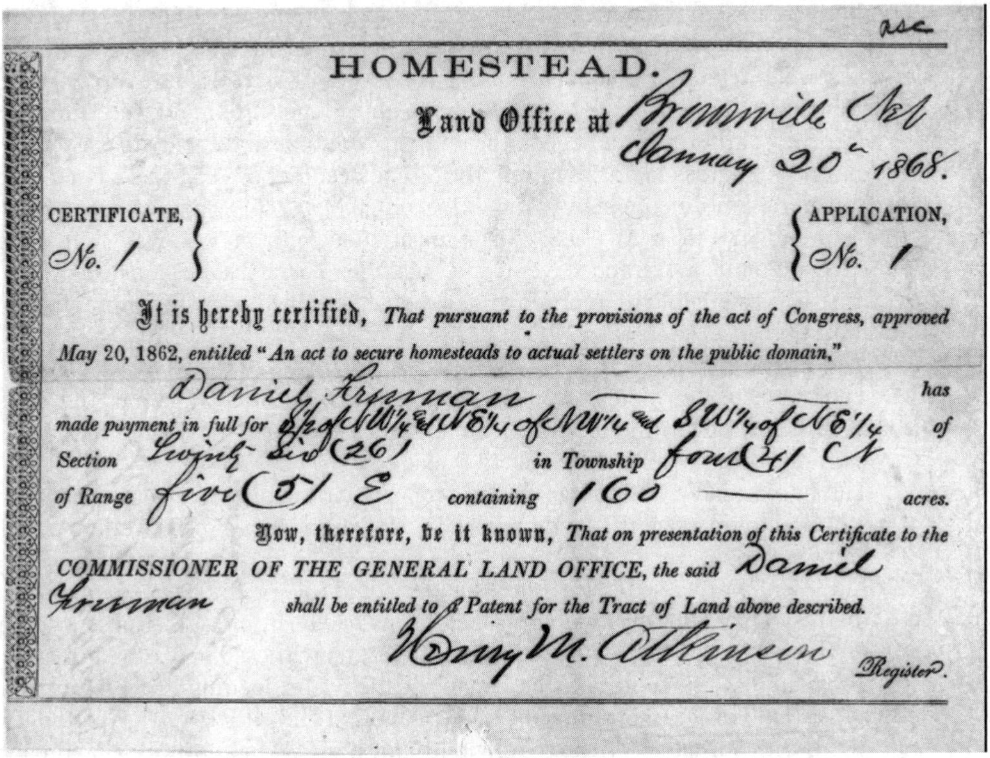

asc

HOMESTEAD.

Land Office at Brownville Neb
January 20th 1868.

CERTIFICATE, No. 1

APPLICATION, No. 1

It is hereby certified, *That pursuant to the provisions of the act of Congress, approved May 20, 1862, entitled "An act to secure homesteads to actual settlers on the public domain,"*
Daniel Freeman has *made payment in full for* S½ of NW¼ & NE¼ of NW¼ and SW¼ of NE¼ *of Section* Twenty Six (26) *in Township* four (4) N *of Range* five (5) E *containing* 160 *acres.*

Now, therefore, be it known, *That on presentation of this Certificate to the COMMISSIONER OF THE GENERAL LAND OFFICE, the said* Daniel Freeman *shall be entitled to a Patent for the Tract of Land above described.*

Henry M. Atkinson *Register.*

FIGURE 9-7 The final Homestead Certificate for Daniel Freeman, the first applicant under the Homestead Act of 1862

Locate Land and Property Records

Subsequent sales and transfers of titles for Public Domain Land property occurred as private transactions without the participation of the U.S. federal government unless a question concerning the original patent or title arose. Agreements of sale, indentures, mortgages, surveys, receipts, and deeds are usually the most common documents found.

Land and property documents may be located almost anywhere. Some documents will be in the possession of the individual or family, while others will be found in courthouses, recorder of deeds' offices, registrars' offices, tax assessors' offices, county offices, state archives, NARA, the BLM-GLO, and other places. As mentioned, copies of applications for bounty land can often be found in veterans' military service and/or pension files. Remember that city directories, voter registration lists, jury lists, and many other records may provide clues to property ownership and associated records.

Learn About Types of Records

Deeds are used to transfer title of property from the grantor to the grantee. Deeds are perhaps the most common document you will find in your property research, and they can contain extensive genealogical information. In the case of a piece of property owned by someone who has died, the transfer of property as part of an estate in probate may contain a great deal of information. The name of the deceased and his or her date of death are often shown to designate the reason for the transfer of ownership. In times before laws required death certificates, a deed may be one of the only sources of a death date. The names and relationships of the devisees/heirs can also be a gold mine in your research. However, this information also serves as a pointer to other records, such as a will and probate packet, marriage documents, and more.

Another important piece of genealogical information that appears in land records is that of "dower release." In referencing Figure 9-1 earlier in this chapter, I called attention to the "dower line" shown on that particular survey report. When a woman had a legal interest in the ownership of property, laws in earlier times required that the woman sign a dower release in order to allow her husband to sell a piece of property. The woman appeared in a court and was interviewed by a judge, separate from her husband. She was asked if she voluntarily exercised her right to relinquish ownership or interest in the property to allow for its sale or transfer. Figure 9-8 shows a copy of a deed recorded in the deed books of Alachua County, Florida, dated 7 June 1873. At the bottom of the document is a record of Priscilla McCall's dower release for that piece of property.

Warranty deeds are those instruments used in property transactions in which the grantor fully warrants good clear title to the property. A warranty deed offers the greatest protection of any type of deed, and you will find references to and copies of these warranty deeds among the land and property records you research. Figure 9-9 shows an example of a cover page of a warranty deed. The remainder of the text of the warranty deed is virtually identical to other deeds but, in this case, proof of title has been presented at the time of transfer to ensure the veracity of the title.

Another type of deed is a "deed of gift" in which one person transfers ownership of property to another person without benefit of any compensation or remuneration. Figure 9-10 shows the original deed of gift from my great-great-grandfather, Goodlow W. Morgan, to his son, my great-grandfather, Rainey B. Morgan, dated 17 December 1885. This deed transfers ownership of the home tract of land to Rainey but reserves Goodlow's right of use and control for the remainder of his life. The deed is registered in a deed book in Caswell County, North Carolina.

There are other documents associated with land and property ownership in the United States that you may find helpful to your research. Particularly useful are those documents that point you to the original land records. These include property tax bills such as the example shown in Figure 9-11.

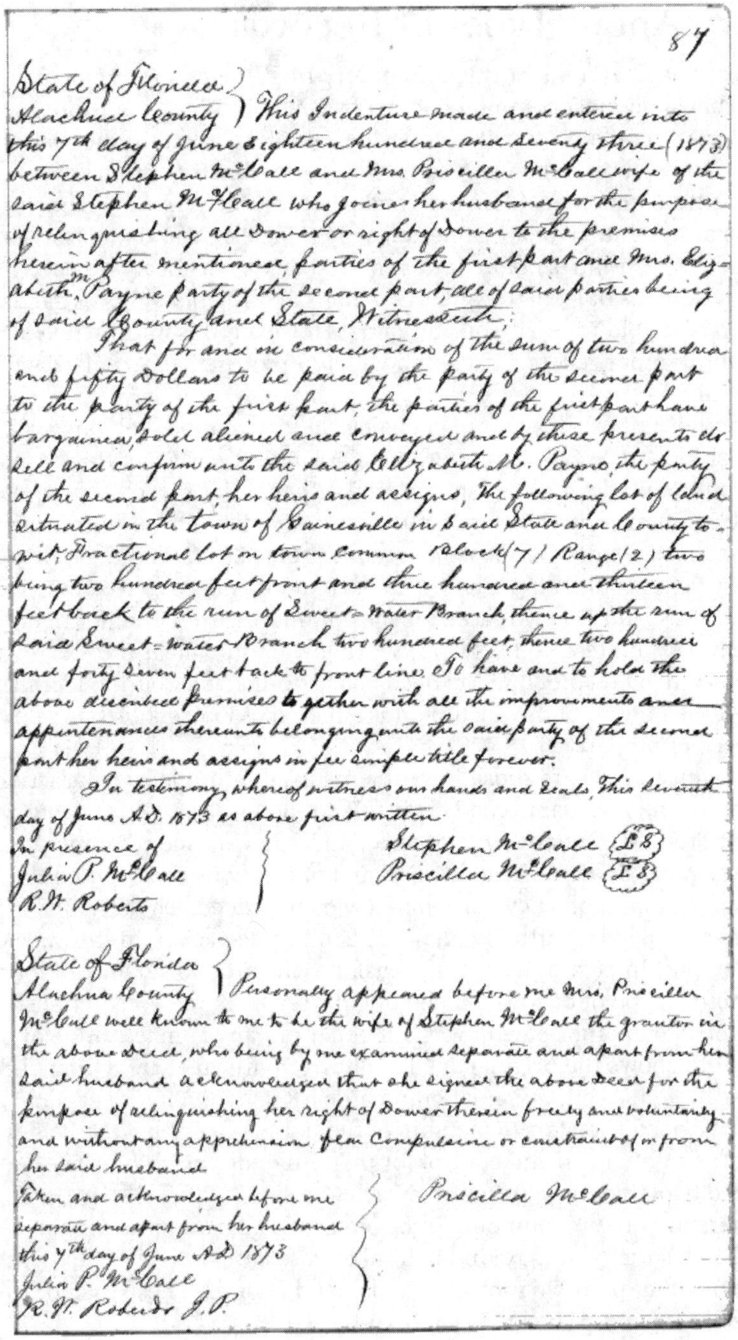

87

State of Florida }
Alachua County } This Indenture made and entered into this 7th day of June Eighteen hundred and seventy three (1873) between Stephen McCall and Mrs. Priscilla McCall wife of the said Stephen McCall who joins her husband for the purpose of relinquishing all Dower or right of Dower to the premises herein after mentioned, parties of the first part and Mrs. Elizabeth M. Payne party of the second part, all of said parties being of said County and State, Witnesseth;

That for and in consideration of the sum of two hundred and fifty Dollars to be paid by the party of the second part to the party of the first part, the parties of the first part have bargained, sold aliened and conveyed and by these presents do sell and confirm unto the said Elizabeth M. Payne, the party of the second part, her heirs and assigns, the following lot of land situated in the town of Gainesville in said State and County to-wit; Fractional lot on town common Block (7) Range (2) two being two hundred feet front and three hundred and thirteen feet back to the run of Sweet-Water Branch, thence up the run of said Sweet-water Branch two hundred feet, thence two hundred and forty seven feet back to front line. To have and to hold the above described premises together with all the improvements and appurtenances thereunto belonging unto the said party of the second part her heirs and assigns in fee simple title forever.

In testimony whereof witness our hands and seals, this seventh day of June A.D. 1873 as above first written

In presence of
Julia P. McCall
R.W. Roberts

Stephen McCall (L.S.)
Priscilla McCall (L.S.)

State of Florida }
Alachua County } Personally appeared before me Mrs. Priscilla McCall well known to me to be the wife of Stephen McCall the grantor in the above Deed, who being by me examined separate and apart from her said husband acknowledged that she signed the above Deed for the purpose of relinquishing her right of Dower therein freely and voluntarily and without any apprehension fear compulsion or constraint of or from her said husband

Taken and acknowledged before me separate and apart from her husband this 7th day of June A.D. 1873
Julia P. McCall
R.W. Roberts J.P.

Priscilla McCall

FIGURE 9-8 This deed includes a record of the wife's interview and her dower release.

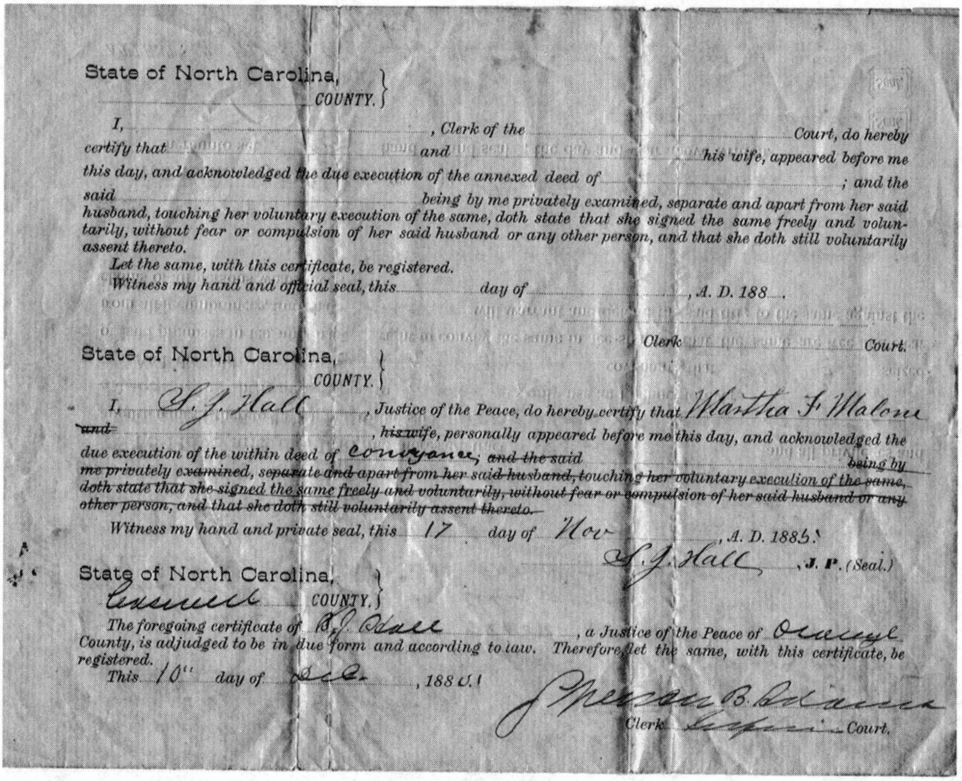

State of North Carolina,
COUNTY.

I, ..., Clerk of the ... Court, do hereby certify that ... and ... his wife, appeared before me this day, and acknowledged the due execution of the annexed deed of ...; and the said ... being by me privately examined, separate and apart from her said husband, touching her voluntary execution of the same, doth state that she signed the same freely and voluntarily, without fear or compulsion of her said husband or any other person, and that she doth still voluntarily assent thereto.

Let the same, with this certificate, be registered.

Witness my hand and official seal, this ... day of ..., A. D. 188...

Clerk ... Court.

State of North Carolina,
COUNTY.

I, S. J. Hall, Justice of the Peace, do hereby certify that Martha F. Malone ~~and~~ ..., ~~his~~wife, personally appeared before me this day, and acknowledged the due execution of the within deed of conveyance; ~~and the said ... being by me privately examined, separate and apart from her said husband, touching her voluntary execution of the same, doth state that she signed the same freely and voluntarily, without fear or compulsion of her said husband or any other person, and that she doth still voluntarily assent thereto.~~

Witness my hand and private seal, this 17 day of Nov, A. D. 1885.

S. J. Hall, J. P. (Seal.)

State of North Carolina,
Caswell COUNTY.

The foregoing certificate of S. J. Hall, a Justice of the Peace of Caswell County, is adjudged to be in due form and according to law. Therefore let the same, with this certificate, be registered.

This 10th day of Dec, 1885.

Jefferson B. Adams
Clerk Superior Court.

FIGURE 9-9 Cover page of a warranty deed

Other documents that may point to land ownership include tax lists, tax liens, court judgments, and auction records, to name just a few. You may find some of these among papers at home, or you may conduct research at a courthouse. You can see that the wide range of documents and their possible contents may provide you with a great many clues. It should be obvious by now, though, that there is a lot to learn about U.S. property records. You will want to learn more about the records available in the areas where your ancestors lived at the times they lived there. By doing so, you can begin to tap these marvelous resources.

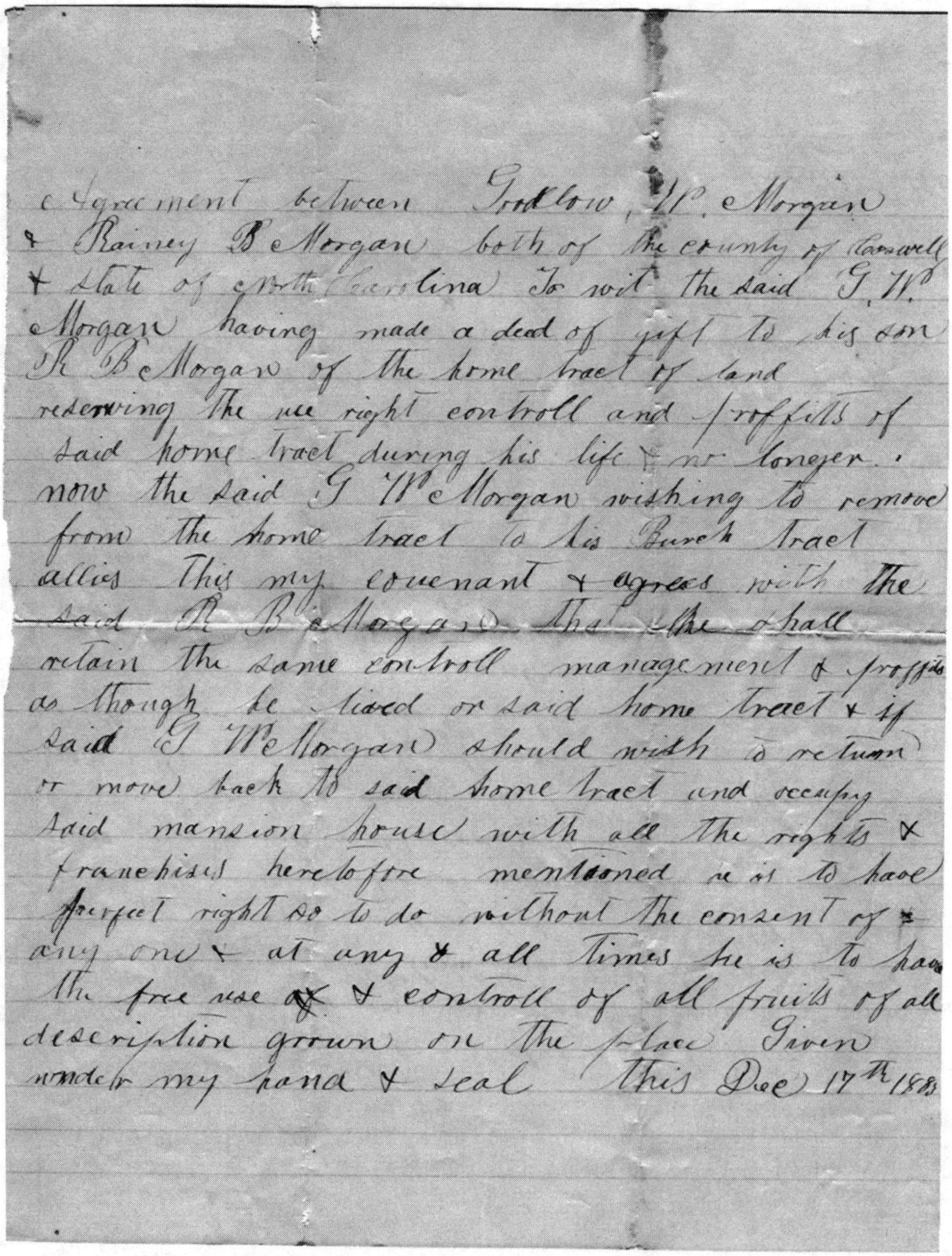

Agreement between Goodlow W. Morgan & Rainey B. Morgan both of the county of Caswell & state of North Carolina To wit the said G. W. Morgan having made a deed of gift to his son R. B. Morgan of the home tract of land reserving the use right controll and proffitts of said home tract during his life & no longer. now the said G. W. Morgan wishing to remove from the home tract to his Burch tract allies This my covenant & agrees with the said R. B. Morgan that he shall retain the same controll management & proffits as though he lived on said home tract & if said G. W. Morgan should wish to return or move back to said home tract and occupy said mansion house with all the rights & franchises heretofore mentioned he is to have perfect right so to do without the consent of any one & at any & all Times he is to have the free use & controll of all fruits of all description grown on the place Given under my hand & seal this Dec 17th 1888

FIGURE 9-10 Deed of gift from the author's great-great-grandfather giving ownership of the home property to the author's great-grandfather

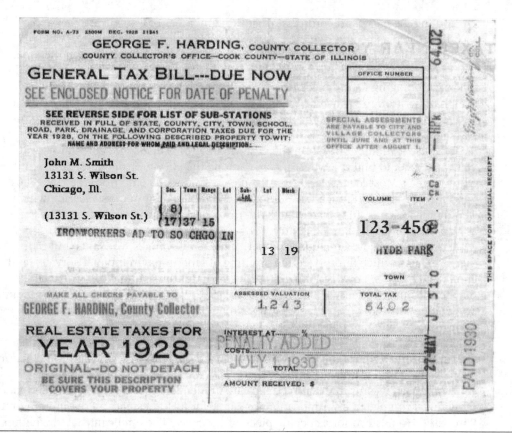

FIGURE 9-11   Sample of a real estate tax bill, which can direct you to the address of a specific piece of property and confirm the name(s) of the owner(s) of record

Learn About Land and Property Records in Canada

Canada was an attractive destination for people from France, Britain, Ireland, and elsewhere. Over the centuries, people were drawn to immigrate by the availability of land. In fact, both the French and British governments recruited people to settle there, and examples of advertisements for emigration to Canada exist in the holdings of the archives of France, Ireland, and the United Kingdom. Many parcels of land were granted in payment for military service. Additionally, people migrated northward from the 13 American colonies and, later, from the United States.

Among the earliest records that exist in many areas of Canada are the land records created as people migrated westward and settled. In many cases, land records are the only records available that document people who lived in the area. What is interesting is the high percentage of early settlers who did own land. While this is encouraging for genealogy research, remember that these records may have been handwritten in French or English by persons whose literacy and knowledge of legal affairs were not always the best. As a result, you may find that some records are particularly challenging to read and use.

Because settlement began in the eastern areas of Canada and spread westward, you can expect to find the oldest records among the surviving documentation in those eastern areas. Most formal land records in eastern Canada date from the late 1700s. Land records in New France were based on the feudal system of *seigneuries*, which were landed estates. In Canada, the holder of a *seigneurie* was referred to as a *seigneur*, as in a member of the landed gentry.

These land records include land petitions, conveyances, warrants and fiats (permissions), which authorized the granting of land in payment for a service, land grants and patents, Loyalist land grants, deeds, indentures, quit-claim deeds, titles, transfer documents, leases, mortgages, liens, and a variety of other land instruments. The documents that are available for research will vary based on the time period, the government having jurisdiction at the time, and the laws of the period.

Transcriptions of the documents were recorded in the government land offices in the various areas where the transactions occurred. Records of legal claims and actions may also be found in court records.

Homestead records in western Canada are tremendously rich in personal information. Individuals completed an Application for Entry for a Homestead, a Pre-emption or a Purchased Homestead for a specific piece of property. The applicant stated whether he was a Canadian citizen, a naturalized citizen, or an alien. He included the number of persons who would be living on the property. He also stated his age, the age of his wife, and the ages of children. He listed his country of birth, the sub-division of that country, the last place of residence, and previous occupation. He signed a formal sworn affidavit in support of his application. There may be other documents in the file as well, such as a statement as why he could not maintain the homestead property. There is then usually a Declaration of Abandonment document, such as the one shown in Figure 9-12, detailing the reason(s) for giving up the property. At the time of this writing, FamilySearch (**https://familysearch.org**) has placed thousands of images of homestead file records online. These are not yet indexed but are well organized and can be browsed.

Land grants have been made for soldiers since the 1600s by both the French and English governments. Loyalists were given land grants following the American Revolution, and Canadian soldiers were given land grants following the War of 1812. The tradition continued with passage of the Soldier Settlement Act in 1917, expanded in 1919, and the Veterans' Land Act in 1942. These allowed veterans of World War I and World War II to apply for government loans to purchase land.

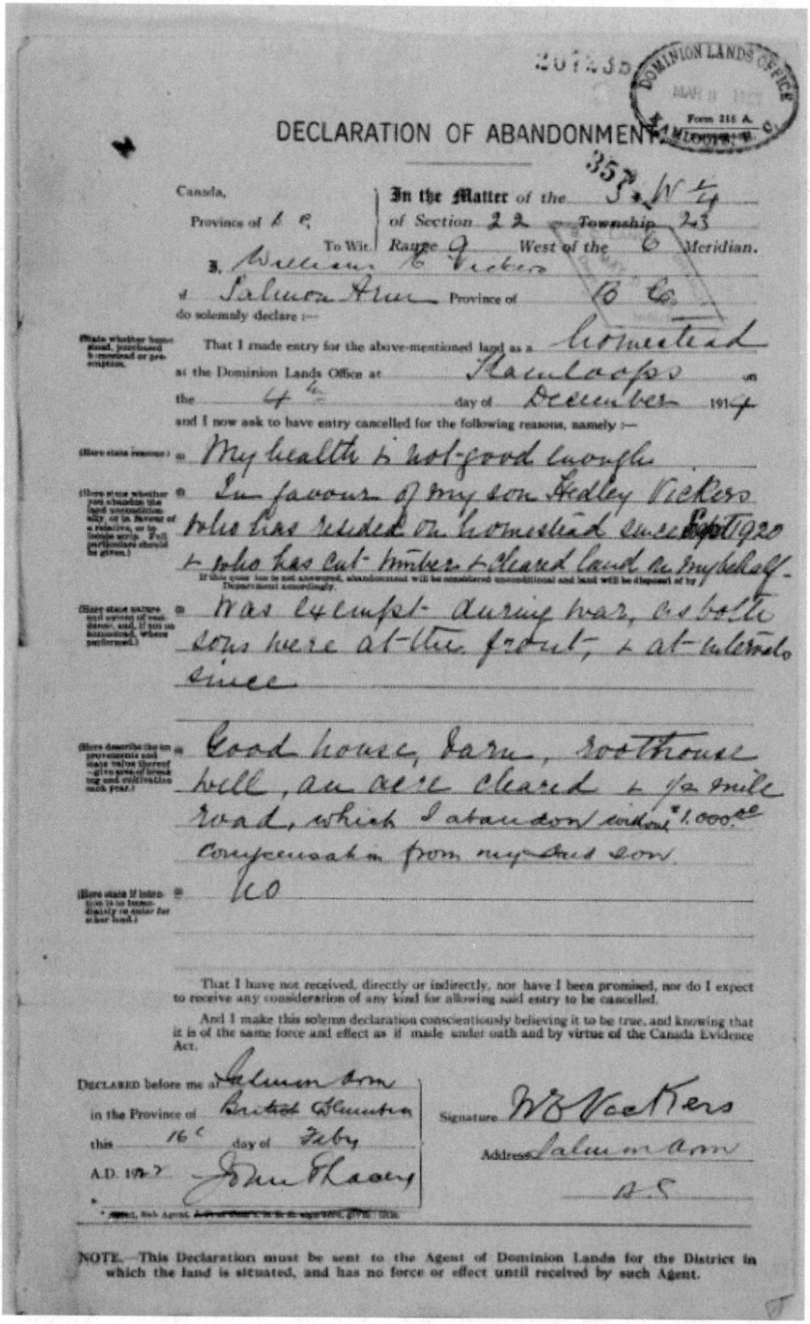

DOMINION LANDS OFFICE

Form 215 A.

DECLARATION OF ABANDONMENT

Canada,

Province of B. C.

To Wit:

In the Matter of the S. W. ¼ of Section 22 Township 23 Range 9 West of the 6 Meridian.

I, William E. Vickers

of Salmon Arm Province of B. C.

do solemnly declare :—

That I made entry for the above-mentioned land as a homestead

at the Dominion Lands Office at Kamloops on

the 4th day of December 1914

and I now ask to have entry cancelled for the following reasons, namely :—

(1) My health is not good enough

(2) In favour of my son Hedley Vickers who has resided on homestead since Sept 1920 & who has cut timber & cleared land on my behalf.

If this question be not answered, abandonment will be considered unconditional and land will be disposed of by Department accordingly.

(3) Was exempt during war, as both sons were at the front, & at intervals since

(4) Good house, barn, roothouse well, an acre cleared & ½ a mile road, which I abandon without $1,000.00 compensation from my said son.

(5) no

That I have not received, directly or indirectly, nor have I been promised, nor do I expect to receive any consideration of any kind for allowing said entry to be cancelled.

And I make this solemn declaration conscientiously believing it to be true, and knowing that it is of the same force and effect as if made under oath and by virtue of the Canada Evidence Act.

Declared before me at Salmon Arm

in the Province of British Columbia

this 16th day of Feby

A.D. 1922

Signature W E Vickers

Address Salmon Arm

B.C.

NOTE.—This Declaration must be sent to the Agent of Dominion Lands for the District in which the land is situated, and has no force or effect until received by such Agent.

FIGURE 9-12 A Declaration of Abandonment document filed in 1922 for a homestead in British Columbia

You can learn a great deal about Canadian land records in the FamilySearch Wiki at **https://familysearch.org/learn/wiki/en/Main_Page**.

Land Measurement in Canada

As you work with property records in Canada, you will undoubtedly encounter the use of surveyors' measurements, just as in the State Land States in the United States. Surveyors used units of measurement based on the length of a surveyor's chain. Refer again to Table 9-1 for a brief overview of conversions from surveyors' measurements to feet and inches.

Land Systems Used in Canada

Several land systems have been used in Canada throughout the centuries. In the course of your research, you may encounter these systems and will need to understand a little about them in order to successfully work with the land records. There are four organizational systems you are likely to encounter:

- **Dominion Land Survey**   This is by far the most common organizational system used in Canada. It is based on the U.S. Public Land Survey System and began being used in Canada in 1871. The basis of this system is the use of townships and sections. A township consists of 36 square miles and is subdivided into 36 sections, which are one mile square. Each section is subdivided into four 160-acre areas referred to as quarter sections. This is the smallest unit of this land system. A parcel of land is typically described in its deed or other document as lying in a particular township, section, and quarter section.
- **Patchwork System**   This system used natural land features such as rocks, rivers and streams, and trees to indicate the beginning and end of a specific boundary. For example, a boundary might be described as "beginning at the large oak near the edge of Twenty-Mile Creek and traveling west, ending at the eastern edge of the creek." Canada is not unique in its use of such descriptive land measurements; this system also was used in areas of the United States for many years, and you will find later physical features noted, along with surveyors' measurements, to more fully describe a piece of property. This system was widely used in Newfoundland and Labrador, Nova Scotia, New Brunswick, and Prince Edward Island.
- **River Lot System**   The use of this system is generally attributed to the land holding system developed and used in New France. Lands along rivers and streams were defined as long, relatively slender lots running perpendicular to the waterway.

- **Rectangular Lot System**   This system uses a Township or Parish system, which should not be confused with the designation of the use of township, section, and quarter section used in the Dominion Land Survey described previously. Used primarily in Ontario, Québec, and the Maritimes, this system employs the use of a formal Township or Parish as its largest unit, and then subdivides individual parcels into individual lots of a uniform size and rectangular in shape. The size of the lot might range from 100 acres on up, and common sizes were 100 or 200 acres.

The land office with which you are working can help you to understand and locate a specific parcel of property. They typically have produced information sheets or leaflets that describe the system or systems in use in their records and will provide them to you on request. In addition, they will also have detailed land maps of the area going back a long time and can help you pinpoint the precise physical location of a parcel by using the property description found on a document.

Taxation and Duty Records

Throughout your research for the land records themselves, don't overlook the taxation and duty records associated with the land in Canada. Property taxes and duty records associated with land transactions can provide another source of information for you. In addition, those records may include names and references to military service, land descriptions, previous and subsequent residences, wills and estates, and other clues that can further your research.

Locate the Land Records

The most logical place to start your land and property research is in the area where you think your ancestor lived. That means making contact with Library and Archives Canada (LAC) to determine what they may have in their possession. Start at their website at **http://www.collectionscanada.gc.ca**.

Next, you will want to make contact with the appropriate provincial or territorial archives to determine what records are in their possession, or for recommendations of additional contacts in their area. LAC maintains a complete list of addresses and web links to the provincial and territorial archives, and to major genealogical societies in those areas, at **http://www.collectionscanada.gc.ca/genealogy/022-802-e.html**.

Be sure to use your local public and academic libraries as reference resources, and visit the nearest LDS Family History Center for help determining what materials you can access at FamilySearch (**https://familysearch.org**) and/or through microfilm that can be ordered from the Family History Library in Salt Lake City. FamilySearch has microfilmed Canadian land records over the decades, and these are being digitized and placed online at their website over time. At the time of this writing, there were a number of collections of British Columbia land records available. While not yet indexed, the records are organized and browsable. Look for additional Canadian land records to be added to the site.

Learn About Land and Property Records in the United Kingdom

Some of the more complicated land and property records, from the perspective of organization, are those found in the United Kingdom. The manorial system in use in England dates back to before the *Domesday Book*, which was commissioned in 1085 and which can be viewed online at **http://www.nationalarchives.gov.uk/domesday**. The manorial system is an amalgamation of an agricultural estate system and a feudal system of military tenures. In effect, the king owned all of the land. A tenant-in-chief received his ability to "hold" a large piece of land from the king. The tenant-in-chief could grant the privilege of "holding" to those persons who might be his retainers or valued representatives. These retainers are also referred to as *mesne lords*. The mesne lord could also grant "holdings" to his persons. Throughout the structure, however, each of these persons could and did create their own manorial area, complete with tenants, servants, and other lower-status persons.

A lord and his manor at any level owed his existence to the person from whom he received his holding, and his tenants and other residents of the manor owed their service and existence to the lord of the manor. That included fields for farming and the raising of livestock, forests for hunting, cottages, the church, and common necessary services such as mills and smithies. Tenants, both free and non-free, and other residents not only provided service to the lord, but also contributed a portion of the produce of the labor to support the lord and the manor. The lord, in turn, paid taxes and tribute to the king and provided men, materials, and service to the monarch as required. These services were originally called "tenures" and there were multiple types of these, including the lowliest of the tenants, the free tenures and non-free tenures. These persons were also known as serfs, bondsmen, or *villeins*.

Tenures were slowly replaced by monetary payments, known as *socage*, and military tenures were abolished in 1660.

How Many Manors Were There?

You might be surprised to learn that there were tens of thousands of manors in England in medieval times. By some calculations, there may have been as many as 25,000 to 65,000 manors. There were approximately 11,000 parishes in the 1500s and 1600s. There were manors of various sizes and with varying numbers of people affiliated with each one. Some parishes often had more than one manor associated with them.

One point of confusion with English land records concerns the fact that manorial lords were often more than simply landlords. In many cases they acted as the administrative and judicial authority, hearing and ruling on all types of claims and complaints. Further, some of the lords also claimed jurisdiction to rule on and administer the wills and estates of their tenants. Beginning in the 14th century, however, the responsibilities of the manorial courts were transferred to other bodies. These included church courts, secular courts, ecclesiastical parish authorities, and finally to the local authorities. Manorial courts still operated into the 19th century for the purpose of handling property transactions on the manor itself.

There actually were three types of manorial court. The Court Leet was the most common court, established by the lord of the manor. Its purpose was to assist in the administration of activities in the manor, and its functions included acting as a court of minor law and, in some cases, monitoring the quality of the produce of the manor. The Court Customary dealt with feudal matters, and particularly with disputes and other matters between the unfree tenants, or *villeins*. The Court Baron dealt with matters of tenure, feudal services, feudal dues, and disputes between free tenants. Obviously, there was more to these courts than this, and their functions varied from manor to manor, in different places, and at different periods. However, this should give you a brief idea of their purposes.

Manorial Records

The good news is that many manorial records have survived for centuries, going as far back as the 13th and 14th centuries. These manorial rolls consist primarily of the minutes of the courts dealing with a vast array of issues. The bad news, however, is that the earliest of these records are written in Latin. With the exception of some records dating from 1653–1660, it was not until the early 1730s that manorial court records began to be written in English, albeit they include many Latin abbreviations and subsidiary notations.

All that said, however, manorial records can contain a great deal of important and helpful genealogical information. The National Archives maintains the Manorial Documents Register (MDR). Not all of the counties' registers are online yet, but work is underway. (Please note that, at the time of this writing, work is also underway at TNA to migrate the indexing of these records to the new catalog, Discovery. Discovery, at **http://discovery.nationalarchives.gov.uk**, will soon be the only place to access descriptions of records held at TNA and other archives around the country.)

The MDR was established by passage of the Law of Property Act 1922. This legislation replaced the medieval system of land law and is important because it resulted in the abolishment of the use of "copyhold" in British property law. Copyhold was a form of feudal land tenure according to manorial law, and this form of ownership was used until it was abolished. Proof of property ownership, however, was primarily defined and registered in the original books and rolls of the manorial courts. Property was therefore seldom included in an individual's will.

In accordance with the 1922 legislation, it was imperative that references to the original copyhold entries be easily locatable in order to expedite the handling of land and property transactions. The MDR is maintained by TNA on behalf of the Master of the Rolls. It maintains a record of the locations of all manorial records throughout England and Wales. Manorial records survive today in many national and local record offices and, in some cases, in private hands. The MDR, therefore, is an essential tool for locating the records you might be seeking.

Some of the MDR is available online at **http://www.nationalarchives.gov.uk/ mdr**. A detailed description of the MDR and Manorial Lordships records is available at **http://www.nationalarchives.gov.uk/records/research-guides/manorial-documents-register-lordships.htm**. However, you may (at the time of this writing) search the MDR for every county in Wales and for many of the English counties. A search of the database will provide you with information about the number and types of available manorial records and where they are located. Manorial Lordships records are of little genealogical help as lordships could be sold and records are incomplete in many ways.

Some more recent land records may be found at Familyrelatives.com at **http:// www.familyrelatives.com**. (See Figure 9-13.) Their Land Records collection in the England group includes the *Return of Owners of Land* books for England, Wales, Scotland, and Ireland for years in the late 1800s, and *Great Landowners of Great Britain and Ireland* from the same period, which includes England, Wales, Scotland, and Ireland. A page from the latter is shown in Figure 9-14.

Your research into British land and property records will require you to do some historical research into the locations and periods in which your ancestors lived. There are many excellent reference works available concerning manorial records and other land records. Among the best are Mark D. Herber's *Ancestral Trails: The Complete Guide to British Genealogy and Family History*, Second Edition (Genealogical Publishing Co., 2006) and Denis Stuart's *Manorial Records* (available in softcover by Phillimore & Co., Ltd., 2010 and available at **http://www.amazon.uk**).

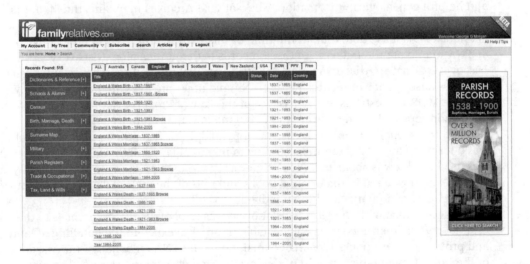

FIGURE 9-13   The search page for the England collection at Familyrelatives.com

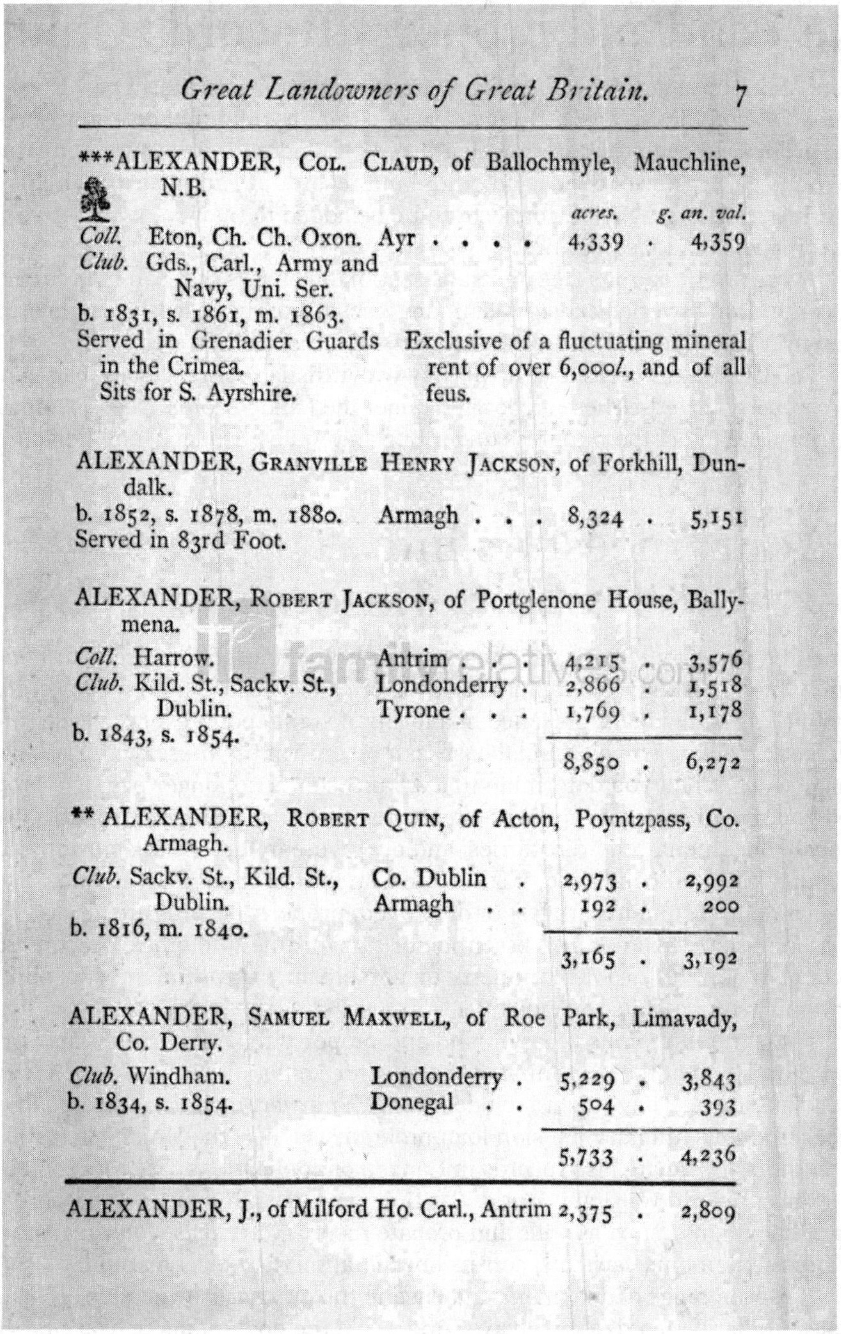

Great Landowners of Great Britain.   7

***ALEXANDER, Col. Claud, of Ballochmyle, Mauchline, N.B.

		acres.		g. an. val.
Coll.	Eton, Ch. Ch. Oxon. Ayr	4,339	.	4,359

Club. Gds., Carl., Army and Navy, Uni. Ser.

b. 1831, s. 1861, m. 1863.

Served in Grenadier Guards in the Crimea. Exclusive of a fluctuating mineral rent of over 6,000*l.*, and of all

Sits for S. Ayrshire. feus.

ALEXANDER, Granville Henry Jackson, of Forkhill, Dundalk.

b. 1852, s. 1878, m. 1880.   Armagh . . . 8,324 . 5,151

Served in 83rd Foot.

ALEXANDER, Robert Jackson, of Portglenone House, Ballymena.

Coll.	Harrow.	Antrim . . .	4,215	.	3,576
Club.	Kild. St., Sackv. St.,	Londonderry .	2,866	.	1,518
	Dublin.	Tyrone . . .	1,769	.	1,178

b. 1843, s. 1854.

8,850 . 6,272

** ALEXANDER, Robert Quin, of Acton, Poyntzpass, Co. Armagh.

Club.	Sackv. St., Kild. St.,	Co. Dublin .	2,973	.	2,992
	Dublin.	Armagh . .	192	.	200

b. 1816, m. 1840.

3,165 . 3,192

ALEXANDER, Samuel Maxwell, of Roe Park, Limavady, Co. Derry.

Club.	Windham.	Londonderry .	5,229	.	3,843
		Donegal . .	504	.	393

b. 1834, s. 1854.

5,733 . 4,236

ALEXANDER, J., of Milford Ho. Carl., Antrim 2,375 . 2,809

FIGURE 9-14   Page from *Great Landowners of Great Britain and Ireland* (1879) showing listings for Alexanders

Locate Land and Property Records Online

More and more materials are being made available on the Internet each month. The MDR and the Nebraska Homestead Documents are only two examples of land and property reference materials that may be found online. Be sure not to overlook the huge collections of deeds and other land records at FamilySearch (**https:// familysearch.org**). New records continue be added to their website every month, and indexing will be done over time.

There are numerous free and subscription databases that can help further your research. Don't overlook the government websites of the places your ancestors lived; they may have indexed and/or digitized many or all of their documents.

The Cyndi's List website at **http://www.cyndislist.com** includes many links to land and property records. These are located under the Land Records, Deeds, Homesteads, Etc. category and under the resources under England, Wales, Scotland, and Ireland.

Place Your Ancestors into Context with Property Records

Land and property records can most emphatically be used to place your ancestors and family members into geographical and historical context. While a census record may establish an individual's presence in a location at one point every decade, property tax records created on an annual basis can reconfirm the presence (or absence) of an ancestor. When you determine that an ancestor is no longer paying a property tax, you may then direct your research toward deed and property indexes, wills and probate documents, city directories, and other research paths to determine if the property changed hands and, if so, the reason for the change. In addition, when other government documents are lost or destroyed, property records are almost always re-created in some manner. It is essential for a government to quickly reconstruct these records in order to establish property ownership and to continue the taxation that is a primary source of its revenue.

There are numerous types of land and property records that you may encounter. As I mentioned at the beginning of the chapter, some of these may be linked to military service. They might include bounty land warrants, homestead and other tax exemptions, military pension loan programs such as the United States' G.I. Bill, and others. There are also records in Canada of applications for property loans to the veterans of World War I and World War II. You also can link property records with other documents, such as wills and probate records, jury lists, voter registration, divorce settlements, lawsuits, census enumeration districts, and more.

The wide range of documents attached to the purchase, ownership, sale, and transfer of land records is extensive. And while the documents may at first glance seem complicated or convoluted, the processes employed and the documentation created are actually quite logical. Now that you have an understanding of the types of land and property records that are used and where they might be found, you are prepared to begin searching for those that have been created for your ancestors and their families. Remember to invest the time in researching the place and time when your ancestors lived in a location so that you understand what land and property records were used at the time. This will make you more knowledgeable and help your research be more successful. Combine your study of history and geography with your genealogical research skills and you really can expand the chronicle of your family's history in a given area.

10

Locate and Use Immigration and Naturalization Records

HOW TO...

- Understand why people migrate
- Locate and use U.S. immigration and naturalization records
- Locate and access Canadian immigration records
- Locate and access Australian immigration records
- Use strategies for determining your ancestor's ship
- Use other strategies for determining your ancestor's place of origin
- Expand your family's story by tracing their migrations
- Understand the naturalization process and work with those documents

Let's step back for a moment and look how far you've come. You've discovered that there are literally hundreds of different record types that may contain information of value in documenting your forebears' lives. You have built a strong foundation for researching your family history, and you've learned how to examine and analyze the evidence that you uncovered along the way.

You've learned a great deal about your family so far by locating and examining home sources, vital records, and civil records. Chapter 6 has made you aware of all the types of census records available and what they include. You've delved into many of the advanced record types, including will and probate files, newspapers, obituaries, military records, and land and property records.

You now also know how important it is to place your family into context, to conduct scholarly research, to analyze every piece of evidence you uncover, and to properly document your source materials.

This chapter discusses some important documents that help you trace your ancestors' migrations. It presents successful methodologies for locating records of emigration, immigration, and naturalization and for evaluating their content. Working with these documents will provide evidence about your ancestors' movements. In the process, you will want to study history and discover the reasons for leaving one place and settling in another. A variety of other, less commonly used materials will be referenced in this chapter, along with recommendations for where to locate them and how to incorporate their contents into your family research and documentation.

Understand Why People Migrate

Since the dawn of time, it is a natural state of affairs for all creatures to migrate from place to place in order to survive. It is the natural order of things, and humankind is no different. People have moved from one place to another for a variety of reasons, sometimes moving multiple times during their lives until they found a place that suited them. While there are many reasons for moving from one place to another, the following are some of the principal motivations:

- **Establishing a Family**   People establish relationships with one another and pair up. This generally involves setting up a residence of their own, and that may involve one or both people moving to another place. As their families grow, they may need to find another residence, or they may migrate to another location where they can better provide for their family.
- **Accompanying or Following Family and Friends**   Many people accompanied or followed other family members or friends who moved somewhere else. The lure of employment opportunities, better living conditions, and political and religious freedom is often irresistible.
- **Adoption**   Adoption forces the movement of the adoptee from one place to another without his or her control. Single-child and multiple-sibling adoptions have been common, especially when one or both parents died. The Orphan Trains carried children from across the United States and placed as many as 150,000 to 200,000 children in new homes in 47 states, Canada, and South America. Orphaned and indigent children were transported from Britain and Ireland to Canada and Australia for adoption at various times. And during World War II, children from Britain, Holland, Belgium, and other countries were often evacuated to relatives or through social agencies to other locations in order to protect them.
- **Slavery**   Slave trade was responsible for destroying families and entire communities, and for the forced relocation of hundreds of thousands of persons over the ages. Human trafficking removed people from Africa to the New World, and then from place to place as a result of sale, barter, kidnapping, and theft. Invading Spanish conquerors enslaved native peoples of the Americas, and substantial numbers also were transported back to Europe as curiosities and as victims of enforced servitude.
- **Forced Relocation of Native Americans**   Native American tribes were often perceived as an imminent danger to settlers and an impediment to progress. Armed conflicts between them and white settlers, and later the U.S. Army, ultimately resulted in treaties calling for the ceding of Native American lands and

permanent relocation of Native Americans to parcels referred to as "reservations." Many died in the relocation marches, such as those who were removed to the Oklahoma Territory in the notorious "Trail of Tears," and in other tribal relocations.

- **Natural Disasters**   Droughts, floods, earthquakes, volcanoes, fires, tornadoes, hurricanes, and other natural disasters are life-altering catastrophes that cause people to leave one place and move to another. Floods in Germany in 1816 and 1830, for example, displaced thousands of people. Hurricane Katrina in August 2005 and the earthquake and subsequent tsunami in Japan in March 2011 are examples of more recent natural disasters that dispersed thousands of people, many of whom may never return to their original homes.

- **Drought, Crop Failure, and Famine**   Drought and plant diseases are common natural causes of famine; wars, land mismanagement, and other human-caused disasters also result in famine. Famine in Ireland in 1816–17 and the potato famines in 1822, 1838, and between the years 1845 and 1850 caused tens of millions of people to emigrate, particularly to the United States and Canada. Famines in France in 1750, 1774, and 1790 and then the general famine across Europe in 1848 caused French, German, Italian, Dutch, and Scandinavian people to immigrate to the United States.

- **Economic Difficulties**   Financial problems endanger survival. The loss of employment demands a search for a new job, and people often relocate to find a new economic opportunity. Economic recessions and depressions in a geographical area are more severe, and may cause people to migrate in larger numbers. Consider the mass migrations in the United States resulting from the Great Depression of the 1930s when people relocated to any place they could find work.

- **Political Turmoil or Oppression**   Millions of people emigrate from their native lands in search of asylum in another place in order to avoid political instability, conflict, persecution, violation of personal rights or freedoms, and other troubles.

- **War**   War is unquestionably one of the greatest catalysts of change. Colonization, land hunger, economic advantage, ideological and social disagreements, armed civil conflicts and military actions, and the disruption and destruction they cause have long been a primary incentive for migration, relocation, and evacuation. Residents of a war-torn area may seek refuge in other locations, never to return. Military personnel and their families may be forced to relocate. A soldier, in the course of service, may also travel to areas to which he or she may later choose to relocate.

- **Religious or Ethnic Persecution**   One overwhelming reason for the migration by our ancestors was their desire to live in freedom, to practice their religious beliefs without persecution, or to pursue the lifestyle of their ethnic group. The Pilgrims are an excellent example of the early settlers who emigrated from England to Holland and then to the American colonies. In the 20th century, the emigration of Jews and other persecuted peoples from Continental Europe to Britain, the United States, Australia, South America, and Israel provides vivid examples of persons fleeing persecution.

- **Criminal Incarceration/Deportation**   Criminals, debtors, and political dissidents were transported to colonial settlements to eliminate them from society and serve sentences of hard labor. Others were offered the option of relocating to a colony rather than face execution or prolonged imprisonment in their homeland.

- **Primogenitor or Ultimogenitor**   It was common in the Middle Ages (and later) for the eldest son to inherit most or all property on the death of his father. In laws or societal rules, the eldest son could then allow his mother and other siblings to remain or he could force them to leave. In some places, a separate custom called *borough-English* or *ultimogeniture* required that the youngest son inherit all the property. In either case, sisters were typically married off and other brothers were encouraged to leave and fend for themselves or become indentured apprentices or servants.

These reasons cannot possibly encompass the universe of factors that influenced our ancestors to make a move. However, placing your own ancestors into context goes a long way toward understanding their motivations. One of my favorite reference websites for a chronological representation of historical events is the Timelines of History website at **http://timelines.ws**. You can also use your favorite web browser to search for historical timelines for specific geographical areas. Simply enter the word **timeline** and the name of the state, province, or country for which you want to find a timeline. Chronological timeline information can help add rich context to your understanding of your ancestors' lives.

Locate and Use U.S. Immigration and Naturalization Records

The desire to trace one's ancestors back to a place of origin is one of the principal motivations for family history researchers. Many of us will spend our entire genealogical research career investigating family members in the country in which they settled, and that is also commonly the same one in which we live and with which we are familiar. However, the impetus to continue the quest backward to our ancestors' native land(s) will take many of us on another, more rigorous research trek.

Placing your ancestor in geographical and historical context becomes a research imperative when you begin retracing his or her migration path across an ocean and back to the place of birth. It is essential that you consider the country and place of origin *and* the destination country, their geographies, the social and historical environments at the time, and the motivations for both leaving the old country *and* choosing to go to a particular location in the new country. For many of us, the knowledge of the place of our family's origin has been lost to time and we will have to use all sorts of clues to reconnect a migration path backward. The pointers we'll use may include letters, photographs, books, family stories or traditions, immigration records, passenger lists, naturalization documents, census records, passports and visas, and a host of other primary and secondary information. This may seem a daunting task, but making that connection is certainly one of the most rewarding and insightful experiences you can imagine.

We earlier discussed some of the motivating factors that compelled our ancestors and their family members to migrate to a new place. Deciding to undertake a move of this magnitude was no small matter; it took a great deal of courage and planning, and it usually meant leaving family, friends, and everything familiar forever. Our ancestors were literally risking everything, including their lives. Under extreme circumstances, some people fled their homes with little preparation. However, a majority of the emigrants left their ancestral home place for another part of the world with some plan for where they would go and what they would do to survive when they arrived. These people were courageous and often endured terrible conditions in order to make a new life for themselves and their families.

Learn About How Our Ancestors Traveled

For most of us, our immigrant ancestors arrived in ships. One of the most familiar images to many immigrants or first-generation Americans is that of the immigration processing station Ellis Island. Millions of people, such as those shown in Figure 10-1, arrived there between 1 January 1892 and 12 November 1954. These immigrants may have left their hometowns on foot, in wagons and carts, in canal boats, and even on trains, to reach a seaport from which they departed to cross an ocean. Millions upon

FIGURE 10-1 Immigrants arriving from Italy at Ellis Island in New York, ca. 1911

millions of people traveled in ships and, depending on the time period, the type of ships on which they traveled determined the duration of the voyage and the living conditions in which they traveled. It was not until well into the 20th century that people emigrated via airplane and, when they began doing so, many of the records we seek were no longer created—in particular, the ships' passenger lists and manifests.

You will find that immigration and naturalization are inextricably linked together, not just because one event occurred before the other but also because, for your ancestors to become naturalized citizens in the new country, proof of when, where, and how they arrived there was required. We're going to concentrate on immigration to the United States and the naturalization process to become an American citizen. However, we also will explore the wealth of records concerning immigration to Canada and Australia from Britain and Ireland and resources for tracing ships from other countries to these destinations as well.

Many migration routes have been used throughout the centuries. You will need to study history to determine the events taking place in their location origin at that particular time. The available modes of transportation and the migration paths used at the time played very significant roles in migrations. This is true not only in the place of origin but also at the destination. Once your ancestors arrived at a point in the new country, they had to travel overland. This may have been done on foot, on horseback, in a wagon or stagecoach, a boat, a train, an automobile or motor coach, an airplane, or a combination of any of these.

There are many excellent websites about emigration for your review, depending on your area of interest. They include the following:

- German emigration to the United States at
  http://spartacus-educational.com/USAEgermany.htm
- Irish emigration to the United States at
  http://spartacus-educational.com/USAEireland.htm
- Italian emigration to the United States at
  http://spartacus-educational.com/USAEitaly.htm
- Russian emigration to the United States at
  http://spartacus-educational.com/USAErussia.htm
- Swedish emigration to the United States at
  http://spartacus-educational.com/USAEsweden.htm
- Immigrants to Canada at
  http://jubilation.uwaterloo.ca/ ~ marj/genealogy/thevoyage.html
- Museum Victoria's "Immigration to Victoria [Australia] - A Timeline" at
  **http://museumvictoria.com.au/discoverycentre/websites-mini/
  immigration-timeline**

For United States research, I have two favorite collections of historical maps online. The first is the Perry-Castañeda Library Map Collection at the University of Texas at Austin, located at **http://www.lib.utexas.edu/maps**. Once at that site, click the first half of the link labeled "Maps of The United States including National Parks and Monuments," and then click the link labeled "Historical Maps of the United States." The menu bar near the top of the page contains links to several interesting groups of maps on this page, including "Exploration and Settlement" and "Territorial Growth," excellent references for migration routes. Also on this page, under the section labeled "Later Historical Maps," are a number of maps compiled from the 1870 U.S. federal census that show concentrations of population settlements of Chinese, English and Welsh, British American, German, Irish, and Swedish and Norwegian people. All of these were prepared in 1872.

My other favorite collection is the David Rumsey Map Collection at **http:// www.davidrumsey.com**. It includes thousands of maps of North America and South America, and historic maps of Europe, Asia, Africa, and other places around the world. You have a choice of a number of viewer tools with which to view the maps. The LUNA browser is simple to use and provides splendid viewing results. It runs in the Internet Explorer, Firefox, Safari, and Google Chrome browsers. The Insight Java Client, which requires a free download of software that installs on your computer, is another excellent viewing option. This collection is searchable in a variety of ways and the images are exceptionally good. (You may need to turn off any pop-up blocker software on your computer in order to access the map images.) Of particular interest is the ability to use Google Earth and Google Maps to overlay in particular areas. Specific historic maps have been interlinked with these two Google facilities and provide excellent geographical context for your research.

Learn About the History of Ships' Passenger Lists

Passenger lists, also referred to as "passenger manifests," will vary in format and content, depending on who created them, why they were created, the time period, and other factors. For example, persons transported in bondage from England—that is, prisoners transported to a colony as punishment and/or to permanently get rid of them—may be documented in court records in the country of origin. The person may also be listed on a prisoner ship's records. In other places, there may be no immigration lists available at the destination location but there may well be emigration lists and/or ships' manifests at the point of departure.

In addition, and perhaps most important of all, it is imperative to remember that you must always look for the obvious records *and*, in the event that you can't find those, investigate the possibilities that there may be alternative record types that can help document the migration. For example, if there are no ships' passenger lists, look for both emigration records from the country of origin and immigration and/ or naturalization records in the destination country to document the arrival. Also, in the United States, you can use the decennial federal census records starting in 1850 to help document and trace your immigrant ancestors. For example, the 1850 census was the first to ask for the place of birth (State, Territory, Country). The 1880 census asked for the place of birth of each person as well as of his/her father and mother. The 1900, 1910, 1920, and 1930 federal censuses each asked for the year of immigration and whether the person had been naturalized. The 1940 census asked for place of residence as of 1 April 1935, but it also asked for the person's place of birth. The enumerator was instructed to ask foreign-born individuals the name of the country in which the person's birthplace was located as of January 1, 1937, and citizenship status. (This census did not ask for the year of arrival in the United States.) Census Population Schedules for some enumerations also asked for the language spoken, or "mother tongue," and that can help lead you to the place of origin. These records can therefore be the bonanza you need in the way of pointers to other records and/or can be used as alternative, supplemental, and corroborative evidence and documentation.

Figure 10-2 shows detail from the 1910 U.S. federal census for the John Scullion family in Patterson Ward 8, District 0138, in Passaic County, New Jersey. John and his wife, Catherine, were born in Ireland. Their four sons and one daughter living were born in New Jersey. To the right of these birth locations is a two-column set of critical information for your search. The year of arrival in the United States is listed in the first column. You can see that John arrived in 1891, and it appears that Catherine arrived in 1881. (Other censuses may show that Catherine arrived in other years, therefore presenting a discrepancy that needs to be addressed. You may therefore need to check ships' passenger lists and naturalization records.)

In the next column for John is a notation "na." This indicates that he has been naturalized. That should be a clue to begin tracing his naturalization records. It appears that his wife was not naturalized by 1910. Subsequent searches of the 1920 and 1930 censuses show that Catherine had not become a naturalized citizen.

Figure 10-3 shows detail from a 1940 census in Ward 3, Boston, in Suffolk County, Massachusetts. Natale Capuano and his wife, Catherine, are shown as born in Italy. The code NA in the Citizenship column for Mr. Capuano indicates that he has been naturalized, but the code AL in the column for Mrs. Capuano indicates that she is still an alien. For the next couple, Augustino and Mary Santanielli, the census shows that he was born in Italy and has been naturalized and that she was native-born in Massachusetts. The next two people, Anthony and Alfred Carpenito, are shown as brothers-in-law of Augustino Santanielli and that they were born in Massachusetts.

Let's look at the United States and ships' passenger arrival lists that you may want to research and examine. In order to understand what is available, we need to briefly examine the history of these records.

A Chronology of Ships' Passenger Lists in the United States

Prior to the Revolutionary War in the American colonies, there was no formal attempt in most areas to require passenger arrival lists. Indeed, any requirements were instituted by the colonies themselves as they had control over their own affairs. Because the 13 colonies were, in fact, British, and close to 80 percent of the white

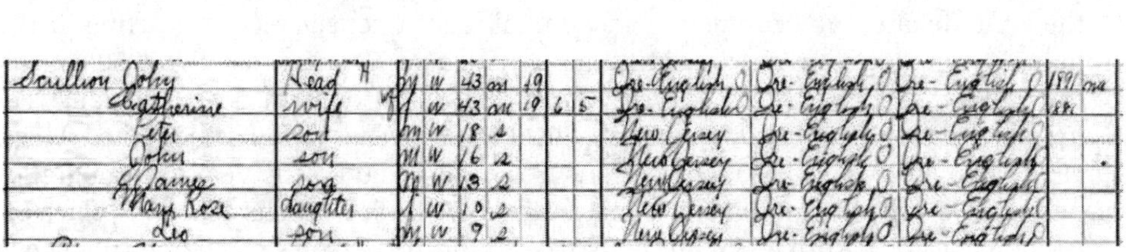

FIGURE 10-2 1910 U.S. federal census detail showing places of birth, arrival year, and naturalization status

NAME	RELATION	PERSONAL DESCRIPTION				EDUCATION		PLACE OF BIRTH	CITIZENSHIP	
Name of each person whose *usual place of residence* on April 1, 1940, was in this household. BE SURE TO INCLUDE: 1. Persons temporarily absent from household. Write "Ab" after names of such persons. 2. Children under 1 year of age. Write "Infant" if child has not been given a first name. Enter ⓧ after name of person furnishing information.	Relationship of this person to the head of the household, as wife, daughter, father, mother-in-law, grandson, lodger, lodger's wife, servant, hired hand, etc.	CODE (Leave blank)	Sex—Male (M), Female (F)	Color or race	Age at last birthday	Marital status— Single (S), Married (M), Widowed (W,O), Divorced (D)	Attended school or college any time since March 1, 1940? (Yes or No)	Highest grade of school completed	CODE (Leave blank)	If born in the United States, give State, Territory, or possession. If foreign born, give country in which birthplace was situated on January 1, 1937. Distinguish Canada-French from Canada-English and Irish Free State (Eire) from Northern Ireland.	CODE (Leave blank)	Citizenship of the foreign born
7	8	A	9	10	11	12	13	14	B	15	C	16
Capuano Natale ⓧ	head		M	W	61	M	No.	4	4	Italy	26	NA
―――, *Catherine*	wife		F	W	61	M	No		10	Italy	26	Al
da anul, Augustin ⓧ	head	0	M	W	25	M	No	H3	20	Italy	26	NA
―――, *Mary*	wife		F	W	23	M	No	H4	9	Massachusetts		
Carpenito, Anthony	mother-in-law	M	W	32	S	No	7	7	Massachusetts		53	
―――, *Alfred*	brother-in-law	M	W	26	S	No	8	8	Massachusetts		53	

FIGURE 10-3   1940 U.S. federal census detailing country of birth and naturalization status

immigrants arriving before 1790 came from England or from other British-governed countries, there was little or no need to record the arrivals. Any documentation about passenger movement was created or maintained by the ships' owners and operators; the colonial governments maintained any information concerning shipping commerce. Their primary concerns were the regulation and taxation of incoming and outgoing goods. Government officials had little interest in passenger arrivals other than those of Crown prisoners and indentured servants.

Pennsylvania was an exception in that it recorded the arrival of Continental Europeans at the Port of Philadelphia, primarily German, French, Dutch, and Swiss, in the years 1727–1744, 1746–1756, 1761, 1763–1775, and 1785–1808. Prior to the American Revolution, British subjects arriving at the port were not recorded because the colonists were also considered British subjects. There were essentially three lists compiled, consisting of: 1) the ship's captain's list, made on board the ship, of names from the passenger manifest; 2) lists of oaths of allegiance to the British king that were signed by all males over the age of 16 who could walk to the local magistrate at the port of arrival; and 3) lists of the signers of the oath of fidelity and abjuration, a renunciation of any claims to the throne of England by "pretenders," also signed by males over the age of 16 who could walk to the courthouse. One estimate is that only about two-fifths of the ships' passengers actually signed these oaths, but not all of the ledgers and documents have survived. These passenger lists and related documents have been microfilmed and are in the possession of the Pennsylvania Historical & Museum Commission. You can learn more about these documents at **http://www.portal.state.pa.us/portal/server.pt/community/naturalization_and_immigration/3851/ships'_passenger_lists/387311**.

If you are seeking information about early immigrant arrivals in the other colonies, it is important to look for alternative records, as previously mentioned, such as "lists of departure" in the original country. Some of these are in national archives, local archives or libraries, or in local government record repositories near the port of departure. (In Spain and Portugal, there are extensive archival holdings relating to shipping and passenger movements that trace back in some cases into the 1300s, and hence we have a solid historical record of much of the global exploration from those periods.) Histories of individual colonies and settlements may also provide you with information about arrivals of individuals or families and their participation in the community affairs. The individual state archives may have other records to help document the arrival of foreign-born individuals. These might include documents concerning bounty colonists (those whose passage was paid as an incentive to settle in the colony), papers of indentured servants, or arrivals of criminal deportees. Land and property records may also provide you with clues to your ancestor's time of arrival.

The year 1820 is a bellwether for U.S. historians and genealogists from an immigration perspective. In that year, Congress passed legislation calling for passenger lists to be filed by each ship's master with the customs officer in the port of arrival. Manifests of goods being brought into port were already being prepared and delivered to the customs officer. However, passenger manifests were something new. These documents are sometimes referred to as the "customs passenger lists" or "customs passenger manifests." Two copies of the passenger list, like the ones shown in Figures 10-4 and 10-5, were created either just prior to the ship sailing or onboard the

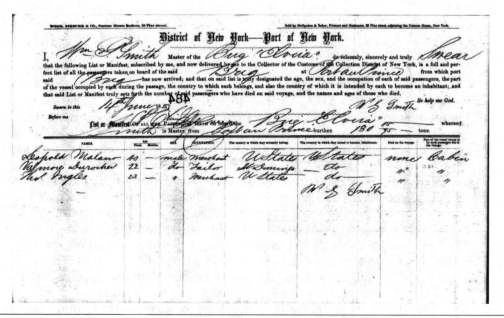

FIGURE 10-4 Passenger list of the Brig *Elvira*, which arrived in New York on 14 June 1855

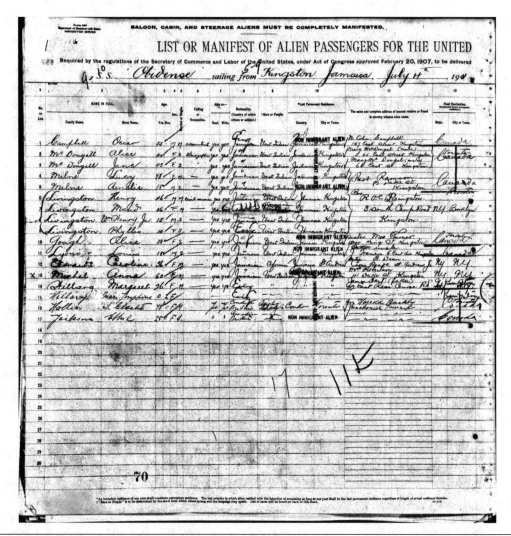

FIGURE 10-5 Manifest of the *Obidense*, which arrived in New York on 10 July 1910

ship, and listed each passenger. The ship's master was also required to record on the list any births and deaths that occurred during the voyage. The names of members of the crew were not required until much later. On arrival at port, the ship's master was required to deliver both copies of the document to the customs collector. The master then swore under oath that the lists were complete and correct, and then both he and the customs officer signed the documents. One copy remained with the customs collector, and the ship's master retained the other copy. The customs officer was required to prepare a summary list of all passenger arrivals at the port on a monthly or quarterly basis and send it to the Secretary of State in Washington, D.C.

The summary included the name of every vessel; the port of origin; any intermediate ports of call; the date of arrival; each respective ship's master's name; and the names, gender, and ages of all passengers.

A Congressional act passed in 1882 required that federal immigration officials record all immigrants arriving in the United States. There are lists that were produced dating from 1883 for the port of Philadelphia and from 1891 for most other ports, and these have been microfilmed by the National Archives and Records Administration (NARA). These lists include the name of the master; the name of the ship; the ports of departure and arrival (including intermediate stops); the date of arrival; the name, place of birth, last residence, age, occupation, and gender of each passenger; and any other remarks. The intermediate ports of call may be important for tracing your ancestors' stages of migration.

The year 1891 was important to U.S. immigration and naturalization for a number of reasons. In that year, a separate federal governmental agency was formed whose purpose was specifically to oversee immigration. This was the Office of the Superintendent of Immigration, and it was a division within the Treasury Department. For the first time, this new bureau strictly oversaw immigration. As a result, the records created called for more detail.

Between 1891 and 1903, responsibility for the collection and maintenance of the forms passed through several federal departments, finally becoming the province of the Immigration and Naturalization Service (INS), which was formed in 1933 as part of the Department of Labor (in 1940 transferred to the Department of Justice). The INS immigration service functions were transferred to the new U.S. Citizenship and Immigration Services (USCIS) in 2003 as part of the Department of Homeland Security (DHS).

Standardized forms, such as the one shown in Figure 10-5, began to be used in every embarkation port around the world and were to be prepared *before* the departure of the ship. Therefore, any changes would have been noted *prior* to entry into any U.S. port. Only births, deaths, and the discovery of a stowaway would have caused the manifest to be changed en route.

Again, the forms were to be presented to the customs and immigration service officers at the port of arrival. The forms became known as Immigration Manifests or Immigration Passenger Lists. When these forms were introduced in the early 1890s, they required more information than ever before to be provided. (Please see Table 10-1.) Further columns were added in later years, all of which provide more information for our genealogical use.

The new Bureau of Immigration formed in 1933 requested that all of the earlier passenger arrival records from all ports of arrival be sent to their office in Washington, D.C. Unfortunately, however, that was easier said than accomplished. The original documents had been stored in customs houses, courthouses, customs collectors' homes, and other places. Some had been damaged, destroyed, or simply lost. Fortunately, a vast majority of the original customs passenger lists from 1820 to 1905 survived, as did the majority of the customs collectors' monthly reports. These are in the possession of NARA and have been microfilmed. In fact, where the original passenger list had not survived, NARA used the customs officers' reports as

TABLE 10-1   Required Contents for Passenger Manifests Arriving in the United States

Time Period	Passenger List Columns/Contents
1820–1891	Passenger Name Age Gender Occupation Nationality
1892	Passenger Name Age Gender Occupation Nationality Marital status Last residence Intended final destination in the U.S. Whether ever in the U.S. before and, if so, where, when, and for what duration Name, address, and relationship of any relative in the U.S. who the immigrant planned to join Whether able to read and write Whether in possession of a train ticket to the final destination Who paid the passage to America Amount of money (in dollars) the immigrant was carrying Whether the person was a convict, indigent, insane, or a polygamist State of the immigrant's health
1903	All of the information as in 1892, plus race or people
1906	All of the information as in 1903, plus personal description (height, complexion, hair color, eye color, and any other identifying marks)
1907	All of the information as in 1906, plus name and address of the closest living relative in the native country

substitutes to fill in gaps in chronological sequence in the microfilmed records. While these abstracts don't contain as much detail as the original passenger manifests, they do supply critical nominal information and other details.

Through the 1800s and 1900s, passenger lists were prepared with more forethought to their clarity and accuracy. Many of these documents were completed using a typewriter, such as the example in Figure 10-6, which certainly makes for easier reading. However, because the typewritten passenger lists were likely prepared from other handwritten documents, the possibility of transcription and typographical error increased.

For more extensive information about ships' passenger lists and manifests, you will want to read John Philip Colletta's definitive book, *They Came in Ships: Finding*

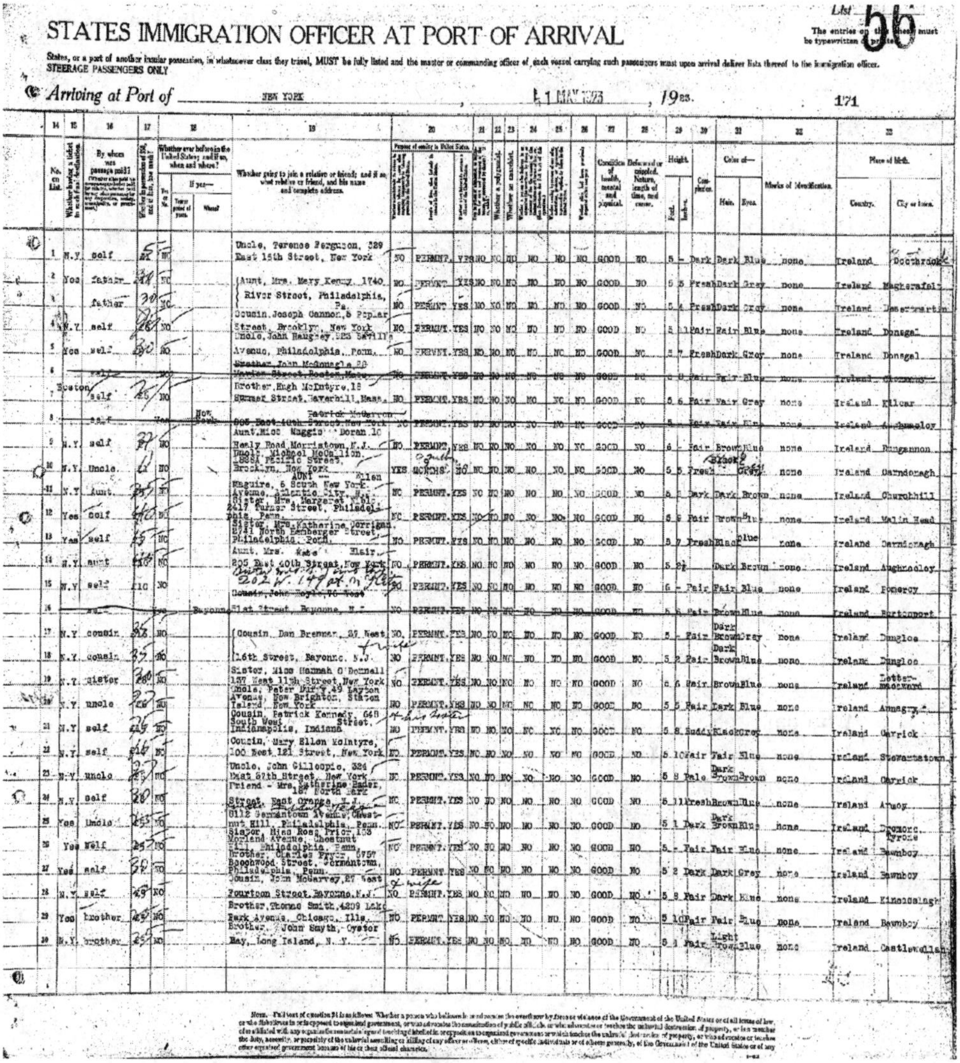

List 56

STATES IMMIGRATION OFFICER AT PORT OF ARRIVAL

The entries on this sheet must be typewritten or printed.

States, or a port of another insular possession, in whatsoever class they travel, MUST be fully listed and the master or commanding officer of each vessel carrying such passengers must upon arrival deliver lists thereof to the immigration officer.
STEERAGE PASSENGERS ONLY

Arriving at Port of NEW YORK, 1 MAY 1923, 1923. 171

No. on List	14 Ticket to final destination	16 By whom was passage paid	17 Money in possession	18 Ever before in U.S. (Yes/No)	18 Where?	19 Whether going to join a relative or friend; name and complete address	20	20 Purpose / length of stay	20	21	22	23	24	25	26	27 Condition of health	28 Deformed or crippled	29 Height Feet	29 Inches	30 Complexion	31 Hair	31 Eyes	32 Marks of identification	33 Country	33 City or town
1	N.Y.	self	[illegible]	NO		Uncle, Terence Ferguson, 329 East 15th Street, New York	NO	PERMNT.	YES	NO	NO	NO	NO	NO	NO	GOOD	NO	5	-	Dark	Dark	Blue	none	Ireland	Doothrdok
2	Yes	father	[illegible]	NO		Aunt, Mrs. Mary Kenny, 1740 River Street, Philadelphia, Pa.	NO	PERMNT	YES	NO	NO	NO	NO	NO	NO	GOOD	NO	5	5	Fresh	Dark	Grey	none	Ireland	Magherafelt
3		father	30	NO			NO	PERMNT	YES	NO	NO	NO	NO	NO	NO	GOOD	NO	5	4	Fresh	Dark	Grey	none	Ireland	Desertmartin
4	N.Y.	self	26	NO		Cousin, Joseph Cannon, 5 Poplar Street, Brooklyn, New York	NO	PERMNT.	YES	NO	NO	NO	NO	NO	NO	GOOD	NO	5	11	Fair	Fair	Blue	none	Ireland	Donegal
5	Yes	self	30	NO		Uncle, John Haughey, 223 Saville Avenue, Philadelphia, Penn.	NO	PERMNT.	YES	NO	NO	NO	NO	NO	NO	GOOD	NO	5	7	Fresh	Dark	Grey	none	Ireland	Donegal
6		~~self~~		~~NO~~		~~Brother John McGonagle 28 [illegible] Street, Boston, Mass.~~	~~NO~~	~~PERMNT.~~	~~YES~~	~~NO~~	~~NO~~	~~NO~~	~~NO~~	~~NO~~	~~NO~~	~~GOOD~~	~~NO~~			~~Fair~~	~~Fair~~	~~Blue~~	~~none~~	~~Ireland~~	[illegible]
7	Boston	self	25	NO		Brother, Hugh McIntyre, 18 Sumner Street, Haverhill, Mass.	NO	PERMNT.	YES	NO	NO	NO	NO	NO	NO	GOOD	NO	5	6	Fair	Fair	Grey	none	Ireland	Kilcar
8		~~self~~		~~Yes~~	New York	Patrick McGarron ~~805 East 40th Street New York~~	~~NO~~	~~PERMNT.~~	~~YES~~	~~NO~~	~~NO~~	~~NO~~	~~NO~~	~~NO~~	~~NO~~	~~GOOD~~	~~NO~~	~~5~~	~~-~~	~~Fair~~	~~Fair~~	~~Blue~~	~~none~~	~~Ireland~~	~~Aughnacloy~~
9	N.Y.	self	27	NO		Aunt, Miss Maggie Doran, 10 Healy Road, Morristown, N.J.	NO	PERMNT.	YES	NO	NO	NO	NO	NO	NO	GOOD	NO	6	-	Fair	Brown	Blue	none	Ireland	Dungannon
10	N.Y.	Uncle	[illegible]	NO		Uncle, Michael McCullion, 1883A Pacific Street, Brooklyn, New York	YES	MONTHS	NO	NO	NO	NO	NO	NO	NO	GOOD	NO	5	5	Fresh	Black	Grey	none	Ireland	Carndonagh
11	N.Y.	Aunt	25	NO		Aunt -- Ellen Maguire, 6 South New York Avenue, Atlantic City, N.J.	NO	PERMNT.	YES	NO	NO	NO	NO	NO	NO	GOOD	NO	5	[illegible]	Dark	Dark	Brown	none	Ireland	Churchhill
12	Yes	self	40	NO		Sister, Mrs. Margaret [illegible], 2417 Turner Street, Philadelphia, Penn.	NO	PERMNT.	YES	NO	NO	NO	NO	NO	NO	GOOD	NO	5	6	Fair	Brown	Blue	none	Ireland	Malin Head
13	Yes	self	25	NO		Sister, Mrs. Katharine Corrigan, 2741 North Hemberger Street, Philadelphia, Penn.	NO	PERMNT.	YES	NO	NO	NO	NO	NO	NO	GOOD	NO	5	7	Fresh	Black	Blue	none	Ireland	Carndonagh
14	N.Y.	aunt	[illegible]	NO		Aunt, Mrs. Kate Blair, 205 East 40th Street, New York	NO	PERMNT.	YES	NO	NO	NO	NO	NO	NO	GOOD	NO	5	2½		Dark	Brown	none	Ireland	Aughnacloy
15	N.Y.	self	10	NO		[illegible] 202 W. 149 St. [illegible]	NO	PERMNT.	YES	NO	NO	NO	NO	NO	NO	GOOD	NO	6	-	Fair	Fair	Blue	none	Ireland	Pomeroy
16		~~self~~		~~Yes~~	Bayonne	~~Cousin, John Boyle, 76 West 51st Street, Bayonne, N.J.~~	~~NO~~	~~PERMNT.~~	~~YES~~	~~NO~~	~~NO~~	~~NO~~	~~NO~~	~~NO~~	~~NO~~	~~GOOD~~	~~NO~~	~~5~~	~~6~~	~~Fair~~	~~Brown~~	~~Blue~~	~~none~~	~~Ireland~~	~~Burtonport~~
17	N.Y.	cousin	25	NO		Cousin, Dan Brennan, 37 West 16th Street, Bayonne, N.J.	NO	PERMNT.	YES	NO	NO	NO	NO	NO	NO	GOOD	NO	5	-	Fair	Dark Brown	Gray	none	Ireland	Dungloe
18	N.Y.	cousin	35	NO			NO	PERMNT.	YES	NO	NO	NO	NO	NO	NO	GOOD	NO	5	2	Fair	Dark Brown	Blue	none	Ireland	Dungloe
19	N.Y.	sister	20	NO		Sister, Miss Hannah O'Donnell 137 West 11th Street, New York	NO	PERMNT.	YES	NO	NO	NO	NO	NO	NO	GOOD	NO	6	6	Fair	Brown	Blue	none	Ireland	Lettermacaward
20	N.Y.	uncle	25	NO		Uncle, Peter Duffy, 49 Layton Avenue, New Brighton, Staten Island, New York	NO	PERMNT.	YES	NO	NO	NO	NO	NO	NO	GOOD	NO	5	5	Fair	Dark	Blue	none	Ireland	Annagry
21	N.Y.	self	25	NO		Cousin, Patrick Kennedy, 648 South West Street, Indianapolis, Indiana	NO	PERMNT.	YES	NO	NO	NO	NO	NO	NO	GOOD	NO	5	8	Ruddy	Black	Grey	none	Ireland	Carrick
22	N.Y.	self	[illegible]	NO		Cousin, Mary Ellen McIntyre, 100 West 121 Street, New York	NO	PERMNT.	YES	NO	NO	NO	NO	NO	NO	GOOD	NO	5	10	Fair	Fair	Blue	none	Ireland	Stewartstown
23	N.Y.	uncle	25	NO		Uncle, John Gillespie, 324 East 57th Street, New York	NO	PERMNT.	YES	NO	NO	NO	NO	NO	NO	GOOD	NO	5	8	Pale	Dark Brown	Brown	none	Ireland	Carrick
24	N.Y.	self	20	NO		Friend - Mrs. Katharine Bader, 187 North Park Street, East Orange, N.J.	NO	PERMNT.	YES	NO	NO	NO	NO	NO	NO	GOOD	NO	5	11	Fresh	Brown	Blue	none	Ireland	Armoy
25	Yes	Uncle	25	NO		6112 Germantown Avenue, Chestnut Hill, Philadelphia, Penn.	NO	PERMNT.	YES	NO	NO	NO	NO	NO	NO	GOOD	NO	5	1	Dark	Dark Brown	Blue	none	Ireland	Dromore, Tyrone
26	Yes	self	25	NO		Sister, Miss Rose Prior, 153 Morland Avenue, Chestnut Hill, Philadelphia, Penn.	NO	PERMNT.	YES	NO	NO	NO	NO	NO	NO	GOOD	NO	5	-	Fair	Fair	Blue	none	Ireland	Bawnboy
27	Yes	self	30	NO		Brother, Charles Pryor, 5757 Beechwood Street, Germantown, Philadelphia, Penn.	NO	PERMNT.	YES	NO	NO	NO	NO	NO	NO	GOOD	NO	5	2	Dark	Dark	Grey	none	Ireland	Bawnboy
28	N.Y.	self	[illegible]	NO		Cousin, John McGarvey, 27 West Fourteen Street, Bayonne, N.J.	NO	PERMNT.	YES	NO	NO	NO	NO	NO	NO	GOOD	NO	5	8	Fair	Dark	Blue	none	Ireland	Kincasslagh
29	Yes	brother	25	NO		Brother, Thomas Smith, 4209 Lake Park Avenue, Chicago, Ills.	NO	PERMNT.	YES	NO	NO	NO	NO	NO	NO	GOOD	NO	5	10	Fair	Fair	Blue	none	Ireland	Bawnboy
30	N.Y.	brother	25	NO		Brother, John Smyth, Oyster Bay, Long Island, N.Y.	NO	PERMNT.	YES	NO	NO	NO	NO	NO	NO	GOOD	NO	5	1	Fair	Light Brown	Blue	none	Ireland	Castlewellan

FIGURE 10-6 Page from a passenger manifest of a ship arriving in New York on 1 May 1923

Your Immigrant Ancestor's Arrival Record, Third Edition (Ancestry Publishing, 2002), articles in *The Source: A Guidebook to American Genealogy*, Third Edition (Ancestry, 2006) and in the Ancestry Family History Wiki (**http://www.ancestry.com/wiki/index.php?title=The_Source:_A_Guidebook_to_American_Genealogy**), and Loretto D. Szucs's definitive reference book for immigration and naturalization reference, *They Became Americans: Finding Naturalization Records and Ethnic Origins* (Ancestry.com, 1998).

There are any number of indexes and finding aids to these records, and the resources cited previously provide excellent guidance to help you locate these indexes. Perhaps the most definitive is the mammoth set of books by P. William Filby, the *Passenger and Immigration Lists Index* and the annual supplements (Gale Group, 1985 to present). These books are part of an ongoing project to index as many resources of ships' passenger information from as many sources as possible. This work and its annual supplements may be found through libraries and archives with larger genealogical book collections. It also is available (through 2008 at this writing) at WorldVitalRecords.com (**http://www.worldvitalrecords.com**; search for **"Passenger and Immigration Index"** in the Keyword box).

NARA's microfilm of the complete chronological set of ships' passenger lists and/or customs officers' reports for all U.S. ports of arrival has been digitized and indexed by Ancestry.com (**http://www.ancestry.com**). FamilySearch (**https://familysearch .org**), at the time of this writing, is in the process of digitizing and indexing these records and placing them online. Passenger arrivals at the Ellis Island processing facility in New York, NY, between the years 1892 to 1924 have been transcribed and indexed by the Statue of Liberty-Ellis Island Foundation at **http://www .libertyellisfoundation.org**, and are free to search online. Information displayed on a search result record includes: first name, last name, ethnicity, last place of residence, date of arrival, age at arrival, gender, marital status, ship of travel, port of departure, and line number on which the person's name appears on the ship's manifest.

Learn About the American Ports of Entry

Although passengers arrived at about 100 different U.S. shipping ports over the centuries, most ports saw only intermittent traffic. Sometimes only a few ships with passengers would arrive in a given year. During the early years, most of the immigration traffic coming into the United States tended to be directed to one of five major ports: Boston, New York, Philadelphia, Baltimore, and New Orleans. Although Philadelphia had been the most popular of these ports during the colonial era, within the first two decades of federal immigration regulation, New York emerged as the preferred port of arrival. One of the reasons for this transformation was the construction of the Erie Canal, which provided faster and more economical travel inland than other forms of transportation. The canal provided an excellent migration route to upstate New York, Pennsylvania, Ohio, and into the Great Lakes areas.

By 1850, more immigrants arrived in New York than in all other ports combined. By the 1850s, New York was also a major railroad hub offering access to nearly every part of the country. Because of the waves of immigrants entering the city, New York was the first port to open an immigration arrival and processing depot. Castle Garden, shown in Figure 10-7, was located at the Battery in lower Manhattan. It was the processing center for the Port of New York and was the predecessor to Ellis Island, which opened on 1 January 1892. Castle Garden was a massive stone structure originally built in 1808 as a fort. It later served as an opera house, and New York State authorities transformed it into an immigration landing and processing station beginning on 1 August 1855.

FIGURE 10-7　View of Castle Garden in New York

Castle Garden's primary purpose was not only to receive and inspect immigrants, but also to help protect them from the thieves, swindlers, confidence men, and prostitutes who prowled the piers looking for easy marks. Inside Castle Garden, immigrants could exchange money, purchase food and railway tickets, tend to baggage, and obtain information about boarding houses and employment. More buildings were erected outside the original Castle Garden to handle the additional volume of people as immigrant arrivals increased. Brick walls were constructed to enclose the large complex. On 18 April 1890, the last immigrants were processed through Castle Garden. During these years, more than eight million immigrants had passed through Castle Garden.

Control over the immigration processing in New York shifted to the U.S. Superintendent of Immigration, and the Barge Office became an interim arrival depot for the immigrants, pending the opening of a new immigrant-processing center on Ellis Island on 1 January 1892. Immigrants such as those shown in Figure 10-8 arrived at a modern, well-organized facility where they were given physical examinations, helped with completing forms by interpreters who spoke their language, and processed efficiently through customs.

On 14 June 1897, however, fire destroyed the Ellis Island facility, and with it went the administrative records of Castle Garden (1855–1890), the Barge Office (1890–1891),

FIGURE 10-8   A group of immigrants is shown arriving at Ellis Island

and Ellis Island (1890–1897). These were administrative records only, and it is believed that very few passenger list documents, if any, were lost. The passenger lists that had already been handled over Ellis Island's years of operation to that date were perfectly safe and already in the custody of the Bureau of Customs and the Bureau of Immigration. The Ellis Island facility was reconstructed, this time using fireproof materials, and it reopened on 17 December 1900. It served as the immigration-processing site for New York until 1954. During reconstruction, immigration processing returned to the Castle Garden location, and all records produced were collected with the Ellis Island recordkeeping system. Again, you will want to research passenger arrivals at the Ellis Island Foundation site at **http://www.libertyellisfoundation.org**. Stephen P. Morse has developed an excellent website that can help you get past some of the limitations of the official Ellis Island Foundation site, and his site can be accessed at **http://stevemorse.org**. Here you will find numerous search tools for both the Castle Garden and Ellis Island immigrant arrivals.

New immigration forms were implemented at different times in different ports depending upon a number of factors, most notably who was in charge of the port at the time. Federal immigration officials began regulating many ports of arrival starting in 1891. Other ports were regulated and administered by local officers contracted by federal officials. Any lists created under the authority of the Bureau of Immigration are considered and referred to as "immigration passenger lists." This distinguishes their content and handling from that of the customs collectors and the "customs passenger lists" and the associated processing that was used from 1820 until 1891.

Contrary to popular myth, the employees of the immigration processing centers did not arbitrarily change immigrants' names as they arrived. You may have seen photographs of immigrants queued up for interview or inspection in which paper tags were attached to their clothing. Each tag actually bore the name of the ship on which the person had arrived and the line number on the passenger manifest on which his or her name was listed. The processing stations used these tags to facilitate the expeditious processing of persons who spoke little or no English. The tags assisted in directing the new arrivals into proper lines for processing. There also was a small army of translators available to assist in the arrival and inspection process. Many immigrants actually changed their own names prior to sailing, on arrival in the new country, or later in order to become more quickly assimilated into American society. Two of the naturalization forms that we will discuss later in this chapter and that were used in the United States at various times have included a place to indicate the name under which the person arrived in the country.

Virtually all of the later immigration passenger lists survived and were eventually acquired by NARA after its creation. As mentioned before, thousands of bound volumes of these lists (about 14,000 volumes of Ellis Island records alone) were microfilmed by NARA during the 1940s and 1950s. Since much of the project was completed comparatively early in the history of microfilming, the quality is not always good. Some estimates indicate that as much as 6 percent of the lists are difficult or impossible to read, with that number reaching as high as 15 percent for the pre-1902 lists. The source documents were destroyed after microfilming, though, making it impossible to create new digital images from the originals.

Locate Ships' Passenger Lists for Immigrants Arriving in the United States

There are several sets of indexes to the ships' passenger lists. You can begin by using indexed digital images at Ancestry.com and FamilySearch. You can use the indexes such as those produced by P. William Filby that were mentioned earlier. There may also be colonial, state, and local histories, and transcriptions in both print and on the Internet to locate ships whose port of origin and time period seem appropriate candidates to search. State archives and libraries may also hold documents that may help you locate the names and ships of arrival of your immigrant ancestors.

Don't forget that U.S. federal census Population Schedules, too, can be a boon as part of your research strategy. For example, the following years' U.S. federal census Population Schedules contain important clues:

- **1880** Nativity columns ask for place of birth for the named person on the census form, as well as his or her parents.
- **1885** This census taken for five states and territories (Colorado, Dakota Territory, Florida, Nebraska, and New Mexico) includes Nativity columns that ask for place of birth for the named person on the census form, as well as his or her parents.
- **1890** Nativity information is once again requested for the named person on the census form, as well as his or her parents. The number of years in the United

States, whether naturalized, and whether naturalization papers have been taken out are also requested. If English was not spoken, the language or dialect spoken was requested.

- **1900** Nativity information is again requested. In addition, the year of immigration is requested, as well as number of years in the United States and status of naturalization.
- **1910** Nativity information is again requested. In addition, the year of immigration, whether naturalized, and language spoken if not English are included.
- **1920** Year of immigration, naturalization status, and year of naturalization are requested. Place of birth and mother tongue are requested for the named person on the census and his or her parents.
- **1930** Place of birth of named person on census and of parents are requested, as well as language spoken in home before coming to the United States. Year of immigration and naturalization status are included.
- **1940** Place of birth of each individual and the citizenship status are requested.

All of these years' census Population Schedules can provide pointers to the person's nativity. The census Population Schedules of 1910, 1920, 1930, and the surviving fragments of the 1890 census, requested language spoken or "mother tongue." A response of "Yiddish" would point to a Jewish background, and a reply such as "Polish," "French," or "Urdu" would indicate another national or ethnic origin. Remember that multiple languages could have been spoken by different groups in a single country of origin.

Naturalization documents, which we will discuss later in the chapter, include the date of arrival, port of arrival, and name of the ship on which the person arrived.

If you are unsure of the ship on which your ancestor arrived, it is possible to use other clues such as language, place of birth, or spelling of the surname to help narrow your search. If you have a good idea of the country of origin, you may be able to use microfilmed or digitized newspapers and read the shipping news. Ships' arrivals, name of the port of origin, intermediate ports of call, and shipping company can help you avoid having to read every entry for every ship in a given year. In addition, by identifying the names of shipping lines arriving from your ancestor's country of origin, you may also be able to locate ships' manifests created and filed on the other side of the ocean.

The Immigrant Ships Transcribers Guild (ISTG) at **http://www.immigrantships .net** is an all-volunteer effort and is making great strides in locating, accessing, and producing accurate transcriptions of ships' passenger lists and manifests from the 1600s to the 1900s from all over the globe.

Learn About U.S. Passport Records

A passport is an official document issued by the government of a country to one of its residents that certifies that person's identity and citizenship. It entitles them to travel under that country's protection in a foreign country through diplomatic agreements. A visa is an endorsement of a passport by a foreign country that allows the holder to enter, leave, or stay in a country for a specific period of time. An authorized representative official or agency of that specific country issues a visa. There may be specific conditions applied to a visa, such as requirements for vaccinations.

Until 1775, citizens in the 13 American colonies who traveled to foreign countries used British passports since they were, in fact, British subjects. The early American passports were issued by consular officials during the American Revolution, between 1775 and 1783, and were valid for up to six months. There was no passport requirement in the new nation between 1783 and the 1787, at which time Congress approved legislation establishing the Department of Foreign Affairs on 21 July 1789 and George Washington signed it into law on 27 July 1789. This was the first federal agency created under the new U.S. Constitution. The name was later changed to the Department of State. The passports created in up to the mid-19th century were issued by the Department of State as well as by states, certain cities, and notaries public. It was not until 1856 that Congress legislated that the Department of State was the exclusive authority that could issue and regulate passports.

Different passport applications were used over time. Early passports, like the one shown in Figure 10-9, were handwritten documents using different wordings, and physical descriptions were included. Preprinted forms were later introduced to standardize the verbiage. By 1888, there were separate application forms for native citizens, naturalized citizens, and derivative citizens (wives who became citizens through their husband's naturalization and children who became citizens through their father's naturalization). A husband and wife, along with their children, were frequently included on the same application form and passport.

Still later forms may also have included multiple individuals; a photograph of the applicant(s) was required. As you can see, not all of the information may be consistent for all applicants at all periods. Likewise, there may be additional information written on the form by the applicant or the reviewing officials. Other supporting documents such as letters and signed affidavits may have been submitted with the application and may be part of the individual's application file. Because these may include valuable information, it is therefore important to personally view the image of the application and any accompanying documents and determine what documentary content exists in the file. Figures 10-10 and 10-11 show both sides of an application from 1924, including a written physical description and a photograph. It provides her name, birthdate, birthplace, and address in New York, New York; informs us that her husband died at sea in 1898 and that she has lived abroad; and states that she plans to visit England and France and will sail on the *President Harding*.

In addition, an accompanying document is a signed and notarized affidavit (shown in Figure 10-12). It provides the invaluable information of the woman's maiden name, her date and place of birth, and the names of her parents.

The U.S. passport applications for 1795 to 1925 were microfilmed by NARA (series M1372 and M1490) and these are now digitized and accessible online. Ancestry.com (**http://www.ancestry.com**) provides access to the images and searchable name indexes. FamilySearch (**https://familysearch.org**) has digitized the images and placed them online but, at the time of this writing, these have not yet been indexed. They can be browsed by microfilm roll, by date range, and by certificate number (where present).

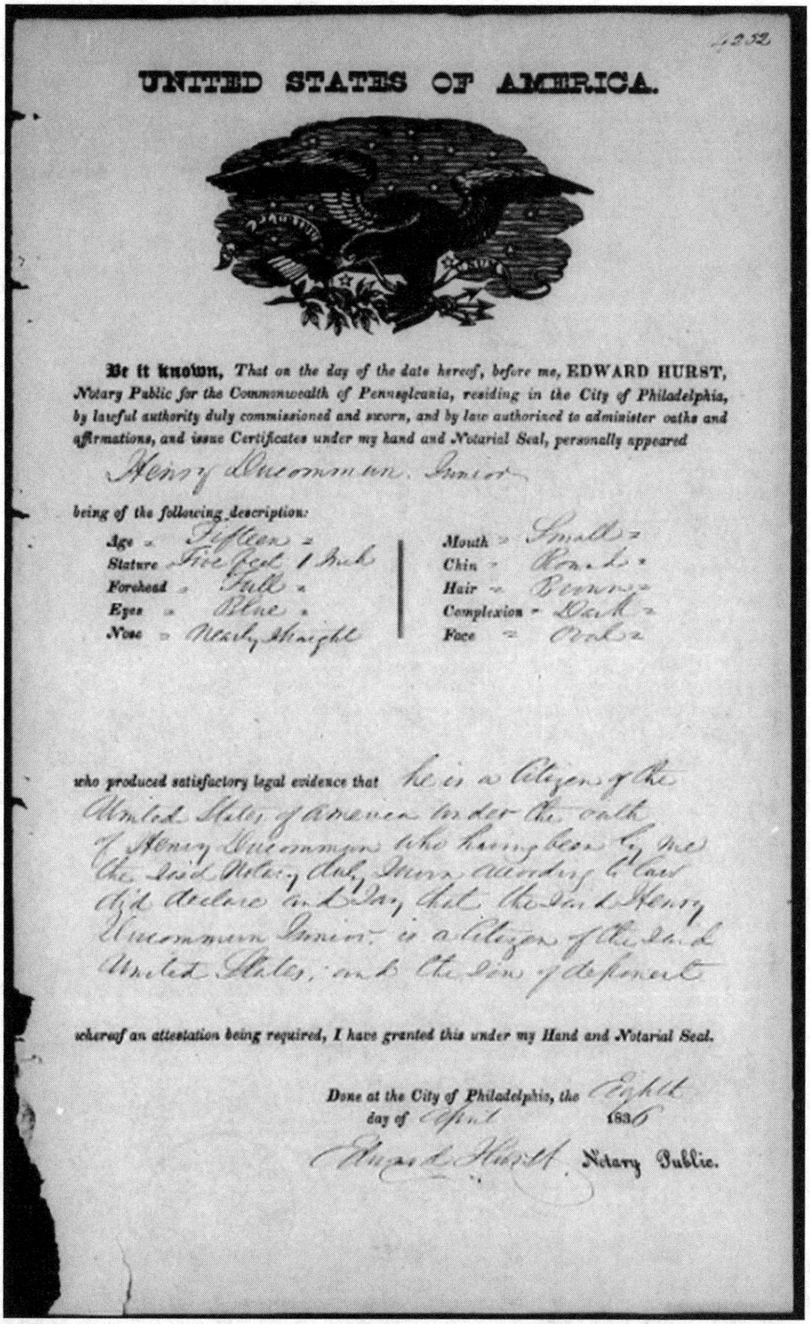

UNITED STATES OF AMERICA.

Be it known, *That on the day of the date hereof, before me,* EDWARD HURST, *Notary Public for the Commonwealth of Pennsylvania, residing in the City of Philadelphia, by lawful authority duly commissioned and sworn, and by law authorized to administer oaths and affirmations, and issue Certificates under my hand and Notarial Seal, personally appeared*

Henry Ducommun Junior

being of the following description:

Age	Fifteen	Mouth	Small
Stature	Five feet 1 Inch	Chin	Round
Forehead	Full	Hair	Brown
Eyes	Blue	Complexion	Dark
Nose	Nearly straight	Face	Oval

who produced satisfactory legal evidence that he is a Citizen of the United States of America under the oath of Henry Ducommun who having been by me the said Notary duly sworn according to law did declare and say that the said Henry Ducommun Junior is a Citizen of the said United States, and the son of deponent

whereof an attestation being required, I have granted this under my Hand and Notarial Seal.

Done at the City of Philadelphia, the Eighth *day of* April 1836

Edward Hurst Notary Public.

FIGURE 10-9 This handwritten passport application was generated by a notary public in Philadelphia, Pennsylvania, on 8 April 1836 for Henry Ducommon, Junior.

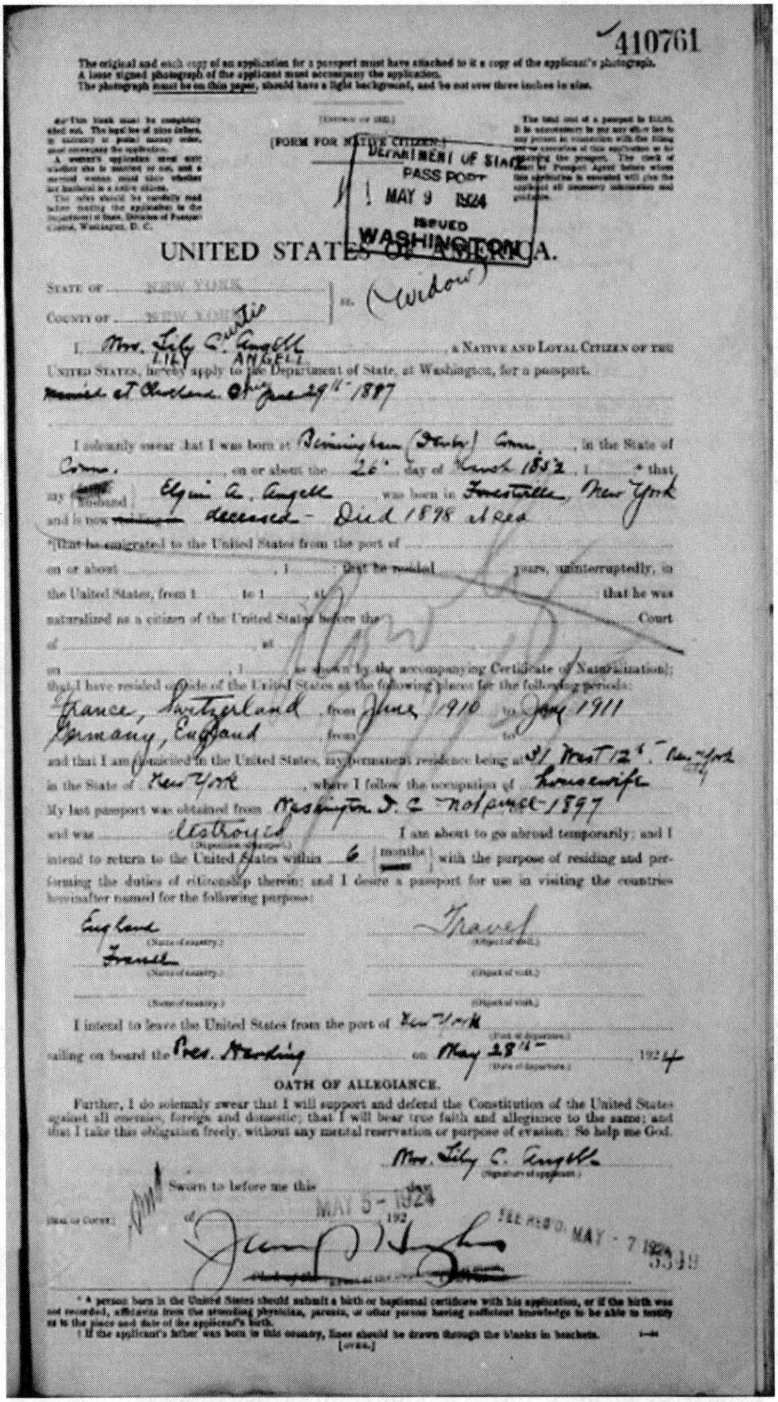

410761

The original and each copy of an application for a passport must have attached to it a copy of the applicant's photograph. A loose signed photograph of the applicant must accompany the application. The photograph must be on thin paper, should have a light background, and be not over three inches in size.

[FORM FOR NATIVE CITIZEN.]

DEPARTMENT OF STATE PASS PORT MAY 9 1924 ISSUED WASHINGTON

UNITED STATES OF AMERICA.

STATE OF NEW YORK
COUNTY OF NEW YORK } ss. (widow)

I, Mrs. Lily Curtis Angell LILY ANGELL, a NATIVE AND LOYAL CITIZEN OF THE UNITED STATES, hereby apply to the Department of State, at Washington, for a passport.

married at Cleveland, Ohio Jan 29th 1887

I solemnly swear that I was born at Birmingham (Derby) Conn., in the State of Conn., on or about the 26th day of March 1862; that my husband Elgin A. Angell was born in Forestville, New York and is now deceased – Died 1898 [illegible]

that he emigrated to the United States from the port of ......, on or about ......, 1......; that he resided ...... years, uninterruptedly, in the United States, from 1...... to 1......, at ......; that he was naturalized as a citizen of the United States before the ...... Court of ...... at ...... on ......, 1......, as shown by the accompanying Certificate of Naturalization; that I have resided outside of the United States at the following places for the following periods:

France, Switzerland from June 1910 to Jan 1911
Germany, England from ...... to ......

and that I am domiciled in the United States, my permanent residence being at 31 West 12th, New York in the State of New York, where I follow the occupation of housewife. My last passport was obtained from Washington D.C. [illegible] 1897 and was destroyed. I am about to go abroad temporarily; and I intend to return to the United States within 6 months with the purpose of residing and performing the duties of citizenship therein; and I desire a passport for use in visiting the countries hereinafter named for the following purpose:

(Name of country.)	(Object of visit.)
England	Travel
France	

I intend to leave the United States from the port of New York sailing on board the Pres. Harding on May 28th 1924

OATH OF ALLEGIANCE.

Further, I do solemnly swear that I will support and defend the Constitution of the United States against all enemies, foreign and domestic; that I will bear true faith and allegiance to the same; and that I take this obligation freely, without any mental reservation or purpose of evasion: So help me God.

Mrs. Lily C. Angell
(Signature of applicant.)

Sworn to before me this MAY 5 - 1924 day of 192

FEE REC'D. MAY - 7 1924 3349

* A person born in the United States should submit a birth or baptismal certificate with his application, or if the birth was not recorded, affidavits from the attending physician, parents, or other person having sufficient knowledge to be able to testify as to the place and date of the applicant's birth.

† If the applicant's father was born in this country, lines should be drawn through the blanks in brackets.

[OVER.]

FIGURE 10-10 Page 1 of the passport application of Mrs. Lily Curtis Angell

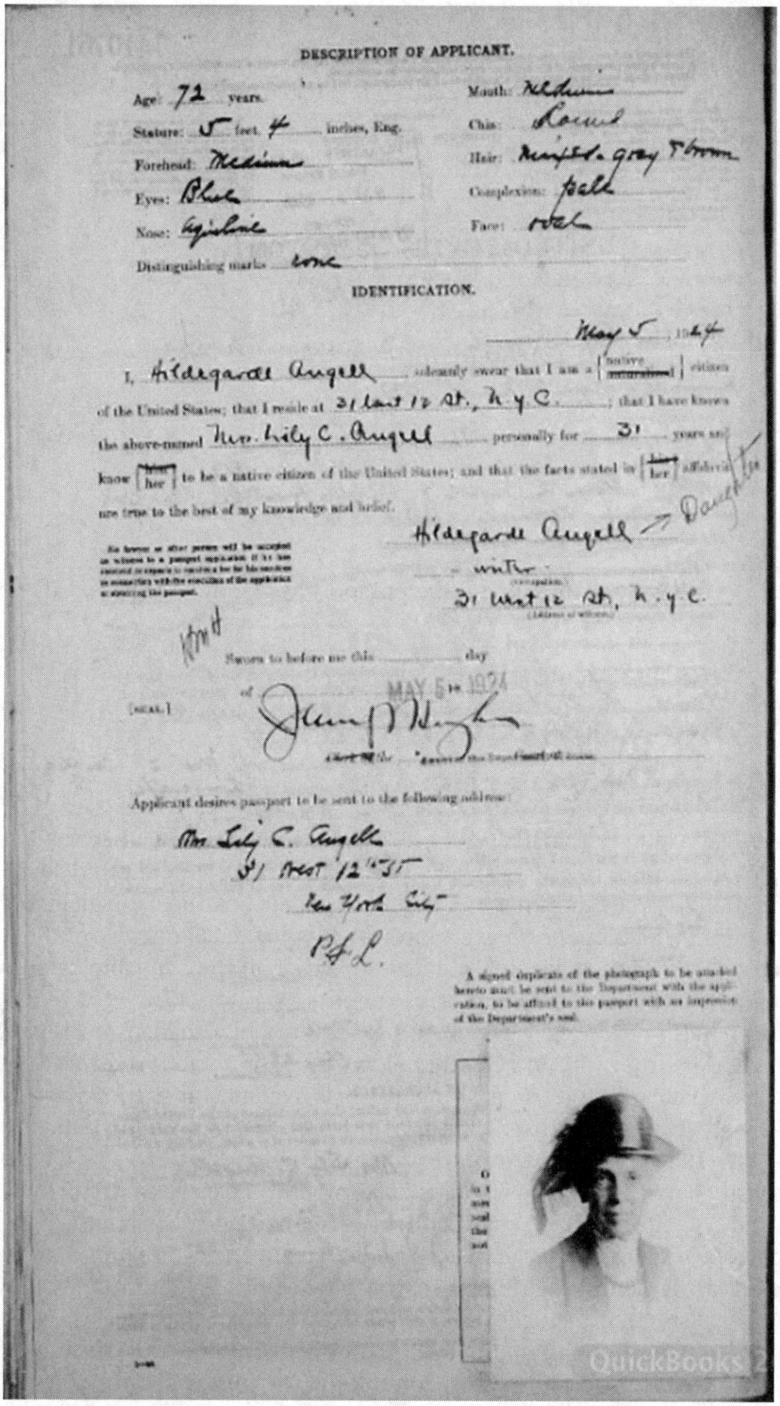

DESCRIPTION OF APPLICANT.

Age: 72 years. Mouth: Medium
Stature: 5 feet 4 inches, Eng. Chin: Round
Forehead: Medium Hair: Mixed gray & brown
Eyes: Blue Complexion: Pale
Nose: Aquiline Face: Oval
Distinguishing marks: none

IDENTIFICATION.

May 5, 1924

I, Hildegarde Angell solemnly swear that I am a [native / naturalized] citizen of the United States; that I reside at 31 East 12 St., N.Y.C.; that I have known the above-named Mrs. Lily C. Angell personally for 31 years and know [him / her] to be a native citizen of the United States; and that the facts stated in [his / her] affidavit are true to the best of my knowledge and belief.

Hildegarde Angell → Daughter
writer
(Occupation.)
31 West 12 St., N.Y.C.
(Address of witness.)

Sworn to before me this ____ day of MAY 5 1924

[SEAL.]

Applicant desires passport to be sent to the following address:

Mrs. Lily C. Angell
31 West 12th St
New York City
P.J.L.

A signed duplicate of the photograph to be attached hereto must be sent to the Department with the application, to be affixed to the passport with an impression of the Department's seal.

FIGURE 10-11 Page 2 of the passport application of Mrs. Lily Curtis Angell listing her physical description and including a photograph

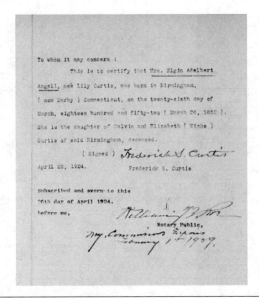

FIGURE 10-12   Affidavit accompanying the passport application of Mrs. Lily Curtis Angell

Locate and Access Canadian Immigration Records

Library and Archives Canada (LAC), at **http://www.collectionscanada.gc.ca**, provides its content in both English and French. Here you will find a wealth of information for your research. On the main page, click the Genealogy & Family History link, which opens a page from which you can search any of the databases related to genealogy. You can also view the list of all the available databases. Click a link and explore the available information.

Immigration passenger lists were not required in Canada until 1865. The originals from that time from 1865 to 1922 are held by the Library and Archives Canada (LAC). A searchable database of those passenger lists is available at **http://www.bac-lac.gc.ca/ eng/discover/immigration/immigration-records/passenger-lists/passenger- lists-1865-1922/Pages/introduction.aspx**. The images have also have been digitized at Ancestry.com (**http://www.ancestry.com**) and Ancestry.ca (**http://www.ancestry .ca**). The LAC site at **http://www.collectionscanada.gc.ca** is an excellent site at which you can learn more about the history and context of these records. FamilySearch (**https://familysearch.org**) has a searchable database of digitized images of Canada Passenger Lists, 1881 to 1922.

Another website with many links is Immigrants to Canada, located at **http:// jubilation.uwaterloo.ca/ ~ marj/genealogy/thevoyage.html**. Included are scores of links, including compilations of ships for specific years, written/transcribed accounts

FIGURE 10-13   Canadian passenger list from 1934

describing the voyages, emigrant handbooks, extracts from government immigration reports of the 19th century, and many, many nationalities' emigration/immigration website links. Don't miss this one. Figure 10-13 shows an example from 1934.

Please note that records from 1 January 1936 are still in the custody of Citizenship and Immigration Canada. Privacy of individuals is protected, and certain restrictions exist. Border Entry records also are available for immigrants arriving across the U.S./Canadian border between April 1908 and December 1935. However, not all immigrants were recorded. Some persons immigrated without being processed through ports when the ports were closed or where no port or governmental station existed. Others, for whom one or both parents were Canadian or who had previously resided in Canada, were considered "returning Canadians" and were not listed.

There also are registers of Chinese immigrants to Canada who arrived between 1885 and 1949.

It is important to know that the records are arranged by name of the port of arrival and the date of arrival, with the exception of the years 1923 to 1924 and some records from 1919 to 1922 when a separate governmental reporting Form 30A (individual manifest) was used. In addition, the Pier 21 Society of Halifax, Nova Scotia, has worked with LAC in inputting passenger list data from 1925 to 1935 and other border entry records data.

LAC provides an Ancestors Search facility at its website that allows you to enter the surname and given name and search one or all databases related to genealogical data. The direct link is **http://www.collectionscanada.gc.ca/lac-bac/search/anc**, and the search template is shown in Figure 10-14.

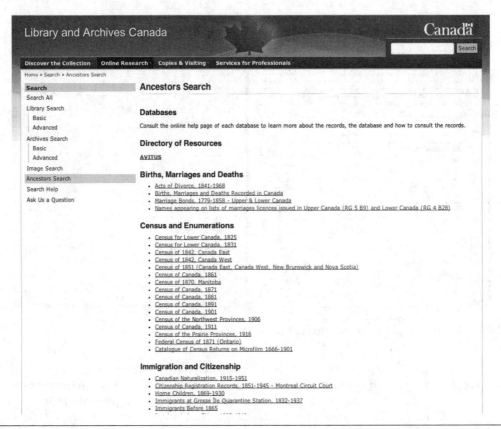

FIGURE 10-14 The top of the web page for the Ancestors Search facility at the Library and Archives Canada site

Home Children is a term used to designate the more than 100,000 children who were sent from Great Britain to Canada between the years of 1869 and the late 1930s. The intent was to provide a better, healthier, and more moral life for them. These were primarily poor or orphaned children, and rural Canadians welcomed them as cheap labor for their farms. (You may learn more about this phenomenon at the Young Immigrants to Canada website at **http://www.dcs.uwaterloo.ca/ ~ marj/genealogy/ homeadd.html**.) The archive contains a great deal of correspondence from sponsoring and administrative agencies for these children. Members of the British Isles Family History Society of Greater Ottawa are locating and indexing the names of these Home Children found in passenger lists in the custody of LAC. Details about the record holdings and a searchable database of these children are accessible on the web page at **http://www.collectionscanada.gc.ca/genealogie/022-908.009-e.html**.

Passenger lists and other records from before 1865 may exist in the provincial or territorial libraries, archives, and/or at maritime museums. The passenger arrival records in the custody of LAC that date from 1865 to 1935 have been microfilmed. They can be accessed in person by visiting LAC at 395 Wellington Street in Ottawa, through interlibrary loan among Canadian libraries, and/or through the LDS Family

History Center nearest you. As mentioned before, digitized images are indexed and accessible at Ancestry.com (**http://www.ancestry.com**) and Ancestry.ca (**http://www.ancestry.ca**).

An excellent strategy for researching immigrants into Canada would be to start with LAC and then seek additional resources in the appropriate province or territory. Please note that Canada *does not* maintain records of emigrations from Canada to other countries. If you are searching for an ancestor who immigrated to the United States, for example, you will need to refer to U.S. immigration records.

Locate and Access Australian Immigration Records

The history of Australia is a rich one, and it is the story of two peoples: the indigenous Aboriginals and the immigrants, primarily from England, Wales, Scotland, and Ireland. The records of emigration from other countries and the immigration records into the country are mostly organized by geographical region. However, understanding some historical background can help you in understanding what is available and how to access the records.

Learn About Australian History

Most people know that Australia was originally used by Britain as a penal colony. Most of the original colonial settlers were, in fact, convicts who were transported from the United Kingdom since 1788, along with the military personnel assigned to the colony.

Many criminal offenses in England during previous centuries could be punished by the imposition of extremely harsh and cruel sentences, ranging from public floggings to an appointment with the hangman, or to an executioner with an axe, if you were a "special" prisoner. During the 17th century, a more humane method of punishment was sought, and *transportation* to a distant wilderness environment was seen as an ideal solution. Thus, transportation began from the United Kingdom to the American colonies. Debtors' colonies and criminal settlements existed for those condemned to penal servitude for a term of years or for life.

The outbreak of the American Revolutionary War halted transportation of criminals and undesirables to North America in 1775. While sentences of transportation were still passed by the courts, the convicts were remanded to prison. Before long, prison overcrowding created dire conditions. The government began to acquire older, perhaps no longer seaworthy ships, which were referred to as "the hulks." These were fitted to house criminals, and thousands of convicts were sentenced to terms of imprisonment in these floating jails moored in coastal waters. The deplorable living conditions in both the prisons and on board the hulks reached a crisis stage, with rampant disease and escalating death tolls. The government sought a new location for a penal colony as a solution to the situation. In 1787, what has been called the "First Fleet" set sail from England for Botany Bay in Australia. A number of penal colony settlements were founded and maintained over the next 70 years. The military personnel assigned to administer the new penal colonies also brought their wives and families to settle there.

Emigration of free settlers from Britain and Ireland did not really begin until the early 1800s, and the number of emigrants was small in comparison to those migrating to the United States and Canada. In the 1830s and 1840s, a major exodus from Ireland saw many Irish farmers headed to both America and Australia. The gold rush in the 1850s provided another impetus for migration to Australia. The mining of opals became an important industry, with Australia now providing 97 percent of the world's supply of opals. Therefore, opal mining also became an important draw for immigrant settlers.

Transportation as a punishment was effectively stopped in 1857, although it was not formally abolished until 1868. As you begin your research for Australian ancestors, you will want to familiarize yourself with the history of the judicial system in the United Kingdom at the time in question, and about the history of the penal colonies in the various areas of Australia. You also will want to try to locate the records of the criminal proceedings against your ancestor, the details of sentencing, and to what colony he or she was transported. This will help you trace the migration path.

Nowadays it is an "in thing" to claim descent from an early convict. In fact, Australian citizens often express the sentiment that the more convicts in the family tree, the merrier—and the more "ocker" (Australian) one becomes. So let's look at convicts first. The earlier your ancestor arrived in Australia, the greater the probability that you are descended from a convict or from a member of the Crown government, an army or naval person, or a member of a ship's crew.

You can often trace the path backward, although it may be more complicated to make that leap without understanding the ancestor's circumstances and his or her offense. The database at the State Library of Queensland may provide details that can facilitate locating the criminal records in the court in the country of origin. Any additional information you can glean in advance may be crucial in distinguishing *your* ancestor from another person bearing the same name. Again, most of these records will be in the possession of the respective state or territory to which the person was transported.

Locate the Existing Australian Immigration Records

It is important to recognize early on that the National Archives of Australia (NAA) on Queen Victoria Terrace in Canberra is the archives of the Commonwealth government. The records in that collection therefore date mostly from the Federation in 1901. That facility does not possess the records of convicts, of colonial migration, or of 18th and 19th century Australian history concerning such periods as the early exploration, the gold rushes, or colonial administration. They also do not have information about functions administered by the state and territory governments such as births, deaths, and marriages registers, or land titles. To obtain further information on these topics, it is necessary to contact the relevant state or territory registrar.

The National Archives of Ireland (**http://www.nationalarchives.ie**) has a searchable index database of transportation of Irish convicts to Australia between 1788 and 1868. Click the Genealogy link on the main page and then click Genealogy Records to locate the link for "Ireland-Australia transportation records (1791–1853)."

What the NAA does have, however, are immigration records relating to the 20th century dating primarily from 1924. The NAA does have some older records dating to the 1850s, but most of the records will be found in the respective state and territory archives. The NAA's Fact sheets page can be accessed at **http://www.naa.gov.au/ collection/fact-sheets**. You will also want to review specific fact sheets for records held in other offices of the archives as follows:

Fact sheet 38	Passenger records held in Canberra **http://www.naa.gov.au/collection/fact-sheets/fs38.aspx**
Fact sheet 56	Passenger records held in Perth **http://www.naa.gov.au/collection/fact-sheets/fs56.aspx**
Fact sheet 64	Passenger records held in Sydney **http://www.naa.gov.au/collection/fact-sheets/fs64.aspx**
Fact sheet 172	Passenger records held in Melbourne **http://www.naa.gov.au/collection/fact-sheets/fs172.aspx**
Fact sheet 184	Passenger records held in Hobart **http://www.naa.gov.au/collection/fact-sheets/fs184.aspx**
Fact sheet 190	Passenger records held in Brisbane **http://www.naa.gov.au/collection/fact-sheets/fs190.aspx**
Fact sheet 256	Passenger records held in Adelaide **http://www.naa.gov.au/collection/fact-sheets/fs256.aspx**

Fact sheet 2, located at **http://www.naa.gov.au/collection/fact-sheets/fs02 .aspx**, is perhaps your most valuable online reference in the search for historical documents related to your genealogical research. It contains the addresses, contact information, and web address links for all of the major Australian archival institutions.

The State Library of Queensland has created the Convict transportation registers database at **http://www.slq.qld.gov.au/resources/family-history/convicts**. It contains details for over 123,000 of the estimated 160,000 convicts that were transported to Australia. The search results for individuals contain a substantial amount of information, which can include name, details of the crime and court, term of the sentence, date of transportation departure, name of the ship, and the place of arrival. The individual's name and the court may be used to locate the extant court records in England or Ireland.

A database project to index names from the NAA's many passenger arrival records from the 20th century (Record Series K269: *Inward passenger manifests for ships and aircraft arriving at Fremantle, Perth Airport and outports*, 1898–1978) is under way and currently includes arrivals from January 1921 to March 1951. The database is accessible through the NAA's RecordSearch facility at **http://recordsearch.naa.gov .au**. You may search as a Guest, and there are several collections that you can access. One choice is the "Immigration and naturalisation records" group.

You will find extensive information about immigration to and emigration from Australia in the FamilySearch Wiki at **https://familysearch.org/learn/wiki/en/ Australia_Emigration_and_Immigration**.

Use Strategies for Determining Your Ancestor's Migration Path

By now, you should have a much better idea of the types of information that are available for the various time periods and what records you may be likely to find. Remember that your early ancestors migrated across country from their places of birth and residence to ports from which ships sailed. They may then have sailed on one of these ships to emigrate across oceans. Also remember that, if an ancestor perhaps arrived in Canada and later relocated to the United States, there may have been several methods of travel and migration routes that were available at that time. Your ancestor may have crossed the border on foot or by some form of wheeled transportation, depending on the time period. These might include wagon, stagecoach, train, automobile, truck, or motor coach. Additionally, travel by boat, ferry, or ship might also have been an option. A combination of methods is also likely. You therefore will want to research the migration routes and transportation methods of the time for the geographical areas where your ancestor traveled.

The actual *locating* of the records is, of course, the real challenge. The following are some strategies you may consider employing in order to locate these records for your ancestors.

Start with What You Know

As with all effective family history and genealogical research, start with the most recent period and work your way backward. Any other approach, especially when researching back "across the pond," can be unsuccessful. As you proceed backward, start with what other family members may know about immigrant ancestors. Look for home sources, including documentary materials that may have recorded immigration and/or naturalization details. These include family Bibles, letters, naturalization papers, voter registration documents, obituaries, and other documents. Another, older relative may even recall having heard Grandpa or Grandma discuss his or her trip to the new country, or something they recall having heard from another family member. While the intervening years may have dimmed or distorted the memory, there is likely to be a basis in fact with which to begin your research.

Locate and Use the U.S. Federal Census Population Schedules

Census records provide milestones for establishing locations at regular time intervals. National censuses and state, territorial, and provincial censuses should be checked from the last census taken before the person's death and tracked backward in time to locate the person at every enumeration, back to the parents' home. Don't overlook the information included on U.S. federal census records from 1880 forward, for example. Gather information on age, place of birth (if available), language spoken (if indicated), marital status, occupation, level of education, property ownership, and any other details. These can provide important biographical and historical context to help establish citizenship. The information you find about migration may point to immigration and country of origin.

Remember to be aware that a stated place of birth may have been in a different geopolitical jurisdiction at the time of birth than was listed on the census. Census enumerators' instructions in the United States, for instance, stated that a foreign-born person was to tell where he or she was born and that the enumerator was to ask for the *current* name of the country in which that place was located. Boundaries and political jurisdictions did change over time. If you discover the country of birth for your ancestor in one census is different from that listed in a previous or subsequent census, it may indicate that a boundary change had taken place. Your understanding of the history and of geographical boundary changes is crucial to your successful research. These changes can help you home in on a specific geographical area. Furthermore, this knowledge enables you to determine the governmental entity in charge of generating official documents at the time. That entity and the places where its government offices were located then will help you determine where documentary evidence is to be found now.

Use City and Telephone Directories

In the absence of census records, and for the years between censuses, city directories and, later, telephone directories may help you establish locations. Addresses may help you identify property that your ancestor may have owned, and you may be able to follow up with government offices that maintain deeds and property tax records for additional information. Business listings that include proprietors' names may help you determine where your ancestor worked.

Refer to Vital Documents and Ecclesiastical Records

Marriage and death certificates, as well as any ecclesiastical records, may provide crucial information concerning your ancestor's origins. Church membership rolls and church minutes can direct you to other churches and locations from which membership may have been transferred. These may include congregations in the previous country of residence. This information may point you to a specific location or geographic area. You can then study migration patterns of the time when your ancestor lived there. These patterns may also point to commonly used ports of emigrant ships' embarkations. You may also study the history of the area to help determine motivations for migrations.

Don't Overlook Voter Registration and Jury Records

One important record overlooked by many researchers is the voter registration record. These records typically are maintained at the county level across the United States and in governmental offices in other countries. Most times they are in a list format but sometimes the original voter registration application cards still exist. In order to vote in an election, an individual was supposed to be a citizen, and the voter registration records may include spaces to indicate the place of birth, when and where naturalized, how many years a resident lived in this voting precinct or ward, and so on.

Voter registration lists provide the court system in the area with the names of citizens who can serve as jurors. Jury lists may still be in the possession of the courts and may help verify the location of an ancestor at a specific time. Remember that women were not legally permitted to serve on juries until later times, and so you should consult the laws in effect at the time that your ancestor resided in an area before searching jury lists for a female ancestor.

Look for Passport Records

We discussed passport records in the United States earlier in the chapter. Certainly other countries issued passports for their citizens' use in traveling abroad. Remember that it also is possible that your ancestor had to obtain a passport to return to and visit his or her homeland (and even to bring other relatives to America). Be sure to determine what passport application records might exist for your ancestor and how to access them. Figure 10-15 shows the passport application for Samuel L. Clemens, also known as author Mark Twain, from 5 May 1891.

Study Published Histories

It is important to locate histories of the country and the locale from which your ancestor(s) may have come. Some of these published chronicles include the names of emigrants, their reasons for emigration, the migration paths they took, the time periods in which they relocated, and, in some cases, the names of the shipping lines (and ships) used.

One category of histories that should not be overlooked is the British genealogies that mention relatives who have gone to the New World. In the 16th and 17th centuries, heralds from the College of Arms would visit the various counties and record the pedigrees of families who aspired to *armigerous* status (meaning that they would have a coat of arms). Occasionally, there would be references to younger sons who had migrated or emigrated elsewhere.

In the 18th and 19th centuries, ambitious compilers of county histories would include pedigrees of the principal families of the county. Again, there might be the occasional reference to a relative who had gone to America, and perhaps even to a specified destination.

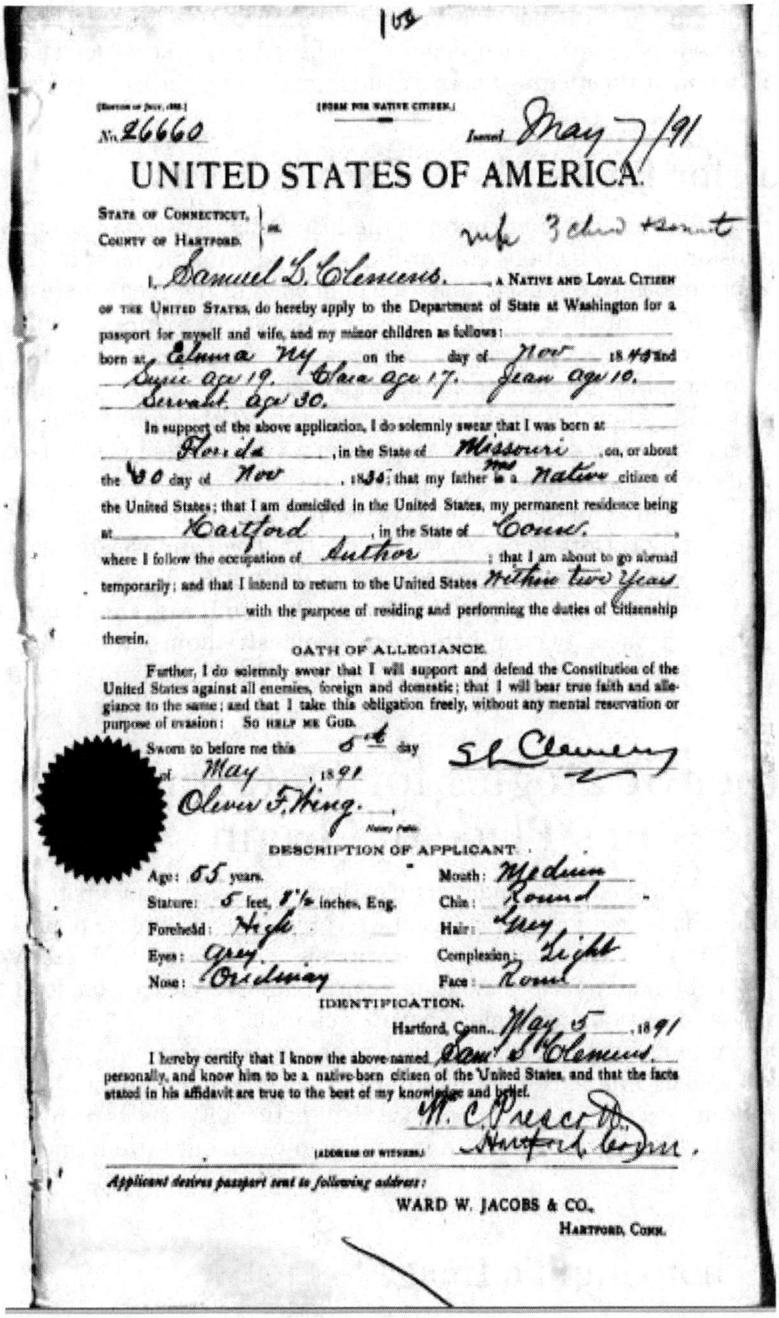

108

[Edition of July, 188.] [FORM FOR NATIVE CITIZEN.]

No. 26660 Issued May 7/91

UNITED STATES OF AMERICA.

STATE OF CONNECTICUT, COUNTY OF HARTFORD. } ss.

wife 3 child + servant

I, Samuel L. Clemens, a NATIVE AND LOYAL CITIZEN OF THE UNITED STATES, do hereby apply to the Department of State at Washington for a passport for myself and wife, and my minor children as follows: born at Elmira NY on the day of Nov 1845 and Susie age 19. Clara age 17. Jean age 10. Servant age 30.

In support of the above application, I do solemnly swear that I was born at Florida, in the State of Missouri, on, or about the 30 day of Nov, 1835; that my father was a Native citizen of the United States; that I am domiciled in the United States, my permanent residence being at Hartford, in the State of Conn., where I follow the occupation of Author; that I am about to go abroad temporarily; and that I intend to return to the United States within two years with the purpose of residing and performing the duties of citizenship therein.

OATH OF ALLEGIANCE.

Further, I do solemnly swear that I will support and defend the Constitution of the United States against all enemies, foreign and domestic; that I will bear true faith and allegiance to the same; and that I take this obligation freely, without any mental reservation or purpose of evasion: SO HELP ME GOD.

Sworn to before me this 5th day of May, 1891

S L Clemens

Oliver F. Wing, Notary Public.

DESCRIPTION OF APPLICANT.

Age:	55 years.	Mouth:	Medium
Stature:	5 feet, 8½ inches, Eng.	Chin:	Round
Forehead:	High	Hair:	Grey
Eyes:	Grey	Complexion:	Light
Nose:	Ordinary	Face:	Round

IDENTIFICATION.

Hartford, Conn., May 5, 1891

I hereby certify that I know the above-named Sam'l L Clemens personally, and know him to be a native-born citizen of the United States, and that the facts stated in his affidavit are true to the best of my knowledge and belief.

W. C. Prescott

[ADDRESS OF WITNESS.] Hartford Conn.

Applicant desires passport sent to following address:

WARD W. JACOBS & CO., HARTFORD, CONN.

FIGURE 10-15 Passport application for Samuel L. Clemens (also known as Mark Twain) from 5 May 1891

Finally, in the 19th and 20th centuries, the various volumes of pedigrees of landed gentry, peerage, and baronetcies, published by Burke's Peerage and Gentry (**http://www.burkespeerage.com**), contain many references to American settlers.

Look for Books About Early Settlers

By the same token, the companion to the histories discussed previously would be the historical publications concerning arriving immigrants at the other end of your ancestors' journey. Local histories published in the area where your ancestors settled can also provide clues to your ancestors' origin. While they may or may not include your ancestors' names, they may provide details about the places of origins for specific groups of residents in the area. These may be important clues to neighborhoods, churches, local newspapers, and other resources for your research.

Google Books (**http://books.google.com**) is an excellent place to search for print and electronic books referencing your ancestors and their relatives. Google has digitized many thousands of older books that are out of copyright, and these are free. The Family History Books collection provided by FamilySearch contains almost 18,000 digitized and searchable family and local histories. The search template for this collection can be found at **https://books.familysearch.org**. Other digital collections can be found at Ancestry.com (**http://www.ancestry.com**), in the HeritageQuest Online databases, at MyHeritage (**http://www.myheritage.com**), and at other sites.

Use Other Strategies for Determining Your Ancestor's Place of Origin

By now, you should understand more clearly that there are more paths to follow than just one in the search for your ancestors' records. When the place of birth, previous residence, or other indication of native origin is conveniently and clearly marked, you can be thankful for more modern records. However, when you don't have such crystal-clear directional markers, what are you to do?

Determining your ancestral origin can be a tricky thing but it is not always impossible to ascertain. Numerous strategies are employed, so let's look at a few. This list can never be complete because each nationality has its own nuances, but you must invest some thought and ingenuity to reach out to your ancestors' stories and traits.

Use Photographic Images

If your ancestors came to America between 1850 and the present, photographs of them may very well exist, especially in family photographic collections. An examination of clothing, hairstyles, shoes, jewelry, and other objects in the picture may be helpful in determining your ancestral origin. On older photographs mounted on cabinet card stock, there may even be the name of a photographer and a location. Researching the photographer or studio can be an interesting study as well, and it is not unusual to find a particular photographer having taken photos in a specific area or neighborhood in which a national or ethnic group lived.

Look at Home for Letters Written in Another Language

If you encounter letters written in another language among the family possessions, or Bibles and books in another language, start asking questions. These may be indicative of the nativity of members of your family or your ancestors. It may also be possible to have these items translated into your language so that you can understand them and potentially gain more clues.

Consider Family Customs

Are there specific customs in your family you don't understand? One researcher wondered why the family always ate marinated herring at Christmastime, only to discover later that it was a residual custom from her maternal grandmother, whose family always ate it at their home outside Uppsala, Sweden. And are there songs in another language that are sung, such as hymns or lullabies? They might provide other important clues.

Find Clues in Culinary Styles

Ethnic or national cooking is always an interesting tip-off, though not always. Your grandmother's goulash may be indicative that she had ancestors in Hungary.

Pay Attention to Family Physical Traits

One African-American friend heard a lecture at the National Genealogical Society Conference in Denver, Colorado, in 1998, by Tommie Morton-Young, Ph.D. In that lecture, "African American Genealogy: New Insights Using Traditional and Less Traditional Methods," Dr. Morton-Young discussed that there are physical characteristics of some African peoples that may be used to trace ancestry of slave ancestors back to a particular geographical area and perhaps even to a specific tribal group. The physical traits in this case were the size and shape of the ear, the shape of the nose, and the physical size of the ulna. It is a very interesting approach, and it might really matter.

Use the Resources at the U.S. Citizenship and Immigration Services Website

The U.S. Citizenship and Immigration Services website, as mentioned before, provides some of the most important historical and reference materials for your immigration and naturalization research. USCIS is located at **http://www.uscis.gov**. However, access the Genealogy Notebook at **http://www.uscis.gov/history-and-genealogy/ genealogy/genealogy-notebook**, which contains a number of excellent articles. The "Our History" section and the "History and Genealogy News" section provide important educational materials for you. Look for the link to the Historical Library, where you will find a link labeled Legal History Resources. The immigration and naturalization laws for different time periods from 1893 forward can be studied here.

Understand the Naturalization Process

The naturalization process has varied in every location we will discuss here, and has evolved over time to produce more consistent practices with more standardized and detailed records. The focus of this section is United States naturalization, but your study of naturalization practices in England and Wales, Scotland, Ireland, Canada, Australia, and other locations can provide you with the knowledge and legal background to help understand those places' laws and requirements.

As our forebears began their new lives in new communities, they strove to "fit in" and to normalize in the new environment. Most realized they would never return to their previous lives, and they eagerly embraced their new circumstances. This meant renouncing their political ties to their motherland and applying to become citizens of their new country.

Naturalization in the United States, like the ships' passenger lists and manifests, has changed through the centuries of the country's existence. Different methods of handling the process, different laws and requirements, different forms, and different places where the process was handled all add up to what can be a challenging research effort. There are many intricacies and exceptions and, as a result, we have to do some self-education to learn the details of the history of naturalization in the United States. To that end, Loretto D. Szucs's book *They Became Americans: Finding Naturalization Records and Ethnic Origins* (Ancestry.com, 1998) wins my applause for the best volume on the process, and is illustrated with scores of document examples. However, in short, there are four principal documents associated with naturalization in the United States:

- **Declaration of Intention** This document (also sometimes referred to as *first papers*) is signed by the immigrant, renouncing citizenship in his/her previous country and any allegiance to the country and/or its ruler or sovereign. It expresses the individual's intent to petition the United States to become a citizen after all requirements are met. The format varied over time, as you can see from the examples in Figures 10-16 and 10-17.

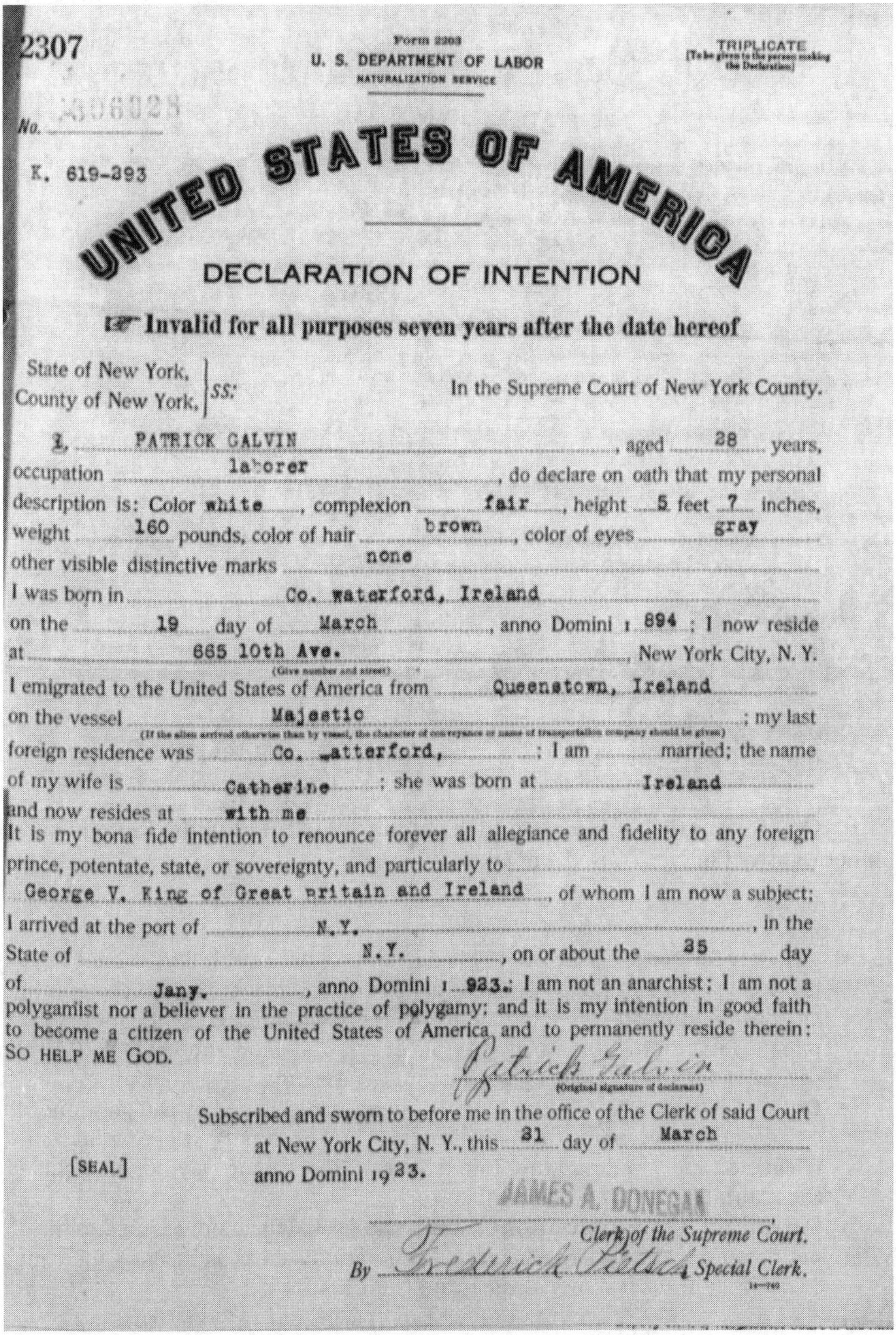

2307

Form 2203
U. S. DEPARTMENT OF LABOR
NATURALIZATION SERVICE

TRIPLICATE
[To be given to the person making the Declaration]

No. 306028

K. 619-393

UNITED STATES OF AMERICA

DECLARATION OF INTENTION

☞ Invalid for all purposes seven years after the date hereof

State of New York, County of New York, } SS: In the Supreme Court of New York County.

I, PATRICK GALVIN, aged 28 years, occupation laborer, do declare on oath that my personal description is: Color white, complexion fair, height 5 feet 7 inches, weight 160 pounds, color of hair brown, color of eyes gray other visible distinctive marks none

I was born in Co. waterford, Ireland on the 19 day of March, anno Domini 1894; I now reside at 665 10th Ave. (Give number and street), New York City, N. Y.

I emigrated to the United States of America from Queenstown, Ireland on the vessel Majestic (If the alien arrived otherwise than by vessel, the character of conveyance or name of transportation company should be given); my last foreign residence was Co. waterford,; I am married; the name of my wife is Catherine; she was born at Ireland and now resides at with me

It is my bona fide intention to renounce forever all allegiance and fidelity to any foreign prince, potentate, state, or sovereignty, and particularly to George V, King of Great Britain and Ireland, of whom I am now a subject; I arrived at the port of N.Y., in the State of N.Y., on or about the 25 day of Jany., anno Domini 1923; I am not an anarchist; I am not a polygamist nor a believer in the practice of polygamy; and it is my intention in good faith to become a citizen of the United States of America and to permanently reside therein: SO HELP ME GOD.

Patrick Galvin
(Original signature of declarant)

Subscribed and sworn to before me in the office of the Clerk of said Court at New York City, N. Y., this 31 day of March anno Domini 1923.

[SEAL]

JAMES A. DONEGAN,
Clerk of the Supreme Court.

By Frederick Pietsch, Special Clerk.

FIGURE 10-16 Declaration of Intention (from 1923)

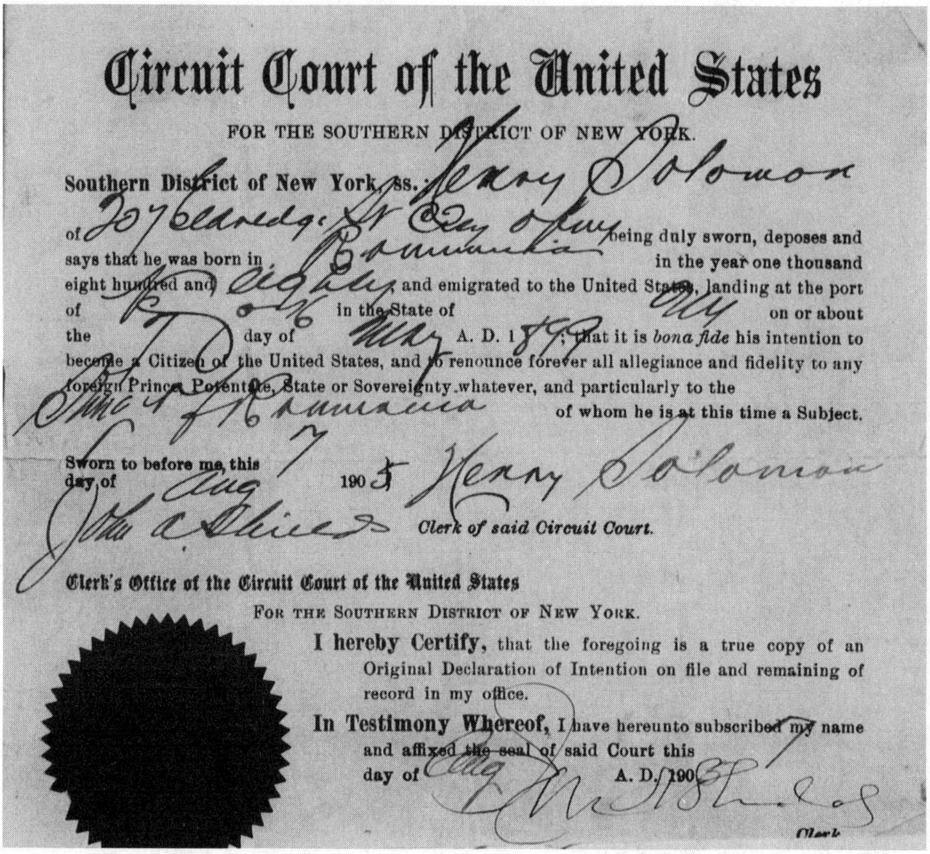

Circuit Court of the United States

FOR THE SOUTHERN DISTRICT OF NEW YORK.

Southern District of New York, ss.: Henry Solomon

of 207 Eldridge St N. City of N.Y. being duly sworn, deposes and says that he was born in Roumania in the year one thousand eight hundred and eighty, and emigrated to the United States, landing at the port of New York in the State of N.Y. on or about the 1 day of May A. D. 1899; that it is *bona fide* his intention to become a Citizen of the United States, and to renounce forever all allegiance and fidelity to any foreign Prince, Potentate, State or Sovereignty whatever, and particularly to the King of Roumania of whom he is at this time a Subject.

Sworn to before me, this 7 day of Aug 1905 Henry Solomon

John A. Shields Clerk of said Circuit Court.

Clerk's Office of the Circuit Court of the United States

FOR THE SOUTHERN DISTRICT OF NEW YORK.

I hereby Certify, that the foregoing is a true copy of an Original Declaration of Intention on file and remaining of record in my office.

In Testimony Whereof, I have hereunto subscribed my name and affixed the seal of said Court this 7 day of Aug A. D. 1905

Clerk

FIGURE 10-17 Declaration of Intention filed at the Circuit Court of the United States for the Southern District of New York (from 1905)

- **Petition for Naturalization** This document (also referred to as *final papers*) is the application that the person completes and submits to request the granting of citizenship, typically after satisfying residency requirements and after filing first papers. Figure 10-18 shows an example of this document, and Figure 10-19 shows the court document granting permission to take the oath of allegiance.
- **Oath of Allegiance** This is the document that is signed by the petitioner for citizenship at the time citizenship is granted (or restored), swearing his/her allegiance and support to the United States. This may or may not be included in the naturalization file for your ancestor.
- **Certificate of Naturalization** This is the formal document issued to the petitioner to certify that he/she has been naturalized as a citizen of the United States. Figure 10-20 shows a certificate from 1940.

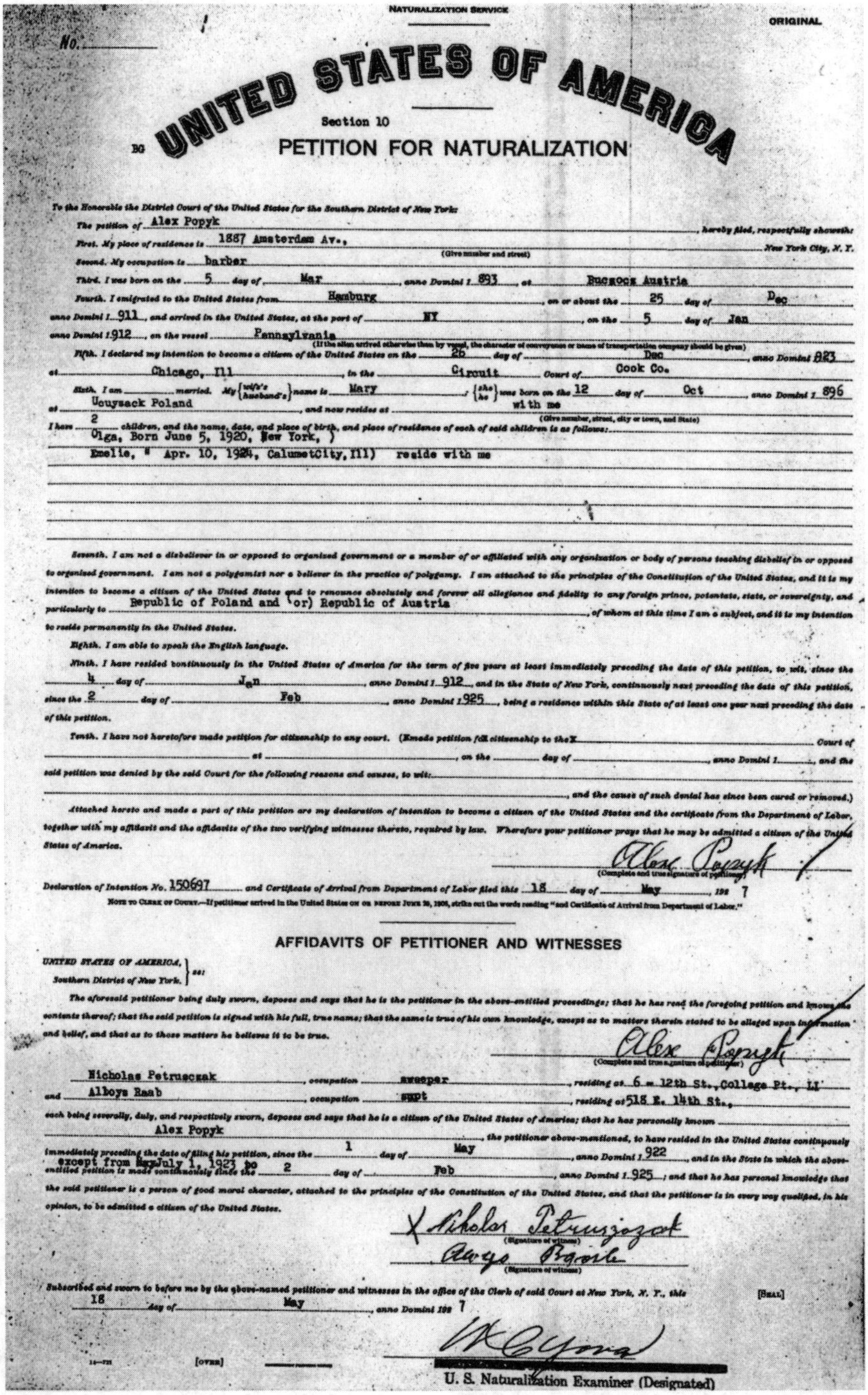

NATURALIZATION SERVICE

ORIGINAL

No.

UNITED STATES OF AMERICA

Section 10

BG PETITION FOR NATURALIZATION

To the Honorable the District Court of the United States for the Southern District of New York:

The petition of Alex Popyk, hereby filed, respectfully showeth:

First. My place of residence is 1887 Amsterdam Av., (Give number and street) New York City, N. Y.

Second. My occupation is barber

Third. I was born on the 5 day of Mar, anno Domini 1893, at Bucgocz Austria

Fourth. I emigrated to the United States from Hamburg, on or about the 25 day of Dec anno Domini 1911, and arrived in the United States, at the port of NY, on the 5 day of Jan anno Domini 1912, on the vessel Pennsylvania (If the alien arrived otherwise than by vessel, the character of conveyance or name of transportation company should be given)

Fifth. I declared my intention to become a citizen of the United States on the 26 day of Dec, anno Domini 1923 at Chicago, Ill, in the Circuit Court of Cook Co.

Sixth. I am married. My {wife's / husband's} name is Mary; {she / he} was born on the 12 day of Oct, anno Domini 1896 at Ucuysack Poland, and now resides at with me (Give number, street, city or town, and State)

I have 2 children, and the name, date, and place of birth, and place of residence of each of said children is as follows:
Olga, Born June 5, 1920, New York,)
Emelie, " Apr. 10, 1924, CalumetCity, Ill) reside with me

Seventh. I am not a disbeliever in or opposed to organized government or a member of or affiliated with any organization or body of persons teaching disbelief in or opposed to organized government. I am not a polygamist nor a believer in the practice of polygamy. I am attached to the principles of the Constitution of the United States, and it is my intention to become a citizen of the United States and to renounce absolutely and forever all allegiance and fidelity to any foreign prince, potentate, state, or sovereignty, and particularly to Republic of Poland and (or) Republic of Austria, of whom at this time I am a subject, and it is my intention to reside permanently in the United States.

Eighth. I am able to speak the English language.

Ninth. I have resided continuously in the United States of America for the term of five years at least immediately preceding the date of this petition, to wit, since the 4 day of Jan, anno Domini 1912, and in the State of New York, continuously next preceding the date of this petition, since the 2 day of Feb, anno Domini 1925, being a residence within this State of at least one year next preceding the date of this petition.

Tenth. I have not heretofore made petition for citizenship to any court. (I made petition for citizenship to the Court of at, on the day of, anno Domini 1, and the said petition was denied by the said Court for the following reasons and causes, to wit:, and the cause of such denial has since been cured or removed.)

Attached hereto and made a part of this petition are my declaration of intention to become a citizen of the United States and the certificate from the Department of Labor, together with my affidavit and the affidavits of the two verifying witnesses thereto, required by law. Wherefore your petitioner prays that he may be admitted a citizen of the United States of America.

Alex Popyk
(Complete and true signature of petitioner)

Declaration of Intention No. 150697 and Certificate of Arrival from Department of Labor filed this 18 day of May, 1927

NOTE TO CLERK OF COURT.—If petitioner arrived in the United States on or before June 29, 1906, strike out the words reading "and Certificate of Arrival from Department of Labor."

AFFIDAVITS OF PETITIONER AND WITNESSES

UNITED STATES OF AMERICA, Southern District of New York, } ss:

The aforesaid petitioner being duly sworn, deposes and says that he is the petitioner in the above-entitled proceedings; that he has read the foregoing petition and knows the contents thereof; that the said petition is signed with his full, true name; that the same is true of his own knowledge, except as to matters therein stated to be alleged upon information and belief, and that as to those matters he believes it to be true.

Alex Popyk
(Complete and true signature of petitioner)

Nicholas Petrusczak, occupation sweeper, residing at 6 - 12th St., College Pt., LI and Alboys Raab, occupation supt, residing at 518 E. 14th St., each being severally, duly, and respectively sworn, deposes and says that he is a citizen of the United States of America; that he has personally known Alex Popyk, the petitioner above-mentioned, to have resided in the United States continuously immediately preceding the date of filing his petition, since the 1 day of May, anno Domini 1922, except from July 1, 1923 to and in the State in which the above-entitled petition is made continuously since the 2 day of Feb, anno Domini 1925; and that he has personal knowledge that the said petitioner is a person of good moral character, attached to the principles of the Constitution of the United States, and that the petitioner is in every way qualified, in his opinion, to be admitted a citizen of the United States.

(Signature of witness)

(Signature of witness)

Subscribed and sworn to before me by the above-named petitioner and witnesses in the office of the Clerk of said Court at New York, N. Y., this 18 day of May, anno Domini 1927

[SEAL]

[OVER]

U. S. Naturalization Examiner (Designated)

FIGURE 10-18 Petition for Naturalization to the Circuit Court of the United States for the Southern District of New York (from 1927)

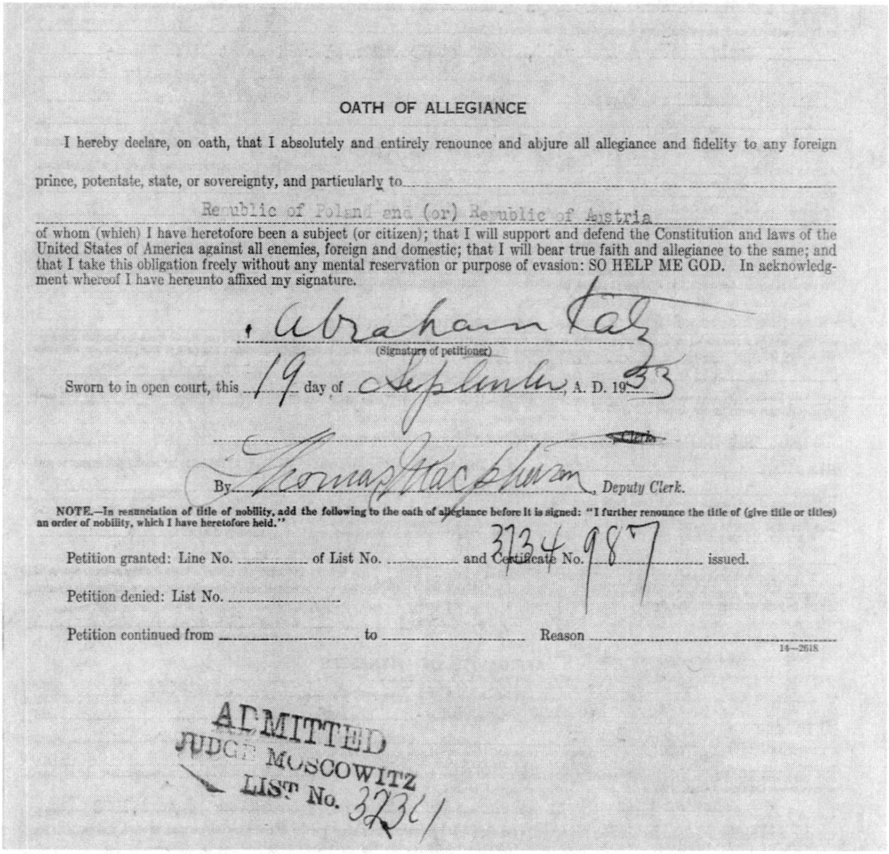

OATH OF ALLEGIANCE

I hereby declare, on oath, that I absolutely and entirely renounce and abjure all allegiance and fidelity to any foreign prince, potentate, state, or sovereignty, and particularly to

Republic of Poland and (or) Republic of Austria

of whom (which) I have heretofore been a subject (or citizen); that I will support and defend the Constitution and laws of the United States of America against all enemies, foreign and domestic; that I will bear true faith and allegiance to the same; and that I take this obligation freely without any mental reservation or purpose of evasion: SO HELP ME GOD. In acknowledgment whereof I have hereunto affixed my signature.

Abraham Katz
(Signature of petitioner)

Sworn to in open court, this 19 day of September, A. D. 1933

Clerk.

By Thomas MacPherson, Deputy Clerk.

NOTE.—In renunciation of title of nobility, add the following to the oath of allegiance before it is signed: "I further renounce the title of (give title or titles) an order of nobility, which I have heretofore held."

Petition granted: Line No. .... of List No. .... and Certificate No. 3734987 issued.

Petition denied: List No. ....

Petition continued from .... to .... Reason ....

14—2618

ADMITTED
JUDGE MOSCOWITZ
LIST No. 32361

FIGURE 10-19 Oath of Allegiance (from 1933)

One change required by the revised statute of 1906 was the addition of a step in the process to verify the arrival/admission of the immigrant in the United States. On the Declaration of Intention document, the individual was required to state the place from which he/she emigrated, the arrival point in the United States, the name under which he/she arrived, the date of arrival, and the vessel on which he/she arrived. Copies of the form were forwarded to the port of arrival, where clerks verified the data against the immigration manifests. If the record was found, the INS issued an additional document: the Certificate of Arrival, a sample of which is shown in Figure 10-21. Between its institution in 1906 and 1 July 1924, the Certificate of Arrival was an essential document to process a Petition for Citizenship. Beginning in 1924, the INS began collecting immigrant visas, and these documents ultimately replaced the need to have verification clerks search the immigration manifests. The visas were presented to an immigration inspector on arrival in the United States, and were filed. Visas for nonimmigrants were filed in the port of arrival, while visas for immigrants were forwarded to the INS in Washington, D.C., for filing and future reference.

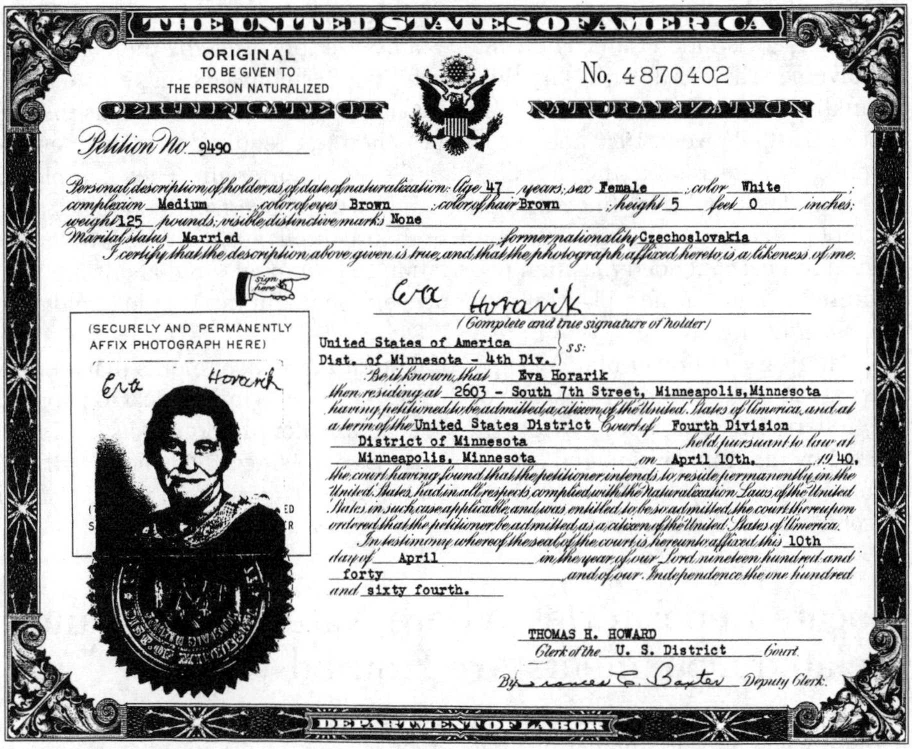

THE UNITED STATES OF AMERICA

ORIGINAL
TO BE GIVEN TO
THE PERSON NATURALIZED

No. 4870402

CERTIFICATE OF NATURALIZATION

Petition No. 9490

Personal description of holder as of date of naturalization: Age 47 years; sex Female; color White; complexion Medium; color of eyes Brown; color of hair Brown; height 5 feet 0 inches; weight 125 pounds; visible distinctive marks None

Marital status Married; former nationality Czechoslovakia

I certify that the description above given is true, and that the photograph affixed hereto is a likeness of me.

Eva Horavik
(Complete and true signature of holder)

(SECURELY AND PERMANENTLY AFFIX PHOTOGRAPH HERE)

United States of America
Dist. of Minnesota - 4th Div. } SS:

Be it known, that Eva Horarik then residing at 2603 - South 7th Street, Minneapolis, Minnesota having petitioned to be admitted a citizen of the United States of America, and at a term of the United States District Court of Fourth Division District of Minnesota held pursuant to law at Minneapolis, Minnesota on April 10th, 1940, the court having found that the petitioner intends to reside permanently in the United States, had in all respects complied with the Naturalization Laws of the United States in such case applicable, and was entitled to be so admitted, the court thereupon ordered that the petitioner be admitted as a citizen of the United States of America.

In testimony whereof the seal of the court is hereunto affixed this 10th day of April in the year of our Lord nineteen hundred and forty and of our Independence the one hundred and sixty fourth.

THOMAS H. HOWARD
Clerk of the U. S. District Court.
By Frances E. Baxter Deputy Clerk.

DEPARTMENT OF LABOR

FIGURE 10-20 Certificate of Naturalization (1940)

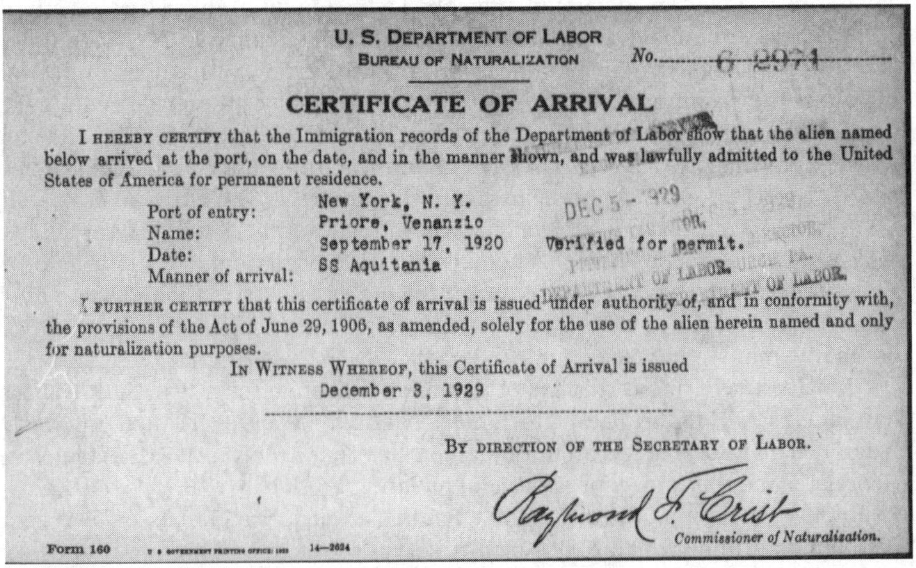

U. S. DEPARTMENT OF LABOR
BUREAU OF NATURALIZATION

No. 6 2971

CERTIFICATE OF ARRIVAL

I HEREBY CERTIFY that the Immigration records of the Department of Labor show that the alien named below arrived at the port, on the date, and in the manner shown, and was lawfully admitted to the United States of America for permanent residence.

Port of entry: New York, N. Y.
Name: Priore, Venanzio
Date: September 17, 1920
Manner of arrival: SS Aquitania

DEC 5 - 1929
Verified for permit.
DEPARTMENT OF LABOR.

I FURTHER CERTIFY that this certificate of arrival is issued under authority of, and in conformity with, the provisions of the Act of June 29, 1906, as amended, solely for the use of the alien herein named and only for naturalization purposes.

IN WITNESS WHEREOF, this Certificate of Arrival is issued December 3, 1929

BY DIRECTION OF THE SECRETARY OF LABOR.

Raymond F. Crist
Commissioner of Naturalization.

Form 160 14—2624

FIGURE 10-21 Certificate of Arrival (1929)

Another important document that may possibly be of help to your research is the Alien Registration Card. The United States was concerned by the possibility of involvement in World War II and the possibility of espionage. Congress and President Franklin D. Roosevelt enacted the Alien Registration Act (also known as the Smith Act) in 1940. Between 1940 and 1944, every alien was required to register as they applied for admission to the country, regardless of their origin. They completed a two-page form and were fingerprinted, and they were given an alien registration receipt card to present if asked to confirm their compliance with the law. Subsequent legislation has amended the alien registration requirements, and aliens are still required to register their place of residence, employment information, and other details annually.

There are a number of other types of naturalization documents that were used during the 20th century. The scope of this book makes it impractical to list all of them here. However, Loretto Szucs provides an excellent reference list of documents issued by the Immigration and Naturalization Service since 1906, along with their abbreviations, on page 169 of her book, *They Became Americans: Finding Naturalization Records and Ethnic Origins*.

Locate Repositories Where Naturalization and Related Documents Are Housed

Locating the original documents and personally examining them is your goal. You certainly will hope to find definite data or clues as to the origins of your ancestor and how he or she traveled to America. As you conduct your research, please remember that an individual may begin the naturalization process, filing a Declaration of Intention, in one place and complete the naturalization process in another place. Therefore, the physical documents may be located in different areas altogether.

The sheer volume of naturalization indexes and documents described previously can be mind-boggling. You should be aware that a significant number, but certainly not all, of the extant naturalization documents themselves that have been unearthed have been forwarded to the INS and, in turn, to NARA for microfilming and storage. As a general rule, NARA does *not* have naturalization records created in state or local courts. However, some county court naturalization records have been donated to the National Archives and are available as National Archives microfilm publications. NARA, for example, has none of the naturalization documents for the State of Utah. These reside with the U.S. District Court for the District of Utah, and some of the older records reside with the Utah State Archives and Records Service. There certainly are many, many other exceptions.

What you will find is that the original naturalization records in NARA's possession have been stored in the National Archives facility that serves the state in which the federal court is located. As an example, the National Archives at Atlanta in Morrow, Georgia, is the repository for documents relating to Alabama, Florida, Georgia, Kentucky, Mississippi, North Carolina, South Carolina, and Tennessee. It is important that you determine which NARA facility serves the state in which your ancestor would have lived at the time he or she filed the Declaration of Intention and/or Petition for Citizenship. Then you need to determine if the NARA facility does, in fact, have the documents you seek. You can begin your research by visiting the NARA website at **http://www.archives.gov**, and then visit **http://www.archives.gov/ locations** for the NARA facilities. Within the pages for each facility, you will find information about their holdings, directions, and more. Not every NARA facility has genealogical records.

In the process of your research, it would be prudent whenever you are preparing to conduct a search for naturalization documents to visit the NARA website, check the holdings list of microfilm publications and/or in their online catalog, and consider making a telephone call to their reference desk. The reference staff can help you determine if the records you seek are or are not part of NARA's holdings, whether those documents have been indexed and/or microfilmed, and how to obtain copies. Be sure to check in advance of making a trip to a NARA facility to confirm that they do, in fact, have the microfilm and/or records you might want to view.

For a reference to the holdings of naturalization materials at NARA, please refer to their website on the topic located at **http://www.archives.gov/research/ naturalization/index.html**. This is essential reading for the researcher, and the link at that site to the video, *Coming to America: Celebrating the Immigrant Experience*, provides some additional insight into the immigration process.

Don't overlook the use of your local LDS Family History Center as a resource to borrow the NARA microfilm from the Family History Library in Salt Lake City. This is an economical means of accessing and working with the materials locally, rather than traveling to a NARA facility.

Finally, Fold3 is, at this writing, in the process of digitizing the indexes to U.S. naturalization indexes and records and placing the images in a searchable database at their subscription website at **http://www.fold3.com**. FamilySearch (**https:// familysearch.org**) is also actively digitizing and indexing the U.S. naturalization records and adding them to their website. These collections are growing over time, so it is recommended that you check back often.

In any event, inasmuch as naturalization records research can involve searching in multiple facilities and potentially working with both archives *and* court repositories, the NARA facility staff can provide excellent guidance for your research.

Work Immigration, Naturalization, and Census Records in Tandem

You will find it natural to work between the use of the immigration and naturalization records for your ancestors and family members, and U.S. federal census records for many clues. Working backward, you can use the naturalization records to isolate the date of arrival, the port, and the name of the vessel. If your ancestors arrived during the implementation of the Certificate of Arrival (1906–1926), this document can provide a strong piece of evidence for you because the arrival date, place, and ship were researched at the time of naturalization. In addition, if the person had changed his or her name since immigration, the name under which he or she arrived would have had to be provided in order to locate and verify the arrival on a passenger list. With naturalization information in hand, tracing the ship can be greatly simplified. You can then trace to the port of departure to determine if other documents exist. These might contain more information to help you trace your immigrant to the hometown.

Once you have the name of the ship on which your ancestor traveled and the date and port of arrival in the United States, you should be able to locate a digitized image of the ship's passenger list. That will provide you with the port of departure, and that may help you trace the migration path back to the place of origin. Depending on the time period, too, a passenger list may include the name of the place from which your ancestor traveled.

Once you have discovered the ship on which the person traveled and the port of arrival, you can begin to look for other evidence about them in that vicinity. Use the port of arrival as a central point, and seek other documents, including city directories and newspapers. Focus on other relatives or in-laws, both of the immigrant and a spouse, in the place to which they immigrated and check census records, city directories, court records, and other documents in their areas. Your immigrant ancestor may have settled temporarily or for an extended period in that vicinity too. Another strategy for locating the origin of your immigrant ancestor is to identify a relative who may also have immigrated—a parent, sibling, aunt or uncle, and/or cousins—and sidestep your research to one or more of them. It may be easier to locate information about *their* place of origin, and then you may also find your ancestor in that same area.

Using the knowledge you are already developing about genealogical record types and research methodologies, you can incorporate immigration and naturalization documents into your work. You're increasing your knowledge of each individual you study *and* you are constantly expanding the overall story of your family. As you do so, remember to apply your critical thinking skills to locate and evaluate the evidence and formulate reasonable hypotheses.

11

Discover Where to Locate Evidence About Your Family

HOW TO...

- Determine where to look for different documents and evidence
- Use indexes and other finding aids
- Use libraries and archives
- Use an LDS Family History Center
- Consult reference books and other resources
- Deal with closed or limited access to materials
- Order document copies by postal mail, email, and online
- Keep track of your correspondence
- Use a research log
- Set up and use a filing system

The previous chapters addressed the foundations of your genealogical research and discussed a broad selection of record types. By this time, you should have a good idea of what you want to do with your genealogical research and how to approach the records. You now know about a variety of the most common document types and how to use your critical thinking skills to evaluate and assess them.

In this chapter, we will discuss processes you can use to locate the appropriate repositories where documents or exact copies are held, and how to access those materials. We will concentrate on traditional research methods and sources. And while this includes some Internet-based resources, we will focus on electronic materials and research methods in Chapter 12. We will discuss social media and mobile apps in Chapter 15.

Advance preparation is essential for your success in accessing and obtaining documentary evidence, and there are many tools available to you. These include indexes, compilations, and other printed finding aides. Electronic tools include the Internet, online databases, library and archive catalogs, and other products.

You will always want to gain access to the original primary source documents whenever possible and obtain copies for your reference and documentation. Photocopies and reproductions can usually be obtained if you make an on-site visit to a facility. Many original documents (or microfilmed images of them) have been digitized, indexed, and made available online. Some of the places you visit may have digital images of original documents that you can access and save to a flash drive. You also can write letters and email to request copies if you cannot make a trip to the repository, and many online facilities make electronic ordering available. If you are an active researcher, your correspondence may be extensive, and it is not uncommon in such situations to lose track of the status of all of your requests for copies. A correspondence log and a little dedication to maintaining it can provide a process you can use to maintain control and to generate follow-up letters, email messages, and/or telephone calls.

You will visit many research facilities and examine literally hundreds of books, journals, other periodicals, indexes, and documents in the pursuit of your family's genealogical history. As a result, it is easy to forget what you have already examined and, consequently, waste both time and money conducting duplicate research. A research log allows you to keep track of what materials you have already researched and what you did or did not find in those resources. It can also help you avoid purchasing books you may already own.

As you acquire more and more copies of documentary evidence in both paper and digital form, you will need to organize a filing system and regularly file those things. We will discuss that topic at the end of the chapter.

The topics covered in this chapter will provide you with some methodologies for becoming a more efficient and effective researcher. Over time, each strategy will become second nature in your standard research process.

Determine Where to Look for Different Document Types

You began your family history research when you began looking for home sources such as Bibles, letters, diaries and journals, scrapbooks, and copies of original records. Having only one place to search is a lot easier than having to conduct investigations to locate places where you *can* conduct research. Yet that is what we have to do.

We can expect to find particular documents in specific places. For example, we know we can usually find probate files at the courthouse where the probate court conducts its business. In other cases, however, the place where document copies reside may not be where we might at first expect to find them. For example, a birth record might be found at a county health department office, a courthouse, a state or provincial vital records or vital statistics office, or elsewhere. The challenge we face as researchers is not just evaluating the records; it very often involves tracking down the records themselves so that we can perform the analysis.

We already discussed the importance of studying geography and history to place our ancestors into context. However, studying history can be equally as important when trying to locate the documents for our family members. The type of record, the person or organization that generated it, the reason(s) for the document's production, the place it was created, and the time period all contribute to our determining the location.

The place where a document was once stored might not be where it is stored today. The document may have been moved elsewhere, such as to another storage location. This is common when one facility exhausts its storage space or when older documents are needed infrequently for reference. They may be packed up and sent to a warehouse or other off-site storage facility. Some documents created by one governmental entity may have been generated in one place and then sent to a central governmental archive or storage facility. For example, the U.S. government in 1830 requested all states to forward their 1790 to 1820 census schedules to Washington, D.C., to replace the summaries that were destroyed when the British burned the city on 24 August 1814 and to create a central repository for all censuses to that time. The 1830 census documents and those for all subsequent censuses have been sent to Washington, D.C.

In some cases, there have been multiple copies of certain documents produced, possibly as exact duplicates or as supposedly exact transcriptions, and one or more copies forwarded elsewhere for someone else's use. A good example of this would be a death certificate. The original and at least one copy are typically produced. The issuing governmental office retains the original and a copy is forwarded to a central office, such as a state or provincial records bureau. Other copies may have been provided to the undertaker, to the executor or administrator of the estate, to the probate court, to the coroner, and to other persons or organizations. If you know that duplicates were produced and held by different official organizations, and you know when that process began, you can begin planning to obtain a copy of a particular document from one or the other office.

In other cases, documents may have been relocated for safety and preservation purposes. During World War II, for instance, original ecclesiastical parish registers were removed from churches in parts of England and placed at universities' libraries or in other locations in order to prevent their being destroyed during German bombing raids over the country. Many of those parish registers have remained in those archival storage facilities ever since.

A document may have been microfilmed and the original placed in storage or destroyed. This, too, is something you will find to be a common practice, especially in courthouses and other government facilities that have storage problems but still need to refer to those records on a frequent basis.

Some of the documents that were microfilmed may have been digitized in recent years, and others that were never microfilmed may also have been scanned. You've already seen that billions of digital records have been added to online sites. However, it is essential that you recognize that not everything has been digitized and made available online. For that reason, traditional research skills are essential to your success because you will need them in order to find the original records and other resources that have not been made available electronically.

Use Indexes and Other Finding Aids

There are many published materials to help you with your search. Some are available through traditional publishers and commercial companies, while genealogical or historical societies and individuals publish others. Libraries and archives also create "pathfinders," short informational reference documents (in print or on their websites) to help patrons understand specific holdings in the collection and how to use them. Other indexes and finding/reference aids are published in the form of databases and/ or on the Internet. Let's explore some examples of these resources.

Use Indexes

An *index* for genealogical purposes can be defined as an ordered listing of people, places, topics, or other data that includes references allowing the user to quickly locate specific information. The format of the listing is dependent on the data being indexed; the content of the index will vary depending on how finitely the data will be index-searchable. We're all familiar with the index found in the back of a book. This book's index is arranged alphabetically by subject, type of document, and so on, with page number references that point you to specific information. There are at least four major categories of indexes that will be of interest to every genealogist. Let's briefly discuss each of these.

Indexes in Courthouses and Government Facilities

We've discussed a number of types of records that you will find in courthouses. This includes: marriage and divorce records; wills and probate packets; judicial records of all sorts; jury lists; voter registration records; land and property records, including deed indexes, property maps, taxation maps, surveys, public auctions, and others; guardianship records; poorhouse records; lunacy records; and many more. Depending on the location you are researching and the time period, the responsibilities of the government in that locality will determine what records were created at the time. As boundaries and jurisdictions changed, the records usually remained in the possession of the original governmental entity. Some of the records may have been physically transferred to (or copies or indexes made for) the new jurisdictional entity, depending on the record type and the need for the new office to have immediate access to the documents.

Most courthouse records are organized and filed in some manner, and indexes have been prepared to facilitate the clerks' ability to quickly locate and access the records in their possession. An index is typically prepared at a later date than the original entries are made. You will encounter both handwritten and typed indexes, and these indexes may have been computerized at some later date. Marriage records are usually indexed twice: once in an alphabetical list of grooms' names and again in an alphabetical list of brides' names. Both are created in *surname sequence*, and then in forename or given name order. These indexes reference the document in the government-held records so that it can be easily found. Women's surnames in these indexes are entered as they were listed on the original marriage record, using the maiden surname for a single woman or the surname from a previous marriage for a divorced or widowed woman. Also, don't be surprised to find a previously married woman's maiden name sometimes listed in the bride index. That means that you should always check for *both* possible surname entries for the bride if you know them. Land and property entries also are typically indexed in two ways, once in grantor sequence and once in grantee sequence. The indexes you find in courthouses and other governmental facilities will point you to specific places where you will find the material you want to use. Figure 11-1 shows the detail of a grantor index. If you were searching for evidence of the transfer of property from Jno. W. Burroughs to Harriet C. Berrien, for example, investigation into the grantor index would indicate the transaction was filed on 16 December 1882 and that the detail can be found in an entry on page 946 of Deed Book N.

There are two good books written by Christine Rose concerning U.S. courthouse research and using indexes there: *Courthouse Research for Family Historians: Your Guide to Genealogical Treasures* (CR Publications, 2004) and *Courthouse Indexes Illustrated* (CR Publications, 2006).

Indexes in Libraries, Archives, and Other Research Facilities

Libraries and archives are veritable gold mines for your research. The most common items you will use in these research facilities are the printed books, journals, periodicals, and electronic databases to which they may provide access. Be sure to check online for pathfinders that describe their holdings in detail, or look for printed

GRANTORS				GRANTEES	KIND OF INSTRUMENT	Date of Filing			Where Recorded	
FAMILY NAMES	ABCDEFGH	IJKLMNO	PQRSTUVWXYZ			Mo.	Day	Year	Book	Page
Burge,		Louisa C.		Williams, M. D.					M	384
Buffington,			T. A.	Darby, Thos. A.					M	514
Butler,	Geo. A.			Thomas, Joseph					M	941
Burt,		James		Calhoun, Wm. L.					M	958
Buffington,			T. A.	Darby, T. A.	W D	June	25	1881	M	514
Burke,		M. A.		Tucker, Mamie W.	W D	Feb	17	1882	N	72
Bunker,		L. V.		Tison, W. O.	W D	July	19	1882	N	568
Bush,	Eliza J			Sikes, W. W.	W D	Sept	6	1882	N	692
Burroughs,		Jno. W.		Carroll, Eliza A/	W D	Oct	7	1882	N	784
Burroughs,		Jno. W.		Bevill, Francis B.	W D	Oct	9	1882	N	787
Burroughs,		Jno. W.		Berrien, Harriet C.	W D	Dec	16	1882	N	946
Burge,		L. C. extx		Mc Ewen, Chas A.	W D	Feb	21	1883	O	124

FIGURE 11-1   Detail of a grantor index to deed entries

pathfinders when you arrive at a facility. There are thousands of indexes that have been published to many original records. Let me provide a few examples for you, along with bibliographic citations.

Census Indexes

Gibson, Jeremy and Mervyn Medlycott. *Local Census Listings: 1522–1930: Holdings in the British Isles.* 3rd ed. Baltimore, MD: Genealogical Publishing Co., 1997.

Register, Alvaretta Kenan. *Index to the 1830 Census of Georgia.* Baltimore, MD: Clearfield Co., Reprint, 2010.

Immigration Lists

Glazier, Ira A., ed. *Germans to America (Series II): Lists of Passengers Arriving at U.S. Ports in the 1840s.* 7 vols. to date. Wilmington, DE: Scholarly Resources, 2002–to date.

Glazier, Ira A. and P. William Filby, eds. *Germans to America: Lists of Passengers Arriving at U.S. Ports 1850-1897.* 67 vols. Wilmington, DE: Scholarly Resources, 1988–2001.

Land and Property Records Indexes

Hughes, B. H. J. *Jottings and Historical Records with Index on the History of South Pembrokeshire: Manorial Accounts*, 1324–33. Pembroke Dock, Wales: Pennar Publications. 1996.

Shuck, Larry G. *Greenbrier County, (West) Virginia, Records.* 8 vols. Athens, GA: Iberian Publishing Co., 1988–1994.

Wills and Probate Records Indexes

Johnston, Ross B. *West Virginia Estate Settlements: An Index to Wills, Inventories, Appraisements, Land Grants, and Surveys to 1850.* Baltimore, MD: Genealogical Publishing Co., 2010.

Webb, Cliff, comp. *An Index of Wills Proved in the Archdeaconry Court of London, 1700–1807.* London, UK: Society of Genealogists, 1996.

As you can see, there are published indexes for many types of records from around the world. The preceding examples represent only a tiny fraction of the record types that have been indexed in printed form. (Note that some of these books are out of print but are still available in libraries for reference.)

Use Other Finding Aids

The term *finding aid* shouldn't confuse you. It simply refers to any resource you can use to further your genealogical search, and includes tools such as the following:

- Maps
- Gazetteers (or place name dictionaries)
- Surname dictionaries by national, ethnic, or religious group
- Dictionaries of contemporary and archaic terminology

- Dictionaries of abbreviations and acronyms of different areas and time periods
- Language translation dictionaries
- Dictionaries of old medical terminology
- Histories of geographic areas, towns and communities, different population groups, and cultural histories
- Reference works to instruct reading old handwriting (paleography)
- Genealogy references, "how-to" books, and guides to working with record types
- Compilations of Internet sites related to genealogy
- Online indexes and databases

Anything that you can use to gain insight into your ancestral search and access quality source materials/evidence can be considered a valid finding aid. Look around you, and use your knowledge and imagination to identify materials that may help you.

Use Libraries and Archives

Libraries, archives, and their staff are among the very best resources you can have. I consider a good librarian to be a "personal information broker." While you can't expect every librarian to know everything about genealogical research and records, you can always rely on a librarian's willingness to help you and his or her ability to conduct quality research on almost any topic. A well-trained librarian or archivist understands research methods and resources of many types, and knows how to locate and access information. We refer to that as "information literacy." Furthermore, he or she is always willing to share his or her skills with you if you are willing to invest the time to listen and learn.

The facilities that libraries and archives provide to their users, or patrons, vary significantly depending on the content of their collection, their service population, and their stated mission. Special collections such as genealogy and local history materials usually are not circulated but are, instead, reserved for use in the facility. There are ways, however, to gain access to the materials without physically visiting the facility, and we'll discuss those shortly.

Learn How to Use the Library Catalog

It has not been too many years ago that libraries and archives had no computers. The primary finding aid for a facility's holdings was a card catalog. There were card catalog cabinets located in a central area and filled with small paperboard cards, all hand-typed and filed in alphabetical sequence by author, title, and subject. Each item in the collection for which there was a card also was coded with a reference code using the classification system employed by that library. Items were shelved or filed using this organizational scheme.

Public libraries in North America and the United Kingdom typically use the Dewey Decimal Classification system, while most North American academic libraries use the Library of Congress Classification system. Academic libraries in the United Kingdom may use a combination of systems. Other archives and repositories may use another system based on the types of holdings in their collections, including one of their own devising that fits the unique needs for organizing and accessing their types of special collection materials. It is to your advantage to learn a little about the Dewey Decimal and Library of Congress systems. Understanding these systems helps you understand how any library is physically organized, and you can then quickly and effectively locate and access materials in their collections. You can learn about the Dewey Decimal Classification system and its contents at the Online Computer Library Center (OCLC) website at **http://www.oclc.org/dewey/resources/summaries/default.htm**, and about the Library of Congress Classification scheme at **http://www.loc.gov/catdir/cpso/lcco**.

Some libraries have adapted the Dewey Decimal Classification system in their genealogical collections, using what some refer to as the "modified Dewey system." This organizational scheme regroups some materials, especially geographical books and journals, into a single area. The reference codes, or call numbers, are changed so that these materials are shelved or filed together.

Some things in libraries and archives have changed over time while others have remained static. Computers have changed information storage and retrieval expectations, and libraries and archives well understood the importance of changing over their printed and typed card catalogs to computerized systems. Standardized online catalog computer programs were developed and have been implemented in most libraries.

Online catalog software can be and has been integrated into libraries' websites, and multimedia capabilities have been added. It now is not unusual for a library to have incorporated graphic and sound files of their holdings into their online catalogs, complete with links to directly access digitized versions of those materials. Helpful pathfinder information is often linked to specific areas of the collection or individual items in the catalog.

Throughout this evolution, the principles of organization, cataloging, and standardizing catalog entries for resources have been maintained and expanded. There are standards in place within the library industry to utilize technology to its maximum, integrate as many materials as possible into the online systems, and provide excellence in customer access and customer service.

Start with What Has Already Been Done

Many of us conduct a substantial amount of our genealogical research, or pre-research, from the comfort of our homes. Perhaps you find yourself sitting in front of the computer, searching on the Internet for records concerning your ancestors. Perhaps it is three o'clock in the morning; you're there in your pajamas, sipping a glass of milk, and munching on chocolate chip cookies. What a life!

Fortunately for us, the Internet and the online catalogs of libraries and archives are accessible 24 hours a day, 7 days a week, and 365 days a year. If you are conversant with the use of the catalog, you can make a tremendous amount of headway with your research into the available resources without assistance.

For a genealogist, one of the first steps in doing research is to locate any published family histories and/or local histories that may contain information about ancestors and other family members. Family histories and many local histories are not usually the type of books that you're likely to find in your neighborhood bookstore, or even in some online bookstores. Instead, to locate such books, you'll have to visit a library, or remotely look in their online catalogs. The next step is to locate the indexes and other finding aids that help you find the resources you want or need. Fortunately, the Web has made that process easier.

If you don't know which library or libraries have a copy of a particular book, contact your reference librarian in your local library and ask for help. You can also search a free online database called WorldCat at **http://www.worldcat.org**. Figure 11-2 shows the main page at WorldCat. You can search for books, DVDs, CDs, and articles, and the search results will provide you with the locations of facilities that hold a copy. I recommend that you create a free ID and password for WorldCat and sign in. When you conduct a search, you can enter your home location (name or postal code) and WorldCat will sort the list of libraries for you from nearest to farthest. Using this feature, you can find libraries nearby that you can visit to locate the availability of the item you want, or you can check its availability near to a place you might be visiting.

Once you have the information on a specific book, a sample of whose record from the John F. Germany Public Library in the Hillsborough County Public Library Cooperative (**http://www.hcplc.org**) based in Tampa, Florida, is shown in Figure 11-3, you have all you need to visit the library and locate the book.

If you are unable to visit the library, there is another option open to you: interlibrary loan, also referred to as ILL in the United States and Canada. (In the United Kingdom, this is often spelled as Inter-Library Loan.) ILL is a service that allows patrons of one library to request the loan of a book from its owning library to their own. However, since most genealogy and local history collection materials are non-circulating reference materials, it is unlikely that you can actually have your library borrow the book. But all is not lost! ILL can be used to request that *photocopies*

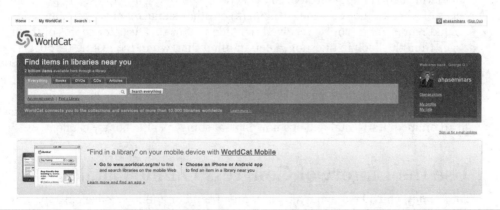

FIGURE 11-2   The main page at WorldCat

FIGURE 11-3 The catalog record at the Hillsborough County Public Library Cooperative shows the book, *Advanced Genealogy Research Techniques*, at the John F. Germany Public Library.

or digital scans be made of certain pages and sent to you or to your library for pickup or emailing. You will probably want to make two ILL requests for copies from a non-circulating book inner genealogical collection. The first will request a copy of the pages of a book's index for the surname(s) or other subject you are seeking, and a second request after you've received the index pages that asks for copies of the text pages from the book in question. Keep in mind that, when requesting text pages, you might want to request one two additional pages *before and after* the pages shown in an index. This helps alleviate the problem that arises when meaningful descriptive text begins on a previous page or continues onto a subsequent page.

As you can see, there is tremendous value to having performed advance research in an online library catalog. Let's now look at some specific library catalogs.

Use the Library of Congress Online Catalog

Sometimes, you'll hear about a book from a friend or a fellow genealogist, or you may see it referred to in some publication. Unfortunately, you may find that you are missing either the author's name or the title of the book, or that one of those is incorrect or incomplete. Your first step should be to pin down the exact title of the book and the full name of the author. This will make later searching much easier and more productive.

The online catalog of the Library of Congress (LC) at **http://catalog.loc.gov** is often a good place to begin searching for unusual materials for which you don't necessarily have all of the information you need. The LC does not lend (or circulate) their materials classified as genealogy or local history. Unless you are planning a trip to Washington, D.C., in the near future, the primary purpose of your use of the LC online catalog is to obtain information about the book so that you can then look for it in a closer library. Remember, you can identify a book at the LC and then use WorldCat to locate the nearest library with a copy of the book.

Use the FamilySearch Catalog and the LDS Family History Centers

The largest collection of genealogy manuscripts, printed materials, and microfilm in the world is undoubtedly at the Family History Library (FHL) in Salt Lake City, operated by the Church of Jesus Christ of Latter-day Saints. The FHL has microfilmed many family and local histories and, for a small rental fee, lends the film from the FHL through its system of local Family History Centers (FHCs) throughout the world. In order to identify what books the FHL has, visit the FamilySearch website at **https://familysearch.org**. Once there, click on the Search option and, on the dropdown list, select Catalog. The "Search by" options allow you to search on titles or author, just like the LC online catalog. The FHL catalog also makes the following search options available:

- **Places** allows you to search for items in the FHL holdings that have been cataloged to include names of places.
- **Surnames** allows you to search for materials related to specific surnames.
- **Call Number** allows you to locate the catalog record for a specific book or other print item if you know the number.
- **Film/Fiche Number** allows you to locate the catalog record for a specific reel of microfilm or sheet of microfiche if you know the number.
- **Subjects** and **Keywords** are similar to the same search options in other library and archives catalogs.

In addition to the catalog search, the FamilySearch site includes another link at the top of the search template labeled Books. Click that link and you will be presented with another page titled Family History Books (**https://books.familysearch.org/ primo_library/libweb/action/search.do?vid = FHD_PUBLIC**). Here you will find links to online book collections at major genealogical libraries with significant digitized book collections. There are more than 150,000 digitized genealogy and family history publications catalogued among these facilities at the time of this writing.

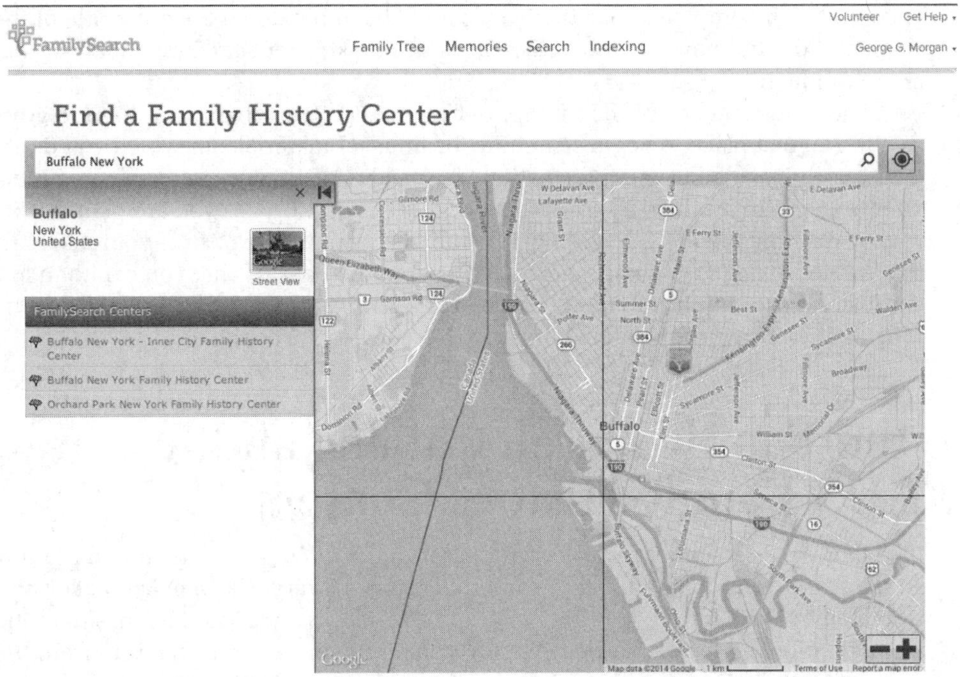

FIGURE 11-4 The FamilySearch website page showing results for a search of a FamilySearch Center in the Buffalo, New York, vicinity

If you do not know the location of the nearest FHC to you, there is a "Find a center" link at the bottom of the main FamilySearch web page. Enter a place name or postal code in the search box shown on the next page. A satellite map will be displayed with tree icons of each FHC. Zoom in or out on the map as needed. A list of links to nearby FHCs will be displayed. Click the link for an address. Figure 11-4 shows an example of a search for FHCs in the Buffalo, New York, area. The people who work at the FHC can help you learn how to use their physical materials, how to request the loan of microfilm from the FHL in Salt Lake City, and how to use the LDS databases and commercial databases to which they have access.

Consult Reference Books and Other Resources

Some of the best resources at your disposal are reference books that focus on different record types and the locations of those records. Among my personal favorites for general reference are the following titles:

- *The Family Tree Sourcebook: Your Essential Directory of American County and Town Records*, produced by the editors of *Family Tree Magazine* (Family Tree Books, 2010), provides a state-by-state reference. Historical background about the formation of each state is provided, along with descriptions of all major record types, when they began being created, and where they reside. For each state, there is a county boundary map and a table showing each county, its contact information, details about its formation, and the years when each of the following record types began being created: birth, marriage, death, land, probate, and court. (This book can be used instead of both Ancestry Publishing's *Red Book* and Everton Publishing's *The Handybook for Genealogists*, both of whose publishers have discontinued publication.)

- *French-Canadian Sources: A Guide for Genealogists*, by Patricia Keeney Geyh et al. (Ancestry Publishing, 2002), is a compilation of scholarly chapters written by experts in French-Canadian research. The book covers the entire history of the French in Canada from establishment in 1605 of Port Royal in what is now Nova Scotia, and it details the many types of records created over the centuries by the French, English, and Canadian governments. Among the elegant appendixes are: a collection of French vocabulary words and phrases you are likely to encounter; charts and descriptions of Canadian census records and substitutes; and an extensive compilation of French-Canadian research addresses.

- *Ancestral Trails: The Complete Guide to British Genealogy and Family History*, Second Edition, by Mark D. Herber (Genealogical Publishing Co., 2006), is the most extensive guide to tracing your British heritage at this writing, presented in an orderly fashion and in easily understandable language. It provides clear descriptions of all major records and many obscure records, and will help you understand the church and governmental structures employed over the centuries in creating and maintaining the records.

- *Tracing Your Irish Ancestors: The Complete Guide*, Third Edition, by John Grenham (Genealogical Publishing Co., 2012), provides an excellent primer on how to begin your ancestral quest, and examines the major sources such as civil records, censuses, church records, land and property documentation, wills, emigration papers, deeds, registry sources, newspapers, and directories. A complete table of Roman Catholic parish registers' reference information is included, as are detailed materials about available research services, genealogical and historical societies, and contact information for an array of libraries and record repositories.

- *Tracing Your Scottish Ancestors: A Guide for Family Historians*, Second Edition, by Ian Maxwell (Pen & Sword, 2014), is an excellent guide for Americans tracing Scottish immigrant ancestors. The book covers every aspect of Scottish history and all the relevant resources. In addition to covering the records held at the National Records of Scotland (NRS) (formerly the General Register Office for Scotland and the National Archives of Scotland), the author examines information held at local archives throughout the country. He also describes the extensive Scottish records that are now available online.

The preceding books form a strong core of reference works for your use. You may decide to purchase some of these as components of your personal genealogical reference collection. Your local public library also may own a copy of each of these books in its own collection. However, if not, you certainly can recommend acquisition to the person responsible for the library's collection development. Don't overlook asking your library about the availability of electronic books (eBooks) in its collection or its online access.

Locate the Repository on the Internet

Web pages typically provide the most current information about a facility or document repository you might want to access. Just as libraries and archives maintain a Web presence, usually with an embedded online catalog, government agencies, companies, organizations, societies, and other entities create and maintain websites. If you know the web address of the facility, you can quickly access their site and check on their holdings. If you don't know the address, you can use your favorite Internet search engine to locate the site. For example, I decided I wanted to locate information about local government offices in the area near the town of Chelmsford, located northeast of London in the United Kingdom. I entered the following in the Google search engine:

chelmsford government

I was rewarded with search results that included a number of links, including those for Chelmsford, Massachusetts. However, I accessed a direct link to the Chelmsford Borough Council's site at **http://www.chelmsford.gov.uk**. Another search result was that of the LocalLife site for Chelmsford at **http://www.locallife.co.uk/chelmsford/governmentoff3.asp**, which included links to government offices' sites. Knowing that Chelmsford is located in Essex, I used my browser and searched for the words **essex government uk**. The first item in the search results list was the Essex County Council website at **http://www.essex.gov.uk**.

Researchers seeking information about vital records in the United States and its territories will want to visit the website at **http://www.vitalrec.com**. Instructions for locating and obtaining copies of birth, marriage, death, and divorce records (and sometimes others) and prices are provided.

Contact the Repository

While we hope that the "official" websites of government agencies and other entities are maintained with up-to-date information, the truth is that a vast number of websites are sometimes less than current. The old adage of "phone first" certainly applies here, especially before making a visit.

Another complication that occurs is when the facility withdraws the materials temporarily because of scanning/digitization, repair, remodeling, or other maintenance. By contacting the repository in advance, you can learn if the materials you want to access will, in fact, be available when you visit or if you request copies from them by telephone, mail, or email.

You will frequently find that some materials of genealogical interest may not have been cataloged. You have already learned about catalog records in this chapter and can understand the effort required to create a single catalog database record. Imagine, then, the loose documents, correspondence, maps, folders, and other materials that may be a part of a library or archive's holdings. It is expensive and labor-intensive to catalog each and every item. Sometimes there may be a single catalog entry to reference a *group* of related materials, such as the correspondence files of a local historian. In many archives, you may find that the collected papers of an individual or family have been stored in one or more files or boxes. The catalog record may refer to the number of boxes or linear shelf feet occupied by the boxes. The record may also include only references to key contents, such as surnames, the names of heads of household, or other predominant information. In other cases, there may be no catalog record at all. For these and other reasons, it is important that you *always* ask the question of a reference professional at the library or archive, "Are there any materials of genealogical or local historical significance in your collection that have not been cataloged?" More often than not, the answer will be in the affirmative. It's then time to form a strong bond with this reference person to learn what is available, the content and scope of those holdings, and how to access the materials. There may be materials stored in vertical files (file cabinets) or in individual family or newspaper clipping files.

Making individual contact with the repository in advance of a visit also allows you to confirm the location, travel directions, hours of operation, costs of printed copies of materials, availability of scanners, and policies for security, access, use of the materials, and use of personal digital cameras and portable scanners. Obtaining that information in advance helps you plan your research visit and your time there more efficiently.

In addition, if you believe there are specific materials that you want to use, you can confirm that they will be available. If you find that they are unavailable, you may be able to adjust your schedule or your research plan. If you find out that the materials you are seeking have been relocated elsewhere, you can then pursue details about where the records are located and how to gain access to them at the new location.

Seek Help from a State, Provincial, or National Library or Archive

The personnel at a local repository may be unable to tell you about specific materials of genealogical importance. The individual may not have the knowledge or training to help you, or may just be overwhelmed with his or her duties and unable to give that little extra something to help you make your connection with the materials you want. Don't overlook the use of the expert professionals who staff libraries and archives that have a broader focus than local ones. Their collections are most often substantially larger than those of local libraries or county governments and they usually have received more intensive training than their local counterparts, so they may have a broader perspective of documents, records, books, journals, microfilm, and digitized materials.

When I have been unable to locate specific geographical locations on maps of a particular state, I have called on the state library or state archive for assistance. Their collections of historical maps, gazetteers, and other reference materials are extensive and the staff members are well trained in effectively using these resources. In addition, I have used the telephone and email reference services of academic libraries, the National Archives and Records Administration (NARA), the Library of Congress, the U.S. Geological Survey, and other types of facilities to obtain answers to questions and to locate materials either that were difficult to find or that had been relocated.

Contact Genealogical and Historical Societies at All Levels

Genealogical and historical societies are among your best resources. They are actively involved with the study of history, culture, society, and documentation in their respective areas. Their focus is on research and, in many cases, preservation of information, documentation, and artifacts. Think of these societies as "networks" of individuals with knowledge and experience in the materials in their area. If you contact one person who does not have an answer to your question, he or she usually knows where to look or who to put you in contact with to help you. It is possible that a society may have acquired records, photographs, or artifacts that have not been accessible to researchers before. The society may be indexing or cataloging records or preparing indexes in preparation perhaps for publishing them or donating them to a library or archive. They also may be involved with collecting and organizing information that is not yet available in any other way. Many societies are involved in digitizing documents and collections.

There are two excellent examples in Florida that immediately come to mind. One is a genealogical society's ongoing project of indexing articles concerning individuals who lived in or passed through their county in the territorial period prior to Florida statehood in March 1845. The other is an ongoing project by one county's genealogical society to canvass and document every gravestone in every cemetery in the county, and to publish indexes for all of those cemeteries. The Florida State Genealogical Society hosts announcements and status reports of ongoing genealogical projects of this type on its Florida Projects Registry at **http://www.flsgs.org/cpage.php?pt = 49**. The products of the work by both of the societies mentioned may be unique and found nowhere else.

It also is not unusual for these societies' members to respond to your problem by jumping in to help you with the research. They may look up records for you, make copies, scan documents, take photographs, or provide assistance in other ways.

Engage a Professional Researcher

Finally, if you are seeking records that you believe should exist somewhere but have been otherwise unable to locate them, you may want to engage the services of a professional genealogical researcher. You will want a person who has the experience and credentials to conduct a scholarly research effort for you, and provide status reports and a final report with copies and fully documented source citations as the final project deliverable. There are a number of organizations that test and accredit professional researchers, and other membership organizations that promote standards of professional ethics. Some of these are listed here:

- Board for Certification of Genealogists (BCG)
  http://www.bcgcertification.org
- International Commission for the Accreditation of Professional Genealogists (ICAPGen)
  http://www.icapgen.org
- Accredited genealogists who became accredited through The Church of Jesus Christ of Latter-day Saints Family History Department prior to October 2000
- Association of Professional Genealogists (APG)
  http://www.apgen.org
- Association of Professional Genealogists in Ireland (APGI)
  http://www.apgi.ie
- Society of Australian Genealogists
  http://www.sag.org.au

Deal with Closed or Limited Access to Materials

Some records are not accessible to the public, or access may be restricted. Since the terrorist attacks in the United States on 11 September 2001, many legislators and government agencies around the world have taken steps to prevent or limit access to information and records that they believe might be used to falsify an identity or to otherwise engage in illegal activities. As a result, a number of official documents previously available for research may now be off-limits or require verification or certification of your identity in order to use them. Vital records or civil registration records, including birth certificates, are highly protected because of their use in obtaining identity cards, driver's licenses, passports, and other official documents. The U.S. Social Security Death Index (SSDI) described earlier in the book was a subject of Congressional legislation in 2013 that limited publication of an individual's death for three years from the date of the event. In other places, such as the State of Florida, the cause of death is redacted from copies of death certificates ordered from its Department of Health/Office of Vital Statistics.

Some government documents are completely closed to the public and may never be opened, regardless of anything you might do. For example, in many cases adoption records cannot be accessed by anyone, even by the adoptee or the adoptive parents, without a court order or the intervention of a judge or magistrate. Other restricted documents may include court-ordered, sealed files concerning some divorce settlements, civil lawsuit settlements, coroners' reports, inquests, and trust documents.

Private companies and organizations also are unwilling to release any information about their clients, employees, or members for whatever reason. Some may divulge information and provide copies of records to persons who are immediate relations of an individual and who can provide official documentary proof; however, many will refuse inquiries and requests unconditionally. As private entities, they have the right to hold information confidential and there is little you can do to circumvent their position. Some funeral homes and private cemeteries have also adopted similar positions.

Religious institutions also may choose to maintain the privacy of their records and those of their members, even former members who have been deceased for many years.

These brick walls can certainly seem like insurmountable problems. There are, however, several methods you may take to help gain access to otherwise restricted or closed records. Let's explore a few of these approaches.

Be Prepared to Provide Proof of Your Relationship

You will almost always be asked to explain the reason for requesting someone else's information, even though that person may have been deceased for some time—even decades or centuries. Your best response will be that you are researching your family and that you can provide proof of your relationship to the individual whose records you are requesting. As an effective genealogist, you will already have traced your family backward from yourself and will have collected documentation concerning your lineage. It is important to be able to present your identification credentials wherever you go but, if your surname is different from that of the person you are researching, you may have to present some additional proof. Be prepared by carrying a copy of a pedigree chart with you, along with copies of birth certificates, marriage licenses, death certificates, obituaries, and any other documentation for other relatives that will prove your relationship. The fact that you *are* prepared to prove your relationship speaks volumes to the people from whom you make these requests. They are usually so impressed by your preparation, your openness, and the evidence that you present that they may open access to otherwise closed or restricted materials.

Offer to Pay All the Expenses

Demonstrate your seriousness about the subject by offering to pay for the expenses associated with making copies or scanning images, mailing or emailing them to you, and whatever else might be required. Be sure that the person you are dealing with knows this from the beginning. If you are working with a religious institution or a nonprofit organization, such as a genealogical or historical society, offer to make a financial donation as a gesture of your appreciation and to help offset the person's time and effort.

Provide Letters of Authorization or Permission to Access

Your relationship to the individual you are researching may not be a direct one. This is common for professional researchers who might work on another person's behalf. Perhaps you are searching for records for your grandfather's brother's children. Since you are not a direct relative or descendent, you may be challenged and possibly blocked from access to some or all records. This can sometimes be resolved by providing a letter of authorization or affidavit from a descendant or other direct blood relative. The letter or affidavit should be signed, dated, and notarized by a registered notary public. It can also help to be able to prove your relationship to the family in the same way described previously, only this time you should be able to show your ancestral connection to this collateral family line.

Invoke the Use of the Freedom of Information Act

In the United States, the Freedom of Information Act (FOIA) requires government agencies to disclose records requested in writing by any person. Certainly there are some restrictions that relate to national security, and certain privacy laws pertaining to living individuals may apply. However, it is important to recognize that you can invoke the FOIA in certain circumstances to overcome artificial obstacles and refusals.

The Office of Information Policy (OIP) of the U.S. Department of Justice (DOJ) maintains at its website quite a bit of information that specifically addresses FOIA issues. You can visit that site at **http://www.usdoj.gov/oip**. Consult their DOJ FOIA references for specific details concerning what can and cannot be accessed and the procedures for making your request. The U.S. Department of State's FOIA web page at **http://foia .state.gov** provides an extensive overview and additional FOIA reference materials.

Different countries' governments will also have legislation that regulates access to information. It is wise to research these laws in each location in advance of making information requests so that you will understand and can satisfy their requirements.

Obtain a Court Order

Some documents are closed or restricted to the public by governments, organizations, and individuals. One effective approach is to apply to a court of law in that jurisdiction for a court order to open records or to provide copies of specific items. You must be prepared to present a convincing argument of your need to access the materials and to provide proof of your relationship to an individual or your authorized representation of an individual. One of the most persuasive arguments presented in contemporary court hearings of this sort is the necessity of medical information. The need to identify blood type, genetic predisposition to a disease or medical condition, or similar reason can often be an effective argument for the issuance of a court order. You may or may not require a legal representative's help in preparing and presenting your request to the court. The use of a legal professional can be expensive, but the cost may be justified if this is your only opportunity to obtain particular information.

Order Document Copies by Postal Mail, Email, and Online

Letter writing has become something of a lost art, and people tend to forget the importance of using effective correspondence to get results. Younger genealogists also may not know what informational components are required in order to get the best results, and some older genealogists may not be using modern technology to achieve success.

It isn't always convenient or cost-effective to make a visit to a particular place to obtain copies of documents you want or need for your research. Therefore, you will do what genealogists have done for decades: write letters and/or complete forms to obtain copies of documents. The difference between the way we handle this now and the way we handled it years ago is that email is available in addition to traditional postal mail. Furthermore, many websites include electronic ordering facilities that use fill-in-the-blank forms. Email is so fast that the slower postal mail has acquired the nickname of "snail-mail." Online ordering also streamlines the process of obtaining materials. Many government offices, libraries, archives, and other repositories have embraced electronic ordering online to facilitate and automate the process.

Your first step, as always, is to determine the correct place to inquire about the records you want to obtain. You certainly can use the Internet and a search engine to locate the website of a particular facility. For example, if you were looking for the contact information for Augusta County, Virginia, governmental offices, you might enter the following into your favorite search engine:

"augusta county" virginia government

The search results list includes the county government's website at **http://www .co.augusta.va.us**. From that page, you could navigate to other pages containing the addresses and telephone numbers of the Circuit and District Courts. You could then write a letter to the clerk of the appropriate court and mail it, along with a self-addressed, stamped envelope (SASE). This is a professional gesture that encourages a response. You may instead send an email or place a telephone call.

You also can obtain copies of required document request forms from some archives and libraries. NARA requires you to use their preprinted, multipart forms to request searches for and order copies of specific records, or use their online ordering facilities. You can obtain these forms by visiting NARA's website at **http://www .archives.gov**, clicking the Research Our Records link, and then clicking the Order Copies of Records link, which takes you to the Obtaining Copies of Records page (**http://www.archives.gov/research/order**). There you will find all the information you need to order copies of many of the records in NARA's possession. Don't forget, though, that many of their older records have been digitized and indexed at Ancestry .com (**http://www.ancestry.com**), Fold3 (**http://www.fold3.com**), and other websites.

When generating a request by mail to any person, organization, or institution requesting anything, use the standard business letter format. Include your complete return address and the date of your letter. The heading should include the name and complete address for the entity to whom you are writing. If you have the name of a specific contact individual, include that name, preceded with the title (Mr., Ms., Mrs., etc.), in the header. See the two examples here:

Alamance County Offices
Attn.: Department of Vital Records
124 W. Elm Street
Graham, NC 27253

The Honorable David Barber
Alamance County Clerk of Court
Alamance County Courthouse
124 W. Elm Street
Graham, NC 27253

Next comes the salutation, followed by a colon. Use the person's name and title, if you know it. If you don't know the name, use the title or a generic salutation. Look at the following examples:

Dear Mr. Barber:
Dear Clerk of Court:
Gentlemen and Ladies:
To whom it may concern:

The body of the letter must clearly communicate what you are seeking. Include the full name of the person whose record you want to obtain. Include any nickname and, for women, the maiden name, and define these alternative names as what they are. Here is the text from the body of a letter that I wrote concerning my parents' marriage record:

I am seeking a copy of the marriage record for my parents who were married on 24 January 1933 in Mebane, Alamance County, North Carolina. Their names and information are as follows:

Groom: Samuel Thomas Morgan (born 18 December 1909)
Bride: Sara Edith Weatherly (born 10 July 1911)

Both parties were residents of Alamance County. I have tried to provide as much information as possible above. I hope it will be enough for you to locate this record for me. Please advise me of the cost of locating and providing me with copies of these records. I will send a check immediately or provide credit card information, whichever you prefer. I am enclosing a SASE for your reply or you can contact me via email at george@george.com or by telephone at (813) 555-1212.

If you do not have these records, please advise me if they have been transferred to another location, the state archive, to a library, or other facility so that I may continue my search there.

Thank you in advance for your invaluable help with my family quest.

You will notice that I included a paragraph asking that, if the records are no longer in that facility, the person should let me know where the records may have been sent or transferred. Many clerks are overwhelmed with work and, if you don't ask the question, they may not automatically supply you with that invaluable information.

The signature block of your letter should include a complimentary closing such as "Yours" or "Sincerely." Include your full name and, if you wish, your title (Mr., Mrs., Ms.) and any professional or educational credential abbreviations that are appropriate (MD, PhD, etc.). Sign your full name.

Address your mailing envelope clearly so that it matches the header block of your letter, and be certain to include your return address. Enclose a clearly addressed SASE with ample postage to encourage a reply.

Another way to streamline the letter-writing process is to create a template in your word processor and save it. This can reduce the amount of typing you have to do. You might consider creating a separate letter template document for use in requesting marriage records, one for death certificates, another for wills and probate records, and yet another for land and property records. Each template will have the specific verbiage you need to specify and obtain copies. You also might consider a mail merge document in your word processor, which is one in which you can define specific fields of the letter and code them in such a way that you simply enter data into one document and then cause it to be merged into the template, creating multiple documents. Check the Help facility of your word processor program for detailed instructions for how to create document templates for these letters and/or mail merge documents. You actually could create multiple mail merge documents. Use the data entry document as the single place you type in information, and then allow it to produce the letters and produce a sheet of mailing labels for envelopes. You also can create a number of self-addressed envelopes at one time and then you only need to add adequate postage and enclose your letters in them. It really is simple to automate the process. It requires a little time investment in the beginning to set everything up. However, after that, the letter-writing process itself can be very simple.

Keep Track of Your Correspondence

My genealogy correspondence used to be a terrible mess. I would write letters to courthouses for copies of documents, send off forms to obtain copies from NARA, and fire off email messages to other researchers. I was so busy sending things out that I wasn't really sure what I had done and what I had not. I ended up duplicating my efforts, and never followed up on anything because I didn't keep track of it. It is particularly embarrassing when you send the same request two or three times to the same person, and it gets expensive sending money multiple times to the same courthouse or archives and receiving the same documents more than once. Yes, it *can* happen to you!

The simple solution is to maintain a correspondence log and get into the habit of entering information about all of your correspondence, including both postal mail and email. The correspondence log is merely a formatted record of what you have written to someone else about, when you wrote it, when you received a response, and what results you obtained.

Some people choose to maintain a record of their correspondence at the surname level and, by doing so, have only one place to check for every letter or email sent and received for an entire family. I know other people who maintain a control log based on geography, or even surname and geography, to get a little more granular. There are a number of options for setting up and maintaining a correspondence log. You will have to choose the format and organizational scheme that works best for you based on the people you are researching.

You have a number of options in terms of format. Ancestry.com provides a free downloadable Correspondence Record form at **http://c.ancestry.com/pdf/trees/ charts/correc.pdf**; RootsWeb offers another format at **http://www.rootsweb .com/ ~ cokids/forms/pics/corresp.jpg**; and *Family Tree Magazine* provides yet another document at **http://www.familytreeuniversity.com/free-forms-family -correspondence-log**. There are other examples on the Internet that you can find by typing **genealogy forms** into your favorite search engine.

Another option is to create your own form using a word processor or spreadsheet program. You can define whatever columns you would like and format them to suit your own research needs. At a minimum, you will want to keep track of the following data fields:

- Date on which you made the request
- Name and address of the person or institution
- Type of information requested
- Type of information received
- Any money that you sent along with the request

I use a spreadsheet program for my genealogy correspondence log. Microsoft's Excel is a good choice for Windows and Apple's Numbers is a good choice for OS X. By setting up multiple columns for surname, forename/given name, and middle initial, I can sort the data in the spreadsheet into whatever sequence I like. The spreadsheet program allows me to sort in ascending or descending order for every field. For example, perhaps I want to see all correspondence I've generated for all persons in alphabetical order. I could sort the surnames alphabetically as the primary sort, then by forename as the secondary sort, and middle initial as a third sort. That would present a spreadsheet in all alphabetical sequence by name. I also could add another sort to place the correspondence in date sequence within person—or in surname. Perhaps I want to see what correspondence I've sent to a specific person or organization. I could sort the spreadsheet in addressee name sequence and then, if I like, add additional sorting within that by date and by surname. As you can see, using a spreadsheet program can provide a great deal of flexibility in viewing the data. That way you can generate follow-ups for correspondence for which you have received no reply.

Using a correspondence log requires a little investment in setup time and a commitment to the process of setting it up and maintaining it. The payback, however, comes in the elimination of redundant written correspondence and in being able to maintain control over what can be an overwhelming activity.

Use a Research Log

Keeping track of all the places you have conducted research and all the resources that you have consulted can be difficult. The danger is that you may duplicate your research, which can be a terrible waste of time and money. It is important to know which resources you have investigated in the past, even those that yielded nothing of value. A research log or research calendar can help you record your progress. You can maintain your log by surname, by individual, by geographic area, in a combination of any of these, or in whatever organizational structure makes you most effective.

A good research log form for use in online databases can be found at **http:// freepages.genealogy.rootsweb.com/ ~ kidmiff/online%20research%20log.pdf**.

All of the information discussed in this chapter will help you home in on different record types in all types of locations. In the process, using correspondence and research logs can help you identify the materials you have already used and thereby avoid an enormous duplication of work effort and waste of money making photocopies, ordering document copies, and purchasing books.

Set Up and Use a Filing System

There are few things worse for a genealogist than to be unable to find some piece of evidence that you just *know* you have and want to re-examine. Perhaps it's a census record, a deed, an obituary, or a photograph. You may have a citation in your genealogy database that tells you what your source of information is. You may have developed a hypothesis based on one or more pieces of evidence that you found, and you need to look at those items again. Perhaps, too, you posted your family tree online at Ancestry.com (**http://www.ancestry.com**), MyHeritage (**http://www.myheritage.com**), FamilySearch (**https://familysearch.org**), findmypast (**http://www.findmypast.com**), or another site on the Internet, and another researcher contacts you to ask what is the source of a piece of information you posted.

You will want to set up a filing system so that you can organize all the evidence you acquire during the research process. The earlier you begin, the less intimidating the filing will be. I urge you to file materials as you go, and that means establishing a routine. I suggest making time on the day that you work with documents and digital files to also file them.

You have many options available to you, and some will depend on whether you are organizing paper documents or digital files. Let's look at each of these organizational schemes.

Paper Documents

The paper documents you will acquire are usually originals or copies of originals, especially because you always want to see and analyze the original source documents for yourself. These might include any of the documents we've discussed in this book and more. Here are some examples of filing schemes for paper documents:

- *Create a binder for each surname you are researching.* Place each paper document in an archival safe storage sheet protector. Polypropylene sheet protectors are available in all office supply stores. Within the surname, file documents together by forename/first name, and then in chronological sequence by the date the document was created. File documents for women in the binder for their maiden name. You can always place a cross-reference document in the binder under her married name that points you to her documentation in the binder under her maiden name.

- *Create a binder or large file folder by geographical area.* You may, for instance, be researching a family or a group of families who resided in a state, territory, county, province, or township. You could group all of these records together and organize them in various ways such as:
  - By surname, then by forename/first name, and then in chronological sequence
  - By small physical location, and then by some organizational system of your choosing within that location
  - In chronological sequence
  - In another organizational system of your devising

- *Make a folder by surname for miscellaneous individuals' records that don't otherwise fit into the family.* For example, you may find people of the same surname as your family in a geographical area but you may not necessarily be able to find the familial link to confirm that they are related.

- *Create a file folder system using a number representing each individual, and then maintain an index of numbers that have been assigned.* That index could be created in a spreadsheet program. You might use a number associated with an individual in your genealogy database. If you have posted your family tree to FamilySearch (**https://familysearch.org**), you could also use the number that is generated and used by their system for each individual.

- *Set up a color-coded filing system.* Create a folder for each individual coded with red dots or file labels to indicate ancestors in your paternal line and blue dots or labels for ancestors in your maternal line. You may also wish to use color-coded hanging files as part of your organizational system. (Other colors can be used for different organizational needs.) Mary E. V. Hill's website at **http://www .genrootsorganizer.com** provides details of how to create and maintain a color-coded genealogy filing system.

You will want to set up an organized filing system for paper documents that works for you. The options listed are not the only ones available.

Digital Files

Digital files have become an integral part of our genealogical research. Digitized images of original documents are available in many places on the Internet, and you can download and store those as part of your documentation. You should also generate source citations for digitized files so that you know where you found them and when.

With storage space at a premium in our lives, many genealogists have been scanning and digitizing their original source materials. They are storing these on their own computer and linking them into their genealogy database programs. They are also using cloud computing facilities, software backup programs, and off-site backup facilities to store their digitized materials. The digitized items may include documents, photographs, audio and video files, and other materials.

One of the greatest challenges for genealogists using digital files is establishing naming conventions for files you create, scan, or download. It is important to develop and use meaningful filenames so they can be easily recognized, and this can help you locate files when you need them. You may want to link a single file to multiple individuals in your genealogy database program. For example, a digitized family photograph of your grandparents and their three children may be linked as "media" to your grandfather's database record, your grandmother's record, and to the records of each of their children's records in your database. Because a single file can be linked to one *or more* individuals in your genealogy database program, establishing a naming convention that indicates that the image file relates to multiple persons can certainly help you locate a group image later. This is all the more reason to make time in your routine to regularly store the files. Backing up to an off-site storage resource is also an essential task.

You will want to develop a filing system for your digital media items that works for you. Here are some suggestions for filename conventions:

- For files related to a specific individual, use the capitalized surname, followed by an individual's initials or forename/first name, and then some descriptive text. You can use a combination of text and punctuation marks, such as hyphens and tildes, to separate different types of data in filenames, and use them consistently for the names of all your digital files. Please note that there are several punctuation marks that Windows doesn't permit to be used in filenames. Examples:

  HOLDER-GB ~ Portrait-ca-1910.jpg
  WILSON-JosephMcKnitt ~ Gravestone.jpg
  SWORDS-John ~ RevWarPension-Page1.tiff
  MORGAN-SamuelGoodloe ~ Obituary-4March1953.pdf

- For files related to a family, use the capitalized surname, followed by the word Family or FAMILY or some other designation, and then some descriptive text. (These can be linked to each of the appropriate individuals in your database.) Examples:

  WEATHERLY-FAMILY ~ FamilyPhoto-1918-MebaneNC.jpg
  HOLDER-Family ~ 1900Census-FloydCountyGA.jpg
  WILSON-SISTERS ~ Ca1890.tiff

When you are saving document images from a website, the filename will usually be meaningless in your overall organizational scheme. You might therefore change the filename, employing your naming convention, before you save it to your computer. You can certainly go back after the fact and change the filename as necessary.

Be sure to check the documentation for your genealogy database program to determine what file formats are acceptable for use and supported. The JPG format is the most commonly used graphic format on websites, and most genealogy programs support it as part of their media. The TIFF format is great for archival-quality images because there is no loss of data. However, this format is not used on websites and may not be supported for viewing in your database. The bitmap, or BMP, format likewise is not used on websites, nor is it supported in most databases. The GIF format is used for low-resolution line art or clipart, and while it is supported on web pages, its low quality is less than desirable for your digitization purposes.

Summary Regarding Filing Systems

Your first filing system may not be optimal initially; you may need to adjust, revise, and replace it as you gain more experience. Don't be afraid to make changes to optimize your system for your needs. You will find many resources about filing systems at Cyndi's List by following the links provided on the Organizing Your Research > > Filing Systems page at **http://www.cyndislist.com/organizing/filing**. These resources can help you make decisions about what system or systems might be right for you.

Now that we have covered so many different record types, and discussed various printed references and finding aids, let's proceed to the next chapter and discuss how to effectively locate information on the Internet about your ancestors.

PART III

Employ Advanced Strategies and Electronic Tools

12

Assess Internet Websites to More Successfully Research Your Ancestors

HOW TO...

- Categorize the major types of genealogical resources on the Internet
- Structure effective searches to locate information
- Use another way to fine-tune your Google searches
- Use online message boards to share information and collaborate with others
- Subscribe to and use genealogy mailing lists
- Write effective messages and postings that get results
- Locate and use additional Internet resources to help your research

Genealogy is one of the top uses of the Internet, and the exponential growth of web-based genealogical source materials on the Internet has attracted tens of millions of people around the world to become involved in investigating their family history. There are many thousands of online indexes, millions of transcribed records, billions of digitized images of original documents, vast collections of scanned and indexed books, millions of uploaded personal family trees, hundreds of millions of pages of digitized newspapers, and so much more on the Internet, and the volume of these materials grows each year. Collaboration between genealogists has become intensified, including volunteers working on projects to scan and/or index records by the millions.

It should be no surprise that many people are confused by all the options available and overwhelmed by the huge volume of information that they find. Making sense of what you find on the Internet means understanding what you are looking at. Understanding the different types of Internet resources is not unlike visiting your local public library and recognizing that dictionaries are vastly different from fiction and nonfiction books, magazines are different from journals, and microfilm is different from the Internet. You use your critical thinking skills every day as you encounter different kinds of materials. When you read a printed or online newspaper, you differentiate throughout between stories concerning politics, a house fire in the area, school activities, entertainment and sports events, between obituaries and stock market reports, and between news items and advertisements, both classified and commercial. Your personal knowledge and experience related to each of these informational items provides you with a unique perspective. You assess the information presented to you and interpret the details as you formulate an opinion. Each time you visit a library or archive to locate documentary evidence, it is essential to differentiate between the types of materials you want to use. You have to recognize what is current versus noncurrent information, and discern between quality, authoritative, and unbiased information and that which is not.

We talked earlier in the book about original source materials versus derivative materials such as indexes, transcripts, extracts, abstracts, and web pages created by individuals. We also mentioned that family trees submitted to online sites should be subjected to intense scrutiny. Information posted with source citations provides you the opportunity to retrace someone else's research and personally examine the materials they used to develop their hypotheses; information without citations is always suspect, and you must use the clues you find to completely re-create the research for yourself.

The array of information available on the Internet today presents us with both challenges and opportunities. This chapter focuses on the different types of Internet resources, how to evaluate them, and how to incorporate them with the "traditional" documents, print materials, and other non-electronic resources that you use. Ultimately, you will work *all* of these sources in tandem to obtain more comprehensive results and to make yourself a more effective researcher.

The emergence of social media such as Facebook, Genealogy Wise, Google +, Twitter, and similar resources in the past few years has added even more tools for genealogists to collaborate with one another. These will be discussed in Chapter 15.

Categorize the Major Types of Internet Resources

Many people equate "the Internet" only with web pages. It is, however, much more than that. Certainly there are tens of billions of web pages, but the Internet really is a collection of copious numbers of tools. These can be grouped into three main categories as they relate to genealogical research:

- Web pages
- Electronic mail (email)
- Message boards and mailing lists

Within web pages are other subsidiary contents, including text, graphics files, sound files, video files, forms for inputting data, search templates, archives of files that can be transferred or downloaded, chat rooms, and a number of other resources.

Email is the most widely used form of communication on earth today. Many billions of electronic messages are sent and received each day. Some are individual person-to-person messages while others are one-to-many messages, such as those sent to an email mailing list or a distribution list. Email has, like web pages, become more than just a way to disseminate textual material. Messages can contain multimedia graphics, sound, and video files within the body of the message, and attachments in many forms can be shared.

Message boards and mailing lists are Internet tools that allow you to reach many persons at once who share an interest in a particular topic. Electronic genealogy message boards have been in use for decades, and they are still used by many thousands of persons each day to post queries concerning persons with a specific surname, post questions about a geographical area, or engage in discussions concerning some other subject area. A mailing list uses email messages to communicate to persons who have subscribed to that particular list whose messages are focused on a specific surname, geographical area, or topic. Message boards and mailing lists are discussed in greater detail later in this chapter.

Web pages, email, message boards, and mailing lists are different media that are used for different purposes. If you understand their formats and uses up front, you are better prepared for what you may *and* may not expect to find when you use them.

One of the best pieces of advice I can give you is to look for "help" resources on the websites you use in your research. Most websites and Internet resources include a "Help" facility. This may also be titled "Tips and Tricks" or some other name. You may also discover a Frequently Asked Questions (FAQ) page that provides more information to assist your use of the site. You can always become more conversant and effective in the use of any online facility by accessing and reading the Help text provided. This area will explain what is and is not available in the way of functionality. Often you will find examples of how to access content effectively and, if there is a search facility available, how to optimize your use of it. These "mini-tutorials" are intended as primers for you and usually are not long, drawn-out, dry narratives.

Some websites include online forums for users (or members), which allow the discussion of almost any pertinent topic. These may be "discussion message boards" where a question or comment is posed, and people respond on that specific topic. That focused discussion is typically referred to as a "thread."

Categorize the Major Types of Genealogical Web Page Resources

No matter whether you're just starting your genealogical adventure on the Internet or you're a seasoned web researcher, there is always something new to be discovered there. I've been involved with researching my family's history since 1962, and I literally find something new every single day. You must remember that Internet websites change over time. New content is added, content is updated, materials are rearranged, dead links and outdated materials are removed (hopefully!), and websites evolve to become easier to use. Let's explore the major types of websites you will encounter and assess what you can expect to find there.

Compilation Sites

Compilation sites are those websites that gather significant resources together in an organized fashion. The materials are presented in a format that allows you to locate materials by reviewing the logical groupings of materials or hierarchical structures to find what you want. Some of these sites may include a search function that allows you to locate specific resources by keyword or phrase. Following are some examples of compilation websites and suggested areas to explore at each.

Ancestry.com at http://www.ancestry.com   We have discussed Ancestry.com and its various international sites throughout the book. It is the world's largest commercial subscription-based genealogy website. However, it also offers a great deal of content that is free. Set up your free login ID and password, and take advantage of some of the great resources. First, the Family Tree facility allows you to upload and share your own family tree with others, and this can be a first start to attract attention by other researchers and begin collaborative efforts. Next, the message boards, which we will discuss later, provide you the opportunity of posting queries for other researchers' responses and to share information with others. Finally, the Learning Center provides a compilation of free resources that you can use for your self-education. Visit Ancestry .com's main page and hover your mouse over the Learning Center link in the menu bar at the top of the page. A drop-down menu lists a number of resources. These include

- **What's New**   This area contains information about new content at the site and new features of the service that can help you get the most out of your use of Ancestry.com. You'll also find links to their Social Network, to the Ask Ancestry Anne column, and to their Livestream Videos, where you can watch live presentations and previously recorded ones to learn tips from Ancestry.com professional historians.
- **First Steps**   Learn the basics about genealogy and about using Ancestry.com in this area. You can find instructional articles, a collection of charts and forms in PDF format, and interesting articles about record types and research methodology.
- **Next Steps**   Here you will find resources that explain how to get the most from the record collections at Ancestry.com, including census records, immigration and naturalization records, military records, and more.
- **Webinars: Online Seminars**   Webinars are online seminars conducted online that include both audio and video content. Ancestry.com has produced many of these educational broadcasts. Here you will find the archive of all past webinars.

- **Help – FAQ** Here you will find resources to answer your questions about using Ancestry.com, its products, and its services.
- **Family History Wiki** Ancestry.com's wiki includes thousands of articles about genealogy topics that have been written by Ancestry.com's staff and independent writers, and contributed to by other members of the genealogical community. We will discuss wikis later in this chapter. In addition, the company has placed the content of two seminal reference books online in this area. The first is *The Source: A Guidebook to American Genealogy*, which describes in exceptional detail all of the major record types available in the United States and how to use them. The second is the *Red Book: American State, County, and Town Sources*, which describes the history of each state, the record types generated there, and details about research in the state. Of particular interest are the state-by-state tables of the counties with contact information, date of formation, and the oldest date of several record types in the county courthouses.

Canadian Genealogy & History Links at http://www.islandnet.com/~cghl Visit the main page and click, for example, the Newfoundland link, and then scroll through the categorized links to locate more information about the area and its records.

Cyndi's List at http://www.cyndislist.com Cyndi Ingle's site has been around for more than 18 years and has over 332,000 categorized website links related to genealogy at this writing. Information is indexed by subject/topic and is searchable by keyword.

GENUKI at http://www.genuki.org.uk Visit the main page (shown in Figure 12-1) and click the link labeled UK and Ireland. Enter this large collection of genealogical information pages for England, Ireland, Scotland, Wales, the Channel Islands, and the Isle of Man. Scroll down to the next page and visit the links in the section "Church History," for example, to see the extensive collection of information there.

JewishGen at http://www.jewishgen.org Visit the main page (shown in Figure 12-2), hover over the button labeled Get Started, and click the link in the drop-down list

FIGURE 12-1 GENUKI is an extensive compilation of UK and Ireland genealogical resources.

FIGURE 12-2 The JewishGen site provides the most comprehensive set of links to Jewish genealogical resources on the Internet.

labeled InfoFiles. Scroll down the page to view the many links to learn about Jewish genealogical research around the world.

Linkpendium at http://www.linkpendium.com   Linkpendium is a vast online directory of genealogical resources that was created by Karen Isaacson and Brian (Wolf) Leverich, the creators of RootsWeb. The site has been extensively updated and expanded in 2014. There are links for localities in the United States, United Kingdom, and Ireland, and for surnames around the world. This is just the beginning.

Origins.net at http://www.origins.net   Origins.net is a British-based, fee-based database website. It includes component areas for British Origins, Scots Origins, and Irish Origins with many unique databases.

RootsWeb at http://www.rootsweb.ancestry.com   RootsWeb is one of the oldest genealogical resources on the Internet (see Figure 12-3). Although owned by Ancestry.com, RootsWeb is entirely free. It is filled with instructional articles, search templates, databases, family trees, and websites hosted at RootsWeb. RootsWeb is host

FIGURE 12-3   The main screen at RootsWeb

to more than 32,500 genealogy mailing lists. It also has more than 198,000 message boards with more than 25 million posts. Both of these facilities are the largest in the world and are a boon to genealogists connecting and collaborating with other researchers.

USGenWeb Project at www.usgenweb.org   The USGenWeb Project is an all-volunteer effort that provides access to information about all 50 states and their counties. Visit the site, whose main page is shown in Figure 12-4, and view the list

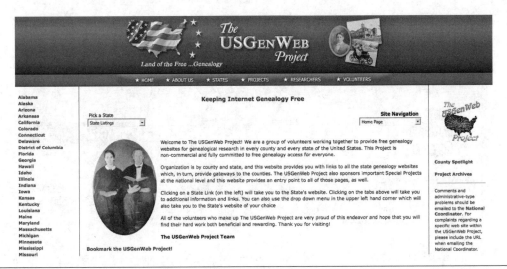

FIGURE 12-4 Main page of the USGenWeb Project site

of states on the left side of the page. You might click on Oklahoma, for example, and then explore what is there. A list of county links is shown on the left side of the page, and links to specific Oklahoma GenWeb (OKGenWeb) Projects are listed on the right side of the page.

WorldGenWeb Project at http://www.worldgenweb.org   This site is the international counterpart to the USGenWeb Project. Visit this site and click the link for CenEuroGenWeb, located on the left side of the page. On the next page, click the link for Germany or the subsidiary list of German states and visit the page for the resources listed there.

As you can see, each of these websites is a compilation of many different types of information. Within some of these are "how-to" materials, databases, maps, dictionaries, and links to other sites. While Cyndi's List offers an exceptionally comprehensive collection of reference links spanning many subject areas across the Internet, a compilation by topic area provides an excellent focal point for your research concerning a specific topic area. The esteemed JewishGen site, for example, provides categories of general and geography-specific information and links, making it the preeminent website for Jewish ancestral research guidance.

"How-to," Educational, and Reference Sites

This category includes "how-to" articles that provide instruction, as well as articles, columns, tips, and other online reference materials. The following are representative examples of this category.

Genealogy at About.com at http://genealogy.about.com   Kimberly Powell regularly writes about all things genealogical for About.com. She is a well-respected genealogist and writer in the genealogy community, and each of the subjects that she covers will add to your knowledge about record types and research methodologies.

AfriGeneas (African Ancestored Genealogy from Africa to the Americas) at http://www.afrigeneas.com   Visit the main screen and click Records at the top of the page for a drop-down menu. Click Library Records. Select one of the items on the page to investigate.

RootsWeb Guide to Tracing Family Trees at http://rwguide.rootsweb.ancestry .com   Visit this web page and select one or more subjects that are of interest to you in your research. You might want to try the Land Records (U.S.A.) link for interesting information.

In addition to these and similar websites, you will find instructional information on some of the compilation sites mentioned previously and in wikis that we will discuss later in this chapter.

Genealogy Charts and Forms

In the course of your research, you will probably find various types of forms to be useful in recording information you uncover. In particular, census transcription forms and forms for abstracting wills, deeds, and other documents can be great tools. You certainly can create forms for your own work style, but there also are free forms available at a number of sites.

About.com at http://genealogy.about.com/od/free_charts   Kimberly Powell, author of genealogical articles at About.com, has made several genealogy charts available for free download.

Ancestry.com at http://www.ancestry.com/trees/charts/ancchart.aspx   Some of the best charts and forms are available at the Ancestry.com site. These include census forms for the United States, United Kingdom, and Canada, and other forms. These are in Adobe PDF file format and are downloadable here.

Cyndi's List at http://www.cyndislist.com/free-stuff/printable-charts-and-forms/?page=2   Cyndi's List contains a large list of sources for free charts and forms.

Family Tree Magazine online at http:// www.familytreemagazine.com/ freeforms   *Family Tree Magazine* has perhaps the most complete collection of free genealogy forms on the Internet, available in PDF and/or plain text formats. The list includes pedigree charts, family group sheets, worksheets for all the U.S. federal censuses, immigration passenger lists, deed indexes, military records, and more.

**National Archives and Records Administration at http://www.archives.gov/
research/genealogy/charts-forms**   NARA has a comprehensive collection of
genealogy forms, including an Ancestral Chart, a Family Group Sheet, U.S. Federal
Census Forms (1790–1940), Non-Population Census Forms, Supplemental Forms for
the 1880 Defective, Delinquent, and Dependent Classes, Immigration Forms, and
Military Forms for the draft registrations of World War I and World War II, all in PDF
format.

These are just a few of the many places on the Internet where you can obtain
free forms to download and/or print. Additional free forms can be found by entering
genealogy forms in your favorite search engine.

Online Databases

The explosive growth of the Internet in the past 30 years has taken already popular
genealogical research to new heights. Individuals have created their own websites to
display their genealogical data and/or have uploaded the contents of their databases to
genealogy service providers' sites. The area of largest Internet growth for genealogists,
however, has been in the number of online databases. These databases include indexes
to original source records, digitized images of original documents, and other content.
There are both free databases and fee-based databases. Various payment options are
available to access data at the fee-based sites. The options include access on an annual
or monthly subscription basis, pay-per-day, pay-as-you-go, or pay-per-record downloaded
or printed. A number of the database sites will give you a free demonstration or sample
subscription. It is wise to first use the site only on a trial basis before committing yourself
to a lengthy and possibly expensive subscription.

In this category of web resources, you should consider exploring as far as you
possibly can, *and* returning often to these sites for new and updated materials. Some
of the best of the databases are listed here.

Ancestry.com at http://www.ancestry.com   Ancestry.com is a company that offers a
subscription site that has placed literally tens of thousands of indexed and searchable
databases online. Some of the databases are free to access, but most are available
only on a subscription basis. Ancestry.com's collections are truly international in
scope and are simple to search. A search will yield a full list, such as that shown in
Figure 12-5 of every database at Ancestry.com that contains that name. Among their
premier subscription databases are the U.S. Federal Census Collection, the UK Census
Collection, U.S. Immigration Passenger Lists, World War I Draft Registration Cards,
and the impressive Historical Newspaper Collection containing hundreds of indexed,
searchable newspapers dating from the 1700s to 2000 from the United States, Canada,
and the United Kingdom. Ancestry.com's Ancestry Library Edition database offering is
marketed to libraries as an institutional subscription, and can often be found as part
of public and academic libraries' subscription database collections. That edition does
not provide access to all the databases available at Ancestry.com because of licensing
arrangements made by the company with some of their database providers. (Other

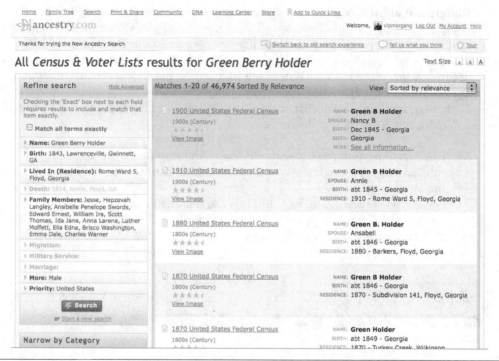

FIGURE 12-5   Search results list at Ancestry.com

Ancestry subscription sites include, at this writing, Canada [in French and English], the United Kingdom, Australia, France, Germany, Italy, Mexico, and Sweden.)

FamilySearch (free databases) at https://familysearch.org   The FamilySearch website is a fast-growing resource for your genealogical reference. FamilySearch is working to digitize, index, and make available on this site nearly all of the microfilmed records they have captured over the decades. Visit the Search Records page. Here you can search across all of the databases, click a geographical area in the map on this page, browse through all the available databases, or search for a collection by name. Click a specific database to search it. Many databases already have digitized images; some of these may already have been indexed, while others have not yet been indexed. If a database of images has not yet been indexed, you will only be able to browse through the images.

Click the link labeled Catalog at the top of the screen to find details of everything available through the Family History Library (FHL) in Salt Lake City, Utah. When you search and locate items in the catalog, you will find detailed information about each item is provided. If a book or set of records is available in a microfilmed format, a film number is included in the catalog record. You can present these film numbers at your nearest LDS Family History Center (FHC), and the staff can work with you to arrange to order the rental microform materials from the FHL in Salt Lake City.

findmypast at http://www.findmypast.com A DC Thomson Family History company, findmypast has been a well-known genealogy subscription database service in the United Kingdom for a number of years. It entered the U.S. market over two years ago and has added vast collections of records. Their database collections include, at this writing, more than 1.6 billion international genealogical records, including British, Irish, Australian, and U.S. materials. Figure 12-6 shows a search template for Birth, Marriage, and Death (Parish Registers) records at findmypast.com. They offer two especially important collections:

- The British Newspaper Collection includes thousands of local and regional publications from England, Wales, and Scotland, dating from 1710 to 1953, and later.
- The Periodical Source Index (PERSI) is the searchable index to genealogical and historical magazines, periodicals, and ethnic publications, with more than 205 million fully searchable entries.

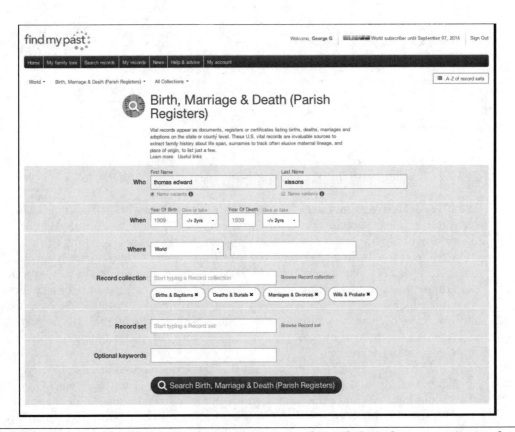

FIGURE 12-6 Search template for Birth, Marriage, and Death (Parish Registers) records at findmypast

Fold3 (subscription databases) at http://www.fold3.com   Fold3, which belongs to Ancestry.com, offers a subscription site that provides access to millions of digitized U.S. document images, specializing in military service and pension records, widows' pension records, naturalization records, city directories, photographs, and much more. It is adding approximately more than a million new images to its website each month. Many of these images come from microfilmed records at the National Archives and Records Administration (NARA), and the company also digitizes on-site at NARA. Their content includes U.S. Revolutionary War, War of 1812, and Civil War documents for service, pensions, and more. Naturalization index cards, city directories, and many other document types are also available. Figure 12-7 shows one page from a search result for the author's ancestor, John Swords. The Revolutionary War Pension database includes the complete file of 45 pages of digitized original pension documents for him.

JewishGen (free databases) at http://www.jewishgen.org   As mentioned earlier in this chapter, this site contains excellent databases, which are available with a simple registration.

Library and Archives Canada (free databases) at http://www.collectionscanada .gc.ca   LAC was discussed in some detail in Chapter 6 concerning census records. LAC has, in its online Genealogy and Family History area, a variety of articles and links and a good number of digitized image databases.

MyHeritage at http://www.myheritage.com   MyHeritage is one of the fastest-growing genealogical database sites on the Internet. The company boasts 5 billion records, 27 million family trees, and 200 million photographs, and the site supports 40 different languages. Records include census records, vital/civil registration records, immigration and travel records, naturalization materials, military records, cemetery

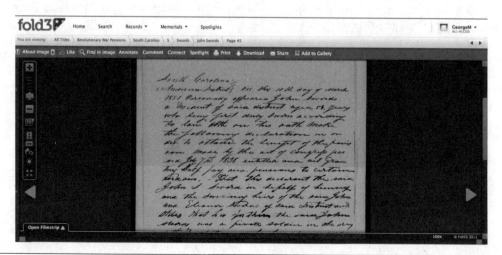

FIGURE 12-7   Revolutionary War Pension file for John Swords at Fold3.com

FIGURE 12-8 The main page at MyHeritage

and obituary records, government documents, public records, court records, books, and more from around the world. You can start working on the site for free, and later upgrade to a premium subscription. They offer a smartphone app for use on the go. The main page in shown in Figure 12-8.

The National Archives (UK) at http://www.nationalarchives.gov.uk The National Archives (TNA) is the primary repository for records of England and Wales and contains over 11 million publicly available documents, some dating back more than 1,000 years. The former Public Record Office (PRO) and the Historical Manuscripts Commission (HMC) were merged in April 2003 to form TNA, and the staff and remaining services of the Family Records Centre (FRC) were relocated to TNA in 2008. The TNA website is a wonderful compendium of information, online exhibits, educational tutorials, and much more. TNA's main web page is shown in Figure 12-9 with its Menu displayed. Of special interest to family history researchers are the many digitized census images from TNA's collection—currently approximately 5 percent of their holdings. A new online catalog, Discovery, was implemented in 2014 and encompasses the holdings of archives around the country.

Origins.net at http://www.origins.net A DC Thomson Family History company, Origins.net provides genealogical databases about Britain and Ireland, including

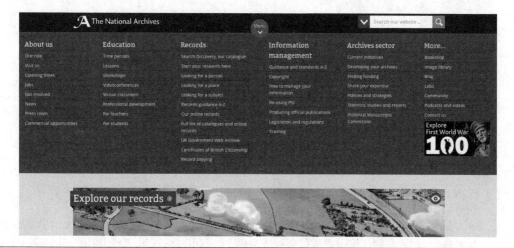

FIGURE 12-9 Main page of website of The National Archives (UK), with drop-down menu shown

British Origins (**http://www.britishorigins.com**), Irish Origins (**http://www .irishorigins.com**), and Scots Origins (**http://www.scotsorigins.com**).

WorldVitalRecords at http://www.worldvitalrecords.com   WorldVitalRecords, a MyHeritage company, is a subscription website that includes many record collections from around the world. National, state, and provincial censuses are represented, as are birth, marriage, and death records, parish records, military records, and a large newspaper collection.

Some governmental agencies have also provided online databases of materials in their possession, although concerns for individuals' privacy and identity theft may have spurred legislators to pass legislation to either prevent making many records accessible to the public, limit access to them, or withdraw them altogether from public access.

Genealogical Societies

Genealogical societies can offer a wealth of information to you, including reference and referrals, education, companionship, and publications, and may well possess important genealogical records found nowhere else. You will want to investigate the societies at the national, regional, state or provincial, county, parish, and local levels where your ancestors and family members lived. The following are some of the major ones of interest to researchers.

Canadian Genealogical Societies at http://www.collectionscanada.gc.ca/022/ 022-801-e.html   This web page is a subsidiary of the Library and Archives Canada website and provides a list of links to the provincial genealogical societies' websites.

There are, however, hundreds of genealogical societies in Canada, and you may locate information for and links to a more extensive list of local societies at the provincial societies' sites.

Federation of Family History Societies (FFHS) at http://www.ffhs.org.uk This international organization, based in the United Kingdom, has more than 180 member societies representing more than 180,000 members worldwide. It provides education and support to individuals and to genealogical societies, and coordinates a number of national projects in order to integrate the efforts of multiple societies, publish the efforts, and publicize the results.

Federation of Genealogical Societies (FGS) at http://www.fgs.org This international organization consists primarily of U.S. and Canadian genealogical societies but also includes some overseas members. Individual societies join FGS and it, in turn, provides a forum for society education and communications, and hosts an annual conference. Visit the Society Hall area of the site at **http://www.fgs.org/ cstm_societyHall.php** to locate member societies and their contact information.

You can also search for a particular genealogical society by using your favorite search engine and typing the name of the area and the quotation mark–enclosed phrase **"genealogical society"** or **"genealogy society"** in the search box. You can further narrow your search by adding the name of a location, such as **"new york" "genealogical society"** or **Canada "genealogical society"**.

Structure Effective Searches to Locate Information

The Web is an enormous place, currently consisting of tens of billions of individual pages. In reality, we can only guess at its actual size, but it continues to grow at a rapid pace. Because it is relatively easy for anyone to put information on the Web, there is a good possibility that somebody, somewhere, has created a web page that contains information you might find useful for your genealogical research. The trick, then, is to locate that one useful page among the billions of pages out there.

It is important that you learn how to use, in a logical, structured way, the two primary search tools on the Internet: search engines and directories. We're going to explore each one in detail, after which you should practice, practice, and practice in order to become an expert Internet searcher.

Define the Difference Between Search Engines and Directories

Early in the development of the World Wide Web, directories were the way of the world. Individuals created structured, categorized links to websites.

A *search engine* is a tool that accesses an index of web pages that has been created by a mechanical software contrivance known as a spider, a robot, or simply a "bot." The key here is that the index is mechanically created, with very little human intervention. There are three indexed components in a web page that a search engine index indexes: the title, the metatags, and the body text of the web page.

When you enter a single word for a search, it might be located anywhere within these areas of the web pages. As you'll see later, the Advanced Search facility of many search engines may allow you to specify where in the web page the word or phrase is to be sought.

Search engines employ the use of structured searches, using words, keywords, and phrases to match entries in their indexes. Search engines typically offer both a simple and an advanced Search facility, the second of which allows you to select criteria to narrow your search results.

The leading search engines today are Google (located at **http://www.google .com**, **http://www.google.co.uk**, and other addresses in many other countries) and Microsoft's Bing (**http://www.bing.com**).

A genealogy-specific search engine called Mocavo (**http://www.mocavo.com**) made its debut in 2011 and claims to search billions of free genealogy records. You will note that a link to the Advanced Search facility of Mocavo is available to registered members.

A *directory* is another Internet tool that, unlike the search engine, is created entirely by human editors who look at web pages and assign them to logical or appropriate categories. (A web page may be assigned to multiple categories when appropriate.) A directory is essentially a manual compilation. Broad categories can be broken down into narrower subcategories and sub-subcategories. This hierarchical structure can be used to browse deeper and deeper to narrow your focus and to locate materials you seek. A directory may also embed a search facility, which enables you to search in just that hierarchical category or to search the entire directory. Some hybrid directories also may allow you to expand your search onto the Web to locate non-categorized materials that are not included in the directory, graphic files, audio files, news wire services, and other resources.

Yahoo! used to be the largest directory on the Internet, but the company discontinued that directory at the end of 2014. One of the largest directories today is the Open Directory Project (**http://dmoz.org**). Another important reference directory you will want to include in your Favorites list is ipl2 at **http://www.ipl .org**, formerly known as the Internet Public Library. Each of the large directories has links to several million different web pages that have been compiled by their human editors. Because editors add new links to a directory, it may take some time (months, perhaps) before a new web page will appear in a general directory.

There is one more search tool that should be mentioned: the *metasearch engine*. A metasearch engine is another hybrid creature, one that allows you to enter a search in one place and have that engine simultaneously search multiple search engines for you. Does this seem like the answer to a prayer? Hardly! The results may be overwhelming. The search results may be less than relevant to the search terms and keywords you submitted. They also may yield duplicate search results and/or omit important leads. Many experienced researchers use metasearch engines only to learn which of the individual search engines has the most or the better search results. However, a metasearch tool can save a great deal of time and can often locate higher-quality results very quickly. Among the major metasearch engines in use today are Dogpile and Mamma (**https://mamma.com**).

Use a Search Engine to Get Great Results

The Simple Search or Basic Search screen is typically the main screen you reach at any search engine website. It allows you to type in a word or two or a phrase, press ENTER, and off you go. Too often, though, a researcher may believe that this is all there is to using a search engine. And while it may give you results, those results may be so massive as to be overwhelming, and may contain a whole lot of results that are useless to you. You may get a sense of all this from the first screen of your search results list. No one I know has the time to cull through 3,920,101 results, and I personally would be skeptical of a search result from Billy Ray Bob's Down Home Page of Genieology! (And yes, that would be misspelled, wouldn't it?) You need to narrow the field. That's where the Advanced Search screen options may help. For Google, you can access the Advanced Search page at **http://www.google.com/advanced_search?hl = en**. Look at the Advanced Search screen from Google in Figure 12-10.

FIGURE 12-10 The Advanced Search page of the Google search engine

Don't forget to look for the Help link on the page. The following are the fields on the Advanced Search page:

- **all these words**   Entering a single word asks for a search for all web pages that have that word anywhere in the page. Entering multiple words asks for a search for web pages that have *both or all* those words located anywhere in the page and in any order.
- **this exact word or phrase**   Entering multiple words here will have the same effect as you would have had on the Simple Search screen had you enclosed them in double quotation marks. Here, however, you don't have to enclose them in double quotation marks. You simply enter the words you want treated as a phrase and they will be automatically enclosed in quotation marks when the search begins.
- **any of these words**   Entering multiple words asks for a search for web pages that have *at least one* of those words located anywhere in the page.
- **none of these words**   Entering one or more words here has the effect of excluding from your search results any pages in which one or more of these words might be included anywhere in the page.
- **numbers ranging from**   You may narrow your search using numbers, and Google will search for web pages with numbers with values from the beginning number through the ending number that you specify. This can be helpful if you want to specify a search for web pages in which a span of years might be included.

The Advanced Search screen also gives you the option of narrowing your search to only web pages written in a specific language.

You may opt to have the search engine return only certain document types (or exclude web pages with those types). These include Adobe PDF files, Adobe PostScript files, Microsoft Word files, Microsoft Excel spreadsheets, Microsoft PowerPoint presentations, and Rich Text Format (RTF) files.

There are some simple rules of thumb to follow when using a search engine to search the Web. These apply to most search engines. However, read the Help materials for your favorite engine to get the best results.

- To enter a word, simply type it in the box. The search directories and search engines don't care whether you type it in uppercase or lowercase.
- Avoid the use of a plural if you can avoid it. If you are searching for matches about bluebirds, enter the word as a singular **bluebird** and most search engines will give matches for both bluebird *and* bluebirds. When entering a surname that ends in an "s," you may want to enter it *without* the "s" in order to see what matches you will get in your search results list.
- To enter an exact phrase in which two or more words must be contiguous to one another in the precise order you type them, make sure you enclose them in double quotation marks to make them one entity. This might include place names, such as **"west virginia"**, **"muskogee oklahoma"**, or **"east riding" yorkshire England**. You may also want to use this search technique for a full

name so that the search engine doesn't just search for the individual components. As an example, instead of entering **john scott trotter**, you might enter it as **"john scott trotter"** or **"john trotter"** or **"john s trotter"** so that your search results are more likely to only include web pages that include a person by that name.

- If you want to force a search engine to *include* in its search results any pages that have one *or* another of the words and/or exact phrases you enter as search criteria, insert the word **OR** in uppercase letters between the search words or phrases. For example, you might want to search for a person named Edward Holder in either Georgia or South Carolina, in which case you might enter the following:

  "edward holder" georgia OR "south carolina"

- If you want to force a search engine to *exclude* from the search results any pages that include a particular word or exact phrase, insert the word **NOT** in uppercase letters. You can also indicate *exclude* by placing a minus sign (–) immediately before the term or phrase you wish to exclude. There should be no space between the minus sign and the term you wish to exclude. For example, you may have searched for Margaret McKnitt and found results from a place you knew she never lived. You might enter one of the following to exclude the unwanted place:

  "margaret mcknitt" maryland NOT "north Carolina"
  "margaret mcknitt" maryland - "north Carolina"

- Your search engine may offer the use of one or more "wildcard" characters. Some facilities, such as Google, allow you to use an asterisk (*) as a replacement for a character that you're not sure about. For instance, you might be unsure of the spelling of a surname and you might enter **jens*n** to represent the spellings of Jensen or Jenson. Google also allows you to use the * as a wildcard for a word in an exact phrase. Enter **"with a * in my heart"** and your search results will include several links for the song or movie titled "With a Song in My Heart." Be sure to check the Help facility in your favorite search tool to see how it handles searches and whether it offers the use of wildcard characters.

Use Another Way to Fine-Tune Your Google Searches

Did you know that Google operates more than 150 versions of its search engine? Yes, there are different versions of the search engine for different geographies, such as the United Kingdom, Australia, Brazil, Canada, France, Germany, Ireland, Italy, Sweden, Spain, Switzerland, and more. The websites and content that each national version of the search engine searches will vary. What that means to us as genealogists is that, if we are searching for ancestors and records in another country, we might want to use the Google search engine for that nationality. Let's see how this works.

On the Internet, each country has been assigned a two-character country code top-level domain (ccTLD), and these are used at the end of URLs to distinguish the country of origin of the website. For example, the code for the United States is **.us**; the code for Canada is **.ca**; and the code for the United Kingdom is **.uk**. (Note that most U.S.-based companies, organizations, and educational institutions do not use **.us** as part of their website URLs, but instead use **.com**, **.org**, or **.edu**.)

So where do you get the list of two-letter country codes? One site, hosted by the Information Technology Associates, is located at **http://www.theodora.com/ country_digraphs.html**. This site lists the codes in two alphabetical formats: by country and by code.

Search for a version of Google for a specific nationality by entering the following, and substituting the name of the country you are seeking:

google italy

Alternately, if you already know the country code, you can enter it as follows, substituting the two-letter country code for the **xx** shown here:

www.google.com.xx

or

www.google.xx

Please note that the URL for Google may include a **.com** or a **.co**, followed by the country code to indicate a commercial site.

The nice thing about visiting these Google pages is that Google has a facility called Google Translate. When you arrive at a page for a country whose language is different, Google will offer to translate it for you. A bar will appear at the top of the page that looks like the one shown in Figure 12-11. The translate facility will work on text in web pages, but it will not work on text within images. For example, if you were working with a Dutch website that had indexed images of original documents, Google would be able to translate the text in the indexes. However, when you click on a link from the index to view an image, there would be no translation. You would still need to read the language or engage the services of someone who could translate for you. However, by using a national version of Google to locate materials for ancestors and family members who may have come from that country, you may locate resources you might not have otherwise found.

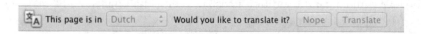

FIGURE 12-11   Google automatically offers to translate a web page to your native language or to any other language you specify by making a selection in the drop-down menu.

Use Mailing Lists and Message Boards to Share Information and Collaborate with Others

Collaboration with other researchers is an ideal way to advance your genealogical research. You can make connections with other people who are researching the same lines as you or who have specific knowledge to share about a geographical area, specific record types, research methodologies, and more. Genealogy mailing lists and message boards have been around for a long time, and they are still as vibrant and viable as ever.

Before there was an Internet, genealogists turned to genealogical periodicals (magazines, newsletters, etc.) as a way to publish a question concerning the ancestors they were trying to learn more about. These messages, usually referred to as "queries," were sometimes successful, but they usually were not, since the odds weren't typically very high that the right person (a person who knew the answer to the question) would stumble upon the query. Few genealogists would have the patience to scan every genealogy publication to read every query, especially if that required culling through a backlog of issues going back many years.

Fortunately, the Internet brought a new tool: the electronic mailing list. A query could be sent to a single email address, and it would be automatically re-sent to every mailing list "subscriber." By itself, this was not necessarily a huge improvement over printed queries appearing in subscription magazines or newsletters. However, electronic mailing lists can be archived, and often are. In other words, the older messages can be saved in a database and, as you've already learned, databases can be searched. This means that you can periodically go to the mailing list's archive and search for information of interest.

Online services such as Prodigy, CompuServe, GEnie, and America Online provided another way to exchange queries: a message board (also called a "bulletin board"). Similar message boards could be found on Bulletin Board Systems (BBSs) and as part of another, older messaging system known as Usenet. Eventually, message boards devoted to genealogy were established on the Web at such places as Ancestry .com (a merger of the RootsWeb message boards and the newer Ancestry.com boards, located at **http://boards.ancestry.com**).

A message board works like a cork bulletin board typically found in an office or school. Someone posts a message and hopes that interested parties will see it (and perhaps respond appropriately to it). As with a physical bulletin board, the messages may not remain posted forever. However, as a general rule, genealogy message boards archive messages so that they can be accessed indefinitely. Just to make certain that you clearly understand the differences between a mailing list and a message board, let's explore and discuss both.

What Is a Mailing List?

A mailing list is a facility on the Internet that uses email to distribute a single message to all subscribers. There are tens of thousands of genealogical mailing lists to fulfill almost every interest you may have. These include mailing lists dedicated to the following topics: surnames, geographical locations, record types, ethnic groups, religious groups and records, fraternal organizations, immigration and naturalization, military records, cemeteries, genealogical software, search methodologies, and more.

The organization that hosts the vast majority of genealogical mailing lists is RootsWeb, and you can access their directory of available mailing lists at **http://lists .rootsweb.ancestry.com**.

It is easy to subscribe to a mailing list. For example, let's say that I am researching my ancestors who lived in Rome, Floyd County, Georgia. The Floyd County mailing list would be a good place to learn more from people who also are researching there. I might learn about the history of the area, learn about archives of records of various types, and even meet someone who also is researching the same surnames that I am researching.

From the RootsWeb mailing list directory (see previous URL), I entered **georgia floyd** in the "Find a mailing list" field, clicked Find, and, on the next page, clicked the list for Floyd County, GA. Figure 12-12 shows the web page that is displayed.

If you study Figure 12-12 for a few minutes, you will note several important pieces of information:

- The mailing list is named GAFLOYD-L.
- There are instructions for subscribing to:
  - The GAFLOYD-L mailing list (individual messages)
  - The GAFLOYD-D mailing list (digest mode)
- There are instructions for unsubscribing.
- There is an archive of older messages that may be browsed or searched, using the links shown here.

Georgia Mailing Lists

Floyd County

GAFLOYD-L
lists3

Topic: Floyd County, Georgia. Interested individuals may want to check out the Floyd County GAGenWeb page at http://www.geocities.com/Heartland/Plains /3242/floyd.htm.

There is a Web page for the **GAFLOYD** mailing list at http://www.geocities.com/Heartland/Plains/3242/floyd.htm.

For questions about this list, contact the list administrator at GAFLOYD-admin@rootsweb.com.

- **Subscribing.** Clicking on one of the shortcut links below should work, but if your browser doesn't understand them, try these manual instructions: to join **GAFLOYD-L**, send mail to GAFLOYD-L-request@rootsweb.com with the single word *subscribe* in the message subject and body. To join **GAFLOYD-D**, do the same thing with GAFLOYD-D-request@rootsweb.com.
  - ○ Subscribe to GAFLOYD-L
  - ○ Subscribe to GAFLOYD-D (digest)
- **Unsubscribing.** To leave **GAFLOYD-L**, send mail to GAFLOYD-L-request@rootsweb.com with the single word *unsubscribe* in the message subject and body. To leave **GAFLOYD-D**, do the same thing with GAFLOYD-D-request@rootsweb.com.
  - ○ Unsubscribe from GAFLOYD-L
  - ○ Unsubscribe from GAFLOYD-D (digest)
- **Archives.** You can search the archives for a specific message or browse them, going from one message to another. Some list archives are not available; if there is a link here to an archive but the link doesn't work, it probably just means that no messages have been posted to that list yet.
  - ○ Search the GAFLOYD archives
  - ○ Browse the GAFLOYD archives

RootsWeb is funded and supported by Ancestry.com and our loyal RootsWeb community. Learn more.

About Us | Contact Us | Acceptable Use Policy | PRIVACY STATEMENT | Copyright
Copyright © 1998-2008, MyFamily.com Inc. and its subsidiaries.

FIGURE 12-12   Detail page for Floyd County, Georgia, mailing list

The difference between the GAFLOYD-L mailing list (individual messages) and the GAFLOYD-D mailing list (digest mode) is important to you as a subscriber. Subscribing to the mailing list whose name ends in *L* will result in your receiving a copy of every message as an individual message. This could bury you with email if this turns out to be a busy mailing list. Subscribing to the mailing list whose name ends in *D* will result in your receiving a digest version. This consists of a single email in which all the messages generated in a specific period will be included. There typically is a list of subject headers at the top of the message so that you can tell what types of information are in these messages, followed by the actual messages.

You can use the Find function to quickly search through a long digest for a word or phrase. You can access the Find facility by going to the menu bar on your browser, selecting Edit, and clicking the Find option in the drop-down list. You can also access this using a keyboard shortcut. On a PC, press the CTRL-F keys; on a Mac, press the COMMAND-F keys. When you subscribe to a digest version of a mailing list and receive a potentially lengthy email with a number of messages inside, the Find function allows you to quickly search for surnames or specific words in which you are interested. This can be a real timesaver.

When you subscribe to a mailing list, you will receive a welcome message. Print and save that message! I personally maintain a file folder labeled "Mailing Lists" in which I keep these messages. The welcome message will provide important information to you to help you maximize your use of the mailing list:

- The purpose of the mailing list and some of its most important rules for use
- How to subscribe and unsubscribe
- How to contact the list administrator
- How to browse and/or search the list archives (if available)

By keeping the welcome message, you will be able to quickly locate important information about the mailing list when you need it. In particular, if you decide you want to get off the list, you will have instructions about how to unsubscribe. If there are problems with the list, such as a nasty person who is abusing his or her privilege of participating, the email address of the list owner is invaluable.

When you join a mailing list, it is a good idea to "lurk before you leap." In other words, watch the exchanges of information and messages for a week or two before you jump in. You may find that this isn't really the mailing list you want, and you can unsubscribe.

When you subscribe, also browse or search the archives, if there is one, for answers to any basic questions you have. People on mailing lists cringe when a new person (a "newbie") jumps in and asks a question that has been asked and answered a hundred times.

Last but not least, there are three important rules you should follow:

- *Never send an email of a commercial nature unless the description of the list expressly permits it.* Sending commercial email on a mailing list is considered to be spamming and is offensive to subscribers.
- *Always be polite and patient.* There are always "newbies" and your courtesy is expected and appreciated.

- *Never type in all capital letters.* It is, in the Internet world, considered to be "shouting," not to mention that all caps are more difficult to read. The only exception is that you *should* type surnames in all caps in order to make them stand out.

What Is a Message Board?

A message board, as explained before, is a place on the Internet where people who share an interest in a topic post electronic messages. The difference between a mailing list and a message board is that, for a mailing list, people subscribe via email and messages arrive in their email mailbox. With a message board, the onus is on you to visit the board, to search out information, and to read the postings there yourself.

The Ancestry.com Message Boards at **http://boards.ancestry.com** are among the best available. Figure 12-13 shows the main screen at the Ancestry.com Message Boards. As you can see, it is easy to locate specific surnames, localities, and topics. It also is easy, using the search template toward the top, to either search *all* message boards for a name or text *or* to find a specific message board. Finding a message board is easy: just fill in the name and go from there.

I entered the surname **Weatherly**, simply clicked the link and was taken to the page displayed in Figure 12-14. If you study this screen of the Weatherly message board

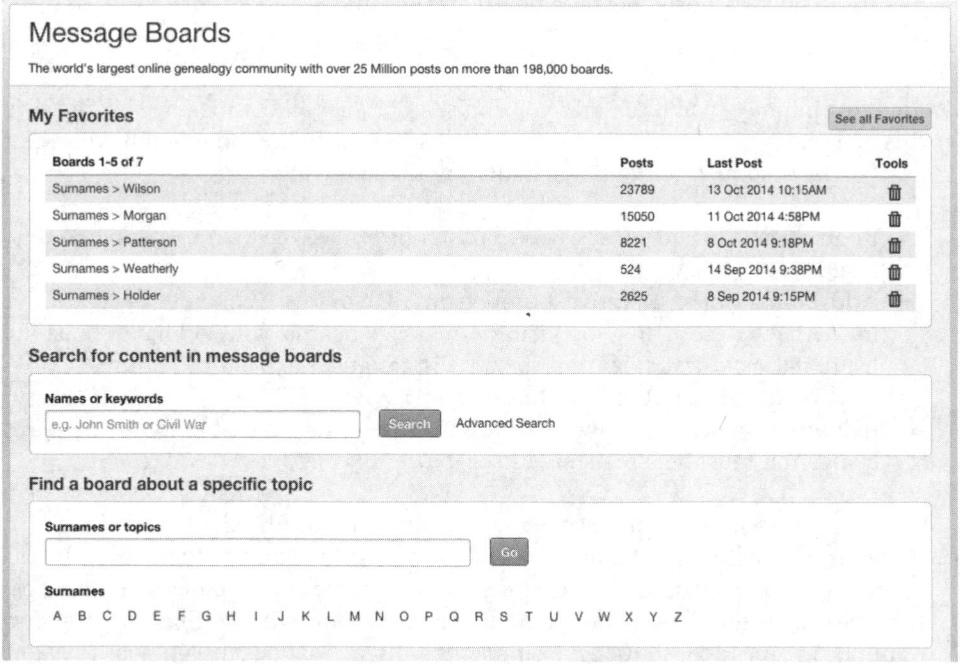

Message Boards

The world's largest online genealogy community with over 25 Million posts on more than 198,000 boards.

My Favorites   See all Favorites

Boards 1-5 of 7	Posts	Last Post	Tools
Surnames > Wilson	23789	13 Oct 2014 10:15AM	🗑
Surnames > Morgan	15050	11 Oct 2014 4:58PM	🗑
Surnames > Patterson	8221	8 Oct 2014 9:18PM	🗑
Surnames > Weatherly	524	14 Sep 2014 9:38PM	🗑
Surnames > Holder	2625	8 Sep 2014 9:15PM	🗑

Search for content in message boards

Names or keywords

[e.g. John Smith or Civil War]   [Search]   Advanced Search

Find a board about a specific topic

Surnames or topics

[   ]   [Go]

Surnames

A B C D E F G H I J K L M N O P Q R S T U V W X Y Z

FIGURE 12-13   Main page at the Ancestry.com Message Boards

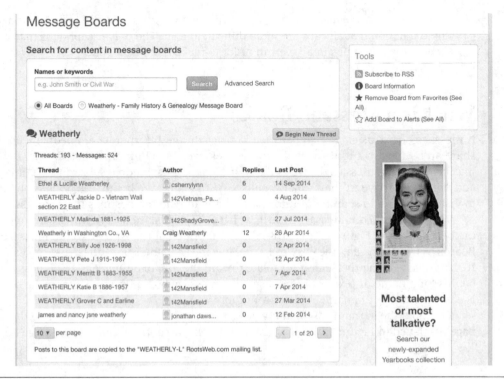

FIGURE 12-14 The Weatherly message board at Ancestry

for a few minutes, you'll see that you can search *either* all the message boards *or* just this one for specific words or terms or names. Just click the radio button you want.

You have some other options, including the following:

- **Begin New Thread** Click this to post a new message on a new topic to this board.
- **Add Board to (or Remove Board from) Favorites** Whenever you are signed in to Ancestry.com and you visit the message boards, you will have a customized list of places to visit. You must be a registered user to use this feature.
- **Add Board to (or Remove Board from) Alerts** Allows you to set up a system that sends you an email every time someone posts a message to this message board. You must be a registered user to use this feature.

What you will see in message board postings is something called a "thread." A thread is nothing more than "a thread of conversation" about a single topic. It consists of an original posting and all of the responses to it and the responses to the responses. Each posting is further indented to indicate the response in the thread chain. For example, Figure 12-15 shows an example of a thread that began 1 August 1999 and that has continued through a series of message postings.

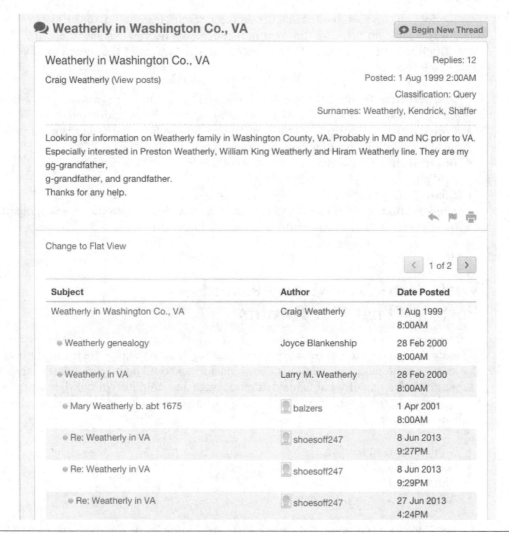

FIGURE 12-15   Messages on the Weatherly message board displayed in "thread view"

There are two display options available when working with the Ancestry.com Message Boards. The first is the "thread view." The page shown in Figure 12-15 is a thread view. The second is the "flat view" in which each message is displayed in its entirety. Either view can be sorted into oldest first or newest first sequence. You can switch from one display option to the other at will, and this makes reading the entire correspondence in a whole thread easier than having to click through each one individually. In flat view they are shown on a single screen. What's more, you can use the browser's Find facility to quickly search an entire web page for a specific name or word you want to locate.

Again, you can search either all the Ancestry.com Message Boards or just the one for this topic, in this case, the Weatherly surname. As you can see, there are some options to help you narrow your search. At the bottom of the screen are five additional important links:

- **Request New Board**   You use this if you wish to submit a request to have a new message board established when a surname or topic is not addressed.
- **Community Guidelines**   This contains guidelines for what is and is not a proper use of the message boards.
- **Board Help**   As always, this is your best friend when you need help and guidance.
- **Board FAQ**   This contains frequently asked questions and answers.
- **Send Feedback**   You can comment on your experience with the message boards by clicking this link, completing a comment form, and sending it.

Write Effective Messages and Postings That Get Results

Well-constructed, well-written messages get results. However, you need to know how to create an effective message. A great message really starts with a great subject line that captures the reader's attention. The subject line should be brief but descriptive. It should tell the reader what is inside the message and help him or her determine whether to read the message at all. The subject line content should include details such as the following:

- Name of person sought
- Location
- Time period
- All of the above or other data

Let's look at three examples of potential subject lines. The first is for Rebecca MONFORT who lived in Greene County, Georgia, and her life dates were 1819 to 1886. Please note that the surname is in all uppercase letters to make spotting the surname simpler. This subject line tells the reader who, where, and when. This should be enough to help the reader decide if this is a person about whom he or she would like to learn more or if he or she has something to share. The reader *will* open this message.

Rebecca MONFORT—Greene Co., GA—1819-1886

The second example tells the reader that the author has or wants information concerning a church in a particular location: Madison, North Carolina, in the county of Rockingham.

Zion Baptist Church—Madison, Rockingham, NC

In the third example, the subject tells the reader a lot of information. In this case, the author is seeking information about Brisco HOLDER, who was born in 1879 and who is believed to have died in the mid-1920s. Mr. Holder was in Georgia, and then moved to Alabama, and then to Kentucky, and then to some unknown place until his death certificate was located in the city of St. Louis, Missouri. (The greater than character, >, indicates that the person moved.) Reading just this header, you might determine (correctly) that the author is seeking to learn exactly where and when Mr. Holder died and where he was buried.

Brisco HOLDER — 1879-ca. 1925 — GA > AL > KY > ? > MO

These are all examples of good subject headers. A subject line that reads "Help!" or "Wilson Family" or "Want Grandpa's Dates" is not effective.

The body of the message is just as important as the subject line. It should be concise and should indicate the following:

- The full name (and any nickname or alias) of the individual
- The location in which the person was located
- The time period about which you are interested
- What it is specifically that you are seeking
- Any research you have already conducted or sources you have checked, regardless of whether they helped your search or not
- What else you might be willing to share with another researcher
- How someone can contact or respond to you

Let's look at an example of the body of a good message in Figure 12-16. The author wrote a subject line that clearly provided the surname and the location of the query. The body of the message indicated that the author was seeking information on one John N. (or M.) SWORDS, his wife, and other members of the family. He provided a detailed description of what he knew, and hoped that this would help the reader determine what he or she might be able to share with the author.

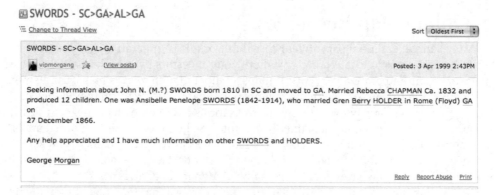

FIGURE 12-16 Example of a good message board posting

As you can see, the use of electronic mailing lists and message boards can really expand and extend your research range by providing the ability to advertise the fact that you are seeking information. You will be surprised how many other researchers, even your own cousins, are out there using these electronic queries. Mailing lists and message boards, along with other Internet resources, provide you with opportunities to share information and to collaborate with other researchers.

Locate and Use Additional Resources in Your Research

Everything we have discussed so far can contribute to your understanding of how and where to locate important genealogical resources for your research. However, there are so many, many more materials available to you! Consider for a moment that you are visiting your local public library to conduct family history research. You certainly will spend time in the genealogy collection. However, you are sure to encounter material that will cause you to want to use additional library materials that are not physically located within the genealogy and local history department. You will want to consult maps and atlases, and these may be in another part of the library. Encyclopedias, biographies, dictionaries, and language translation books are also in another area. Calendar and timeline books are elsewhere, as are telephone directories and other people-finder materials. The list goes on and on. And hopefully, in the course of your library visits, you are now utilizing *all* of the resources there already, and not just the genealogy books.

Let's explore a number of additional Internet-based resources that may be of help to you in your research. In the following sections, I will suggest some examples of Internet searches to help you locate materials for that genre, and will include some of my favorite sites for your review and enjoyment. Your job in all of this is to search for materials that will be of use in your own research, *and* to incorporate these tools into your search strategies.

Online Map Resources

Maps are an essential part of your research work. It is imperative that you use historical maps to locate precisely where your ancestors lived at the time they were there. Contemporaneous historical maps, compared with today's maps, can help you focus in on the places where documents may now reside. Political boundaries have altered tremendously over the centuries. Nations have come and gone, counties and provinces have been formed and divided into smaller, more easily governed areas, towns have been founded and disappeared, places have been renamed, and some places have simply disappeared. It is therefore important to be able to locate historical maps, atlases, and gazetteers (place name dictionaries) of all types.

Following are some examples of Internet searches that might be of help to you. Substitute the place name you are seeking for the one(s) shown in the following examples. Please note that the minus (–) character is being used to exclude results with a particular word or from a particular type of site, as are the double quotation marks (" ") that form an exact phrase. You may use any search engine you like, and may want to use the Advanced Search facility to exclude some materials. For example, for the map searches, perhaps you will want to exclude commercial sources and therefore use the Advanced Search facility to exclude the .com sites from your results. (Remember: You've learned a lot already about how to search the Internet more effectively. Don't slip back into your old ways!)

> **map "south carolina"**
> **map persia**
> **atlas Georgia 1895**
> **gazetteer ireland 1800s -site:.com**

(This search was conducted using Google, and locates pages with the words "gazetteer," "Ireland," and "1800s," and excludes the commercial [.com] sites. Be sure to check the Help of your favorite search engine to verify the correct format for including and excluding specific domains and other data.)

I have a number of favorite websites where I find historical maps. I encourage you to try some of these terrific resources for yourself.

Perry-Castañeda Library Map Collection at http://www.lib.utexas.edu/maps   The map collection in the Perry-Castañeda Library at the University of Texas-Austin includes more than 250,000 maps, and approximately 50,000 of these have been digitized and made available online. They include historic and modern maps from around the world. They can provide you with perspective of the places your ancestors lived.

David Rumsey Map Collection at http://www.davidrumsey.com   The David Rumsey Map Collection contains more than 51,000 images of maps, atlases, globes, and prints from his massive collection. There are several image viewers embedded in the website, and digital overlays from Google Maps and Google Earth are available. These allow comparisons between historic views and contemporary views of the same areas.

Library of Congress Geography & Map Division at http://www.loc.gov/rr/ geogmap   The Library of Congress Geography & Map Reading Room website is an excellent place to begin searching the facility's extensive collection. Be sure to visit the American Memory Map Collections page at **http://lcweb2.loc.gov/ammem/ gmdhtml/gmdhome.html**.

Dictionaries

There are hundreds of sources for dictionaries online for English and for other languages that may be helpful for translation purposes. Some excellent dictionaries may be found in the following sites:

- ipl2, under Resources by Subject   **http://www.ipl.org**
- Wikipedia, the largest online reference compendium   **http://www.wikipedia .com**

Language Translation

We already discussed Google Translate earlier in this chapter. There is, however, another version of this translation facility. The Google Language Tools page at **https://translate.google.com** includes a language translation tool. Here you may enter text and have it translated from one language to another, or you may simply enter a URL and that single web page will be translated to the language of your choice.

Please recognize that no online translation is ever going to be perfect. The idiomatic variations and vernacular may not translate well. However, the translation you obtain should be sufficient to help you gather the meaning of the text. For more precise translations, you may want to seek a professional or contact a college or university where students are learning the language. A professor may be willing to have a student assist you as a for-credit project.

Historical and Biographical Resources

Information abounds on the Internet about history and about the lives of notable or historical figures. The databases at Ancestry.com (**http://www.ancestry.com**) and at Fold3 (**http://www.fold3.com**) and the HeritageQuest Online databases available in libraries and archives include a number of important digitized book resources in this area. The Family History Books page at FamilySearch (**https://books.familysearch.org**) provides links to digitized book collections in important genealogical libraries that you can use.

Wikipedia (**http://www.wikipedia.com**) is a good place to begin to locate historical and biographical reference articles. In addition, you can use your favorite search engine to search for information. (Remember to use your critical thinking skills to evaluate the information you find on websites, and look for source citations that can help you locate authoritative materials to verify and extend your research.) Here are some examples of searches you might employ using your Internet browser and a search engine:

> **"george washington" biography**
> **"george washington" genealogy**
> **"richard ball" genealogy**
> **pedigree "mark twain"**
> **life "queen Victoria" –albert**

Note in the last example that the minus sign (–) was placed immediately in front of the word or phrase to be excluded. In this case, the search would attempt to exclude details about Prince Albert.

Calendars

You may find good use for calendars in your research. Remember that there was a switch from the Julian calendar to the Gregorian calendar in 1752 in Britain and the British Empire. The changeover in other parts of the world occurred at different times.

A good place to find a reference table for the changeover is located at **http://en.wikipedia.org/wiki/Gregorian_calendar#Timeline**. You also can search the Internet for calendar converters using the keywords **julian gregorian jewish** and others as needed.

Perhaps you want to know on what day of the week an ancestral event occurred, in which case a perpetual calendar is just what you want. There are many on the Internet, but one of the easiest to use is at **http://www.searchforancestors.com/ utility/perpetualcalendar.html**.

People Finders and Telephone Directories

In the course of your research, you are going to want to try to locate "lost relatives" and others. There are many online telephone and people finder resources on the Internet and most are geographically specific. Be aware that there are a couple of drawbacks to using these facilities:

- People with unlisted telephone numbers are not included in the telephone number and people finder databases.
- People's cellular telephone numbers are not included in these databases.
- Email addresses are seldom if ever updated. Therefore, if you find an old email address for someone, a message you send may not be delivered, and some email service providers do not generate "postmaster" messages indicating a failed delivery attempt.

Among the most prolific of the people finder facilities for U.S. residents and businesses are the resources shown in the following list. You will want to search regional versions of Yahoo! and Google for other countries to locate online telephone, email, and people finder services. There may be a cost for more than just the basic search in some of these facilities.

- The New Ultimates   **http://www.newultimates.com**
- PeopleSearch.net   **http://www.peoplesearch.net**
- PeopleSpot   **http://www.peoplespot.com**
- superpages.com   **http://www.superpages.com**
- Veromi   **http://www.veromi.net**
- Zabasearch   **http://www.zabasearch.com**

13

Research and Verify Your Ancestors Using Genetic Genealogy (DNA)

HOW TO...

- Learn about DNA and its place in genealogical research
- Discover the difference between paternal testing, maternal testing, autosomal testing, and the results
- Learn about test processes and results
- Determine what tests are appropriate for you and other family members
- Learn about genetic testing services
- Join a DNA surname project on the Internet
- Learn more about genetic genealogy

You've probably read or heard other genealogists talking about using DNA to assist with their research. One of the most recent additions to the genealogist's toolkit is genetic testing. Like learning how to use the Internet and databases, you'll want to learn about DNA and genetic testing in order to understand it and apply it in your own research. Because this chapter cannot possibly address everything about genetic genealogy, I'll discuss some basic concepts and then refer you to other books at the chapter's end that will provide you with an in-depth understanding.

We all have physical traits that distinguish us from one another. You've often heard the comment that someone has his mother's eyes, her father's hair coloring, or some other physical attribute. We know that genetics, the science of biology and heredity, plays a central role in how we are formed. Our genes provide the template for our physical development, from the single-cell fertilized egg to the human form that we become. The basis of this genetic template is DNA.

Learn About DNA and Its Place in Genealogical Research

DNA is an acronym for deoxyribonucleic acid, a chemical that is the blueprint for every cell in all living organisms and in some viruses. DNA molecules store the information and instructions for all the components of cells. DNA carries the genetic information, called genes, that is involved with how the entire organism is formed.

You may have heard the structure of DNA referred to as a "double helix." DNA physically consists of two long strands of organic material called nucleotides. The nucleotides are formed from sugars and phosphate groups that are joined together. These long strands run in opposite directions and form the twisted double helix. One of four types of molecules is attached to each sugar in each strand, and these molecules are called "bases." The sequence of the bases is the coding that determines the genetic coding for each cell. The coding is replicated into ribonucleic acid, known as RNA, a single strand of nucleotides.

DNA is organized into structures called chromosomes, and these building blocks are duplicated before cells divide and replicate themselves. All of this information is essential to the creation of life. Scientists have been working for decades to decode the genetic sequences and understand the function of each gene. The Human Genome Project began in 1990 with the goal of identifying all of the human genes and studying their physical structures and their functions.

Although this is a relatively simple description of DNA, it will suffice for the rest of the discussion in this chapter. I have also included at the end of the chapter a concise bibliography of reference books that can help you learn even more.

Both genetics and genealogy focus on heredity:

- *Genetics* is a branch of biology that concentrates on the scientific study of the heredity of an individual organism's physical traits. It also is used to demonstrate relationships between individuals.
- *Genealogy* is the study of families and includes tracing the lineage and history of families and demonstrating kinship and history. It seeks to establish proof of relationships from one generation to another.

As you can see, the two research disciplines share a somewhat common goal. DNA has been used in medical and forensic applications for quite some time. Amniocentesis is a method in which a small amount of a pregnant woman's amniotic fluid is removed and tested. It is an important procedure used to diagnose chromosomal irregularities and infections and employs genetic testing. Paternity tests also use DNA to confirm or refute the relationship of a man to a child. We've seen many episodes of television dramas in which DNA evidence has been used to identify a body, to determine the relationship between individuals, or to link a suspect to a crime scene or a victim.

DNA in your genealogy research can similarly be used to prove or disprove relationships between individuals and family groups. While not as precise as forensic DNA analysis, modern DNA testing for genealogical purposes has advanced to include more genetic marker tests. These provide a broader range for comparison with other people's test results.

There are three timeframes with which DNA testing can help genealogists:

- **Modern Era**   This period covers the last 500 years, which encompasses the time when the first surnames began being used in England and elsewhere.
- **Historical Era**   This period includes the time before surnames were commonly used; generally speaking, before the year 1500 A.D. back to the beginning of written history.
- **Ancient Era**   This period extends backward before the historical era. This is often referred to as the period of "deep genealogy" or "deep ancestry" when it is possible only to trace migrations of groups.

The modern era is the period in which you are most likely to be able to achieve the most value from DNA testing in your genealogical research. However, some kinds of testing can also identify your paternal line or maternal line haplogroup. *Haplogroups* are the main branches of the human genealogical tree, and they consist of haplotypes. *Haplotypes* are closely linked genes and genetic markers that are shared by a closely related group of people. These people typically are from a specific geographical area and/or part of the same ethnic origin. Haplogroups correspond to early human migrations between distinct geographical regions. Your haplogroup is indicative of your deep ancestral origin. Figure 13-1 shows an example of a haplogroup report from Family Tree DNA.

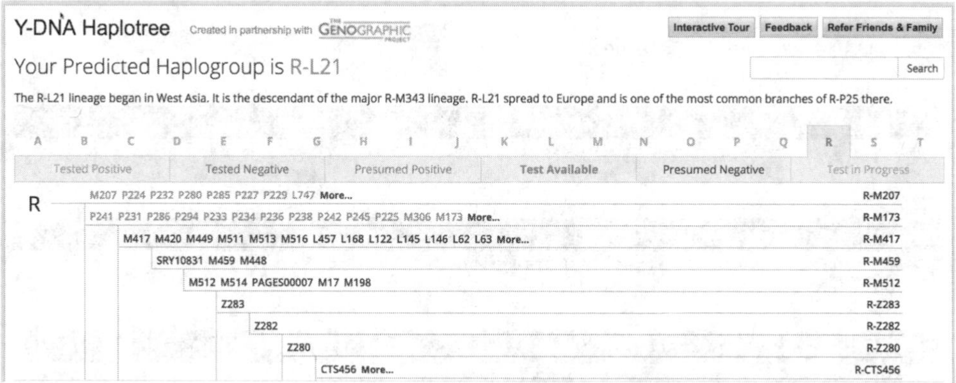

FIGURE 13-1   Sample of haplogroup results from Family Tree DNA

Discover the Difference Between Paternal Testing, Maternal Testing, Autosomal Testing, and the Results

It is important to know that humans, as well as most other mammals, have one pair of sex-determining chromosomes in each cell. Males have one Y chromosome and one X chromosome, while females have two X chromosomes. The Y chromosome is present only in males and can therefore reveal information only about the paternal line. The test for the Y chromosome is referred to as a Y-DNA test. Figure 13-2 shows the results of a Y-DNA test from Family Tree DNA.

For a Y-DNA test, the test determines the values of a set number of markers, and the resulting values can be compared against other people's results. The Y-DNA test uses highly variable repeat sequences that can identify closely related individuals *or* differentiate between unrelated individuals. It also is used to study mutations in the marker values. Both the similarities *and* the mutations help determine the number of generations backward that there may be to reach a "most recent common ancestor" (also referred to as the MRCA). The mutations occur at a comparatively regular rate, and these changes can be used to project statistically the number of generations between you and the MRCA that you share with another person.

A Y-DNA test can reveal that a man is related in some degree to other males—with the same surname or not. It indicates that there is a common male ancestor, but there may be no way to determine exactly how many generations back that the MRCA lived. The value, however, is in comparing your Y-DNA test results with other people's results. We'll discuss this later in the chapter when we cover DNA surname projects.

Y-DNA - Standard Y-STR Values

+ Page Help | Interactive Tour | Feedback | Refer Friends & Family | A A A

PANEL 1 (1-12)

Marker	DYS393	DYS390	DYS19**	DYS391	DYS385	DYS426	DYS388	DYS439	DYS389I	DYS392	DYS389II***
Value	13	24	14	11	11-15	12	12	13	13	13	29

PANEL 2 (13-25)

Marker	DYS458	DYS459	DYS455	DYS454	DYS447	DYS437	DYS448	DYS449	DYS464
Value	17	9-9	11	10	25	15	19	28	15-16-17-17

PANEL 3 (26-37)

Marker	DYS460	Y-GATA-H4	YCAII	DYS456	DYS607	DYS576	DYS570	CDY	DYS442	DYS438
Value	11	11	19-23	15	15	18	19	36-36	13	12

FIGURE 13-2 Sample of Y-DNA test results from Family Tree DNA

Mitochondria are structures within cells that convert energy from food into a form that the cells can use. The mitochondria contain a small amount of their own DNA. This genetic material is known as mitochondrial DNA, or mtDNA. This mtDNA is passed only from mother to child, and there is usually no change from parent to child. It is therefore a powerful tool for tracing ancestry through the female line.

The mtDNA test allows you to undertake research into the records of your mother's maternal ancestors. This can be a daunting task. However, the mtDNA test results can be used to definitively confirm your research and the relationships in your maternal lineage (see Figure 13-3).

The rest of your DNA, the part that isn't the sex-determining chromosomes and the mitochondrial DNA, represents a mix of DNA from *both* your parents, and is known as autosomal DNA. In recent years, this has become the most popular type of DNA testing, because it can match so many potential cousins on all ancestral branches of your family. An autosomal DNA test is most effective, however, when people share comparatively recent common ancestors.

It is important to know that we inherit, on average, 50 percent of the DNA from each of our parents. Since our parents also inherited, on average, 50 percent of each of *their* parents' DNA, we can be certain that the DNA we inherited from our parents contains markers reflecting approximately 25 percent of our grandparents' DNA. The autosomal DNA test is used to study the marker code values of those 22 additional pairs of chromosomes, and then it is possible to compare those values against other

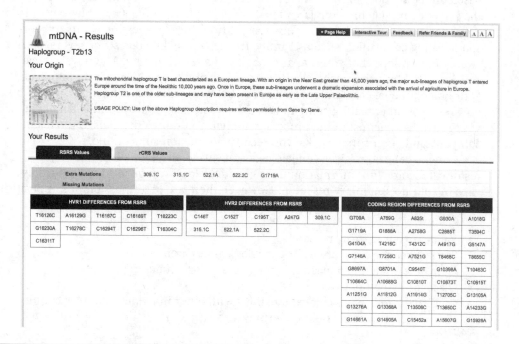

FIGURE 13-3   Sample of mtDNA test results from Family Tree DNA

people's test results to check for cousinship. First- and second-cousin relationships are almost certain to show up. The percentage of DNA from great-grandparents, great-great-grandparents, and more distant ancestors diminishes in each successive generation. Therefore, matches with third, fourth, and more distant cousins are still possible, but they are less likely than matches to closer relatives.

To summarize, there are three common types of DNA test available to assist in your genealogical research:

- **Y-DNA Test** This is a test available only for males to help determine their direct paternal line.
- **mtDNA Test** This is a test available to anyone (male or female) to help determine their direct maternal line.
- **Autosomal Test** This is a test available to anyone (male or female) to help determine all ancestral lines, but back only to a limited number of generations.

Test Processes and Results

You begin by deciding which DNA test you want (usually either Y-DNA, mtDNA, or autosomal DNA) and then investigating the companies that provide that type of test. In the case of a Y-DNA test, another consideration will be the number of genetic markers you want tested and reported on, because the price of the Y-DNA test is based on the number of markers tested. The more markers that are tested, the greater the accuracy in matching the DNA test results of other people. Once you have made these decisions, you can then order a test kit from the DNA testing company. For some testing companies, such as Family Tree DNA, the kit consists of several sterile swabs, an envelope that you seal and label, and a return mailer. The physical test consists of rubbing the swabs inside your mouth and then placing them into vials. Your oral epithelial cells and saliva contain DNA, and it is that which is captured on the swab. For other testing companies, such as Ancestry.com, you fill a small vial with your saliva, but the rest of the process is similar. You return the vials to the testing company and, after some weeks, you receive your test results online.

Genetic genealogy gives genealogists a means to check or supplement the historical record with information from genetic data. It can be used to help resolve gaps in your documentary research. However, there are other possibilities. A positive test match with another individual may

- Validate your existing research
- Suggest geographical areas for genealogical research
- Help determine the ancestral homeland and/or ethnic origin
- Discover living relatives
- Confirm or refute possible connections with other individuals and/or families
- Prove or disprove theories concerning ancestry

As you can see, Y-DNA and mtDNA tests can trace ancestry on the paternal and maternal lines, respectively. The autosomal DNA test, however, can take your research into a more precise area. It also will provide you with matches from *both* sides of your family at once.

You should know that there is resistance to DNA testing by some individuals. The reasons may include

- Uncertainty about which testing company to use
- Cost of the test
- Quality of the testing
- Variation in the number of markers tested by the companies
- Privacy issues
- Identity theft concerns

You may want to seek the participation of other relatives to help expand your genetic genealogy research. Many genealogists encourage cousins, aunts, and uncles to submit DNA test kits, even offering to pay for the testing in order to gather more sample data. You may want to consider this incentive approach in order to extend the range of your genetic research.

Learn About Genetic Testing Services

There are many commercial DNA testing services available. For each service you are considering, you will want to conduct research about the types of tests and the number of markers tested, the price of the tests, and any affiliations they may have with other companies and/or with surname DNA projects on the Internet. You may, in fact, be able to obtain a lower price as part of a surname group, discussed in the next section. Prices differ between the different types of testing, and prices also may vary between testing services. Some of the companies offer a combination of tests together in a bundle at a package deal price. You want to select a testing service whose results are specifically used for genealogical purposes. A DNA paternity test kit or a forensic DNA testing service is not going to be of value to your genealogical research.

The following table lists the three major DNA testing services for genealogists in the United States:

23andMe	**https://www.23andme.com**
Ancestry.com (AncestryDNA product)	**http://dna.ancestry.com**
Family Tree DNA	**https://www.familytreedna.com**

Join a DNA Surname Project on the Internet

Genealogists who have had their DNA tested want to locate genetic matches to other researchers. This is particularly true of those who have had their Y-DNA tested and are seeking matches with others with the same surname and those who have had their autosomal DNA tested and wish to connect with cousins. A surname DNA project is the ideal place to make connections with other researchers.

A surname project is a genetic genealogical project in which the results from Y-DNA testing are used to trace male lineage. Surnames are passed down from father to son in many cultures, and Y chromosomes are passed from father to son with a predictable rate of mutation. People who share the same surname can use Y-DNA testing to determine if they share a common ancestor within recent history. It is certainly possible for persons with a different surname to share the same Y-DNA test results. Don't jump to any conclusions, however. Yes, there may have been an illegitimate child, but other factors may also account for the discrepancy. There may have been a change of surname due to adoption; a man may have taken his wife's name; frequent misspelling of an earlier surname may have resulted in a man taking another surname; a surname may have been changed by a male immigrant in order to "fit in"; or a nickname or alias may have been used and was then taken as the surname.

The results of a Y-DNA test checks the values of Y-chromosome markers. Depending on the number of markers tested, the results can be compared to someone else's results and can reveal whether the two individuals share a common male ancestor. The number of markers tested and the number of matches at those markers can help determine the range of generations until their MRCA would be expected. Let's say that two men are tested using 37 genetic markers. If the two tests match exactly on 37 markers, there is a 50 percent probability that the MRCA was no more than two generations ago and a 90 percent probability that the MRCA was no more than five generations ago. A further comparison with other persons' test results might indicate a familial relationship.

A DNA surname project takes the comparison another step. By joining such a project on the Internet, you not only share your test results, but also provide documentation of that surname in your ancestry back to your earliest known male ancestor in that surname line. The administrator of the project adds your test results into a grid that allows for easy comparison of each marker's value with that of other people. The name of each participant's earliest documented ancestor is included, as is the haplotype. The results are typically grouped together by haplotype in order to create clusters of more closely related individuals. You can make contact with other researchers, usually with the project administrator acting as intermediary to help protect each person's identity and privacy until both researchers indicate their desire to communicate directly. You can then share more detailed genealogical information and collaborate to further one another's research.

Learn More About Genetic Genealogy

There is obviously much more that you can learn about genetic genealogy and using DNA test results in your research. There are several books available on the subject. I personally recommend the following titles:

- Aulicino, Emily D. *Genetic Genealogy: The Basics and Beyond.* AuthorHouse, 2013.
- Dowell, David R. *NextGen Genealogy: The DNA Connection.* Santa Barbara, CA: Libraries Unlimited, 2014.
- Pomery, Chris. *Family History in the Genes.* Kew, Richmond, Surrey, UK: The National Archives, 2007.
- Smolenyak, Megan, and Ann Turner. *Trace Your Roots with DNA: Using Genetic Tests to Explore Your Family Tree.* Emmaus, PA: Rodale, Inc., 2004.

Another excellent place to learn more about DNA is the How-To DNA blog at **http://howtodna.com**. This is a multimedia blog that includes videos, podcasts, and other types of postings to help you learn about genetic genealogy and how to understand and use the DNA test results. The author is Dr. Blaine T. Bettinger, professional genetic genealogist and author of the long-running blog, "The Genetic Genealogist" (**http://www.thegeneticgenealogist.com**).

The possibilities offered by DNA testing are increasing and improving each year. You will want to incorporate genetic genealogical research into your research toolkit, and gain another strong research facility for your family history.

14

Use Alternative Research Strategies to Locate Difficult-to-Find Ancestors

HOW TO...

- Recognize when you have hit a "brick wall"
- Look for alternate record types
- Take a fresh look at your evidence
- Reevaluate the quality of your sources
- Widen the scope of your search to include new and different sources
- Use photographs
- Develop an ancestor profile/timeline
- Switch to another family member to bypass your roadblock
- Seek help from libraries, archives, and societies
- Engage the help of a professional researcher
- Consider some common brick walls

Inevitably you will confront the genealogist's worst nightmare: the dreaded "brick wall." Despite all your best research efforts, your careful assessment of the evidence, documentation, and facts, the quality of your source materials, and your best hypotheses, you'll find you just can't progress any further. It happens to all of us, but the situation isn't always hopeless.

We have explored the most common record types, and you have learned about methodologies for using them to discover and document more about your ancestral families. There are literally hundreds of other types of records and artifacts that may provide valuable clues or data to expand your research. This chapter will provide an introduction to some of these resources.

Drew Smith and I wrote a book, *Advanced Genealogy Research Techniques* (McGraw-Hill, 2013), in which we address many ways of getting around research roadblocks. In addition to what you have learned here, I recommend that book as another resource to extend your genealogical research.

Recognize When You Have Hit a "Brick Wall"

Sometimes a person you think is going to be the simplest to locate becomes a dead end. Every avenue you explore seems to come to an abrupt halt. One of the most frustrating things is not being able to locate even the most basic vital or civil records that should have been where you expected to find them. Worse yet is the discovery that the person who you *thought* was your ancestor and in whom you've invested a great deal of research effort actually is not related to you at all. You've been researching someone *else's* ancestor!

Unfortunately, it is easy to become so consumed with the "ordinary" search that you may not even realize you've hit the proverbial "brick wall". The work you've done to hone your critical thinking skills can now provide the biggest payoffs.

There are several keys to solving your problem. The first thing to do is to recognize the fact that you really *do* have a brick wall, and that you haven't just made an oversight. Identify and literally describe the scope and symptoms of the problem. Write a description of your problem, including what you know to be fact and the sources of every fact in evidence. Also list pieces of evidence that are very solid or don't quite fit, and write the reason(s) why you believe as you do. Include in your description what you *want* to find out, what you *already* have searched, and the results you have *or* have not achieved. Finally, describe the brick wall and why you think it has stopped your research. Often, just putting the facts and the actions you've already taken into words on paper can help focus your attention on the real issues. Here are examples of just a few of the more common categories of research brick walls you can expect to encounter:

- Your ancestor's name is a common one, or there are numerous people of the same name in the same geographical area.
- You can locate no records for your ancestor—anywhere!
- You cannot identify your ancestor's parents or cannot link him or her with people who you believe are or might be the parents.
- Records have been lost, stolen, destroyed, or transferred elsewhere, and you can't absolutely determine what happened to them.
- Records that you want to access are private, restricted, or entirely closed to the public.
- No resources can be found on Internet web pages, in Internet-based free or subscription genealogical databases, and/or in those databases accessible through libraries and archives.
- Books or manuscripts are not readily available or are located far away.
- You are unable to confirm that a person you think is your ancestor really is *your* ancestor.

Using your written description of the problem *and* the resources you have already researched, now develop a list of alternative research paths, records, and other sources that might help resolve the problem. You may need to conduct some additional research to put your ancestor into geographical, historical, and/or social context and to determine what records might or might not exist to help you locate more information. You may not know about all the various alternative resources that might be available. Your continued reading, research, and collaboration with other genealogists can help you learn about these resources and how to maximize your use of them. We will look at some examples of problems and possible solutions in this chapter's final section, "Consider Some Common Brick Walls."

Look for Alternate Record Types

Alternate record types encompass many different types of materials, as you have seen. You are sure to encounter many materials in the course of your family history odyssey that can reveal facts or clues. We discussed in Chapter 7 the many types of death-related records (see Table 7-1), and I suspect you were astonished at the extensive number of source materials listed there.

American researchers lament the loss of the 1890 U.S. federal census population schedules. They understand that they have to look for other documentary evidence to help place their ancestors in a specific geographical location in the years between the 1880 and 1900 censuses. Here are just a few of the alternate records that can be used for this purpose, in alphabetical order:

- Cemetery records
- Church membership lists, bulletins, and other publications
- City directories
- College and university records and yearbooks
- Family Bible
- Family photographs
- Grantor and grantee indexes to property deeds
- Jury lists
- Letters, postcards, diaries, and journals
- Licenses (business, dog, professional, and other)
- Local histories
- Lodge and fraternal organization records
- Newspapers (local and trade union)
- Property tax rolls and tax lists
- School records (censuses) and yearbooks
- Telephone directories
- Voter applications and registration lists
- Wills and probate records (of the person and/or other family members)

English and Welsh researchers are fortunate to have civil registration records dating back to 1 July 1837 that record births, marriages, and deaths. Prior to that and back to the reign of King Henry VIII, parish records for Church of England congregations have been kept for christenings, marriages, and burials. Americans are not so fortunate in that there was no national law requiring registration of births, marriages, and deaths. That legislation was up to the various states' legislatures. Marriage records were maintained early on to document legitimacy of children and their legal right to inherit. However, governments in many states did not record births and deaths until well into the 20th century. American researchers therefore must rely on alternative records to help establish/document the date of birth for an ancestor. Here are some examples, in alphabetical order, of alternate records that might be used to *help* determine an individual's date of birth:

- Baby book
- Birth announcement (printed)
- Census population schedule (age or month/year)
- Church christening or baptism records
- Church membership record or church minutes
- Death certificate
- Family Bible
- Funeral home records
- Letters between family members
- Licenses (business and driver)
- Life insurance applications and redemption documents
- Military records (draft registration, enlistment, service records, pension records)
- Newspaper account of baby shower
- Newspaper birth announcement
- Obituary
- Photographs (labeled/dated)
- School records (enrollment and school censuses)
- Social Security Death Index (SSDI)
- Synagogue records; *bar mitzvah/bat mitzvah* records
- Tombstone
- Will and probate records and probate court minutes

Be sure not to ignore artifacts found among home sources and heirlooms. Family Bibles can provide clues to other records, even if the Bible itself is a secondary source. Other materials however can be of significant value. They may or may not be dated, but they can provide clues about your ancestors, including their level of education, their talents and skills, and other information, all of which can help you build context for their lives.

Take a Fresh Look at Your Evidence

One strategy that I consistently use is the reexamination of documentation and other evidence that I have previously collected. It amazes me how much information can be gleaned from taking a fresh look at something that I thought I knew so well.

Remember that over time you will gather new evidence of many types; learn more about history, geography, and other influences; and become acquainted with new people in your family history.

Reevaluate the Quality of Your Sources

Scholarly work is one of the goals of genealogical research and we are therefore always searching for the best evidence we can find. It is certainly gratifying to locate an original marriage certificate, created at the time of the marriage and bearing the actual signatures of the bride and groom. Few things are as exciting as holding and touching a document that was handled and signed by our ancestors and that was as important to them as a marriage certificate. The next best thing, of course, is seeing a facsimile of such a document on a photocopy, on microfilm, or as a digitized image. You already know that there are more and more digitized images being made available on the Internet every month.

Not all of our source materials, however, can be such excellent forms of evidence. As you've learned, genealogists work with sources of both primary *and* secondary information; with data transcribed, extracted, and abstracted from original documents; and with a vast array of published materials in all types of formats. In our quest to locate facts about our family, we often must use sources that may be one or more times removed from original source material, and often this information is less than 100 percent accurate. There may be something lost in the transfer, diluted as it were, and it is for that reason that we must maintain a keen awareness of primary *vs.* secondary information and be prepared to carefully analyze the quality of our sources.

An original marriage license would, indeed, be a great find. For most of us, however, the closest we will get is the entry in a county marriage book. Remember that the clerk transcribed that entry from the original marriage return document, and that errors might have been introduced.

Another problem we have occurs when all of the pieces of evidence we have acquired are not original or primary in nature. I often tell genealogists, "Two secondary sources do not a primary source make." Perhaps it sounds a little corny, but it is emphatically true. I recommend maintaining a healthy skepticism of almost any information until its authority can be proved, and then evaluate the weight that it may provide to the big picture.

One major factor contributing to many of our research brick walls can be a problem with the quality of the information we may have obtained from source materials. It is important to take a giant step back from a problem and reexamine all of our evidence. I don't mean "just" the sources of secondary information, but everything. As I said earlier, a great way to do this is to arrange every piece of evidence you have in the chronological sequence as it may have occurred in the ancestor's life. Reread everything in the chronological order of the events as they occurred. You are sure to find gaps in what you know. In the meantime, reexamine where your information was derived. What you may think is a solid fact may be well documented by a less than excellent source. Let me give you an example.

A friend in Georgia hit a brick wall in her search to prove the identities of the parents of her grandmother and locate other documentation about them. She had a death certificate for her grandmother that documented the date of death as 4 October 1935 and indicated the place of burial was to be in Munford, Alabama. The certificate stated that her grandmother had been born on 22 June 1859 in Atlanta, Georgia, and that she was 78 at the time of her death. The only information my friend had about the names of her great-grandparents came from the death certificate, and she inferred from the place of birth listed on her grandmother's death certificate that her great-grandparents had lived in Atlanta.

You will remember that a death certificate can be one of those "combination" sources: a source of primary information about the death and a source of secondary information about almost everything else. My friend knew that well, but still had entered the information she found on the death certificate into her genealogical database and documented the source. However, in her concentration on locating documentation on her great-grandparents, she failed to recognize that the *only* information she had about their names and the place they lived was the information from this death certificate. It turned out that the informant who provided the information for the death certificate was a nephew, and that he really did not know the facts about the date and place of birth, the names of the parents, and their place of residence. One glaring error was in the age shown on the certificate. Wait a minute! When I subtract 1859 from 1935, I come up with 76, not 78! Something was amiss here. And why was she to be buried in Alabama?

My friend backed up and began her research again, this time with a fresh perspective. She knew that she had made an error in judgment in assuming that the names, dates, and locations on the death certificate were "probably correct." She now knew that she needed to search for additional source materials. Her next step was to begin again with what she really knew to be factual based on primary information. She developed a list of document sources that might be available and that might help her solve her research problem. She did some research to determine where those documents might be located, and then began making contact with those locations to see what she could obtain by mail or email. She ultimately arranged to make two short trips to conduct on-site research.

After about a year, she told me that she had solved some problems and had finally gotten around her brick wall. There were four important pieces of information she had obtained from other materials that helped her:

- She located a copy of her grandmother's obituary, which indicated that she grew up in Greensboro, Georgia. It listed her age as 78, and not 76, and confirmed that burial was to occur in Munford, Alabama.
- She traveled to Alabama and located the cemetery where her grandmother was buried. Her grandmother's grave was next to that of her grandfather in *his* family's cemetery lot. That made sense. She also noted on her grandmother's gravestone the birth date of 22 June 1857, yet another confirmation of the age of 78 and not 76 years. While information carved on tombstones is definitely secondary in nature, in this case the information contradicted what the nephew had provided for the death certificate.

- She reexamined her grandparents' marriage certificate and noted the marriage date of 24 November 1881 and the place of issue as Greene County, Georgia. As it was often customary for a bride to be married at home or in her church, my friend believed it made sense to pursue research in Greene County and not in Atlanta.
- She traveled to Greensboro in Greene County to search for records of her grandmother's family. She located microfilmed copies of the local newspaper in the public library and began searching for marriage announcements. She found the announcement in a newspaper dated Thursday, 8 September 1881, and the notice included her grandmother's name, the name of her fiancé, and the names of *both* sets of parents and *their* places of residence.

Armed with the new information, my friend continued her research in Greene County and located a vast amount of information about her grandmother's family. She found church records, land and property records, tax rolls, and a probate packet for her great-grandfather in which his children's names were listed. Now knowing the correct state and county, she continued by working with the 1880 federal census records for Greene County to verify the family's residence there, the names of the children, and their ages. Furthermore, my friend learned that her great-grandfather had been the county sheriff for many years, including at the time that her grandmother had been born in 1857. She has been trying to determine whether her grandmother really was born in Atlanta or in Greensboro.

My friend's story is not uncommon. Even though her brick wall was a comparatively simple problem, it illustrates how a small error in judgment or an assumption can result in a major blockage in a person's research. This case required stepping back and reexamining the source material, followed with the development of an additional research plan, and some concentrated research to get around her brick wall. Since that time, she has extended her research to include other of her grandmother's siblings and has been able to identify and document her great-grandmother's parents and grandparents. She is still on the right research track, and she has extended her factual evidence by three generations.

Dissect Obituaries

Obituaries can offer tremendous clues for genealogical research. And even though they are distinctly sources of secondary information and prone to errors, they can provide pointers to a wide array of resources. Unfortunately, though, many researchers fail to get the most from an obituary.

A method of mining information from an obituary that really works involves dissecting the obituary. The process involves identifying every possible component that states or infers a fact, determining what evidentiary sources might exist to document or substantiate the fact, and then identifying where each source might be located.

Figure 14-1 shows a transcription of the obituary for a Tampa, Florida, resident who died on 30 December 1998. You can use a photocopy of an original obituary for

St. Petersburg Times - January 2, 1999

CANNON, NATHANIEL, SR., 81, of Port Tampa, died Wednesday (Dec. 30, 1998) at a local hospital. Born in Leesburg, he came here from Sanford more than 50 years ago. He was a retired exchange manager for the federal government. He was a member of St. Mark Missionary Church. He served in the Navy during World War II. He served as chairman of the deacon board of his church. He was Sunday school superintendent, president of Usher Board No. 1 and a member of Ushers' Union No. 3 at his church. He was a member of the board of directors for Old St. Mark Community Air Center, Port Tampa. He was a member of the NAACP and Mayor's Awareness Task Force for the city of Tampa. Survivors include four sons, Nathaniel, Jr., Norman T., Tyrone and Gilbert, and a daughter, Gisele Jones, all of Tampa; and five grandchildren. Wilson Funeral Home, Tampa.

FIGURE 14-1   Transcription of the obituary of Nathaniel Cannon, Sr., from the *St. Petersburg Times* on 2 January 1999

your dissection. I have underlined each component that might point to sources of evidence about Mr. Nathaniel Cannon, Sr.'s life.

The following table shows the component pieces of information that may point to other information, what that evidence may be, and where it might be located. Some of these records may be sources of distinctly secondary information, such as the tombstone, directories, and so forth. They should not, however, be overlooked as they can provide another source of corroboration of the fact in consideration.

Obituary Content	Type of Evidence	Where Evidence Might Be Found
Cannon, Nathaniel, Sr.,	Name	Birth document Death certificate Social Security application (SS-5 form) Social Security Death Index (SSDI) Tombstone Other documentary sources
81	Age	Same as above
Port Tampa	Residence	City directory Telephone directory Voter registration list Land and property tax records Jury list
died Wednesday (Dec. 30, 1998)	Date of Death	Death certificate Probate records Tombstone
local hospital	Place of Death	Death certificate You probably will not be able to obtain copies of medical records or other confirmation of death in a medical facility

Obituary Content	Type of Evidence	Where Evidence Might Be Found
Born in Leesburg	Place of Birth	Birth document Christening or baptism records Birth announcement in newspaper School enrollment U.S. federal census Military records Death certificate Family letters, diaries, or journals
came here from Sanford more than 50 years ago	Previous Place of Residence	School records City directory Church membership records
retired exchange manager for the federal government	Employer	Social Security Application form (SS-5) Paycheck stubs Income tax returns Employee directory Family members
member of St. Mark Missionary Church	Church Membership	Church membership roll Home sources
He served in the Navy during World War II	Military Service	Military service records available through the National Personnel Records Center (NPRC) in St. Louis, Missouri Military documents among home source materials Photographs Copy of military discharge in the county courthouse in the county in which he lived when he returned from military service Pension records available from NPRC or from the U.S. Department of Veterans Affairs
chairman of the deacon board of his church	Church Service	Records of St. Mark Missionary church, including church minutes and bulletins Fellow members of the church
Sunday school superintendent	Church Service	Same as above
president of Usher Board No. 1	Church Service	Same as above
member of Ushers' Union No. 3 at his church	Church Service	Same as above
member of the board of directors for Old St. Mark Community Air Center, Port Tampa	Community Service	Contact the Old St. Mark Community Air Center, Port Tampa, Florida, to learn more about his involvement and participation Check local newspapers

(Continued)

Obituary Content	Type of Evidence	Where Evidence Might Be Found
member of the NAACP	Membership	Contact the NAACP, and locate the local unit in the Port Tampa, Florida, area for membership information Check local newspapers
member of Mayor's Awareness Task Force for the city of Tampa	Community Service	Contact office of the Mayor of Tampa, Florida, for information Check local newspapers
list of survivors and place of residence	Survivors	Investigate each person in the location cited in the obituary for his or her information
Wilson Funeral Home, Tampa	Funeral Home	Obtain details about services provided for the deceased and his family Determine place of interment Determine date of interment Follow up with cemetery administrator or sexton for other death-related records

You can see that this obituary is packed with informational details that provide clues to other evidence. Some of this evidence will take the form of documents, while other sources will include making contact with family members, friends, fellow church members, and other people. Don't ever overlook a cemetery's office; its files may contain letters, a burial permit, records of the installation of a marker, a copy of a death certificate, and possibly a transit permit.

Once you have dissected the obituary for types of alternative records, take the time to consider the places where each of those records might be found. Next, determine how you might access the records from the places where they are located. Remember that exact copies in various formats such as microfilm and digitized may be available in multiple places. You can then prepare your research plans to locate the records and access them for your personal examination. This may involve making a visit to a specific repository, writing letters or making phone calls, working with a database of digitized images, or some other form of accessing copies for your personal examination and evaluation.

Widen the Scope of Your Search to Include New and Different Sources

One of the joys of genealogy is learning about different resources that can be used to document your family history. Discovery of these materials is exciting and invariably leads to a desire to learn more about them. I remember my excitement at learning about transit permits, those documents that are used to facilitate the transport of bodies across state or national borders to a hometown or some other place of interment. A transit permit can contain a great deal of information about the individual and, prior to the use of official death certificates, can provide details about the cause of death. In the course of my research, I have encountered transit permits in cemeteries' files for soldiers in the U.S. Civil War who died in battle or from disease. I even found a death certificate for my great-uncle, Luther Moffett Holder, who died of tuberculosis en route by train from New Mexico to Georgia. A digital image found on Fold3 gave me the documentary proof I needed to confirm his death in 1908 (see Figure 14-2).

I've also seen transit permits for a woman killed by a train, people killed by gunshot wounds, several suicides, and for people who died from any number of different diseases. Transit permits that allowed the transport of Civil War soldiers' bodies from one state to another may still be inside cemeteries' administrators' files or inscribed in interment books. These may be the only records of the causes of death of these soldiers. This certainly is not unusual in the offices of administrators and sextons in Canada, the United Kingdom, Australia, and other places worldwide.

There are literally hundreds of documents you may never have imagined existed that could help you document your ancestors and family members. Beyond the record types I've covered in this book, you will want to consider other sources. How do you find out about them? Well, there are all sorts of books available that can introduce you to descriptions and samples of these records. Let me share a few of my favorites.

Hidden Sources: Family History in Unlikely Places, by Laura Szucs Pfeiffer, is a compilation of more than a hundred different record types that may be of help to your personal research. Each record type is described in detail, along with information about places where it can be located and how it can be used. You will find an illustration included for each record and a bibliography for additional reading and reference. Some of the more interesting records are almshouse records, coroner's inquests, bankruptcy records, Freedmen's Bureau records, name change records, orphan asylum records, passport records, school censuses, street indexes, post office guides and directories, patent records, and voter registration records.

FIGURE 14-2 Death certificate of the author's great-uncle, Luther Moffett Holder

Another excellent compilation is *Printed Sources: A Guide to Published Genealogical Records*, edited by Kory L. Meyerink. This impressive book contains authoritative chapters concerning different record categories, written by a number of eminent genealogical experts. For example, if you are looking for a more thorough understanding of U.S. military records, David T. Thackery's chapter, "Military Sources," is a comprehensive study of what types of records are available and a selective description of published sources for major military conflicts. Records at the federal, colonial, and state level are addressed in detail; histories, rosters, and important reference works are described; and a vast, definitive biography is included.

A study of English parish records requires some understanding of the structure of the parish system *and* of the social responsibilities of the parish officer. *The Compleat Parish Officer* is a reprint by the Wiltshire Family History Society of a 1734 handbook for those persons "who had to apply and interpret the increasingly complex laws enacted to deal with the various social problems as they arose, its starting point being the Great Poor Law Act of 1601 and its various amendments." This compact little book details the authorities and responsibilities of parish constables, churchwardens, overseers of the poor, surveyors of the highways and scavengers, and other officials in the parish operational hierarchy. It is an invaluable primer for genealogists and family historians in understanding the English parish environment and the records that are found documenting your ancestors.

A companion to *The Compleat Parish Officer* is Anne Cole's *An Introduction to Poor Law Documents Before 1834*. This volume describes the parish documents, explaining the reasons for each one's creation, the contents, and what can be gleaned from them. The settlement certificate, for example, was an exceptionally important document for those to whom it was issued. It provided legal proof of residence in the parish and thus, in time of need, entitled the person to financial assistance. However, more importantly, the settlement certificate was used to provide permission to persons to relocate their place of residence from one parish to another. These two books, used together, provide excellent insight for the researcher of English parish records.

The few examples I've provided here merely begin to scratch the surface of the wide range of record types that can be found and used for your genealogical documentation. I urge you to use the resources of library and archive catalogs, particularly the subject and title search facilities of their online catalogs, to locate books of interest for these topics. In addition, you will find that using the bibliographies included in many genealogical and historical publications will lead you to more reference materials. Further, be sure to check out digitized books available at Google Books (**http://books.google.com**) and other online venues that have been discussed earlier in this book.

Use Photographs in Your Family Research

If you're like most people, you have a collection of photographs stored somewhere in your home. Many of these may be identified and labeled, but you probably have a substantial group of unlabeled photographs, and I refer to these in my home as "the unknowns." You will find that photographs can, indeed, be helpful in identifying persons and placing them in a specific place at a particular point in time.

Photographs have been around since the production of the first photographic image in the summer of 1826, which is universally credited to Frenchman Joseph Nicéphore Niépce. Over time, other processes and methods of mounting or displaying photographs were developed and introduced. You will find that the type of photograph and its physical attributes, the mountings used, the clothing and hairstyle worn by the subjects, and the background or surroundings can be used to date your photographs with surprising accuracy. It is important to understand a little history of photography first.

Learn About the Types of Photographs

Louis Daguerre's technique of capturing an image on a silver-clad copper plate was officially announced in 1839. These first commercially successful photographs were known as *daguerreotypes* and were, at the time, quite expensive. A daguerreotype was usually attached to a sheet of glass using a decorative frame made with a sheet of gold-colored heavy foil. The decoration was usually embossed into the foil material before enclosing the daguerreotype and its glass. This unit was then press-fitted into a wooden case specifically designed to hold a daguerreotype and sometimes padded with satin, silk, or velvet. The case also may have been a two-piece, hinged affair with a clasp that closed and protected the daguerreotype.

The *calotype* was the first paper photograph, and it was made using a two-step process. The first step involved treating smooth, high-quality writing paper with a chemical wash of silver nitrate. This wash process was performed in a dim, candlelit room and the paper was then exposed to a little heat until it was almost dry. While still somewhat moist, the paper was soaked in a solution of potassium iodide for several minutes, then rinsed and gently dried. The chemical processes in effect iodized the surface of the paper to prepare it for its ultimate exposure to light. The slow drying process preserved the smooth texture of the paper, preventing wrinkling and puckering of its surface. The iodized paper could be stored for some time in a dark, dry place at a moderate temperature. The second step occurred almost immediately before the iodized paper was to be used for a photograph. The photographer mixed a solution of equal parts of silver nitrate and gallic acid that, because of its inherent instability, had to be used right away. Once again, in dim candlelight, the iodized paper that had been prepared in the first step was dipped in this solution, rinsed with water, and blotted dry. It was then loaded in complete darkness into the camera and the calotype photographic image was captured. While the paper treated to the second solution could be dried and stored for use a short time later, the most reliable images were captured using paper still moist with the solution. Calotypes were made for perhaps a decade, from approximately 1845 until 1855. The main problem with them was that because the silver nitrate–gallic acid solution was not chemically stable, many of the images faded over a relatively short time. The surviving examples of many of these early calotypes appear as shadows or "ghosts" on the paper.

The *ambrotype* was introduced in 1854 and became very popular throughout the United States during the Civil War period. An ambrotype is a thin negative image bonded to a sheet of clear glass. When the negative image is mounted and displayed against a black background, the image appears as a positive. Ambrotypes were mounted in display cases much like those used for daguerreotypes.

Photography gained huge popularity in Great Britain when it was showcased at the Great Exhibition of 1851 in London. Both Queen Victoria and her husband, Prince Albert, were fascinated with photography and there are numerous photographs of the couple and other members of the Royal Family dating back to the 1840s. The public was introduced to several displays of photographs in various locations at the Exhibition, and a subsequent increase in photographers' business in England has been attributed to that event.

The *tintype* was introduced in the early- to mid-1850s and was in use until the early 1930s. It became hugely popular in both the United States and Great Britain because it was cheap to produce and therefore accessible by almost everyone. Advertisements of the time touted them as the "penny photograph," and street photographers became commonplace sights in towns, cities, and at resort areas such as Brighton, England, and Atlantic City, New Jersey, and also at carnivals and fairs. Tintypes were extremely popular during the U.S. Civil War when soldiers wished to have a picture made of themselves in uniform with their rifle or sword to send home to loved ones. Since a tintype is an image made on metal instead of on a glass plate, it could be mailed without concern for breakage. There is no "tin" in a tintype; it actually is a thin sheet of black iron. The original name for the tintype was *melainotype*, but the more common name is *ferrotype*, which refers to the ferrous (iron) base on which the image is recorded. It has been suggested that the term "tintype" was derived from the use of tin sheers used to cut and trim the images on the metal plates. Many tintypes will be irregular in shape, because of the imprecise trimming work. It is possible to narrow the dating of tintype photographs produced during this extensive period based on a number of criteria, especially in the United States:

- **1856–1860** The iron plate stock used in this period is thicker than at any other time, and plates are typically stamped on the edge with "Neff's Melainotype Pat 19 Feb 56." They may be found in gilded frames reminiscent of those used with ambrotypes or in leather sleeves.
- **1861–1865** During the Civil War years, their paper display sleeves may help to date tintypes. These "frames" may bear patriotic symbols such as stars and flags, and early ones bear the imprint of Potter's Patent. After 1863, the paper holders became fancier, with designs embossed into the paper holder rather than printed. In an effort to raise revenue to help fund the Union Army, the U.S. Congress imposed a tax to be collected on all photographs sold between 1 September 1864 and 1 August 1866. A revenue stamp was required to be adhered to the reverse side of the photograph, either on the photographic plate itself or in the case. The tax was based on the amount of the sale, and these revenue stamps are highly prized by stamp collectors. Some photographers initialed the stamps to cancel them and included the day's date and this provides a precise date for the completion of the sale of the photograph.

- **1870–1885**   This period is referred to as the "Brown Period" because one company, the Phoenix Plate Company, introduced a ferrous plate with a chocolate-tinted surface. Soon photographers across the United States were clamoring to use this new style of plate. You should also know that photographers began using painted backgrounds reflecting a "country" look, with fences, trees, stones, and other rural images, in this time period. The painted rural background in these photographs is a telltale indicator that the photograph was made after 1870.

- **1863–1890**   Photographer Simon Wing patented a multiplying camera that captured multiple images on a single plate. These photographs measured approximately .75" × 1" and became known and marketed as "Gem" or "Gem Galleries" photographs. These tiny portraits were typically mounted in ovals and attached to a larger mounting card. Some were even cut to fit into pieces of jewelry, such as lockets, cameo frames, cufflinks, and stickpins.

- **Circa 1866–1906**   A new method of mounting photographs was introduced and is referred to as the "cabinet card." The photograph was adhered to a piece of cardboard stock. Early cabinet card stock is rather plain, with designs printed on the card. The type and color of the card stock and its decoration changed over the years, with embossed designs, colored inks, beveling, gilded or silvered card edges, and scalloped corners and edges being used at different periods. Photograph mountings were a point of high fashion, and you can use these distinctive traits, card sizes, and card thicknesses to date the period in which the photograph was made. The example shown in Figure 14-3 can be dated by the

FIGURE 14-3   This photograph of the author's great-grandmother, Ansibelle Penelope Swords Holder, was taken circa 1885.

card stock to the period between 1880 and 1890 because the card stock is quite heavy, the front and reverse sides are of different colors, and the front surface is textured, rather than smooth. The woman's hairstyle indicates a bun worn high in the back. The not-so-high collar, the ornamental pleating on the shoulders of her dress, and the detailed, raised embroidery along the neckline and down the front of the bodice are indicative of fashion three to five years prior to the explosive couture of the 1890s.

- At the same time that cabinet cards were being used, other sizes and styles of photographic mountings came into use. One very popular format was a smaller mounting referred to as the *carte-de-visite*, or visiting card. These cards, like the example shown in Figure 14-4, typically measured 4 1/4" × 2 1/2" and were made of heavy, often glossy card stock. They became the rage and were used as souvenirs and, true to their name, were left as calling or visiting cards.
- Other popular styles and sizes included the Victoria (5" × 3 1/4"), the Promenade (7" × 4"), the Boudoir (8 1/2" × 5 1/4"), the Imperial (9 7/8" × 6 7/8"), the Panel (8 1/4" × 4"), and the stereograph (3" × 7").
- The stereoscope became a tremendously popular form of entertainment and education, beginning in approximately 1849 and continuing until the

FIGURE 14-4   A typical *carte-de-visite*

FIGURE 14-5   A stereograph looking east from the intersection of Ellis and Jones Streets in San Francisco, California, following the devastating earthquake on 18 April 1906

mid- to late-1920s. The apparatus consisted of a viewing hood with two lenses and an attached arm on which a sliding holder was mounted. The stereoscope was used to view *stereographs* such as the one shown in Figure 14-5, which depicts destruction following the San Francisco earthquake of 18 April 1906. A stereograph is a card on which two almost identical photographs are mounted side by side. When viewed with the stereoscope, the effect is that of a three-dimensional view of the subject. Tens of thousands of stereographs were made for the huge consumer demand for more and more subjects. In fact, you might draw an analogy between the stereograph and a modern television/DVD setup. People could not seem to get enough of them. Subjects included Civil War battlefields and scenes, world travel photographs, public figures, expositions such as the St. Louis and Pan-American Expositions, Americana, African-American subjects, children's games and antics, costumes, cemetery tours, and even series of stereographs telling a story.

- **Circa 1889 to Present**   Photography historians argue about who invented photographic film. However, an Englishman named John Carbutt, who also was an accomplished stereographer living and working in the United States, is credited with coating sheets of celluloid with a photographic emulsion while working in Philadelphia in 1888. In that same year, George Eastman introduced a new camera called the Kodak that used a roll of photographic film. The camera with the film still inside was sent to his company for processing, and the camera and a new roll of film were returned to the customer. Within a year, the Kodak name was a household word in the United States, Great Britain, Canada, France, and elsewhere, and the public was hooked on photography. People even had a choice of the way photos were printed, including as a face side for a postcard.

- Over the years, several film base materials and a number of emulsion processes were used, each having specific attributes. You can learn more about 20th-century photography and fashions in books on the subjects and on the Internet.

You probably never knew there was so much to learn about photographs, did you? One of the best books on the subject of dating photographs is Maureen A. Taylor's *Uncovering Your Ancestry Through Family Photographs*.

Date Photographs Using Clothing and Hair Fashions

Don't overlook the fact that clothing and hairstyles shown in photographs can be very important research clues. Studio photographs were often made with the subject wearing his or her very best clothing, sometimes purchased specifically for the occasion. A photograph of a woman wearing a dress with a wasp waist and balloon sleeves, mounted on a cabinet card with a buff-colored, matte front and a dark-gray back, with gold beveled edge can be dated to within a year or so of its creation date. Examine the paper stock or card stock for a printed or embossed studio name (and location), which helps to narrow the focus of your genealogical search to a time and place.

Be sure to examine photographs for tiny details that might yield clues. Pay attention to buildings, signage, the presence or absence of electric and telephone wires, the styles of wagons and carriages, the sizes of trees and shrubs, and every detail that might communicate location and time period. Look at military insignia on uniforms, name badges or sewn-on patches, and other clothing details. Researching an old photograph is much like reading between the lines in a book. Enlarge and enhance photographic images to bring out details.

An excellent book on the subject of fashions over the centuries is *Out-of-Style: A Modern Perspective of How, Why and When Fashions Evolved*, by Betty Kreisel Shubert (Flashback Publishing, 2013), which contains hundreds of illustrations and descriptions of clothing fashions. The book can be used to help you identify the time period during which a photograph was made.

You can also search the Internet using general phrases such as "history of photography" or "costume history" or conduct more specific searches such as "Victorian clothing"; "women's dresses" + 1830s; history + "men's clothing" 1860s; or other combinations of keywords and/or phrases. There is a wealth of information available to help you narrow the date and place of your photographs.

Switch to Another Family Member to Bypass Your Roadblock

Sometimes, despite all your research, analysis, and troubleshooting efforts, an ancestral brick wall will just be entirely too contrary. Every effort at direct research may be thwarted. What can you do now?

One of my favorite techniques is what I call "Sidestep Genealogy." This can be comparatively simple to perform, and involves locating another close family member and switching your research focus. There have been times when I have encountered a brick wall in my research for one person and could not progress to the next generation. What I do then is review all I know about the person through compiling an ancestor profile. If I can identify a sibling or some other blood relative, I move to that person and begin conducting detailed research. I often have found that, while my ancestor may not have left a very good paper trail, his or her brother or sister may have. As a result, by researching a sibling, I have sometimes been able to trace the sibling's parents and then, from one or both parents' records, have been able to make the connection downward to my own ancestor.

If you cannot locate or identify a sibling to use in your research sidestep, look for another relative such as an aunt, uncle, cousin, and so forth. If you can identify one person as a focal point, you may just be able to blaze a new research path, albeit sometimes convoluted, up, down, and across the family tree, to locate the link that can then be connected downward to your own ancestor.

Seek Help from Libraries, Archives, Museums, and Societies

It may seem intuitive but genealogists often overlook the services that can be obtained from librarians, archivists, museums, and all types of societies. Librarians and archivists are among my favorite people. They are intelligent and have a nearly unquenchable thirst for knowledge. They love to research interesting and difficult questions and to provide help and instruction to their patrons. These unsung heroes of our communities are trained and skillful professional researchers. They may not know where my great-grandmother Penelope Swords Holder was born, but they know how to employ their research skills, techniques, and tools to help me locate print and electronic reference materials.

If I have a particularly impossible question about the location of a place that no longer appears on any map, I certainly try to search the materials at my disposal. That includes my own collection of maps, atlases, and gazetteers; online databases and map collections; and any possible Internet resource that I am creative enough with search terms to locate. After my own exhaustive searches, however, I have been known to contact an academic library with a good map collection, a state library or archive, and even the cartographic division of places like the Library of Congress, the National Archives and Records Administration, the National Geographic Society, and The National Archives in the UK. The staffs at these places are experts in locating this type of information and are always willing to help.

I encourage you to join genealogical societies in the places in which your ancestors lived and where you are conducting research. The cost is comparatively small but the benefits can be great. The publications of these societies, such as journals, magazines, and newsletters, often contain articles that provide contextual insight about your ancestors' lives and the events in the area. A genealogical or historical society may have conducted a project to identify, document, or otherwise produce a compendium of names, locations, or events in a specific area. They may even have published some or all of the information in a book or journal, but other materials may not yet have been made publically available in any widespread way. These materials may significantly extend your research. In addition, there is the opportunity to connect with other researchers who might be researching your family or connected collateral lineages.

Genealogical *and* historical societies are excellent resources to assist in your research. Even if you are not a member, you may still make an inquiry of such a group to request information. The society can check its own collection of information and reference material and respond with information for you. Often, too, a society member will make an extra effort to help by heading to a local library, courthouse, government office, cemetery, or other facility to do a quick look-up for you. These "genealogical angels" perform extraordinarily kind services, and while it often is not expected or requested, I always offer to reimburse the person for the cost of their mileage, photocopies, postage, and other expenses. Don't overlook the Federation of Genealogical Societies (FGS) at **http://www.fgs.org** and the New England Historic Genealogical Society (NEHGS) at **http://www.americanancestors.org** in the United States, and the Federation of Family History Societies (FFHS) at **http://www.ffhs.org.uk** in the United Kingdom as resources to help connect you to important organizations and resources in their areas.

Heritage and lineage societies are another excellent source of information. Their staffs and members often maintain extensive collections of printed materials, as well as genealogical records and data submitted by members. These people are experts in genealogical problem solving and know how to address difficult questions and help find answers to obscure facts. There are scores of different such societies, many with regional chapters, lodges, or branches.

You may also determine that your ancestor or another family member was a member of a particular professional, fraternal, trade, alumni, or similar membership organization. If so, consider locating their headquarters and inquiring about any records that may exist about your ancestor, a website where those records might be located, and how to proceed to request them. Almost all of these organizations will have a website that you may locate using an Internet search engine.

All of these entities exist to serve their members, and their membership operational staffs may be able to help you locate information on your ancestor. They provide yet another resource to help you locate information to get past your brick wall.

Engage the Help of a Professional Researcher

There may come a time when you simply cannot get past your most stubborn brick wall. After trying everything you can think of and following every link you can discover, you may realize that you need the help of a professional genealogical researcher.

A professional genealogical researcher can help you in one of two ways. First, he or she can perform research for you on a fee basis, or second, he or she can act as a paid consultant to you and provide guidance and advice. Before engaging a professional, it is important to identify one who is qualified to provide the service(s) you wish performed, reach agreement on the scope of the work, and define the guidelines that will govern the arrangement.

Locate a Qualified Professional Genealogical Researcher

Anyone who has experience in genealogical research can assist and advise you. However, your best guidance will come from an individual who has been professionally trained and/or has successfully passed tests administered by a professional genealogy credentialing body. There are a number of organizations whose genealogical credentialing standards are held in high esteem. Let me share some of those with you, along with their websites at which you can learn more.

Association of Professional Genealogists (U.S.)

The Association of Professional Genealogists (APG) is not an accreditation or credentialing body, *per se*. It is, instead, a membership organization consisting of more than 2,000 members in the United States, Canada, and 20 other countries whose primary purpose is to support professional genealogists in all phases of their work, from the amateur genealogist wishing to turn knowledge and skill into a vocation, to the experienced professional seeking to exchange ideas with colleagues and to upgrade the profession as a whole. Headquartered in Westminster, Colorado, the association also seeks to protect the interests of those engaging in the services of the professional. Their website at **http://www.apgen.org** presents a good primer at their link labeled "Hiring a Professional," located under the Publications menu. In addition, the site contains a searchable database of all current APG members, their titles and/ or certification, organizations with which they are associated, and their area(s) of expertise or specialization.

Association of Professional Genealogists in Ireland

The Association of Professional Genealogists in Ireland (APGI) acts as a regulating body to maintain high standards among its members and to protect the interests of clients. Its members are drawn from every part of Ireland and represent a wide variety of interests and expertise. Applicants are required to submit samples of their work in the form of a report on research conducted over a period of not less than five hours, exclusive of report preparation time. The association's website is located at **http://www.apgi.ie**.

The Board for Certification of Genealogists

The Board for Certification of Genealogists (BCG) is an independent, internationally recognized organization headquartered in Washington, D.C., that certifies qualified individuals in the field of genealogy. They define their mission as follows: "To foster public confidence in genealogy as a respected branch of history by promoting an attainable, uniform standard of competence and ethics among genealogical practitioners, and by publicly recognizing persons who meet that standard." Certification involves preparing a portfolio of materials, which is independently reviewed by a panel of three or four judges. BCG requires different materials for each of the following certification categories (the credential designations are shown in parentheses):

- Certified Genealogist (CG)
- Certified Genealogical Lecturer (CGL)

BCG has published the *BCG Genealogical Standards Manual*, which details the requirements for certification in each category. Certification is for a period of five years, after which time the researcher may apply for renewal of his or her certification.

The BCG website at **http://www.bcgcertification.org** maintains a current roster of certified individuals, searchable by where they are located and by special interests (Irish, English, Jewish, African-American, church records, and more).

Genealogical Institute of the Maritimes

The Genealogical Institute of the Maritimes (Institut Généalogique des Provinces Maritimes) is a nonprofit organization that examines and certifies persons wishing to establish their competence in the field of genealogical research. The first level of certification is that of Genealogical Record Searcher [Canada] [GRS (C)]; the second is that of Certified Genealogist [Canada] [CG (C)]. By completing a preliminary application form that assigns points for education, genealogical research experience, and publication, a candidate is evaluated through a points system to determine if he or she possesses the qualifications required to apply for certification at either of these two levels. More information is available at their website at **http://nsgna.ednet.ns.ca/gim**.

International Commission for the Accreditation of Professional Genealogists

The International Commission for the Accreditation of Professional Genealogists (ICAPGen) is a professional credentialing organization that is involved in testing an individual's competence in genealogical research. Originally established in 1964 by the Family History Department of The Church of Jesus Christ of Latter-day Saints (LDS), the program was transferred to ICAPGen in 2000. At the time of the transfer, ICAPGen was affiliated with the Utah Genealogical Association (UGA).

Each applicant for the ICAPGen Accredited Genealogist (AG) credential must demonstrate through extensive written and oral testing, and through production of high-quality, well-researched documentation, that he or she is an expert in a particular geographical or subject area. The current areas of geographical testing are the United States, the British Isles, Scandinavia, Canada, Continental Europe, Latin America, and the Pacific Area. You can learn more about the specific countries and regions included by visiting the ICAPGen website at **http://www.icapgen.org**.

The ICAPGen website also provides a database of accredited researchers, searchable by name, their place of residence, or area of specialization. PDF files of North American and International researchers are also available for printing.

Other Credentials

Individual genealogical researchers may have been awarded other credentials than those previously listed. Some colleges and universities offer courses in genealogical studies, and there are any number of specialized genealogical lecture programs and institutes offering individual classes or immersion conferences. These all may entitle the student or attendee to receive the award of a certificate, diploma, or another document attesting to his or her successful completion of the curriculum. These may be weighed in your decision-making process to determine if an individual has the education, experience, and expertise to perform the service(s) you require.

Define the Scope of the Work to Be Performed

Once you decide which professional researcher you want to hire, he or she will likely ask you to define exactly what you are seeking. You should prepare a written report on the individual or family group for which you want research performed, and provide all the information you have gathered. Include names, dates, and source materials you have located, and a description of each item's contents. Here is where an ancestor profile can really come in handy. What you are doing, in effect, is preparing for your potential researcher a complete picture of what you know.

Once that is prepared, you must decide what it is you want to know, and what you want the professional researcher to find for you. These two items may not be one and the same. For example, you may believe that identifying the parents of one ancestor may be all you need in order to continue your research beyond that point.

On the other hand, you may decide that you want the researcher to accept the commission and pursue your research farther. For example, you may have traced your ancestors back to a point at which they arrived from another country or continent, and you want the researcher to first locate the passenger arrival records to determine their port of departure, and then to trace your ancestors back to their native town or village.

Establish Guidelines, Goals, and Milestones

It is important to be precise in determining the goal or goals of your research. Your goal(s) will determine the scope of the work to be performed, and you should also define the scope in writing. This document complements the documentation of your research to date, that is, the ancestor profile.

The professional researcher will now be able to review your research materials and evaluate the scope of your project goals. Request a written research plan, an itemized estimate of research time and expenses, a reasonable timetable for the project, and a list of project deliverables. For example, the researcher may determine that locating your immigrant ancestors' passenger arrival may take 15 hours' work, tracing the ancestors to their native village may take another 30 hours' work, and preparation of the final report may take another 5 hours' work, a total of 50 hours' work. In addition, costs of document copies, photocopies, telephone calls, postage, mileage, travel, lodging, and meals may be itemized to present an itemized grand total. A good researcher will generally offer you a list of references, and may provide a sample of a final report to give you an idea of the quality of the final product you would receive.

Take your time to review the researcher's proposal and weigh the expenses against what it might cost you in time and money to perform a similar job. Contact the references the researcher provided and discuss their experience with the researcher. Describe at a high level to each reference what it is you want the researcher to do for you, and ask if the person believes the researcher could and would be able to satisfy your need. Take notes and prepare additional questions for your potential research candidate.

Schedule a time to meet with or talk by telephone with your researcher about any questions you have. Make sure that they are all answered to your satisfaction. At that time, consider all the information you have at hand and make your decision. Investing in a professional researcher's services is much like buying an automobile. It pays to do your advance research and to shop around as necessary for the right researcher. Requesting proposals from two or more researchers is not a bad idea. This advance work may save you money and frustration as the project progresses.

Document the Relationship

Let's say that you have decided to accept the proposal of one professional researcher. The association between the two of you should be a formal contractor-contractee relationship. As such, it should be documented in the form of a contract. A good contract will detail the scope of the work. It also will specify the exact amount of time the researcher will spend and the precise amount of money that you authorize for the project. Be sure to establish benchmarking milestones in the project schedule. These facilitate communication of status reports from the researcher so that you know what is happening. It will help alleviate surprises later on and will allow you both to determine early on whether the scope and goals of the project need to be adjusted.

The contract should include payment terms, and it is not unusual to use a graduated payment schedule. For example, you might choose to pay 25 percent of the total fee as an advance before the project commences; incremental payments payable at certain milestone points, such as written status reports or some mutually agreeable criteria; and the remainder as a final payment when the final report and documentation are delivered. Include a contract cancellation clause that protects your and the researcher's interests.

A good contract is mutually acceptable to both you and your researcher. It should be designed to provide legal protection for both of you. With the project goals and deliverables clearly defined, and the authorized expenses clearly itemized, your expectations and those of the researcher are set.

Conclude the Relationship

When the research project is completed, and you have received your final report and accompanying documentation, make time to read and study its contents. Prepare a list of any questions you have about the contents or outstanding issues. At that point, you should schedule and conduct a final recap meeting with your researcher. Discuss the report and any questions you have about it, the documentation, the source materials found, where they were located, the source citations, and any other pertinent issues. You may learn a great deal from the researcher's recounting of the research process, including information that he or she may have encountered about other individuals that is not included in the report. These may be leads that you can pursue on your own at a later date.

If your experience with your professional researcher has been a positive one, you can offer to be a reference for his or her future clients' inquiries. In the event that the experience has been problematic or the researcher has not performed in a professional or ethical manner, you should consider contacting the certifying or regulatory body that awarded his or her genealogical credentials and file a formal report. This action will help the organization keep track of problems and consider them when reviewing the renewal of the individual's certification or continuation of accreditation. It also helps protect other genealogists from an unsatisfactory researcher.

You will find that professional genealogical researchers are eager to help you and subscribe to a code of high professional ethics and behavior. Seeking out a credentialed individual with the qualifications and experience in the field of specialization you require is a solid first step to getting what you want from a professional research experience. Carefully setting the goals and establishing the contractual relationship with your researcher is essential. You can encourage the progress of the project by establishing and following up on the milestone status reports along the way.

All of the methods and resources discussed in this chapter should make you feel more confident about the various research routes you have open to you. Difficult-to-trace ancestors will invariably show up in your family tree. However, as long as you know how to conduct scholarly research, learn about and work with all kinds of alternative records, and employ the strategies and methodologies defined here, the chances are excellent that you can knock down those brick walls and keep moving your genealogical research forward.

Consider Some Common Brick Walls

Be prepared for research brick walls to appear anywhere and at any time. A roadblock may occur because of a lack of evidence, spelling and transcription errors, multiple people in the same area with the same name, and a wide variety of other reasons. Let's look at a few examples to give you some ideas of possible solutions.

Problem: A Person's Parents Cannot Be Identified

The person's parents cannot be identified or traced. This is perhaps the most common brick wall genealogists face. Moving backward one more generational step can be exceptionally challenging.

Possible Solutions Search for ecclesiastical records for your person that may indicate previous membership in another congregation elsewhere. I was able to trace one of my grandfathers from the church in North Carolina in which he was a member at the time of his death back to the church in which his family were members in Georgia, then back to another church in Alabama, and finally to the church in Tennessee in which he was christened. That church's membership roll also included his parents' transfers of membership from other churches, thus directing me to those churches for their families. Another possible solution, discussed in detail earlier in the chapter, involves researching one or more other family members.

Problem: A Person's Previous Place of Residence Can't Be Identified

The person's previous place of residence cannot be identified or traced. This is perhaps the second most common brick wall genealogists face.

Possible Solutions The ecclesiastical membership record search could work here as well. Common alternative records to help locate previous places of residence include voter registration records, school records, census indexes and population schedules, immigration and naturalization documents, land and tax records, probate packet inventories and heir lists showing property ownership and/or the residences of heirs in other locations, military service records, and obituaries.

Problem: Records Are Missing or Have Been Destroyed

The records you wanted or expected to find are missing, lost, or have been destroyed. Records do disappear, sometimes through misfiling and sometimes by having been removed or stolen. A common problem, too, is that the courthouse or other repository burned at some time and the records were lost. Consider my dismay to find evidence of an ancestor's considerable estate documented in probate court minutes, only to find that the entire probate packet was not in the probate clerk's files. The will and the executor's/administrator's documentation could have provided definitive proof of the names of my ancestor's children and whether they were living or deceased at the time of his death. It also could have identified other relatives, land and property holdings, and other pointers to other documentation.

Possible Solutions Locate all the probate court minutes for hearings concerning the estate. Some of the probate file materials may actually have been read into evidence in the probate court minutes when the report was introduced. Seek newspaper announcements concerning the settlement of the estate. Determine the name(s) of the executor/administrator(s) of an estate through the use of probate court's minutes, and then check the probate files in the event your ancestor's packet was incorrectly filed under the executor/administrator's name rather than under your ancestor's or another family member's name. In addition, it is not unheard of to find that a probate packet was removed by a lawyer or other representative and retained in that person's professional files. Investigate the possible existence of transcriptions, extracts, or abstracts of the original will in books, genealogical society publications, and elsewhere. Contact libraries, archives, and genealogical and historical societies to determine if they are aware of the existence and/or disposition of the records you are seeking.

Some of the records you seek may actually have been microfilmed after they were separated, and your research may require that you reunite and reconstruct the different materials from different locations. Further, those records may have since been digitized and may be online at a county website, at FamilySearch, or on another commercial database site.

Problem: Records Have Been Discarded or Destroyed

The records you are seeking have been discarded or destroyed. Perhaps the courthouse or other government repository ran out of space and determined that records older than a certain date were no longer needed. Originals of records may have been microfilmed and then destroyed, and then the microfilm might have been lost. There may have been a fire, tornado, hurricane, earthquake, flood, or other calamity in which the courthouse or archive was damaged or destroyed, and records were lost.

Possible Solutions   Consider substitute records that might provide identical or similar information. Contact archives, libraries, and genealogical and historical societies that might have acquired or salvaged any records. Investigate the possible existence of transcriptions, extracts, or abstracts of the original materials made or published prior to the records' loss. Don't overlook the possibility that records could have been duplicated and sent/transferred to another agency. Tax lists are usually published annually in a newspaper. These may help identify land ownership for your ancestor from the time the property was purchased until the time it was sold or ownership was otherwise transferred.

Problem: Records Were Destroyed During Wartime

Records were destroyed during a time of war. Contrary to what you may have heard, General William Tecumseh Sherman did *not* destroy every courthouse in his march through Georgia during the U.S. Civil War. However, some county government buildings and their records were lost. During World War II, there was so much bombing and fire damage in Antwerp, Belgium, that only a few pages of passenger lists survived.

Possible Solutions   Look for possible duplicate or substitute records. Investigate the possibility that the records were copied or microfilmed prior to their loss, that transcripts were published elsewhere, or that indexes survived when the actual records did not.

Problem: No Evidence Exists That a Person Lived in a Certain Place

There is no evidence the person ever lived in that place. Your research has pointed you to a specific place where, no matter what type of records you investigate, there are no records that your ancestor was ever there.

Possible Solutions   Perhaps the lead you had was incorrect. Or maybe the governmental jurisdiction has changed and the records are really in another place. Be sure to check historical maps from the time period you believe your ancestor was there, and verify the correct jurisdiction. Stop and reexamine all of your information to look for clues you may have missed or information that may have been incorrect.

Problem: Names and Dates Don't Fit

The names and/or dates are all wrong. I was searching for the origin of one of my great-great-grandfathers, Jesse Holder. I knew he lived in Georgia after he was married, but U.S. federal censuses indicated he was born in North Carolina. Searches of records in North Carolina yielded nothing, and so I transferred my attention to the possibility that he may have lived in South Carolina during some period. I found a Jesse Holder in Laurens County, South Carolina. Unfortunately, his year of birth didn't seem to fit. I then was able to find evidence that this Jesse Holder had married another woman and that he had died prior to when my great-grandfather was born in Georgia. My own Jesse Holder had been born on 13 August 1810 in North Carolina, and the other Jesse Holder had been born well before his inclusion as a head of household in the 1790 U.S. federal census. My further research revealed that the Jesse Holder in South Carolina was, in fact, the uncle of my great-grandfather. He was the person after whom *my* maternal great-great-grandfather was named.

Possible Solutions   Retrace the research steps to determine if you are on the right track or took a wrong turn. Look also in the same area for other branches of the same family that really might be yours. Naming patterns sometimes show that children may have been named for one of the parents' parents, an aunt or uncle, or a sibling.

Problem: You Can't Link Your Ancestor with Possible Family Members

There is no discernible link between *your* ancestor and the people you think could be the parents, siblings, spouse, and/or other relatives.

Possible Solutions   Examine census records in the area in which your person lived. Look for other persons in the vicinity with the same surname, and begin to research them. Examine obituaries, wills, probate records, and ecclesiastical records and look for any family relationship or common denominator linking them together. Examine land and property records to look for names of family members between whom property was bought, sold, given, or inherited. Consider cemetery records and monumental descriptions to help you relate persons to one another, and then conduct research on those people. Be alert to burials of individuals adjacent to one another that might infer family relationships, and be prepared to research these.

Problem: Person Has Vanished

The person has just simply vanished into thin air. (I call this the "my ancestor was abducted by an alien spaceship" problem.)

Possible Solutions   Reexamine census records for your ancestor and for the four to six neighboring families on either side of your ancestor. Locate your ancestor in the last census where you found him or her. Look, then, at the next available census for the neighbors. If *they* are all still in the same place and your ancestor is gone, you know you have looked in the correct place. If one or more of the neighbors also is gone, start looking for your ancestor *and* the neighbor in available census indexes in that location and surrounding parishes, counties, provinces, or states. Work in concentric circles, using a map and considering the migration routes and social trends of the time, and move outward seeking your ancestor in records that might likely have been created at the time. For example, if you know your ancestor was a Methodist, start looking at Methodist church membership records. Look for voter registration records if the period coincides with a major national election year. Check land and property records to determine if there was a change in property ownership—property sold, different property purchased, relocation to another location, or reference to the death of the property owner and the inheritance by an heir.

    Don't forget to look at census mortality schedules in the U.S. federal censuses of 1850 through 1880. If your ancestor died in the 12 months prior to the enumeration date of the census, he or she should be listed on the mortality schedule, along with his or her age, the reason for death, and other information.

Problem: Adoption Records Are Sealed

Adoption records are sealed by a court and not accessible to the public.

Possible Solutions   Formally petition the court in whose jurisdiction the adoption took place for access to names and dates of the parties. Be prepared to demonstrate your relationship to any and all parties. (Be sure to check the more recent legislation of the locations involved, as some of these adoption records are being made available, especially in the United States.)

Problem: Records Are Private

The records you want are the property of a private corporation and you are refused access to them.

Possible Solutions   Prepare evidence of your relationship to the person whose records you require and a solid reason for your request. Instead of access to the entire body of records, request an exact extract of the content you want to obtain. If you are refused, be prepared to escalate your request to the headquarters and/or executive officer(s) of the corporation. I have used this tactic in order to access personnel records and funeral home/mortuary records of individual family members.

These examples are not, of course, comprehensive in the scope of possible alternative sources and strategies, but they will give you some ideas to contemplate. Again, it is important to understand your ancestor in context, *all* of the record types that might have been created, possible repositories, and individuals and organizations that may be of help to you.

Do not ignore published case studies just because they do not specifically address your ancestors. There are many professional genealogists who write case study articles for publication in magazines and journals. These can be highly informative and educational because they illustrate how to approach research problems in a logical and methodical way. They typically start with a description or definition of the research problem in the question(s) that they want answered. Each research step is described in detail including: the type of record or alternative record being sought; the information expected to be found in each of these records; the place(s) where the record(s) might be found; how the records were accessed; whether this was an original or derivative record; what was actually found in the records, and how good was the information in it; which questions were answered and which ones were not; and what hypotheses or conclusions were drawn from the records. Case studies can be found in many professional journals, society journals, and commercial genealogy magazine publications. Carefully read these articles and study the documents used and the processes applied. You are guaranteed to learn a great deal from other people's research.

15

Incorporate Social Networking into Your Genealogy Research

HOW TO...

- Locate and use blogs
- Use wikis and collaborate with others
- Enjoy podcasts and web-based radio programs
- Learn more about genealogical research with Internet videos
- Attend live webinars and access recorded webinars
- Learn about and use the latest social networking resources
- Learn about hardware for the tech-savvy genealogist
- Use smartphone apps for genealogy-on-the-go

The Internet and the use of new technologies have grown and evolved over the past few years beyond our wildest expectations. We discussed DNA in Chapter 13 and how it can be used to complement your traditional research and to connect with others to collaborate.

New resources and tools have become available and genealogists have seized the opportunities they present to learn more, create content, communicate with other people, collaborate with other researchers, expand their research horizons, and take their genealogy files and research tools with them wherever they go. This chapter provides information about some of the most important Internet-based resources available to genealogists at this writing. It also looks at mobile telephones and a group of apps available for those devices.

Locate and Use Blogs

We briefly discussed blogs and how to locate them in Chapter 3. Let's explore them in a little more depth now.

The term *blog* is short for "web log." A blog can be created and maintained by an individual (*blogger*) and is somewhat like a diary or journal. Entries can include commentaries, descriptions of events in which the blogger is participating, and possibly graphics and video. Blogs have also become a popular medium for companies and organizations to communicate with the public. (Check for blogs on the websites of online database collections, genealogy software program providers, libraries and archives, genealogical and historical societies, and others.)

After the introduction of blogging technology, genealogists quickly began blogging on a wide array of subjects: their research experiences; surname research; geographical research; record types and/or methodologies; cemeteries; ethnic and religious research; obituaries; technology; DNA and genetic genealogy; photography; preservation; and many more. Unlike message boards and mailing lists that focus their attention on similar subjects, a blog primarily contains the writings and supplemental media of a single author. Readers may often add comments if the author enables that feature. Genealogy blogs offer a tremendous amount of information to the reader, and you will find blogs that mirror your interests so closely that you will eagerly anticipate every new entry.

Each blog entry is referred to as a *post* or *posting*, and postings are usually displayed in reverse chronological order—from most recent to oldest. Archives of older entries are typically stored in groups by month, and the majority of blogs incorporate a search facility that allows you to locate postings with the term(s)/keyword(s) you enter. In addition, a blogger will often try to organize his or her postings by adding one or more labels or keywords, also referred to as *tags*, to each posting. These help to organize blog postings about a single subject and quickly search to locate all such entries.

You can quickly establish your own blog. Free blogging services are available on the Internet, and they employ simple WYSIWYG (What You See Is What You Get) formatting similar to what is available in a word processor. Two of the most popular free blog hosting services are Blogger (**http://blogger.com**), which is a product of Google, and WordPress.com (**https://wordpress.com**), a product of Automattic. (Blogger requires that you be logged in to your free Google account before you can use that facility.) Figure 15-1 shows a Blogger page into which you type your blog content. Notice the toolbar over the body of the text and the similarity to that of a word processor. Note, too, the labels box at the bottom. This is where you enter the tag(s) that you want to be associated with this blog post.

Now that you know what a blog is, how do you find those that might be of interest to you? There are two excellent resources to help locate blogs. Chris Dunham's Genealogy Blog Finder website at **http://blogfinder.genealogue.com** and the GeneaBloggers website's Genealogy Blog Roll at **www.geneabloggers.com/genealogy-blogs** are the two best websites to search for blogs written by other genealogical researchers.

Individual blogs are as different from one another as snowflakes. Each author has his or her individual focus, schedule, and writing style. Some bloggers post a new entry each day or each week, while others post at another frequency. When you find one that is of interest to you, you may want to read it whenever there is a new posting. You can subscribe to a blog by examining its web page for the subscription button or link. Look for an orange icon labeled RSS (Really Simple Syndication),

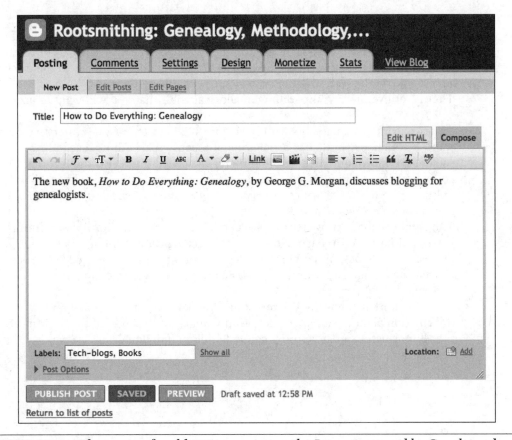

FIGURE 15-1   Blogger is a free blogging service on the Internet, owned by Google, and this is the WYSIWYG template it uses.

a link labeled "Entries RSS," or some notation about subscribing. Click the icon or link and you will usually be given the option to add the subscription to this blog to your favorite blog reader. Or you may need to copy and paste the RSS subscription link to whatever application you are using to read blogs, such as the blog reader at Feedly (**https://feedly.com**).

Use Wikis and Collaborate with Others

A wiki is a website that allows the creation and editing of a collection of interlinked web pages using a web browser and software embedded in the wiki. The term *wiki* comes from the Hawaiian word for "fast" or "quick," and the term was chosen to point out that anyone can quickly update the wiki website. A wiki is usually the result of collaborative work among many people. A person starts an informational article entry on a new web page in a wiki site, and then other people contribute to it and/or edit it. More details may be added, graphics may be inserted, and source citations and attributions may be added. While not every contributor may be an authority on the subject, the group collaboration tends to increase the quality and authority of the content. A wiki is created and edited using wiki software on the Internet. There are several software providers, and each uses a WYSIWYG template. You are probably already familiar with the largest wiki on the Web, Wikipedia, at **http://en.wikipedia.org**.

There are several very important genealogical wikis that you will want to use:

- Ancestry.com has created its Family History Wiki at **http://www.ancestry.com/wiki**. It contains over 33,000 articles about record types, ethnic research, societies, libraries and archives, and more. Of special interest is the fact that the company placed all of the content of its two most important genealogical books online in the wiki: *The Source: A Guidebook to American Genealogy* and *Red Book: American State, County, and Town*.
- The FamilySearch Family History Research Wiki at **https://familysearch.org/learn/wiki/en/Main_Page** is the largest genealogical wiki for articles about places, record types, and other genealogical content, with nearly 80,000 articles concerning research all over the world. Figure 15-2 shows the main page of this wiki.
- WikiTree at **http://www.wikitree.com** is the largest genealogical wiki for information about specific ancestral individuals. At the time of this writing, it has information about approximately 8 million individuals.

FIGURE 15-2 The main page of the FamilySearch Family History Research Wiki

Enjoy Podcasts and Online Radio Broadcasts

The growth of transmission bandwidth on the Internet has allowed for faster and more data-intensive communications. Online radiocasts have been available for a number of years. There are two types of broadcasts: podcasts and live radio broadcasts.

A *podcast* is a recorded audio program that you can listen to at the broadcaster's website, download from the same website, or subscribe to and receive the file electronically from iTunes or similar tools. There are a number of great podcasts that you can access:

- *The Genealogy Guys*^{SM} *Podcast* at **http://genealogyguys.com** is hosted by George G. Morgan and Drew Smith. It is the oldest continuously running genealogical podcast and is free to access. It presents news for the genealogical community, responds to listeners' email questions, and provides book reviews, interviews, and lively discussions of many topics of genealogy interest.
- *Genealogy Gems Podcast* at **http://lisalouisecooke.com/podcasts/** is hosted by Lisa Louise Cooke, and includes news, interviews, and genealogical discussions.
- *African Roots Podcast.com* at **http://africanrootspodcast.com** is hosted by Angela Walton-Raji and includes discussions, interviews, and other features.
- The National Archives in the United Kingdom presents excellent podcasts, video, and other audio programming at **http://media.nationalarchives.gov.uk** about history and TNA's record holdings.
- *Family Tree Magazine* produces monthly podcasts hosted by Lisa Louise Cooke. The podcasts are accessible at **http:// www.familytreemagazine.com/info/ podcasts**.

Learn More About Genealogical Research with Internet Videos

Bandwidth growth has also made it possible for explosive growth in the availability of video files on the Internet, and this also stretches to genealogy. You will find that there are several places where you can access instructional videos for free or for a small fee:

- The National Genealogical Society has produced a number of videos, many of which are free at **http://www.ngsgenealogy.org/cs/videos_online**. Others are available only to its members.
- YouTube at **http://www.youtube.com** contains scores of videos that can expand your knowledge. Visit the site and enter the term **genealogy** in the Search box. You will receive thousands of search results. You can limit the search to specific types of materials by adding one or more words. If you enter **genealogy basics**, your search results will include many videos about getting started with family history research. Enter **genealogy census** and you will find

videos about researching the U.S. federal census records and census records in the United Kingdom. Other terms you might want to enter include **genealogy military** for military records, **genealogy immigration** for videos about ships' passenger lists, or **genealogy Ireland** to learn more about Irish research and records. Enter **family history library** and you'll find a video tour of the library in Salt Lake City.

Attend Live Webinars and Access Recorded Webinars

The webinar is another fast growing resources of the Internet, and genealogists are actively involved. The time and expense involved with attending one class or an entire conference has grown. People are more and more willing to attend online educational classes, and this includes webinars.

A *webinar* is an online training class, most frequently presented live. These virtual classes can include PowerPoint or Keynote presentations with accompanying audio and video of the instructor. The presenter can share with the audience anything that he or she can bring up on the computer screen. Students can ask questions via a chat room message board, via audio in the webinar, or via telephone call-in, depending on the webinar software used and the presenter's preference. Many webinars are also recorded for later access and playback.

You usually have to register in advance to attend a live webinar. Many are free while others are accessible for a fee. You will receive an email confirmation of your registration that contains a link to the webinar. Be sure to keep this email until the webinar is over. The organizer usually will send a reminder email during the week before the event. Because the webinar's presenter or hosting organization may be in a time zone different from your own, be sure to figure out when you need to be online to attend the webinar. On the day of the webinar, use the confirmation email you received and click the link to connect to the online meeting room. Make sure you arrive early, especially if it's a free webinar, because some free webinars are limited as to how many attendees can attend. Arriving early to any webinar also gives you extra time to test your own video and audio hardware so that you can be sure to see and hear everything being offered.

When you go to the virtual meeting room, you may be automatically prompted to download and install a small piece of webinar software. You will listen to the audio portion of the webinar using your computer speakers, via headset, or by telephone (if that option is available).

There are many webinar resources available to you. First of all, GeneaWebinars at **http://blog.geneawebinars.com** is a blog that publishes news about genealogy webinars and a calendar. This site will alert you to upcoming events and will also allow you to home in on webinar providers whose previous webinars were recorded. You can always go back to download and enjoy them. Some of the best genealogy webinars available are listed here:

- Ancestry.com has broadcast and archived a number of webinars featuring good how-to instruction. This webinar archive is located at **http://www.ancestry.com/cs/us/videos**.
- Legacy Family Tree, maker of the genealogy software by the same name, produces a broad selection of webinars at **http://www.familytreewebinars.com**. Some of the archived webinars are free while others require a fee for viewing.
- The New England Historic Genealogical Society has produced some great webinars for beginning genealogists and for researchers wishing to learn more about the contents of the NEHGS collection that could benefit their research. Visit **http://www.americanancestors.org/online-seminars** to access these webinars.
- RootsMagic, maker of the genealogy software by the same name and other titles, has produced a collection of excellent webinars concerning the RootsMagic product and how to get the most from it. The webinars are accessible at **http://rootsmagic.com/Webinars**.

Look for other webinars at the GeneaWebinars site and take advantage of these excellent online learning opportunities.

Learn About and Use the Latest Social Media Resources

A *social network* can be defined as a social structure consisting of individuals who are acquainted with one another and share some type of relationship. This may be a friendship, a familial or professional relationship, or some other type of connection. Regardless, the individuals share some common interest or other link. A family is a social network. A church is a social network. A workplace is a social network, as is a neighborhood, a school, and more. We could go on and on to identify and describe many, many other types of social networks.

The Internet provides us with electronic tools with which to communicate with other people. Starting with email, mailing lists, and message boards, we genealogists have been networking with one another to expand our research reach, to share information, and to collaborate with one another. However, the past several years have seen rapid development of new *social media*—those electronic tools that facilitate communication and interaction with other people. That includes computer-based tools *and* mobile device–based tools. Let's explore the most prolific of these social media resources that are available at this writing.

Facebook

Facebook (**http://www.facebook.com**) is the largest single social media site on the Internet. At this writing, Facebook estimated that as of 30 June 2014 there were 1.32 billion active monthly Facebook users. They also estimated that there were 654 million mobile Facebook users as of that same date. Genealogists are very active using Facebook, both for individual personal interaction with others and as active members of Facebook groups for genealogy.

Facebook allows you to create a profile for yourself, engage in live chat with other users who you have accepted as "friends," post messages to those friends, upload photos and group them into "album" collections, create and join groups of people sharing a common interest, play online games, and otherwise stay in touch with one another. It is not unusual for a genealogist to post a message asking for opinions and suggestions about a research problem. The collaboration and support can be very helpful. The site is free and the mobile app for Facebook is free.

Genealogy Wise

Genealogy Wise (**http://www.genealogywise.com**) is another free social networking site, and it began operations in 2009. The National Institute for Genealogical Studies (NIGS) acquired the site in 2010. Like Facebook, Genealogy Wise is a social networking site that allows you to set up your own profile page, invite people to be your "friends" on the site, upload photos, chat, and more. Of particular interest are the more than 4,400 user-defined Groups on the site. These groups include photographs, a discussion forum (message board), a common wall for user comments, and external links. You can visit a group and/or you can join it. By joining a group, you can always quickly find it again whenever you log in by clicking the link to My Groups. The company also offers many high quality genealogy courses and certificate programs in a variety of genealogy-focused areas.

Google+

Google+, also written as Google Plus, debuted on the Internet at **https://plus.google .com** in June of 2011. Within one month, more than 20 million people had joined and begun using it. Google+ is a social networking site, owned and operated by the same company that runs the ubiquitous Google search engine.

Google+ is free and is another Google resource available when you log in to Google. All you need to do to start is to register to use Google+. It allows you to log in and create a profile for yourself and upload photographs. You can also invite friends, but, unlike Facebook and Genealogy Wise, you assign them to one or more "circles." The predefined circles are Friends, Family, and Acquaintances. You can, however, also create new circles. People can be added to circles in multiple ways, including via drag-and-drop.

Google+ on its website features a facility called Hangouts. Hangouts allow you to create or participate in a live video chat with up to nine other people. There is a facility that allows you to search for pages, people, and posts (with search terms or keywords), just like in a search engine. You can search for **genealogy** and find many different types of Google+ interests. Enter **irish genealogy** and narrow your search to just posts with both those terms.

An excellent place to learn all about Google + is at **https://www.google.com/ +/learnmore**. This site will help you get started and learn about all the features of Google +.

Twitter

Twitter (**http://www.twitter.com**) is a social networking website that offers a messaging or micro-blogging service. Twitter was launched in July of 2006 and has experienced explosive growth. At the time of this writing, the company estimates are that there are at least 271 million Twitter users in the world, and that approximately 350 billion tweets are delivered each day.

Twitter users send short text messages, or posts, up to 140 characters in length, which are known as *tweets*. Messages are addressed and grouped together using what are known as *hashtags*. A hashtag is a word or phrase preceded by the "#" character. Corporations and organizations define a hashtag for themselves and begin using it to help group traffic. They also can submit it to a directory where it can be listed and people can find it.

What do Twitter and hashtags have to do with genealogy? A genealogical society that is planning a conference may be interested in allowing attendees and interested parties to exchange messages in real time about the event. The conference planners can define a hashtag to identify the conference. They will then probably publicize that there is a Twitter hashtag for the conference, or about specific events during the conference, and people can then send tweets addressed to that hashtag. All of the tweets will be grouped together so that when an interested person searches for the hashtag in Twitter, he or she will be able to see all the recent tweets made that contain that hashtag. Please note that a tweet can contain multiple hashtags, and that makes the posting available to search using multiple terms.

You can learn all about Twitter at a number of places on the Internet. One good starting point is *The Twitter Guide Book* at Mashable.com (**http://mashable.com/ guidebook/twitter**). This primer includes text, video tutorials, instructions on how to find people on Twitter, and more.

Learn About Hardware and Software for the Tech-Savvy Genealogist

Genealogists are among the quickest to latch onto and become effective users of new technologies. There are so many hardware options available that it would require a separate book just to scratch the surface of the topic.

Laptops and tablets have been developed and improved upon a great deal in the last few years. Prices have also gone down, putting them within the reach of many people. Computer manufacturers have reported declines in the sales of desktop computers and increases in the sales of the laptop and tablet computers.

Portable scanning devices and all-in-one printers are also immensely popular among genealogists, and new choices and upgrades are introduced each year.

Genealogy software programs and apps for desktop computers, laptops, and tablets are abundantly available. Even more apps are available for smartphones, and some of these are discussed in the following section.

There are many choices of hardware and genealogy software/apps for these portable computers, and the market changes quickly. I am therefore not going to address this segment of the genealogy marketplace. Rather, I suggest that you consult the leading genealogical periodicals on the market, since they regularly review your options. Those periodicals include *Family Chronicle* and *Internet Genealogy* (Moorshead Magazines at **http://www.moorshead.com**), *Family Tree Magazine* (F + W Media at **http://www.familytreemagazine.com**), and *Your Family Tree* (Immediate Media Company Bristol Limited at **http://www.yourfamilytreemag.co.uk**). Cyndi's List (**http://www.cyndislist.com**) also has categories for Software & Computers, Scanners & Scanning, and other topics related to help you learn more. Genealogical societies' publications and online bloggers may also review hardware and software options.

Use Smartphone Apps for Genealogy-on-the-Go

Society is changing dynamically, and people are increasingly on the move. We live in an on-demand world and have become accustomed to accessing, receiving, and exchanging information almost instantaneously. Cellular phones have become the ubiquitous way to communicate in many ways.

One of the most exciting changes for family historians in the last several years has been the development and availability of genealogy software apps for cellular telephones. Our telephones have evolved into powerful computers, doing much more than simply handling telephone calls and a personal address book. They incorporate high quality photograph and video capabilities; text messaging using Twitter and other tools; online meetings using Google + and Skype; GPS; and other sophisticated tools. In addition, there are tens of thousands of apps available for just about every interest. There is no lack of genealogy apps, and we will examine a number of them for the iOS (iPhone) and Android platforms that are available as of this writing. (There are no genealogy apps for the Windows or Blackberry phones.)

It is important to understand that there are two primary cell phone application (app) platforms. Apple has developed the iOS platform, which is the operating system running on the iPhone, iPad, and iPod. Genealogy software developers have created apps that run on the iPhone or iPad, and these are separate versions of the same programs. Google developed the Android platform that runs on Android phones, and there are some genealogy apps for that operating system.

You can obtain apps (programs) for iOS devices at the App department of the iTunes Store on iTunes. iTunes is a downloadable program available at

http://www.apple.com/itunes. You download and install iTunes on your computer, and then can use it to purchase, manage, and play audio and video files, and to access the iTunes Store. The store is the place where you locate music, movies, TV shows, apps, books, podcasts, digital periodicals, and more. It is also where you search for, purchase, and download these items to your computer or cell phone. Materials that you download to your computer can be synched to your iPhone. You can also access the iTunes Store from your iPhone and purchase and download files directly to your phone. These are then synched with your computer or with the iCloud, if you choose, the next time they connect. It should be noted that a software app may be available for free or for a small price. Likewise, a version of the app may be free and a full-feature version may be available for a price.

Apps for the Android are available at Google Play at **https://play.google.com/store/apps**. Unlike iTunes, Google Play is not a computer program with an interface to an online site. Google Play is an Internet website where you can search and download apps, movies and TV, music, video, books, and newsstand items for Android devices. Like iTunes, this is where you search for, purchase, and download these items to your cell phone, install, and run them.

First of all, you should know that many of the desktop-based genealogy database software program companies have developed apps for the iPhone and/or Android phone. There are currently apps for both iOS and Android available for Family Tree Maker, Heredis, Legacy Family Tree, MyHeritage, Reunion, and RootsMagic. If you use one of these programs or others, I encourage you to visit the respective company's website to learn if an app exists for your phone and, if so, how to obtain it.

There are a number of useful apps available at this writing for both the iOS and/or Android platforms, and we will briefly discuss each one.

BillionGraves Camera App (Free & Fee)

BillionGraves is a website at **http://billiongraves.com** that is working to compile an expansive database of world cemeteries. Membership is free, with an additional fee-based upgrade for a service to watch specific records and the facility to perform virtual walk-throughs of cemetery interments. You can earn watch credits by participating as a volunteer by capturing photographs of graves, uploading them, and transcribing inscriptions.

The BillionGraves Camera App, shown in Figure 15-3, is available for both iOS and Android and allows you to capture and view photos, transcribe inscriptions, upload data to the website, search records to locate burials in the database, view maps of cemeteries, and more.

CousinCalc (Free)

CousinCalc is an iOS app (but not available for Android) produced by Ack Me Software that helps you determine the correct term for a relationship, such as great-great-great-grandfather, first cousin once removed, and so forth.

FIGURE 15-3 A screen from a name search using the BillionGraves Camera App

FamilySearch Memories (Free)

FamilySearch Memories is an iOS app (not available for Android) that interacts with FamilySearch on the Internet (**https://familysearch.org**). A sample screenshot is shown in Figure 15-4. The app allows you to capture new photos, type new stories, and record audio on your phone and upload them to your FamilySearch account. Likewise, you can view photos and stories and listen to audio recordings you have saved to your FamilySearch account. It's a great way, indeed, to capture and share memories.

FamilySearch Tree (Free)

The FamilySearch Tree app available for both iOS and Android allows you to access your free FamilySearch account at **https://familysearch.org** and view your pedigree chart file, list all the persons in your online pedigree file, and view and work with the data on individual people. Figure 15-5 shows the History List with each person in my tree. You can search for individuals, and you can click on the individual's name to see their full record. In addition you can save photos taken on your phone to your tree, and even download your six-generation pedigree chart to the app for off-line viewing.

FIGURE 15-4   A screenshot from the FamilySearch Memories app showing photos on my FamilySearch account

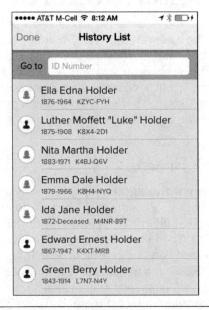

FIGURE 15-5   The FamilySearch Tree app allows you to view your pedigree file and individual people's information on your phone.

FIGURE 15-6 A screenshot from the Family Tree History and Genealogy Coat of Arms of Last Names app

Family Tree History and Genealogy Coat of Arms of Last Names (Free & Fee)

The Family Tree History and Genealogy Coat of Arms of Last Names is an iOS app (not available for the Android) from Adv Webbing, Inc., and is a database of the meanings of surnames and, if available, a coat of arms. A description of the meaning of the surname, such as the one shown in Figure 15-6, can be displayed in English, Italian, French, Spanish, German, or Portuguese. You can share the result via email, Facebook, or Twitter. There is a free version of the app available, and an advertisement-free version available for $4.99.

Find A Grave (Free)

Find A Grave (**http://www.findagrave.com**) is a website composed of information about cemeteries and burials, all contributed by volunteers over a number of years. It includes more than 116 million entries online as of this writing. Ancestry.com acquired the site in 2014. The Find A Grave app, shown in Figure 15-7, allows you to search for records already on the website or search for a cemetery. The iOS app uses your location to display a map with surrounding cemeteries. (The app is not available for Android.) Each cemetery map includes links to all the memorial records that have been added for those interred there. You can add information to the website, take photos and upload them, enter the GPS location of a grave, and request headstone photos from a volunteer (or become a volunteer yourself).

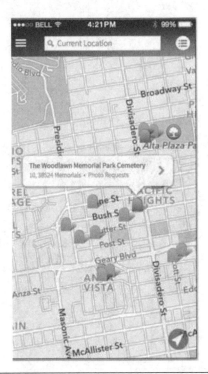

FIGURE 15-7   This screenshot from Find A Grave shows a map of an area with surrounding cemetery locations highlighted.

National Geographic World Atlas (Free)

The National Geographic World Atlas is more than just a high-resolution map app only available for the iOS. First, it provides a strong search facility to locate countries and towns, and enables you to move the map and to zoom in by pinching the screen. Measure distances between locations. You can click-and-drag the map, double-click a location to zoom in, place marking pins, access a currency calculator, save maps for off-line use, and more. When you search for country, there are demographics such as area (square miles or square kilometers), population, languages spoken, religions, government, an historical overview, details about the capital (including GPS location, population, local time, weather, and temperatures in Fahrenheit or Celsius), and other facts. See Figure 15-8 for a screenshot example.

Atlas 2014 (Free)

Atlas 2014 is an app for the Android that provides high-quality political world maps, large regional maps, and World Time Zone maps. These maps are stored on your phone and do not require an Internet connection. See Figure 15-9 for a screenshot example.

FIGURE 15-8   A screenshot from the National Geographic World Atlas app showing infographics about Panama

FIGURE 15-9   A screenshot from Atlas 2014 showing a large regional map

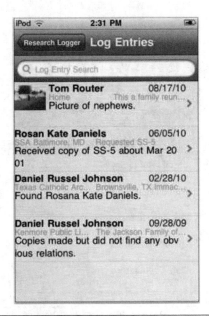

FIGURE 15-10 Research Logger allows you to set up to-do lists by ancestor, and then click on an ancestor to see all active items in detail.

Research Logger (Free)

We talked earlier in the book about the importance of maintaining a research log. Research Logger is an iOS app (not available for Android) created by Spencer T. Hall that allows you to keep track of your research. There is a to-do list that can be sorted/ displayed by uncompleted items, completed items, or all items. (See the example shown in Figure 15-10.) You can maintain log entries by ancestor, and you can view all blog entries as a list and select from that. Each to-do entry (ancestor) appears as a separate item, and you can view that item in detail: ancestor name, date and time, source location, source description, media, and comments. Under media, you can select and link photos and can also record and play back an audio recording for each item.

Wolfram Genealogy & History Research Assistant (Fee)

Wolfram Alpha (**http://www.wolframalpha.com**) is a sophisticated computational knowledge engine on the Internet. It collects objective "curated data" and then performs dynamic calculations based on its built-in data, algorithms, and computational methods. The Wolfram Genealogy & History Research Assistant app,

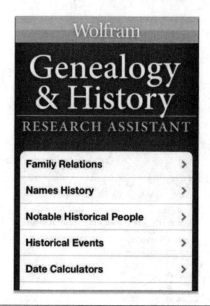

FIGURE 15-11 The main screen of the Wolfram Genealogy & History Research Assistant app

shown in Figure 15-11, is tailored for use by genealogical researchers. It includes a wealth of tools, including: a relationship calculator; names history for first names, surnames, and even name variations; information about notable historical people by name, birthplace, and location, and even calculates the age of these individuals at a particular time; historical events and timelines with multiple views; an extensive date calculator and a Gregorian-Julian calendar converter; astrology and weather; geographical and demographic information; and financial data, including a comparison calculator for the value of U.S. money between now and past years. It also includes a word interpreter, a unit converter, a Roman numeral converter, and several other tools. At this writing, the app sells for $4.99.

You'll want to explore the iTunes Store and Google Play for other apps that may be useful tools in your genealogy research. New apps are added frequently and existing ones are updated, so check back often to see what's new.

Index